KARL KRAUS
APOCALYPTIC SATIRIST

Frontispiece: The original cover of *Die Fackel*

KARL KRAUS
APOCALYPTIC SATIRIST

Culture and Catastrophe in Habsburg Vienna

EDWARD TIMMS

YALE UNIVERSITY PRESS
NEW HAVEN AND LONDON

For Saime

Designed by Robert Baldock.

Set in 11/12 pt Bembo by Alan Sutton Publishing Ltd., Gloucester, and printed in Great Britain at The Bath Press, Avon.

Library of Congress Cataloging-in-Publication Data
Timms, Edward
  Karl Kraus, apocalyptic satirist.

  Bibliography: p. 431
  includes indexes.
  1. Kraus, Karl, 1874–1936—Criticism and interpretation.
  2. Kraus, Karl, 1874–1936—Contemporary Austria.
  3. Vienna (Austria)—Intellectual life.   I. Title.
  PT2621.R27Z83 1986   838'.91209   86–1665

  ISBN 0–300–03611–6 (cloth)
       0–300–04483–6 (pbk)

Contents

List of Illustrations

Maps and Figures

xi

SOURCES OF ILLUSTRATIONS

Permission to reproduce illustrations from the following sources is gratefully acknowledged:

Frontispiece: F [*Die Fackel*] 1: cover. 1, *Das Wiener Kaffeehaus* (Verlag der Museen der Stadt Wien). 2, Elisabeth Springer, *Die Wiener Ringstraße: Geschichte und Kulturleben* (Wiesbaden: Franz Steiner Verlag, 1979). 3, *Adolf von Sonnenthals Briefwechsel* (Stuttgart: Deutsche Verlags-Anstalt, 1912). 4, postcard from the collection of Reinhard Urbach (Vienna). 5, Österreichische Nationalbibliothek. 6, Leopold Liegler, *Karl Kraus und sein Werk* (Vienna: Richard Lanyi Verlag, 1920). 7, F 852–6: 49. 8, F 182: 15. 9 and 10, Hans Jochen Irmer, *Der Theaterdichter Frank Wedekind* (Berlin: Henschel Verlag, 1975). 11, Nike Wagner, *Geist und Geschlecht* (Frankfurt: Suhrkamp Verlag, 1982). 12, *Memoirs of the Countess Potocka* (London: Grant Richards, 1901). 13, Charles Brison, *Pornocrates* (London: Charles Skilton, 1969). 14, First edition of *Sprüche und Widersprüche* (1909), collection of J. P. Stern (Cambridge). 15, Österreichische Nationalbibliothek. 16, Wiener Stadtbibliothek, Plakatsammlung. 17, *The Graphic Work of Félicien Rops* (New York: Léon Amiel, 1975). 18, F 326–8: frontispiece. 19, F 137: 17. 20, *Unser Conrad: Ein Lebensbild*, dargestellt von einem Österreicher (Vienna: Historisch – politischer Verlag, 1916). 21, Österreichische Nationalbibliothek. 22, *Zeit im Bild*, April 1913 (Bayerische Staatsbibliothek, Munich). 23, Wiener Stadtbibliothek. 24, Deutsches Literaturarchiv, Marbach. 25, Rupertinum, Salzburg, and Cosmopress, Geneva. 26, Österreichische Nationalbibliothek. 27, collection of Friedrich Pfäfflin (Marbach). 28, *Reichspost*, 29 July 1914. 29, Bezirksmuseum Währing (by kind permission of Rudolf Becska). 30, *Reichspost*, 2 July 1914. 31, F 499–500: frontispiece. 32, *Die letzten Tage der Menschheit* (1922): frontispiece. 33, collection of Friedrich Pfäfflin (Marbach). 34, *Die letzten Tage der Menschheit* (Akt-Ausgabe, 1919). 35, F 501–7: frontispiece. 36, Maria Pötzl-Malikova, *Die Wiener Ringstraße: Die Plastik* (Wiesbaden: Franz Steiner Verlag, 1976). Additional photographic work by Don Manning (Cambridge).

Preface

'Why are there no really *critical* writers in German?' asked a student from England during a visit to Bavaria in 1960. 'Try reading Karl Kraus,' replied a more knowledgeable German friend. Thus was I introduced to Kraus's satire, which takes fin-de-siècle Vienna as its point of departure but culminates in a vision of the collapse of western civilization. The aim of this book is to make that vision more comprehensible.

During its long gestation the book has benefited from the research of several generations of scholars. Its findings may nevertheless come as a surprise. For my approach diverges from the main tradition of Kraus criticism, which has insisted on the unity of man and work. This book offers an alternative reading which emphasizes the discrepancies between Kraus's personal position and his satirical voice. And he emerges as a writer of divided allegiance, conservative in personal outlook but radical in his satirical strategy.

The paradoxes of Kraus's career, which are related to his Jewish background, became particularly pronounced during the First World War. Reluctantly relinquishing his conservative allegiances, he became a militant pacifist and radical democrat. The seismic shift of history, which brought about the collapse of the Habsburg Empire, is memorably recorded in his great documentary play *Die letzten Tage der Menschheit*, which emerges from this analysis as a faulted masterpiece.

Kraus's literary development forms a complex story, which has taken twenty years to unravel. Even so the argument has been carried through only to the end of the First World War and the founding of the Austrian Republic. To do justice to the second half of his career would require a second volume.

My preoccupation with the study of satire dates back to student days in Cambridge, where I benefited from the guidance of a number of gifted teachers. My interest in German literature was kindled by E. K. Bennett, and I was initiated into the systematic study of satire by F. J. Stopp. A more substantial debt is owed to J. P. Stern, who greeted me when I returned to Cambridge as a research student by saying: 'Of course you will have to read every word of Kraus's magazine *Die Fackel*.' This advice has stood me in good stead, and I have benefited from Peter Stern's guidance and inspiration ever since.

In the early stages of my research I was fortunate to meet a number of people who were willing to share with me their memories of Karl Kraus: Heinrich Fischer, Kraus's literary executor and editor of the Kösel edition of his works; Gertrud Jahn, who assisted Fischer with the preparation of that edition; Leopold Ungar, who made me feel welcome at the Caritas student hostel on the Kahlenberg in Vienna; Friedrich Torberg, who greeted me in the Café Raimund with sheaves of articles from his magazine *Forum*; and Paul Schick, who provided such kindly guidance during my early visits to the Vienna City Library.

My thanks are also due to other friends and colleagues: to Hans Keith (the friend who introduced me to Kraus's work); to Reinhard and Katharina Urbach for their welcome during my repeated visits to Vienna; to Sophie Schick for sharing with me her unique knowledge of Kraus's life and letters; and to Gila Kunze for many stimulating conversations. Others who have kindly assisted me on points of detail include Murray Hall, Friedrich Jenaczek, Leo Lensing, Eda Sagarra, Sigurd Paul Scheichl, Wendelin Schmidt-Dengler, Jonathan Steinberg, Gerald Stieg and W. E. Yates.

Particular gratitude is due to those who have read and commented on sections of this book: Gilbert Carr, who so generously assessed a very bulky typescript; John Halliday, who read the sections dealing with the First World War (and allowed me to incorporate his discoveries about Kraus's dealings with the censorship); Peter Bayley and Sally McMullen, who read individual chapters; and Hugh Salvesen, whose research has helped to clarify Kraus's complex relationship with Frank Wedekind. I am also grateful to my father, John Timms, for reading my research in an earlier form and for providing (together with my mother) a background conducive to study.

Among institutions which have facilitated the writing of this book, pride of place must go to the Vienna City Library, which has allowed me access to the rich resources of its Karl Kraus Archive. The Austrian National Library in Vienna and the German Literary Archive in Marbach have also enabled me to consult valuable material. The Cultural Office of the City of Vienna have been helpful in providing accommodation. And I am grateful to the Austrian Institute in London, and to its Director Bernhard Stillfried, for generous support.

The Vienna City Library and the German Literary Archive have kindly allowed me to quote unpublished material. And I am grateful to the administrator of the Karl Kraus copyright, Friedrich Pfäfflin, for permission to quote unpublished letters and for help in obtaining photographs. Professor Franz Stoessl has also kindly allowed me to quote from the manuscript of a letter from Kraus to Otto Stoessl.

Thanks are due to the University of Cambridge, and to Gonville and Caius College, for periods of study leave and grants towards travelling expenses. Gratitude of a different kind is due to my wife Saime and children, Yusuf, Defne and Sebastian, for cheerfully tolerating my absence – or simply my absent-mindedness.

At various stages during the revision of my typescript I have received secretarial assistance from Irmgard Kapner, Rosemarie Baines, Ann Hughes and Edna Pilmer. The intervention of Robert Baldock (of Yale University Press) provided the final incentive which enabled me to complete the book. I am grateful to Catharine Carver for her sensitive and meticulous copy-editing; and to John Halliday and Ritchie Robertson for help with proofreading.

My interest in Kraus was originally inspired by his revival of the myth of Pandora. But my research would never have been completed if it had not been sustained by the patience of Penelope. Hence my dedication.

Gonville and Caius College   Edward Timms

Abbreviations

Works by Karl Kraus cited in the text

F   *Die Fackel* (1899–1936)
References are to the 922 numbers of the journal, followed by the page, e.g. *F* 400–3: 2–5.

FS   *Frühe Schriften*, ed. J. J. Braakenburg, 2 vols. (Munich 1979). Kraus's writings of the 1890s, reprinted in this edition, are cited in the text by volume number and page, e.g. *FS* II. 277–97.

BSN   *Briefe an Sidonie Nádherný von Borutin: 1913–1936*, ed. Heinrich Fischer and Michael Lazarus, 2 vols. (Munich 1974). Kraus's letters to Sidonie Nadherny, together with excerpts from her diaries and notes, are cited from this edition by volume number and page, e.g. *BSN* II. 113.

W   *Werke*, ed. Heinrich Fischer, 14 vols. (Munich 1952–67), cited by volume number and page, e.g. *W* III. 27–9. An account of the contents of each volume of this edition is given in the Bibliographical Note at p. 432.

PART ONE

CITY, MASKS AND TORCH

CHAPTER 1

Vienna 1900

The silhouette of Vienna, darkly illuminated on the cover of *Die Fackel* (see frontispiece), marks out the horizon of Kraus's world. Great cities have always inspired the satirist — from Juvenal's Rome to Joyce's Dublin. But the link between Kraus and Vienna is exceptionally close. He was not actually Viennese by birth — he was born in 1874 in northern Bohemia, the youngest son of a Jewish paper manufacturer, and was three years old when his family moved to the capital. But it was in Vienna that he spent his childhood, among the bustle of the metropolis and the tranquillity of the surrounding woods and vineyards. It was here, in the flourishing literary coffee-houses of the 1890s, that he served his apprenticeship as a journalist. And it was here that he wrote, edited and published the 922 numbers of *Die Fackel* which contain his life's work.

This lifelong attachment to the city which he reviled is one of the paradoxes of Kraus's career. It also defines the nature of his achievement. It is not the great world of European politics but the local affairs of Vienna that provide his theme. His critical focus may be intensified, his response heightened into visionary satire; but he does not often venture beyond the suburbs of Vienna in quest of material. Even in *Die letzten Tage der Menschheit*, his great satirical panorama of the First World War, it is the home front, the streets and conversations of Vienna, that bulk most largely. Like Freud (though on a more public plane) Kraus diagnoses the psychopathology of everyday life, as it is reflected in the language of the Viennese and the jargon of their newspapers. Even when his theme is the breakdown of western civilization, it is still in the Kärntnerstrasse that he finds the motifs for his satire.

This passionate parochialism constitutes the primary fascination of Kraus's writings. More vividly than any other writer of the period,

he captures the grotesque and frivolous features of life in Vienna
during the final decades of the Habsburg Empire. But is he merely
the satirical chronicler of Vienna, or is he (as has been claimed) 'the
first European satirist since Swift'?[1]* Kraus's attachment to an
apparently eccentric locale seems to militate against this more
universal perspective. But was Vienna really such a special case?
What were the essential features of that city culture which nourished
Kraus's satirical imagination?

Conflict and Creativity: The Vienna Circles

The first advantage the city offered was an audience. However
problematic the politics of the multinational Empire, there can be no
doubt that by 1900 Vienna had emerged as one of the great artistic
capitals of the world. The Viennese were uniquely receptive to music
and the theatre and insatiably curious about the lives of the city's
actors and musicians, writers and artists. The emergence of this
audience can be traced back to the early nineteenth century, when the
authorities encouraged the popular passion for the theatre as a policy
of bread and circuses. Patronage for the arts, no longer an aristocratic
preserve, ranged from the cultivation of higher things in the salons to
grass-roots enthusiasm for the popular theatre in the suburbs. A
writer on the Vienna of Grillparzer suggests that these different social
groups met on common ground in their passion for the theatre and
that 'here for once it is legitimate to speak of a — more or less
genuine — popular culture'.[2] In the organization of choral societies
and public concerts the fusion of bourgeois cultural aspirations with
popular musical traditions was especially evident.[3] An official report
records that in 1828 (when the population of the city numbered
about 300,000) the five principal theatres could together accommo-
date almost 10,000 people.[4]

In the late nineteenth century the emergence of a prosperous
bourgeoisie gave a new impetus to the cultural life of the city,
shifting its centre of gravity away from the popular theatre towards
more sophisticated art forms. For the satirical writer this
sophisticated city culture offered a fertile field. Satire flourishes
where it can appeal to an initiated audience, sensitive to the oblique
reference and the esoteric joke. Kraus was the inheritor of a rich
tradition of parody and burlesque, which found in the comedies of
Johann Nestroy its most verbally inventive expression. This tradition had in the later decades of the nineteenth century taken
sophisticated form in the satirically tinged feuilleton, of which
Daniel Spitzer was the most notable exponent. Kraus invoked these

* Superior figures in the text refer to the Reference Notes at p. 405.

writers as his forerunners. He was also indebted to them for the
existence of an audience schooled in the appreciation of satire. By the
end of the nineteenth century the tradition of wit had entered the
currency of social intercourse, with the coffee-house as the exchange
for well-worn anecdotes and new-minted puns. This congenial
atmosphere is reflected in the painting by Reinhold Völkel of the
most celebrated literary coffee-house, the Café Griensteidl (Pl. 1).
And memoirs of this period, like those of the conductor Bruno
Walter, emphasize 'the part played by the Viennese coffee-house in
the stimulation of conversational genius'.[5] The Jewish contribution
to this exchange of wit constituted an additional enrichment.

1   *Café Griensteidl* by Reinhold Völkel

The success of Kraus's first pamphlet, *Die demolirte Literatur*
(1897), inspired by the demolition of the Café Griensteidl, was a
product of this milieu (*FS* II. 277–97). In this satire on the
mannerisms of Viennese writers such as Schnitzler, Hofmannsthal
and Hermann Bahr, none of Kraus's victims is named. But the satire
appealed to an initiated audience able to identify the targets of attack
on the evidence of a stylistic or sartorial mannerism. The pamphlet
rapidly ran through five impressions, and one of Kraus's victims,
Felix Salten — derided for his shaky grasp of grammar — resorted to
physical violence in reply.[6] The spectacular success of the early
numbers of *Die Fackel*, with their witty attacks on prominent local
personalities, is also only explicable in terms of a receptive milieu.

On the day when *Die Fackel* hit the news-stands, its brilliant cover turned the whole town red. The first number sold almost 30,000 copies.

The existence of an audience for satire proved in the long run an ambiguous asset. For a witty satirist there was indeed a reputation for the making in fin-de-siècle Vienna (and *Die Fackel* soon found many imitators). But the interaction between author and audience was problematic. The picture of felicitous collaboration offered in Stefan Zweig's classic account, *The World of Yesterday*, is clearly a simplification. The more problematic aspects of Viennese culture have been emphasized in a number of studies.[7] Few cities can boast such a flowering of artistic and intellectual life. But this must not lead us to underestimate the tensions between cultural avant-garde and conservative environment. Conflict rather than conciliation was the keynote, not only for Kraus but for his whole generation of Austrian iconoclasts.

The city which feted Johann Strauss the younger responded with chilling incomprehension to the more radical innovations of Bruckner or Schoenberg. The most original minds of Vienna had to contend with a public predominantly hostile to dissonant forms of creativity. The letters and diaries of these iconoclasts vividly record the derision with which their work was received in the city which Schoenberg (writing to Mahler) called 'our beloved and hated Vienna'.[8] The compositions of Bruckner were ridiculed, the architectural visions of Otto Wagner denounced as a ludicrous extravagance. Public petitions were organized against the paintings of Klimt, and the City Council took out an injunction against Adolf Loos's threateningly modernist building on the Michaelerplatz. Freud was ostracized by his colleagues and his follower Otto Gross actually imprisoned by his own father for deviant conduct. Schoenberg's concerts were disrupted by a scandalized audience and the goings-on in Egon Schiele's studio so shocked his neighbours that he was arrested for immorality. Kokoschka's paintings also provoked an outcry. And the open-air production of his first play would have been wrecked by enraged spectators, if Kraus had not been there to call the police.[9]

Within this climate of incomprehension there was nevertheless an audience of the initiated prepared to support avant-garde activity. Jewish patrons were particularly significant. 'Most of my sitters were Jews,' Kokoschka recalls. 'They felt less secure than the rest of the Viennese Establishment, and were consequently more open to the new and more sensitive to the tensions and pressures that accompanied the decay of the old order.'[10] Loos, who was so active in Kokoschka's support, also received the majority of his early commissions from Jewish patrons. But when the crisis arose over his building on the Michaelerplatz, Loos was able to mobilize a larger body of public opinion behind his project. His illustrated lecture in December 1911 in defence of his controversial building attracted an audience of 2,700 people. Thus however isolated these radical dissenters may have felt amid the splendours of the Habsburg capital, they could in a crisis rally supporters to their cause.

The great strength of the Viennese avant-garde lay however in its internal organization. The 'Vienna Circle' of logical positivists led by Moritz Schlick has become well known in the history of philosophy. But the whole structure of avant-garde culture in Vienna can be pictured as a series of intersecting 'circles' (see Fig. I).

Each of the dominant personalities gathered around him a circle of adepts: Wagner's school of radical architects, Theodor Herzl's Zionists and Victor Adler's Social Democrats, Freud's exclusive Psychoanalytic Society and Schnitzler's more loosely-knit circle of literary acquaintances. In this same period Eugen Böhm-Bawerk was conducting his seminar on economic theory at the University, Mahler was inspiring a revival of creativity at the Opera, Schoenberg instructing his pupils in the principles of atonality, Rosa Mayreder rallying the feminists, Josef Hoffmann popularizing the exquisite designs of the Wiener Werkstätte. In many cases these were literally circles – groups of people meeting round a table, at a particular time (Freud's Wednesday evenings) in a specified place (Kraus's table in the Café Central). The circles tended to be esoteric and intensely inward-looking. They had to fortify themselves against the easy conviviality of the city in order to sustain their more puritanical endeavours. They formed tiny élites within the cultural élite, all the more distinctive for the predominance of Jewish intellectuals among them.

But if the circles had been merely inward-looking, they would never have achieved that contribution to twentieth-century civilization which has made the Vienna of Freud and Herzl, Schoenberg and Wittgenstein so renowned. The crucial feature which distinguishes these Vienna circles from the cultural élites of other cities is that the circles intersected. Certain people were members of two or more different circles, which ensured a rapid circulation of ideas. Fritz Wittels linked the circles of Kraus and Freud, Robert Scheu maintained contact between Kraus and the socialists. There were Marxists like Otto Bauer and Rudolf Hilferding in Böhm-Bawerk's economics seminar, while poets like Richard Beer-Hofmann were actively interested in Zionism. Loos designed austerely elegant covers for Kraus's books. Alfred Roller used the flowing colours of the Klimtian palette in his stage designs

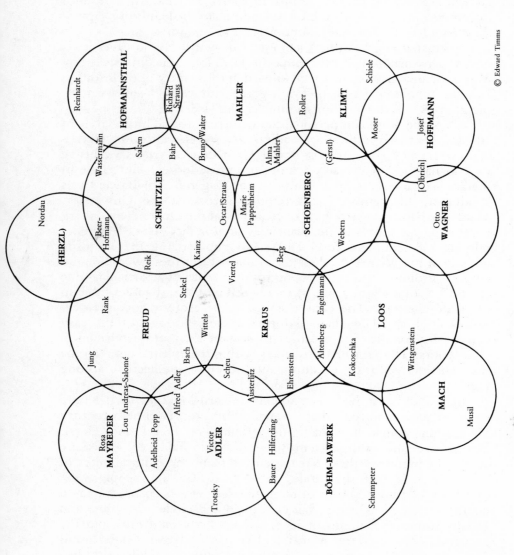

Fig. I: The Vienna Circles: a diagram of creative interaction in Vienna around 1910

© Edward Timms

for Mahler's operatic productions, while Richard Gerstl (before his suicide in 1908) taught Schoenberg how to paint. The ideas of Mach and Freud sparked off a creative response in writers as diverse as Hofmannsthal and Kraus, Musil and Wittgenstein.

The cross-fertilization between different disciplines was particularly significant within Freud's own circle, which included an extraordinary diversity of talent: Hugo Heller, the bookseller who organized the first exhibition of Schoenberg's pantings; Marie Pappenheim, who wrote a depth-psychological libretto for Schoenberg's composition *Erwartung*; Max Graf, a musicologist who wrote a study of Richard Wagner; Otto Rank, noted for his contributions to aesthetics and literary theory; and Theodor Reik, who wrote a pioneering study of Schnitzler. Most versatile of all was David Bach, a member of Freud's circle who was also a Social Democrat, a musicologist — and later one of Kraus's most active supporters. Bach, though not a significant figure in himself, formed one of those points of multiple intersection which generated such extraordinary creative energy. The Vienna circles may thus be pictured as a condensed system of micro-circuits.

Kraus's circle was at the centre of the system. His work had a decisive influence on Schoenberg and Wittgenstein, Loos and Kokoschka, as well as a galaxy of minor talent. Although he adopts in *Die Fackel* a stance of embattled isolation, he was in truth a convivial person who by 1910 had gathered around him an amazingly gifted circle of writers and artists. The fact that these circles were in the habit of sending cards of collective greetings to absent friends makes it possible on occasion to be quite precise about who was present on a particular evening in the Café Frauenhuber. But relations were not always so cordial. Rival factions sat at separate tables, and artistic antagonism sometimes erupted into physical violence, as when Kraus was assaulted in the Casino de Paris by members of a cabaret he had criticized.[11]

Against the enduring hostility of the journalists of Vienna Kraus was able to set the artistic integrity of allies like Altenberg and Wedekind, Loos, Kokoschka and Schoenberg. His position is paradoxically poised between the exclusivity of this élite and the appeal of *Die Fackel* to a wider audience. In insistent declarations he claims for his writings an artistic autonomy which transcends the mundane concerns of his readers. But if he was writing his magazine for posterity, he was selling it to his contemporaries. However much the satirist may inveigh against his readers, the author was well aware of the advantage of his position at the centre of this city culture. A letter to Maximilian Harden written shortly after the founding of *Die Fackel* shows that Kraus was consciously appealing to a metropolitan audience (rather than to readers in the provinces). And a letter to Wedekind seven years later suggests that the many aggravations of life in Vienna actually have the effect of making him more productive![12]

The Austrian Crisis of Identity

Kraus's creativity was further enhanced by the conflicts which were convulsing the Habsburg political system. This sprawling dynastic empire with its multitude of different nationalities, its retarded (but rapidly accelerating) industrial development, its predominantly rural and Catholic population, its autocratic government led by an octogenarian Emperor, seems at first an erratic outline on the otherwise orderly map of Europe before the First World War (see Fig. II). And its dual system of government, dividing responsibilities between Vienna and Budapest according to a complicated schema, further underlines its eccentricity. There were fifteen officially recognized languages in Austria-Hungary (not counting Yiddish). And in the supposedly 'Austrian' half of the Monarchy, the politically dominant German speakers were actually outnumbered by the supposed ethnic minorities. So acute was the crisis of political identity that the Austrian half did not even have an official name, but was known constitutionally as 'the kingdoms and territories repre-sented in the Reichsrat'. The word 'Austria' was commonly used to denote not the provinces of the modern Republic, but an enormous sweep of territory stretching from the ghettos of Galicia to the minarets of Sarajevo.

Beneath this eccentric surface, however, a more significant pattern may be discerned, which made Austria-Hungary (in Kraus's prophetic phrase of July 1914) an 'experimental station for the end of the world' ('Versuchsstation des Weltuntergangs', *F* 400–3: 2). The historian who analyses the disintegration of Austria-Hungary may see this as a problem peculiar to that multinational Empire.[13] But this same phenomenon can also be discussed in terms of a more fundamental loss of centre. Seen in these terms, the problems which bedevilled the Austro-Hungarian Empire may not be so peripheral to modern civilization after all. Even the problem of dissenting minorities was one which other European powers had to face in this same period. There was the Irish question in Britain, the Polish minority in the German Reich, the position of the Jews throughout Europe. Austria-Hungary was merely the extreme case.[14]

The key to this situation lies in an ideological disorientation which affected the whole Empire. In the German Reich we can identify a pervasive corruption of values. The humanistic vision of Kant, Lessing, Herder, Goethe, Schiller and Humboldt had pointed the

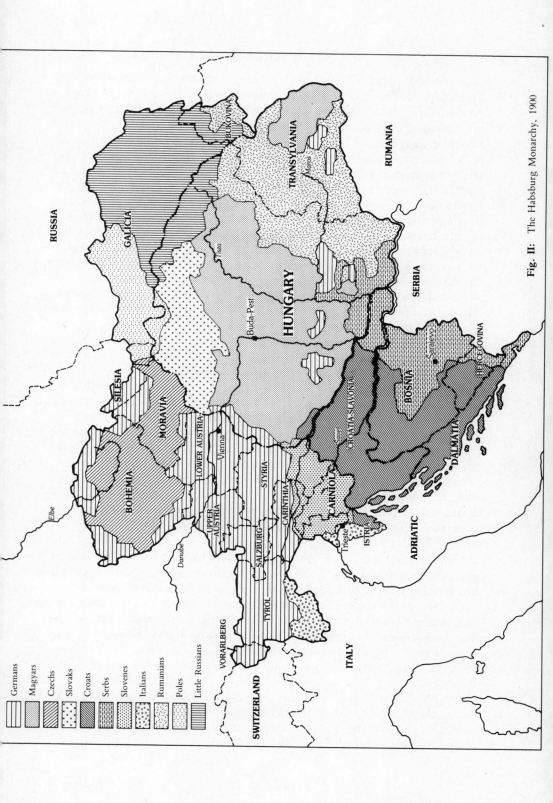

Fig. II: The Habsburg Monarchy, 1900

Germans
Magyars
Czechs
Slovaks
Croats
Serbs
Slovenes
Italians
Rumanians
Poles
Little Russians

RUSSIA

GALICIA

BUKOVINA

SILESIA

MORAVIA

BOHEMIA

Elbe

Danube

LOWER AUSTRIA

Vienna

UPPER
AUSTRIA

SALZBURG

STYRIA

CARINTHIA

CARNIOLA

VORARLBERG

TYROL

SWITZERLAND

ITALY

Trieste

ISTRIA

ADRIATIC

Tisza

Buda-Pest

HUNGARY

TRANSYLVANIA

Maros

RUMANIA

SERBIA

CROATIA-SLAVONIA

Save

BOSNIA

Sarajevo

HERCEGOVINA

DALMATIA

way towards an ideal civilization. The constitution drawn up by the Frankfurt parliament of 1848–9 had indicated how these principles could be put into practice. All of this was betrayed by the power politics of Bismarck and the imperialism of the Kaiser. But the situation in Austria-Hungary was more complex. Here we can speak of an endemic confusion of values, arising from the fact that no coherent model of the state existed. The Habsburg territories had traditionally derived their sense of identity — as bastion against heretic and infidel — from Catholic and dynastic loyalties. These loyalties, like the rural economy on which the Habsburg state was traditionally based, were essentially medieval in character. Since the two decisive intellectual movements of modern Europe — the Reformation and the Enlightenment — had left the Habsburg Empire intact, a multinational state based on anachronistic principles survived into a century which was fundamentally hostile to them. The more enlightened reforms of Joseph II were largely undone after his death, and the conservative reaction after 1815 and again after 1848 left Austria unprepared for the dynamic political pressures of the late nineteenth century. Economic and social changes which in Britain had been spread over three centuries were in Austria crammed into a period of forty years. As a result the movement from a medieval to a modern society took the form not of a gradual transition, but of a head-on collision between the old order and the new. The process of modernization, far from strengthening the state (as in the German Reich), accelerated the tendency towards disintegration, as each national group asserted its own identity.

In 1848 the system of political absolutism perfected by Metternich had come into violent collision with the emerging ideology of liberal democracy. This conflict, fought out with much bloodshed on the streets of Vienna, was resolved not by compromise but by brute force. The city surrendered to the army of Windischgrätz, and among those executed was the delegate from the Frankfurt parliament, Robert Blum. The same methods were used to suppress the Italian, Czech and Magyar separatist movements which threatened the unity of the Empire. The subsequent compromises of Dualism (the granting of self-government to the Hungarian-dominated part of the Empire) and of a more liberal constitution in 1867 left these conflicts unresolved. The nationalities problem continued to exert a disruptive influence at every level of Habsburg society.

An equally bitter trial of strength, which cut across the lines of nationality, was meanwhile taking place between liberalism and clericalism. Attitudes became increasingly intolerant as the religious fervour of liberal leading articles was answered by political slogans from the pulpits. As the ideals of liberalism passed into the hands of a predominantly Jewish bourgeoisie, clericalism was joined by economic jealousy and antisemitic prejudice in a militant Christian Social alliance. The triumph of this Christian Social Party in Vienna under the leadership of Karl Lueger was one of the most disturbing features of Vienna in 1900.[15] The situation was further disrupted by the rise of a Pan-German movement both antisemitic and anti-Catholic in inspiration, whose chauvinistic leader Georg von Schönerer competed with Lueger in popular demagogy and so obstructed the proceedings of the Reichsrat that he had to be removed by force. The Social Democratic movement too was distorted by contradictions between 'class' and 'national' loyalties, which contrasted grotesquely with its internationalist ideology. And it had to contend with a dyed-in-the-wool peasantry who would have been the last to believe that their interests could be served by Marxist intellectuals in Vienna.

At every point this ideological confusion was compounded by a Jewish diaspora far more significant than in other European countries. Traditionally, the Jewish population had been confined to the remoter provinces, especially Galicia and Bukovina. But successive waves of migration resulted in a concentration of the Jewish population in the capital cities, approaching 10 per cent of the population in Vienna (and almost one quarter in Budapest).[16] Their predisposition to cultural pursuits, reflected in the exceptionally high figures for Jewish enrolment in academic education, certainly contributed to the creative ferment.[17] And in banking, commerce and journalism they acquired an influence out of proportion to their numbers. Like other migrants, the majority of Jews were anxious to assimilate with the metropolitan culture of the capital. But the situation had by 1900 become so unstable that the continuing influx of Jewish settlers only served to exacerbate it. The Jewish community itself was riven by faction. Westernized Jews felt alienated by the beards and kaftans of recent arrivals from the eastern provinces. Assimilationists were affronted by the increasingly strident propaganda for Zionism. Kraus's pamphlet *Eine Krone für Zion* (1898) reflects the dismay with which he — like others bent on assimilation — reacted to the Zionist programme (*FS* II. 298–314). The Jewish population of Vienna experienced the crisis of Austrian identity in its most acute form. Indeed Kraus's self-definition as satirist, to be analysed in Part Three, must be seen as a response to this dilemma. Like other leading Jewish intellectuals, he sought personal salvation by converting to Catholicism. But he was to find that the society in which he lived denied all possibility of stable affiliation.

The paradox of the Austrian situation was that despite apparent concessions (such as the introduction of universal male suffrage in 1907), effective control of the increasingly centrifugal state remained in the hands of the traditional ruling class. The government of the Empire was conducted by an army of professional bureaucrats, principal among them the Emperor himself, and by an equally unrepresentative group of rather less professional politicians. Since parliament was paralysed by the conflict of nationalities, successive administrations had no more substantial basis for their authority than the favour of the Emperor (and the backing of a venal press) and could offer no more sophisticated political method than government by imperial decree. The suicide of Crown Prince Rudolf in 1889 had removed the one Habsburg prince committed to a programme of reform. And a heavy shadow was cast over affairs of state by the enigmatic personality of the heir apparent, Archduke Franz Ferdinand, whose policies upon accession promised to be authoritarian and reactionary.

If ever a political system succumbed to its own inner contradictions, it was the Austro-Hungarian Empire in 1918. It is true that there were also strong forces working for cohesion — not merely the bonds of dynastic loyalty, but also more practical factors like mobility of population between the provinces and urban centres, the expanding network of communications, the increasing commercial interdependence of different parts of the Empire. The ethnic minorities on the periphery were in some cases more loyal to the Empire than the Germans at the centre, whose envious gaze was drawn towards Bismarck's Reich. Some commentators even believed that by 1910 the threat to the unity of the Empire had been dispelled and that 'great security' and a 'mighty new strength' could be predicted for Austria-Hungary in the future.[18] But in Wickham Steed's study of 1913 sufficient evidence is assembled to justify far more 'catastrophic hypotheses'. It was with a sense of impending disaster that he left Vienna in July 1913, after a decade as correspondent of *The Times*.[19]

The Austrian conflict of ideologies found most concentrated expression in Vienna itself. To speak of a 'loss of centre' in the Habsburg capital itself may seem paradoxical. The historical developments of the late nineteenth century brought Vienna unprecedented prosperity. The final decades before 1914 are regarded as Vienna's Golden Age — an age of commercial prosperity and imperial splendour, but also of outstanding social and cultural achievement. Stefan Zweig has suggested that the population of the city, for all its heterogeneity, formed a harmoniously integrated city culture. The different social, economic and ethnic groups, hierarchically distributed in circles radiating out from the Hofburg, found their sense of unity in the public festivals and the rich cultural life of the city. And the tensions and conflicts latent in this situation were (he maintains) fused into a flexible and conciliant harmony through the unifying consciousness of being Viennese.[20] Certainly, the cult of 'being Viennese', which dates well back into the eighteenth century, reached a climax in Vienna around 1900. It flourished at all social and cultural levels, creating a local mythology immortalized by entrancing popular melodies. And a strong sense of historical continuity found visible embodiment in an Emperor who had been on the throne since 1848. As regular as clockwork the Emperor's carriage would drive through the streets of Vienna. And every summer for sixty years the unalterable rhythm of the seasons would carry him on his summer vacation to Bad Ischl (where Kraus's family, like other members of the Viennese bourgeoisie, had a holiday villa). There can be no doubt that the predominant Viennese self-image around 1900 was one of security and ease.

It is easy for the historian, wise after the event, to show how foolish the Viennese were before it. A more legitimate procedure is to reconstruct the Viennese situation in terms of events and documents that were public property at the time. It might seem an offence against decorum to suggest that the question of what 'being Viennese' really meant can be answered by statistics. But the fact remains that during the decade ending in 1890 the population of Vienna virtually doubled, rising (as the city boundaries were extended) from 705,000 in 1880 to 1,340,000 ten years later. By 1910 that population had passed the 2,000,000 mark.[21] The coherent community of the Metternich period may perhaps have survived the revolution of 1848 and even the levelling of the old city ramparts in the 1860s; but the subsequent increase in the city's population created a radically new situation.

As a result of a rapid influx of settlers (many of them not German-speaking), less than half of the city's population was now Viennese by birth; and a new sense of working-class militancy began to disrupt social cohesion. Two Viennas now existed side by side, at times in open confrontation. The luxurious new apartments of the Ringstrasse constituted a different world from the miserable tenements, with their multiple-family occupancy, of the working-class suburbs. A large proportion of the population lived in destitution and was condemned to a lifetime of sweated labour. Social Democrats like Victor Adler had turned the spotlight on these problems. Some of Lueger's municipal reforms were designed to alleviate them. And the investigations of Emil Kläger (1908), supported by stark documentary photographs, had exposed this substratum of urban destitution to public scrutiny.[22]

The unified city culture was essentially a myth, concocted by writers encapsulated in their coffee-houses. The reality of working-class experience hardly impinged on their pages, although it is clearly enough recorded in the memoirs of less privileged contemporaries.[23] Kraus, like other members of the intellectual élite, had no contact with the cultural aspirations of the working class, until he swung his support behind the socialist cause after the collapse of the Empire. But the strength of the Social Democratic movement was nevertheless unmistakable. On 1 May 1890 the burghers and shopkeepers of Vienna retired behind their shutters while the first great procession of workers, part of an internationally organized demonstration for shorter working hours, marched through the streets of the city. This show of strength was repeated in even more impressive form in November 1905 at the time of the agitation for universal manhood suffrage. A rift had become apparent in the life of the city which the purveyors of local mythology, still dreaming of the Vienna of Schubert, Beethoven and Grillparzer, were reluctant to acknowledge. Sentimental authors like Felix Salten were still cultivating the traditional myths.[24] But at the general elections of 1907 the Social Democrats captured almost a quarter of the national vote. Only the fact that they too were divided into ethnic factions, with the Czechs at loggerheads with the Germans, prevented them from becoming an effective parliamentary force.[25]

Caught between the political militancy of the working class and the commercial power of the bourgeoisie was a third social group which rendered the situation even more unstable. Small businessmen, shopkeepers and traders constituted in Vienna a particularly numerous class. As a result of the late onset of industrialization in Austria, enterprises employing less than five workers were still a preponderant feature of the city's commercial life. And these small traders vigorously asserted their political identity under the charismatic leadership of Karl Lueger. Campaigning under the slogan 'The small man must be helped!', Lueger's Christian Social Party in 1897 gained control of the Vienna City Council from the Liberals (under a system of limited franchise that effectively excluded the Social Democrats). But for all the impressive municipal works completed in Vienna under Lueger's regime, it can hardly be said that his party was the expression of positive aspirations. Rather, it was a compound of negative attitudes – of the fears and insecurities of the lower middle classes. Lueger appealed to the hostility among these groups to large-scale capitalist enterprises. Given the prominence of Jewish entrepreneurs in Viennese commerce, banking and the stock exchange, this hostility assumed a crudely antisemitic form, which Lueger did not scruple to exploit. A fierce resentment against the supposedly unpatriotic and irreligious Social Democrats constituted a further negative pole of Christian Social ideology. It was the void created between the working class of the suburbs and the capitalists of the inner city that Lueger exploited with such demagogic flair. And his success foreshadowed a more sinister future, for it was the Vienna of Karl Lueger that provided Adolf Hitler with his political education.

The first part of *Mein Kampf* contains a perceptive account of Lueger's popular success – his mobilization of the lower middle classes, his exploitation of antisemitic prejudice, his skill in gaining the support of the Catholic Church, his demagogic appeal to the common man. In Vienna Hitler found his political horizon already essentially complete, particularly since he was able also to imbibe the fanatical ideology of Schönerer. Virulent antisemitism (partly as a cover for anticapitalism), fierce hostility to 'Jewish' socialism and Marxism, and the Pan-German commitment to a crusade against the Slavs – these forces that were to sweep the National Socialists to power in Germany in the 1930s had all erupted in Vienna thirty years earlier. The tactic of boycotting Jewish shops did not originate in Berlin around 1930 but can be found in Vienna around 1910. In the Habsburg capital (and in the provinces which sent their deputies to parliament), the struggle to maintain German hegemony over the Slavs already dominated the political scene. And it was perhaps only in Vienna, where the leadership of the Social Democratic Party was in the hands of Jewish intellectuals like Victor Adler, Otto Bauer and Friedrich Austerlitz, that Hitler could so easily have reached his conclusion that socialism represented a conspiracy of the Jews against the German people. Even Hitler's cult of racial purity found in Vienna its theoretical antecedents (in the publications of Lanz von Liebenfels, editor of *Ostara*); and vivid passages in *Mein Kampf* record Hitler's hysterical reaction to the degree of racial assimilation and intermarriage in Vienna, which led him to the conclusion that the purity of the German race was being defiled. For the fanatical visionary of a new Germanic world order, no other city of Europe could have offered so portentous a political initiation.[26]

Kraus too was a reader of portents. And it will by now be clear that the situation in Vienna before the First World War offered him material for a prophetic style of satire pregnant with wider implications. Reviewing the conflict of nationalities in May 1899, Kraus concluded that the problems of Austria-Hungary were not soluble by conventional political means. Dynastic loyalty and the law of inertia might help the Empire to withstand the storms, but a definitive remedy would require the dissolution of the state (*F* 6: 13–16). The First World War was tragically to confirm his image

of Austria-Hungary as an 'experimental station for the end of the
world'. But even after the ravages of 1914–18 Kraus's prophecy was
not fulfilled. It was only in the 1930s, when Hitler began to put into
force the political lessons he had learnt in Vienna before 1914, that
the full significance of that prediction became clear.

Kraus's satire is the expression of a civilization inwardly disintegrating. It reflects the incipient anomie which Durkheim detected
in societies which offer no stable social attachments. Durkheim too
sees the ethnic diversity of Austria as constituting 'a complete
laboratory' for the investigation of sociological problems. He
emphasizes the high suicide rate in Vienna at the turn of the century,
which in his theory of 'anomic suicide' is related to the loss of social
equilibrium. The suicide rate in the Austrian army was exceptionally
high, reflecting the insufferable contradictions between a rigid
military system and disintegrating social norms.[27] The suicide in
1913 of Colonel Alfred Redl, a homosexual member of the Austrian
Secret Service who was exposed as a Russian spy, revealed a conflict
of loyalties which had become insoluble. But there were equally
spectacular suicides among the intellectual élite, most notably that of
Otto Weininger. In short, the Austrian crisis of identity imposed
intolerable stresses on members of minority groups. It is hardly
surprising that in Kraus's writings (as we shall see) suicide becomes a
recurrent symbolic motif.

Ideologies and Façades

The stability of traditional loyalties was undermined in Vienna by a
profusion of disruptive ideologies. Even full-scale studies of these
ideological currents do not exhaust their complexity.[28] For they
leave out of account the more ephemeral cults and crazes, such as
Robert Musil recalls in the early chapters of *Der Mann ohne
Eigenschaften*. And this ideological ferment created increasing
instability as it spread to potentially dissident groups in the provinces. Sacher-Masoch and Weininger were debated in the intellectual
coffee-houses of Trieste. Ibsen, Strindberg and Kropotkin had their
adherents in the depths of Bosnia. It was these heady ideas, blended
with resurgent national pride, which inspired the secret societies of
'Young Bosnia' and led Gavrilo Princip in June 1914 to fire the pistol
shot which precipitated the collapse of the Empire.[29]

This disintegration on the horizontal plane was compounded by an
even more serious vertical disjunction – the contradiction between
the given social structure and the forms of consciousness in which it
was apprehended. Late-nineteenth-century Austria saw an
unprecedented acceleration in the growth of population and the
spread of industry. The development of the railway system, from

3,000 kilometres of track in 1860 to well over 20,000 in 1910, was the most spectacular measure of industrial enterprise.[30] But the effort to modernize social institutions and attitudes lagged far behind, hampered by obstruction in parliament and by anachronistic attitudes in public administration. Hermann Bahr put the matter very neatly when he observed that laws passed in 1900 were being administered by officials with a mentality of the year 1750. Adolf Loos, an even more acute critic of these retarding tendencies, noted that while he was living in the year 1908 his neighbour was living in 1880, while there were peasants in the Austrian provinces still living in the twelfth century.[31] This discrepancy became spectacularly evident during the Imperial Jubilee of 1908, which brought to Vienna the representatives of remote and quasi-feudal communities who paraded through the streets in their traditional folk costumes. There could hardly have been a greater contrast to the aspirations of the cultural avant-garde, displayed at the Kunstschau exhibition of that same year.

There were two factors – the army and the dynasty – which appeared to guarantee the cohesion of the Empire. But neither could escape the pervasive historical contradictions. A unified army command embraced all the nationalities of the Empire, and a system of compulsory military service supposedly instilled the principles of loyalty. But in practice the army was ethnically so diverse and so underfunded that it was more of a ceremonial institution than a modern war-fighting machine.[32] Moreover loyalty to the dynasty had to be accommodated to such a wide variety of national, factional and class interests that there was a disturbing lack of correlation between the theory of the Austrian state and its practice. And reciprocally we find institutions that were nominally independent, like parliament, the judiciary and the press, tending to subordinate the imperatives of justice, good government and factual reporting to the supposed interest of the dynasty. Wickham Steed, whose ten years as correspondent in Vienna give his book a unique value, observes that 'on paper, most things in Austria-Hungary are regulated by ordinance or by law. [. . .] But, in practice, few institutions discharge precisely the functions theoretically assigned to them.' And he concludes that 'the problem of Vienna as, indeed, the problem of Austria and the Monarchy is how to adjust appearances to reality and to bring more sincerity into life.' The essential error of Austrian policy lay in the unavailing attempt to adjust reality to appearances.[33] Perhaps only the Social Democrats grasped that the situation required radical remedies. But they too had grasped this only in theory. In practice their leaders were becoming part of the Austrian establishment, and tended to sneer at radicals like Lev

Bronstein who were plotting revolution at another table in the Café Central. Bronstein, a refugee from Tsarist Russia who wrote under a pseudonym for a variety of obscure journals, was also not quite what he seemed. For as Leon Trotsky he was to emerge in 1917 as the organizational genius of the Russian Revolution.[34]

The discrepancy between traditional allegiances and the requirements of modern society became particularly apparent in the contradictions between Austrian civil and canon law. Liberal reforms had been introduced to facilitate divorce; but under canon law it remained a heinous offence. A Catholic who wished to marry a divorced person in a civil ceremony was compelled to leave the Church. This not only caused great personal anguish but left fundamental problems unresolved. For liberalism and clericalism were not simply matters of personal belief. They were all-embracing ideological systems, each of which sought to impose itself upon the state. Inspired by the papal encyclical *Rerum Novarum*, the Christian Social movement acquired a dynamic political momentum. And the Catholic Church exerted a powerful attraction on those who longed for a consolidation of traditional values – like Kraus himself during the final years before the First World War. But the subordination of pastoral to political imperatives led to what has been called the 'tragedy of Austrian Catholicism'.[35] The battle between clericalism and liberalism was fought with particular bitterness in the spheres of science and education. It is memorably dramatized in Schnitzler's *Professor Bernhardi* (1912), the play in which a Jewish doctor, concerned to protect a patient from the knowledge that he is about to die, prevents a Catholic priest from administering the last sacrament.

The case of Liberalism is more complex. At its inception it had been a modernizing movement. The Liberal ministries of the 1860s and '70s, together with the Liberal city administrations of Vienna, could claim important reforms, notably the education act of 1869. And through important legal and constitutional reforms they had begun to redefine Austria as a modern secular state. But these reforms had only shallow roots. The full legal emancipation of the Jews was not achieved until 1867. All too soon it was threatened by the resurgence of antisemitism which accompanied the stock exchange scandals of 1873. By 1900 the Liberals had lost power not only in the Austrian parliament but also in Vienna itself; and a growing discrepancy had become evident between the Liberal world-view and the world which it purported to describe. The Liberal ideals of freedom, progress and equality had increasingly become a façade for the property interests of capitalist entrepreneurs. Liberalism also provided ideological camouflage for the extension of German political and economic influence into the Slav areas of

central Europe. There can be no doubt as to the powerful hold
exerted by this Liberal scheme of ideas over the minds of the
educated Austrian middle class. It found its vehicle in technically
advanced and immensely influential newspapers, of which the *Neue
Freie Presse* was the most prominent. And it was the inspiration for
that passionate cultivation of music, literature and the arts which
flourished not merely in Vienna itself but extended its tendrils into
the theatres and coffee-houses of remote garrison towns. For Jews
emerging from the ghettos of the provinces, Liberalism was the
radiant new creed which drew them irresistibly towards Vienna:
Bruno Bettelheim has described how his grandfather walked bare-
foot to the capital to seek his fortune.[36] Kraus's own father seems to
have been a stout believer in the Liberal virtues of self-improvement
sustained by financial probity.[37] But as Austrian Liberalism became
increasingly divorced from political power, it lost its pragmatic
vigour and degenerated into a set of slogans.

The rift between the façade of Austrian life and its inner reality
expressed itself in every sphere of public activity. The streets of
Vienna, which yielded such rich material for Kraus's satire, offered a
daily enactment of this theme. Distinctions of dress have reality
enough in a stable society. But in a world of rapid economic change
the elaborate clothes sported by the upper classes were the costumes
of a public masquerade. The uniforms of army officers had an
aristocratic panache. They were designed to divert attention from the
fact that military pay was appallingly low and that army officers
were finding it necessary to marry the daughters of bourgeois
businessmen whom they despised, in order to secure their dowries.
The colourful artifice in civilian dress as well concealed an
underlying instability. These were clothes designed with a minimal
respect for natural contours and a maximal concern for keeping up
appearances: high starched collars and top hats for gentlemen,
whalebone corsets and improbable bustles for the ladies,
anachronistic dress swords for army officers. This resplendent
sartorial façade was echoed on a more monumental scale by the
architecture of the city itself. The front of a Venetian palace adorned
the premises of a bank, the Stock Exchange was built in Renaissance
style, the City Hall in ponderous neo-Gothic. The commercial
bourgeoisie of late-nineteenth-century Vienna established itself
behind aesthetic façades borrowed from pre-industrial eras.

In a polemical essay first published in 1898, the architect Adolf
Loos described Vienna as a Potemkin's City of artificial façades, as
remote from reality as the pasteboard villages said to have been
constructed by Potemkin to simulate prosperity in a desolate area of
Russia.[38] Until Otto Wagner's Post Office Savings Bank (1904–6)

and the department store designed by Loos himself for a prominent site on the Michaelerplatz (1908), the façades of Imperial Vienna were moulded and embellished according to the principle that opulent appearance was more important than functional design. The applications of this principle can be studied in the Burgtheater (1888). Its design was reputedly technically rather advanced, since electric lights were used to illuminate the stage. But in its ground-plan the auditorium was shaped like a lyre, with the stage at the top. The resulting design looks very elegant on paper and no doubt helped Semper and Hasenauer to win the competition. In practice it meant that some of the boxes were so positioned that they actually faced *away* from the stage. The wealthy families who subscribed to these boxes were evidently less interested in drama than in self-display.[39] The grandeur of the Burgtheater, like that of the Ringstrasse as a whole, expressed the triumph of façade over function.[40]

The buildings of the Ringstrasse were designed to harmonize with a life centred on ceremonial. The Ring itself provided a magnificent setting for military cavalcades, and its junction with the Kärntnerstrasse was the scene of the daily Corso – the leisurely parade of members of Viennese society who wished to see and be seen. The painting of this social parade by Theodor Zasche (Pl. 2) includes Gustav Mahler (foreground, third from right). But many of the figures portrayed are pretentious nonentities, like Angelo Eisner von Eisenhof, frequent butt of Kraus's satire (foreground, fifth from right, with his back to the viewer).

A casual observer of such occasions had the impression of a city untouched by the coarser realities of life, devoted to carnivals, flower festivals and masked balls. It was a city centred partly on the Court, partly on the theatre. Indeed the theatre became the focal point for a redefinition of social experience. The theatricality of public life was noted by many contemporary observers and forms one of the leitmotifs of Kraus's satire. In the theatre the Viennese were not merely transported into an aesthetic realm. They also found there models for a style of life, dress and manners to be cultivated in their social relationships.

The Theatre as a Social Paradigm

It may sound implausible to ascribe to the Viennese theatre this exemplary function. But this is fundamental to the history of the German theatre, whose revival in the late eighteenth century was inspired by an Enlightenment concern with education. In Vienna, where the Burgtheater had been reconstituted by Joseph II in 1776 as a national theatre, these aims assumed a special importance. The ideal (as a late-eighteenth-century writer put it) was that the theatre should

2 The Social Parade on the Ringstrasse by Theodor Zasche

become 'a school of good conduct and morals'. This intention is repeatedly restated in official policy documents of the nineteenth century, though the emphasis may vary from the refinement of taste to a more pragmatic concern with keeping discontented citizens off the streets.[41]

The actors of the Burgtheater came to be regarded as exemplars of a certain life-style. This style was modelled on the aristocratic salons to which many of the actors had access and into which a surprising number of them actually married. As members of what was technically still a court theatre they enjoyed considerable social status. They were annually received in audience by the Emperor (who indeed chose an actress, Katharina Schratt, as his own companion). An outstanding actor like Sonnenthal, whom Kraus greatly admired, exemplified the aspirations of a whole era. From humble origins as a Jewish tailor's apprentice in Budapest, Adolf von Sonnenthal rose to become the outstanding actor of the Burgtheater, where he made an exceptional impact from 1889 onwards in the role of King Lear (Pl. 3). He appeared on the stage of the Burgtheater every year without exception from 1856 to 1908, was ennobled towards the end of his career, and received such adulation that he might almost have been a real king, rather than the impersonator of Shakespearean monarchs.[42]

The elevated status of the actors was enhanced by the idealized mode of performance which predominated in Burgtheater productions of the nineteenth century. It seems to have served as a model of social decorum for a bourgeois audience with aspirations to be accepted in polite society. In a discussion of the Burgtheater of the 1880s Zerline Gabillon, Sonnenthal and Ernst Hartmann are cited as actors whose clothing and behaviour were particularly admired and imitated. A decade later it was Josef Kainz whose diction was echoed in the discourse of barristers and other public speakers.[43] Kainz too became a cult figure, photographed in elegant evening dress in widely circulated picture postcards of the Burgtheater (Pl. 4). An even more vivid account of the Burgtheater's influence is given by Stefan Zweig, who concludes: 'The stage, instead of being merely a place of entertainment, was a spoken and plastic guide of good behaviour and correct pronunciation.'[44] That influence also extended far into the provinces. Elias Canetti records that for his parents, living in a small town in Bulgaria, the experience of its productions was so memorable that they spoke together a 'secret language' based on the diction of the Burgtheater.[45]

At a more popular level it was the actor Alexander Girardi whose gestures and inflections were imitated outside the theatre. Kraus was a great admirer of Girardi also, and saw his death in 1918 as symbolic

3 Adolf von Sonnenthal as King Lear

5 Alexander Girardi as Valentin in *Der Verschwender*

4 Josef Kainz and the Burgtheater

of the passing of an era (*F* 474–83: 120–2). But it is Felix Salten who
explores the social implications of the Girardi cult: 'People have
learnt from him in the theatre how to be Viennese, and have
subsequently copied him [. . .]. Ultimately every second person
one met on the street was a Girardi-role: every cab-driver, every
postman, every petit bourgeois.'[46] This analysis is confirmed by
Hermann Bahr, who notes that if a young man in Vienna wants to
please a girl, he models his approach on Girardi, speaks with a
Girardi drawl, walks with a Girardi swagger. The Viennese, Bahr
concludes in another context, is an actor playing out carefully studied
roles. 'The theatre is not a representation of life. Life is an imitation
of the theatre.'[47] With due allowance made for the Wildean
undertones of this paradox, Bahr provides a plausible explanation for
Girardi's popularity. It is significant that the actor was actually a
native of Graz, and that the roles he played with such conviction
were those of a Viennese of the old style, of the pre-industrial period.
As the faithful servant Valentin in Raimund's *Der Verschwender* (Pl.
5), Girardi remained one of Kraus's treasured memories until his
dying day (*F* 917–22: 42). Amid the anomie induced by the impact of
new forces upon a conservative society, the actor seems to have
provided a reassuringly stable model of Viennese identity. But as a
means of coming to terms with a changing world the Girardi cult
had regressive implications.[48]

So pervasive was the Viennese sense of cultivated artifice that the
theme of 'play-acting' becomes a recurrent literary motif. The early
poetry of Hofmannsthal, particularly his Prologue to Schnitzler's
Anatol, reflects the artificial life-style of a select minority of aesthetes.
And later he was to revive the traditional conception of *theatrum
mundi*. But Hofmannsthal, as Hermann Broch has shown in his
pioneering account of the 'vacuum' of Viennese culture, lacked the
rigour to turn the play-acting motif into a penetrating critical
theme.[49] Indeed Hofmannsthal became one of the primary
purveyors of the Viennese myth. His text for Strauss's opera *Der
Rosenkavalier*, first performed in January 1911, celebrates a timeless
Vienna of amorous intrigues and disguises. But Hofmannsthal
shrinks from expressing in public that awareness of the disintegration of Austria-Hungary that is evident in his private letters.[50] It
is Schnitzler who explores more critically the Austrian masquerade,
showing that it extends through the whole social hierarchy. And the
motif finds definitive expression in the satire of Kraus and Musil.

The image of the world as a stage is an age-old literary topos. But
in German and Austrian writing from Nietzsche onwards this motif
becomes exceptionally prominent. The generation of authors who
came to maturity around 1900 was acutely aware of the discrepancy

between official ideology and inner identity, between private self and
public role. In Imperial Germany (as the historian Fritz Stern argues)
hypocrisy had become a 'governing system' – a system of 'villainous
dissembling'.[51] In Austria-Hungary the need for systematic
'dissembling' was even more acute, though perhaps less villainous.
For the strategy of dissembling had a practical purpose,
corresponding to unresolved tensions in the social and political
fabric. The forgeries concocted by the Austrian Foreign Office,
which came to light in the Friedjung case of 1909 (to be analysed in a
later chapter), were certainly despicable. But the archaic paradigm of
dynastic centralism excluded the possibility of plain dealing with the
South Slavs and made such subterfuges seem necessary. Only a
complete change of paradigm, the abandonment of the attempt to
maintain German and Magyar hegemony over the other nationalities
of the Empire, could have eliminated such practices. But when such
a change was attempted, through Badeni's proposals to make
concessions to the Czechs in 1897, it was frustrated by the
ungovernable violence of the Germans themselves.[52]

Structural dissembling was evident at every level. In the German
Reich the discrepancies were perhaps more dramatic: the public
pomp of Bismarck's German Empire, and the covert operations of
the Jewish financier Gerson Bleichröder who provided funds for the
ruling élite; the histrionic proclamations of Wilhelm II in favour of
peace, and the secret councils at which he and his advisers resolved
upon the need for war.[53] In Germany the inner instability was
concealed by a brash ostentation, in Austria by a 'nervous splendour'.[54] But at almost any point in Habsburg society, even in the
intimate sphere of sexual mœurs, there was a discrepancy between
theory and practice. In theory sexual intercourse with a girl under the
age of consent was punishable by twenty years' hard labour; in
practice child prostitution seems to have been widespread. In theory
homosexuality was a crime; in practice it flourished, not least in
all-male institutions like the army, though it was fear of exposure
that led Colonel Redl to betray Austrian military secrets to the
Russians. In theory (under the civil code) duelling was a criminal
offence. In practice (under the military code of honour) it was an
inescapable obligation for an officer who had been insulted. If he
fought and died in a duel, his widow received a state pension. But if
he obeyed the law and refused to fight, he was hounded out of his
regiment.[55] Small wonder that in the literature of Habsburg Austria
the duel became such a crucial subject. It was the point at which
military and civil ideologies collided head-on.

In this historical situation the satirical method could hardly fail.
Ideological contradictions created states of mind that were self-

evidently absurd, as Schnitzler shows in *Leutnant Gustl* (1901), his portrait of an officer contemplating a duel. In trivial details it was possible to detect symptoms of a fundamental disorder. Politics, displaced from parliament itself by the tactics of obstruction, over-flowed into other channels of communication and created a kind of ideological saturation. Schnitzler records that before one joined a cycling club, one had first to ascertain whether it was a Progressive, Christian Social, German Nationalist or antisemitic organisation.[56] Kraus notes in the very first number of *Die Fackel* that political discussion has taken refuge from parliament in the courts of law (*F* 1: 11). The ideological saturation of everyday life meant that it was possible to diagnose the Austrian malady in the proceedings of the provincial court. Hence the obliqueness of Kraus's style of satire, which debates the fundamental issues of his age in displaced forms. The spheres of activity on which this book focuses – journalism, the theatre, prostitution and the enforcement of morals, theories of the unconscious, architectural design, advertising, technology, the problems of language, and the role of the artist – are only apparently 'unpolitical'. Each of these spheres contributed to the masquerade of Austrian public life, which reached its climax during the First World War in the 'Tragic Carnival'.

Eros in Vienna

The principle of displacement finds its most profound expression in the debate about sexuality. In turn-of-the-century Vienna sexuality became the 'symbolic territory' where the fundamental issues of the age were debated: the crisis of individual identity, the conflicts between reason and irrationalism, between domination and subservience.[57] Given the leading role which Jewish writers played in this debate, the problem of sexual adjustment became inextricably entangled in the counter-current of antisemitism (as the tragic example of Weininger shows). The great realistic novel of Vienna, Schnitzler's *Der Weg ins Freie*, does not deal with social problems of the kind portrayed by Balzac, Dickens or Fontane. It portrays a pre-marital sexual relationship in an environment suffused with antisemitic prejudice. The contradictions of the Viennese situation, which created such political instability, also seem to have engendered the most disturbing psychological insights. Was it because sexual repression was so stifling among the Viennese middle classes that it provoked such critical insight? Or was it on the contrary because sexual libertinism was so freely displayed that the psychologist enjoyed an unprecedented wealth of material? 'Both of these asser-tions cannot be true at the same time,' one critic has insisted in an investigation of Freud's Viennese background.[58] But that is precisely

the point: they *were* both true at the same time. It was the
simultaneous existence of incompatible forces which made the
Vienna of 1900 such a uniquely fertile environment. A frock-coated
Victorian moralism coexisted with blatant erotic displays – by army
officers in full fig or women of the *demi-monde*. The most respectable
restaurants had *chambres séparées* to facilitate intercourse after dinner.
On its front page the *Neue Freie Presse* printed edifying articles about
the sanctity of family life. But the small advertisements on the back
page revealed that marriage was a financial transaction; and that
those who could not afford the bride-price could nevertheless find
consolation with 'Miss Birch, Box no. 69'. Rarely can institutionalized promiscuity have so blatantly coexisted with the
proprieties of bourgeois moralism and religious conformity. Such
discrepancies characterized the public life of Austria–Hungary in
every sphere.

The significance of the emblems which Kraus placed on the cover
of *Die Fackel* in April 1899 will by now be clear. The mask is the
all-pervasive symbol of fin-de-siècle Vienna. In Kraus's design the
grinning mask of comedy and the goatish face of the satyr not only
proclaim the intention of comic and satirical stylization. They also
convey an acute awareness of the elements of theatricality and
disguise in Austrian affairs. And the rays emanating from the flaming
torch are thrown forward in a pattern that suggests the boards of a
stage. The aim is clearly to break through the clouds of mystification
and shed light behind the scenes. But the configuration of images
leaves open the question of the role the editor himself will play in the
satirical masquerade.

CHAPTER 2

Journalism, Duplicity and the Art of Contrasts

The Critique of the Press: Early Aims and Models

For Kraus the primary source of mystification is the daily newspaper. During his lifetime the press gained a greater domination over public affairs than in any period before or since. Mass literacy, improved communications and advances in technology gave unprecedented power to the printed word. Techniques of printing had been revolutionized by the introduction of rotary presses and linotype composing machines. The railways, telephone, telegram and teleprinter were transforming communications. The collection of news was becoming systematized through news agencies and official press bureaus. Funds were available through the stock exchange for a vast expansion of journalistic operations. Mass circulations were achieved as a result of the increase in population and literacy. New techniques of journalistic presentation were introduced to gain the attention of this mass audience of semi-educated readers.[1]

The ownership of the press, however, was still in the hands of individual entrepreneurs, rather than the anonymous financial corporations of a later period. It was the era of the 'newspaper baron' — the owner-editor who had control both of share capital and of editorial policy.[2] Individual owners could exercise almost feudal power over an apparatus whose technological sophistication belonged to the modern age. Men like Hearst, Northcliffe and Hugenberg were able to pressurize democratic governments into adopting policies of their own choosing, even on questions of peace and war.[3] And they willingly colluded with regimes which shared their own imperialist outlook.[4] Their mass circulations gave them power without responsibility. Until the advent of radio and television they collectively held a monopoly over the distribution of news.

The newspaper press has a long and complex history. In the British press there is a vigorous tradition of independence from government influence. And even in the heyday of British imperialism this nonconformist tradition still survived, notably in the *Manchester Guardian* under the editorship of C. P. Scott.[5] But in Germany the press never attained that degree of critical independence. There was a proliferation of national, regional and factional newspapers, some of them (like the *Frankfurter Zeitung* and the *Berliner Tagblatt*) noted for their liberalism of outlook.[6] But during the final decades before the First World War the press department of the German Foreign Office exerted a continuous influence on the newspapers of the Reich, effectively frustrating the formation of an informed public opinion and systematically building up support for a future war. Only the minority press of the German Social Democratic Party offered sustained opposition to militaristic policies that were carrying Germany to the brink of disaster.[7] In Austria-Hungary, where government policies were no less fraught with danger, the function of the press was essentially similar. 'The history of the Austrian press', comments Wickham Steed, 'is largely the history of a struggle to widen the field of activity that lies between official inspiration and official confiscation.' Writing in 1913, after his ten-year study of Austrian affairs, he sees the Viennese newspapers as 'instruments working to manufacture public opinion, primarily in accordance with the wishes of the State authorities, and secondarily in the interests of financial and economic corporations'.[8] The deadlock in parliament led Austrian administrations to rely on the newspapers as an agency of government. This method was made possible by Article 14 of the constitution, which enabled the Emperor to govern by decree. The administration of Ernst von Koerber (1900–4) institutionalized this method of issuing decrees and having them 'debated' and 'ratified' not by parliament but by the press.[9] A contemporary political observer characterizes the effects of Koerber's press politics as 'totally demoralizing'.[10] This demoralization was all the worse for being reciprocal. If the press sacrificed its independence to the interests of the government, the government in its turn had to make concessions to the vested interests controlling the press. The net result of this collaboration was to subvert democratic government, falsify public opinion, and add a further dimension of unreality to Austrian life.

In foreign affairs the Austrian newspapers acted as a front for government policies. In the domestic sphere they provided a screen of an equally distorting kind. The freedom of speech proclaimed by the dominant German-language press did not extend beyond the economic, social and national interests which it represented. The

links between editorial offices and the great banks and finance
corporations were particularly close. The founder of *Die Presse*,
August Zang, is quoted as saying that his ideal would be 'a
newspaper that did not contain a single line that had not been paid
for'.[11] The device of printing advertisements disguised as news items
was accepted journalistic practice; subsequent attempts to legislate
against it were shamelessly circumvented. The role played by the
Viennese press in promoting dubious enterprises became
spectacularly evident at the time of the financial crash of 1873.
Reviewing the influence of the Austrian press during the final
decades of the nineteenth century, the cultural historian Hans Tietze
remarks not merely on the extent of the financial corruption, but
more particularly on the fact that this venality was taken for
granted.[12] The outstanding example was the *Neue Freie Presse*, the
bible of the economically dominant bourgeoisie. Through its
feuilleton section it exerted a powerful hold on the culture of Vienna.
Its supplement, the 'Economist', dictated the terms of financial life
throughout the Habsburg Empire. And politically, it was the most
influential newspaper in central Europe. 'The greater part of what
does duty for "Austrian opinion"', observes Wickham Steed, 'is
dictated or suggested to the public by the editor-proprietor of the
Neue Freie Presse.'[13]

The aspiring critic of this press found himself faced with a
dilemma. The dominant newspapers cried out for attack; but they
effectively muzzled criticism. Although the number of newspapers
published in Austria rose very rapidly during the late nineteenth
century, so that every ideological faction had its own journalistic
voice, there was no forum for the independent-minded critic.[14] The
official censorship continued to harry critical publications by
confiscation or by banning distribution through the state-licensed
news-stands. The internal censorship applied by the newspaper
proprietors themselves was equally stifling. And professional solidarity was maintained by the 'Austrian Association of Journalists and
Writers', which lived up to its name 'Concordia' by acting as a mute
on discordant voices. In the Austria of the 1890s there was no
tradition of independent critical journalism. The Liberal era, though
it lifted some of the restrictions on the press, proved hardly more
favourable to independent criticism than the repressive regime of
Metternich. The most outspoken critic of Austrian affairs before
1848, Charles Sealsfield, spent the greater part of his life in exile.
Grillparzer himself, frustrated by the censorship and by the intrusive
attentions of the police, withdrew into a kind of inner emigration
and vented his spleen over Austrian public affairs in the privacy of his
diaries. The flood of publications released by the revolutionary

events of 1848 was followed by a further decade of rigid censorship. In 1858 we find the social critic and dramatist Eduard von Bauernfeld complaining: 'If I'm not supposed to write as I feel, I'd rather not write at all.'[15]

The career of Ferdinand Kürnberger illustrates this dilemma. Born in 1821, Kürnberger became in 1848 an active partisan of the Vienna revolution. On 10 November 1848, the day after the execution of Robert Blum, he fled from Vienna into an exile that lasted for seven years. Even after his return to a more liberal Austria, his former membership of the Academic Legion made him a marked man. The chicaneries of the police obliged him as late as 1867 to spend ten days in prison for an infringement of passport regulations.[16] Even during the '70s Kürnberger still found himself in an isolated position, a resolute upholder of the values of 1848 in a situation overshadowed by the scandals of 1873. This was the period when he wrote his most memorable feuilletons, distinguished by a vigour of style that never softened into the more characteristic Viennese mode of resigned irony.

To readers who objected to the intrusion of politics into the aesthetic sanctuary of the feuilleton Kürnberger was ready to answer in their own terms: 'Am I writing about politics? [. . .] I am writing the theatre review of the Austrian tragedy.'[17] But his attack, though it may be oblique, never wavers in its aim. Two essays published in 1872 astringently exposed the methods of Austrian government officials who were conspiring to sell off tracts of the Vienna Woods for commercial development. These essays, together with the polemical articles of Kürnberger's friend Joseph Schöffel, succeeded in frustrating the deal and saving the Woods for posterity. In the face of the sell-out of Liberalism to capitalist speculators Kürnberger's language certainly does not lack directness. In an article about the consequences of the financial crash of 1873 he writes: 'Since the year 1872 there has established itself an *Austrian stock-exchange patriotism*, in which the whole nation seems to have been bribed and bought. [. . .] Whole swarms of educated people, who had previously stood upright, are now prostrating themselves and kissing the patriotic soil of the share index.' This article, like many of Kürnberger's most penetrating feuilletons, was published in a North German newspaper. For he was writing about a society intolerant of outspoken criticism. In January 1872 he acutely characterized this situation:

> The delicate and profound sense of Austrian criticism is thus 'as follows: Criticize in every affair some marginal aspect, not the affair itself; this itself must be cunningly avoided. Criticize further in such a way that you do not set yourself apart from those whom you criticize, do not claim to be of different fibre from them, do not in proud and self-imposed isolation make truth and bitter earnest of your crusade.[18]

The most deft exponent of this marginal style was Daniel Spitzer. The contrast between Kürnberger and Spitzer defines a polarity that runs through the work of Kraus himself — the tension between vigorous polemical commitment and self-absorbed verbal artistry. Kraus respected Kürnberger as the greatest 'political writer' that Austria ever possessed (F 214–15: 5), but Spitzer was for him a 'great satirist', comparable even to Nestroy (F 912–15: 4–6). Spitzer was not however a satirist who defied the dominant values of his day. He established himself in the Hofburg of Viennese journalism, the *Neue Freie Presse* itself, and was content to set out on his weekly strolls through Austrian public life from that solid but limiting base. In these *Wiener Spaziergänge* he shows himself to be a master of verbal artistry – of the ingenious pun, the ironic period, the delicate culminating point. But his writing lacks the imaginative energy to transcend its local occasions and never rises to the pitch of *saeva indignatio*.[19]

That Spitzer's weekly column in the *Neue Freie Presse* should have been offered to Kraus in 1898 (F 5: 10) was by no means as incongruous as it seems. The Kraus of the 1890s had closely followed Spitzer's path. His initial ambition had been to secure a position as theatre critic.[20] And in these early years we find him trying his hand at almost any kind of literary journalism, from theatre notices and book-reviewing to criticism of cultural trends. But it was as a satirical raconteur in the style of Daniel Spitzer that he showed greatest flair. He writes about the carnival season and describes the reception accorded to an esoteric new poem by Hofmannsthal. He ironizes the elegant clientele of Bad Ischl and mocks the municipal authorities for their incompetence in dealing with unexpected summer rains. He describes a craze for puns, a cookery exhibition, and the closing of a literary café. He records the public response to the death of a popular actor, to the appointment of a new director at the Burgtheater, and to the retirement of a singer whose carriage was drawn home by her admirers after a last performance. He elaborates the theme of the assaults on his privacy by the 'tip-receiving classes'. In all of this there is little sign of polemical individuality. Indeed his style is at times indistinguishable from that of Spitzer, his model.

In the first numbers of *Die Fackel* Kraus was to complain that he had been muzzled by cowardly editors. Even when writing for the supposedly independent journal *Die Wage*, he had spent the better part of his time pondering the things he was not permitted to say (F 5: 10). This complaint does less than justice to *Die Wage*, which under the editorship of Rudolph Lothar was a creditable publication, enlightened and even outspoken in tone (during its first year of publication approximately every second number was interfered with by the censor). It was not merely the various forms of censorship, it was the ironic manner of Spitzer that by the end of 1898 had become unbearably irksome to Kraus. He was increasingly aware that his new social-critical insights could not be expressed in the prescribed tone of 'professional jocularity' ('berufsmäßige Schalkhaftigkeit', *FS* II.113). Moreover he was beginning to realize that this style of writing was incommensurate with the political crisis building up within the Habsburg Monarchy. The violent scenes in the Austrian parliament in November 1897, at the time of Badeni's language decrees, vividly brought home to Kraus the parlous situation of the Monarchy. After witnessing the upheavals in parliament, Kraus notes that there is now no place for writers of feuilletonistic causeries ('Plauderfeuilletonisten', *FS* II.132). Events can no longer be accommodated within the framework of the feuilleton ('sprengen den Feuilletonrahmen', *FS* II.113). The victory of the antisemitic Christian Social Party in the elections of 1897 also revealed the dangerous drift of Austrian affairs. A speech by an antisemitic Councillor such as Gregorig was so self-evidently absurd that it put a hundred humorists out of a job! (*FS* II.166–7).

The violent political events of 1897–8 marked the end of twenty-five years of comparative stability. The assassination of the Empress Elisabeth by the anarchist Lucheni, the retrial of Dreyfus in Paris, and the launching of Theodor Herzl's Zionist movement were events full of portent. These were developments of a different magnitude from those that had preoccupied Daniel Spitzer in a period which Kraus, looking back, described as a 'paradise lost' (*F* 912–15: 9). For a writer not wholly serious in his criticisms of the feuilleton, the invitation to take over Spitzer's column would have been irresistible. But Kraus's attitude was becoming increasingly uncompromising. In 1897, through the satirical pen-portraits of *Die demolirte Literatur*, he had sharply distanced himself from that convivial coffee-house milieu. In 1898 he took the even more significant risk of alienating the feuilleton editor of the *Neue Freie Presse*, Theodor Herzl, by the pamphlet *Eine Krone für Zion*. When at the end of 1898 the offer of a position on the *Neue Freie Presse* finally came, Kraus proved unapproachable. For it was the corrupting influence of the press itself that he now wished to attack. He was indeed a critic of a 'different fibre'.

Critical Independence: The Strategy of Die Fackel

The founding of *Die Fackel* was inspired by the example of Maximilian Harden, editor of *Die Zukunft* in Berlin. Harden had shown that it was necessary to become owner and editor of a journal of one's own, if one wished to speak with an independent voice.

Kraus's father was able to guarantee the publication costs of the first number of *Die Fackel*, and its immediate success made the journal self-financing. The fact that Kraus, after his father's death in 1900, inherited a substantial private income, further guaranteed his independence. He was thus financially as well as ethically immune to the pressures which generated malpractices among his contemporaries. The high moral tone he adopted was made possible by his strong financial base. He never had to make the concessions to wealthy patrons that had inhibited the greatest satirist of the nineteenth century, Heinrich Heine.[21] He was in a position to defy society and adopt the motto of that great crusader for social justice, Ferdinand Lassalle: 'aussprechen, was ist' – 'declaring the facts' (*F* 2: 1).

Kraus's initial targets lay in the sphere most familiar to him – the journalistic cliques which dominated cultural life. But the field of his critical crusade rapidly widened. After the sensational success of his first numbers, he found himself being supplied with inside information about corrupt practices in almost every sector of Austrian public life. And *Die Fackel* became a forum for the expression of the accumulated dissatisfaction of informants previously denied the possibility of ventilating their grievances. It also attracted contributions from men distinguished in various fields of public life. The German Socialist leader Wilhelm Liebknecht and the veteran political crusader Joseph Schöffel were among early contributors. Others equally distinguished, such as the jurist Heinrich Lammasch and the Serbian political leader Milovan Milovanovic, sent in contributions to be published anonymously. And Kraus found himself in the position of champion of public morality, exposing corruption, inefficiency and petty tyranny in every field. The bureaucracy, the Church, the judiciary, the stock exchange, the banks, the political parties, the universities, the Ministry of Education, the army, the police, the Foreign Office, the railway companies, the theatres, and above all the press – all were revealed to the scandalized gaze of Kraus's readers as venal and incompetent. The healthy circulation of *Die Fackel* made him independent of the influence of advertisers, which stifled criticism elsewhere. *Die Fackel* was indeed outselling some of the leading daily newspapers. No wonder it found so many imitators – one of whom even tried to pirate Kraus's original cover design.[22]

For upwards of five years Kraus waged a running battle against corruption in public life. The 150 numbers of *Die Fackel* issued during this period constituted an exemplary achievement in the field of social-critical journalism. Kraus's intention is at this stage explicitly reformist. Despite the polemical vitality and wit that enliven his work, his aim is amendment, not entertainment. In an article on Austrian banking institutions Kraus emphasizes that his crusade is not being conducted for the entertainment of a scandal-hungry mob of idlers, but will increasingly win practical successes in the public interest (F 33: 22). In February 1901, dealing with the press and the problem of advertisements, he again insists that his aim is to promote amendment (F 66: 18). Eight months later we find him in a less optimistic mood, conceding that the number of practical successes that he has been able to achieve during the first two and a half years of publication of Die Fackel has been limited. But, undeterred, he declares that it is an ethical task to vex scoundrels, even if they cannot be reformed: 'Die Schurken, die nicht zu bessern sind, zu ärgern, ist auch ein ethischer Zweck' (F 82: 2). This may remind us of the programme of Jonathan Swift: 'to vex rogues, though it will not amend them'.[23] Both formulations reflect the difficulties inherent in any attempt to set the world to rights by means of the pen.

In retrospect it is clear that there was a quixotic element in Kraus's crusade right from the start. The ethical strength of his position lay in the complete independence of Die Fackel. But for a reformer this independence also meant isolation and ultimately ineffectiveness. Kraus's ethical absolutism led him to spurn alliances which might have enabled him to integrate his campaign into an effective movement for social reform. His ideal is that of 'a writer without preconceptions who observes things without party spectacles' ('das Ideal eines voraussetzungslosen, die Dinge ohne Parteibrille betrachtenden Schriftstellers', F 90: 17).

Kraus not only avoids ideological affiliation, but attacks it in all its manifestations: Liberalism and clericalism, Zionism and anti-semitism, Pan-Germans and Pan-Slavs, doctrinaire socialists and rapacious capitalists. This is not to deny that his writings betray certain underlying political sympathies. But a determined effort is made to subordinate these to the obligations of what he conceived as his 'public office' (F 147: 27). His mission as a satirist was to attack ideological thinking in all its forms, not merely those he happened personally to dislike. Thus the Social Democrats, with whom at this early stage he sympathized, were at times attacked as fiercely as the Liberals, against whom he felt a strong revulsion. The aim was to counteract partisan imbecility ('Parteiverblödung'), slogan-mania ('Schlagwörterwahn') and the befogging of the brain ('Benebelung der Gehirne') in whatever quarter they might originate (F 38: 25; 90: 17; 147: 23). But this set up a contradiction between Kraus's two main aims. His reformist campaign could only be implemented with political support. But his intransigence towards organized factions effectively precluded it.

This contradiction is exemplified by his relations with the Social Democrats. In the second number of *Die Fackel* he expresses great admiration for the Socialist leader Victor Adler and the editor of the *Arbeiter-Zeitung* Friedrich Austerlitz. And he prints in *Die Fackel* a number of articles by leading Socialists, including Wilhelm Liebknecht's commentaries on the Dreyfus Affair, attacks by Wilhelm Ellenbogen on the Southern Railway Company, and anonymous articles dealing with a weavers' strike in Brno. In Kraus's own essays of this period we also find outspoken attacks on the exploitation of industrial workers by ruthless capitalists. On one occasion, in May 1900, he suggests that those of his readers who intend to vote in the municipal elections should support the Social Democrats (*F* 41: 1–4). But even in this period of loose association with the socialists, he maintains a position of critical detachment. Indications of *embourgeoisement* in the party, and of an undercurrent of German nationalism, do not escape him. And the fact that the *Arbeiter-Zeitung*, to alleviate its financial difficulties, regularly accepted advertisements from capitalist enterprises seemed to him particularly suspect. In a series of articles he attacked this practice, arguing in particular that the appearance of the advertisements from the Danube Steamship Company had suspiciously coincided with the termination of a series of attacks on that company (*F* 47: 12–22; 49: 9–16). Victor Adler responded by denouncing Kraus for his insinuations, and the loose association between *Die Fackel* and the Social Democratic movement was soon dissolved.

A detailed analysis of Kraus's relationship with the Social Democrats, has suggested that there were failures on both sides. The party leadership was at fault in not responding to his criticisms in a more constructive spirit. Kraus for his part failed to grasp that socialism was not merely a movement of ethical inspiration but rested on a systematic analysis of the economic structure of capitalism.[24] It is certainly true that Kraus was not a systematic social analyst. But the view that he was ignorant of political theory arises from an over-literal reading of passages in which he casts himself in the role of *ingenu*. Kraus was familiar with the argument that an unjust 'social order' was to blame for the corrupt practices of banks, press and stock exchange (*F* 82: 1). But this did not square with his experience of Austrian affairs, where power seemed to lie in the hands of a relatively small number of corrupt individuals. Moreover Kraus had grasped the fundamental flaw in Marxist theory. His active interest in socialism coincided with a period of intense controversy among the theorists of the Second International. The reformism of Eduard Bernstein was being fiercely contested by defenders of revolutionary Marxism like Karl Kautsky and Rosa Luxemburg. But in this controversy one essential proposition went unchallenged, since it was shared (with varying emphasis) by all factions. This was the assertion that the ideological superstructure is determined by the economic base.[25]

Kraus attacks precisely this dogma in his commentary on the 1900 municipal elections. The problem is how to explain the electoral success of the Christian Socials and the failure of the Social Democrats to make the expected gains. Initially, he writes, the Christian Socials had appealed only to a particular economic stratum: the petty bourgeoisie, minor officials and civil servants, and schoolteachers with economic grievances. Now the party has extended its appeal to sections of the population not primarily interested in its economic programme:

> Das ist nichts Auffallendes: den Gläubigen des Marxismus, der im Sieg ideologischer Momente über wirtschaftliche Interessen eine Anomalie erblickt, mag eine Rundschau über die europäische Politik belehren, dass solche Ausnahme fast die Regel ist. (F 43: 4)

> (There's nothing remarkable about that. Adherents of the creed of Marxism, which regards the victory of ideological factors over economic interests as an anomaly, might learn from a survey of European politics that such exceptions are virtually the rule.)

Kraus does not ignore the Marxist theory of material determinants, he challenges it. And in so doing he shows a more realistic grasp of the historical situation than those socialists who believed that economic class interests would determine the pattern of Austrian politics.

One further alliance offered itself to Kraus during this early social-critical period. In October 1902 the weekly magazine of current affairs *Die Zeit*, edited by the Liberal journalists Heinrich Kanner and Isidor Singer, was reconstituted as a daily newspaper. The aims of this new venture were on the surface very similar to Kraus's own: to break the hold of the *Neue Freie Presse* over the educated public and to create a more truthful climate of opinion. Kanner and Singer sought to make their newspaper independent of financial control, free of government influence, and radical in its perspective on the social and political problems of the Monarchy. Although it never achieved a large circulation, *Die Zeit* did represent a significant attempt to raise the standards of journalistic integrity. Wickham Steed, a severe judge, concedes that *Die Zeit* 'approximated, at times, to what an independent organ of public opinion should be'; and a more recent historian has also singled out *Die Zeit* (along with the *Arbeiter-Zeitung*) as the only Austrian daily newspaper not at the disposal of the government.[26] *Die Zeit* was particularly noted for its independence on foreign policy. Almost alone among Viennese daily newspapers it advocated a conciliatory attitude towards Russia and Serbia, and resolutely opposed the alliance with Germany. No one who reads the leading articles which appeared in *Die Zeit* during July 1914 can fail to be impressed by their grasp of the political situation and their resolute opposition to any attempt to use the assassination of Franz Ferdinand as a pretext for war with Serbia. On 14 July *Die Zeit* warns that this policy can only lead to a great European war in which the Central Powers will be decisively defeated.

The launching of *Die Zeit* as a daily newspaper nevertheless elicited from Kraus a hostility verging on vindictiveness. His opposition was based on the conviction that in the given socio-economic situation a daily newspaper could only maintain itself by making concessions to the commercial interests of its supporters and advertisers. The programme of integrity proclaimed by *Die Zeit* was thus compromised from the start, Kraus held, by the inescapable conditions under which daily newspapers have to be produced. Its radicalism could at best be no more than a radicalism sustained by commercial cunning ('ein geschäftsschlauer Radicalismus', *F* 124: 6). In his critique of the press Kraus shows a firm grasp of historical determinants, recognizing that the press is an element of the capitalist world-order ('Element der capitalistischen Weltordnung', *F* 28: 6). It is not simply a question of the moral defects of individual editors. But his vendetta against *Die Zeit* in the period 1902–4 is unedifying. Kraus descends at times to the level of mocking the Jewishness of Isidor Singer's name and of his origins in Galicia. Anyone who tried to form a judgement of the merits of this newspaper on the evidence assembled in *Die Fackel* would be grievously misled. Even Kraus's verdict, after Kanner and Singer had found themselves obliged to sell their newspaper in 1917, is very ungenerous (*F* 474–83: 132).

This campaign must, however, be understood in the context of his critique of the whole institution of the press. For the proponent of this structural critique, the attempt to establish an improved and progressive daily newspaper merely confused the issue; for it seemed to confound Kraus's general proposition that the non-socialist press constituted a single reactionary mass ('*eine* reactionäre Masse', *F* 124: 5). In Benedikt and Bacher, the proprietors and editors of the *Neue Freie Presse*, he found spectacular and in a sense welcome confirmation for this general hypothesis; they provided 'sublime examples of corruption' – 'erhabene Corruptionstypen' (*F* 118: 4). On the evidence of the manifest corruptness of this one newspaper, he felt it was possible to prove 'the pernicious nature of *the* newspaper, the corrupting influence on culture of the press as an institution' ('die Verderblichkeit *der* Zeitung, die culturwidrige Macht der Pressinstitution', *F* 124: 5). The success of *Die Zeit* would have compromised this general argument. Here we encounter a paradox which runs right through Kraus's writings. As a reformist critic he certainly wished to raise the standards of Austrian journalism; but as satirist he proclaims that the press is irredeemably corrupt.

To contemporary readers Kraus's campaign against *Die Zeit* seemed to add force to the objection that he was a writer who could 'only negate'. But social reform was not his primary aim. Above all he wanted to teach people to read — to read the public prints with scepticism and mistrust. It was in this immunization of the reading public that he saw the productive content of his work of destructive criticism (*F* 56: 11). In the growth of an attitude of critical mistrust he saw salvation beckoning for a civilization corroded by printer's ink: 'Werde *misstrauisch*, und einer von Druckerschwärze fast schon zerfressenen Cultur winkt die Rettung' (*F* 98: 4). Clearly this is an ambitious aim. For the German word 'Kultur' means not only artistic culture. Kraus seems to entertain the hope that a revival of civilization as a whole might be achieved though the growth of critical enlightenment. Thus even when he was directing his attack against Liberalism, he was still working within one of its essential paradigms: its faith in the immense power, for good or evil, of the printing press. In his fundamental aim Kraus is thus closer to Voltaire than to Karl Marx. But his writings illuminate a problem that the Marxists of his day grievously underestimated: the phenomenon of false consciousness.

Satire as the Art of Contrasts

In the first five years of *Die Fackel* the problem of consciousness is not yet Kraus's overriding concern. The attack on the language of ideological thinking is indeed already announced in the very first number of the journal, which proposes a 'draining of the vast swamp of slogans and clichés' ('Trockenlegung des weiten Phrasensumpfes', *F* 1: 2). But at this stage Kraus's attention is still engaged by a multitude of more practical problems. Against the folly of Austrian relations with Serbia and the injustice of the administration in Bosnia, specific changes in government policy are advocated. Taking issue both with the propaganda of antisemitism and with the programme of Zionism, Kraus argues for the assimilation of the Jews into the national cultures in which they live. Discussing the administration of Austrian universities and the curriculum of the grammar schools, *Die Fackel* advocates educational reforms. And in the attack on injustices in the social and economic system, the aim is

to obtain shorter working hours and better conditions for workers
and employees. In his criticism of the dubious practices of banks and
finance corporations Kraus expresses the hope that his disclosures
will promote institutional reforms. And to rectify abuses inherent in
the practice of the courts he argues for specific changes in the law. So
diverse are his critical themes that a reader of the early numbers of
the journal is left with an impression of fragmentation and incoherence.

There is however a unifying principle underlying these writings —
one which has not received the attention it deserves. This is the motif
of the mask, emblazoned on the cover of the early numbers of *Die
Fackel*. Kraus's attitude is shaped by a sensitivity to masks — to
duplicity and disguise, to discrepancies between theory and practice.
His treatment of the strike of coal miners at Mährisch-Ostrau provides a good example. In a series of articles beginning in February
1900 he defends the claims of the miners for a shorter working day
and denounces the obduracy of the mine owners. But where a
socialist would have attacked the whole system of ownership which
sets capitalists and workers in opposition to each other, Kraus's eye is
caught by an antithesis of a different kind: the contrast between the
ruthlessness with which the mine owners exploit thousands of workers and the self-righteous generosity of their contributions to charity
balls and festivals (*F* 31: 3). It is not simple inhumanity, it is the more
complex phenomenon of duplicity that Kraus attacks. This motif
becomes even more explicit when he turns his attention to the role of
the government, which was expected to act as mediator between
owners and workers. The government mediators are denounced as
merely representatives of the mine owners in disguise. Their
pretence at impartiality is a 'carnival mask' — ('Carnevalsmaske',
F 32: 1).

It is this seminal image of the mask which gives a structural
coherence to Kraus's early writings, particularly to his critique of the
press. What he attacks most forcefully is not its financial corruptness,
but the discrepancy between its shady financial dealings and its
resplendent cultural prestige. The press is a prostitute which in
Austria wears the robes of a priestess ('kleidet sich hier in das
Gewand der Priesterin', *F* 28: 6). Its true financial aims are concealed
behind editorials which are a paper disguise ('Blätterhülle', *F* 28: 7).
Economic aims should be declared in a form that is undisguised
('unverhüllt', *F* 28: 7). To reveal the shady dealings of the *Neue Freie
Presse* it is necessary to tear off its hypocritical mask
('Heuchlermaske', *F* 82: 27). Almost as pernicious is the device of
concealing the authorship of anonymous libels behind an editorial
front-man ('Strohmann', *F* 84: 27). For this world of specious

pretences and usurped ideals Kraus is even able to find a definition in Tacitus: 'speciosa nomina praetexuntur' (*F* 108: 1).

Once one is alerted to this motif of masks and disguises, one finds it in every conceivable context. The socialism professed by former German Nationalist Engelbert Pernerstorfer is a badly acted role ('schlechtgespielte Rolle', *F* 75: 16). It is folly to try to conceal irrepressible sexual urges behind the mask of morality ('die Maske "Moral"', *F* 115: 6). When journalists make their raids on the public purse they use the ideals of Freedom and Patriotism as a front ('Mauer', *F* 118: 3). There is an element of play-acting in the hostility of the Christian Socials towards Jewish journalists; they are all good friends behind the scenes ('hinter den Coulissen', *F* 5: 18). The superior airs of the theatre critic Paul Goldmann are merely a layer of make-up ('angeschminkt', *F* 155: 19). When theatre director Max Burckhard tries to impress people as a poet, he is wearing a mask ('die Maske eines Dichters', *F* 32: 30). And what is it about Theodor Herzl that particularly catches the eye of the satirist? Precisely the fact that the clothing which he rends in agony over the sufferings of the Jewish people has been supplied by such an elegant tailor (*F* 2: 14).

This theme of duplicity finds its most intense focus in the problem of Jewish identity. Herzl's clothes had a metropolitan panache which belied his revivalist programme.[27] The Jews of Vienna found themselves caught between two cultures: the traditional Judaic community and modern secular society. This was made embarrassingly evident by the fact that many Jews had two different names. A decree signed by Joseph II in 1787 had imposed German surnames on Austrian Jews.[28] And many of the surnames chosen had a resoundingly Jewish association, like Baruch, Löwy or Salomon. Others were implausibly poetic, like Rosenfeld and Blumenthal. For Jews anxious to become assimilated it thus became the fashion to further Germanize their names, especially if they were converting to Christianity, or if as writers they were looking for a flattering pseudonym. For Kraus these assimilated names were a disguise. When Felix Salten tries to establish himself as authentically Viennese, readers of *Die Fackel* are reminded that behind that aristocratic-sounding name there lurks an immigrant from Budapest called Zsiga Salzmann (*F* 86: 16). Indeed, there were so many Samuels masquerading as Siegfrieds that Kraus could with some justice speak of a 'pseudonymous civilization' ('eine pseudonyme Kultur', *F* 333: 9).

Kraus's satire on the duplicity of names is so rich — and so problematic — a subject that it deserves a monograph in itself. It was not only Jewish names that caught his critical eye. In the polyglot Empire almost any name could have secondary associations (indicating social status or pretension, ethnic or regional origin).

Decoding the names in *Die Fackel* is an art in itself. Who on earth is
Prohaska? And why should it be an affront to the Emperor to invoke
this name? (*F* 207: 29–30) Such questions are left unanswered by a
factual index.[29] In many cases Kraus is less interested in the
individual bearer of a name than in its humorous associations.
Sometimes the principle is *nomen est omen*. More often it is the
discrepancy between the associations of a name and the activities of
its bearer that yield a satirical effect. The disruption of the traditional
order meant that names, like words, no longer corresponded to
realities. Names like Angelo Eisner von Eisenhof, designed to give
an aristocratic flourish to recently ennobled social climbers, formed
part of the public masquerade.

We have already noted the theatricality of Austrian public life,
which made this masquerade motif so apposite. But there is also a
more subjective factor. Kraus's whole mode of perception seems to
have been shaped by a sensitivity to masks and disguises. He later
recalled that he had an acute eye for the pretentiousness of his teachers,
even while he was still a schoolboy (*F* 283–4: 19). This may also be
related to the very early development of his interest in satire. His first
literary project, conceived with his school friend Anton Lindner, was
to edit a satirical anthology. At this date (1892–3) his conception of
satire was as uncertain as his spelling of the word — sometimes
'Satire', sometimes 'Satyre' (*FS* II. 65, 71). The goat-like satyr featured on the front cover of *Die Fackel* also suggests that for the Kraus
of the 1890s satire was a vaguely defined primitive force disrupting the
civilities of a philistine society. The vigour of Wedekind and
Liliencron and of other dynamic North German authors was to be
invoked against the effeteness of Vienna. But at the same time Kraus
admired the more restrained and elegant style of satirical 'unmasking'
that he found in the writings of Gustav Schwarzkopf (*FS* I.208–10).
He seems to be wavering between what he calls 'social' satire and a
more 'literary' style that would be modeled on the work of earlier
authors (*FS* I.85). This uncertainty is expressed in a letter of 13 July
1897 to his mentor Maximilian Harden, asking how it is possible to
establish a 'satirical rapport' with the world of politics: 'Wie wirft man
sich in die Politik, [. . .] wie setzt man sich möglichst rasch in eine
satirische Beziehung zu ihr und ihren Männern?'[30]

It was not until ten years later that Kraus was able to give his own
definitive answer. By this date (October 1907) he was able to derive a
definition of satire from his own accumulated experience:

> Ich bin Satiriker und mein Blick bleibt an Kontrasten hängen. Nicht wie
> ich über den Ausgleich denke, aber wie ich über die Menschensorte
> denke, die über den Ausgleich denken sollte, ist erheblich.
>
> (*F* 232–3: 2)

(I am a satirist, and my gaze is caught by contrasts. What matters is not what I think about the Austro-Hungarian Compromise, but what I think about the type of person who ought to be thinking about the Compromise.)

The aim of his satire is not to comment directly on political problems, but to expose the discrepancy between ideologies and events.

Kraus was not the kind of writer who sits down with a blank sheet of paper to compose. Like the great satirists before him, he was a man of antithetical disposition. He needed an irritant to provoke his creativity. He would begin, characteristically, by pasting a newspaper clipping on a larger sheet of paper, to define an opponent's position. That position would then be encircled — penned in by Kraus's minute handwriting. This caused headaches for his printer (and for the critic who examines the many proof corrections which survive in the Vienna City Library). But this method yielded that multitude of satirical glosses which are Kraus's most characteristic achievement. He is the master of ironic juxtaposition — that techique of unmasking intellectual and social pretentions which was being classically defined in Henri Bergson's theory of 'Laughter'.[31] This approach became formalized in Kraus's favourite device of reprinting contrasting news items in parallel columns. This mode of demystification was to be used most effectively during the First World War in his repeated confrontations of complacent patriotism with anguished human suffering (F 405: 1–2; 418–22: 2–6). And the experiences of the war led him to the conclusion that civilization had been destroyed not by the events themselves, but by the irreconcilable contrasts which had rendered them so unmanageable: 'An den Kontrasten, nicht an den Dingen sollten wir zugrundegehen' (F 501–7: 37). This dictum formalizes the pattern which we have seen emerging from Kraus's earlier writings: the preoccupation with discrepancy and disguise. But in his early work he characteristically relies on inside information obtained from 'behind the scenes' ('Hinter den Coulissen', F 59: 5). The contrasts explored in his later work are already the public property of newspaper readers, who are too brainwashed to comprehend them. In short, Kraus later becomes less interested in the 'mask' of hypocrisy than in the 'veil' of ideology.[32]

There is one further reason why Kraus's preoccupation with duplicity deserves special emphasis. It provides a *structural* explanation for what appears to be an *ideological* bias. In practice Kraus never succeeded in sustaining his ideal of impartiality. Although *Die Fackel* does contain outspoken attacks on right-wing

factions, its main target is the ideology of Liberalism. This bias is
particularly marked towards the end of the first decade. Some
commentators have taken this as evidence that Kraus's impartiality
was only notional, and that his work was shaped by
unacknowledged political prejudices. Kraus's own explanation was
that the Liberal press necessarily commanded most attention because
its influence was far more corrupting than that of the less talented
proponents of reactionary ideologies (F 156: 18). The important
question, however, is *why* he should have believed this — and
continued to believe it even in the 1920s, at a time when the greater
dangers of right-wing propaganda should have been evident.

Kraus's political prejudices may have less bearing on the problem
than the particular mode of perception which we have identified. A
writer sensitive above all to duplicity, and expert in the demolition of
façades, will understandably be inclined to discount the danger of
political movements which make no secret of their aims. A racialist
who blatantly proclaims his hostility to the Jews may in this view
appear less sinister than a liberal intellectual who deceives the public
for his own financial gain. For the language of the one is
unequivocal, that of the other replete with mystification. Essays by
Houston Stewart Chamberlain are thus printed in *Die Fackel* of this
early period without critical reservations. Kraus clearly respected the
uncompromising bluntness of Chamberlain's polemics.[33] The journalists Bahr and Benedikt on the other hand (as we shall see in the
following chapter) attract his unremitting critical attention precisely
because their real aims are concealed behind such plausible
camouflage. The same pattern is repeated fifteen years later, when
Chamberlain's crude Pan-German war propaganda is ignored, while
the attempts by Bahr and Benedikt to wrap up a rather similar
political programme in layers of idealistic verbiage are incisively
exposed. For the amateur of ideological disguises a self-righteous
hypocrite, of whatever political persuasion, will always seem a more
interesting target than a plain-speaking fanatic. Thus it becomes
comprehensible that in the 1920s Kraus should have regarded the
forthright fascism of Adolf Hitler as less sinister than the spurious
pacifism of Alfred Kerr. At times Kraus's sensitivity to disguises
obstructs his perception of the historical balance of forces. And it
certainly impairs his political judgement. But for one task it left him
admirably equipped: for the writing of satire and polemic. It is here
that his antithetical sensibility comes into its own. For satire is the art
of contrasts.

CHAPTER 3

Polemical Targets and Satirical Archetypes: The Apocalyptic Perspective

From Factual Polemic to Imaginative Satire

When *Die Fackel* was founded in April 1899, Kraus's aim was factual disclosure. From about 1904 onwards this aim was displaced by more imaginative forms of satire. This gives rise to a disconcerting blend of documented fact and imaginative fantasy. His attacks on named individuals (as in the following example, from March 1904) may originate in the context of polemical journalism; but they increasingly invoke a literary frame of reference:

> Johann Feigl, Hofrat und Vizepräsident des Wiener Landesgerichts, hat als Vorsitzender einer Schwurgerichtsverhandlung am 10. März 1904 einen dreiundzwanzigjährigen Buben, der in trunkenem Zustand eine Frau auf der Ringstraße attackiert und ihr 1 K 20 h zu entreißen versucht hatte, zu lebenslänglichem schweren Kerker verurteilt. (*F* 157: 1)

> (Johann Feigl, Hofrat and Vice President of the Vienna Provincial Court, presiding over a trial by jury on 10 March 1904, sentenced a twenty-three-year-old youth, who in a drunken state had attacked a women in the Ringstrasse and tried to snatch from her the sum of 1 Crown 20 Hellers, to life imprisonment with hard labour.)

In a single sentence Kraus declares the facts of the case. His aim is to demand action – the reduction of the life sentence to a more reasonable term. The article also unmasks the judge himself. The sentence passed by Feigl presents a formal appearance of legitimacy: the maximum penalty for attempted robbery with violence was indeed life imprisonment. However, a close study of the transcript enabled Kraus to bring to light the judge's actual motives. During the trial the accused man, Anton Kraft, had spoken up impudently in his own defence. He had thereby antagonized the judge and provoked him into imposing life imprisonment as a punishment for 'insolent behaviour in court': 'Am 10. März 1904 wurde in Wien lebenslänglicher schwerer Kerker wegen frechen Benehmens im Gerichtssaal diktiert!' (F 157: 6)

This article is a hard-hitting individual polemic. Kraus's style is functional and free of idiosyncrasies (he even resists the temptation to play on the name 'Feigl'). He wishes to mobilize public opinion, and in this the article was indeed partly successful. So great was the public outcry that the life sentence was reduced, on appeal (although Kraft was still imprisoned for twelve years). Polemical journalism of this kind has an important function in its own day. But its significance does not transcend the fragment of social history which it records. It lacks the complexity which we associate with the concept of satire.

Even as a piece of journalism the focus of this article is restricted. It is considerably less informative than the two reports on this case which had appeared in the *Arbeiter-Zeitung* a week earlier (11 and 12 March 1904). Kraus shows no interest in the social background of the young delinquent Anton Kraft. His denunciation of the judge is so sweeping that the social implications of the case are obscured. The spectacle of the courts defending the handbags of ladies on the Ringstrasse from penurious young men with empty stomachs might have stimulated a more profound type of social criticism. The *Neue Freie Presse* (10 March 1904) had described the life sentence as appropriate to the seriousness of the assault. One might have expected Kraus to react with a denunciation of the hypocrisy of the bourgeoisie. He was indeed aware that the sentence imposed on Kraft was all the more severe because the young man's offence was a threat to the social order – 'ein Verbrechen gegen die Gesellschafts-ordnung' (F 213: 4). But this insight is peripheral to his argument.

The attack on Feigl invokes not socio-economic but literary categories. Kraus's mind was steeped in Shakespeare: by the age of thirty he had seen *King Lear* performed on no less than twelve occasions (F 191: 22). A tendency to interpret contemporary social issues in terms of Shakespearean analogies is characteristic of his whole *oeuvre*. Kraus juxtaposes the facts of the Feigl case with a quotation from *Hamlet* (III.iv): 'Heaven's face doth glow [. . .] With heated visage, as against the doom.' In Schlegel's translation this is quite explicitly the Day of Judgement – 'der jüngste Tag'. The Shakespearean reference thus sets up a confrontation between two spheres of justice, one human and corrupt, the other cosmic and absolute. And even in this short and unassuming article there is a movement of the imagination away from the Wiener Landesgericht towards 'eine höhere Instanz'. Feigl will have ultimately to answer for a life which has spanned 'about ten thousand years' – 'etwa zehntausend Jahre, die andere im Kerker verbrachten' (*F* 157: 6). This intensification of moral perspective is characteristic of Kraus's writing. The attack moves from individual polemic towards apocalyptic satire. But the intermediate dimension of socio-economic analysis remains unexplored.

In this article Kraus also invokes Shakespeare's *Measure for Measure*. Since the action of that play is set in Vienna, it provided him with apt analogies. And in certain respects his writings gain from this literary frame of reference. 'Shakespeare hat alles vorausgewußt', he writes in September 1902, introducing the great theme of 'Sittlichkeit und Kriminalität' (*F* 115: 3). The frankness of Shakespeare's treatment of sex reinforces Kraus's attack on hypocritical moral codes. But the assumption that Shakespeare had 'foreknowledge of everything' has a limiting effect when Kraus turns his hand to social and political themes. For it leads him to narrow his focus on Feigl's motives, so that these are summed up by Shakespeare's archetypal image ('urkräftig' is the word Kraus uses). Feigl is seen as Shakespeare's 'petty officer' who 'dressed in a little brief authority [. . .] plays such fantastic tricks before high heaven as make the angels weep' (*F* 157: 3; *Measure for Measure*, II. ii. 113–23). It is simply a matter of the disproportion between a little man and a great office. Here Kraus's reliance on a literary analogy tends to pre-empt analysis in more concrete historical terms.

In this article we can already discern the movement beyond factual polemic towards imaginative satire which is so characteristic of Kraus's work. This may be clarified by recalling the fundamental distinction between polemic and satire, on which Kraus himself insists. Polemic requires that the figure represented in the text should be congruent with the person under attack: 'daß die Gestalt mit der Person kongruent sei' (*F* 267–8: 25). The attack should be grounded in verifiable evidence. Thus polemic is rooted in a specific historical situation, and its interest for later readers tends to be documentary rather than imaginative. In any evaluation of polemic, its effect within the given historical situation has to be taken into account. Polemical battles are 'lost' and 'won'. We can all think of polemical crusades that were crowned with success: Swift's campaign against the debasing of the coinage in Ireland, Schöffel and Kürnberger's battle to save the Vienna Woods, Kraus's campaign during the 1920s to drive Bekessy out of Vienna, the exposure of the Watergate affair by journalists from the *Washington Post*. In these polemical campaigns (as Swift himself puts it) corrupt men were defeated 'by the Shame of having their Crimes exposed to open View in the strongest possible Colours, and themselves made odious to Mankind'.[1]

With satire, the aim of attacking an individual is no longer in the foreground. Satire is 'on' a theme, rather than 'against' a person. The material of Kraus's satire may appear to be the same as that of his polemics – actual contemporaries, referred to by name. But the figures of his satire are no longer targets significant in themselves. They now serve as stimuli to the imagination, becoming significant through what the writer makes of them. The aim of satire is less to 'declare facts' than to 'explore possibilities': 'aussprechen, was möglich ist' (F 336–7: 42). And Kraus's satire emerges as a mode of writing that is essentially creative or rather 're-creative' ('nachschöpferisch', F 360–2: 55). Like Swift, he offers even in the act of negation 'the spectacle of creative powers'.[2] His ethical astringency generates through the play of wit a paradoxical sense of exhilaration. The satirical animus yields 'a fantastic vision of the world transformed'.[3]

This commitment to creativity transforms the nature of Kraus's enterprise. The imaginative mode projects the figures of his satire into a dimension of fictionality. This may seem paradoxical. More closely than that of any other European satirist, Kraus's work seems to be attached to the events and personalities of his day. It is not Voltaire's fictional Doctor Pangloss but the historical Professor Friedjung who figures in Kraus's satire as the bearer of vacuous platitudes. No fictional Leutnant Gustl but an actual general, Conrad von Hötzendorf, typifies the posturings of the officer class. The multitude of names that people the pages of Die Fackel are not fanciful inventions in the manner of Dickens or Nestroy. The journal forms a critical encyclopaedia of the public life of central Europe. It is thus an invaluable source-book for the cultural historian. Its range is extraordinary (the index prepared by Franz Ögg lists more than 10,000 names). And one of Kraus's aims was to give as faithful a picture as possible of Viennese intellectual life: 'ein möglichst getreues Abbild der Wiener Geistigkeit' (F 657–67: 169).

Die Fackel will always be read partly for its documentation of historical events: the decline of Austria-Hungary, the emergence of antisemitism, the pervasive influence of the press, the horrors of the First World War, the political struggles of the Austrian Republic and the rise of National Socialism. But to read Kraus's work solely in terms of its historical references would be to ignore its imaginative dimension. Kraus himself repeatedly warns against this kind of near-sighted reading:

> Nur jenen, die fern in Zeit oder Land,
> wird der Inhalt meiner Satiren bekannt.

(F 472–3: 17)

(Only those distant in time and nation
will grasp my satire's implication.)

And it is Kraus who introduces the notion of fictionality, claiming that historical individuals are transformed into dramatic and fictional characters in his satirical glosses: 'in szenische Gestalten und in die Romanfiguren meiner Glossenwelt transformiert' (F 676–8: 51–2). These named contemporaries (he paradoxically claims) are figments of his imagination (F 338: 1), significant as 'paradigms' (F 462–71: 70).

The reader's task would be easier if it were possible to draw a clear line between polemic and satire, historical target and fictional character. But Kraus's writing characteristically hovers between the two modes:

HERMANN BAHR
–das ist ein etwas schlichter Titel für eine Glosse [. . .] indes ich halte gerade den schlichten Namen für wirksam, denn wenn ich 'Hermann Bahr' setze, so weiß man ohnedies, daß eigentlich 'Glaube und Geschäft' zu stehen hätte, während, wenn ich 'Glaube und Geschäft' schriebe, sich viele getroffen fühlen könnten, ehe sie durch die Lektüre der Glosse darüber beruhigt werden, daß ausschließlich Hermann Bahr gemeint ist.
(F 363–5: 56)

(–that is a rather plain title for a gloss [. . .] however, I consider precisely the plain name to be most effective, for if I put 'Hermann Bahr', everyone knows anyway that it really should be 'Conscience and Commerce', whereas if I were to write 'Conscience and Commerce', many people might feel themselves to be under attack, until they reassure themselves by reading the gloss that it is Hermann Bahr alone who is meant.)

Obviously it is *not* Hermann Bahr alone who is meant. Like Alexander Pope, Kraus plays both with his victims and his readers, using what 'by good luck happens to be the name of a real person' in order to 'multiply' the satire.[4]

Hermann Bahr, the initiator of the Austrian literary revival of the 1890s, was a gifted critic and essayist. It was precisely because he was so influential that Kraus could treat him as a representative figure. Bahr exemplifies the Austrian cultural malaise – the subordination of literature to journalism. He is the man of letters who has betrayed his calling by scribbling away at the dictates of the daily newspaper (FS I.108). Kraus believed that literature should be an independent force, counteracting the pernicious influence of the press. But in Vienna (as he wrote to Harden in 1899) 'the reporter has devoured the writer' ('bei uns hat der Reporter den Schriftsteller verschlungen', F 2: 8). The problem was of course not confined to Vienna, as readers of

Gissing's *New Grub Street* will know. The spread of the newspaper-reading habit created market pressures which few writers were able to resist.[5] Bahr thus exemplifies a general trend towards the debasement of artistic standards and the sell-out of ethical integrity.

This subordination of conscience to commerce was exemplified by the double role Bahr played in 1900. As a theatre critic his brief was to write regular reviews of the Deutsches Volkstheater. But as a dramatist he aspired to have his own plays staged at the same theatre, with whose director Emerich von Bukovics he was on friendly terms. Thus Bahr was in a position to promote the production of his own plays by giving a favourable slant to his reviews. And Bukovics, to retain the good offices of such an influential critic, was under pressure to accept Bahr's plays on favourable terms. For Kraus, Bahr's double role was improper in principle. But information also reached him that Bahr had received from Bukovics a substantial financial inducement – a plot of building land in a fashionable suburb. This led him to suggest that Bahr had received such benefits from Bukovics that he not only had every reason to praise his theatre but also 'good grounds – for building a villa' ('guten Grund – zum Bau einer Villa', F 43: 25).

This proved to be one of the most expensive puns in literary history. In February 1901 Bahr and Bukovics brought a libel action against Kraus. And Bahr was able to lay before the court a contract proving that he had obtained the land from Bukovics by purchase, not as a gift. The fact that this contract was not registered until November 1900, five months after Kraus had published his allegation, failed to sway the jury in his favour. He lost the case and was ordered to pay a fine of 1,800 Crowns plus a further 1,200 in costs.[6] The severity of the penalty can be gauged from the fact that the fine was greater than the annual salary of the presiding judge. But although defeated on a technicality, Kraus was able to show that he was justified in principle. For he demonstrated that when in 1899 Bahr republished his theatre reviews in book form, he altered reviews of the Volkstheater which had originally been hostile in order to give them a favourable slant. Thus a passage from one of these reviews which had been published in *Die Zeit* on 27 October 1894, describing one of Bukovics's adaptations as the work of an illiterate ('Analphabet'), was now tactfully deleted (F 69: 45). The views of the supposedly independent critic were retracted once Bahr had himself become a dramatist earning royalties from the Volkstheater. Theatre historians have subsequently confirmed that the practice of combining the positions of dramatist and drama critic was one of the most damaging features of the German and Austrian theatre at the turn of the century.[7]

In attacking Bahr Kraus was condemning the system. Bahr's biographers have often complained that Kraus's attacks were unjust, but it is worth pointing out that his analysis is corroborated by an unimpeachable source: Bahr himself. Kraus's central point was that Bahr's undoubted literary gifts were compromised by his work as a journalist. Bahr (in a diary note of 8 January 1904) describes himself as a man 'whose spirit links him with the highest achievements of contemporary culture, but whose journalistic profession shuts him up in the same stable as disreputable, envious idiots'. Similar outbursts can be found in the diaries of other leading literary journalists of the day. Theodor Herzl deplores his 'vile servitude to the *Neue Freie Presse*, where I am not allowed to have an opinion of my own'.[8] The conflict of values which Bahr and Herzl conceded in the privacy of their diaries, Kraus insisted on ventilating in public.

In Kraus's treatment of Bahr the individual author becomes a representative target. And there are again hints of an underlying literary archetype – the figure of Proteus (*FS* I.107). This tendency towards imaginative stylization is even more evident in Kraus's characterization of Felix Salten. Salten, one of the best-known Viennese journalists of his day, was noted for his elegant feuilletons on current affairs. But to read Kraus's satire on the figure of Salten as if it were aimed at an individual target would be to miss the point. In a series of glosses in *Die Fackel* of October 1909 the journalist is imaginatively transformed:

> Der beste Journalist Wiens weiß über die Karriere einer Gräfin wie über den Aufstieg eines Luftballons, über eine Parlamentssitzung wie über einen Hofball zu jeder Stunde das Wissenswerte auszusagen. In Westungarn kann man nachts Wetten abschließen, daß der Zigeunerprimas binnen einer halben Stunde mit seinem ganzen Orchester zur Stelle sein wird; man läßt ihn wecken, er tastet nach der Fiedel, weckt den Cymbalschläger, alles springt aus den Betten, in den Wagen, und in einer halben Stunde gehts hoch her, fidel, melancholisch, ausgelassen, dämonisch und was es sonst noch gibt.   (*F* 289: 12)

> (The best journalist in Vienna knows at any moment what is worth knowing and saying, whether about the career of a countess or the ascent of an air balloon, a session of parliament or a court ball. In Hungary one can lay bets at night that the gypsy band leader will be on the spot with his whole orchestra within half an hour; you send someone to wake him up, he gropes for his fiddle, wakes the cymbals player, they all leap out of bed and into the carriage, and in half an hour the show is on, gay, melancholic, uninhibited, demonic, or whatever mood you care for.)

No doubt the image of the Hungarian gypsy orchestra suggested itself because Felix Salten was born in Budapest. But as a metaphor

for the arts of journalistic versatility it transcends the actual person to
whom it is applied. Salten is assimilated into the archetype of the
Trickster, the mercurial shape-shifter who acts out the fantasies of
society.[9] We do not need to know anything about the historical Felix
Salten in order to appreciate the imaginative power of Kraus's
pen-portrait. Indeed when this gloss was republished as an aphorism
in *Pro domo et mundo* (*W* III.217), the contextual references to Salten
were erased.

In Kraus's satire on Salten the individual becomes a type, one of
the 'Grundtypen des geistigen Elends' (*F* 289: 8). The individual
target is re-created in terms of a satirical typology which can be
traced back to Juvenal.[10] Salten becomes the demonic fiddler of folk
mythology, capable of conjuring up any mood at the drop of a hat:
'fidel, melancholisch, ausgelassen, dämonisch'. Kraus's imagination
characteristically projects his targets on to a mythopoeic plane. This
process reaches its climax in his treatment of Moriz Benedikt, editor
of the *Neue Freie Presse*, whose chauvinistic propaganda made him
for Kraus the evil genius of the First World War. In the epilogue to
Die letzten Tage der Menschheit Benedikt is re-created not merely as a
predator (Lord of the Hyenas) but as the Antichrist himself (*W*
V.750–4).

The four examples we have considered make it possible to draw
up a satirical charge-sheet, showing the four primary modes of
treatment meted out to Kraus's victims:

name	offence	perspective	paradigm
Feigl	personal vindic- tiveness	individual target	'petty officer'
Bahr	journalistic duplicity	representative type	Proteus
Salten	feuilletonistic versatility	imaginative re- creation	demonic fiddler (Trickster)
Benedikt	destruction of civilization	archetypal myth	Antichrist

The neatness of these categories is however deceptive. Bahr may at
one moment be the target of representative polemic, the next
moment a stimulus to satirical fantasy. Feigl is both attacked as an
individual target and projected on to the archetypal plane of the Last
Judgement. Kraus's style does not move sedately from factual
polemic towards imaginative satire. His texts are polysemous. He is
continuously playing with different linguistic registers. It is indeed
this interaction between different 'codes' which gives his work its
exceptional vitality. It invites a structuralist reading even at those
points where it seems most historically specific.

A full reading must be alert both to archetypal resonance and to historical specificity. The productive intensity generated by this mode of writing arises (as Walter Benjamin observed in another context) from the tension between archetypal pattern and modern variant: 'die Spannung zwischen Urform und Variante'.[11] The power of Kraus's gloss on Felix Salten is that it gives memorable form to a crucial historical diagnosis: his attack on the feuilleton for trivializing political events and ultimately preparing the way for war. In 1909 Kraus pinpoints a journalistic versatility which deals with equal ease with parliamentary debates and court balls. By 1912 this trivialization of public affairs is seen as threatening the peace of Europe. Kraus now denounces journalists who are capable of 'launching a première one day and a war the next' ('heute eine Premiere und morgen einen Krieg lancieren', F 363–5: 71). This phrase prophetically anticipates the transformation of public opinion from carefree frivolity to militaristic fervour that was orchestrated by the Austrian press in July 1914.

The attack on Felix Salten thus combines accurate historical analysis with creative literary expression. The individual author is transposed into a figure exemplifying the irresponsibility of modern journalism. And during the First World War Salten is repeatedly cited in Die Fackel to show up the spuriousness of this feuilletonistic support for the patriotic cause. Moreover the dishonesty of Salten's writings, which Kraus attacks in public, can also be confirmed from a private source. The diaries of Arthur Schnitzler record conversations with Salten which show that Salten's private views about the war were very much at odds with the patriotic sentiments of his journalism: 'Welch ein problematisches Individuum'.[12] But Kraus is not concerned with Salten as an individual. His satirical vision has far wider implications. The figure of Felix Salten, assimilated into the archetype of the Trickster, exemplifies the hallucinatory powers of modern propaganda.

Archetypes and Apocalypse

In Jungian psychology the word 'archetype' ('Urbild') is used to denote recurrent patterns of perception that are independent of human consciousness and may even be genetically transmitted. But in literary theory the term has more precise connotations.[13] Kraus himself, from a very early stage, uses the word 'Urbild' to identify literary paradigms applicable to recurrent social phenomena. To characterize the amorphous resistance in the early 1890s to innovations at the Burgtheater, he invokes 'das Urbild des "Großen Krummen"' – 'the archetype of the Great Boyg' in Peer Gynt (FS 1.17). This indicates how profoundly Kraus's imagination was

shaped by the theatrical experiences of his early years. The image of
the 'Great Boyg' became so deeply lodged in his mind that we find it
recurring in *Die Fackel* thirty years later (*F* 730–1: 1–2 [July 1926]), at
the climax of his polemic with Bekessy.[14] Above all, it was
Shakespeare whose writings shaped Kraus's histrionic imagination.
Certain Shakespearean phrases seem to have been so completely
assimilated that they became second nature to him. Kraus acknowledges that the writer who thinks for himself is likely to find that his
most daring ideas have already been formulated by others before him
(*F* 462–71: 94). And this is reinforced by his prefigural conception of
language itself. In a series of aphorisms he suggests that literary
creativity articulates patterns of perception which pre-exist in the
materials of language (*W* III.236). The skilful writer will establish the
richest possible network of associations between words (*W* III.122),
but this does not preclude the existence of unconscious archetypes
which elude rational definition. Language encompasses the quest for
a primal image which has been lost – 'ein verlorenes Urbild' (*W*
III.338).

In Kraus's writings we find both unconscious archetypal
patterning and conscious mythological references. It is indeed when
archetypes acquire specific definition in the form of myth that they
are most readily identifiable. Such mythic patterns repeatedly
reinforce Kraus's satire. From Judaic scripture he derives the myths
of Creation and Primal Innocence, the Garden of Eden and the Fall of
Man, the Dance around the Golden Calf and Driving the Money-
Changers from the Temple, Apocalypse and Judgement Day, Antichrist and the Great Whore of Babylon. From Greek and Roman
sources he derives the figures of Timon and Proteus, Thersites and
Pandora, the myth of Thebes, the opposition of city and countryside, the topoi of *theatrum mundi* and *miles gloriosus*, not to mention
Ephialtes, demon of nightmares. From Germanic literature and
folklore he takes the motifs of Carnival and Dance of Death, Witch
Hunts and Walpurgisnacht, the Sorcerer and his Apprentice, Earth
Spirit and Primal Woman. Some images are a synthesis of disparate
sources: the fable of the Tortoise and the Hare combining with a
mystical vision of life as a race to be run in his enigmatic poem 'Zwei
Läufer'. Others have a more specific historical source, like the
witchcraft motifs borrowed from Scherr's *Geschichte der deutschen
Kultur und Sitten* to characterize modern outbursts of sexual and racial
persecution. Kraus's satirical vision is shaped by such archetypal
images, though they may not be consciously perceived by the reader.
The most obvious image of all, though it has never attracted any
critical attention, is the torch emblazoned on the front cover of *Die
Fackel*. This bears little resemblance to any actual torch that might

have been used in Vienna in Kraus's day. It is the Torch of Prometheus the Firebringer, shedding light upon a benighted civilization. But it is also (as Kraus made clear when he used key verses from the Book of Revelation in a reading given in November 1914) the Torch which heralds the apocalyptic End of the World.[15]

Kraus's writings (like those of Joyce) abound in mythopoeic references. But the concealed literary allusions are so skilfully blended into the narrative that fifty years after the author's death they still elude exegesis. Who are those 'Figures Dressed in Green' who make such a haunting impression in Kraus's poem 'Die Grüngekleideten' (F 406–12: 155–6)? The context suggests that they are Austrian customs officials in green uniforms. But the subtext reveals that they too (like the Great Boyg) hail from the mythopoeic mists of Scandinavia.[16] Such archetypal motifs characteristically enter Kraus's work through pre-existing literary structures: plays by Shakespeare or Schiller, poems by Goethe, the literature of Romanticism (E. T. A. Hoffmann and Jean Paul), even the libretti of Offenbach. Thus their mythic origin may not be immediately apparent. But this merely adds to the complexity of the patterns of reference. Timon, who embodies the archetype of misanthropy, is no less resonant a figure for being invoked through the mediation of Shakespeare. Nor do Kraus's re-enactments of the myth of the Sorcerer's Apprentice lose their magic for being derived from Goethe's poem 'Der Zauberlehrling'. Beneath the layers of literary sophistication lurk residues of primitive ritual. Satire has its roots in magical incantation.[17]

Kraus is so celebrated for the rigour of his writings that this imaginative dimension has often been underestimated. His response to the modern world is shaped not merely by a sceptical intelligence but by a mythopoeic imagination. The present book elucidates the most fundamental of his mythologems, from Primal Woman through to Last Days. It is wrong to suppose that this reliance on myth is necessarily 'regressive'.[18] A more discriminating approach will show that Kraus's satirical vision is enhanced by this mythopoeic dimension. But at moments of political crisis his reliance on prefiguration does lead to errors of judgement. The antithesis of the Sword and the Pen, which shaped Kraus's response to the outbreak of war in 1914, certainly led to oversimplifications. But what is not in doubt is the structural significance of these motifs. Kraus's borrowings from literature and myth are not a superficial embellishment. They contribute to the deep structure of his writings and cumulatively generate what Kraus himself consciously disowned: an underlying philosophy of history.

Kraus lived in a period when philosophies of history were two-a-penny. Although the Christian world-view seemed to have broken

down, it had been replaced by a variety of secular creeds: the
Hegelian view of the nation state leading the march towards
freedom; the Whig view of history, in England; the American sense
of manifest destiny. Social Darwinism seemed to justify a ruthless
struggle for power between nations and for economic domination.
Marxism offered the opposite view of a civilization impelled towards
revolutionary change by its own economic momentum. What all
these ideologies had in common was their technological optimism.
Of course there were undercurrents of doubt, particularly among
writers sensitive to the growing rift between technocracy and the life
of the spirit. But it was not until the cataclysm of the First World
War that the dominant creed of Progress was discredited.

The Austrian situation around 1900 made it difficult to share this
historical optimism. There was no basis for that sense of mission
which sustained the German Reich. And technological progress was
so unevenly assimilated that it merely enhanced the anachronisms of
the Habsburg Empire. Thus in place of a more orthodox histori-
ography we find Kraus developing a series of interrelated paradigms,
all of which convey a sense of living in End Time. The first is the
motif of Masquerade and Carnival. The cycle of the pre-Lenten
carnival implies the inescapable approach of Ash Wednesday, the
moment of truth when the masks will be stripped away and the
sinner reduced to sackcloth and ashes. The second fundamental motif
is that of the Court of Law. Human life (for Kraus as for Kafka) is
pictured as a protracted judicial inquiry which, however arbitrary the
law's delays, will lead to a final Day of Judgement. And this motif of
judgement is linked to the third and most fundamental of the
archetypes that shape Kraus's vision: the notion of a cosmic pattern
extending from original Creation to imminent Apocalypse.

Kraus was by no means the only writer of his generation to be
inspired by the 'sense of an ending'.[19] But he was by far the most
articulate prophet of impending Apocalypse. The inner disintegration of the Habsburg Empire provided him with abundant
auguries. His task, announced in the very first number of *Die Fackel*,
was to read the writing on the wall – that enigmatic *Mene Tekel*
which signified that the days of the Empire were numbered (*F* 1: 2;
Daniel 5: 26). His method, like that of the prophets, was to discern a
sinister meaning in words which others disregarded. He created for
himself a prophetic role which he sustained through a series of
variations. But even where his tone is jocular, we find him guided
still by the apocalyptic question: 'Is this the promised end?' (*F*
245: 18; *King Lear*, V, iii, 263). His strictures on the ideology of
Progress, at first random and piecemeal, gradually assume the shape
of a coherent apocalyptic myth. The political crisis of autumn 1908,

when war over Bosnia was only just averted, led to his first formal declaration in his prophetic spirit ('Apokalypse', F 261–2: 1–14). After that the omens came thick and fast, as the precariousness of European civilization became increasingly evident. In December 1908 the city of Messina was obliterated by an earthquake, with the loss of 84,000 lives. In May 1910 Halley's Comet appeared, provoking all too plausible predictions that it might collide with the planet earth and bring about a literal 'end of the world'.[20] Kraus had been able to see for himself, during a visit to the ruins of Pompeii, how completely a civilization could be obliterated by act of God. The sinking of the *Titanic* in 1912 provided him with his most eloquent symbol of a technologically triumphant civilization steering headlong towards disaster. Meanwhile war was rumbling in the Balkans and threatening to erupt over Morocco.

Historical events thus lent themselves to interpretation in terms of apocalyptic myth. But Kraus alone had the literary stamina and ethical seriousness to sustain this myth, from the *Mene Tekel* of 1899 to *Die letzten Tage der Menschheit* in 1919. The history of *Die Fackel* in this period is a cumulative process of Revelation. It begins with revelations on a small scale: the unmasking of hypocrites, the exposure of corruption, the critique of the Austrian masquerade. But it ends with Revelation writ large — apocalyptic visions of a civilization capable of bringing about its own destruction through the unrestricted development of military technology. Apocalyptic myth thus proved to be a more reliable guide than the rational systems of historical explanation which it challenged. Writing in May 1918, Kraus was able to foresee that it would soon be possible to destroy whole cities, simply by pressing a button (F 474–83: 43). Thus he is not merely the satirist of a disintegrating empire. His vision portrays a whole civilization, poised on the brink of self-destruction.

PART TWO

THE AUSTRIAN
MASQUERADE

CHAPTER 4

Pandora and the Prostitute

The essay 'Sittlichkeit und Criminalität' (*F* 115: 1–24) [September 1902]) marks the beginning of a sustained attack by Kraus on the 'mask' of moralistic attitudes towards sex. His targets were provided by attempts to enforce morals through the courts of law. His articles on this theme appeared in book form in 1908 under the general title *Sittlichkeit und Kriminalität*. And his preoccupation with sexual themes, which also inspires some of his finest aphorisms, reached its climax in the apocalyptic premonitions of the essay 'Die chinesische Mauer' (July 1909).

Kraus's basic attitude was that of an advocate of reform. He argues for a more liberal attitude towards sex and for specific changes in the law. There should be a clear separation of spheres between 'Sittlichkeit' and 'Kriminalität' – sexual morality and criminal justice. Sexual behaviour (he argues) belongs to the private sphere. Every person is entitled to privacy in the pursuit of sexual satisfaction. And what consenting adults do together in private is no concern of the public prosecutor. The law should provide social, not moral protection. It should regulate sexual behaviour only where it is necessary to protect the interests of minors, to prevent the spread of disease, and to punish the committing of a public nuisance. No legal constraints should be placed on homosexuality, adultery, prostitution, or other extramarital forms of sex. Least of all should the law condone a double standard of morality, denying to women sexual freedoms readily conceded to men. Information about contraception should be available. Abortion should cease to be a criminal offence. Laws which punish unconventional sexual behaviour are not only an intolerable invasion of privacy; they also have the noxious side-effects of encouraging blackmail and bribery, the corruption of the police and the victimization of prostitutes. And the attempts by

forensic psychiatrists to provide a scientific justification for locking
up sexual deviants are sheer humbug.

The arguments of *Sittlichkeit und Kriminalität* have lost little of their
relevance over the years. Kraus's articles relate in the first instance to
specific court cases. But he succeeds in enunciating general principles
for enlightened legislation. His attitude was far ahead of his times. It
was many decades before the reforms which he proposed finally
began to be implemented. It was not until 1971 that homosexual acts
between consenting adults ceased to be a criminal offence in Austria.
And abortions performed during the first three months of pregnancy
were only decriminalized with the introduction of a new Austrian
Penal Code in January 1975.[1] Kraus's campaign thus entitles him to
an honourable position among the pioneers of a more permissive
attitude towards sex. But *Sittlichkeit und Kriminalität* is not simply the
work of a forceful advocate of reform. The polemical attack on the
legal system is infused by the imaginative vision of the satirist. It is
the intersection between these two perspectives which gives the
book its disconcerting force.

The Witch-Hunt at Leoben

Kraus's articles on 'The Witch-Hunt at Leoben' (July and November
1904) show how his critique of the law is reinforced by a mythopoeic
imagination. In August 1903 Bezirkshauptmann Franz von Hervay,
District Administrator in the Styrian provincial town of
Mürzzuschlag, had married an exotic foreign wife. Scandalous
rumours began to circulate about this marriage in the provincial
press – particularly about Frau Hervay's compromising past. Hervay
himself was suspended from his post, and in June 1904 his wife was
arrested and taken into custody, pending the fuller investigation of
the case. As she was being taken to prison, she was exposed to hostile
and abusive demonstrations. Shortly after the scandal became public,
Hervay himself committed suicide. Frau Hervay was then held in
custody for five months, before being put on trial in the provincial
town of Leoben. She was charged with bigamy, and it transpired
that she had indeed gone through a form of marriage with Hervay at
a time when her divorce from a previous husband had not become
final. Although this had happened with Hervay's knowledge and
indeed at his instigation, she was convicted of bigamy and sentenced
to four months' imprisonment.

During the trial the judge allowed the submission of lurid evidence
about Frau Hervay's past. The case thus provided salacious material
for scandal-hungry newspapers. The fact that Frau Hervay proved to
be of Jewish descent elicited particularly virulent coverage from the
antisemitic press. Although the charge of bigamy was tenuously

made to stick, it was clearly the immorality of Frau Hervay's conduct that antagonized both the public and the court. It turned out that she had been four times divorced. And during her relationship with Hervay she had misrepresented her age and the extent of her sexual experience, her family antecedents and her fortune. The vindictiveness of the public response illustrates that confusion of 'immorality' with 'criminality' which is the fundamental theme of *Sittlichkeit und Kriminalität*.

Kraus introduces imaginative motifs to bring out the representative significance of the case. His article begins with an imaginative prelude – the description of a scene in a Parisian night-club, in which the sophisticated eroticism of the cancan is contrasted with the heartiness of a Tyrolese clog dance. Kraus's theme is the collision between two incompatible worlds – the provinciality of the unfortunate Hervay and the cosmopolitanism of his wife. In Hervay he sees the typical product of a system which leaves Austrian civil servants disablingly ill equipped to face the realities of emotional and sexual experience. His tragedy lies in the fact that he is the victim, not of a designing woman, but of his own education. His emotional immaturity exemplifies the restricted horizon of a whole class of similarly trained government officials and civil servants. The cart-horse of bureaucratic routine begins to shy (Kraus writes) the moment an attractive female passes by. It so happened that Frau Hervay was the daughter of a professional conjurer. This provides Kraus with the motif for a more fundamental confrontation:

> Und einen fesselnderen Anblick als [. . .] der beim ersten Anprall des Lebens gefällte Normalmensch Hervay bietet diese Zaubererstochter immerhin, die die Ehepakte wie Spielkarten verschwinden läßt, Männer in Esel verwandelt und erst scheiterte, als sie die Frage stellte, ob jemand von den Herrschaften in Mürzzuschlag zufällig ein reines Taschentuch bei sich habe.   (F 165: 7)

> (And a more captivating sight than [. . .] Hervay, the normal man felled by the first impact of life, is after all offered by this magician's daughter, who makes marriage contracts disappear like playing cards, changes men into donkeys and only comes to grief when she asks whether one of the gentlemen in Mürzzuschlag happens to have a clean handkerchief on him.)

Both Hervay and his wife are given representative status, with strong symbolic undertones.

This imaginative mode of representation raises certain difficulties. For Kraus's characterization of Hervay as 'Normalmensch' leaves a great deal out of account. According to more circumstantial reports

in the *Arbeiter-Zeitung*, Hervay was a special case. He had gained
unusually rapid promotion through having friends in high places.
This had aroused the envy of less favoured colleagues and even of
senior officials in Graz. His unconventional marriage had provided
them with a pretext for cutting Hervay down to size. The *Arbeiter-
Zeitung* identifies the Governor of Styria, Count Clary, as the key
figure. It suggests that he instigated the newspaper articles which
started the scandal and was also responsible for the decisions to
suspend Hervay and arrest his wife. What might otherwise have been
a happy if unconventional marriage was thus turned into a disaster
by a malicious intrigue within the provincial civil service.[2]

Kraus's imaginative response to the case leaves these factors out of
account. His second article carries the 'magician's daughter' motif a
stage further:

> Leontine von Hervay war auf einem Besenstiel nach Mürzzuschlag
> durch die Luft geritten, wobei ihr seidener Unterrock sichtbar wurde. Ein
> ahnungsvolles Barchentgemüt rief sofort: 'I durchschaudi'. Was nützte es,
> daß sie den Bezirkshauptmann glücklich gemacht hatte? Eine Zauberers-
> tochter und fremder Sprachen mächtig. Also 'teuflischer Buhlschaft'
> dringend verdächtig. Dem einen erkrankte wohl das Vieh, dem andern
> verdarb vielleicht das Getreide. Der ganze Ort wird rebellisch. Dem
> Bezirkshauptmann hat sie einen Liebestrank eingegeben.   (F 168: 3)[3]

(Leontine von Hervay came riding through the air to Mürzzuschlag on a
broomstick, and thus her silk petticoat became visible. 'I.C.Thruyou' was
the immediate cry of a numskull, full of presentiment. What help was it
that she had made the District Administrator happy? A magician's
daughter with the mastery of foreign tongues. Thus under strong
suspicion of 'devilish intercourse'. One man no doubt found that his cattle
had fallen sick, the next perhaps that his corn was ruined. Soon the whole
place is up in arms. She gave a love potion to the District Administrator.)

In a further extension of this motif, Kraus transposes the proceedings
of the court at Leoben into the terms of a medieval witch-hunt
('Hexenprozeß'). Johannes Scherr's *Geschichte der deutschen Kultur und
Sitte* supplies the archetype. The president of the court is seen as
'Hexenrichter', entitled by virtue of this office to ignore normal legal
procedures and subject the accused to the most painful inquisition.
She herself is being treated as a 'woman possessed' ('eine Besessene'),
who must undergo the processes of exorcism. And the hostile mob
at Mürzzuschlag, who were only just restrained from physical
violence, fit into the same pattern. The trial (Kraus argues) is
designed to satisfy the deep nostalgia of the popular soul for the
time-honoured institutions of branding, torturing and executing
witches. In Scherr's account it is the Church which was responsible
for such outbreaks of popular hysteria. For Kraus the technique of

the witch-hunt has been perfected by the black arts of journalism. And in a substantial passage he documents the treatment of the case by the antisemitic press, which denounces Frau Hervay as a 'modern vampire' and a 'Jew-woman of devilish nature' ('teuflisch geartetes Judenweib'). Here (he concludes) the connection between modern publicism and a belief in witches is clearly established (F 168: 2,8,16).

In these articles we can already discern that romantic archetype of womanhood which was soon to figure so prominently in Kraus's writings. But the intuition which led him to the image of a witch-hunt was no mere fantasy. So close a match does he establish between medieval precedent and modern example that his image ceases to be a metaphor. It becomes a graphic transcription of the forces of racialism, sexual hysteria and xenophobia lurking in the Austrian provinces. Above all, it enables him to take the measure of a collective phenomenon. His target is here not simply an individual judge (Feigl) or a journalistic Mafia (represented by Bahr). He neglects the bureau-cratic clique which instigated the intrigue. But his archetypal method enables him to take a deeper sounding – to go to the very bottom of the well of Austrian popular feeling ('den tiefsten Brunnengrund österreichischen Volksempfindens', F 168: 3). With prophetic accuracy Kraus identifies that vindictive antisemitism which was later to emerge as such a terrifying force in European affairs.

Writing elsewhere in a more sceptical mood, he sometimes seems to underestimate the threat of antisemitism. In his references to notorious cases like the re-trial of Dreyfus (1899) and the Hilsner 'ritual murder' trial (1900), Kraus tends to mock the self-righteousness of Jewish apologetics rather than confront the brutish prejudices of antisemitism head-on (F 6: 18–20; 59: 1–4). Here, however, his vision achieves prophetic force. It was in a similar environment in the Austrian provinces that Adolf Hitler spent his formative years. At the time of the Hervay trial Hitler was just completing his schooling in Linz and Steyr. And this same blend of sexual revulsion and antisemitism can be found in the pages of *Mein Kampf*. The sinister possibilities which Kraus perceived in the victimization of the 'Judenweib' at Leoben were to be program-matically fulfilled thirty years later when women denounced as 'Judendirnen' were subjected to organized violence on the streets of Nazi Germany (F 890–905: 299). In the Hervay articles, as in so much of Kraus's satire, his subjective flights of fantasy land uncom-fortably close to the realities of the future.

'Weib' and 'Frau'

Kraus's preoccupation with the position of women emerges logically enough from his critique of sexual hypocrisy. From the beginning he

recognizes that the moral codes of his time bear particularly
oppressively on women. His target is quite explicitly a 'brutal male
morality' ('brutale Männermoral', *F* 115: 22). In case after case he
defends the position of women who are victimized as a result of a
hypocritical double standard. At first sight this seems to align him
with the movement of female emancipation which was gaining such
momentum during the first decade of the twentieth century. But
although he argues for equal treatment in the courts of law, he is far
from being an advocate of women's emancipation in the social and
economic sphere. Only in the very early numbers of *Die Fackel* do
we find any hints of sympathy with the progressive women's
movement. In April and May 1899 the magazine carried advertisements for the series *Dokumente der Frauen*, edited by the Austrian
feminist Rosa Mayreder. And an article of April 1901 refers
approvingly to Rosa Mayreder's art criticism and to the career of the
Swiss jurist Emilie Kempin. This unsigned article even looks
forward to the day when the barriers inhibiting women's
participation in intellectual life will have completely fallen (*F*
74: 18–20).

Kraus's later writings, however, are disrespectfully satirical about
those for whom female emancipation means equality of access to the
institutions of the male world (*F* 345–6: 1–4). Emancipation in this
sense he sees as self-defeating: the social and economic goals of
contemporary society are too impoverished to be worth aspiring to;
and a woman who seeks to assume the functions of a man can only
do so at the cost of suppressing her femininity. Thus women, in
order to rise in public estimation, are obliged to 'disguise themselves
as men' ('sich als Männer zu verkleiden', *F* 229: 15). Against this
Kraus sets an ideal of womanliness which emphasizes emotional
spontaneity and sensuous self-expression. He lays great emphasis on
the physiological factors which distinguish the sexes. But
paradoxically he ignores the reproductive functions which they
serve. The cult of Motherhood propagated by the Swedish feminist
Ellen Key is dismissed as sentimental twaddle (*F* 178: 1–4). And one
of the rare contributions to *Die Fackel* by a female author is a poem in
which a woman laments the alienating effect of her pregnancy (*F*
219–20: 23).

The literary provenance of Kraus's cult of the sensuous woman is
not difficult to trace. His formative years were the 1890s, a period
when the myth of the amoral woman was enjoying a revival. The
Victorians had nurtured an ideal of woman as the lofty embodiment
of purity and solicitude. Closeted and corseted, sexless and
unbending, women were assigned a position aloof from the mundane spheres of professional and commercial activity. The economic

and legal constraints imposed upon women during this period had indeed gone a long way towards making this idealization a social reality. The imaginative writers of this same period, however, cultivated a more primitive image of woman which reflected the Victorian underworld of illicit sexuality. Female beauty was endowed with demonic powers. From Poe through Baudelaire and Flaubert to Zola, Swinburne and D'Annunzio the *femme fatale* had many reincarnations. And her seductive powers were enhanced by the work of visual artists in morbidly sensuous variations on the Sphinx and Vampire, Judith and Salome motifs.[4]

Although this cult could be found in almost every country in Europe, there were regional variations. In the German–language area it acquired a particularly misogynistic emphasis. The stridently masculine ethos of Wilhelmine Germany and the repressive moralism of official attitudes created a situation in which women became the scapegoats for sexual disorder. And this attitude appeared to gain philosophical sanction from the writings of Schopenhauer and Nietzsche.[5] The final decades of the nineteenth century saw a remarkable revival of the cult of the demonic woman, luring men to destruction in the thrall of promiscuity.[6] And the social themes of Ibsen were displaced by sexual antagonism in the plays of Strindberg and Wedekind. The obsession with sexuality, epitomized in the self-destructive theories of Otto Weininger, reached its climax in Vienna around 1900.[7]

Kraus's involvement in this debate is evident from the prominence he gives in *Die Fackel* to Wedekind and Strindberg, Weininger and Altenberg. As early as 1892 Kraus had struck up a friendship with Peter Altenberg, whose impressionistic prose poems celebrate the 'aesthetic genius of women', which he puts on a par with the 'intellectual genius of men' (*F* 81: 19). But the decisive influences were Wedekind and Weininger. Kraus read Weininger's *Geschlecht und Charakter* as soon as it appeared in May 1903 (*F* 169: 7). The profound impression which this book made on him is indicated by an aphorism published four years later, in which he pays tribute to Weininger's 'insight into the otherness of woman' ('Erkenntnis der Anderswertigkeit des Weibes', *F* 229: 14). This notion soon became associated in his mind with the work of Wedekind, a writer whom he had admired since the early 1890s (*FS* I. 71, 161). When *Erdgeist* was staged in Vienna in June 1903, Kraus reproached the play's critics for failing to understand 'the polygamous nature of woman' ('die polygame Frauennatur', *F* 142: 17). The conception of woman as 'polygam' derives directly from *Geschlecht und Charakter*.[8] The contrast Wedekind drew between the sensuous appeal of Lulu and the requirements of bourgeois society particularly impressed Kraus.

And his admiration for Wedekind led him to organize a production
of *Die Büchse der Pandora* before an invited audience, at a time (May
1905) when public performance of the play was forbidden. The
success of this production marked a turning-point in Wedekind's
career. But it also led to a reorientation of Kraus's programme as a
publicist. The address 'Die Büchse der Pandora' which he delivered
before the performance is his first great achievement in a new mode:
a synthesis of literary criticism and satirical vision.

Similar stimuli were received from other sources. Kraus prints a
series of contributions by Strindberg, whose reflections on the theme
'Mann und Weib' (published in *Die Fackel* in November 1907) he
particularly praises (*F* 236: 9–15). He admired the conception of the
courtesan as an active and dominant figure in the third volume of
Heinrich Mann's *Die Göttinnen oder die drei Romane der Herzogin von
Assy* (1902–3). And a short prose text by Heinrich Mann dealing
with a romantically conceived *femme fatale* is included in *Die Fackel* in
February 1906 (*F* 196: 12–17). Kraus also admired the work of Jens
Peter Jacobsen, particularly the historical romance *Marie Grubbe*
(whose aristocratic heroine finds her salvation in the arms of a lusty
ostler) (*F* 148: 27). And lurking in the background are those
progenitors of the Romantic Agony: the Marquis de Sade, whose
ideas are given prominence in *Die Fackel* in June and July 1906 (*F*
203: 1–5; 206: 1–4); and Edgar Allan Poe, whose sketches Kraus
singles out for special praise in December of the same year (*F*
213: 17).

'Influence' is never a simple matter. And Kraus's response to
almost all these writers involves critical discriminations which are
forcefully made. But it is clear that his ideas ripened in a climate of
literary bohemianism permeated by notions of the amorality of
woman. The literary flavour of this conception deserves special
emphasis. It is to the realm of imaginative archetypes that it
primarily belongs, rather than of social observation. Of course,
Kraus frequented cafés and night-clubs where women of easy virtue
were readily available. 'Je suis libre tous les soirs à partir de 9 heures,'
writes one young woman in a billet-doux which has survived among
Kraus's early correspondence.[9] 'The sidewalks were so sprinkled
with women for sale', Stefan Zweig recalls, 'that it was more
difficult to avoid than to find them.'[10]

The favours of a prostitute could be purchased almost as easily as a
packet of sweets at the corner store. If this sounds like an exagger-
ation, we should recall the story Kraus told later in life about an
experience he had at the age of sixteen. As he emerged from a
sweet-shop in the Krugerstrasse, the sixteen-year-old was asked by a
porter whether he wouldn't like to accompany one of the 'ladies' of

the street to her home. He did so, only to find that the change left
over from buying sweets was not sufficient to pay for her favours.
The outraged prostitute threw him out, but the memory of this
experience remained with Kraus to the end of his days.[11] The chaste
daughters of the bourgeoisie, on the other hand, had to repress their
desires until a marriage could be arranged. There was thus a basis in
experience for the sharp juxtaposition between women's social and
sexual identities — between 'Frau' and 'Weib' — which we find not
only in Kraus's writings but in the work of many European
contemporaries.

The English language lacks a word to distinguish 'Frau' from
'Weib'. Thus James Joyce had to borrow from the German in order
to define the womanliness portrayed in the final chapter of *Ulysses*:
'perfectly sane full amoral fertilisable untrustworthy engaging
shrewd limited prudent indifferent *Weib*'.[12] The debate about
sexuality at the turn of the century relied heavily on these antithetical
categories. 'Weib' denoted the sexual, 'Frau' the social aspect of
women's existence. 'Weib' is female, whereas 'Frau' is merely
feminine. Although Kraus's word-choice is not consistent, he is
essentially campaigning on behalf of the sensuous liberation of
'Weib' and against the social emancipation of 'Frau'.

The image of woman in *Die Fackel* is filtered through a mind
steeped in literary associations. The theatre once again was Kraus's
particular source of inspiration. The notion of 'weibliche Dämonie'
invoked in the Hervay essays of 1905 reflects a vogue for plays about
demonic female sexuality which had swept the German stage in the
previous years. The sensations of the Berlin theatre in autumn 1902
had been the premières of Strindberg's *Rausch*, Wilde's *Salomé* and
Wedekind's *Erdgeist*, followed in 1903 by Gorky's *Nachtasyl* and
Hofmannsthal's *Elektra*. The spectacular effects achieved by Max
Reinhardt's new style of production reinforced the impact of these
plays, while the actress Gertrud Eysoldt was celebrated for her
portrayal of 'weibliche Dämonie'. Indeed, it was apparently her
sensuous style of acting which inspired Wedekind, after the Berlin
première of *Erdgeist*, to add the famous lines in the Prologue
describing Lulu as 'die Urgestalt des Weibes' ('the primal figure of
woman'). These plays find a vibrant echo in *Die Fackel*. The essay
which Kraus wrote in defence of *Salomé*, after witnessing three
different productions, shows how theatrical experience reinforced
his satirical perspective. In *Salomé* he hailed a masterpiece which
blended voluptuousness with terror. And he was delighted that the
play scandalized the philistines of all ideological factions (*F*
150: 1–14). Against the 'brutal male morality' of his age Kraus sets
his alternative ideal of 'Weiblichkeit' which is 'ethically scarcely

definable' (*F* 165: 7). This image is the precipitate of literary reading, passion for the theatre, and poignant personal experience.

The Voice of Antonia: Annie Kalmar

For Kraus even the experience of love was mediated by the theatre. The fact that his early love relationships were with professional actresses leaves an unmistakable imprint on his writings. We are told that while still at school he had fallen in love with an actress.[13] And his love for Annie Kalmar is of particular significance. Annie Kalmar (the stage name of Anna Elisabeth Kaldwasser) was born in Frankfurt on 14 September 1877. It is her beauty that is celebrated, and her death lamented, in Altenberg's letter about the 'aesthetic genius of woman' (June 1901; *F* 81: 18–21). Kraus, characteristically excluding his most intense personal experiences from the polemical pages of *Die Fackel*, gives no hint of his own bereavement. The significance of his relationship with Annie Kalmar was not that it enabled him (as has been claimed) to base his image of woman on 'a real, positive experience of love'.[14] On the contrary, it is far more likely to have encouraged his myth-making tendencies.

Kraus's acquaintance with Annie Kalmar was of very brief duration and came about under unusual circumstances. It was as an actress on the stage of the Deutsches Volkstheater that she first caught his attention, in the spring of 1899. Her gifts made a deep impression on him; and he wrote an admiring notice in *Die Fackel* (*F* 2: 29). She responded with an appreciative letter (dated 22 April 1899). But it seems that they did not become personally acquainted until the summer of 1900. Photographs from this period (Pls. 6 and 7) convey something of the attraction the young actress must have held for the aspiring author. But by this time Annie was seriously ill with tuberculosis. She spent the summer of 1900 in a sanatorium near Vienna, where Kraus paid her frequent visits. By the autumn of that year she seemed sufficiently recovered to take up an engagement at a theatre in Hamburg. Kraus himself, through his friendship with the director of the Hamburg theatre, Alfred von Berger, had helped to arrange this opportunity for her. She fell ill again shortly before the première of Schiller's *Maria Stuart*, in which she was to have played the title role. And although Kraus made arrangements for her to have the best possible treatment, at a hospital in Hamburg (where he visited her frequently during the following months), she died on 2 May 1901. The effect of her death on Kraus may be gauged from the fact that by the end of June his own health had broken down. Complete nervous exhaustion was diagnosed, and he suspended publication of *Die Fackel* for three months.

6   Karl Kraus, 1898

7   (*right*) Annie Kalmar

Whatever general conclusions Kraus may have drawn from such a brief and poignant relationship, it is hardly surprising that they acquired a romantic aura. Neither his first image of Annie Kalmar, radiantly beautiful on the stage, nor his later impressions of her in the equally artificial context of a sanatorium, can have offered a very realistic view of female personality. Kraus's aphorisms show him to be aware of the subjectivity of perception in love. He recognizes that the person loved is in part an ideal image projected by the lover. And the experience with Annie seems to have lent itself particularly to such idealization.

The process through which lived experience becomes assimilated into imaginative archetype is not difficult to reconstruct. Six months after Annie's death Kraus attended a performance of Offenbach's *Tales of Hoffmann* at the Vienna Opera. And he was particularly impressed by the singer who played the three main female roles (*F* 86: 28). She achieved greatest dramatic impact in the role of Antonia, the singer whose frail health is undermined by her singing, which finally brings about her death. In Kraus's memory, Annie seems to have become so closely associated with Antonia that in the poem 'Annie Kalmar', published thirty years later, their two voices are indistinguishable: 'so ist's, als ob's Antonias Stimme sei' (*F* 852–6: 48). In a less transparent reference (in the play *Traumstück*) memories of Annie again appear to be associated with the music from *Tales of Hoffmann* (this time the Olympia act). And in more general reflections about Offenbach's operettas Kraus suggests that his imagination may have received more decisive impulses from this source than from more formal modes of education (*F* 270–1: 10).

To say that Kraus's love for Annie Kalmar inspired his treatment of sexuality is to put the matter too simply. It inspired him to perceive the relationship between the sexes in terms of romantic paradigms. In this imaginative patterning Offenbach is of course only one formative influence among many. But it is worth noting that the three acts of *Tales of Hoffmann* introduce three of the principal roles which Kraus assigns to woman: Olympia — the woman (actually an automaton) who becomes beautiful in the eyes of the poet through the power of his subjective perception; Giulietta — the courtesan who is irresistibly attractive to the poet despite his awareness of her promiscuity; and Antonia, whose beauty is too frail to survive in a hostile world. Only the first and the last are explicitly associated with Annie Kalmar in Kraus's writings. But even with Giulietta the association would not have been inappropriate. After Annie's death Kraus supported legal actions instigated by her family to protect her name from the smears of gossip columnists. One such allegation was that her estate included a large amount of jewellery given to her by admirers in return for sexual favours. Kraus fiercely condemned these intrusions into the private life of an actress. And to refute allegations about Annie Kalmar's accumulated possessions, he noted that her estate in fact amounted to 15,000 Marks (F 84: 21–9; 107: 15–24). But elsewhere (particularly in the play *Traumtheater*, which is dedicated to Annie) Kraus suggests that it is part of the natural endowment of the actress to be able to satisfy the sexual desires of a variety of admirers. It seems that in Annie Kalmar he found a living embodiment of the 'polygamous' nature of woman.[15]

Speculation about the biographical sources of Kraus's writings is bound to peter out in conjecture. The attempts (by Margarete Mitscherlich and others) to trace his attitude towards women back to childhood experiences of emotional deprivation exemplify this. The biographical evidence is too sparse to justify firm conclusions. Kraus was born with a slight curvature of the spine. It is thus possible that he felt a greater need for maternal reassurance than the average child. But the claim that during infancy Kraus felt deprived of his mother's love because of the birth of a younger sister is mere speculation. More plausible is the report that he was deeply affected by the death of his mother, who died in October 1891 when he was seventeen. But this is an insufficient basis for the claim that these early traumas determined all his subsequent relationships with women, since he remained dependent on his mother 'in a repressed sexual sense'. And the attempt (by Manfred Schneider) to explain Kraus's creativity in terms of the Oedipal configuration of paternal hatred and maternal bond seems sadly misconceived.[16] The poignant circumstances of his love for Annie Kalmar, so vividly reflected in his letters, elude such reductive categories.[17]

No doubt Kraus found the third act of *Tales of Hoffmann* all the more resonant because at the climax of the opera it is the voice of Antonia's mother which calls on her to sing and die. Perhaps there is an echo of both voices in that line from the poem 'Annie Kalmar' which refers to a song from the undefined past which has faded away: 'Mir ist ein Lied von irgendwann verklungen' (F 852–6: 48). This may contain the hint that for Kraus, as for any sensitive lover, the experience of love echoes the original maternal bond. But the voice of Antonia is nevertheless quite distinct from that of Jocasta.

Playing Pandora: Wedekind and Bertha Maria Denk

The literary assimilation of emotional experience can be traced even more precisely in another instance. About a year after the death of Annie Kalmar, Kraus became attracted to another actress, Bertha Maria Denk. But he lost trace of her until May 1905, when they were reintroduced by Frank Wedekind on the occasion of Kraus's production of *Die Büchse der Pandora*. Bertha Maria was one of the actresses considered for the demanding role of Lulu, as a letter from Wedekind to Kraus of 9 May 1905 reveals: 'Sie hat sich auch mit dem Problem Lulu beschäftigt, gesteht aber selber der Rolle, auf der Bühne wenigstens, nicht gewachsen zu sein. (She too has occupied herself with the Lulu problem, but herself admits that the role is beyond her capacity, at least on the stage.)' (*F* 521–30: 111) Off-stage her powers must have been considerable, for Wedekind was on the point of becoming engaged to her. And she travelled to Vienna to attend *Die Büchse der Pandora*. But another Lulu possessed even greater powers. On 29 May 1905 the actress Tilly Newes, playing Lulu, was lustfully done to death by Wedekind, as Jack the Ripper, on the stage of the Trianon Theatre. A distinguished cast list (Pl. 8)

TRIANON-THEATER

===== (Nestroyhof) =====

Wien, 29. Mai 1905

Einleitende Vorlesung von Karl Kraus

Hierauf:

DIE BÜCHSE DER PANDORA

Tragödie in drei Aufzügen von Frank Wedekind.

Regie: Albert Heine.

Lulu	Tilly Newes
Alwa Schön	O. D. Potthof
Rodrigo Quast, Athlet	Alexander Rottmann
Schigolch	Albert Heine
Alfred Hugenberg, Zögling einer Korrektions- anstalt	Tony Schwanau
Die Gräfin Geschwitz	Adele Sandrock
Marquis Casti-Piani	Anton Edthofer
Bankier Puntschu	Gustav d'Olbert
Journalist Heilmann	Wilhelm Appelt
Magelone	Adele Nova
Kadéga di Santa Croce, ihre Tochter	Iduschka Orloff
Bianetta Gazil	Dolores Stadlon
Ludmilla Steinherz	Claire Sitty
Bob, Groom	Irma Karczewska
Ein Polizeikommissär	Egon Fridell
Herr Hunidey	Ludwig Ströb
Kungu Poti, kaiserlicher Prinz von Uahubee	Karl Kraus
Dr. Hilti, Privatdozent	Arnold Korff
Jack	Frank Wedekind

Der erste Akt spielt in Deutschland, der zweite in Paris, der dritte in London.

Die Vorstellung findet vor geladenem Publikum statt.

Anfang präzise ½8 Uhr.

---

8   Cast list for Kraus's production of *Die Büchse der Pandora*

included Kraus himself in a minor role. The paradox of this production is that Wedekind was soon under the spell of the woman who portrayed his own fiction. In June and July 1905 he was still entertaining Bertha Maria in Munich, and he visited her at the Bohemian spa of Franzensbad in August. But by the autumn he was in Berlin, performing in another play with Tilly Newes as his partner. Tilly was even more alluring as the young Lulu in productions of *Erdgeist* (Pl. 9) than she had been as *femme fatale* in *Die Büchse der Pandora* (Pl. 10). Meanwhile another admirer, Karl Kraus, was visiting Bertha Maria in Bohemia. He too fell in love with her, and their relationship reached its first climax during a holiday together in Italy at the end of August 1905.

The resulting emotional triangle can be traced through Kraus's correspondence.[18] In December 1905 he wrote to Wedekind in some detail, explaining that his relationship with Bertha Maria was 'not flirtation, merely predestination' ('kein Verhältnis, nur ein Verhängnis'). At this stage Bertha Maria was hesitating between her two lovers. But when she visited Wedekind in Berlin in January 1906, she found him firmly attached to Tilly Newes (they were married later that year on 1 May). On her return to Vienna Bertha Maria became seriously ill. Kraus tended her during her stay in a sanatorium and wrote her solicitous letters during her convalescence in the Austrian provinces. This correspondence continued when she later lived in Italy and in Paris. The letters indicate that they met only intermittently, that their relationship underwent many fluctuations, and that she had other lovers. At times Kraus writes with the detachment of a sympathetic friend, at times in a mood of erotic elation, at times in almost suicidal despair. Although some of his letters cannot be dated precisely, they suggest that the relationship was passionately renewed in the spring of 1908.

There can be little doubt that this experience contributed significantly to Kraus's reorientation as a writer during the years 1905–8. The first number of *Die Fackel* to be published after their Italian journey of 1905 proudly announces the magazine's 'moral decline' ('moralischer Niedergang'). Aesthetic and erotic preoccupations are to take precedence over the campaign against corruption. The satirist has begun 'to court the wicked woman' ('um die schlimme Frau zu werben', F 185: 1–9). Kraus characteristically conceals the actual erotic experience which lay behind this transformation. Even when he published Wedekind's letters in *Die Fackel*, many years later, he suppressed Bertha Maria's identity. But a number of the aphorisms about erotic experience which appeared in *Die Fackel* from the autumn of 1905 onwards can be traced back to Kraus's letters to the actress.[19]

9   Tilly Newes as Lulu and Wedekind as   10   Tilly Newes as Lulu in *Die Büchse der*
     Dr Schon in *Erdgeist*   *Pandora*

Several of these groups of aphorisms appeared under the title
'Tagebuch'. But to read them simply as diary transcriptions of
private experience would be a misconception. Kraus's letters show
that Bertha Maria was too complex a person to fit into his
preconceived scheme of the relationship between the sexes. With this
complexity he had to come to terms, both in his private experience
and in his published writings. She certainly seems to have fulfilled his
ideal of the polygamous woman. Reflecting on this relationship in a
letter to Wedekind dated 29 February 1906, Kraus insists that 'we
really *did* play Pandora's Box' ('daß wir *wirklich* die Büchse der
Pandora gespielt haben'). But in other respects Bertha Maria seems
to have been less easily assimilated into the archetype of the
all-giving woman.

In another letter to Wedekind, dated December 1905, there is a
description of Bertha Maria knitting socks for her grandmother.

This cosy domesticity is not allowed to obtrude upon the published aphorisms. And Bertha Maria possessed one gift which Pandora has never been allowed in any version of the myth: intelligence. Kraus's letters repeatedly betray the perplexity which this caused him. In her he has to love a quality which in other women he claims to hate: 'Dein Verstand – ein Aphrodisiacum'. He has to acknowledge that her letters are well written and that she is a discerning reader. He sends *Die Fackel* to her and welcomes her comments. He also sends her lists of recommended reading: Dostoevsky, Stendhal, Edgar Allan Poe, Bernard Shaw, Johannes Jensen, even Musil's *Törless*. How then is he to reconcile her acknowledged intellectual gifts ('Geistesgaben') with his preconceived notions of brainless 'Weiblichkeit'?[20]

The solution suggested in Kraus's letters is ingenious. Here as so often he insists on the subjectivity of emotional perception. It is a matter of bringing illusions to life ('Illusionen verlebendigen').[21] The circumstances of their journey to Italy seem particularly to have favoured the formation of such 'illusions', as his letter to Wedekind of 17 December 1905 records:

Sie kennen Bertha Maria nicht, da Sie sie nicht im mondbeleuchteten Colosseum gesehen haben, auf einem Trümmer des Marmorsitzes der Kaiserin; der ganze Zauber des Gewesenen, den diese Ruinen einschließen, schien leibhaftig aus ihren schönen Augen zu treten, bis ein Thränenflor ihn verhüllte. Seit damals bete ich sie an.

(You don't know Bertha Maria, since you have not seen her in the moonlit Colosseum, on the marble remains of the empress's throne; all the magic of the past which is enclosed by these ruins seemed physically to emanate from her beautiful eyes, until covered by a veil of tears. Since that moment I have worshipped her.)

The passage exemplifies Kraus's sensitivity to theatrical atmosphere and to the archetypal resonance underlying a given moment of experience. He evidently responded to women who had the ability to dramatize emotions and to play the role in which he cast them. Indeed, in an aphoristic reminiscence of Annie Kalmar he identifies the source of her attractiveness as the 'unity of woman and actress' ('das Einsein des Weibes und der Schauspielerin'), which gave a 'theatrical quality' ('Bühnenhaftigkeit') to her natural charm (*W* III.104–5). Kraus's letters also emphasize Bertha Maria's 'capacity for play-acting in real life' ('Fähigkeit, im Leben Komödie zu spielen'). His emotional development seems to have owed less to the maternal bond than to the lure of the theatre.[22]

In the relationship with Bertha Maria Denk this element of dramatic type-casting seems more contrived. She may not be a Roman empress, but she seems to have cultivated an aristocratic identity, calling herself (in a letter to Kraus) 'Madame la Comtesse Maria Rota' and even signing herself (in a joint missive to Wedekind) 'Gräfin Potocka' — an allusion to a Polish countess of the Napoleonic period. Wedekind had evidently been so struck by the resemblance between Bertha Maria and the portrait of the countess by Angelika Kauffmann (compare Pls. 11 and 12) that he entitled one of his poems 'An Bertha Maria, Typus Gräfin Potocka'. Like the countess Bertha had expressive eyebrows, to which Kraus himself paid tribute in an aphorism (F 251–2: 41). And he went on to encourage her to follow the example of the great courtesans of the past by writing her memoirs. It is by *this* means that she will be able to put her intellectual gifts in the service of her sensuality. The seriousness of this suggestion is shown by the fact that Kraus sent a list of erotic narratives to inspire her, including Brantôme's *Vie des dames galantes* and Sade's *Juliette*. He offered to read through her manuscript and even suggested a title: *Tagebuch einer nie Verlorenen*.[23] As an unashamed celebration of the erotic life, it was to counteract the influence of the diary of a penitent prostitute which had been published under the title *Tagebuch einer Verlorenen* ('Diary of a Lost Woman'). Whether anything came of this suggestion is not clear. Kraus's relationship with Bertha Maria seems to have petered out around 1910.

A striking contradiction is apparent between Kraus's private relationship with an intelligent woman and his public emphasis on women's 'brainlessness' ('Hirnlosigkeit', F 229: 14). This dogma was uncomfortably at odds with his private acknowledgement that the woman he was in love with had considerable gifts as a writer.[24] Only obliquely is his insight into the more complex dimensions of female personality reflected in the published aphorisms (as in the 'kompliziertes Räderwerk' image of F 251–2: 40).[25] And even in private letters we find Kraus trying to assimilate the personality of Bertha Maria into his nature myth. One of the emotional climaxes in their relationship seems to have coincided with the great eruption of Vesuvius in April 1906. When their passion was renewed in the spring of 1908, Kraus suggests in a letter that the fire must have been glowing all the time under a layer of volcanic lava. He is thus able to claim that she does, after all, fit into his preconceived philosophy of life ('fertige Lebensanschauung'): as an elemental force of nature which inspires his hatred of banality. Kraus had actually climbed Mount Vesuvius in 1907, a year after the eruption, and this spectacle seems to have blended with his passionate experiences with Bertha Maria in Italy into a private myth.[26] The image of sexuality as a volcanic eruption was later to be magnified into a vision of a whole civilization built on a crater which threatens to engulf it (F 285–6: 2).

1   Bertha Maria Denk

12   *Countess Potocka* by Angelika Kauffman

Variations on the Myth: Goethe and Bachofen

Biographical arguments direct our attention towards the source of a given motif, not its function. It is the strategy of Kraus's satire which gives the image of woman in *Die Fackel* its special charge of meaning. Individually, the women whose cause Kraus defends are the victims of a hypocritical male ethic. Symbolically, they become assimilated into the myth of Pandora. The pattern is closely aligned to the structure of Wedekind's plays, in which Lulu functions both as childlike victim and as destructive *femme fatale*. In Wedekind, however, it is unclear whether Lulu is a woman more sinned against than sinning – an ambiguity for which Kraus reproaches him (*F* 142: 17–18). Wedekind's text contains strong echoes of the Hesiodic myth in which woman is created merely to inflict suffering. Kraus's commentary hints at an earlier version of the myth, in which

Pandora's gifts are not yet confined within the fatal box.[27] His essential point is 'that in this narrow world the source of joy necessarily becomes Pandora's box' ('daß der Freudenquell in dieser engen Welt zur Pandorabüchse werden muß', *F* 182: 13). It is the constraints of civilization which are at fault.

Kraus never retracted his admiration for *Die Büchse der Pandora* (although as Wedekind moved into the ambit of Max Reinhardt, their relationship became more distant). He reprinted his essay 'Die Büchse der Pandora' in *Die Fackel* in 1925 and again in the volume *Literatur und Lüge* (1929). But it is understandable that later in life he came to feel an even stronger affinity with Goethe's version of *Pandora*. For Goethe's play inverts the Hesiodic myth, insisting (through the words of Pandora's lover Epimetheus) that her gifts brought joy not suffering. Beauty is certainly transient, for Pandora has now departed leaving Epimetheus alone with his memories. And it may engender tragedy, as is shown by the fate of their daughter Epimeleia, caught between two lovers. But even her agony of spirit possesses for Kraus as affirmative charge. *Pandora* was one of the texts which he read most frequently at his public recitals. And in May 1918 he published a poem inspired by Goethe's play, identifying in Epimeleia the 'origin of all womanly power' ('Ursprung/aller Weibmacht', *F* 474–83: 85).

This archetypal imagery is characteristic of Kraus's mode of representation. 'Freudenquell', 'Urquell', 'Ursprung', 'Urkraft', 'Urgesicht', 'Naturgewalt' are recurrent epithets associated with woman. Avoiding the artifice of formal mythology, he invokes a nature myth in which the free-flowing female principle is constricted by male civilization:

> Der Mann hat den Wildstrom weiblicher Sinnlichkeit kanalisiert. Nun überschwemmt er nicht mehr das Land. Aber er befruchtet es auch nicht mehr.   (*F* 275–6: 26)

> (Men have canalized the torrent of womanly sensuality. Now it no longer floods the land. But it doesn't make it fruitful any longer either.)

This echoes a myth so ancient that it cannot simply be taken as a transcription of personal experience. The fullest exposition of the myth occurs in Bachofen's celebrated study of matriarchy, *Das Mutterrecht*, published in 1861 and reprinted in 1897. Although Kraus does not mention Bachofen in *Die Fackel*, he was probably acquainted with his ideas through the mediation of Weininger.

Bachofen argues that the earliest forms of Mediterranean civilization were guided by female principles of natural wisdom. The transition to male-dominated forms of society subordinated the sensuousness and fecundity of women to the male principles of intellect and aggressive energy. Although Bachofen accepts this as an evolutionary process, his eloquence and erudition are devoted to foam-born Aphrodite, not form-giving Apollo. It is this rich body of nature myths which is echoed in Kraus's satire. In *Die Fackel* the relationship between the sexes is pictured in terms of the strongest possible contrast between 'male' and 'female':

> Ein Weib, dessen Sinnlichkeit nie aussetzt, und ein Mann, dem ununterbrochen Gedanken kommen: zwei Ideale der Menschlichkeit, die der Menschheit krankhaft erscheinen.   (*F* 272–3: 40)

> (A woman whose sensuality is inexhaustible and a man continuously fertile in ideas: two ideals of humanity which seem unhealthy to mankind.)

The echo of Bachofen is unmistakable: 'Der Sieg des Mannes liegt in dem rein geistigen Prinzip. [. . .] Denn an Sinnlichkeit überragt ihn das Weib, das der Begierde Stachel stärker antreibt, und das den zehnfachen Geschlechtsgenuss empfindet. (The victory of the man lies in the purely intellectual principle. [. . .] For in sensuality he is surpassed by the woman, who responds far more strongly to the goad of desire and experiences tenfold sexual pleasure.)'

Such passages from *Das Mutterrecht* suggest that Kraus was probably influenced by Bachofen, who at times even anticipates his aphoristic style: 'Nicht um in den Armen eines Einzelnen zu verwelken, wird das Weib von der Natur mit allen Reizen, über welche sie gebietet, ausgestattet. (It is not for the purpose of withering away in the arms of a single man that woman is equipped by nature with all the charms of which she disposes.)'[28] But where Bachofen pictures the relationship between male and female in terms of inescapable conflict, Kraus emphasizes an ideal of harmonious interaction:

> Des Weibes Sinnlichkeit ist der Urquell, an dem sich des Mannes Geistigkeit Erneuerung holt.   (*W* III. 13)

> (The sensuality of woman is the primal spring at which the intellectuality of man finds renewal.)

This motif is given pride of place in *Sprüche und Widersprüche* (1909) and runs right through Kraus's aphorisms and lyric poetry.

Prostitution: Natural Force or Social Problem?

In Bachofen's historical scheme the phase of ordered matriarchy is preceded by a primal condition of anarchic promiscuity. The Hetaera – 'Pandora, das Urweib' – precedes the Mother as the primal archetype.[29] In Weininger's *Geschlecht und Charakter* 'Prostitute' and 'Mother' become equally baleful forces. Kraus read this section of

Weininger's book with particular admiration (*F* 157: 19). But his own writings revive the original polygamous myth. It is the prostitute that Kraus's writings celebrate, as the great antagonist of Christian chastity and bourgeois repression. Around this figure he constructs some of his most pungent arguments. 'Das Ehrenkreuz' (February 1909) reduces to absurdity the legal categories by which society attempts to regulate prostitution. And the treatment of prostitutes becomes the test of civilization in a wealth of polemical essays and satirical glosses.

In the Vienna of 1900 it was only the bohemian *demi-monde* that was sexually liberated. Middle-class women, as well as sexually inhibited males, remained trapped within a repressive moralism. A whole chapter in Zweig's *World of Yesterday* is devoted to this extraordinary dualism. Schnitzler's diaries and memoirs show that respectable society set definite limits to what was permitted by way of flirtation. The sexual exploits which he records almost invariably took place with girls lower down the social scale. Kraus, writing from a critical perspective, sharply distinguishes between the bourgeois 'social order', in which a crippling moralism prevails, and the sphere of sexual indulgence provided by prostitution. In 'Der Prozeß Riehl' (November 1906) he identifies this division as profoundly destructive. Sexuality, the most elemental part of human nature, has been placed beyond the pale. And self-respecting men despise by day the women whose favours they crave at night. This institutionalized hypocrisy leads to a mindless licentiousness.

How far this falls short of Kraus's ideal of harmonious interaction between sexual and mental life is made clear in his peroration to 'Der Prozeß Riehl':

> Fort mit der Schamhaftigkeit, die die körperliche und geistige Gesundheit der Völker seit fast zwei Jahrtausenden untergräbt! Auch die geistige. Denn die Natur hat dem Weib die Sinnlichkeit als den Urquell verliehen, an dem sich der Geist des Mannes Erneuerung hole. Die Gründer der Normen aber haben das Verhältnis der Geschlechter verkehrt, die habituelle Sexualität der Frau in die Konvention geschnürt und die funktionelle Sexualität des Mannes schrankenlos ausarten lassen. So ist die Anmut vertrocknet und der Geist. Der Frau sind Würde und Bewußtheit vorgeschrieben, dem Mann ein tierisches Sichausleben gestattet. Darum kanalisiert er den herrlichen Wildstrom weiblicher Sinnlichkeit für seine uninteressanten Bedürfnisse, und sein Gehirn geht leer dabei aus.
>
> (*F* 211: 27–8)

> (Away with the prudishness that has been undermining the physical and mental health of the nations for almost two millennia! Including their mental health. For nature has endowed women with sensuality as the primal spring at which the minds of men may find renewal. The founders

of norms however have reversed the relationship between the sexes, constricting the habitual sexuality of women by convention and allowing the functional sexuality of men to run wildly to seed. As a result both physical grace and mental energy have dried up. Dignity and self-possession are prescribed for the middle-class woman, while the man is permitted a bestial self-indulgence. He therefore canalizes the splendid torrent of female sensuality for his own uninteresting needs, and his brain is left empty in the process.)

The identification of mental energy as male and sensuality as female raises problems to which we shall return. But Kraus's argument discredits with equal force both repressive moralism and mindless hedonism. Although his satire is framed within a repressive civilization, it still has application to societies in which the balance has tilted the other way.

The satirical overstatements of 'Der Prozeß Riehl' do not diminish its force. Reprinted in pamphlet form, it was widely read and must still count as one of the most inspired attacks on bourgeois sexual hypocrisy. Freud read it with particular admiration. But Kraus's arguments become problematic when he raises the basic question of why prostitutes, despite the persecution to which they are subjected, continue to exist.

The tremendous spread of prostitution before the First World War was a consequence of market forces. On the one hand, the concentration of wealth in the hands of sexually frustrated males created the demand. On the other, rapid population growth in a situation that offered restricted employment opportunities for women guaranteed the supply. These social factors, which Kraus largely ignores, are clearly identified in the study of Viennese prostitution by Heinrich Grün (1907).[30] And the economic causes are emphasized in August Bebel's *Die Frau und der Sozialismus* (first published in 1879 and repeatedly reprinted). Kraus was certainly familiar with the Marxist view that prostitution was a bourgeois institution which would be eliminated in the socialist state of the future. But he mocks this as a typical Marxist simplification ('Nur immer schön marxistisch gedacht!'). And he brushes aside Stefan Grossmann's argument in the *Arbeiter-Zeitung* that to represent prostitutes as glamorous 'Lustweiber' is to falsify the facts of social deprivation (*F* 190: 15–16). Bebel's book too is criticized in *Die Fackel* for its dogmatism and lack of psychological insight (*F* 248: 13). And Kraus had no sympathy with those who saw the cult of sensuousness as a historical variable, forced upon women by their position of financial dependence (as his friend Adolf Loos argued in a brilliant article on 'Ladies' Fashions').[31]

Kraus consciously sets such pragmatic questions aside in his

defence of sensuous energy against the 'phantom of morality' (*F*
211: 18). Instead, he invokes a nature myth with echoes of Rousseau.
For the radical critic of civilization the problem is to identify that
original naturalness which has been destroyed by socialization.
Rousseau finds his answer in the sensitive child, Kraus in the
sensuous woman. He argues that prostitutes who ply their trade with
such heroic endurance are fulfilling their 'natural destiny'. For a
woman it is a 'natural right' to turn her aesthetic advantages into
hard currency (*F* 211: 24–5).

Kraus's most revealing treatment of this theme occurs in 'Prozeß
Veith' (October 1908). The essay deals with the case of a prostitute,
Mizzi Veith, who committed suicide after her stepfather had been
arrested for soliciting on her behalf. In this essay Kraus concedes that
there may be prostitutes whose trade is merely a social necessity.
Perhaps Mizzi Veith was one of these. But for the satirist this more
sober perspective is inadequate. To bring out the fundamental
implications of this tragedy, he feels compelled to 'stylize her case'
('ihren Fall stilisieren', *F* 263: 8). It is transposed into the terms of a
mythic struggle between Nature and Civilization:

> Manches zur Liebe bestimmte Geschöpf wird das Opfer des großen
> christlichen Nächstenhasses. Sie setzen sich allen Pfeilen aus, die die
> soziale Welt für ihre Leugner bereit hält, leisten der Natur Gefolgschaft
> und gehen in dem Vernichtungskriege unter, der das hehrste Schauspiel
> dieser subalternen Zeit vorstellt. Was weiß ein Staatsanwalt davon?
> Verstände er es, wenn ihm ins Hirn gebrannt würde, daß das Hurentum
> das letzte Heroentum einer ausgelaugten Kultur bedeutet?
>
> (*F* 263: 6–7)

> (Many a creature destined for love becomes the victim of the great
> Christian principle of brotherly hatred. They expose themselves to all the
> arrows which the social world holds ready for those who disavow it,
> follow the command of nature and are destroyed in the great war of
> annihilation which represents the most sublime spectacle of this inferior
> age. What does a public prosecutor know of this? Would he understand it
> if it were burnt into his brain that whoredom signifies the last heroism of
> a washed-out civilization?)

The theme is reinforced by the identification of the prostitute's
souteneur as the heroic adversary of bourgeois society. And Kraus
romanticizes the relationship between them by attributing their love
for each other to a 'force of nature' ('Naturgewalt', *F* 263: 26).
Prostitute and pimp thus bestride the world of his satirical vision like
the figures in an allegorical print by Félicien Rops, *La Prostitution et la
folie dominant le monde* (see Pl. 13). It can scarcely be a coincidence that
Kraus had etchings by Rops hanging in his study (*F* 187: 26).

The strengths and weaknesses of Kraus's imaginative satire are

13   *Prostitution and Folly Dominating the World* by Félicien Rops

particularly evident in this essay. It may not do justice to the individual case of Mizzi Veith. But this mythopoeic perspective forms part of a conscious rhetorical strategy. If Aphrodite herself were to come down to earth (he writes), witnesses with names like Obletal, Hlawatschek and Schabetsberger would be called before a Viennese court to give evidence that illicit intercourse had taken place (*F* 263: 17). The contrast between *petit-bourgeois* Vienna and a legendary Olympus echoes one of the stock devices of the nineteenth-century popular theatre. But the use of a formal mythology is no longer plausible in a twentieth-century polemical essay. To reinforce the attack Kraus has to create a myth of his own. Since Aphrodite cannot come down to earth, Mizzi Veith must stand in for her.

Paradoxes and Prejudices: The Affirmation of a Bisexual Universe

Kraus's account of the relationship between the sexes abounds in aphorism and hyperbole. The aphorism (according to his own definition) is 'either a half-truth or a truth-and-a-half' ('entweder eine halbe Wahrheit oder anderthalb', F 270–1: 32). He was aware that the personalities of individual women may blend sensuousness with intellect. 'Der Geist Deiner Sinnlichkeit' is acknowledged in a letter to Bertha Maria Denk.[32] But in a published aphorism of the same period he mocks the idea of 'Das Gehirn der Frau'. For the satirical aphorism is not merely a transcription of experience. It thrives on antithesis: 'mein Stil liebt Antithesen' (F 229: 7). And it incorporates within its own structure that tension between author and reader which is presupposed in any form of rhetorical discourse. Kraus may declare (in the first essay of Sittlichkeit und Kriminalität) that he wishes his work to be taken as the expression of his innermost convictions ('der reine Ausdruck innerster Überzeugung', F 115: 5). But this underlying seriousness of purpose does not preclude the stratagems of pun and paradox:

> Ein Paradoxon entsteht, wenn eine frühreife Erkenntnis mit dem Blödsinn ihrer Zeit zusammenprallt.   (F 274: 24)

> (A paradox comes into being when a precocious insight comes into collision with the idiocy of its age.)

Such paradoxes express not simply the opinions of the author, but the tension between a set of received ideas (presupposed in the reader) and a challenging alternative. A complex aphorism may pursue this collision of ideas through a sequence of dialectical stages without ever reaching a fixed conclusion. One aphorism, for example, suggests that under certain circumstances a woman may be quite a tolerable substitute for the pleasures of masturbation — though it needs a lot of imagination:

> Ein Weib ist unter Umständen ein ganz brauchbares Surrogat für die Freuden der Selbstbefriedigung. Freilich gehört ein Übermaß von Phantasie dazu.   (F 229: 2)

For the literal-minded reader this becomes an 'unambiguous personal confession' which reveals Kraus's pathological inclinations.[33] But aphorisms are not confessions of anything. The author (as Freud put it when he cited this aphorism in an essay of 1908) 'turns the tables' on the reader in order to reveal a paradoxical truth. Far from supposing that Kraus must himself have been suffering from pathological tendencies, Freud praises him as a writer of intelligence and wit.[34] Kraus's aphorisms undermine the resistance of the reader by appealing to his sense of humour. Only the most solemn feminist will take offence at this definition of the female soul (F 288: 15):

Die Frauenseele =

$$\frac{x^2 + \sqrt{31{\cdot}4 - 20 + 4{\cdot}6} - (4 \times 2) + y^2 + 2xy}{(x + y)^2 - 3{\cdot}8 + 6 - 6{\cdot}2} - (0{\cdot}53 + 0{\cdot}47)$$

If such formulations leave us unimpressed, it is because their wit is schoolboyish, not because their sentiment is anti-feminist. The joke is that when one works out the apparently complex equation, the result is zero.

The element of 'collision' ('zusammenprallen') is also important in Kraus's reflections on authors he admired. His response to Weininger's *Geschlecht und Charakter* is characteristic: 'Ein Frauenverehrer stimmt den Argumenten Ihrer Frauenverachtung mit Begeisterung zu (An admirer of women assents with enthusiasm to your arguments for despising women)' (F 229: 14). The sexuality which Weininger despises becomes for Kraus a superabundant sensuousness, and women are assigned an active role as initiators of emotional liberation. By inverting the traditional paradigm and celebrating the 'otherness' of women, Kraus's aphorisms open up a new range of possibilities.

What those possibilities might be is spelt out in the unexpected context of a polemic against male chauvinism, *The Female Eunuch* by Germaine Greer:

If women understand by emancipation the adoption of the masculine role then we are lost indeed. If women can supply no counterbalance to the blindness of male drive the aggressive society will run to its lunatic extremes at ever-escalating speed. Who will safeguard the despised animal faculties of compassion, empathy, innocence and sensuality? What will hold us back from Weininger's fate?

Although Greer makes no reference to Kraus, the parallels are striking. Like him, she sees Weininger's *Geschlecht and Charakter* as a pivotal work; and like him she takes Weininger's book and 'turns all the defects which it defines into advantages'.[35] The harnessing of female labour to the service of a competitive, technocratic society seems to both authors likely to eliminate that counterweight of innocence and sensuality. Viewed in this perspective, Kraus's repudiation of conventional notions of women's emancipation cannot be dismissed as mere chauvinism. Indeed, the matriarchal myths of Bachofen might provide the inspiration for a qualitatively different society.

Weininger's arguments betray the belief that the processes of reproduction are loathsome ('ekelhaft'). To escape from the burden of their sensuality women should become like men. And sexual intercourse should cease. Even the propagation of the species is no justification for coitus, since it reduces human beings to means to an end. This exalted idealism leads Weininger to conclude that a morally courageous person will not fear physical extinction (a belief to which, on 4 November 1903, he set the seal of his own suicide).[36] Weininger's arguments reinforced that life-denying asceticism which formed such a dominant feature of western thought from St Paul through to Schopenhauer and Tolstoy. Against this, Kraus's aphorisms affirm a harmonious interaction between sensuous and spiritual experience.

Kraus's insistence on the reciprocal enrichment of mind and body is quite distinct from the cult of sexual pleasure as an end in itself. This also becomes clear when he takes issue with the writings of Schnitzler. As a young reviewer Kraus had written admiringly of Schnitzler's *Anatol* (*FS* I. 68–70). And it is possible to detect echoes of Anatol's epigrams in some of Kraus's more playful aphorisms. It may indeed be argued that he was unduly harsh in his judgements on the subsequent development of Schnitzler's work, which explores the position of women with considerable psychological and social insight.[37] But Kraus senses the void which underlies Schnitzler's view of sexuality. Schnitzler's treatment of erotic love has none of the mythic resonance which in different ways enriches the writings of both Wedekind and Kraus. For Schnitzler the satisfaction of the sexual urge is a repetitious and ultimately rather melancholy business, ending in spiritual emptiness. As Kraus writes in the essay 'Schnitzler-Feier': 'Wenn auf solch amouröse Art die Zeit vertrieben ist, folgt nichts nach, und Herzklopfen ist nur eine physiologische Störung. (When the time has been whiled away in this amorous fashion, nothing follows, and the beating of the heart is merely a physiological disturbance.)' (*F* 351–3: 79) It is indeed striking that although Schnitzler addresses himself so frequently to erotic themes, he so rarely succeeds in endowing them with existential value. His diaries, which record the experience of coitus with monotonous regularity, reinforce this impression.[38]

The reduction of the value of sexual experience is challenged in Kraus's aphorisms wherever it is encountered. He is equally hostile to the religious belief that sexual experience is damaging to the soul and the secular fear that it may contaminate the body. He certainly does not ignore the problem of venereal disease, which loomed so large in this period. The horrific consequences of such diseases, often transmitted with a criminal irresponsibility, are indicated in Schnitzler's autobiography. And the scourge was so widespread that James Joyce could remark in the same period: 'I presume there are few mortals in Europe who are not in danger of waking some morning and finding themselves syphilitics.'[39] It even seems from Kraus's correspondence that he himself picked up a dose of gonorrhoea. And one of his closest friends, Ludwig von Janikowski, became insane, apparently as a result of what was euphemistically called 'the French disease'.[40] But Kraus's response was to argue for a more frank and vigorous medical approach to venereal disease and for legislation to make its witting transmission an offence (F 211: 26–7). He did not allow the fears and traumas which haunted sexual experience in this period to cast a shadow over his vision of sensuous liberation.

It is this affirmative emphasis which distinguishes Kraus from his contemporaries. At the turn of the century the relationships between the sexes were predominantly portrayed in terms of conflict: Wedekind's elemental antagonism between Lulu and Jack the Ripper, Weininger's self-destructive opposition of Male and Female, Kokoschka's image of love as war-to-the-death (in his plays) or at best an uneasy truce (in his pictures), Hofmannsthal's hysterical *Elektra* and Wilde's sadistic *Salomé* (so powerfully evoked in the music of Richard Strauss), Heinrich Mann's 'Blue Angel' wreaking vengeance on society, Klimt's *femmes fatales* and the threateningly erotic waifs portrayed by Schiele, the links between sexuality and sadism in Musil's stories, and the insistence on a fundamental affinity between Love and Death which is prominent in the work of both Schnitzler and Freud. Freud was truly the presiding genius of this generation, with his image of sexual relations governed by penis-envy on the one hand and castration anxiety on the other. And every schoolboy knew from Nietzsche that when he went to his woman, he should not forget the whip. Wedekind was ringmaster in this sexual circus, actually appearing on stage whip in hand at the start of *Erdgeist* to proclaim the need to tame the female predator. While in an alternative version, associated with Sacher-Masoch, it was the woman who wielded the lash.

From this sombre context Kraus's writings emerge with luminosity. For him, male and female principles are complementary; it is the social order which generates antagonism. His aphorisms envisage a harmonious interplay between the extremes. Despite his admiration for the plays of Hauptmann, Kraus repudiated the turgid pessimism of the Naturalists, who rediscovered sexuality as a literary theme only to portray it as a corrupting force, leading to physical and

moral degeneration (*F* 232–3: 30). But he was equally sceptical about
the aesthetes who saw female beauty as an object for detached
contemplation, creating (as he observes of Peter Altenberg) 'an
aesthetic world of dolls' ('eine ästhetische Puppenwelt', *F*
259–60: 52). Equally, Kraus tries to strike a balance between the
contending visions of the two Scandinavian dramatists who
dominated the European intellectual horizon around 1900. Although
an admirer of Ibsen's visionary early plays, Kraus is sharply critical
of the desexualized heroines of his social drama (*F* 205: 4–5). The
writings of Strindberg exerted a stronger hold over Kraus's
imagination, but this did not lead him to endorse the dramatist's
misogyny. In a review of *The Father* in May 1897, he emphasized the
one-sidedness of Strindberg's intellectual position, though he also
saw it as a source of his tragic power (*FS* II.61). Strindberg's writings
make a significant contribution to the image of 'das Weib' that
emerges from the first decade of *Die Fackel*.[41] But when Kraus came
to sum up Strindberg's achievement in an obituary tribute in June
1912, he laments his failure to accept that the opposition of Man and
Woman is a rhythm of nature as fundamental as that of Day and
Night (*F* 351–3: 1).

This obituary tribute forms a culminating point in Kraus's
exploration of the myth of woman. The tribute is expressed in
biblical imagery which suggests that Kraus's cult of sexuality is not
so much anti-Christian as pre-Christian: a vision of harmony before
the Fall. The primal referent is neither Pandora nor Eve but an
archetypal creation myth which embraces them both. The more one
ponders Kraus's aphorisms on the Mann/Weib polarity, the clearer it
becomes that they transcend gender-linked personal characteristics
and become symbolic terms for a more fundamental dualism.
'Mann' and 'Weib' are seen as partners in a bisexual universe, with a
rich range of symbolic associations: mind and body, spirit and
sensuality, culture and nature, day and night, air and water,
constraint and flow, city and garden, goal and origin. There are
anticipations of Jung as well as echoes of Bachofen. But we may also
be reminded of the harmonious interaction of Yin and Yang,
particularly as Kraus was fascinated by what he called the 'dream of
the Chinese' (*F* 261–2: 7). In China Kraus admired a civilization
which was not in a state of civil war with nature (*F* 285–6: 14). In
advanced industrial societies he lamented the tragic division of the
male and female principles:

> Er mit dem Geist und sie mit der Schönheit mußten auseinander und
> hinaus. Es mit der Technik schafft da und dort Ersatz.

(*F* 389–90: 34)

(He with his mind and she with her beauty were forced to separate and depart. It with technology supplies a substitute for both.)

This aphorism appeared in December 1913. The myths which Kraus invokes against a repressive moralism ultimately challenge the even more destructive effects of technocratic society. He shares with Freud the conviction that the analysis of sexual relations can be extended into a critique of civilization as a whole.

CHAPTER 5

Sorcerers and Apprentices: The Encounter with Freud

Kraus has acquired the reputation of being one of Freud's most outspoken opponents. His writings have been used in an attempt to discredit the whole enterprise of psychoanalysis. And followers of Freud have been equally tendentious in their efforts to undermine Kraus's position.[1] To set the record straight it is necessary to show how much the two had in common, even when their paths diverged. They were the two greatest critics of the discontents of civilization to emerge from Habsburg Vienna, and their diagnoses are essentially complementary.

Standing Together
Their first contact can be precisely dated. On 2 October 1904 Freud sent Kraus his visiting card with the following inscription: 'Ein Leser, der nicht sehr oft Ihr Anhänger sein kann, beglückwünscht Sie zu der Einsicht, zu dem Mute und zur Fähigkeit, im Kleinen das Große zu erkennen, die Ihr Artikel über Hervay kundgibt. (A reader who cannot often be your supporter congratulates you on the insight, courage and ability to perceive the larger implications of a small affair which are manifest in your article on Hervay.)' (F 257–8: 40) On 8 November 1905 Kraus returned the compliment, commending to his readers the courage and the insight shown by Freud in arguing that homosexuals should not be treated as criminal or insane (F 187: 21). On 21 December 1905, at a time when Freud was being vilified for his emphasis on infantile sexuality, Kraus published a favourable review (by Otto Soyka) of *Three Essays on the Theory of Sexuality* (F 191: 8–11).

Freud's pleasure at finding his name repeatedly mentioned in *Die Fackel* is recorded in a letter of 12 January 1906, when he remarks to Kraus that their aims and opinions are in 'partial agreement'.

Between 25 September and 18 November 1906 he wrote Kraus a further five letters, asking for his support in the controversy with Wilhelm Fliess over the origin of the theory of bisexuality. It is probable that the two became personally acquainted in this period (Freud certainly proposed a meeting). Kraus responded by publishing in *Die Fackel* of 31 October 1906 a note explaining and justifying Freud's position (*F* 210: 26–7). After the publication of 'Der Prozeß Riehl' he sent Freud a reprint. Freud replied on 18 November 1906 that he had, of course, already read the article in *Die Fackel* and found some of it 'really indescribably beautiful'. Against the solidarity of public opinion (he suggested) 'we few should stand together'.[2]

It is clear that Freud was a regular reader of *Die Fackel*. The extent of Kraus's knowledge of Freud's work is a more difficult question. It certainly cannot be resolved by asserting arbitrarily that Kraus 'did' (or 'did not') read Freud's writings.[3] A useful clue is provided by a letter of March 1907, in which Kraus confides to Bertha Maria Denk that he is attending lectures by Freud, in which 'dreams are interpreted for hours on end (mainly in an erotic sense)'.[4] Clearly, he was not content to form his judgement at second hand. And it is probable that he actually read (at least in part) *The Interpretation of Dreams*, *Three Essays on the Theory of Sexuality* and *Jokes and their Relation to the Unconscious*. Between April 1907 and June 1908 there are repeated references in *Die Fackel* to the principal theories put forward in these books.

The difficulty of identifying precisely what Kraus read derives from the allusiveness of his comments. Thus an aphorism of 2 July 1907, which appears to be a general reflection of Freud's theory of jokes and dreams, contains concealed allusions which show that Kraus had actually read Freud's book on *Jokes* (*F* 229: 4). An even more specific reference lies behind an aphorism of 9 April 1910, which laments the dismal fate of 'children of psychoanalytical parents' (*F* 300: 27). It shows that Kraus was familiar with Freud's 'Analysis of a Phobia in a Five-Year-Old-Boy' (1909). And there are a number of other instances where specific echoes of Freud can be detected.[5] Indeed it is clear from Kraus's mode of expression that he had assimilated such key concepts as repression, sublimation and resistance and was even familiar with the jargon of 'active' and 'passive' analysis, 'erogenous zones', 'polymorphous perversity' and 'anal character'.

From an early stage Kraus's response to Freud took the form of a dialectical 'yes, but . . .'. Thus on 2 December 1907 he comments more sceptically on Freud's method of interpreting dreams, pin-pointing the problem of providing conscious explanations for

unconscious mental processes (*F* 237: 9). Freud seems to have replied
to this criticism, for in *Die Fackel* of 15 January 1908 we read: 'Das
Unbewußte macht aber wirklich schlechte Witze, erwiderte der
Traumdeuter.[. . .] (But the unconscious really does make bad
jokes, replied the interpreter of dreams.[. . .]' (*F* 241: 21) This not
only emphasizes the element of 'dialogue' in Kraus's relationship
with Freud, but even hints at a personal discussion (perhaps arising
from Kraus's attendance at Freud's lectures).

For Kraus the danger is that Freud's relatively rigorous approach
to the unconscious may be abused by his youthful imitators. This
argument is spelt out more forcefully in a series of aphorisms
published on 5 June 1908, which focus on the problems which arise
when Freud's brilliant theoretical discoveries are applied in practice:

> Die sexuellen Kindheitseindrücke sind gewiß nicht zu unterschätzen, und
> Ehre dem Forscher, der mit dem Glauben aufgeräumt hat, daß die
> Sexualität mit der Ablegung der Maturitätsprüfung beginnt. Aber man
> soll nichts übertreiben.   (*F* 256: 20)

> (The sexual impressions of childhood are certainly not to be
> underestimated, and honour is due to the researcher who disposed of the
> belief that sexuality begins with the taking of the School-Leaving
> Examination. But one should not take things to extremes.)

It is these extremes which Kraus attacks. He argues that the hopes
attached to psychoanalysis as a form of therapy are misplaced,
because it encourages in the patient a paradoxical pride in his own
symptoms ('Symptomenstolz'). It is in short 'a method that
obviously makes a layman into an expert more quickly than it makes
a sick person healthy' ('eine Methode, die augenscheinlich schneller
einen Laien zum Sachverständigen, als einen Kranken gesund
macht', *F* 256: 20). And Kraus denounces the reductive effects of
these methods when they are applied to works of literature. During
Freud's absence from Vienna, one of his pupils had been interpreting
Goethe's poem about 'The Sorcerer's Apprentice' as a masturbation
fantasy (the broomstick getting out of control). Taking up this
motif, Kraus calls on Professor Freud himself – 'der alte Meister' – to
return like the Sorcerer in the ballad to banish the apprentices who
are arrogating his powers (*F* 256: 22–3).

These comments of June 1908 mark the end of a period in which
Freud and Kraus did indeed 'stand together'. For they shared certain
fundamental assumptions. Both authors see erotic experience as
quite distinct from the mechanisms of reproduction which it may (or
may not) set in motion. It is this non-reproductive emphasis which
leads Kraus and Freud to defend the homosexual and espouse the
erotic emancipation of women. Both authors challenge the Victorian

ethos which identified female sexuality with procreation. Indeed, the scientist shares the satirist's view of women as pre-eminently sensuous beings, less capable than men of sublimating their erotic drives. Both authors attack a double morality which allows men a dubious licence while condemning women to frustration and hysteria. Kraus (as we have seen) denounces in 'Der Prozeß Riehl' a 'prudishness which has undermined the physical and mental health of the nations for almost two millennia' (F 211: 27). And Freud offers a similar critique of 'the harmful suppression of the sexual life of civilized peoples' in the more measured terms of '"Civilized" Sexual Morality and Modern Nervousness' (1908).[6] A reciprocal interaction stimulates the satirist towards psychological reflection and the analyst towards social criticism. Thus in many ways their positions are complementary. Freud acknowledges that the findings of psychoanalysis have been anticipated by poets.[7] Kraus replies that the scientific investigation of sexual life has its value, providing its results are confirmed by the artistic imagination (F 241: 1).

Kraus was subsequently to find more ominous metaphors for this relationship. But he never retracted his praise of Freud. Indeed, it has not proved possible to find in Die Fackel a single reference to Freud himself which is hostile or derisive. This point deserves particular emphasis. For we are told by Ernest Jones that Kraus was 'one of Freud's bitterest opponents' and by Thomas Szasz that after initial friendly contacts 'the conflict between Freud and Kraus could not have been sharper'.[8] Kraus consistently distinguishes between Freud and his followers, between a brilliant theory and its crude applications. It is when insight hardens into dogma that he turns to the attack. His singular respect for 'der Traumdeuter' is clearly distinguishable from his collective denunciations of 'die Psychoanalytiker'. There is a noticeable change in the tenor of Kraus's comments after the first Psychoanalytical Congress, held at Salzburg in April 1908, which initiated the world-wide dissemination of Freud's ideas. And his most outspoken attacks relate to the period after 1910, when the movement split into factions and Freud's methods began to be vulgarized.

The Unruly Apprentice: Fritz Wittels

When Kraus, after 1910, denounces 'die Psychoanalyse' in general, he is attacking applications of the theory which lack Freud's discrimination and control. For him it was no recommendation that individual analysts (for example Wilhelm Stekel, editor of the Zentralblatt für Psychoanalyse) were becoming 'disloyal to Professor Freud'. What he condemns are 'unauthorized' applications of the theory – 'Unbefugte Psychologie' (F 387–8 [November 1913]:

17–22). To see Kraus's polemic in perspective, we must take account
of the denunciations of 'Adler-Stekel and the whole insolent gang
now throwing their weight about in Vienna' which occur – not in
Die Fackel – but in Jung's letters to Freud. Freud himself deplored
Stekel's 'treachery' and Adler's 'paranoia'. Like Kraus, he defended
the integrity of his theory against its perversion by less principled
practitioners. We repeatedly find him trying to restrain the excesses
of his followers. Thus the key image from 'The Sorcerer's
Apprentice', which Kraus had applied to Freud in 1908, is invoked
by Freud himself in December 1911, when as 'würdiger alter
Meister' he tries to reassert his authority over Jung.[9]

Goethe's 'sublime symbol' of the sorcerer and his apprentices
frames Kraus's whole critique of psychoanalysis (*F* 256: 22–3;
363–5: 27; 668–75: 148). The special interest of this paradigm is that
it applies to both Freud and Kraus with equal force. Both were
compelling personalities who gathered circles of adepts around
them. Their circles intersected in the person of Fritz Wittels. Born in
Vienna on 14 November 1880, Wittels was a doctor with literary
ambitions. He became a member of the Vienna Psychoanalytic
Society on 27 March 1907, and papers written by him formed the
main subject of discussion on ten occasions during the following
three years. Between February 1907 and May 1908 he also
contributed thirteen pieces to *Die Fackel*, some of them literary,
others (printed over the pseudonym Avicenna) on medical and
sexual problems. In this period he was Kraus's most important
contributor and seems to have enjoyed his particular esteem.

For a short time Wittels had the best of both worlds. An article on
'Female Physicians' which he wrote for *Die Fackel* on 3 May 1907
was discussed by the Psychoanalytic Society on 15 May, and a paper
on 'Venereal Diseases' read to the Society on 13 November was
printed in *Die Fackel* of 16 December (and also issued by the Fackel
Verlag as a brochure). Wittels was valued by Kraus for his medical
knowledge and by Freud for his wealth of ideas. He certainly
deserves credit for the cross-fertilization which occurred between the
two groups. And the encouragement which he received in return is
attested by the fact that Kraus arranged for his first book, a volume
of love stories in historical settings entitled *Alte Liebeshändel*, to be
published by Jahoda & Siegel towards the end of October 1908. But
on 30 November Kraus printed in *Die Fackel* a series of aphorisms
under the title 'Persönliches', which deal very astringently with the
problem of the intellectual renegade (*F* 266: 14–28). Although no
names are mentioned, it is clearly Fritz Wittels who is the target.

There has been a great deal of speculation about the causes of this
rupture. One account suggests that it was due to rivalry for the

affections of the actress Irma Karczewska. Irma had played a minor
role in Kraus's production of *Die Büchse der Pandora*, and he was
proud to claim her as one of his 'discoveries' (*F* 203: 18–19). It seems
that they also had a short-lived love affair and that Wittels, who was
one of Irma's admirers, became extremely jealous.[10] But if Wittels
was jealous of Kraus, this does not explain why Kraus should have
attacked a less successful rival. An alternative explanation attributes
the break to an 'Oedipal' antagonism between Kraus and Wittels,
with repressed homosexual components. Kraus's response (we are
told) was that of the threatened father, repudiating the son in whom
he senses patricidal impulses.[11] This is interesting as an example of
vulgar Freudianism, which reduces all relationships to the same
Oedipal schema. But speculations and dogmas are less reliable than
documents – in this case the book which constituted Wittels's
declaration of independence. When a disciple asserts his right to
intellectual independence (as Jung insists in his letters to Freud), it is
not a matter of 'overcoming the father', but is more aptly explained
by Nietzsche's principle: 'One repays a teacher badly if one remains
only a pupil.'[12] The more powerful the personality of the teacher, the
more painful the break is likely to be. The disciple becomes
over-assertive in his new-found independence, the teacher over-
sensitive to the apparent disloyalty. In some instances the disciple
himself may achieve originality. But more often the image of the
apprentice exploiting powers which are not of his own creation
proves valid. The discomfited sorcerer is certainly a more appropriate paradigm than the king slain at the crossroads.

Fritz Wittels fits the pattern almost exactly. He was essentially a
popularizer of other people's ideas: Kraus's satire on sexual hypocrisy, Freudian psychoanalysis, the social theory of Josef Popper, and
related theories of educational psychology and penal reform. The
books which he published on these themes, first in Austria and later
in the United States, are not without merit. But it was this flair for
popularizing the ideas of others which brought about the break with
Kraus in 1908. In the autumn of that year Wittels published *Die
sexuelle Not*, a book which examined the causes of 'sexual deprivation' and propounded possible remedies. The book drew heavily on
articles which Wittels had originally published in *Die Fackel*. It also
contained an account of childhood based on the author's harsh
personal experiences, and a vehement attack on monogamous
marriage. In this book Kraus saw a travesty of his own ideas, a
reduction of erotic insights to propaganda for sexual permissiveness.
He also criticized Wittels for currying favour with the Viennese daily
newspapers in order to obtain cheap publicity. In view of the
privileged position which Wittels had enjoyed, this seemed like

treachery. The book is thus condemned as deficient both in intellectual and ethical integrity (*F* 266: 14–20).

Kraus's reaction fits the pattern of the master discomfited by a disciple's sudden show of independence. He must have felt particularly provoked by the fact that Wittels ostentatiously dedicated his book to Freud: 'Meinem Lehrer Professor Dr. Sigmund Freud verehrungsvoll zugeeignet'. The solitary reference to Kraus is tucked away in an aside. This is grudging indeed, when one considers that about two-thirds of the text of *Die sexuelle Not* had originally appeared in *Die Fackel*. Moreover, the book deals more centrally with Kraus's theme of sexual hypocrisy than with Freud's field of unconscious repression. The section on the family is characteristic.[13] It is an elaboration of Kraus's attack on the crippling effects of the arranged marriage. On balance, it would have been more appropriate if the book had been dedicated to Kraus himself. The tribute to Freud announced a decisive shift of allegiance. Freud's own response to this book is thus of particular interest.

Die sexuelle Not was discussed by the Psychoanalytic Society on 16 December 1908. Freud's comments deserve special attention:

> Wittels' book, which presents proposals for reform, stems from two different sources — from, so to say, a paternal and a maternal source. The first one, represented by the *Fackel*, goes part of the way with us in its assertion that suppression of sexuality is the root of all evil. But we go further, and say: we liberate sexuality through our treatment, but not in order that man may from now on be dominated by sexuality, but in order to make a suppression possible — a rejection of the instincts under the guidance of a higher agency. The *Fackel* stands for 'living out' one's instinctual desires to the point of satiating them [ausleben]; we distinguish, however, between a pathological process of repression and one that is to be regarded as normal.[14]

Freud's parental metaphors are a polite way of indicating that he too regards the book as derivative. More interesting is his recognition of the dialectical relationship between his position and that of *Die Fackel*. But he is mistaken in identifying Kraus with Wittels's programme of sexual hedonism. *Die sexuelle Not* bore on its title-page the slogan: 'Die Menschen müssen ihre Sexualität ausleben, sonst verkrüppeln sie (Human beings must live out their sexuality, otherwise they become crippled).' But this was by no means the programme of *Die Fackel*. It is precisely this slogan that Kraus himself had criticized in one of his aphorisms a fortnight earlier (*F* 266: 20).

If Fritz Wittels deserves attention, it is because he acted as a catalyst. It is the contrasting reactions of Kraus and Freud which are significant. Wittels's most provocative contribution took the form of a paper delivered to the Psychoanalytic Society on 12 January 1910 under the title 'The "Fackel"-Neurosis'. Wittels starts from the assumption that 'pathographies of artists' show 'how art and neurosis are related, and how the one passes over into the other'. The first problem is to identify the 'personal motive' which led Kraus to launch a bitter attack on journalism, especially the *Neue Freie Presse* and the Jewish community it served. The answer came to Wittels when he 'had a vision in which he saw his own father reading the *Neue Freie Presse*'. It dawned on him that the *Neue Freie Presse* is 'the father's paper', perhaps even 'the father's organ', against which Kraus directs his own 'small organ', *Die Fackel*. Moriz Benedikt is thus attacked as a father figure. This is corroborated by the fact that Kraus's father was named Jacob, meaning the 'blessed one' — 'Benedictus'. 'From all this [Wittels concludes] it is evident that it was a *neurotic* attitude towards one particular newspaper that was the starting point of his hatred for journalists. [. . .] In order to understand this neurotic hatred of his, one need only remember that the origin and starting point of every neurosis is the Oedipus motif'.

In the second period of *Die Fackel* (Wittels continues), when Kraus deals with the problem of sexuality, 'his private neurosis has become linked with the general neurosis of the time.' He has thus 'lived through much of what Freud has found out by way of scientific work, and has presented it in an artistic form'. This change of direction may be connected with the death of an actress (Annie Kalmar). Even though this phase of *Die Fackel* is an artistic achievement, 'in a few instances the fundamental neurotic scheme betrays itself.' This is particularly evident in Kraus's view that, except for the woman who gives herself to everyone, 'all women are hysterical'. This may be interpreted in Freudian terms as 'the reversal of a previous overvaluing of the mother and being disappointed in that love.' Wittels adds that in later years 'Kraus had in fact such a wretched attitude towards his mother that his brothers were able to put the blame on him for her death'. The third phase of *Die Fackel*, after Kraus's break with Wittels, is 'the period of artistic sterility'. Kraus 'first sexualized the newspaper, [. . .] now it is *form* that he sexualizes' — the form of the aphorism. In his concluding remarks Wittels touches on 'the problem of the satirist': 'Kraus is a misshapen man, as was Voltaire', but 'differs from Voltaire in the inconsequentiality of his accomplishments'. Kraus's 'great dramatic-parodistic talent' may also be a factor.[15]

What was Freud's reaction to this travesty of the psychoanalytic method? Jones tells us that he found the paper 'clever and just', Szasz speaks even more emphatically of 'Freud's approval' and Schneider suggests that he 'welcomed it in principle'.[16] These judgements are misleading. For Freud begins by warning that 'such a vivisection could justly be reproached as inhumane'. Although he commends Wittels for his sacrifice and self-control, he also suspects that he has not entirely succeeded in overcoming the more painful aspects of his relationship with Kraus. Freud's summing-up offers a more balanced assessment: 'Some of the points Wittels adduced are undoubtedly correct: the father complex, the character of the milieu, Jewishness, the return of enmities as neurotic character, etc. But we forget too easily that we have no right to place neurosis in the foreground, wherever a great accomplishment is involved.' Freud now recognizes that he made an error of judgement in supposing that Kraus might support the cause of psychoanalysis: 'Kraus has an extraordinary talent', but he 'lacks any trace of self-mastery'. But he disagrees with the view that 'Kraus's accomplishments in this most recent period have declined so greatly'. He warns that on the question of the names Jacob–Benedictus 'a certain degree of caution' is needed, and that in order to relate Kraus's enmities to his family background 'one would have to be familiar with the family history'. The most important point in Wittels's account of Kraus is 'the clue that by nature he is an actor'.[17]

These comments cannot be interpreted as an endorsement of Wittels's paper. Almost all the other members of the Society assented to Wittels's assault on Kraus's character. Freud alone insists on Kraus's 'extraordinary talent' and refuses to accept that his accomplishments have recently declined. But Freud's most fundamental point is one of general principle: 'we have no right to place neurosis in the foreground, wherever a great accomplishment is involved.' Although he suggests that Kraus may be too much 'at the mercy of his instincts', he draws a clear line between weaknesses of personal character and quality of artistic accomplishment. The one cannot legitimately be reduced to the terms of the other.

Wittels's paper was thus methodologically unacceptable to Freud himself. Worse still, it proved to be motivated by an underlying vindictiveness. This came into the open a few months later when Wittels published a novel, *Ezechiel der Zugereiste*, in which Kraus is caricatured under the name Benjamin Eckelhaft. In this novel the subject of Wittels's supposedly scientific paper becomes the target of venomous abuse. The references to Kraus (even to his misshapen physique) are transparently obvious and culminate in the imprecation: 'The filthy Jew should be beaten to death.'[18] Freud's reaction to this may be gauged from the fact that he broke off his relationship with Wittels, who resigned from the Psychoanalytic Society that same year. Freud clearly felt that Wittels was bringing the whole movement into disrepute. And he seems to have feared

Kraus's powers of retaliation (the 'Kraus affair' was discussed at a meeting of the Society on 14 April 1910).[19] But although Kraus instigated legal action against Wittels over *Ezechiel der Zugereiste* (*F* 311–12: 56), it is not clear whether he knew of the '"Fackel"-Neurosis' paper at this stage. The aphorisms on psychoanalysis which he published on 9 April 1910 are certainly hostile in tone, but they address themselves to general principles (*F* 300: 26–8).

Art and Neurosis

The attribution of works of art to pathological sources is the perversion of Freudian theory which Kraus most forcefully condemned. But Ernest Jones's statement that Kraus's attacks on psychoanalysis were a response to Wittels's paper is misleading. His attacks on psychoanalytical attempts to 'pathologize' men of genius (notably in *Die Fackel* of 5 June 1908) pre-date that paper by well over a year. He had indeed frequently criticized this view of art in its earlier, less sophisticated forms. It had flourished during the 1890s in the wake of Krafft-Ebing's *Psychopathia Sexualis* (1886), when there was a vogue for books on the decadence of modern art. This theory received pseudo-scientific support from Lombroso's diagnosis of the 'degenerate character' of the man of genius and Möbius's 'pathographies' of Goethe and others. The exponent of the theory whom Kraus most forcefully attacked was Max Nordau, whose *Entartung* (1892) includes Tolstoy, Ibsen and Zola among its 'degenerate writers'. The insanity of Nietzsche, himself a writer obsessed with decadence, gave the theory an added impetus. The instability of Strindberg and the suicide of Weininger were taken as confirmation that the most advanced ideas were pathological in origin.[20]

These prejudices were backed by penal sanctions which placed sexual deviants under the threat of prosecution and imprisonment. The trial of Oscar Wilde created a philistine reaction which inhibited the development of modern art in England for twenty years. In Germany the cultivated diplomat Philipp Eulenburg was dragged through the courts on similar charges. And when Wedekind ventured to portray homosexual characters in print, his books were banned and the plates on which they had been printed were destroyed. In Austria the painter Egon Schiele was imprisoned for alleged immorality and Otto Gross, the eccentric propagandist of sexual freedom, was arrested and sent to an asylum for the insane. Even the popular actor Girardi only narrowly escaped a similar fate. Under these circumstances Kraus's defence of the idiosyncrasies of artistic temperament was not merely personal *parti pris*. It became a pivotal point in his critique of a repressive society. It was all the more galling to find psychoanalysis, originally his ally, now supplying the philistines with modern weapons.

Freud's theory of the unconscious brought a new sophistication to the art of literary analysis. Its applications fell into three main categories. Applied to literary *characters*, the notion of unconscious motivation introduces a new subtlety of interpretation (exemplified by Freud's comments on *Hamlet*). Applied to the creative *process*, it opens up a new understanding of the play of the imagination (initiated by Freud's essay on 'Creative Writers and Daydreaming'). But applied to literary *authors*, it reduces artistic creativity to neurotic impulses and literary texts to pathological symptoms. The author is treated as if he were a patient in the consulting room. Methodologically, this infringes one of Freud's most fundamental axioms: that access to the unconscious is only possible with the active participation of the patient. It was this third approach that Kraus condemned.

The chief exponent of the approach was Isidor Sadger, who published pathographies of *Conrad Ferdinand Meyer* (1908), *Nikolaus Lenau* (1909) and *Heinrich von Kleist* (1909). Wilhelm Stekel offered a more general contribution to this same theme in his *Dichtung und Neurose* (1909), which contained a final section on Grillparzer. Max Graf published a depth-psychological study of *Richard Wagner* (1911). When Kraus denounces the psychopathographical approach to great artists, it is Sadger, Stekel and Graf that he has in mind, not Freud (*F* 300: 27; 376–7: 21; 388–9: 21).

Freud's position can be reconstructed from the *Minutes* of the Psychoanalytic Society, where these subjects were repeatedly discussed. He regarded the work of Sadger with particular distaste. This is hardly surprising, since Sadger's approach adulterates the Freudian 'mother complex' with 'hereditary traits' derived from Möbius and Lombroso. Even in the case of Lenau, discussed at the meeting of 28 November 1906, Freud challenges the concept of 'hereditary neurosis' and warns against a 'too crude' interpretation of the poet's relationship with his mother. On 4 December 1907 he condemns the paper on Meyer even more forcefully: the approach is 'not correct' and the enigma of the poet's personality remains 'unresolved'. And his judgement of the paper on Kleist, discussed on 5 May 1909, is truly devastating. Sadger's paper is 'repellent' in its general approach and 'wholly unreliable' in its handling of evidence. Even the more explicit explanations are 'a complete failure'. In short: 'The general public is right in rejecting this type of analysis — and this refers in part also to Stekel. In such elementary analyses all finer distinctions of structure manage to get completely lost, and so does the understanding of the poet.'[21]

Freud seems to have heeded Kraus's appeal (in *Die Fackel* of 5 June 1908) to call a halt to the activities of his apprentices. His letters to Jung contain repeated references to his desire to restrain his Viennese followers, particularly Sadger (whose writing is 'insufferable') and Stekel (whose contributions to the Society are on occasion 'absolutely frivolous and faulty in method').[22] The fact that he did not prevent them from publishing does not imply that he approved. It is true that he instituted a series of 'Schriften zur angewandten Seelenkunde' devoted to literary and artistic subjects, in which Max Graf's book on Richard Wagner appeared. But Graf's work fell short of Freud's own criteria, as well as those of Kraus. Since psychoanalysis argues that every boy is motivated by rivalry with his father (Kraus writes in May 1913), the question it should be answering in the case of Wagner is which *specific* endowments prepared him for the composition of *The Flying Dutchman* (*F* 376–7: 21). In another context Freud had already enunciated this same principle: 'We know that poets, like other human beings, have had parents and therefore a parental complex; what we want to see is what has become of this complex in the case of the poet, which attitude in his later life we can perhaps trace back to a *specific* constellation of that complex.'[23] Freud's discriminating approach to literary and artistic subjects was unfortunately disregarded by most of his followers.

The guiding principle for both Kraus and Freud is that great accomplishments cannot be reduced to neurotic origins. This principle is not infringed by Freud's own incursion into the field of artistic pathography, *A Childhood Reminiscence of Leonardo da Vinci* (1910). This book has been justly criticized. But it avoids the reductionism of Stekel, Sadger and Wittels. Freud's more sensitive arguments are designed to meet the objections of those who 'find all pathography distasteful'. Leonardo (he concludes) is certainly not to be classified as a neurotic, despite the obsessional elements in his character. The late flowering of Leonardo's genius is due not to neurosis but on the contrary to a *release* from emotional inhibitions. Meeting a woman (the model for the *Mona Lisa*) whose smile awoke repressed memories of his mother, Leonardo achieves his greatest artistic triumphs 'with the help of the oldest of all his erotic impulses' ('mit Hilfe seiner urältesten erotischen Regungen').[24]

The sense that art arises not from the repression but from the release of erotic impulses brings Freud's view of the artist close to that of Kraus himself. The difference is one of degree rather than of principle. An uninhibited exploration of the varieties of erotic experience is for Kraus the quintessential right of the artist ('das ureigenste Recht des Künstlers', *F* 237: 18). But for Freud too, despite his emphasis on sublimation, a sexually abstinent artist is 'hardly conceivable' ('Ein abstinenter Künstler ist kaum recht denkbar').[25] The artist resists the imperatives of renunciation and celebrates the pleasure principle in his creativity. He 'allows his erotic and ambitious wishes full play in the life of phantasy' and is able to 'mould his phantasies into truths of a new kind, which are valued by men as precious reflections of reality'. The potency of art derives from 'hidden sources of instinctual liberation'.[26]

Freud and Kraus both value the artistic imagination for its powers of revelation. Freud may pride himself on his scientific rigour, Kraus on his lack of it. But in practice their rhetorical strategies are not dissimilar. Both of them insisted on 'declaring the facts' with uncompromising candour. Both of them wrote about sexuality in a style that was essentially designed to be provocative ('wesentlich dazu bestimmt, ein Ärgernis zu geben', as Freud puts it in a letter to Fliess).[27] If anything, Freud's scientific sang-froid infuriated his audience even more than Kraus's satirical vehemence. But both were aware of the limits of what could be achieved by frontal assault. It is not a coincidence that Freud wrote a book on jokes which Kraus admired. Both writers were challenging an audience 'secure in its solidarity' (Freud to Kraus, 18 November 1906). Both see verbal wit as a means of getting under the guard of the complacent rationality of the age.

Jokes and their Relation to the Unconscious contains a wealth of observations relevant to the strategy of satire. Freud's notions of 'compression' ('Verdichtung') and 'conflation' ('Mischwortbildung') can indeed be applied very fruitfully to Kraus's own practice. Even more suggestive is the emphasis on the relationship between joke and audience. In tendentious jokes the jester directs his humour not simply against a target, but towards a third person whose assent must be gained. Jokes about respected institutions and moral principles (above all, marriage) achieve their effect by undermining the coercive effects of education on the minds of the audience. They bring about a pleasurable release from inhibition; and this makes possible a recognition of truths which the logical mind would have resisted.

The freakish play of language brings repressed elements of experience to the surface of the mind. In jokes this is a conscious process, promoted by the wit of the jester. In dreams it is unconscious and dependent on the skill of the analyst. The verbal displacements of dream-work are attributed to the 'censorship of conscious thinking', while the techniques of wit serve to overcome 'the objection of critical reason'. But the displacements of the dream are crude and arbitrary, while wit achieves a 'multiplicity of thought-associations'.

It is hardly surprising that Kraus, reflecting on this section of the book, compliments Freud on having 'demonstrated' ('nachgewiesen') the connection between jokes and dreams (F 229: 4). Freud's writings presuppose a psychological, Kraus's an ideological system of resistances. In both cases it is a matter of outwitting the 'censor'.

The imaginative elements in Freud's writings are thus as important as their scientific rigour. In his analysis of psychic conflicts (as in Kraus's account of social disorders) we find a synthesis of critical insight and literary myth. To label Freud a 'rationalist' and Kraus a 'mystic' is as misleading as to praise Kraus's rhetoric as 'noble' and condemn Freud's as 'base'.[28] The fundamental difference lies in the myths which they espoused. From *The Interpretation of Dreams* onwards Freud's writings are haunted by the spirit of Oedipus. In *Totem and Taboo* (1913) he attempts to synthesize the psychoanalytical model of the family with anthropological myths of an original patricide. Modern man still has to come to terms with genetically transmitted traces of his archaic heritage, derived from the killing of a tyrannical father by members of the 'primal horde'. Kraus, on the other hand, suggests that psychoanalytic categories might be synthesized with a very different myth — that of an age of erotic fulfilment:

> Die Menschheit ist im Mittelalter hysterisch geworden, weil sie die bestimmenden sexuellen Eindrücke ihrer griechischen Jugendzeit schlecht verdrängt hat.   (F 229: 4)

> (The human race became hysterical in the middle ages because it had poorly repressed the decisive sexual impressions of its Greek youth.)

The choice is between Oedipus and Pandora. Against Freud's grim myth of patricide we must set Kraus's vision of female sensuousness as the obstructed source of a more harmonious existence.

The Divining-Rod of Language

Just as both Kraus and Freud relate modern experience to primal myths, so too they assign to language quasi-magical powers. It is here that one may detect echoes of that Judaic heritage which they both shared (and both in different ways repudiated). Language is treated as the source of the most profound revelation. When Kraus speaks of the 'Delphic' quality of language, he is emphasizing both its ambiguity and its chthonic resonance. And it is precisely this combination of elements which Freud identifies when he refers to the discourse of one of his patients as 'oracular' ('orakelhaft'). From a very early stage Freud was fascinated by what he calls 'the magic of words' ('der Zauber des Wortes'). The aim of scientific psychotherapy (he writes in a seminal essay) is to 'restore to words a part at least of their former magical power' ('dem Worte wenigstens einen Teil seiner ursprünglichen Zauberkraft wiederzugeben'). The 'ancient magical power' of words is again emphasized in the *Introductory Lectures* (1916) and *The Question of Lay Analysis* (1926). Freud may pride himself on the scientific character of his investigations, but he was aware that psychotherapy has something in common with Christian faith-healing and the magical rites of primitive religions.[29]

The reliance on the suggestive power of words is even more evident in his techniques of diagnosis. Everything that passes between Freud and his patient is within the medium of words. They are the symptoms of neurosis, the clues to its origin, the catalysts which precipitate its release. Freud's psychology is precisely that: a study of psyche through logos. The paradox is that he treats the oracular utterances of his patients both as profoundly revealing and as treacherously ambiguous. The 'word-representation' ('Wortvorstellung') or 'word-memory' ('Wort-Erinnerung') is the point where repressed feelings break through into consciousness. But its essential quality is verbal indefiniteness ('Wortunbestimmtheit').[30] It is these assumptions, first spelt out in a letter to Fliess of 22 December 1897, which explain Freud's reliance on the technique of verbal association.

In *The Interpretation of Dreams*, *The Psychopathology of Everyday Life* and the great case histories this technique is deployed with extraordinary ingenuity. No fragment of verbal evidence is too trivial for attention: the key-words ('Schlagworte') and verbal sequences ('Wortreihen') which randomly occur to a patient, the verbal record ('Wortlaut') of dreams, the verbal residues ('Wortreste') of conscious recollection, the verbal bridges ('Wortbrücken') of morphological and symbolic association, crude puns, clumsy slips of the tongue and subtle plays on words. The most careful attention (Freud insists) is paid to 'every nuance of linguistic expression'. The dream is treated 'like a sacred text' ('wie einen heiligen Text').[31] No wonder Kraus was initially so enthusiastic. For him too metaphor is the matrix of insight. Language is 'the divining-rod which discovers sources of thought' — 'die Wünschelrute, die gedankliche Quellen findet' (F 277–8: 61). This image derives from an earlier tribute to Freud's powers of divination (F 223–4: 7–8). But can this linguistic method be equally valid both for scientific knowledge and for satirical insight?

It is clear that Freud's interpretations owe a great deal to the linguistic ingenuity of the analyst. Of a woman who dreams of a journey to Italy ('gen Italien') we are told that the dream actually expressed a desire for intercourse ('Genitalien').[32] This is comparable to Kraus's comment on the female tendency to confuse the spelling of 'Genus' and 'Genuss' (roughly: 'procreation' and 'recreation') (*F* 198: 1). In both cases verbal associations are used as evidence for a conception of the suppressed sensuality of women which had actually been reached in advance. This focus on language may be fruitful for the satirical aphorist, but forms a flimsy basis for science. It reflects the predisposition of the analyst himself, who combines a particular hunch about the causes of neurosis with a particular gift for playing with words. The sequence of 'verbal bridges' constructed in the case of the 'Rat Man' (1909) ('Ratten-Spielratte-Raten-heiraten' and their symbolic associations) clearly owes more to Freud's intellectual virtuosity than to the mind of his patient.[33]

Freud may reply that the unconscious does make bad jokes, for which science is not to be blamed. But Kraus saw in this disjunction the crucial flaw in Freudian theory. The data of analysis may derive not from the unconscious of the dreamer but from that of the interpreter. In this way a sense of guilt may be projected from analyst to patient (*F* 241: 21). Analysis may then become a form of table-tapping (in which it is unclear who is moving the Ouija board). Kraus explicitly exempts Freud himself from this criticism (*F* 237: 10). But he makes it clear that the abuses of psychoanalysis derive from flaws within the theory itself. Its weakness as a science lies in the fact that it cannot be disproved: 'sie behält in jedem Falle Recht' (*F* 241: 21). Psychoanalysis lacks the 'steady hand' of scientific investigation. Indeed, the analyst may merely be compensating for his own sense of inferiority. In short, psychoanalysis is too fraught with emotion to be called a science: 'mehr eine Leidenschaft als eine Wissenschaft' (*F* 376–7: 20–1).

These doubts about the value of psychoanalysis are synthesized in Kraus's most celebrated aphorism:

> Psychoanalyse ist jene Geisteskrankheit, für deren Therapie sie sich hält.
> (*F* 376–7: 21)

> (Psychoanalysis is that mental illness of which it believes itself to be the cure.)

This aphorism is one of those deftly-thrown pebbles which leave ripples long after the initial splash has subsided. It has been particularly resented for its suggestion that analysts themselves are sick. But we should recall that several of Freud's followers (including Stekel) had originally been his patients and that some were mentally disturbed to the point of suicide. Otto Gross was described by Freud himself as incurably paranoid or schizophrenic (letter to Jung, 21 June 1908). Johann Jakob Honegger died by his own hand on 28

March 1911. And Karl Schrötter committed suicide in Vienna on 16 May 1913.[34] It is hardly surprising that the psychoanalysts were so sensitive to Kraus's criticisms. His aphorism equating psychoanalysis with mental illness appeared on 30 May 1913, only a fortnight after Schrötter's suicide (which may have contributed to its formulation). But the resonance of Kraus's aphorism derives from the fact that he does not personalize the issue. His suggestion that psychoanalysis originates in neurosis and that psychotherapy is a form of projection grasps a more fundamental truth.

Kraus's aphorism identifies the structural paradox of psychoanalysis. If the theory is valid, then the analyst must acknowledge in himself that Oedipal predisposition which he diagnoses in his patient. Every diagnosis must therefore involve an element of unconscious projection. It is significant that Wittels's diagnosis of the '"Fackel" Neurosis' was inspired by a dream of his *own* father (with whom he did have a traumatic relationship) reading the *Neue Freie Presse*. There could hardly be a clearer example of that projection of guilt 'from the unconscious of the interpreter' of which Kraus had spoken two years earlier. A more sophisticated form of analysis will integrate an awareness of this difficulty into its therapeutic practice. But this is a relatively late development in the history of psychoanalysis. In the traditional model of psychotherapy the analyst is an authoritarian figure, reluctant to acknowledge his own limiting subjectivity.

Thus when Stekel, after reprinting Kraus's challenging aphorism in the *Zentralblatt für Psychoanalyse* in 1913, claimed that he was aware of the great dangers of psychoanalysis, Kraus remained unconvinced. Indeed, he cited a specific instance where a confusion between two surnames, which Stekel imputed to the repressed instincts of his patients, was more likely to derive from the conscious mind of the doctor (*F* 387–8: 20). Again, his criticism is on target. We are told by Ernest Jones that Stekel was in the habit of inventing names to fit in with his theories and 'had no scientific conscience at all'.[35] And Stekel's compendium of dream symbols, *Die Sprache des Traums* (1911), is explicitly designed to make dream-analyses more 'independent' of the mind of the dreamer. It is important to realize that Stekel, not Freud, is the central target of that great assault on pschoanalysis which Kraus launched in November 1913. In Stekel he attacks the journalistic vulgarization of theories which he had once admired. The hostile tone of his comments on dream-analysis after 1911 is almost certainly related to the brashness of Stekel's book, which enjoyed a considerable vogue. Kraus recognizes the difference between the 'active' school of psychoanalysis led by Stekel and the 'passive' approach advocated by Freud himself. Freud's dream interpretations had been politely queried (F 237: 9–10). Stekel's approach is denounced for its arrogation of arbitrary powers over the defenceless unconscious.[36]

The Parting of the Ways

Even in the period of Kraus's greatest hostility to psychoanalysis, his references to Freud remain respectful:

> Den Weg zurück ins Kinderland möchte ich, nach reiflicher Überlegung, doch lieber mit Jean Paul als mit S. Freud machen.   (F 381–3: 73)

> (The journey back to children's land I would, after mature reflection, prefer to make with Jean Paul rather than S. Freud.)

This aphorism not only acknowledges an intellectual debt, but allows that Freud's view of childhood may still be valid. Jean Paul is cited in preference, not in refutation. For Jean Paul the most important element in early childhood was not the pleasurable satisfaction of physical appetites ('Genuß') but the joyousness ('Freudigkeit') of the child's impulse to play. His novels repeatedly invoke the 'innocent joys of childhood' ('die unschuldigen Kinderfreuden'). The contrast could hardly be more extreme. In Freudian terms such a selective recall of childhood is a blend of self-deception and amnesia. Kraus's point is that psychological insight is not enough. Even more important is the ability 'to see beyond psychological data' ('über einen psychologischen Bestand hinwegzusehen', F 381–3: 73). It is precisely the selective recall of childhood which can make such memories into an inspirational force.

Freud detects murky meanings in even the happiest dreams of childhood. Jean Paul sees a radiance in even the darkest: 'Die Kindheit, und noch mehr ihre Schrecken als ihre Entzückungen, nehmen im Traume wieder Flügel und Schimmer an [. . .] Zerdrückt uns diese flatternden Funken nicht! Lasset uns sogar die dunklen peinlichen Träume als hebende Halbschatten der Wirklichkeit! (Childhood, its terrors even more than its delights, take wing and become radiant again in dream [. . .] Don't crush these flickering sparks! Leave us even our dark disturbing dreams as hazy shadows which enhance reality!)'[37] In Kraus's writings memories of childhood are celebrated in precisely this spirit. 'Der Weg zurück ins Kinderland' should be a resonant journey, enriched by musical associations (specifically, echoes of Brahms).[38] Kraus's aphorism is directed against those who can no longer hear this music, and for whom dreams are merely symptoms to be reduced to rational components. At this point imagination and analysis finally part company.

Even at this parting of the ways Kraus still acknowledges a fundamental affinity:

> Man sagt mir oft, daß manches, was ich gefunden habe, ohne es zu suchen, wahr sein müsse, weil es auch F. gesucht und gefunden habe. Solche Wahrheit wäre wohl ein trostloses Wertmaß. Denn nur dem, der sucht, ist das Ziel wichtig. Dem, der findet, aber der Weg. Die beiden treffen sich nicht. Der eine geht schneller, als der andere zum Ziel kommt. Irgendetwas ist ihnen gemeinsam. Aber der Prophet ist immer schon da und verkündet den apokalyptischen Reiter.   (F 360–2: 7)

> (People often tell me that something which I have found, without seeking it, must be true, because F[reud] too has sought and found it. This kind of truth would surely be a poor criterion. For the goal is important only for the seeker. For the finder it is the path. The two do not meet. The one moves faster than the other reaches his goal. They have something in common. But the prophet is always there first and proclaims the apocalyptic horseman.)

This aphorism shrewdly identifies a cardinal weakness in Freud's work: the relentlessness with which his arguments drive towards a fixed conclusion ('das Ziel'). For Freud the aim of science was to reduce the complex data of observation to universal principles. This introduces a dogmatic note even into his most imaginative writings: *all* dreams are wish-fulfilments; *all* cases of neurosis have a sexual aetiology; *every* human being has to overcome the Oedipus complex, which is 'the nucleus of *all* neuroses' and the point of origin of 'religion, morals, society *and* art'.[39]

It is this apparent universality of application which gives Freudian theory its popular appeal. But anyone who has immersed himself in Freud's writings is likely to agree that the path of inquiry is more rewarding than the goal of proof. Freud's claim to have discovered the 'Royal Road' to knowledge of the unconscious is less impressive than those many points in his argument where 'the path divides and the finest prospects open up on every side'.[40] For Kraus this dogmatic element is the fatal flaw which turns exploratory insight into an ideology which can be exploited by lesser minds. Thus he pictures himself as prophet and Freud as portent of an intellectual disaster. The nature of that disaster is spelt out more clearly in an essay published a month after this aphorism, 'Untergang der Welt durch schwarze Magie' (December 1912). Psychoanalysis has been absorbed by that journalistic 'black magic' which is destroying traditional culture. Kraus was aware that Jews were as prominent in the psychoanalytic movement as in the press and the stock exchange (F 300: 27). As a result some of his comments have antisemitic undertones: psychoanalysis is defined as the newest Jewish malady — the older generation still has diabetes! (F 387–8: 18). But even in these satirical diatribes one element remains constant. It is still the 'sorcerer's apprentices' who are the target (*F* 363–5: 27).

Kraus's normal polemical method was to aim at outstanding individual targets and to hold the progenitor responsible for any subsequent perversion of his ideas (Heine for the consequences of his style). Why, uniquely in the case of psychoanalysis, does he eschew this method? Why does he not hold Freud personally responsible for the perverted applications of his theories? Why, even in his outraged reactions to the theory of the 'anal character', does he not denounce Freud as its originator? The evidence all points to the same conclusion. Kraus's respect for Freud seems to have endured even through the period of his greatest hostility to psychoanalysis. He refrained from attacking him personally, whatever the provocation. From 1908 right through to 1936 it is repeatedly the apprentices that he attacks. The sorcerer himself comes through unscathed.

Kraus's preoccupation with psychoanalysis represents one of the most interesting dimensions of his work in the decade between 1905 and 1914. His response passes through four phases. The campaigner against moral hypocrisy enthusiastically assents to Freud's frank approach to sexuality, his shrewd observations on wit and his subtle exegesis of dreams. The sceptical aphorist then takes over, reflecting more critically about the methodology of psychoanalysis and its problematic applications. The defender of artistic integrity then launches a counter-attack against the pathographies written by Freud's disciples. Finally psychoanalysis is denounced as one of the destructive ideologies of the age. But even in this final period the two writers still 'have something in common'. That something — as Kraus's apocalyptic image suggests — is the increasing pessimism of their prognosis.

Initially, both Kraus and Freud had believed that their campaign for sexual enlightenment would bring about tangible reforms. A remedial thrust was evident even in their most vigorous assaults. But after 1910 the pessimistic counter-current in their writings became increasingly powerful. Both now found themselves fighting on two fronts. Struggling vainly against conservative moralism, they also had to defend their teachings against 'progressives' who were perverting them. In both cases, faith in a younger generation which might take up the torch of emancipation gave way to disillusionment. Both felt betrayed by disciples who had abandoned them. These personal set-backs coincided with an awareness that the political situation of Austria-Hungary was becoming increasingly stormy.[41] Freud is not usually credited with political insight. But he like Kraus was aware that the resistances with which they had to

contend were paradigmatic of a larger disorder. When Kraus gave
Freud credit for having 'introduced a Constitution into the anarchy
of dreams', he added: 'But things are as bad there as they are in
Austria' ('Aber es geht darin zu, wie in Österreich', F 254–5: 33).
Both Kraus and Freud came to believe that the antagonisms of public
life were related to unresolved tensions in the anarchic underworld of
sexuality. This is the theme of Kraus's essay 'Die chinesische Mauer'
(F 285–6: 1–16, July 1909), which ends with prophecies of the
destruction of western civilization.

Freud too, in his more restrained linguistic register, sounds the
alarm. In 1912 he made the 'gloomy prognosis': 'We may perhaps be
forced to become reconciled to the idea that it is quite impossible to
adjust the claims of sexual instinct to the demands of civilization.'[42]
And in *Totem and Taboo* (1913) he went on to speak of the 'mass
psyche', on which the 'emotional inheritance' of the 'primal horde'
remains indelibly imprinted. Aggression, enmity and guilt are seen
as the repressed impulses with which modern civilization still has to
come to terms.[43] Freud is too conscious of his role as a scientist to
shift into the mode of prophecy. But the pessimism of his prognosis
is unmistakable. And after the outbreak of the First World War he
was able, in a letter of November 1914 to Lou Andreas-Salomé, to
write with some justification:

> I do not doubt that mankind will surmount even this war, but I know for
> certain that I and my contemporaries will never again see a joyous world.
> It is all too hideous. And the saddest thing about it is that it has come out
> just as from our psycho-analytical expectations we should have imagined
> man and his behaviour. Because of this attitude I have never been able to
> agree with your blithe optimism. My secret conclusion was: since we can
> only regard the highest civilization as disfigured by a gigantic hypocrisy it
> follows that we are organically unfitted for it.[44]

Much of this was indeed implicit in Freud's pre-war publications.
But it also forms an apt summary for Kraus's campaign in *Die Fackel*.
The conclusion which Freud had reached in secret, Kraus had
proclaimed from the public platform: that European civilization was
on course for self-destruction. The sexual aspects of this 'gigantic
hypocrisy' formed for Kraus and Freud a common theme. But Kraus
also attacks it in its more public manifestations. Hence the assault on
cultural façades which he launches in alliance with the architect Adolf
Loos.

CHAPTER 6

Façade and Function: The Alliance with Adolf Loos

Imperial Vienna was a city of façades. The architects of the Ringstrasse aimed at monumental splendour, rather than functional simplicity. This grandiose programme of public building coincided with Kraus's most impressionable years. He later recalled how oppressive he found the towering buildings and tumultuous streets, as a sensitive child newly arrived from the provinces. The replacement of the old Burgtheater in 1888 by the opulent building on the Ringstrasse formed a caesura in his personal development. The demolition of the homely Café Griensteidl to make way for the grandiloquent Palais Herberstein constituted a further symbolic landmark, commemorated in his early satire *Die demolirte Literatur*. His ambivalent attitude is expressed in the opening paradox that Vienna is being 'demolished into a great city' ('Wien wird jetzt zur Großstadt demolirt', *FS* II.277). He was by no means a nostalgic conservationist, and he mocked the aesthetes of the 1890s for their cult of 'Old Vienna'. But in his early writings he shows little interest in the physical environment. It was only when he became acquainted with the ideas of the pioneering modern architects, Otto Wagner and Adolf Loos, that he began to incorporate the motifs of ornament and façade into his satire.

Otto Wagner's motto 'artis sola domina necessitas' is quoted in an early number of *Die Fackel* as a guiding principle (*F* 30: 16). Function is to take precedence over artistry. Wagner's plans for the development of Vienna in the 1890s had emphasized the practical needs of modern life, and his designs for the Vienna City Railway (1894–1901) achieved a balance between form and function. In his programmatic textbook *Moderne Baukunst* (1895) he criticized the historicism of the Ringstrasse and called for a more practical approach. Although Wagner's buildings were still embellished with symbolic motifs, they represented a decisive break with tradition. The elegance of his Postal Savings Bank (Postsparkassenamt, 1904–6) derived from functional design rather than ornamental detail. Thus Wagner provides a positive reference point in early numbers of *Die Fackel*. The decorative designs of Joseph Olbrich, architect of the Secession building (1898), are seen as the antithesis to Wagner's 'honest constructivist thinking' (*F* 56: 23). The beauty of Olbrich's interiors is undeniable, but the trouble with his furniture is that it tends to fall apart when you sit down. Honest carpenters have to be called in to make these beautiful objects serviceable (*F* 30: 16).

The designs of the Secession and the products of its offshoot, the Wiener Werkstätte (set up in 1903), are repeatedly criticized in *Die Fackel* for their ornamentalism. And similar arguments are applied to the paintings of the presiding genius of the Vienna Secession, Gustav Klimt. This was the period of Klimt's great public projects: the allegories of Philosophy, Medicine and Jurisprudence, which he was commissioned to paint for the University of Vienna. The ensuing controversy again illustrates that displacement of political debate into aesthetic spheres which was so characteristic of the period. Klimt's daring designs, combining sensuous female forms with allegorical compositions of considerable obscurity, provoked questions in parliament and a protest by eighty-seven university professors. The Minister of Education, a supporter of the Secession, was resolute in Klimt's defence. Through the newly formed Arts Council ('Kunstrat'), the Minister actively encouraged the arts as a means of conciliating the different nationalities at home and raising Austria's prestige abroad. Klimt's paintings, however, had the opposite effect. They alienated almost every ideological faction: the liberal academics, whose principles of rational discourse were obscured by Klimt's murky allegories; the Catholics, who were scandalized by the nudity; and the antisemitic press, which managed to discern yet another Jewish conspiracy in the campaign organized in Klimt's defence.[1]

Kraus's response is hard to disentangle. It is not always clear which articles in *Die Fackel* of this period are written by Kraus himself and which by unnamed collaborators. He certainly took a personal interest in Klimt's work and repeatedly visited the Secession gallery to see for himself what all the fuss was about (*F* 73: 12). In his view Klimt's work was too derivative to be artistically successful. Klimt is seen as a 'Stileklektiker', whose borrowed styles range from the historical pageantry of Makart to the modernistic portraiture of Fernand Khnopff (*F* 36: 16; 73: 10). And the preponderance of decorative motifs in his paintings is attacked in the same way that Kraus attacks the adulteration of literature by journalism. In Austria the painters are being overshadowed by the decorators, just as the writers are being swallowed by the journalists (*F* 139: 18).

Ornament and Crime

Kraus's critique of the Secession indicates that he was assimilating the ideas of a theorist more radical than Otto Wagner, the architect and designer Adolf Loos. Kraus was familiar with the articles on functional design which Loos contributed to the *Neue Freie Presse* during 1898, at the time of the Jubilee Exhibition. He was evidently surprised at finding such advanced ideas in that newspaper. He himself had responded to the Exhibition with superficial persiflage (*FS* II. 220–5). He repeatedly commends Loos in early numbers of *Die Fackel* for the verve and originality of his arguments (*F* 32: 31–2; 161: 9). And soon they had become personally acquainted. This proved to be the beginning of an enduring friendship. Where other allies of this early period drifted away from Kraus (like Wedekind) or became enemies (like Harden), Loos was one of the few who enjoyed his lifelong friendship and support.

At times their relationship was exceptionally close. Anecdotes of the Viennese coffee-houses picture them as habitual companions, with Peter Altenberg as the third prominent member of their circle. And Kraus seems to have helped Loos to secure valuable commissions during the early stages of his career. Loos designed apartments for two of Kraus's brothers, Alfred Kraus (in 1905) and Rudolf Kraus (1907). He also designed an apartment for Otto Stoessl (1900), one of Kraus's most regular contributors. Their friendship also had its more intimate side. When Kraus was received into the Catholic Church in April 1911, it was Loos who acted as his sponsor. And it was through Loos that Kraus was introduced to Max Thun, the eccentric aristocrat whose cousin Sidonie Nadherny was to play such an important role in his emotional life.

Kraus's letters to Sidonie give us revealing glimpses of his relationship with Loos during the First World War. Their contacts were close and continuous, even though there were fundamental differences of opinion. Loos succumbed to the patriotic 'furor teutonicus' of the day, and is also censured in Kraus's letters for a lack of discrimination in the company he keeps. But this was not enough to shake Kraus's respect and affection for him. After November 1918 their roles were reversed. Kraus became a supporter of the new Austrian Republic, whereas Loos was so sceptical that he soon emigrated to Paris. Their cordial relationship continued even during these years of separation. Kraus spoke up for Loos on a number of occasions, criticizing the Republic for its failure to accord him any public recognition. And he published photographs in *Die*

Fackel to mark his sixtieth birthday. When Loos died in 1933, Kraus delivered the obituary tribute.

From the very beginning their careers ran parallel. For in their different spheres they were conducting a campaign against a common enemy: the anachronistic cultural institutions of Habsburg Austria. Their aim was the demolition of façades. Loos's 1898 essay 'Die Potemkin'sche Stadt' was a far more incisive attack on the pretentious façades of the Ringstrasse than Otto Wagner's. These façades are as spurious, Loos argues, as the villages made out of canvas and cardboard by which Potemkin had hoped to deceive Catherine the Great into believing that progress was being made in the Ukraine, since they are designed to make modern apartments look like Renaissance palaces. To satisfy the vanity of the *nouveaux riches*, speculative builders have nailed on to their buildings ornamental façades which imitate Baroque stucco work or Tuscan stone. But in fact they are made of cement.[2] In his essays on the Jubilee Exhibition Loos extended this argument into a comprehensive critique of Austrian design. Everywhere he insists on the need for practical efficiency, rather than ornamental ostentation: in leatherwork and tailoring, furniture, glass and pottery, shoes and hats, printing and not least plumbing. Decorative designs betray the pretentions of the wealthy parvenu. Against this, Loos enunciates his own principles: honest workmanship, a respect for materials, an unobtrusive elegance which derives from functional design. Discussing the furniture of Otto Wagner, he reaches the conclusion that the beauty of a practical object can only exist in relation to its purpose.[3] A more radical challenge to the arts-and-crafts ideals of the period could scarcely be imagined.

It is easy to see why Kraus found these ideas so attractive. His own critique of Austrian journalism sought to achieve a similar separation of façade and function. But it was only gradually that he fully assimilated Loos's ideas. The alliance between them became most significant in the years 1908–14. For both Kraus and Loos this was a period of exceptional creativity. Loos completed some of his most original and influential architectural commissions, above all the building on the Michaelerplatz which caused such controversy. And his ideas began to attract attention abroad through the publication of his essays in periodicals in Berlin and Paris. In this same period Kraus's writings achieved an unprecedented subtlety and incisiveness. The stimulus which he derived from Loos's critique of ornament was an important contributory factor. Loos's principle became the battle-cry for Kraus's intellectual demolition work: 'Ich haue Fassaden ein und mache tabula rasa' (*F* 311–12: 13).

In 1908 Loos wrote the most provocative of his theoretical essays, 'Ornament and Crime'. It earned him his reputation as one of the pioneers of the modern movement whose ideas were only fully realized twenty years later by the Bauhaus in Weimar Germany and by Le Corbusier in Paris.[4] This view of Loos is certainly an oversimplification. But there is no doubting the polemical vehemence of his onslaught against ornament. The ideas tentatively advanced in his articles of 1898 are in the later essay compellingly reformulated within an anthropological framework. Ornament is identified with a primitive stage in the evolution of civilization. The Papuan (Loos claims) tattoos his skin, just as he decorates every other available object. But if a member of a modern society tattoos his skin, it is a sure sign that he suffers from criminal or pathological tendencies. Modern man has transcended ornament. And in an italicized passage Loos insists that the evolution of culture is identical with the removal of ornament from objects of utility. Ornament of this kind is a waste of labour, materials and capital. The rapid tempo of modern technological and economic development requires functional efficiency in every sphere. The dilemma of Austria is that it lags so far behind in this evolutionary process.[5]

There are many echoes of Loos's ideas in Kraus's writings. The most significant is certainly this polemical definition of ornament. It becomes a key concept in several of his most important critical essays. Thus in May 1909, attacking a stylistically elaborate form of journalism which merely obscures the events it purports to describe: 'Der Verschweinung des praktischen Lebens durch das Ornament, wie sie Adolf Loos nachgewiesen hat, entspricht jene Durchsetzung des Journalismus mit Geistelementen, die zu einer katastrophalen Verwirrung führt. Die Phrase ist das Ornament des Geistes. (The debasement of practical life by ornament, demonstrated by Adolf Loos, finds its counterpart in the permeation of journalism by elements of higher culture, which has led to a catastrophic confusion. Phraseology is the ornament of the mind.)' (F 279–80: 8) The same concept is given prominence in Kraus's two most sustained assaults on pseudo-literary journalism, 'Heine und die Folgen' (August 1911) and 'Untergang der Welt durch schwarze Magie' (December 1912). The intellectual gain that would be obtained by eliminating phraseology from journalistic discourse would be infinitely greater than the economic gain to be derived from Loos's programme of 'saving on ornament' ('Ersparnis am Ornament', F 363–5: 4). Kraus saw the parallel between their critical campaigns as so close that he pinpointed it in a memorable aphorism in December 1913:

> Adolf Loos und ich, er wörtlich, ich sprachlich, haben nichts weiter getan als gezeigt, daß zwischen einer Urne und einem Nachttopf ein Unterschied ist und daß in diesem Unterschied erst die Kultur Spielraum hat. (F 389–90: 37)

(Adolf Loos and I, he literally, I in the sphere of language, have done nothing more than show that there is a difference between an urn and a chamber pot, and that it is only by maintaining this difference that there is any scope for culture.)

Amid the ornamental splendours of Habsburg Vienna such pronouncements seemed provocatively original. But like most fundamental distinctions this argument has significant antecedents. Loos acknowledged his debt not only to Otto Wagner but also to the mid-nineteenth-century architectural theorist Gottfried Semper. Nietzsche's denunciations of stylistic masquerade may have been a further source. But Loos is also likely to have been stimulated by his reading of Ruskin, whose *Seven Lamps of Architecture* anticipates Loos's essential argument. For Ruskin it is a 'general law [. . .] not to decorate things belonging to purposes of active and occupied life'. In short: 'You must not mix ornament with business.' He ridicules the tendency to decorate shop-fronts and railway stations with ornaments originally invented 'to adorn temples and beautify kings' palaces'. 'Let the iron be tough and the brickwork solid'; but it is better to 'bury gold in the embankments, than to put it in ornaments on the stations'. Denouncing this kind of decorative design as a form of 'monstrification', Ruskin even anticipates Loos's provocative analogy with the tattooing of the skin: 'I believe that we regard these customary deficiencies with a savage complacency, as an Indian does his flesh patterns and paints.'[6] Of course, Ruskin is also eloquent in defence of ornament — in its right place. Ornament has a pre-eminent value as one of the expressive resources of dedicated craftsmanship or sacramental art. For Ruskin there are *seven* lamps of architecture, whereas for Loos there are only two: Truth and Life. But Ruskin is nevertheless making the same fundamental distinction between sacramental art and practical life.

Kraus's aphorism too seems to have an earlier source — not in Ruskin, but in Lichtenberg. In February 1909 Kraus quotes a letter by Georg Christoph Lichtenberg, which seems to him to support Loos's attack on ornament. Lichtenberg is arguing against a proposal to embellish the town gates of Göttingen with sculpted pineapples and artichokes, urns and flower pots ('Urnen und Blumentöpfe', *F* 274: 22). In his view the building of a gate is a job for the master mason, not the architectural muse. At most, he is prepared to have the flower pots fixed to the wall, provided they are made of the simplest materials and not designed by artists. Since Kraus specifically cites this letter in support of Loos, it is likely that the line which Lichtenberg draws between 'Urne' and 'Blumentopf' stuck in his mind and later became the basis of his own more drastic antithesis between 'Urne' and 'Nachttopf'.

Kraus's aphorism implies that the medium of linguistic expression is analogous to that of architectural design. This claim is put forward with such panache that it has scarcely been questioned. The pioneering account of the subject by Paul Engelmann assumes that Kraus, Loos and Wittgenstein were engaged in parallel activities. And this assumption has provided the basis for a number of further studies.[7] This interdisciplinary approach has certainly illuminated the cross-fertilization between artistic and intellectual spheres which proved so fruitful in Vienna after 1900. The austerely elegant type face Loos used in his designs for the book jackets of Kraus's early publications accentuated their shared conception of intellectual rigour (Pl. 14). But there comes a point where it is necessary to be more discriminating. Kraus's repeated use of the word 'Ornament' for certain kinds of verbal mystification blurs an important distinction. On the one hand we have an architect and designer imposing form on bricks and mortar, plaster or stucco, marble or concrete, wood or metal. On the other we have a writer concerned with words: metaphors and clichés, quotations and allusions, the devices of phonetic and typographic accentuation. Loos's materials are part of the material world (marble is hewn in quarries). But Kraus's materials are merely representations of it, an arbitrary system of signs. Thus when Kraus draws our attention to verbal ornament, ideological façades or the masking function of words, these are themselves metaphors. Words do not really function in the same way as the façade of a building, a decoration on a teacup or a mask in the theatre. The relationship between signifier and signified is abstract and arbitrary.

However, the fact that words are only representations paradoxically gives Kraus's critique of language more far-reaching implications than Loos's attack on ornamental design. If we take away the pseudo-classical façade from the modern public building, what we are left with is still a building. Its structure may have become clearer — reinforced concrete rather than the pretence of marble columns. Techniques and materials may be more honestly displayed. The Post Office and the Stock Exchange may look like places designed for buying stamps and selling shares, rather than Renaissance palaces. There is a certain gain in efficiency and in the open acknowledgement of social practice. But what has been achieved is a better building, not the revelation of some fundamentally different truth. It would, after all, have made little difference historically if the new Austro-Hungarian War Ministry on the Stubenring, built between 1909 and 1913 to the opulently baroque designs of Ludwig Baumann, had been designed by Adolf Loos instead.[8] Even the most inspired architect can do little to make

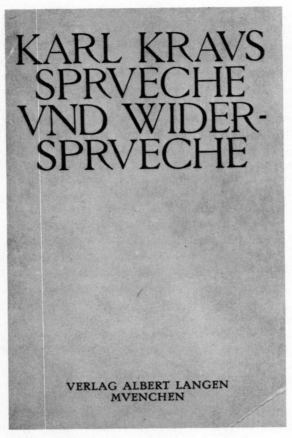

KARL KRAVS
SPRVECHE
VND WIDER-
SPRVECHE

VERLAG ALBERT LANGEN
MVENCHEN

14 Loos's design for the jacket of Kraus's 1909 book

the operations of the military-industrial complex more rational or more transparent.

Verbal façades are different. They are not really façades at all. They are a kind of veil through which our mental eye dimly apprehends the contours of the world around us. Thus Kraus's attempt to disperse the vapours of verbal and ideological mystification has more far-reaching consequences. These are already implicit in his most forceful writings of the period before the First World War. They became fully apparent in his campaign against the ideologies which sustained the war effort itself. The soldiers went into battle with expectations derived from schoolboy romances or patriotic songs or stories of medieval chivalry. Like the vistas of the Ringstrasse, their mental horizons were cluttered by the anachronistic embellishments of bygone eras. But the discrepancy between being a knight on horseback and the actual experience of advancing through barbed wire, poison gas and machine-gun fire — this discrepancy is totally different from the aesthetic disjunction between a brick building and its marble façade. Thus Kraus's application of the concept of 'ornament' amounts to a full-scale critique of ideological mystification.

The special attraction of Ruskin for both Kraus and Loos lay in the social and ethical applications of his aesthetic theory. His approach, like theirs, is holistic. Ornament in the wrong place is a form of 'deceit', an offence against the ethical duty of truthfulness. The false representation of material (for example, the attempt to make brick look like stone) is 'utterly base and inadmissible'. And like Loos, Ruskin tends to draw sweeping conclusions about the health of society at large from apparently insignificant details. A Greek cornice over a shop-front, or a business ledger artistically cased in enamel, is enough to raise doubts about 'our national probity'.[9] Thus it is not surprising to find Ruskin's ideas not only echoed by Loos, but also quoted by Kraus.

In February 1900 Kraus printed in *Die Fackel* an anonymous tribute to Ruskin, featuring a substantial quotation from *Sesame and Lilies*. In this passage Ruskin denounces the vulnerability of public opinion to journalistic propaganda, capable of turning a nation into a mob, which 'thinks by infection, catching an opinion like a cold' (*F* 31: 7–8). It seems quite probable that Kraus was stimulated by this article to take a closer look at *Sesame and Lilies* which (like *The Seven Lamps of Architecture*) appeared in a new German translation that same year. The affinities between his and Ruskin's intellectual positions are very striking. Like Kraus, Ruskin insists on a strict separation between journalism and literature, between 'books of the hour' (which are no more than 'newspapers in good print') and 'books of all time'. Like Kraus, he distinguishes complex 'thought' from transient 'opinion', and denounces the way literary values are being displaced by the spread of 'a shallow, blotching, blundering, infectious information'. Above all, he insists on the value of 'looking intensely at words'.[10]

This principle of 'looking intensely' at words and objects inspired a hyperbolic style of cultural criticism. Both Kraus and Loos excelled in the symbolic decoding of trivia. This kind of cultural extrapolation is indeed characteristic of Viennese intellectual life of the period. Kraus would base his apocalyptic prophecies on the evidence of a small advertisement or a local incident reported in the newspaper. Freud would draw far-reaching conclusions from an individual dream or even a slip of the tongue. Wittgenstein took trivial turns of phrase from everyday speech as the data from which to derive a whole philosophy of language. Loos would draw sweeping anthropological conclusions from the cut of women's clothing, the shape of a button or the design of a salt-cellar. The salt-cellars in Austrian restaurants may have been elegant, but they betrayed a fundamental failure to grasp modern principles of hygiene. For the patron had no option but to plunge his knife into the reservoir of salt, which soon acquired the colour of every item on the menu. When Loos put this argument to an acquaintance, however, he received the reply: 'How disgusting! I always lick my knife off first.'[11]

The mode of argument employed in these examples may seem fanciful and idiosyncratic. But it appealed to a shared perception of objects of everyday experience as emblems of ideological positions. Loos's restrained designs for the interior of the Café Museum in 1899 quickly earned that coffee-house the sobriquet 'Café Nihilismus'. The simple design of his furnishings was seen as a denial of the more traditional plush interiors and the ideology of conspicuous consumption which they embodied. This ideological approach to furniture design was shared by progressive and reactionary theorists alike. Lanz von Liebenfels, campaigning for a revival of Germanic manliness, would print in his periodical *Ostara* pictures of decadent bourgeois chairs, which invited one to slump lethargically against the back-rest. And in contrast to this there would be pictures of the Aryan way of sitting in an upright chair, designed to stiffen the backbone and improve muscular posture. There were even ideological debates about the design of water-closets. The pedestal was felt to be a decadent over-refinement which deprived one of the invigorating naturalness of squatting on one's hams.

The holistic approach to cultural phenomena has been much criticized. There is clearly an implicit Hegelianism in the assumption that every fragment of cultural expression can be related to a general Zeitgeist (or rather: to contradictions underlying its dialectical evolution). And one must be wary of the retrospective ingenuity of the historian who reconstructs the cultural mosaic in a simplified pattern, discarding the pieces which will not fit his design. But in the present case the pattern is not retrospectively imposed. The point is that this is how things were seen at the time. Architecture had become a focal point for the articulation of ideological conflicts.

Architecture and Politics

The battle of the façades reached its climax in the controversy over Loos's building on the Michaelerplatz. The casual passer-by in Vienna today would scarcely see Loos's design as controversial. What is now apparent is the success of his underlying aesthetic intention: to design a building which would harmonize with its environment (by echoing, for example, the portico of the Michaelerkirche in the marble columns of his shop-front). But in the very different ideological climate of 1910, Loos's traditionalism was not perceived. On the contrary, the building was seen as an affront to the traditional values of Habsburg Vienna. The ensuing controversy (admirably documented by Czech and Mistelbauer) lasted from September 1910 until May 1912.[12]

The dispute with the City Planning Department, which took out an injunction against the project and threatened the owners of the site with dire financial penalties, hinged on whether Loos had infringed the terms of the original planning consent. The City Council thus had some formal basis for its attempts to impose on Loos's building a more conventional decorative façade. Professional rivalry was also a factor (one of Loos's main opponents on the City Council was an architect, Hans Schneider, who specialized in revivalist designs). And some of the counter-arguments were indeed formulated in aesthetic terms (the stylistic disjunction between marble shop-front and the austere rendering of the upper storeys was repeatedly criticized). Ultimately the Council climbed down, saving face by getting Loos to agree to place bronze flower baskets beneath the upper windows.

In the heat of this controversy, Kraus pin-pointed the ideological thrust of Loos's design. Loos had affronted the sensibilities of the Viennese (Kraus wrote in *Die Fackel* of December 1910) because he had 'built them an idea' on the Michaelerplatz: 'Er hat ihnen dort einen Gedanken hingebaut' (*F* 313–14: 5). The 'idea' behind the building is defined by Kraus in a sequence of witty antitheses. Loos (he argues) believes in functionalism ('Zweckmäßigkeit'), where his critics are addicted to mediocrity ('Mittelmäßigkeit'). It is a blow struck in the name of progress ('Fortschritt') which is making the Viennese stand rooted to the ground ('Stehenbleiben'). In place of their dearly loved 'façades' Loos has confronted them with a 'tabula rasa' (*F* 313–14: 5). In all of this there is an element of polemical oversimplification. Kraus was aware of the paradox underlying Loos's work (which had been identified in an earlier article by Robert Scheu): that while he preaches 'nakedness', the actual effect of his buildings and interiors is festive and ceremonial ('feierlich', *F* 283–4: 34). Loos was by no means simply an iconoclast. Defending his building in a public lecture on 11 December 1911, he himself emphasized his debt to traditional Viennese building styles. But amid the dust of controversy (which began while the lower storeys of the building were still encased in scaffolding) such refinements passed unnoticed. It was the uncompromisingly plain and square windows of the upper storeys that captured public attention, not the elegant supporting columns. The contrast with the ornate historicism of the adjacent Palais Herberstein, built in 1903, made the challenge of Loos's design even more apparent (see Pl. 15).

The new building stood defiantly opposite the entrance to the Hofburg, completed in neo-baroque style between 1888 and 1893 (after the demolition of the old Burgtheater). For centuries the architectural advisers of the Imperial Family had been concerned to clear the huddle of urban dwellings around the Michaelerkirche, in order to create a magnificent approach to the Hofburg itself. Some very handsome buildings had been demolished in the process. The plainness of Loos's design could only be taken as an affront to the ceremonial values of the Habsburg dynasty. Reverting to its role as spokesman for the establishment, the *Neue Freie Presse* put this argument very eloquently. Here, in the immediate vicinity of the Burg, where Austrian history had been made and the great Maria Theresa had daily driven by, the building (its critic claimed) had the effect of 'a stab in the heart' for old Vienna and 'a declaration of war'.[13] This argument was echoed in the Viennese press in every stylistic register, from purple prose to scurrilous doggerel and caricature. In short, the design was seen as programmatic. Inherent in its austere façade was an ethical imperative. Not merely: 'This is how buildings must be designed in future!', but by implication: 'This is how life must be lived in future!' Both opponents and supporters perceived the ideological import of the aesthetic debate. Loos's building, as Paul Engelmann put it in a poem published in *Die Fackel*, signalled the beginning of a new age (F 317–18: 18).

In retrospect it may seem surprising that so much significance was attached to a single building. Other equally functional buildings were being erected in Vienna in this same period without fuss, for example Otto Wagner's block of shops and apartments on the corner of the Neustiftgasse (1909–10).[14] The difference lay not only in the prominent site of Loos's building, but also in the fact that his writings had given modern design the momentum of an ethical crusade. The programme which he had announced in his short-lived journal *Das Andere* (1903) was 'the Introduction of Western Civilization into Austria' (F 283–4: 34). His evolutionary arguments presented functionalism as an urgent imperative and ornament as the symptom of nostalgic regression. The political implications of this programme only became fully apparent during the 1920s and 1930s in the controversies which surrounded the Bauhaus. But the documentation by Czech and Mistelbauer shows that even in the Vienna of 1910 the connections between aesthetics and politics were being made.

15   The Goldmann & Salatsch building on the Michaelerplatz, designed by Loos

One voice is missing in this documentation of responses to Loos's building, a voice which turned out to be the most powerful of all. There was a student of architecture in Vienna in this period called Adolf Hitler. He can scarcely have been unaware of the controversy, since it was widely reported and became the talk of the town. The young Hitler was passionately interested in all aspects of architecture and design, and spent his idle hours poring over the newspapers in cheap cafés. His favourite reading was the antisemitic *Deutsches Volksblatt*.[15] It is thus more than possible that this controversy helped to shape his own approach to the political implications of architecture.

The way in which the National Socialists used architecture to convey political messages has been analysed by Barbara Miller Lane in her book *Architecture and Politics in Germany, 1918–1945*. But she underestimates the significance of the period before 1918, and fails to analyse Hitler's own architectural ambitions in Vienna before the First World War. This is not entirely due to the paucity of documentation. For there are a number of sources which illuminate the connections between Hitler's frustrated artistic ambitions and his subsequent political career. The memoir *Young Hitler* by August Kubizek is particularly instructive. Kubizek, a close friend of Hitler during his early period in Linz and Vienna, records Hitler's passion for the Ringstrasse. The Ringstrasse was the realization of Hitler's 'boldest artistic dreams'. He would spend hours studying and admiring 'this magnificent exhibition of modern architecture'. Kubizek was puzzled by Hitler's 'one-sided preference for the Ringstrasse'. The explanation he gives is revealing: 'Almost every style was represented. The House of Parliament was in the pseudo-Hellenic style, the Town Hall neo-Gothic, and the Burgtheater, an object of Adolf's special admiration, late Renaissance. Yet they had one thing in common which was especially attractive for my friend: their ostentation.'[16] Hitler's imagination was fired not only by the monumental buildings of the Ringstrasse, but also by the Heldenplatz — the great square in front of the Burg which inspired him with visions of mass meetings and military parades. It was here, thirty years later, that he was to turn fantasy into reality, when he returned to Austria in 1938 to celebrate his greatest political triumph.

Architectural styles made a significant contribution to the development of both progressive and reactionary ideologies in Vienna. The designs of the Ringstrasse may originally have reflected the aspirations of the Liberal bourgeoisie of the 1860s. But for Hitler the imperial splendour of these buildings proclaimed the ascendancy of the German race within the multinational Empire.[17] We may thus conclude that the antithesis Ringstrasse — Looshaus exemplified a fundamental conflict of values. Denouncing the spurious feudal magnificence of the apartment blocks on the Ring, Loos designed a building whose message was functional sobriety and practical adaptation to the needs of modern life. No more regressions to the life-style of primitive savages with their tattoos and war paint! But for Hitler the Ringstrasse spelt out a different message. The monumentality of its public buildings affirmed the possibility of imposing an heroic grandeur on the political events of the modern age.

The architectural controversies of 1910 prefigured the ideological conflicts which were to convulse Europe during the following decades. And the critique of façades provided Kraus with a crucial paradigm for the analysis of regressive tendencies in political thinking, above all his assault on the 'Techno-Romanticism' of German attitudes during the First World War. Moreover Loos seems to have sharpened his eye for the significance of visual motifs, as a means of enriching his satirical discourse. The satirist preoccupied with words becomes the seer for whom the streets of the city acquire visionary implications.

CHAPTER 7

Satirical Eye and Responsible Face

Kraus has often been praised for his acoustic imagination. But his response to visual stimuli is also extremely significant. He himself emphasizes his 'eye for faces and gestures' ('Blick für Gesichter and Gebärden', *F* 426–30: 78). From about 1908 onwards visual motifs become increasingly prominent in *Die Fackel*; and visual stimuli decisively shaped his response to the First World War. On occasion, he reproduces drawings or photographs in *Die Fackel*, in order to strengthen his attack on an individual target or to illustrate some more general aberration. More frequently, he is content to transpose visual impressions into verbal terms. He has a rich repertoire of images for the human face, especially in its distorted forms — 'Fratzen' and 'Grimassen'. The grotesque masks have been removed from the cover of *Die Fackel*, only to reappear in the text.

Kraus's interest in visual images was reinforced by his association with *Simplicissimus*. He had taken a not uncritical interest in this satirical magazine ever since its foundation in Munich in 1896. And he particularly admired the graphic artists Olaf Gulbransson, Rudolf Wilke and Thomas Theodor Heine. At an early stage we find Kraus adapting Heine's visual motifs to Austrian circumstances. A Habsburg dignitary observed clutching his monocle as he flees from the Ischl floods of 1897 is described as a subject for Th. Th. Heine (*FS* II. 96). And when in 1906 he used the title 'Aus dem dunkelsten Österreich' for one of his essays (*F* 214–15: 1), he must have expected his readers to catch the allusion to Heine's 'Durchs dunkelste Deutschland' — a series of drawings in *Simplicissimus* contrasting affluence with poverty. But it was only in 1908, when Kraus himself became a contributor to *Simplicissimus*, that the connection became explicit. The pleasure of seeing his work appear alongside the drawings of such gifted artists is the reason Kraus gives

for agreeing to become a contributor, even though he had little
sympathy for the magazine's democratic viewpoint and had
criticized its literary contributions (F 400–3: 30). Between February
1908 and August 1910 about twenty of his essays appeared in
Simplicissimus, together with more than a dozen groups of his
aphorisms. In these essays, which were also printed in *Die Fackel*,
visual motifs become particularly prominent. The essays mark a
clear advance on his earlier satirical style. The tone is less brashly
aggressive, more elegantly ironic. The guiding spirit is not moral
indignation but aesthetic sensibility.

Faces, Beards and Uniforms

One of the earliest of the essays, 'Von den Gesichtern' (June 1908),
deals directly with faces. It is the plaintive cry of an aesthete pained
by ugliness and confused by similarities. The stress on long noses,
jug-handle ears and pointed moustaches suggests that Kraus was
trying to reproduce that accentuation of prominent features which
we find in the cartoons of Gulbransson and Heine. The attempt was
clearly misconceived. For a literary text requires a more complex
perspective than a line drawing. In a satirical essay such features only
become significant when they are presented not as a freakishness of
nature, but as culturally determined distortions of the natural face. A
second essay, on the theme of 'Human Dignity' ('Menschenwürde',
April 1908), is more successful precisely because it focuses on this
aspect. Dignity is seen here as a form of protective mimicry, a pose
adopted to impress people by means of titles, uniforms and medals.
The celebrated 'Captain from Köpenick', the cobbler who imposed
himself on German bureaucracy by hiring an officer's uniform,
exemplifies this principle. Dignity ('Würde') is in Kraus's definition
the 'conditional form' of human existence: what one 'would be' if
one could ('würde' in the verbal sense) (F 251–2: 33).

The would-be world of dignified appearances is explored in other
essays. In 'Die Malerischen' (September 1908), an essay on the cult of
the picturesque, Kraus recalls the weather-tanned captain of a
steamer whom he caught applying artificial colouring to his face.
This world is a children's nursery, full of toys in beautiful uniforms,
more costume than content ('mehr Kostüm als Inhalt', F 261–2: 23).
In this essay Kraus also makes a more fundamental distinction: 'Zwei
einander feindliche Prinzipe bewegen unser geistiges Dasein: der
Sinn für das Malerische und das Gefallen am Nützlichen. Ich möchte
hundert gegen eins wetten, daß der praktische Mensch, der
sozusagen im Leben steht, also der Philister, dem Malerischen den
Vorzug gibt, während der Dichter sich's am Nützlichen genügen
läßt. (Two mutually hostile principles activate our mental life: the

sense of the picturesque and the pleasure in the functional. I'd wager a hundred to one that the practical man who stands so to speak in the mainstream of life, that is the philistine, gives his preference to the picturesque, whereas the poet is content with the functional.)' (*F* 261–2: 16) The picturesque is a substitute for art, and impedes the smooth functioning of society.

Kraus sees southern European countries, like Italy and Austria, as the centres of this ornamentalism. The Austrian (he argues in 'Von den Sehenswürdigkeiten', November 1908) tends to vanish behind the accoutrements of his official position and becomes a kind of ornamental salad: 'Hier aber gibt es Menschen, die ganz und gar eine Salatexistenz führen. [. . .] das Stigma des Malerischen, vor dem ich gewarnt habe, ist hier Ehrenzeichen und Bürgschaft einer Karriere, und überall verschwinden die Nutzmenschen hinter den Salatmenschen. (But here there are people who live what is entirely a salad existence [. . .] the stigma of the picturesque, against which I have warned, is here a mark of distinction and guarantee of a successful career, and everywhere the functional people are disappearing behind the salad people.)' (*F* 266: 9)

Kraus's satirical glosses abound in examples of these 'salad people'. The outstanding example is the Viennese hotelier Ludwig Riedl, who during a colourful career had collected no less than twenty-seven decorations for his services to the various royal houses of Europe (*F* 366–7: 19). The preponderance of ornament over function reinforces that of the past over the present. In a period of rapid technological change, requiring readjustments both in mental outlook and in life-style, the Viennese (Kraus argues) remain attached to life as it was lived in 1830. This creates a disturbing vacuum (*F* 300: 29). The 'romanticism' of life in Vienna is unfavourably contrasted with the functional sobriety of Berlin:

> Die Straßen Wiens sind mit Kultur gepflastert. Die Straßen anderer Städte mit Asphalt.
>
> (*W* III.146; cf. *F* 266: 8)
> (The streets of Vienna are paved with culture. The streets of other cities with asphalt.)

As Kraus surveys this anachronistic spectacle, his eye is repeatedly caught by one motif — the beard. Beards figure in his satire as emblems of a multiplicity of intellectual and cultural disguises. The pattern which emerges is full of paradoxes. Orthodox Jews were immediately recognizable in this period by the length of their beards. Kraus cites the provisions in Leviticus (19: 27) which imposed this upon them (*F* 187: 5); but these beards are not sacred to the satirist (*F* 326–8: 71–2). On the other hand, the typical liberal free-thinker can

also be identified by his beard (*F* 368–9: 3). Tolstoy's beard betokens
a problematic sanctity (*F* 250: 6), Bernard Shaw's an unpardonable
levity (*F* 418–22: 96). Bohemian artists traditionally wore beards (*F*
324–5: 1), but so do pillars of the establishment. The historian
Friedjung 'hat einen Voll- und Ganzbart' — a beard as 'full and
whole-hearted' as the patriotic support he gave (as we shall see) to
forged documents of the Foreign Office (*F* 384–5: 5). On several
occasions photographs of bearded public figures are actually reproduced in *Die Fackel*: Moriz Benedikt (*F* 326–8: frontispiece); Hermann Bahr (*F* 381–3: 33); and Otto Ernst, exponent of a folksy
literary idiom which Kraus found particularly spurious. Such
photographs (he insists) are far more revealing than the most artistic
caricature by Th. Th. Heine (*F* 398: 27–8).

The symbolism of beards is as varied as the historical
circumstances in which it is formulated.[1] In the Vienna of 1848 the
student revolutionaries had worn beards, which became symbols of
their political fervour. And after the defeat of the revolution it is
reported that the authorities forcibly shaved them off. By the 1880s
those students had become pillars of the Austrian establishment.
Their beards, now grey and venerable, symbolized for the iconoclasts of Kraus's generation a pompous Victorianism that had to be
swept away. A study of Wittgenstein puts the matter very clearly:
'The rebellious young men who were seeking to achieve consistency
and integrity rejected facial hair along with all other bourgeois
superfluities. To them, moustaches and sideburns were mere
ostentation, like velvet smoking jackets and fancy neckties. A serious
uncluttered mind called for a clean-shaven chin.'[2] Since then, the
cycle of fashion has come full circle. In the 1960s, beards once again
became the emblem of radical youth (inspired by Fidel Castro and his
barbarillos). And repressive regimes (such as the military government
of Turkey in the early 1980s) have again tried to curtail intellectual
freedom by imposing a ban on beards.

The symbolism of beards has potent undertones. But Kraus
reverses the conventional pattern. Beards figure in his writings not as
emblems of manliness, but as camouflage for intellectual and sexual
insufficiency. Beards are for Kraus what wigs were for the rebellious
young men of the eighteenth century: an ostentatious attempt to
disguise the inadequacies of the wearer. He tries to endow the word
'Bart' with the associations of the eighteenth-century 'Zopf'
('pigtail'). But Gottsched's wig really was false (as Goethe quickly
discovered), whereas Tolstoy's beard was not.[3] Thus beards can also
be symbols of naturalness or the outward and visible sign of a return
to Christian piety. Kraus's attempt to make Tolstoy's patriarchal
beard into an emblem of mystification falls lamentably short of its

target (*F* 250: 1–10). It is not logical argument, but merely fortunate coincidence, which enables the satirist to connect a fraudulent intellectual position with equally extravagant accoutrements. The photograph of Bahr with beard and flowing beach robe functions in this way. It reinforces our sense of the spuriousness of his posture, both as 'prophet' of the Austrian literary revival and as a convert to simple Christianity. And the hypocrisy of Bahr's feigned indifference to money is all the more effectively exposed (*F* 381–3: 33–40).

Kraus puts the case against beards in a mischievous paradox: 'Ich möchte behaupten: gerade jene Gesichter, die des Vollbartes nicht wert sind, brauchen ihn. (I'm inclined to maintain that it is precisely those faces not worthy of a beard that need one.)' (*F* 384–5: 5) If they had their beards shaved off, they would be 'unmasked' ('entlarvt'). Having fun at the expense of people's appearance may not seem a very sophisticated form of satire. But Kraus's objections form part of a satirical strategy organized around the motifs of masks and façades, beards, costumes and disguises. The aim is to find tangible symbols for the ideological mystifications of his age. Like Loos, he denounces a civilization which decks itself out in anachronistic forms: 'Mich täuscht die Fassade nicht![. . .] Ich kann tabula rasa machen. Ich fege die Straßen, ich lockere die Bärte, ich rasiere die Ornamente! (I am not taken in by the facade! [. . .] I can make tabula rasa. I sweep the street, I loosen the beards, I shave the ornaments!)' (*F* 384–5: 7) But this confident tone is not sustained. At times the 'beardedness' of Austrian culture looms so large that it threatens to blot out the sun, like the black 'sackcloth of hair' which presages the end of the world (*F* 378–80: 71; Revelation 6: 12).

We may wonder at the vehemence of this response to beards. A clue is provided by Kraus's refusal to grow a beard of his own as a matter of 'conviction': 'Es wäre gegen meine Überzeugung' (*F* 389–90: 40). We may also recall his vignette of the barber's shop, in which he is reassured that *his* beard (which the barber is shaving) is the real thing: 'Ja *der* Bart hats *in* sich!' (*F* 577–82: 47). Kraus makes this a symbol for the vigour of his literary style. And it is tempting to associate this with his insistence on the 'masculinity' of his writings. But the psychological explanation of Kraus's preoccupation with beards seems more likely to be ethnic than sexual. If shaving is an act of personal conviction, it is so because *not* shaving was also a matter of conviction, in the Orthodox Jewish tradition which Kraus repudiated. It was the antisemitic ambience of Austria-Hungary which gave beards their symbolic force. Theodor Herzl reacted to the antisemitic sentiment of the 1880s by defiantly growing a beard to accentuate his Jewish solidarity. Kraus's assimilationist attitude led

him in the opposite direction. He mocked the Zionists for the
regressiveness of their 'Assyrian' beards and hair-styles, as well as
their ideas (*FS* II.305). Being clean-shaven was part of his attempt to
divest himself of all traces of Jewish identity. He seems unaware of
Heinrich Heine's definition of the beard as the eternal emblem of
Jewishness, which 'no barber can shave off'.[4]

The moustache had the opposite significance. It was the
unmistakable emblem of the military type and had become a visual
cliché for countless caricaturists. Another satirist of this same period,
adopting the viewpoint of a visitor from Mars, concludes that the
cultivation of the moustache (with its militaristic associations) must
be the principal aim of German education.[5] In Kraus's pre-war satire
this motif is less prominent than the beard, since his main concern is
with the ideological camouflage of liberalism, rather than with the
more blatant threat of militarism. But as the danger of war became
apparent after the Austrian annexation of Bosnia (1908), the bristling
military moustache grows in Kraus's imagination until it too
becomes an apocalyptic portent. The visionary essay 'Apokalypse'
(October 1908) describes a horseman whose moustache 'stretches
from the rising to the setting of the sun' and to whom (in the biblical
phrase) 'it was given to take peace from the earth, so that they should
slay one another' (*F* 261–2: 4; Revelation 6: 4). The moustache of
the German Kaiser is here for Kraus the portent of dynamic German
militarism, just as (retrospectively) he was to identify the fuzzy
side-whiskers of Emperor Franz Joseph as the symbol of Austrian
ineffectiveness (*F* 501–7: 7).

Kraus's exploitation of visual motifs presupposes a knowledge of
what he calls the 'sartorial language' of Austria-Hungary ('die
Kleidersprache des Landes'). The reader unfamiliar with this language is likely to miss the point, like the Englishman in Kraus's
anecdote who made the mistake of wearing a hat when visiting the
headquarters of a Hungarian regiment (speechless with rage, the
Hungarian official knocked his hat off) (*F* 331–2: 22–3). In a hier-
archical society, hats, hair-styles, clothing and uniforms comprised a
highly differentiated semiotic system, and the rituals of Austrian
public life gave minor gestures a profound significance. A man who
refused to take off his hat when the Blessed Sacrament was carried
through the streets of Vienna during a Corpus Christi procession
was sentenced to fourteen days imprisonment. In glossing this
episode, Kraus pin-points the irony that in the synagogue the
wearing of a hat would have been a sign of piety (*F* 210: 1–3).

The clothes and uniforms of Austria-Hungary provided the satirist
with a rewarding spectacle. Like Adolf Loos, Kraus sees the
outmoded accoutrements of Austrian tradition as emblems of the

country's backwardness. But he was equally attentive to clothing which signalled a provocative modernity, as when women began to wear trousers, causing chaos on the streets of Vienna (*F* 319–20: 11). Clothing motifs are not only symbols of ideological confusion. They also become metaphors for intellectual and ideological disguises. Like Carlyle in *Sartor Resartus*, Kraus focuses on 'clothes' which have become 'mere hollow Shapes or Masks, under which no living Figure or Spirit any longer dwells'. Carlyle's 'Philosophy of Clothing' invokes a conception of language which is attributed to a fictive German philosopher named Teufelsdröckh: 'Language is called the Garment of Thought: however, it should rather be, Language is the Flesh-Garment, the Body, of Thought.'[6] The formulation is echoed in Kraus's insistence 'that language does not clothe thought, but thought grows into language' ('daß die Sprache den Gedanken nicht bekleidet, sondern der Gedanke in die Sprache hineinwächst', *F* 389–90: 42). This is the basis for Kraus's attacks on writers for whom language is merely a borrowed 'costume'. The bombastic style of Maximilian Harden is 'an exotic garment' ('apartes Kleid', *F* 234–5: 10), which must be stripped off to reveal the underlying philistinism of Harden's attitudes. 'Kleid' and 'Kostüm' become (like 'Ornament') key concepts in Kraus's critique of spurious modes of communication.

The World of Advertising

There is one point where these visual motifs intersect particularly vividly with the sphere of communications: in Kraus's critique of advertising. The impact of advertising posters is the theme of one of his most suggestive essays, 'Die Welt der Plakate' (June 1909). This essay focuses on the way advertisements reduce human beings to consumers, living at the behest of commercial enterprises. It has a freshness of vision that makes it far more memorable than any sociological treatise. Kraus achieves this by re-creating the impressionability of childhood. The uncomprehending child, who does not realize that the stilted exchanges portrayed in advertisements are merely designed to sell products, imagines that this is how people behave in real life. This naive perspective enables the satirist to picture a world created in the advertiser's image.

The visual impact of the manufacturer and advertiser takes even more direct forms: 'Eines Tages brach die Sintflut des Merkantilismus über die Menschheit herein, Gevatter Schneider und Handschuhmacher gebärdeten sich als die Vollstrecker eines göttlichen Willens, und es entstand die Mode, die Köpfe dieser Leute an den Straßenecken zu konterfeien. (One day the great flood of mercantilism swept over mankind, the Tom, Dick and Harrys of commercial life started behaving as if they were the executors of a divine will, and it became the fashion to put up portraits of these people at street corners.)' (F 283–4: 21–2) The influence of these haunting images is portrayed as inescapable. The whole world (as Kraus's title intimates) has been taken over by commercial interests. Advertising hoardings dominate the townscape and also invade the countryside. They haunt the waking consciousness and even penetrate into the mind as it is falling asleep. The essay reaches its fantastic climax in a series of nightmare visions, in which the faces and voices of advertisers besiege the semi-conscious mind and drive it towards suicidal despair.[7]

The strengths and limitations of Kraus's visually orientated satire are particularly evident in this essay. It is rich in suggestive insights. But no attempt is made at analysis in depth. It is revealing that Kraus uses the old-fashioned word 'Merkantilismus' for the commercial consequences of capitalism. And it is equally characteristic that he offers no explanation of historical causes. 'One day the great flood of mercantilism swept over mankind,' we are told, in the manner of a fairy-tale. Kraus's perspective is impressionistic, not analytical. He disclaims any knowledge of sociology or the history of capitalism (F 303–4: 40). And yet his vision of a world in which commodities have become more powerful than people unwittingly echoes a famous chapter by Karl Marx.[8] The self-destructive tendencies of consumerism reach their climax in Kraus's final nightmare image of a gunsmith, whose slogan for selling his products is 'Murder yourself!'.

This motif is intensified in a short essay of October 1912, 'Momentaufnahmen'. Here Kraus is dealing with the use of snapshot photographs in commercial advertising:

Da ich aber von dem inbrünstigen Glauben durchdrungen bin, daß die heutigen Tags lebende Menschheit wirklich nur [. . .] aus dem Annoncenteil desertiert oder beurlaubt ist, um seiner Idee in Freiheit zu dienen; da ich diese Kärntnerstraßengesichter wirklich in keine andere Rubrik des Lebens tun könnte und absolut überzeugt bin, daß wir am Ende der Zeiten stehen und ein höheres Wesen die irdische Schöpfung nicht mehr als das aufgeschlagene Buch, sondern als ein vielfach verhobenes, von Druckfehlern wimmelndes, nur in den Annoncenbildern lesbares, einem kosmischen Abtritt vorbehaltenes Montagsblatt besieht: so beruhigt alle Schrecken, die die Entwicklung dem Gefühl des Betrachters vorstellt, der Gedanke an das Ende!   (F 357–9: 32)

(Since I am imbued with the fervent belief that the human beings alive today are [. . .] really only deserters or men on leave from the advertising section, in order to serve its idea in freedom; since I would be unable to place these faces seen in the main street under any other rubric of life, and am absolutely convinced that we have reached the end of time and that a higher being contemplates the earthly creation not as an open book, but as a much damaged Monday morning paper, abounding in misprints, legible only in its advertising section, and destined for a cosmic demise: for this reason all the horrors which this development presents to the sensibility of the observer are calmed by the thought of the approaching end!)

The lightness of tone of 'Die Welt der Plakate' has given way to apocalyptic prophecy. The same motif occurs in Kraus's fiercest denunciation of the values of his contemporaries in the final years before the First World War, 'Die Kinder der Zeit' (F 354–6: 72).

The war seems if anything to have intensified his sensitivity to the suggestive power of advertisements. The juxtaposition of three posters shaped his problematic response to the outbreak of war in 1914 (F 404: 3). And during the war itself the leering faces on the advertising hoardings seemed as sinister to the satirist as the shrill cries of the newsvendors announcing military victories. The slogans of commerce, like those of war, celebrate the destruction of a meaningful existence; and the face of the epoch is that of a grinning youth advertising the prophylactic Lysoform (see Pl. 16). 'Indispensable for women', the poster proclaims (hinting at the need for precautions against venereal disease). Plastered larger than life around the streets of war-torn Vienna, this leering face inspired a diatribe against the cynical frivolity of the age (F 418–22: 10–11).

Kraus had a sharp eye for the significance of advertisements, large and small. His most fertile field was provided by the small ads for matrimonial and sexual partners which were such a feature of Austrian newspapers. Dozens of examples are reprinted in *Die Fackel*:

> *Zur Einheirat*
> in großes Textilunternehmen
> wird 45 bis 50 Jahre alter
> Herr aus feiner isr. Familie,
> mit Vermögen gesucht.
>
> (F 370–1: 47)

('Wealthy gentleman, of refined Hebrew family, aged between 45 and 50, and willing to/*Marry into the Firm*/is sought by a large textile business.') The mercenary values of the advertisers are often so blatant that no commentary is required. Many of Kraus's examples derive from the Jewish community, whose traditional system of marriage brokers found a wider sphere of operation through this method of advertising. But his selection is catholic enough to show that marrying for money was an unashamed practice among almost every section of society. Professed Christians, manly 'Aryans' and

16   Advertisement for Lysoform

dynamic Germans from the Reich showed equally few scruples in publicly offering their hand in marriage to the highest bidder. By documenting these practices Kraus makes a valuable contribution to social history.[9]

Those glosses in which Kraus responds with an astringent satirical commentary are even more impressive. Here the play of his imagination strikes a balance between creative wit and destructive vehemence. Picturing the possible encounter between the gentleman of refined Hebrew family and the daughter of that large textile business, he offers us a stereoscopic vision of their courtship, marriage and copulation, and above all of the withering away of the spiritual life of the woman — the nameless victim of this transaction, whose children will in their turn be married off to commercial enterprises (F 370–1: 48). Another example, in which a travelling salesman advertises for a 'Father-in-Law' who will set him up in the clothing business, elicits from Kraus a brilliant image of a woman traded like 'a ready-made garment' ('dieses fertige Kleidungsstück von Weib', F 406–12: 38).

Through these small ads the satirist also catches glimpses of a second, more fundamental impulse: sexual concupiscence in all its abundant variety. We can imagine Kraus's delight in discovering the following in the highly respected Neue Freie Presse (31 March 1900):

Reisegenosse gesucht, jung,
nett, Christ, unabhängig. Briefe unter
'Conträr 69' postlagernd Habsburgergasse.

(F 40: 17)

('*Travelling Companion Sought,*/ young, congenial, Christian, independent. Replies to "Invert 69" poste restante Habsburgergasse.') In the following decade he never tires of tracking down advertisements of this kind, in which cryptic allusions to sexual perversions have escaped the vigilance of the sub-editor. From homosexuality to fellatio, from flagellation to masochistic fantasy, there were few of the furtively pursued varieties of sexual experience which did not surface in the small ads of the Viennese press. It is not the sexual impulse itself that Kraus satirizes, but the hypocrisy of a press which is so prissily moral in its front-page editorials and so ready to satisfy lecherous desires through small ads on the final page.

Even in these marginal glosses we can see a visual imagination at work. For Kraus, a newspaper is like a human being, with a 'face' and a 'behind'. The ideals up front may be false, but on its arse the world 'wears no mask' — 'Auf dem Arsch trägt sie keine Larve' (F 370–1: 47). Kraus responds to the small print of these advertisements with an image which once again seems to have a visual source, the illustration of *Hypocrisy* by Félicien Rops, which shows a curvaceous female bottom with a carnival mask saucily tied around it (see Pl. 17).

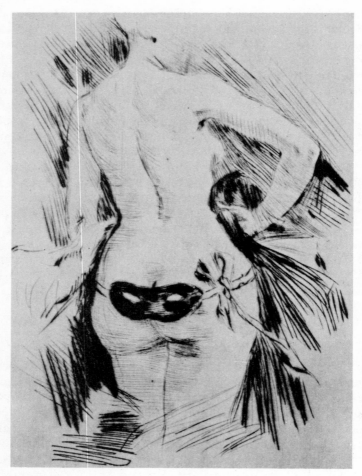

17   *Hypocrisy* by Félicien Rops

The Quest for a Responsible Face

Where the casual reader sees only newsprint, the satirist sees 'faces'. Kraus not only responds to visual stimuli. His imagination also travels in the reverse direction, putting an individual 'face' to abstract phenomena. Here again his method is reminiscent of the cartoonists of *Simplicissimus*, who had to give actual faces to abstractions like Church or Army and allegorical images of Germany or Austria.

Behind the most trivial journalistic utterance Kraus seeks a 'physiognomy' (*F* 232–3: 14).

This habit of mind is illustrated by an essay of March 1909 on the theme of 'Progress' ('Der Fortschritt', first published in *Simplicissimus*). His starting-point here is a newspaper slogan that contains the revealing mixed metaphor: 'Wir stehen im Zeichen des Fortschritts'. How can we be simultaneously 'standing' and 'striding forward'? Kraus sets out in quest of visible manifestations of this self-contradictory spirit of progress. The streets of Vienna abound in such symbols: street-cleaning machines which merely create dust and mud; an automobile taxi whose progress through the city is so laborious that it is overtaken by pedestrians. But above all he seeks to identify Progress in terms of a human face. Amid the political and linguistic confusion of Habsburg Austria, the ideology of Progress has become amorphous: 'Ich fand den Fortschritt in allen [Regionen], ohne in einer einzigen seine Physiognomie zu finden. Ich glaubte, ich sei in eine Maskenleihanstalt geraten. (I found progress in all these regions, without finding its physiognomy in a single one. I thought I must have found my way into a place where they hire out theatrical masks.)' (*F* 275–6: 37) Kraus's image emphasizes the hollowness of Progress, which manifests itself in such a multiplicity of disguises. How much easier it would be (he declares in July 1914) if these sinister forces all had a *single* face: 'Denn die Gefahr hat nur *ein* Gesicht zu haben' (*F* 400–3: 60).

Here we reach a crux in Kraus's account of the destruction of human personality. A combination of social and commercial, journalistic and ideological pressures has generated a subhuman synthesis which Kraus identifies as the 'essential face' of the century:

> Und aus dem letzten Eckchen eines Zeitungsblattes, das noch unter meiner Lektüre liegt, lugt mir, da ich sie durchfliege, schon die Judasfratze des Jahrhunderts hervor, immer dieselbe, ob es sich um den Journalisten oder den Mediziner, den Hausierer oder den Sozialpolitiker, den Spezereikommis oder den Ästheten handelt. [. . .] Ich habe diese unselige Fähigkeit, sie nicht unterscheiden zu können, und ich agnosziere das Urgesicht, ohne daß ich mich um die Entlarvung bemühe.
>
> (*F* 303–4: 39)

> (And from the last little corner of a newspaper, which still forms part of my reading, there peeps out at me, as I glance through it, the distorted Judas-face of the century, always the same one, whether it is a matter of the journalist or the medical man, the hawker or the social politician, the travelling salesman in groceries or the aesthete. [. . .] I have this unfortunate faculty of not being above to tell the one from the other, and I identify the essential face, without troubling to unmask it.)

The 'Judas-face of the century' is that of the modern bourgeoisie — 'die Bürgerfratze' — distorted since birth by an alienated form of society (F 378–80: 71).

It is this bourgeois face, emblem of a confident, progressive, secular and commercial civilization, which is Kraus's central target in the final years before 1914. The more 'picturesque' Austrian institutions, monarchy and aristocracy, Church and army, are treated more marginally. On this score, Kraus cannot be absolved of a certain partiality. In the years before 1914, he certainly underestimated the dangers arising from reactionary political movements (just as he ignored the position of the working class). But in the longer term this preoccupation with the values and institutions of bourgeois civilization is a source of strength. For the late-twentieth-century reader his satire would have far less bite if it confined itself to mockery of decadent Austrian aristocrats, instead of concentrating on the values of the educated, progressive, intellectually sophisticated middle classes (the values of those most likely to be his readers).

One of the paradoxes of the Habsburg situation was that the progressive bourgeoisie were even more eager than the Austrian establishment to equip themselves with titles, dignities and decorations. Die Fackel in this period is full of references to the nouveau riche class of capitalists and entrepreneurs, many of them from Jewish backgrounds, who were thrusting themselves into prominent positions in Austrian public life. Kraus's conservative leanings in the final years before 1914 made him especially sensitive to the way positions of influence were being usurped by commercial counter-jumpers and journalistic interlopers from the eastern provinces. The distorted face of the new bourgeoisie did not become any more attractive when it assumed the trappings traditionally associated with the old aristocracy. This hybrid identity represented the Austrian confusion of values, stigmatized in Die Fackel as an 'aristodemoplutobürokratischen Mischmasch' (F 374–5: 7). Kraus's pursuit of this amorphous physiognomy became increasingly urgent during the final years of the Habsburg Empire, culminating in awesome imprecations against 'the Austrian Face'.

Obviously, there can be no one face that epitomizes all the disorders of Austria-Hungary. But the face that Kraus singles out for most intensive scrutiny is that of Moriz Benedikt, proprietor and editor of the Neue Freie Presse. His printing of a photograph of Benedikt as frontispiece to Die Fackel in July 1911, represents Kraus's most significant attempt to identify the 'essential face' of the age in terms of a named individual. The photograph is in fact a photomontage: a picture of Benedikt taken from an illustrated magazine.[10] This is superimposed on a photograph of the Austrian parliament building (see Pl. 18). By this device Kraus makes a critical point in visual terms: effective political power in Austria lies not with the elected parliamentary representatives, but with the bourgeois press and the financial interests it promotes. The Liberal Party had made significant gains in the parliamentary elections of 1911. Kraus's photomontage suggests that parliamentary government is a façade, and reveals the face of the true victor, the man who really holds power in the land — 'Der Sieger' (F 326–8: frontispiece). By means of a commonplace photograph he claims to have shown 'wie der

DER SIEGER

Nach einer photogr. Aufnahme

DER HERAUSGEBER DER NEUEN FREIEN PRESSE
20. JUNI 1911

18   'The Victor': photomontage of Moriz Benedikt in front of the Austrian parliament

Fortschritt dasteht, wie die Geldgier die Faust ballt, welchen Blick
die Aufklärung hat, welchen Bart der Einfluß und welche Nase der
freisinnige Triumph (how Progress stands, how Avarice clenches
its fist, what sort of look Enlightenment has, what sort of beard
Influence, what sort of nose the Triumph of Liberalism)' (F
331–2: 1–2). The satirist seems confident that he has at last
identified the physiognomy of Progress and the essential face of the
age. But his claims are clearly problematic. For problems arise both
from his personalization of the issue and from his accentuation of
certain features of the person.

Kraus's intellectual outlook predisposed him to attack
contemporary evils in terms of named individuals, rather than
anonymous institutions or amorphous forces of history. His whole
career revolves around the problem of finding what in a key
formulation of October 1917 he called a 'responsible face'. In his
more analytical moments he concedes that there is no such
responsible face: 'Aber da ist kein verantwortliches Gesicht' (F
462–71:171). Indeed, he had acknowledged in July 1914, in a
passage quoted from Theodor Haecker, that the evils of the modern
world are attributable to 'anonymous, completely irresponsible
mass forces which cannot be pinned down' (F 400–3: 58). Nevertheless, it is both the glory and the limitation of his satire that he
never abandons this quest for a 'responsible face'. This is a primary
source of his imaginative and moral achievement. It is the creative
focus on individual targets which makes his writing so vivid and
animated. And it is his insistence under all circumstances on the
moral responsibility of the individual that gives his work its ethical
charge.

If any individual was to represent the power of the press, it
certainly had to be Benedikt. The monopoly of newspapers over
the distribution of information gave him political power
comparable to that of Northcliffe in Britain and Hearst in the
United States during this same period. Indeed the weakness of the
Austrian parliament, which was actually suspended in the spring of
1914 and not even consulted about the fatal decision to declare war
on Serbia, endowed Benedikt's dynamic propaganda for the
German cause with even greater influence. His career was summed
up in 1920 by the obituarist of the London *Times*:

> The death of Herr Benedikt removes from the life of Vienna an
> influence which was as potent in its own way as that of the late Emperor
> Francis Joseph himself. [. . .] Benedikt was unscrupulous, fanatical,
> indefatigable and pernicious. No secret of international finance was
> unknown to him, and very few of the secrets of the Hapsburg State. By
> means of the *Neue Freie Presse* he blackmailed Ministers and State

officials, 'bulled' and 'beared' the stock market, enriched himself, and dominated a powerful section of Austrian opinion. Benedikt, more than any other man, was responsible for the downfall of Austria. [. . .] He may fitly be called the evil genius of the Hapsburg Monarchy in its declining years.[11]

Thus Kraus's diagnosis in 1911 was by no means as eccentric as it seems. But the influence of mass media is so intangible that to attribute its evils to a single representative figure is bound to be misleading. It foregrounds the function of an individual and obscures more complex factors (above all, the manipulation of the press by government agencies).

The problem is compounded by Kraus's emphasis on Benedikt's personal features — his swarthy beard and his prominent nose. The antisemitic undercurrent which runs through Kraus's satire is also evident in the visual motifs he chooses. In his campaign against *Die Zeit* in 1903 he had mocked advertisements which showed the paper being promoted by a vendor with sterotyped 'Jewish' features. When

19   Advertising posters for *Die Zeit*

Die Zeit substituted the features of a round-faced innocent, *Die Fackel* was able to confront the two images in a striking juxtaposition (Pl. 19; *F* 137: 17). The tendency of advertising artists to endow their subjects with Jewish visual characteristics is also evident in the advertisement for Lysoform. Kraus obliquely draws attention to this by applying to the face in the ad the Jewish jargon word 'Ponem' (*F* 418–22: 11). And when he defines the essential face of the century as 'die Judasfratze', he is clearly treading dangerous ground. The accentuation of the noses of prominent journalists such as Benedikt (*F* 331–2: 2) and Alice Schalek (*F* 413–17: 36) comes near to implying that we should despise the press because it is Jewish, rather than because it is tendentious.

The task for the modern reader is to distinguish the objectively valid dimensions of Kraus's critique from the mesh of Jewish associations with which it is entangled. His perspective was clearly distorted by factors which were specific to Habsburg Austria. If Kraus had been familiar with Edwardian Britain, he would have realized that the problems created by mass-circulation newspapers did not stem from their being in the hands of Jewish proprietors. But because the press in Vienna (as in Budapest) was largely owned, edited and written by Jews, the two questions became conflated in his mind. The problem is compounded by Kraus's own Jewish origins, which led some observers to suggest that in his attacks on Benedikt he was trying to exorcise aspects of his own group identity. The aim of the present book is to show that the validity of Kraus's critique of systems of communication is not impaired by that undercurrent of antisemitism. This will become particularly clear when we turn to his response to propaganda for war.

CHAPTER 8

Undertones of War: Friedjung and the Feuilleton

Kraus's critique of the press is reinforced by an awareness of the accelerating pace of technology and the growing threat of war. This theme was prophetically anticipated by the lines from a poem by an unknown Austrian soldier which he quotes in November 1904:

> Auf einmal kommt die Kanon
> Und der Mensch muß davon
>
> (F 169: 22)

('Suddenly the cannon come/And man must be gone'.) After the crisis caused by the Austrian annexation of Bosnia in 1908, it became clear that the struggle for power in the Balkans could easily trigger off a European war. The arguments in favour of war against Serbia nevertheless became increasingly vocal in Vienna, since Serbian nationalism was undermining the loyalty of the two million Serbo-Croats who were Habsburg subjects. The pro-war faction was led by the Chief of Staff Conrad von Hötzendorf and supported by influential voices in the Austrian press, notably Heinrich Friedjung in the *Neue Freie Presse*.

Die Fackel of the years 1908–14 is fraught with undertones of war. The successive crises and mobilizations are memorably portrayed in a novel by an anonymous army officer, published in 1913 under the title *Quo vadis Austria*.[1] Austrian indecisiveness is shown to be having such demoralizing effects on the army that the book was promptly confiscated and the author hauled before a military tribunal. The authorities were reportedly so perturbed that they planned to issue another novel, more robustly patriotic in tone. Kraus's comments on this affair show that he was sceptical of all such attempts to provide a literary or intellectual sanction for war (F 395–7: 65–7). Although he did not align himself with the organized pacifist movement, he had

earlier endorsed the warnings of Alfred Fried about the dangers of
'military romanticism' (F 212: 18).

The Old Ethic and the New Machines

Kraus is sometimes reproached for a lack of historical understanding.
It is true that he does not often comment directly on historical events
and cultivates an attitude of disdain towards politics ('Politik', F
264–5: 1–4). But he had a more fundamental awareness that
technological developments had created a situation of unprecedented
crisis. More had happened during the last thirty years (he wrote in
January 1908) than in the previous three hundred. And the dilemma
of the modern age arises from 'the manufacture of new machines for
the operation of an old ethic' (F 241: 15). This is one of many
passages in which Kraus pin-points the self-destructive tendencies of
modern technology. But this does not lead to a simplistic repudiation
of machines.

The problem is that as a European of the year 1910 he finds himself
living among people who are still attached to the picturesque world
of 1830:

> Es gibt ein Zeitgefühl, das sich nicht betrügen läßt. Man kann auf
> Robinsons Insel gemütlicher leben als in Berlin; aber nur, solange es
> Berlin nicht gibt. 1910 wirds auf Robinsons Insel ungemütlich.
> Automobildroschke, Warmwasserleitung und ein Automat für
> eingeschriebene Briefe beginnen zu fehlen, auch wenn man bis dahin
> keine Ahnung hatte, daß sie erfunden sind. Es ist der Zeit eigentümlich,
> daß sie die Bedürfnisse schafft, die irgendwo in der Welt schon befriedigt
> sind. Um das Jahr 1830 wars ja schöner, und darum sind wir
> Feinschmecker dabei geblieben. Aber indem wir uns bei der Schönheit
> beruhigen, macht uns das Vacuum von achtzig Jahren unruhig.
>
> (F 300: 29)

> (There is a sense of time which cannot be deceived. One can live more
> cosily on Robinson Crusoe's island than in Berlin; but only as long as
> Berlin does not exist. In 1910 Robinson Crusoe's island is no longer cosy.
> One begins to miss automobile taxis, hot water taps and a machine for
> registering letters, even if up to that point one had no inkling that they
> had been invented. It is a characteristic of the age that it creates those
> needs which have somewhere in the world already been satisfied. Around
> the year 1830 life was more beautiful, and for this reason we epicures have
> remained there. But while we are consoling ourselves with beauty, the
> vacuum of eighty years makes us uneasy.)

The epicures are of course the Austrians, whose failure to come to
terms with the new era of electricity and telephones Kraus repeatedly
ridicules. His own attitudes to machines show a functionalist respect

for their utility. He explicitly repudiates the Tolstoyan solution of a 'return to Nature' (*F* 250: 5–6).

This functionalist attitude towards machines is subordinated to a humanistic insistence that they be the servants not the masters of mankind. And at this point Kraus's individual acceptance of the new technology gives way to doubts about the ability of society as a whole to make the necessary adjustments. An updating of mental attitudes is necessary, in order to overcome the dangerous vacuum. But this must not lead to a mindless capitulation to machines. The two extremes, of anachronistic retreat into nature and of futuristic worship of machines, are equally dangerous. The ingenuity that has gone into new inventions must be counterbalanced by qualities of mind which are far more essential to the health of civilization — the qualities Kraus associates with 'Geist'. This is a more profound thoughtfulness, firmly grounded in traditional humanism and in a respect for the harmony of nature.

The signs of the times, as Kraus reads them around 1908, are that mankind is expending its spiritual capital on its inventions and retaining nothing for their operation:

> Kein Atemholen bleibt der Kultur und am Ende liegt eine tote Menschheit neben ihren Werken, die zu erfinden ihr so viel Geist gekostet hat, daß ihr keiner mehr übrig blieb, sie zu nützen.
>
> Wir waren kompliziert genug, die Maschine zu bauen, und wir sind zu primitiv, uns von ihr bedienen zu lassen. Wir treiben einen Weltverkehr auf schmalspurigen Gehirnbahnen.   (*F* 261–2: 1)

> (There is no breathing space for culture, and ultimately mankind lies dead beside its works, whose invention has cost so much intelligence that there was none left to put them to use.
>
> We were complicated enough to build the machine and we are too primitive to put it to our service. We are operating a world-wide system of communication on narrow-gauge lines of thought.)

In the final years before 1914 Kraus therefore denounces a technological civilization which is displacing humanistic culture, destroying the harmony of nature and threatening the survival of mankind. It is not, however, technology in itself that is under attack, but a technology which is plunging out of control.

Kraus's critique of technology becomes even more impressive when he makes the connection with two other still more ominous developments — the techniques of propaganda and the threat of war. In the final years before 1914 he shows that the dangers of technological development are calamitously compounded by the malignant influence of the media. This connection is forcefully made in the aphorism of January 1908, cited above:

Von der fürchterlichen Verwüstung, die die Druckpresse anrichtet, kann man sich heute noch gar keine Vorstellung machen. Das Luftschiff wird erfunden und die Phantasie kriecht wie eine Postkutsche. Automobil, Telephon und die Riesenauflagen des Stumpfsinns — wer kann sagen, wie die Gehirne der zweitnächsten Generation beschaffen sein werden?

(F 241: 14–15)

(Of the terrible devastation which is being wrought by the printing press it is still not possible today to have any conception. The airship is invented and the imagination crawls along like a stage-coach. Automobile, telephone and the mass dissemination of stupidity — who can say what the brains of the generation after next will be like?)

Distorted conceptions of reality do not arise spontaneously from contradictions within the changing structure of society. They are manufactured by mass communications.

The greatest excitement was being generated by the invention of flying machines. The press was enthusiastically celebrating the 'conquest of the skies' and organizing air races between the major cities of Europe. For Kraus these developments were a source of apprehension: the conquest of the skies is one of his apocalyptic portents (F 261–2: 2). He may not have foreseen the military implications as clearly as H. G. Wells.[2] But he was exceptionally sensitive to the disjunction between anachronistic attitudes and technological advances. In March 1909 he published in Die Fackel a prophetic essay by Otto Soyka entitled 'Der farblose Krieg'. The technology of modern warfare, Soyka argues, has become so sophisticated that it has rendered the ethos of heroism anachronistic. Modern artillery requires scientific precision (F 277–8: 47–51). Soyka's plea for a functional attitude towards military technology lacks Kraus's moral perspective. But is is these historical developments which provide the framework for Kraus's increasingly anguished view of technology and his denunciations of the ideology of Progress.

Kraus was not a systematic thinker. His piecemeal perceptions are scattered through countless essays and aphorisms, his most trenchant observations tucked away in marginal notes. The difficulty of piecing together a coherent theory is increased by his satirical mode of utterance, with its reliance on paradox and antithesis, hyperbole and visionary projection. Complex thought cannot be reduced to simplified opinion. But his critique of the press culminates in two essays of exceptional penetration: 'Prozeß Friedjung' (December 1909) and 'Untergang der Welt durch schwarze Magie' (December 1912). In each of these he attacks, from a different angle, the myth of salvation through war.

The Mystification of War

Kraus's analysis of the Friedjung trial is exemplary. The Austrian annexation of Bosnia had provoked a protracted crisis in the Balkans. By March 1909, the Austrian army was mobilized and poised to invade Serbia, and it seemed the conflict could only be settled by war. By defeating Serbia the Austro-Hungarian government hoped to crush the political aspirations of the South Slavs within its own boundaries. But in 1909 (as in 1914) there were two great problems: first to ensure that the war remained localized; secondly to find a moral justification for declaring war on Serbia. Count Aehrenthal, the Austrian Foreign Minister, decided to orchestrate a press campaign and found a willing ally in the patriotic historian Heinrich Friedjung. The *Neue Freie Presse*, which had been stirring up public opinion with a series of alarmist editorials, published on 25 March 1909 an article by Friedjung, justifying military action. Drawing on documents supplied to him by the Austrian Foreign Office, Friedjung accused members of the Croatian Diet (the regional administration of one of the Habsburg provinces) of a treasonable conspiracy with the hostile government in Belgrade.

The article was intended as a fanfare of war. But at the last moment, under pressure from Russia, the government of Serbia abandoned its opposition to the Bosnian annexation. The threat of war receded. And in place of the intended humiliation of Serbia it was Austrian foreign policy that was put on trial. In December 1909 the members of the Croatian Diet brought a libel action against Friedjung, which Kraus regarded as so significant that he attended in person. The action, which lasted for fourteen days, was fulsomely reported in the *Neue Freie Presse* (9–22 December 1909). It began with patriotic bluster and attempts by the prosecution (supported by the judge) to intimidate Serbian witnesses. Friedjung produced copies of his famous documents in which individual conspirators were named. Dr Bozo Markovitch, a university professor in Belgrade, was surprised to discover from newspaper reports of the trial that he had allegedly held secret meetings with the Croatian 'conspirators' and induced them to accept treasonable payments. Risking arrest by the Austrian authorities, Markovitch travelled to Vienna to testify that at the time of these treasonable meetings in Belgrade he had actually been in Berlin, attending lectures on jurisprudence. This testimony was greeted by judge and jury with incredulity. However the Prussian police, famous for their meticulous record-keeping, were able to confirm that Markovitch had indeed been in Berlin on the dates of the alleged conspiracy. The Foreign Office documents were exposed as crude forgeries and Friedjung was ignominiously obliged to retract his calumnies.

Kraus's article 'Prozeß Friedjung' is a trenchant political analysis. He unhesitatingly attacks the irresponsibility of the Austrian Foreign Office and Count Aehrenthal. But his main theme is the susceptibility of public opinion:

> Austria in orbe ultima: in einer Welt, die betrogen wird, glaubt Österreich am längsten. Es ist das willigste Opfer der Publizität, indem es nicht nur glaubt, was es gedruckt sieht, sondern auch das Gegenteil davon glaubt, wenn es auch dieses gedruckt sieht.
>
> (F 293: 1)

> (Austria in orbe ultima: in a deluded world Austria is the last to lose its credulity. It is the most willing victim of publicity, in that it not only believes what it sees in print, but also believes the opposite, if it sees that too in print.)

The case provided a model of political double-think. It showed that the patriotic fervour whipped up by the press by no means lost its hold when the documents on which it was based were shown to be fraudulent. Kraus identifies this willingness to be duped, this inability to draw any conclusions from the political fiasco, as a most alarming sign: 'Österreich ist das Land, in dem man keine Konsequenzen zieht' (F 293: 29).

His analysis also focuses on the individual figure of Friedjung, who exemplifies the political corruptibility of the intelligentsia. The court case left no doubt that Friedjung had acted in good faith. What was it in his attitude of mind that led him to be so easily duped, to be so willing to lend his prestige to a blatant propaganda exercise? Kraus tried to deduce the answer from linguistic evidence:

> Dieser ganze Schnickschnack aus den Achtzigerjahren, dieses Schönbartspiel des Gelehrtentums, diese Inzucht von Staatsgeschäftigkeit und Wissenschaftlhuberei, diese Bereitschaft, wenn's sein muß, für das Vaterland mit Phrasen zu kämpfen und "wenn's zu einem Waffengang mit dem Feind kommen sollte", in der Neuen Freien Presse die Save zu überschreiten und "dem Serben eine Schlacht zu liefern" [. . .]
>
> (F 293: 7–8)

(All this tittle-tattle from the 1880s, this play with the bearded dignity of scholarship, this incest between the bustle of affairs of state and the activities of a scientific busybody, this readiness, if the need should arise, to fight for the fatherland with clichés and 'if it should come to a passage of arms with the enemy', to cross the river Save in the *Neue Freie Presse* and 'do battle with the Serbs').

What Kraus identifies is a mode of thinking remote from lived experience and rendered opaque by anachronistic martial metaphors. The intellectual scruples of the historian are submerged in heroic rhetoric. In the testimony of Professor Friedjung he identifies the sonorous voice of a liberal scholar of the old school, now occupying a front seat on the bandwagon of German expansionism. Kraus's analysis of this phenomenon was to have prophetic relevance to the events of the First World War itself, when German scholarship so readily lent its prestige to patriotic propaganda.[3] Looking back on this essay in May 1918, Kraus was able to claim that his analysis had been vindicated by events (*F* 474–83: 52). The essay should indeed be prescribed reading for anyone studying the problem of intellectuals in politics; for there are still plenty of Friedjungs in the academic community.

'Prozeß Friedjung' is Kraus's most balanced analysis of the manipulation of opinion. In other contexts he tends to understate the role of governments as the instigators of political mystification, and to treat the press in isolation, as an independent force for evil. Here he does justice to all the main factors involved: the Austrian government as instigator of the affair, the press as its willing agency, the connivance of intellectuals, the gullibility of public opinion, and finally the dimension of false consciousness itself (manifest in linguistic forms). And he makes clear the disastrous consequences that are likely to follow from this propagation of patriotic myths: a war in which thousands of lives will be lost.

Through his close focus on language, Kraus is able to show how the thinking of educated people is losing its flexibility and clarity. It is becoming rigid with ideological schemas, opaque with anachronistic metaphor, and automatic in its movement from one cliché to the next. Equally important is another aspect of the journalistic mystification of reality. This is the tendency for factual reporting to be overlaid with the veneer of an ornamental style. The literary feuilleton is for Kraus the main source of this form of mystification. He sees a pseudo-literary style as one of the consequences of the influence of Heine. Whether this judgement does justice to the qualities of Heine's prose is open to question.[4] But there can be little doubt that Kraus's strictures on the feuilleton were justified. The arguments against this form of writing have been concisely formulated by Carl E. Schorske in his study of *Fin-de-Siècle Vienna*:

> The subjective response of the reporter or critic to an experience, his feeling-tone, acquired clear primacy over the matter of his discourse. To render a state of feeling became the mode of formulating a judgement. Accordingly, in the feuilleton writer's style, the adjectives engulfed the nouns, the personal tint virtually obliterated the object of discourse.[5]

Kraus's critique of the feuilleton does not rest on generalities. He is tireless in clipping specific examples, for example a collage of snippets from the press coverage of the social season in 1911, which highlights the sequence of predictable clichés (F 331–2 :30–2). The lavish expanse of newsprint devoted to frivolous activities betrays a loss of all proportion. Worse still is the tone in which such events are reported: the unctuousness of style, the abundance of colourful adjectives. The activities of an ambitious restaurateur or a pretentious socialite are described with a lavishness that would be more appropriate to a royal jubilee.

All this may seem to provide material for light-hearted satire. But for Kraus the inflated reporting of trivialities is a serious matter; for it provides the daily mental nourishment of the educated class. He identifies this style as a soporific which induces a trancelike state of unreality ('Fiebertraum im Sommerschlaf' is his title). And instead of shrugging off the inanities of journalese as being unworthy of serious attention, he raises the vital question: what will be the response of minds saturated in such trivialities when they are confronted with something important? The medium of feuilletonese provides a kind of gauze, which filters out the grit of reality and allows only a soothing unguent to pass through. This may not matter very much when all that is being described is a floral parade in the Prater. But the ubiquitous application of this style tends to reduce all news to the same soothing formula. The impressionistic newspaper reporter superimposes the same feeling-tone on the incidents of a flower show and the events of a war.

Well before 1914 the press coverage of the Balkan wars confirmed Kraus's strictures. In the autumn of 1912, hostilities broke out between Bulgaria and Turkey. In this miniature theatre of war the representatives of the leading Austrian newspapers enjoyed the status of privileged spectators. And in their reports, their subjective impressions of the experience take priority over the sober reporting of facts. 'Österreich ist auf dem Balkan durch Impressionisten vertreten,' Kraus writes in November 1912. And he devotes fourteen pages of Die Fackel to the reprinting of excerpts from the writings of Austrian war correspondents. The following passage (from a feuilleton by Paul Zifferer) exemplifies this style of reporting:

> ### Gefecht vor Adrianopel
>
> Seit zwei Tagen nun schon kann ich mich an dem Schauspiel nicht sattsehen, wie in der Ferne aus dem silbernen Morgen die Festung Adrianopel auftaucht, mit ihren Wällen und Türmen als ein Schimmer am gewundenen Ufer der Maritza hingebreitet . . . . Früh am Tage umhüllen die flatternden Nebel, dann später Pulverdampf die Stadt, wie lichte Schleier das Antlitz einer schönen Frau . . . . man fühlt sich selbst mit geheimer grundloser Sehnsucht zu dieser fernen Stadt hingezogen, man will zu ihr hineilen, sie gleichsam selbst erobern, in Besitz nehmen.
>
> (F 360–2: 47)

(*Battle at Adrianople*/For two whole days now I have been feasting my
eyes on the spectacle of the fortress of Adrianople emerging in the
distance from the silver light of the morning and stretching its glittering
shape along the winding banks of the Maritza, with its ramparts and its
towers . . . . Early in the day the city is wrapped in fluttering mists, later
in the smoke of gunpowder, just like delicate veils around the face of a
beautiful woman . . . . one feels oneself drawn towards this city by some
secret, unfathomable longing, one wants to hasten towards her, to
conquer her oneself as it were, to take possession of her.)

Subjective sensations are offered instead of sober facts. And the
reader is left with the hazy image of a beautiful woman, rather than
with a precise picture of dying men.

In the essay 'Untergang der Welt durch schwarze Magie'
(December 1912) Kraus puts this feuilletonistic style into historical
perspective. He reprints a selection of newspaper reports from the
year 1848, a year of revolution and civil war. What is most
remarkable about these reports is the sobriety with which they
describe sensational events. Kraus quotes a report on the siege of the
city of Milan by Austrian forces:

> *Italien.* Aus dem Hauptquartier S. Donato nächst Mailand (5. August):
> Wir sind noch hier. Diese Nacht sahen wir mit freiem Auge, wie die
> schöne Stadt Mailand an *acht* Orten brannte; außerordentlich aber an zwei
> Orten. Heute früh 4 Uhr kamen 3 piemontesische Generale als
> Parlamentär in's Hauptquartier. Ergibt sich Mailand nicht bis zum
> Abend*, so wird es bombardiert. So eben war auch der Erzbischof an der
> Spitze einer Deputation bei unsern Feldherrn, und erbat, dass mit dem
> Bombardement bis Morgen früh 8 Uhr eingehalten wird.
>
> ───────────────
> *Die Uebergabe ist bereits gemeldet.
>
> (F 363–5: 16)
>
> (*Italy*. From the headquarters at St Donato near Milan (5 August): We
> are still here. Tonight we were able to see with the naked eye how the
> beautiful city of Milan was burning in *eight* places; particularly badly,
> however, in two places. This morning at 4 o'clock, 3 Piedmont generals
> came to headquarters to negotiate. If Milan does not surrender by
> evening*, it will be bombarded. The archbishop has also just visited our
> commanders at the head of a deputation, and requested that the bom-
> bardment should be delayed until tomorrow morning at 8 o'clock.
>
> ───────────────
> *News of the surrender has already arrived.)

The style of this writing — sober, economical and factual —
exemplifies Kraus's ideal of functional journalism. The reporter of
1848 does at one point introduce an ornamental epithet, when he
speaks of the 'beautiful city' of Milan; but this has the function of
underlining the loss that will occur if the city is bombarded.

Zifferer's celebration of the beauty of Adrianople, on the other hand, has the opposite effect. The bombardment of Adrianople is presented as a glamorous romantic conquest.

The consequences of journalistic mystification are made clear in this same number of *Die Fackel*, in a short piece entitled 'Und in Kriegszeiten'. The newspaper-reading public (Kraus argues) responds to the wars in the Balkans in the same way as it responds to the latest operetta; in both it finds an entertaining source of diversion. Public opinion has lost the ability to discriminate between the two phenomena, because both have been reduced by the press to the same level of hazy unreality: 'Eine Operettenkultur rückt zu Zeiten auch mit Kriegsbegeisterung aus. Ihre Söldner sind Schreiber. Völlig verantwortungslose Subjekte, die heute eine Premiere und morgen einen Krieg lancieren. (On occasion, an operetta culture will start parading its enthusiasm for war. Its mercenaries are writers. Totally irresponsible types, who launch a première one day and a war the next.)' (*F* 363–5: 71)

Although Kraus was not nominally a pacifist, this denunciation of irresponsible warmongers in December 1912, supported by an acute analysis of the language of mystification, must count as a significant contribution to the pacifist cause. It culminates in the prophetic warning: 'Im Krieg [. . .] erneuert sich keine Kultur mehr, sondern rettet sich durch Selbstmord vor dem Henker. (Through war [. . .] a civilization no longer renews itself, but merely saves itself by suicide from the hangman.)' (*F* 363–5: 71) Kraus was one of the few at the time to realize that modern technology had rendered war an act of self-destruction. The only military action he was willing to support was intervention by an international force to relieve the besieged Balkan city of Scutari in 1913 (*F* 376–7: 48).

Kraus's critical theme is summed up by the title given to a group of glosses in May 1913, 'Die Katastrophe der Phrasen'. The clichés and distortions of newspaper coverage, he argues, threaten to turn the Balkan crisis into a European catastrophe. In mentally bankrupt ages, when events have become obscured by hollow phrases, war is inevitable. (*F* 374–5: 3) The apparent hyperbole conveys a sombre truth: words, no longer the passive reflections of events, have become active agents of disaster. This argument echoes Ruskin's *Sesame and Lilies*, from which Kraus in February 1900 had quoted a short passage about the effects of propaganda (*F* 31: 7–8). Ruskin's argument, formulated at the time of the Austro-Prussian war crisis of 1865, continued:

> Words, if they are not watched, will do deadly work sometimes. There are masked words droning and skulking about us in Europe just now, [. . .] which nobody understands, but which everybody uses, and most

people will also fight for, live for, or even die for. [. . .] There never
were creatures of prey so mischievous, never diplomatists so cunning,
never poisoners so deadly, as these masked words.[6]

It is quite possible that Kraus read this passage, after the new German
translation of *Sesame and Lilies* (Jena, 1900) was drawn to his
attention by Heinrich Lammasch. The affinities with Ruskin's view
of language are certainly very striking (and were indeed acknowledged in *Die Fackel* at a later date, F 697–705: 92–3). For Kraus, as
for Ruskin, the language of mass communications has turned words
into fetishes for which men will fight and die.

For a critic concerned to combat the influence of masked words,
the obvious method is to unmask them. The outstanding example is
provided by Kraus's critique of the style of Maximilian Harden.
Harden's essays in *Die Zukunft* abounded in ornate circumlocutions
and bombastic displays of erudition. Although Kraus had initially
admired Harden's German (F 136: 15), he later explicitly identifies
this mode of discourse as a mummery and a mask (F 360–2: 70). His
most effective method is to strip away the superfluous verbiage in
order to reveal the simple underlying meaning. On one side of the
page he prints Harden's elaborate sentences, on the other the actual
meaning, translated into plain words. This series of 'Translations
from Harden' and 'Courses in Desperanto', which left Harden's
reputation considerably deflated, still makes entertaining and
instructive reading.

It has been argued that Kraus's attacks on Harden prove merely
that the latter wrote bad German, and that they fail to penetrate
beyond the 'masking function' of Harden's journalism to underlying
political causes.[7] This is to miss the connection between journalistic
style and propagandistic effect. The mystification created in
European affairs by this style of journalism is specifically identified as
a *political* danger. The Kaiser's *Daily Telegraph* interview (Kraus
notes in November 1908) had almost plunged Europe into war. For
Kraus the danger lay not merely in the Kaiser's blunder, but in the
mechanisms of the press which amplify it, so that a few incautious
phrases may suffice to send six million soldiers into battle (F
264–5: 2).

The style of political commentary Kraus found so dangerous is
exemplified in a passage of 'Desperanto' quoted two years later: 'Die
Österreicher dürften ruhig bis nach Saloniki spazieren, wenn dem
fest an die Flanke des Britenleun gebundenen Reussenreich endlich
der Pontuskäfig geöffnet würde.' (F 307–8: 49) The meaning that lies
behind these euphemisms is presumably: 'Austria would be able to
extend its influence in the Balkans if Russia, restrained by an alliance
with Britain, were granted free passage through the Black Sea.'

Kraus argues that in an era of international tension, exacerbated by irresponsible press coverage, politics are characterized by the disproportion between cause and effect (*F* 264–5: 3). But the confusion is worse compounded when the dangers are described not in plain words but in anachronistic euphemisms.

Kraus should perhaps have given Harden greater credit for his campaign for democratic control over an irresponsible autocrat. But Harden shared the nationalistic prejudices of his day, and at the height of the Morocco crisis of 1911 we find him making speeches urging a war with France as the only possible solution to the international crisis (*F* 334–5: 18). Moreover Kraus's analysis of the dangers inherent in Harden's rhetoric was spectacularly confirmed in August 1914, when *Die Zukunft* published a characteristic passage of purple prose justifying the German invasion of Belgium. Struggling through an argument which transposes the military conflict into the terms of pseudo-Darwinistic biology, the hapless reader may fail to recognize the crudity of Harden's actual message, which is in effect: 'To hell with international law! Might is right!'[8]

Subversive Dialogue

Kraus's technique of critical unmasking is supplemented by further, more creative strategies, particularly the construction of satirical dialogues. From about 1910 onwards his writing is permeated by elements of dialogue. And many glosses which appear to be merely verbal juxtapositions prove in fact to be implicitly dramatic in form. To take a simple example (from the 'Katastrophe der Phrasen' series of May 1913):

> *Wie viele gibt es?*
> ' . . . . und dann wird es sich zeigen, daß für uns die Beschlüsse Europas unabänderlich sind. Die Situation ist sehr gespannt, aber a l l e Mächte des Dreibundes stehen zu Österreich-Ungarn . . . . '
> Alle doch nicht. Höchstens Deutschland und Italien. Österreich-Ungarn ist neutral.

> (*F* 374–5: 12)

(*How many are there?*/' . . . . and then it will become evident that for us the decisions of Europe are irrevocable. The situation is very tense, but *all* the powers of the Triple Alliance are standing by Austria-Hungary . . . . ' Surely not all. At most Germany and Italy. Austria-Hungary is neutral.)

This gloss is structured as an exchange between two speakers: the patriotic editorialist who is trying to raise morale by implying that there is wide support for Austrian policies in the Balkans; and the sceptical, deflating voice of the satirist. This incipient dialogue form was later to be developed in *Die letzten Tage der Menschheit* in the conversations between the Optimist and the Grumbler.

The characters in the dialogues are usually re-creations of actual contemporaries. Starting from published documents, Kraus reconstructs the exchanges behind the scenes. Several of his most effective dialogues are set in newspaper offices, for example 'Herbstzeitlose, oder Die Heimkehr der Sieger' (December 1912). The originality of these dialogues lies in a skilful blending of documentary and imaginative elements. Individual journalists are made to speak the words which they have had the effrontery to write. The effect is devastating. It does not stem simply from the discrepancies between the rhythms of spoken and written language. For the dialogues demonstrate that this kind of journalism is, in an ethical as well as literal sense, unspeakable. The heartlessness of war correspondents in the Balkans and the impressionistic self-indulgence of their reporting of the disasters of war are drastically accentuated by the transposition of text into dialogue (*F* 366–7: 37–56). These writers stand condemned by their own words.

The satirical effect is enhanced when these sonorous clichés are embedded in an invented dialogue framed in the most mundane of jargons. It is the slang that might plausibly be spoken by newspaper reporters in the privacy of their own offices, crudely colloquial and distorted by characteristically German-Jewish idioms. Kraus does not claim that the journalists who work in this milieu actually speak this dialect, or speak it with the same distinctness. The named individuals are to be taken as representative types (*F* 360–2: 53–5).

The most significant of these reconstructed dialogues was provoked by the recall of Conrad von Hötzendorf as Chief of General Staff in December 1912. Since his first appointment to this position in 1906 Conrad had been the most powerful advocate of a military solution to Austria's problems in the Balkans. His reappointment in the atmosphere of crisis at the end of 1912 was a signal that the balance of Austrian foreign policy was tilting towards war. Photographs appeared in a number of Austrian magazines showing Conrad, backed by one of his aides, gazing grimly at the map of the Balkans (see Pl. 20). Though war was temporarily averted, Kraus's unerring ear picked up the bugle call with which the name 'Conrad von Hötzendorf' was soon to become associated (*F* 366–7: 1). And his eye for pretentious gesture led him to reconstruct the following dialogue behind the scenes:

In Österreich wurde es ernst. Da wurde Conrad von Hötzendorf Generalstabschef. Da studierte er die Balkankarte. Da siegte am Hofe die

Friedenspartei und da trat der Hofphotograph Scolik ein. "Eine kleine Spezialaufnahme wenn ich bitten darf — !" "Für die Weltgeschichte?" "Nein, für das interessante Blatt." "Aha, zur Erinnerung an die Epoche!" "Ja, für die Woche." "Ich bin aber grad beim Studium der Balkankarte —" "Das trifft sich gut — " "Wirds lang dauern?" "Nur einen histori-schen Moment wenn ich bitten darf — " "Soll ich also das Studium der Balkankarte fortsetzen?" "Gewiß Exzellenz, setzen ganz ungezwungen das Studium der Balkankarte fort — so — ganz leger — nein, das wär' unnatürlich — der Herr Major wenn ich bitten darf etwas weiter zurück — nein, nur ganz ungeniert — kühn, bitte mehr kühn — es soll eine bleibende Erinnerung an die ernsten Zeiten sein — so ists gut, nur noch — bisserl bitte — so — machen Exzellenz ein feindliches Gesicht! — jetzt — Ich danke."

(F 366–7: 3)

(In Austria things became serious. Then Conrad von Hötzendorf became Chief of the General Staff. Then he studied the map of the Balkans. Then the peace party were victorious at court and then Scolik the court photog-rapher walked in. 'Just a small exclusive photograph, if you'll be so kind — !' 'For world history?' 'No, for the *Illustrated News.*' 'Aha, a memento of this era!' 'Yes, for the *Mirror.*' 'But I'm just in the middle of studying the map of the Balkans — ' 'That's a lucky coincidence —' 'Will it take long?' 'Only a historic moment, if you'll be so kind — ' 'Shall I continue studying the map of the Balkans, then?' 'Certainly, your Excellency, continue studying the map of the Balkans quite casually — that's right — quite relaxed — no, that would seem a bit forced — and if the Major would kindly stand a little more in the background — no, don't be self-conscious — look intrepid, please, a little more intrepid — it is to be a lasting memento of these grave times — that's fine, now just — please, just a little — fine — scowl, please, your Excellency! — that's it — Thank you.')

The posturings of the war party could hardly have been more effectively deflated.

Kraus also uses the opposite method of introducing a more elevated linguistic dimension, in order to expose the pretensions of political reportage. The feuilletons of Siegmund Münz provide the best example. Münz was a correspondent of the *Neue Freie Presse* who specialized in interviews with reigning monarchs. Kraus accen-tuates the pretentiousness of these interviews by embellishing them with overtones from Schillerian drama. Thus the conversation between Münz and the King of Bulgaria finds its literary parallel in the famous scene between Marquis Posa and King Philip of Spain in Schiller's *Don Carlos.* Transposed into Schillerian terms, Münz's self-important posturing is rendered ridiculous (F 301–2: 47–51).

Undeterred by these glosses (which Kraus also began to read in public in March 1911), Münz continued to publish his interviews in the *Neue Freie Presse.* And Kraus continued to embellish them with

20   Conrad von Hötzendorf, with his adjutant

his dramatized satirical commentaries. The publication in the *Neue Freie Presse* of 9 April 1911 of an interview between Münz and the Queen of Romania provided Kraus with an ideal opportunity. For now he could recast the journalist as 'Don Münz', modelled on Don Carlos himself, who in Schiller's play has a passionate love affair with Elisabeth, wife of Philip of Spain. The end of Münz's interview can thus be transposed into the terms of Schiller's famous dénouement, Carlos's romantic leave-taking from Elisabeth, which is so cruelly interrupted by the arrival of the King and his grandees. And the editor of *Die Fackel* is himself cast in the role of Schiller's Grand Inquisitor, who leads Carlos/Münz off into captivity (*F* 321–2: 4–5).

These miniature satirical dramas carry serious political implications. They do not merely mock the pretensions of a journalistic nonentity, disporting himself on the stage of European politics. There is a more disturbing irony. For Münz's feuilletons carried political weight. Given the precarious political balance in the Balkans and the prestige of the *Neue Freie Presse*, an unguarded remark recorded in an interview with Münz really was capable of triggering off a war. This became apparent on two separate occasions. In June 1910, after Münz had reported remarks by the King of Greece about Greek claims to the island of Crete, the Ottoman government retaliated by threatening war if this claim was not publicly retracted (F 305–6: 15–16). The second occasion was in August 1911, during the Moroccan crisis, when the *Neue Freie Presse* printed a series of hostile remarks about Germany allegedly made by an English diplomat to one of the paper's correspondents. The diplomat turned out to be Sir Fairfax Cartwright, the correspondent Siegmund Münz (F 331–2: 8–13). In each case the situation was only relieved when the victim of Münz's interview issued a diplomatic *démenti*. Kraus was incensed that a garrulous diplomat should have the power to send the nations of Europe into the slaughterhouse of war. But even worse was the fact that power over life and limb could lie in the hands of irresponsible journalists (F 331–2: 8).

Kraus's response to the writings of Münz represents one of his most finely balanced achievements. Nowhere can we see more clearly the interplay between documentary and imaginative elements that is the hallmark of his satire. The explicit dialogue form, with invented characters, may conform more closely to conventional norms of creativity. But in terms of Kraus's aesthetic of imaginative subversion, this more flexible form with its disconcerting shifts between documentary and dialogue is far more effective. The free flow of imagination (supported by ingenious plays upon words) subverts the reader's expectations. And the variations between different stylistic levels also keep the reader continuously on the alert. There is a close parallel here with Nestroy, whose dialogue also owes much of its vitality to different levels of discourse interwoven within a single speech. Cruder forms of satire may use a method of deflation based on the maxim that from the sublime to the ridiculous is only a single step (this is the method of Heine). In Kraus's re-creative satire we find not this single step, but a complexity of stylistic gradations.

His use of literary allusions often attains a Joycean subtlety. Thus in his attack on the *Neue Freie Presse* over the Cartwright affair, he introduces lines from Goethe's *Faust* which express the complacent bourgeois attitude towards foreign wars:

> Nichts Bessers weiß ich mir an Sonn- und Feiertagen
> Als ein Gespräch von Krieg und Kriegsgeschrei,
> Wenn hinten, weit, in der Türkei,
> Die Völker auf einander schlagen.

('On Sundays, holidays, there's naught I take delight in,/Like gossiping of war, and war's array,/When down in Turkey, far away,/The foreign people are a-fighting.')[9] Kraus transposes the

Neue Freie Presse itself into the character of one of these complacent burghers: '[. . .]und nichts besseres weiß sie sich an Sonn- und Feiertagen als ein Gespräch von Krieg und Kriegsgeschrei, auf die Gefahr hin, daß hinten, weit, in der Türkei, infolgedessen die Völker aufeinanderschlagen. ([. . .] and on Sundays, holidays, there's naught it takes delight in, like gossiping of war and war's array, at the risk that down in Turkey, far away, the foreign people may consequently start a-fighting.)' (*F* 331–2: 11). The preoccupation of the *Neue Freie Presse* with foreign wars reflects the same kind of smugness that Goethe satirized in his burghers of the eighteenth century. But Kraus's interpolation of the word 'consequently', which abruptly breaks the flow of Goethe's verse, introduces the alarming modern perspective: the readiness of the *Neue Freie Presse* to satisfy the idle curiosity of its readers may actually become a cause of war.

One further feature of Kraus's use of dialogue deserves special attention: the voice of the satirist himself. It is by no means simply that of narrator. In these imaginative dialogues the satirist often has the function of a dramatic character in his own right. This is explicit at the end of the 'Don Münz' dialogue, where the editor of *Die Fackel* appears in the role of the Grand Inquisitor. But the satirist also appears in less tangible guise in a significant number of other glosses; and his voice is heard in a wide variety of modulations. At one moment he catechizes an erring reporter from the *Neue Freie Presse* in the voice of a stern schoolmaster ('Schlichte Worte', *F* 341–2: 21–2). But when it suits his purposes he is quite happy to invert the relationship and address the *Neue Freie Presse* in tones of exaggerated humility, as in 'Bitte, das ist mein Recht' (*F* 345–6: 54).

The contrast between these two glosses shows how ludicrous it is to take the satirical voices of *Die Fackel* as the direct expression of Kraus's opinions. Are we to assume that in the three months between January 1912 ('Schlichte Worte') and April 1912 ('Bitte, das ist mein Recht') Kraus's attitude towards the *Neue Freie Presse* changed from serene superiority to cringing submissiveness? The point is that the speaker in each of these glosses is a literary persona — a dramatization of a possible reponse, not the statement of an actual one. In order to bring a critical point home to the reader Kraus uses the voice of enhanced authority at one moment, the voice of exaggerated submissiveness the next.

Between these two extremes we find a wide variety of different voices, some of them quite obviously parodistic impersonations. Thus the attack on Harden is expressed sometimes in the impassioned voice of polemical vehemence, sometimes in the cool voice of the disinterested lexicographer (*F* 261–2: 33–4). The method is reminiscent of the ironic masks used by Jonathan Swift — the pose of gravity and good intentions, adopted in order to achieve a satirical effect (the 'Bickerstaff Papers' provide a good example).[10] This indirect method is not only more entertaining than the strident voice of 'Maximilian Harden — Eine Erledigung' ('Ich trage einen Haß unter dem Herzen', *F* 234–5: 1). It is also more effective. Harden's reputation is more incisively undermined by critical irony than by personal invective.

Kraus had an outstanding gift for ironic impersonation. On several occasions he succeeded in hoaxing the *Neue Freie Presse* by sending in fictitious readers' letters. The aim of these letters was to show up the intellectual pretensions of the newspaper and the gullibility of those who produced it. One of the masks Kraus adopts for this purpose is that of 'Zivilingenieur Berdach', an expert on earthquakes who writes in elaborately pseudo-scientific style about 'tellurian earthquakes' which he measures with the aid of a compass. In another of the letters, he assumes the identity of four Viennese housewives, fanatical supporters of the Liberal Party eager to storm the bastion of clericalism. In both cases Kraus's parody was so skilful that the letter was published in the *Neue Freie Presse* without demur, and later gleefully reprinted in *Die Fackel* (*F* 245: 21–2; 326–8: 14). In his satirical glosses Kraus adopts a medley of different voices in response to different stimuli. The most effective is that of the credulous reader, who feigns to believe all the tendentious nonsense he reads in newspapers or publicity blurbs. The two finest examples are 'Der kleine Brockhaus', which blends the response of the credulous reader with that of the sensitive child, overwhelmed by the useless information disseminated by the sales blurb for an encyclopedia (*F* 339–40: 20–1); and 'Wiener Faschingsleben 1913', in which the misanthropic satirist is suddenly swept away by the slogans of the carnival (*F* 368–9: 21–3).

Any attempt at classifying these ironic voices is bound to do less than justice to their subtlety. Examples like 'Wiener Faschingsleben 1913' or the introduction to 'Übersetzung aus Harden', in which a single ironic persona is consistently maintained, are relatively infrequent. Unlike Swift, Kraus did not make this mode of irony into the central method of his satire. Nor is dialogue between two voices his essential mode. Kraus's characteristic effects are achieved by subtle shifts of intonation: from mockery to moments of pure lyricism; from childlike sensitivity to the voice of *saeva indignatio*; from parodistic cliché to heroic Shakespearean allusion; from the voice of the linguistic pedant to that of the apocalyptic visionary.

The voices used in Kraus's implicitly dramatic glosses are best

thought of as variations on his dominant narrative stance: the role of
the satirist. Ironic inversions subtly refer back to this unifying
narrative identity. Parodistic impersonations gain their effect from
the contrast between assumed voice and habitual style. Dreams and
visions extend the expressive range of the narrative. It is important to
recognize the rhetorical function of these different voices. But this
does not mean that they become self-sufficient fictional creations.
The serial form of their publication in *Die Fackel* imposes an overall
unity on Kraus's multifarious glosses. There are inextricable links
between literary persona and existential identity. Kraus's satire
during the final years of the Habsburg Empire is not merely an
attempt to answer the question 'Quo vadis Austria?'. It is (as we shall
see in Part Three) a sustained attempt to forge his own identity.

PART THREE

THE ROLE OF THE SATIRIST

CHAPTER 9

Literary Style and Histrionic Temperament: The Paradox of the True Mask

Kraus's satire is structured by his own self-image. It is the voice of the satirist which gives coherence to that rambling monologue which fills the thirty-seven years of *Die Fackel*. Even when he uses dramatic form, he still characteristically introduces an image of himself into his play — as Grumbler (Nörgler) in *Die letzten Tage der Menschheit*, as Poet (Dichter) in *Traumstück*, as Arkus in *Die Unüberwindlichen*. So prominent is the figure of the satirist throughout his writings that it has proved peculiarly difficult to discuss them without shifting the focus back to the author. The uniqueness of Kraus's achievement, we are told, arises from the 'unity of man and work'. His impassioned writings, says another critic, are the 'direct expression of his being'.[1]

The reception of Kraus's work has been dominated by this simplistic approach, which attributes the power of his satire to his exceptional moral qualities. In suggesting an alternative reading, the aim is not to question Kraus's sense of mission. It is clear that the editor of *Die Fackel* must have been an exceptionally dedicated writer with a strong sense of moral seriousness. But moral seriousness is not enough. The power of satire depends not on the strength of the author's feelings, but on the effectiveness of their formulation. And the relationship between Kraus's authorial position and his narrative voice is far more oblique than is generally supposed. The 'style' is by no means 'the man himself'.

The Style and the Man
The satirist of *Die Fackel* is a very different figure from the author who emerges from personal memoirs. For the satirist characteristically appears in embattled isolation. He is an ascetic who has renounced the pleasures of social intercourse and freed himself from all personal ties. He is a misanthrope who avoids human company by sleeping during the day and working at night. He is a prophet in

whom the trivialities recorded in the press inspire apocalyptic
visions. His detached position enables him to assess human
behaviour with the rigour of a Last Judgement. His discourse is
impassioned and hyperbolic. What he sees around him appears to
justify his unremitting pessimism about human society. He repudiates all social affiliations — whether with the Habsburg state, the city
of Vienna, his Jewish heritage, his family, or the world of letters.
Correspondence is left unread, invitations spurned, and the judgement of his contemporaries is despised. A consuming egotism leads
him to make extravagant claims for his own artistic achievement. To
his mission as a writer he devotes all his waking hours; indeed it
seems that he has no private life beyond the pages of *Die Fackel*. His
magazine is a 'diary' issued in periodical form.

Now if Kraus's writings are a direct expression of his personality,
we should expect (when we turn to the private memoirs) to find a
lonely, intolerant and misanthropic man, like Schopenhauer — the
philosopher he most admired. In fact, the biographical sources
reveal a sharply contrasting picture. Those who enjoyed his private
acquaintance found (in Georg Moenius's words) 'a human being,
not a satirist'.[2] He is described as a person full of charm and
sympathy; relaxed, friendly and sociable, with a wide circle of
acquaintance. The fiercely negative declarations in *Die Fackel* about
his social life are simply not borne out by the evidence. On the
contrary, the memoirs repeatedly picture him at the centre of what
Erich Mühsam (who met Kraus in 1906) called a 'circle of
sociability'.[3]

Moenius, who knew Kraus towards the end of his career,
emphasizes that his supposed cruelty and vanity were only apparent:
'This man, who had a reputation for vanity, was one of the simplest
and most natural of men.'[4] And the publisher Kurt Wolff also
emphasizes the contrast between the figure on the public platform
and the person he came to know in the privacy of Kraus's
apartment. The private Kraus is described as a person 'without a
mask' — 'relaxed, gay or serious, peaceful or passionate, but always
completely natural'.[5] Like Wolff, though at a later date, Friedrich
Torberg found that in private conversation Kraus was a man of
extraordinary kindness, sympathy and understanding. Torberg tells
us that he had naïvely expected Kraus to display the characteristics
of the satirist in private. But he found that Kraus was by no means
concerned to play the role of authority or judge; on the contrary he
clearly valued the opportunities offered by a small circle of friends
'to relax into a mood of private toleration' ('sich in seine private
Toleranz zu entspannen'). Summarizing his brief but highly
suggestive account, Torberg writes:

He had a kindliness that was frequently and effortlessly captivating, he was a person of a strangely unpolished, indeed most clumsy charm (all the more disarming for that), and his most characteristic, most personal reaction to all the iniquity that pressed around him was to shake his head [. . .]. He knew how to chuckle.[6]

The charm and tolerance that characterized Kraus's private discourse are recorded by other friends of his later years. Edwin Hartl speaks of him as 'warm-hearted, witty and charming as only he could be'. Heinrich Fischer, recording his personal memories of Kraus's contacts with Brecht, recalls that 'Kraus, as nearly always in his private life, was very charming to Brecht and tactfully avoided antagonizing him'.[7]

Similar testimony to Kraus's private kindliness can be found in the memoirs of women who knew him well. Helene Kann, whose acquaintance with Kraus dated from 1904 and lasted until his death, speaks of his gaiety, kindness and warm-heartedness as a friend; and she stresses that he was fundamentally a sociable person. She records a conversation in which the poetess Else Lasker-Schüler, who also knew Kraus well, remarked upon the childlike quality of his character: 'Er ist doch so 'n Kind.'[8] Particularly revealing glimpses of this gentle Karl Kraus are given by Helga Malmberg, in her account of her friendship with Peter Altenberg before the First World War. Among instances of Kraus's tact and kindliness, she describes an encounter in Gmunden, where she was recovering from the strains of her relationship with Altenberg. Kraus is revealed as a warm-hearted and lifeaffirming friend:

He made it clear to me that my life could never lose its content, that I only needed to relax completely in order to find a new meaning in it. This would emerge of its own accord, if I allowed myself to drift, keeping my soul open for all the riches, for all the beauty that lay before me. At that time I found it very difficult to believe him. But he succeeded in dissolving the last remnants of constriction aand bitterness in me and giving me back my confidence and self-assurance.[9]

Kraus's gift for friendship was not eroded by the passage of time. Gina Kaus, who met him twenty years later, has left an even more circumstantial account of his courtesy and charm.[10]

These memoirs are confirmed by the evidence of unpublished correspondence. Letters which survive in the Vienna City Library suggest that he had a particular gift for counselling women, and was remembered with affection even by those he no longer loved. 'You are one of those people', writes Jule Stoeckl in a letter of 1906, 'who are able to bring to the love of a woman an alleviation which has healing power and leads to the rebirth of love in a new form.'[11] It is

Kraus, she suggests, who has restored her self-confidence and enabled her to embark on a new relationship.

Kraus's gift for friendship is even more fully documented in the sequence of over a hundred letters and cards which he wrote to Otto Stoessl between 1902 and 1918. One passage must suffice to convey the tone of this correspondence, from a letter of 5 June 1908 in which Kraus praises Stoessl's essay 'Der Skeptiker' (which had just appeared in *Die Fackel*):

> Ganz besonders danke ich Ihnen — noch einmal — für Ihren 'Skeptiker'. Je öfter ich diesen Essay lese, umso besser gefällt er mir — das schönste Lob, das ich meinen eigenen Sachen wünsche. Ich las ihn kürzlich auf der Fahrt nach Weidlingau wieder und strich mir fast jeden Satz an. Auf dem Rückweg wollte ich Sie besuchen, leider wurde es zu spät. Ein ganzer Tag später kam Ihre freundliche Einladung, der ich nächstens bestimmt folgen werde. Oder könnten wir uns nicht in *Weidlingau* treffen? Dahin zieht es mich immer mehr. Seither habe ich mich entschlossen, den Sommer dort zu verbringen.
>
> Wenn nichts dazwischen kommt, möchte ich Samstag mit Ihnen zusammentreffen. Paßt es Ihnen in Weidlingau? Wir könnten den Mühlberg besteigen — ein kleiner Spaziergang.
>
> Vielleicht haben Sie die Güte mir telephonisch Nachricht zu geben: am besten 12 bis ½1 Uhr.
>
> Die schönsten Grüße und sonstige Empfehlung!
>
> Ihr
> KARL KRAUS[12]

> (I would most especially like to thank you — once again — for your 'Sceptic'. The more often I read this essay, the better I like it — the highest praise I could desire for my own work. I read it again recently during the journey to Weidlingau and marked almost every sentence. I wanted to visit you on my way back, but unfortunately it was too late. Just one day later your kind invitation arrived, which I shall definitely take up very soon. Or couldn't we meet in *Weidlingau*? The place attracts me more strongly than ever. Since then I have decided to spend the summer there.
>
> If nothing occurs to prevent it, I would like to get together with you on Saturday. Would Weidlingau suit you? We could climb the Mühlberg — a modest walk.
>
> Perhaps you would be so kind as to let me know by telephone: preferably between 12 and 12.30.
>
> Warmest good wishes and the usual regards,
>
> Yours
> KARL KRAUS

Kraus clearly had a gift for friendship which is at odds with his reputation. It is precisely his 'friendliness' which is emphasized by those who knew him best, among them Sigismund von Radecki and Berthold Viertel.[13]

The evidence, though incomplete, seems conclusive. To contemporary readers, the power of Kraus's satire seemed to derive from an unsparing commitment to his mission as publicist. His greatest gift lay, for them, in his ability to make enemies. But behind the forbidding public figure lurked a person of delicacy and charm. Thus the biographical evidence reveals not 'unity' but a 'dualism' of man and work. It is this which explains the highly polarized reactions of his contemporaries. Some perceived only the uncompromising aggressiveness of the satirist; others (particularly those with access to his private circle) responded to the more lyrical undertones. The polarization becomes drastically clear when one compares the caricature of Kraus published in the periodical *Zeit im Bild* in 1913 with a photograph of him taken at approximately the same period (see Pls. 21 and 22). The caricature portrays a cynical Jewish intellectual, with sneering face and accentuated nose and ears, declaiming his work from the public platform with exaggerated gestures. It provoked Kraus himself into an attempt to correct the distorted image by juxtaposing with it a photograph of his true face (*F* 374–5: 32).

Some commentators have sought to resolve the dualism by invoking the Schillerian conception of the satirist as inspired by a displaced lyrical impulse. Following Schiller, they argue that it is the horrified experience of the moral corruption of the age that engenders in a man of idealistic disposition the burning indignation of the satirist.[14] Such formulations clearly oversimplify the psychological and artistic impulses which underlie the writing of satire. The question must be framed more precisely. By what psychological and artistic process does the transposition of human being into satirist come about?

The first clue is provided by Kraus's method of writing. His satire may give the impression of an impassioned overflow of feelings. But it was the product of infinitely painstaking craftsmanship. This is evident both from contemporary accounts and from the countless corrected proof-sheets which survive in the Vienna City Library. It is possible to follow the composition of a complete number of *Die Fackel* through a dozen or more stages of proof. Each sheet is embellished by corrections and additions in Kraus's hand, which are then incorporated in the subsequent proof. Every morning (as Helene Kann recalls) the corrected proof-sheets would be fetched from Kraus's apartment by his dedicated printer; and the same evening the new proofs would be on his desk, duly corrected, ready for further revision.

21 Karl Kraus: photograph
by d'Ora Benda, 1908

22 (*below*) Karl Kraus:
caricature by Blix

Karl Kraus

Helene Kann's account of how Kraus worked accentuates the difference between his private and public voice. 'It often occurred', she tells us, 'that people meeting Karl Kraus for the first time were surprised by his simple, natural way of speaking. "People always expect me to speak the language of *Die Fackel*", he said on one occasion.' She emphasizes that Kraus, discussing a problem in the circle of his friends, always used the simplest and clearest means of expression. The contrast between this simple mode of expression and the style of *Die Fackel* was marked. 'It amused him too', she writes, 'when I said to him after reading the great polemic "Warum die Fackel nicht erscheint": "Is that really by you? One would hardly believe it, after the way in which you spoke about the matter previously."'[15]

It may be objected that this account of Kraus's creative method ignores the more passionate feelings of the author at his writing-desk. Where Helene Kann emphasizes his self-control, Heinrich Fischer recalls the powerful emotions which Kraus experienced prior to the process of composition: 'I remember how he would turn pale, how the veins in his forehead would swell, how he gazed with a look of uncomprehending astonishment at the newspaper in whch he now [after the Nazi seizure of power] read day after day of things more frightening than the worst carnage of the last war.'[16] Certainly, it seems that Kraus was a person of intense emotions. But the question is what happens to these emotions in the process of literary transposition. This process has tended to be conceived too naïvely. 'Kraus was often amazed', Helene Kann recalls, 'at the naïvety which pictured him "wrestling" at his writing-desk and saw him in an "intoxication" there, when the one thing that inspired him was the "ecstasy of logic".'[17] It is the intensity, not of the writer's emotions but of the artistic process, that counts.

The Histrionic Satirist

Kraus's method of composition does not fully explain the transformation of the gentle human being into the impassioned satirist. We must also take account of psychological factors. Margarete Mitscherlich-Nielsen has rightly pointed out the inadequacies of an idealized picture of Kraus's creative impulse. The matter is clearly more complex. She seeks to resolve it by vulgar Freudian theories of Oedipal anxiety, but it seems far more fruitful to follow up the clue which Freud himself gives us: that by nature Kraus was 'an actor'.[18]

To become an actor was Kraus's first great ambition. While still attending university he took part in drama-school productions, and in January 1893 he played Franz Moor (to Max Reinhardt's Spiegelberg) in a production of *Die Räuber*. His failure in the role brought home to him that his slightly malformed physical stature debarred him from a career on the stage. In the same year he experimented with public readings of literary texts, notably Hauptmann's *Die Weber*; and he offered his services as suburban drama critic to a newly founded daily newspaper. This youthful enthusiasm for the theatre, so characteristic of the Viennese milieu, continued undiminished throughout Kraus's later life. Although after his early rebuff he abandoned his ambitions in the conventional theatre, it is clear that he had great histrionic gifts. And his talent as a director seems to have been as remarkable as his potential as an actor. Frank Wedekind believed that Kraus was missing his vocation by declining to work in the theatre (*F* 521–30: 125). In the event, Kraus's histrionic energies were diverted into more literary channels — most obviously his 'Theater der Dichtung': recitations of plays by Shakespeare, Goethe, Nestroy, Raimund, Gogol and Hauptmann and of the operettas of Offenbach. The accounts we have of these one-man platform performances testify to his extraordinary histrionic gifts.

The persistence of Kraus's interest in the theatre has been noted by a number of commentators.[19] But they do less than justice to its influence on his *non*-theatrical writings. For histrionic impulses leave a profound imprint on his work. First, the condition of the contemporary theatre furnishes Kraus with highly suggestive symptoms of the decay of civilization in general. The theatre (he declares in January 1914) is a thermometer which registers the 'temperature of life' ('den Wärmegrad des Lebens', *F* 391–2: 33). World and stage are regarded as concentric, and theatre criticism becomes part of the wider satirical indictment. Secondly, the realm of theatre, costume and carnival provides Kraus with a rich source of imagery to express the falsity of the society in which he lives — the 'Operettenkultur' of Austria before the First World War, the 'Köpenickiade' of the war itself, and the 'Walpurgisnacht' of Hitler's Germany. Thirdly, his histrionic temperament leads him to formulate a very substantial part of the satirical narrative of *Die Fackel* in implicitly dramatic form. And most important of all, it provides the impulse behind Kraus's self-dramatization in the role of satirist.

The significance of these last two points can hardly be overstressed. As we have seen, Kraus creates a *theatrum mundi* in which contemporary figures are recreated as characters on an imaginative stage. His remarkable gifts as a mimic leave a profound impression on his written style, which is a rich medley of tones and voices, dialects and jargons. He could rightly describe himself as 'perhaps the first case of a writer who simultaneously experiences the process of writing as an actor' ('vielleicht der erste Fall eines

Schreibers, der sein Schreiben zugleich schauspielerisch erlebt', *F* 389–90: 42). Through this process his frustrated impulses as an actor came to fruition in a vividly dramatic literary style.

The sources of this histrionic impulse can be traced back to Kraus's childhood. We are told that as a sensitive child newly arrived in the metropolis, his most treasured possession was a puppet theatre, which he used to take with him on walks to the park. And a school friend records that he had a particular gift for imitating the mannerisms of his teachers.[20] His mimetic gifts may originally have developed as a 'defence mechanism'. Manfred Schneider argues that this 'psychological dramaturgy' was later extended until it formed Kraus's primary mode of rapport with the outside world. Rehearsing his writings like an actor in the privacy of his study, and later performing them on the public stage, Kraus was able to gain a sense of release from the deep-seated anxieties which beset his personality. Unfortunately, Schneider's potentially fruitful line of argument is hedged in by psychoanalytical dogmas which reduce literary creativity to neurotic sources. Kraus's achievement is presented as if it were a compensation for the 'fear of castration' which derived from his 'Oedipal' relationship with his father. This is the 'unity of man and work' theory on a more sophisticated plane. The nightmarish visions of the satirist are attributed to actual nightmares which afflicted the author. Schneider too readily identifies the literary structure of Kraus's text with the 'psychic structure of the author', disregarding the dimension of conscious literary creativity.[21]

Just as the frustrated ambitions of Kraus the actor found literary expression in the dramatic vitality of his style, so the inherently dramatic qualities of his style led him back to the stage — or rather, to the public platform. In January 1910, seventeen years after his first experiments as an actor and a reader of plays, Kraus began to read his own work in public (his readings from classical literature began two years later). He was to give in all 700 public readings and recitations, almost 400 of which were partly or entirely readings of his own works. Kraus gives no reasons for his decision to strengthen the impact of his satire by public appearances. And it might seem at first paradoxical that he should begin reading in public just when he was cultivating a sophisticated literary style, whose complex associations might escape the notice of an evening audience.

Kraus himself was acutely aware that 'theatrical' gain may imply 'literary' loss. Soon after he began his readings we find him warning: 'When I give public readings, I am not making literature into a performance' ('Wenn ich vortrage, so ist es nicht gespielte Literatur'). At the same time he was aware that a dramatic element in his writing was clamouring for more direct expression: 'But what I write is a performance in written form' ('Aber was ich schreibe, ist geschriebene Schauspielkunst', F 336–7: 41). In the two or three years before his readings began that 'dramatic' element in Kraus's style becomes increasingly prominent. Even the aphorisms of this period, for all their verbal complexity, often have an antithetical structure that lends itself to dramatic delivery. Thus when Kraus decided to read in public, he was not imposing a public form on recalcitrant material. The public appearances from 1910 onwards were the product of intrinsic pressures within the literary style and the artistic temperament of the author.

However strongly Kraus may insist that his public readings were not 'gespielte Literatur', it is very clear from contemporary reports that these were by no means simply recitations. They were performances. The setting itself (as the Danish author Karin Michaelis describes it) created an atmosphere of theatre — the large, darkened hall, the single illuminated table, the frenetic applause of the audience (F 336–7: 42–6). And another reviewer reports: 'This is no reader's table, no lecturer's platform. It is a stage, on which the author performs his works for us. This is the reason for the screen, for the lack of the usual carafe of water, for the darkening of the hall — all techniques of the stage.' (F 339–40: 23)

Kraus's versatility of voice, facial expression and gesture has often been described. And recordings of his readings from plays like *Timon of Athens* and Raimund's *Der Alpenkönig und der Menschenfeind* survive to give an impression of his remarkable expressive range. Even more extraordinary is the film made of one of his readings in 1934. His declamatory utterance, enhanced by histrionic gesture, achieves uncanny effects, especially in his reading of 'Reklamefahrten zur Hölle'.

This declamatory style was modelled on the diction of the Burgtheater in Kraus's youth. The vocal qualities of actors like Adolf von Sonnenthal and Charlotte Wolter were among Kraus's most treasured recollections in later life. Their elevated diction represented for him an ideal of dramatic art which mere 'speakers' of dramatic verse, like Josef Kainz, had betrayed. And Kraus prided himself on his acoustic memory, which enabled him (he claimed) to reproduce the whole range of actors' voices from productions which had been staged several decades earlier (F 341–2: 8). The way he projected his own personality on stage was amost certainly influenced by these models. The stage is indeed one of the sources of that definition of 'personality' which is so central to Kraus's work: 'Man darf auf dem Theater die Natur einer Persönlichkeit nicht mit der Natürlichkeit einer Person verwechseln. (In the theatre one must not confuse the nature of a personality with the naturalness of a person.)' (*F* 275–6: 29) Through the great actor, Kraus insists, we hear the voice of Nature itself speaking, not the natural voice of the ordinary human being. And the impassioned actors of the old Burgtheater provided the models for his own self-dramatization on stage.

To say that Kraus had no formal dramatic training is in a sense misleading. As an impressionable fifteen-year-old he had been profoundly moved by the spectacle of Sonnenthal as King Lear (in the Burgtheater production of 1889). And on seven subsequent occasions he returned to watch that actor in the role, being particularly moved by the power with which Sonnenthal pronounced Lear's curse on Goneril (*F* 191: 22). Kraus had not 'studied' the theatre — he had assimilated it to his own temperament. Productions of Shakespeare, Nestroy and Offenbach experienced in childhood helped to shape his mercurial personality. But there were other influences, less openly acknowledged. Together with Loos and Kokoschka he frequently visited the Jewish theatre in the Leopoldstadt, which must have enhanced his awareness of the incongruities of Jewish identity.[22]

Kraus's histrionic temperament provides the psychological key to his strategy of self-dramatization. This process was mediated by a further sphere of experience, midway between the author's writing-desk and the satirist's platform: the informal auditorium of the coffee-house. In the coffee-house he was able to relax from the solitary labours of composition. It was recreation in a double sense — both relaxation and a re-gathering of the energies that went into his literary work. In this semi-public sphere, the transformation of the charm and gaiety of the private man into the histrionic gestures of the satirist was already evident. Responding to the intimate audience of his coffee-house circle, Kraus would begin to unfold his gifts as an actor. And it is clear that what resulted was already a 'performance'.

Thus Willy Haas, describing a visit which Kraus paid to Prague before the First World War, recalls:

> It is inconceivable what he offered us in a single session, during which we moved from one coffee-house to another, from one night-club to another, in twelve, fourteen, sixteen hours, without interval, without interruption by anyone else: infinitely amusing gossip and scandal from Viennese coffee-house and literary circles, a complete old Burgtheater production of 1890, with all the voices of the actors who had taken part at that time, when he was a young critic, a lecture on Lichtenberg and Heinrich Heine, an act out of Jacques Offenbach's 'Vie Parisienne' [. . .] a tragicomical parodistic portrait of Theodor Herzl, [. . .] dozens of fascinating scenes from the life of his most interesting friend, the poet Peter Altenberg [. . .] all of that was in the programme of an evening and a night far into the small hours of the morning.[23]

A similar picture of Kraus's coffee-house performances is drawn by Heinrich Fischer, writing of a later period:

> Oh, those nights in Berlin, Vienna and Prague, where Hellenic gaiety wafted across a coffee-house table towards us, a never-failing cataract of ideas, voices and gestures [. . .]. The nights after a public reading! The ensemble in his breast seemed never to come to rest [. . .] suddenly he sees an actor before him, whom he had not thought of for more than forty years. In an instant he is imitating his face, re-creating his voice, and now he begins to narrate: the Baden Arena is resurrected, the Offenbach period, a world of masks and tones.[24]

Kurt Wolff has also left an account of Kraus in the coffee-house, all the more significant because it makes the connection between these coffee-house improvisations and their subsequent literary formulation:

> On rare occasions I was witness of another life, which was played out at the coffee-house table, to which Kraus sacrificed many thousands of hours — but sacrificed is perhaps the wrong word: he indubitably needed this atmosphere; before attentive listeners he improvised a great deal that later, carefully worked out over long nights, received its form.[25]

In Kraus as he is recollected in the coffee-house we thus see both traces of the private person, happy 'to relax into his private toleration', and also hints of the satirist, already improvising the role that was later to be played out in public.

Kraus may not have been fully conscious of the traces of actor's vanity which were noted by perceptive observers. But he was well aware of his histrionic powers on the public platform. He knew that he could 'rely on his own suggestive power as an actor' ('seiner eigenen schauspielerischen Suggestion vertrauen', F 370–1: 25). And repeatedly in Die Fackel he discusses the question of audience response. He was proud of being able to weld desultory individuals into a unified 'theatre audience' ('Theaterpublikum', F 384–5: 28). At the same time he was uneasily aware of the ambiguities of the relationship between actor and audience, who are carried along by the 'rhythmical effect' of the performance rather than by intellectual comprehension of the text. Thus in Kraus's own self-analysis we are confronted by a contradiction: an emphasis both on impassioned sincerity and on histrionic performance. This paradox can only be resolved by seeing his public role as a quest for authentic identity.

Social Position and Existential Identity: The True Mask

Kraus's characteristic impulse was to project his personality on to a symbolic plane. He makes of himself — as he so often makes of his adversaries — a representative figure. In a highly dramatic

confrontation between vice and virtue, the stylized figure of the
satirist becomes the embodiment of public conscience — a figure
larger than life. The strategy is enhanced by archetypal symbols,
notably the antithesis between Night and Day. Kraus's personal
habit of working during the hours of darkness becomes highly
charged with symbolic meaning:

> Zerstreuung aller Art hab' ich gefunden
> in siebentausend und dreihundert Nächten,
> die ich bis an den Tag hab' durchgewacht,
> ihn zu belauschen und ihn zu betrachten,
> [. . .]
> doch so verstrickt in tolle Abenteuer,
> von denen ihr am Spieltisch, auf der Jagd,
> im Drange der Geschäfte nichts, ja selbst
> nicht liebend oder betend etwas ahnt.
>
> (F 508–13: 2)

> (Distractions of all natures I have found
> in seven thousand and three hundred nights,
> through which I have kept vigil till the dawn,
> in watchful contemplation of the day,
> [. . .]
> but so caught up in turbulent adventures,
> such as you at the gambling table, on the hunt,
> in the thick of business, even in love or prayer,
> could have no inkling of.)

The implications of these lines go far beyond autobiographical
statement. The contrast between the satirist's vigil and the trivial
distractions of ordinary mortals has archetypal undertones. Similarly, in Sebastian Brant's *Ship of Fools*:

> Ich hab etwann gewacht zu nacht
> Do die schlyeffent der ich gedacht
> Oder villicht by spyl und win
> Sassent, und wenig dochtent myn

('I have worked at night/While snug in bed they slumbered tight/Or
gambled, freely drinking wine,/And never thought of me and
mine.')[26] To note this parallel is of course not to suggest a conscious
borrowing. The two passages illustrate the perennial concern of the
satirist to express the contrast between his values and those of the
world in the sharpest possible terms.

The construction of such an antithetical scheme is not to invent for
the satirist characteristics which have no basis in the personality of
the author. But Kraus is highly selective. Aspects of his private
personality which do not accord with his public stance are

suppressed and withheld. Other motifs are accentuated in this process of selective and symbolic self-mirroring. The figure of the satirist is thus not so much 'true to life' as true to an artistic purpose. The satirist is invested with a maximum of persuasive authority. But it is only because the author is speaking through a persona that his voice acquires such resonance.

The question now arises of the function — indeed the legitimacy — of this elaborately sustained narrative identity. If the figure of the satirist involves self-dramatization, is not the moral seriousness of Kraus's work undermined? How is the satirical stance to be legitimized, if it can no longer be seen as a simple expression of the author's convictions?

The first answer is that satire is rhetoric. Kraus's intention is to persuade his audience, not simply to transcribe his own opinions and feelings. The histrionic heightening of his own identity enables him to endow the voice of the satirist with maximum persuasive authority. It is not merely an individual who is speaking, it is the voice of conscience, of spirituality, of language itself. To awaken his audience to the inadequacy of their civilization, the satirist rejects it out of hand; and he uses a black-and-white scheme of judgement in order to rouse them to the realization that their lives are grey.

To see the figure of the satirist merely as a resource of rhetoric would be to oversimplify the matter. Even more remarkable is the stamina with which this persona is sustained. Kraus never for a moment admits that he is 'playing a role'. Indeed his commitment to this role, both in print and on the platform, is so courageously sustained that it ceases to be merely a rhetorical stance and becomes a kind of existential identity. This paradox was pin-pointed by Walter Benjamin, when he ascribed to Kraus not the true face, but the 'true mask' of the satirist.[27] Benjamin was aware that Kraus's satirical stance was modelled on literary antecedents, above all *Timon of Athens*. His cryptic formulation suggests that Kraus has so thoroughly assimilated these literary paradigms that they have become second nature to him. And it is this paradox of the 'true mask' which conveys the full significance of Kraus's public role.

Kraus's self-image as satirist is an attempt to construct an authentic identity. It is the positive counterpart to his assault on those social and ideological factors which led to the impoverishment of personality — that 'Mangel an Persönlichkeit' with which he indicts his contemporaries (*F* 261–2: 13). On Kraus too the inescapable social nexus imposed accretions of ascribed identity. He was a Jew by birth, an Austrian by nationality, a Viennese by residence, a German by language, a journalist by profession, bourgeois by social status and a rentier by economic position. Amid the ideological turmoil of Austria-Hungary, all of these ascribed identities seemed like falsifications. Kraus's self-mirroring in *Die Fackel* consequently takes the form of a radical self-reconstruction. One by one, the layers of social identity are demonstratively discarded.

Austrian citizenship (he declares in a characteristic outburst) is a 'capital crime' ('ein todeswürdiges Verbrechen', *F* 209: 9). As for the self-image of the Viennese, so complacently cultivated by his contemporaries, this is for Kraus a travesty of human identity (*F* 368–9: 36). He even announces that he has had his name deleted from the city directory: 'Ich bin keine Wiener Adresse mehr' (*F* 474–83: 58). The sense of a 'German' identity, to which he might have felt drawn by language and culture, is equally declined. The situation of the 'Germans in Austria', a vociferous political pressure-group, elicits from him nothing but ridicule; and his fiercest satire is reserved for the Pan-German euphoria of the First World War. Political alignments of any kind are anathema to him. He is 'der fanatische Nichtpolitiker' (*F* 194: 7), for whom membership in a political party, indeed any kind of group activity, seems like a sell-out of individual integrity.

Even more forceful is Kraus's rejection of the identity assigned to him by his profession. Strictly speaking, his profession was periodical journalism; yet the identity of the journalist is the one he most fiercely denounces and disclaims. He would never have acknowledged the unpalatable truth which is expressed by one of his nineteenth-century models, Ferdinand Lassalle: 'There are two kinds of human beings that I despise above all, journalists and Jews — and I am both.'[28]

Most striking of all is Kraus's suppression of his social and economic roles. In economic terms he was a rentier, because he derived a significant part of his income from capital inherited after the death of his father in April 1900. Under Habsburg law the property of a deceased person was shared equally among his children, and Kraus's share would have enabled him to live in idle ease.[29] But it is difficult to detect in *Die Fackel*, in the period before 1918, any indication of these private resources (although the pages abound in denunciations of the money-grubbing tendencies of the age). Only in December 1921 did Kraus reveal that he enjoyed a secure income of a thousand Crowns a month ('tausend sichere Kronen für den Monat', *F* 583–7: 50). The word 'secure' contains the clue (which Kraus himself does not explain) that his income was even safe from the ravages of inflation which were sweeping Germany and Austria: the family paper-manufacturing business from which it derived was situated in financially stable Czechoslovakia. The business letterhead of the firm of Jacob Kraus (see Pl. 23) forms the invisible sub-text of *Die Fackel*.[30] In a full reading of Kraus's satire, its function must be made apparent.

23   Letterhead of the firm of Jacob Kraus

Kraus's income both from his family inheritance and from the sales of *Die Fackel* placed him in a high socio-economic category. He was, whether he liked it or not, a member of the bourgeoisie. His family background had been secure and prosperous: a comfortable town house near the 'Stadtpark', a cottage in the country for summer holidays, governesses and private tutors for the children, and the best education that could be provided. After his father's death in 1900, he was able to afford an apartment of his own in a predominantly middle-class district of Vienna. The palatial block in the Lothringerstrasse, in which he rented an apartment from 1912 until his death, was the epitome of 'bürgerlich' respectability. He was also joint owner of the family villa at Bad Ischl.[31] And he could afford to travel widely and take long holidays abroad in the best hotels. Glimpses of this life of cultivated ease can be gained from his letters to Bertha Maria Denk — for example his description of a holiday in Sorrento, written on the magnificently headed notepaper of the Imperial Hotel (see Pl. 24).[32] And it is more fully reflected in his correspondence with Sidonie Nadherny. This shows that in June 1914, at a time when automobiles were an aristocratic luxury, Kraus could afford to buy a motor car and hire a chauffeur. And when on the outbreak of war that car was requisitioned by the military, he was affluent enough to buy a second car for use during vacations in Switzerland.

In *Die Fackel*, however, we find few traces of this bourgeois identity. Bourgeois values are on the contrary fiercely repudiated, with the disdain of the 'artist' in Kraus's writings before 1914 and with a new-found sense of solidarity with the working class after 1918. Kraus lays particular emphasis on his 'inverted life-style', in order to differentiate his existence from that of the 'Bürger' ('Lob der

TENNIS
IMPERIAL HÔTEL
LUMIÈRE ÉLECTRIQUE
NORTH SIDE
Tramontano & Tasso
SORRENTO
PROPRIÉTAIRE:
G. TRAMONTANO.
SOUTH SIDE
ASCENSEUR DE LA PLAGE À TOUS LES ÉTAGES
Telegr. TRAMONTANO-SORRENTO (A.B.C. Code 5 th. Ed.)
Sorrent, 10. August

4 First page of a letter from Kraus to Bertha Maria Denk

verkehrten Lebensweise', June 1908). The antithesis is one to which
he gives even more forceful expression in his later work. Thus a
poem 'Nach dreißig Jahren' culminates in the line:

> Hier Kämpfer, Künstler, Narr, und dort die Bürger!
>
> (F 810: 12)

> (Here fighter, artist, fool, and there the bourgeois!)

For Kraus the concept 'Bürger' is not a socio-economic category,
but denotes a heartless and philistine set of attitudes. But he himself
was the owner of an economic enterprise — the 'Verlag Die Fackel'
— which under Austrian commercial law was registered alongside
other businesses such as 'Gentlemen's Tailors' or 'Retailers of
Machinery and Spare Parts'. When in November 1913 Kraus's name
was actually published on such a list, and he himself publicly
identified as a businessman ('Kaufmann'), he found the identification
repulsive (F 389–90: 19–20). In fact, it was precisely because his
business was so successful that public registration had become
necessary. By 1913 the profits from the Fackel Verlag exceeded the
maximum allowable for unregistered enterprises.[33]

Kraus's self-image rests on a fundamental incongruity. He derived
his private income from trade, but distances himself ostentatiously
from his elder brothers, who were actually running the family firm
and generating his regular 6 per cent return on capital. He made a
profit from sales of Die Fackel, but prides himself on being an 'artist'
who is aloof from commercial considerations. Of course, he
dedicated himself to his profession as a writer with exceptional
integrity. But his attempt to establish a literary identity free of
compromising affiliations was clearly unrealistic. It is not only
Marxism which emphasizes the inescapability of one's socio-
economic identity. Social psychologists have argued that in all forms
of human interaction there is an element of role-play. 'Role-
expectation' and 'role-performance' form the underlying structure of
social interaction, and individuality expresses itself in terms of
'role-distance'. Even the attempt to detach oneself from the role
required by a given situation may be seen as an inverted form of
role-behaviour — an 'anti-role'.[34]

The relevance of this to Kraus's self-image is clear. His strategy is
to confront his age with a consciously constructed image of himself:
'ein Ich mit der Zeit konfrontieren' (F 557–60: 18). He thus embarks
on the construction of a series of 'anti-roles', which are partly a
response to the pressure of circumstances, partly the expression of
histrionic impulses. Above all, they are shaped by literary models.
Why (we may ask) does Kraus in his letter to Stoessl lavish such
extravagant praise on the essay 'Der Skeptiker'? It is evidently

because Stoessl, drawing on the examples of Chamfort, Lichtenberg and Montaigne, defines being a 'sceptic' not merely as an attitude of mind, but as a way of life ('Lebensrichtung', *F* 254–5: 25). The 'sceptic' in this essay prefigures the 'satirist' of Kraus's self-image.

There were also other models for this evolutionary process. Around 1905, as Kraus was feeling his way into one of the most significant of his anti-roles, that of the 'artist', he turned rather surprisingly to England. For his paradigm was provided by Oscar Wilde.

CHAPTER 10

Wilde, Nietzsche, and the Role of the Artist

The Influence of Wilde

Oscar Wilde receives more attention in *Die Fackel* than any other English author (with the exception of Shakespeare). The interest is concentrated in the years 1905–9 — the crucial period for Kraus's self-definition as 'artist'. The first significant reference to Wilde occurs in *Die Fackel* of December 1903, in an extended essay on *Salomé*. In the same context Kraus expresses his admiration for *The Picture of Dorian Gray*, *The Ballad of Reading Gaol* and Wilde's epigrams. In the following number he prints excerpts from *Dorian Gray* in German translation. And in autumn 1904 we find him quoting both from 'The Soul of Man under Socialism' and 'The Decay of Lying'. In February and March 1905 he prints further excerpts from 'The Soul of Man', and in October devotes a dozen pages to a translation of Wilde's poem 'Ravenna'. In subsequent numbers he prints excerpts from 'Phrases and Philosophies for the Use of the Young' and a series of Wilde's poems, book reviews and letters. He was evidently fascinated not only by Wilde's literary style but also by his tragic destiny, which reminded him of Shakespeare's Richard II, imprisoned in Pomfret Castle (F 204: 1).

It is not only the extent of Kraus's interest in Wilde that is striking, but also the effusiveness of his praise. *Salomé* is described as a masterpiece for which there is scarcely a parallel in world literature (F 150: 6), *Dorian Gray* as poetic, profound and inspired (F 151: 21). Even more extravagant is Kraus's praise for 'The Soul of Man under Socialism'. When a German translation appeared in 1904, he wrote: 'Mir erscheint sie als das Tiefste, Adeligste und Schönste, das der vom Philistersinn gemordete Genius geschaffen, mit ihrer unerhörten Fülle der Leben und Kunst umspannenden Betrachtung als das wahre Evangelium modernen Denkens. (It appears to me the most profound, most noble and most beautiful thing that this genius murdered by the spirit of the philistines has created, with its extraordinary richness of reflection encompassing life and art, the true gospel of modern thinking.)' (*F* 167: 10) In the light of such passages (from a critic normally so sparing in his praise), it is hardly possible to dismiss Kraus's interest in Wilde as a passing phase.

The example of Wilde helped to inspire Kraus's defence of the private life of homosexuals against the sanctions of criminal justice ('Die Kinderfreunde', November 1905, is his first important article on this theme). In more general terms, Wilde's strictures on prevailing theories of crime and punishment, quoted in *Die Fackel* in March 1905, may have stimulated Kraus's interest in the problem of 'Sittlichkeit und Kriminalität'. More important still, however, is the influence of Wilde on Kraus's literary style. The aesthetic perspective tentatively introduced in *Die Fackel* in March 1904, and confidently proclaimed in October 1905, clearly owes a great deal to Wilde.

It is through Wilde that Kraus first seems to have become interested in prose writing as an art form. It can hardly be a coincidence that Kraus's first experiments as a writer of aphorisms (March 1906) follow so soon after his praise of Wilde's work and the printing in *Die Fackel* (November 1905) of 'Phrases and Philosophies for the Use of the Young'. And Wilde's review of Walter Pater, which Kraus printed in *Die Fackel* in December 1907, significantly lays great stress on the artistry of writing in prose. Most important of all is the significance of Wilde in Kraus's quest for a literary identity. It is in the Wildean conception of the 'artist' that he finds, at least initially, his solution.

It is not difficult to see why 'The Soul of Man under Socialism' made such a deep impression. This essay is a synthesis of the aesthetic ideals of the 1890s with ideas that would not be out of place in the work of an intelligent Marxist. The gospel which Wilde's essay preaches is individualism. Instead of the 'sordid necessity of living for others' imposed on one by the prevailing forms of social existence, a man should aim at 'the full realization of his own personality'. The existence of private property enables some people to develop 'a certain very limited amount of Individualism' — 'to realize some form of beautiful and intellectual life'. But a society based on private property is ultimately unacceptable, because it makes such self-realization unattainable for the majority of mankind.

The aim of socialism should be to eliminate poverty, physical hardship and manual labour, to socialize property, and thus to liberate the true personality of man. 'Individualism is what through socialism we are to attain.' In the present condition of society, however, it is only the artists, poets and philosophers who are able truly to realize themselves. Only on the imaginative plane of art is it possible to achieve 'the full expression of a personality'. To be an artist is for Wilde much more than merely a matter of writing books or painting pictures. Being an artist is a 'mode of life', alternative to the 'actual life of fact'. The artist thus becomes an exemplary figure.

The figure of the 'artist' which assumes such a central position in Kraus's writings of the period 1907–14 is Wildean in inspiration. Wilde's key definition (in this essay which Kraus praised so extravagantly) is: 'The present is what man ought not to be. The future is what artists are.'[1] This is echoed six years later in Kraus's own definition of the artist: 'Seine Sache ist es nicht, mit der Gegenwart zu gehen, da es doch Sache der Zukunft ist, mit ihm zu gehen. (It is not his task to go along with the demands of the present, for it is the task of the future to go along with him.)' (F 300: 18–19)

This is not to deny that there may also have been other influences. The antithesis of 'Künstler' and 'Bürger' is a recurrent topos in German literature, from Goethe onwards. In the Romantic period the artist became something of a cult figure. And the figure of the artist gained enhanced prestige as a result of Schopenhauer's theory of the liberating function of aesthetic contemplation. Nietzsche too, though he takes a much more critical view of the matter, gives great prominence to the problem of the artist. By the end of the nineteenth century this problem had indeed become a favourite theme with German authors. It is clear, however, from the way that Kraus treats the figure of the artist, that his inspiration derives from Wilde, rather than from Nietzsche.

To be an artist is for Wilde not so much a creative activity as a mode of life. Indeed, under the prevailing social order, it seems to be the only mode of life through which full development of the personality can be attained. It is understandable that Kraus, concerned as he was with the problem of authentic identity, should have felt drawn to this solution. But Wilde's theory of the artist carries implications that throw an even more suggestive light on the manner of Kraus's self-representation. For Wilde suggests that the artist may mould his own life into artistic form. One of the 'Phrases and Philosophies for the Use of the Young' reads: 'One should either be a work of art, or wear a work of art.' We might be inclined to dismiss this dictum as a piece of elegant frippery. But Kraus himself thought it worth including among the excerpts he prints in *Die Fackel* (F 189: 18). And it expresses a conception of life which Wilde reiterates elsewhere. 'The first duty of life', he writes, 'is to assume a pose.' And again: 'Create yourself; be yourself your poem.' In *De Profundis* he declares: 'I treated art as the supreme reality and life as a mere mode of fiction.' Discussing this aspect of Wilde's work, one critic has concluded: 'For Wilde, the ideal is not the man of unrestrainable passions, but the man whose passions have been tempered and refined into another self, which is consciously fabricated, *posed*.'[2]

Perhaps the most suggestive formulation of Wilde's argument in favour of adopting a mask occurs in his essay on Thomas Wainewright, 'Pen, Pencil and Poison'. The double life of Wainewright, the respected literary man who was secretly a criminal, no doubt had a special appeal for Wilde (himself condemned by the laws on homosexuality to lead a double life). What Wilde sees as most significant in Wainewright, however, is his attempt to make his life into a work of art: 'He recognized that Life itself is an art, and has its modes of style no less than the arts that seek to express it.' In Wainewright's writings he values above all the expression of a strong personality. Wilde's comment on Wainewright's use of pseudonyms is particularly suggestive: 'A mask tells us more than a face. These disguises intensified his personality.' This observation has important applications not only to the work of Wilde, but through Wilde to that of Kraus himself. There can be little doubt that Kraus was acquainted with the essay, which appeared in a German translation in 1903 (in a volume which also contained 'The Decay of Lying', 'The Critic as Artist' and 'The Truth of Masks').[3] The volume was certainly available to Kraus, for in November 1904 we find him quoting from it a passage from 'The Decay of Lying' (F 168: 12). And a polemical essay of October 1907 contains what is more or less a direct quotation from 'Pen, Pencil and Poison' (F 234–5: 6). It is thus by no means improbable that this conception of a mask which 'intensifies the personality' contributed to Kraus's own self-image.

This is not to suggest that Kraus led the kind of 'Doppelleben' for which Wilde is criticized in *Die Fackel* (F 173: 17): an elegant pose concealing a guilty secret. Nor was he influenced by the external trappings of the Wildean pose — orchids, velvet breeches and long hair. On the contrary, he repudiated such supposedly 'artistic' affectations:

> Gewiß, der Künstler ist ein Anderer. Aber gerade deshalb soll er es in seinem Äußern mit den anderen halten. Er kann nur einsam bleiben, wenn er in der Menge verschwindet. Lenkt er die Betrachtung durch eine Besonderheit auf sich, so macht er sich gemein und führt die Verfolger auf seine Spur. [. . .] Je mehr den Künstler alles dazu berechtigt, ein anderer zu sein, um so notwendiger ist es, daß er sich der Tracht der Durchschnittsmenschen als einer Mimicry bediene.

(F 259–60: 41)

(Certainly, the artist is different. But precisely for this reason he should
not dissociate himself from others in his external appearance. He can only
remain solitary if he disappears in the crowd. If he draws attention to
himself through some peculiarity, he makes himself cheap and sets the
pursuers on his trail. [. . .] The more everything justifies the artist in
being different, the more necessary it is for him to adopt the garb of the
man-in-the-street as protective mimicry.

But though Kraus rejects the externals of the artistic pose, he retains
Wilde's more inward conception of the artist as the man who attains
the full realization of his personality.

The Assimilation of Nietzsche

The question of Nietzsche's influence is more difficult. Although so
many German writers of his generation fell under Nietzsche's spell,
Kraus's attitude was extremely guarded. And there is insufficient
evidence to support the sweeping assertions which have been made
about Nietzsche's influence on Kraus's 'Weltanschauung'.[4] The
numerous references to Nietzsche in early numbers of Die Fackel
occur mainly in articles by other contributors. This is certainly true
of the reflections which appeared in August 1900, shortly after
Nietzsche's death (F 51: 19–22), which on more than one occasion
have mistakenly been attributed to Kraus himself.[5] Indeed, as late as
April 1912 Kraus identifies himself as an author who does not know
Nietzsche's work ('ich, der Nietzsche nicht kennt', F 345–6: 37). But
in the same breath he acknowledges that he has read excerpts from
Nietzsche's work. We must take the claim 'not to know' Nietzsche
to mean that Kraus had not read his writings in a systematic way.
Traces of Nietzsche's influence can nevertheless be identified.

Passages from Nietzsche which are actually quoted in Die Fackel
provide the most reliable pointers. Two quotations about the
influence of newspapers, printed in June and July 1902, suggest that
Kraus was reading Also sprach Zarathustra at that time (F 108: 2;
110: 20). The fact that he gives a page-reference to Zarathustra
suggests that he had the book itself to hand, not merely excerpts.
The debate which followed Otto Weininger's suicide the following
year is likely to have further stimulated Kraus's interest. Weininger
and Nietzsche are both included among the men of genius whom
Kraus defends against pathographers (F 169: 6 fn.). It is also clear
that Nietzsche did provide a point of reference for the evolution of
Kraus's art as an aphorist. In early May 1908 he quotes Nietzsche's
definition of the artist as a person for whom form is coextensive with
content (F 253: 20). Later in May 1908, and again in December 1909,
he quotes Nietzsche's adjuration 'to work on a page of prose as if one
were working on a sculpture' ('an einer Seite Prosa wie an einer

Bildsäule arbeiten', F 254–5: 25; 293: 27–8). This passage occurs at a rather unobtrusive point in Menschliches, Allzumenschliches (Section 2, 95),[6] and it thus seems likely that Kraus was acquainted with this work as well. A cryptic invitation to compare his style with that of Nietzsche is even contained in Kraus's choice of the title Sprüche und Widersprüche for his first volume of aphorisms. It implies a familiarity with Nietzsche's 'Sprüche und Zwischenfälle' — the title given to a sequence of aphorisms in Jenseits von Gut und Böse. Kraus chose a title which brings out the contrast between his own densely verbal style of aphorism, where insights arise out of collisions between words, and Nietzsche's more external handling of the German language.

This point is explicitly made in a passage of May 1917, which pin-points Nietzsche's failure to write from within the medium of language, even though he (like Hebbel) had written so suggestively about language (F 457–61: 55). By this date Kraus's attitude was overtly hostile. For the effects of Nietzsche's undisciplined use of language had become abundantly clear: the debasement of German political discourse through slogans like the 'Superman' and the 'Will to Power', and the inflation of literary rhetoric through Nietzsche's influence on the Expressionists. Kraus's critique of Nietzsche's style and influence culminates in November 1921 in a devastating attack (F 577–82: 61–4), which follows one of his rare admissions that he has actually been reading Nietzsche's work (F 577–82: 41).

In a period when that work was being widely debated, Kraus may have assimilated more of Nietzsche's ideas than he realized. There are striking affinities of both theme and attitude: the denunciations of the press, the laments about the weakening of 'personality', the polemical use of quotation to discredit intellectual opponents, the cult of linguistic artistry, and the stance of militant opposition to prevailing cultural norms. Nietzsche defines his intellectual activity (in the Preface to Vom Nutzen und Nachteil der Historie) as being directed against his age ('gegen die Zeit').[7] This is echoed in Kraus's insistence that art should be directed against the values of its day ('gegen heute', F 360–2: 22). Thus it may not be entirely wrong to suggest that Nietzsche was one of the models for Kraus's stance as a publicist.

One of the leitmotifs in Nietzsche's writings is the need to shape one's identity in an artistic way. This is an idea which he explores with far greater sophistication than Wilde. For Nietzsche recognizes that in any system of communication the speaker inevitably assumes a public 'role' for his audience. The self-conscious artist will thus construct this role with flair and finesse. Through the process of time, moreover, this self-conscious pose is likely to evolve into an existential identity. Nietzsche pin-points the paradox in Menschliches,

Allzumenschliches (Section 1, 51): the 'mask' which one adopts when one enters a profession, for example as 'artist' or as 'priest', may ultimately become one's authentic face. The writer of course has exceptional freedom in the range of narrative identities he may adopt — a freedom which Nietzsche exploits with great versatility. 'Every profound spirit needs a mask,' he proclaims ('Jeder tiefe Geist braucht eine Maske').[8] The gentler a person is by disposition, the more abrasive he may become in his mode of utterance, in order to convey his vision to an uncomprehending world.

Kraus may well have been familiar with these ideas from his own reading. Nietzsche had after all put his theories spectacularly into practice through his use of the persona of Zarathustra to amplify his narrative voice and give prophetic force to his utterances. But to the discerning reader it was clear that even when he was apparently speaking in his own voice, Nietzsche's literary identity was endowed with archetypal undertones. Two of the most fundamental of these archetypes, the Quester and the Seer, are identified in an essay by Otto Weininger which Kraus published in *Die Fackel*, 'Sucher und Priester' (*F* 145: 26–30). Nietzsche (Weininger argues) had begun his career as 'Quester' but later, with the publication of *Zarathustra*, assumed the mantle of 'Priest' or 'Seer'. This pattern of transformation, it is suggested, is characteristic of the greatest artists, such as Goethe and Wagner. Kraus was obviously impressed by this typology. And it may well have helped to shape his own self-image, as it evolved from the questioning stance of the 'Artist' towards the prophetic utterance of the apocalyptic 'Satirist'.

It is not fanciful to detect Nietzschean undertones in Kraus's definition (in January 1906) of 'the significance of the literary life-plan to which I have devoted my energy' ('die Bedeutung des literarischen Lebensplanes, dem ich meine Kraft gewidmet habe', *F* 194: 6). The essential principle is formulated in *Die fröhliche Wissenschaft* (Book 4, 290): '*One thing is necessary.* — To "give style" to your character — a great and rare art! This is exercised by the person who has an overall view of all the strengths and weaknesses which make up his nature and integrates them into an artistic plan.'[9] Even if Kraus did not derive his idea directly from a reading of Nietzsche, it would have filtered through to him from the life-style of other authors and acquaintances.

The outstanding example in Kraus's immediate circle was Peter Altenberg. Altenberg's motto was 'to live artistically'.[10] He became just as celebrated for his bohemian life-style as for the impressionistic prose poems in which that mode of existence is reflected. To a sceptical observer like Arthur Schnitzler this bohemianism appeared to be a pose. And Hofmannsthal too, reviewing *Wie ich es sehe*

(1896), detected a histrionic element in Altenberg's narrative voice: 'He stylizes himself as the chap who just wanders around and watches.[. . .] He acts out himself.'[11] But Kraus emphatically denies that Altenberg is a 'poseur'. On the contrary, the aim of his life has been 'to break through conventional pretences' ('die Konvention der Verstellung zu durchbrechen', F 274: 2). The role of the buffoon, which Altenberg played out so publicly in the cafés and night-clubs of Vienna, is so convincingly sustained that it becomes for Kraus the epitome of 'honesty' ('Ehrlichkeit', F 274: 4).

This paradox reminds us of Nietzsche's account of how masks become identities. It also reflects the theatrical model of 'personality' which underlies Kraus's work. Peter Altenberg is 'authentic' in the same way that the actor Alexander Girardi becomes the embodiment of 'authenticity' ('Echtheit', F 246–7: 38–44). Both act out their chosen roles with complete conviction.

The link between literary identity and theatrical performance was even more evident in the case of Frank Wedekind. Wedekind was a celebrity because he appeared as actor in his own plays. The personality of the author made an unprecedented impact when Wedekind himself spoke the outrageous lines of the Ringmaster in the Prologue to *Erdgeist* or played the role of 'vermummter Herr' at the end of *Frühlings Erwachen*. Kraus was well aware of the discrepancy between this 'satanic' public role and the private character of the author, with his *petit-bourgeois* inhibitions, his streak of moral idealism. The audiences which respond only to the 'grotesque' elements in Wedekind's work (he argues) 'confuse the mask with the face' ('Sie verwechseln die Maske mit dem Gesicht'). The grotesqueness of Wedekind's dialogue conceals the 'sense of shame of the idealist' ('das Schamgefühl des Idealisten', F 182: 12).

It is not hard to detect a parallel here with Kraus's own position, as an idealist who adopts an aggressive public pose. But Kraus responded with indignation to any suggestion that in his own public readings he was wearing an 'actor's mask' which could be dispensed with. 'Meine Komödiantenmaske abnehmen!', he writes, in a vehement response to such a suggestion in March 1912. How could that public identity at which he has worked, night after night without sleeping, for thirteen years possibly be a mask? (F 345–6: 39). Against this we must set his admission that he *did* experience the process of writing 'as an actor' (F 389–90: 42). Kraus's own testimony leaves us with a paradox. It can only be resolved by the concept of the 'true mask' — the public role which is played out with such seriousness that it becomes an existential identity.

The Artist and the Flâneur

In a programmatic statement of October 1905 Kraus announced his intention to give the aesthetic sense priority over moral indignation (*F* 185: 8). And from 1906 onwards we find him increasingly defining his position as that of 'Künstler'. This new stance is spelt out most clearly in an exchange of letters with the socialist Robert Scheu in January 1906. Scheu sees Kraus's campaign against the bourgeoisie as an attack on 'the common enemy of the artist, the genius and the people' (*F* 194: 2). Kraus replies that his aim is to defend the artistic personality against mass organizations of any kind. Sceptical of the achievements of the Austrian Social Democrats, he identifies himself as an artist who stands above the political confusions which beset the Habsburg Empire. The claim to be an artist was not an idle boast. For Kraus was able to substantiate it by the imaginative richness of his writing. Yet this self-identification is not simply a statement of fact. It is an attempt to establish a valid identity in an anomic historical situation.

Initially, Kraus had prided himself on the strict separation of his private life from his public office (*F* 147: 27). This, he claimed, was the guarantee of his integrity as a writer. But by 1906 there are signs of frustration about this division of the public from the private self. The aim is increasingly to find a literary stance through which to express the values of the 'inner life' (*F* 194: 11). Hence the highly personal, even confessional tone of his writings in the period 1907–9. He now writes under rubrics like 'Selbstbespiegelung' ('Self-Mirroring'), 'Persönliches' ('Personal Matters'), 'Bekenntnisse' ('Confessions') and 'Tagebuch' ('Diary'). He suggests that *Die Fackel* itself is a kind of diary in periodical form (*F* 267–8: 24). But he insists that even when he is writing about himself, his essential subject is language — the medium through which (like Goethe) he seeks to express his personality in exemplary form (*F* 290: 20–1).

Artistic form is thus the medium in which the public and the private spheres meet. An exceptional linguistic sensitivity entitles the author to present the preoccupations of his inner life as a matter of public concern. The artist (as Kraus represents him) is the whole man, in whom unity of being is restored and the life of the mind no longer divorced from social existence. There is no trace of that defeatism which inhibits the artist heroes of Thomas Mann. For Mann's 'Künstler', art is a curse which deprives him of the healthy vitality of the 'Bürger'. In Kraus's writings the situation is reversed. It is the bourgeois who is seen as half alive, his mind blunted by the media and his personality diminished by the demands of routine.

The artist on the other hand has all the faculties intact. Above all, he exemplifies the synthesis of passionate feeling and creative imagination. The artist (for Kraus as for Freud) is more richly endowed with the capacity for erotic experience than the ordinary mortal. His imaginative endowment enables him to experience life at a higher degree of intensity: 'Der Künstler soll mehr erleben? Er erlebt mehr!' (F 338: 17). The imagination of the artist has the power to transform the experience of love:

> Prinzessin von Gnaden meiner Phantasie — Aschenbrödel meiner Erkenntnis. Der Künstler läßt beide Rollen gleichzeitig spielen. Der Philister ist enttäuscht und zieht die erste zurück.
>
> (F 237: 11)

> (Princess by the grace of my imagination — Cinderella of my perception. The artist can sustain both roles simultaneously. The philistine is disappointed and retracts the first.)

This same imaginative endowment allows the artist to find gratification in homosexual encounters: 'Der Künstler, der das Gebiet der Weiblichkeit schneller abgehaust hat als der Philister, hat vermöge der Gnadengabe einer regenerierenden Phantasie die Kraft, seinen Bedarf am Weib auch beim Mann zu decken. (The artist, who has exhausted the realm of womanliness more quickly than the philistine, has by virtue of the gift of a regenerating imagination the capacity to satisfy his need for woman also with a man.)' (F 237: 20) In Kraus's account of the artist, this extended capacity for erotic experience is quite distinct from the compulsive homosexuality of the invert. It is a kind of bonus over and above the pleasures of normal love. The artist is thus for Kraus 'the full man' ('der volle Mann') who is able freely to explore the possibilities of a bisexual endowment (F 237: 20).

Strengthened through experiences in the sexual sphere, the imagination reaches a kind of take-off point where the gravitational pull of physical experience is transcended and the mind finds fulfilment in the creative act:

> Der Geist hat tiefere Wollust, als der Körper beziehen könnte. Irgendwie lebt er davon, daß Wollust die Mitgift des Weibes ist. Er muß es erlebt haben. [. . .] Schließlich steigt Phantasie vier Treppen hoch, um das Weib nicht zu finden, und bis zum Himmel, ohne es zu suchen. Sie hat sich des Stoffs begeben. Aber sie hat die Form, in der der Gedanke wird und mit ihm die Lust. Sie ahnt, was keiner zu wissen vermag. Sie hat sich an der Wollust gebildet und konnte von da an, durch immer neue Erlebniskreise zu immer neuen Potenzen dringend, nie versagen, wenn ungeistige Begierde längst versagt hätte. Nun bedarf sie des Anlasses nicht mehr und läßt sich an sich selbst, und genießt sich im Taumel der Assoziationen, hier einer Metapher nachjagend, die eben um die Ecke bog, dort Worte kuppelnd, Phrasen pervertierend, in Ähnlichkeiten vergafft, im seligen Mißbrauch chiastischer Verschlingung, immer auf Abenteuer aus [. . .]
>
> (F 323: 22)

(The mind has deeper ecstasy than the body could ever obtain. In some
way it lives from the fact that ecstasy is the dowry of woman. It must
have experienced her. [. . .] Finally imagination climbs four flights of
stairs, in order not to find the woman, and right up to heaven, without
seeking her. It has relinquished matter. But it has form, in which ideas
come and with them delight. It has intuitions of what no one may know.
It has found itself through ecstasy and from now on, thrusting
continually through new circles of experience to new potencies, can never
fail, where desires not of the mind would long since have failed. Now
imagination no longer needs a stimulus, it becomes self-sufficient and
finds its own delight in the rapture of associations, here chasing in pursuit
of a metaphor which has just disappeared round the corner, there
match-making with words, perverting phrases, falling for similarities, in
the blissful abuse of chiastic interwining, always out for adventure
[. . .])

Kraus's account of the creative process, which extends through a
whole series of aphorisms, essays, and later even poems, repeatedly
celebrates this union of the creative and erotic spheres. The effect is
to establish, in the most vivid and dramatic language (above all
through the imagery of erotic pursuit), the validity of the life of the
mind. Through this dramatization of creative experience, the artist is
portrayed as the exemplary man, a synthesis of inspired poet and
romantic lover. Kraus further enhances the exemplary nature of the
artist by introducing hints of a spiritual vigil into his composite
portrait. 'Geist' as he uses the word embraces both intellect and
spirituality. The artist, once again, is the whole man.

The figure of the artist is also enhanced by the social function
which Kraus assigns to art. It is not for himself alone that the artist
seeks salvation. Art (in Kraus's scheme) has for the world at large an
almost redemptive power. It re-creates the world, transforming the
chaotic fragments of experience into a coherent pattern of meaning.
By art Kraus understands a dynamic and militant force, directed
against existing values. The initial function of art, as he understands
it, is disruptive: 'Kunst bringt das Leben in Unordnung. Die Dichter
der Menschheit stellen immer wieder das Chaos her. (Art brings life
into disorder. The poets of mankind continually restore chaos.)' (*F*
329–30: 19)

The prevailing scheme of values, seen as hypocritical and
repressive, must be disrupted in order to release the forces of passion
and imagination. This does not, however, result in an anarchic
chaos, even though Kraus does concede that there is an element of
'anarchisches Denken' in his outlook (*F* 194: 10). Through art —
above all through the almost magical power of language — a new
and more satisfying order of meaning may be established: 'Nur in
der Wonne sprachlicher Zeugung wird aus dem Chaos eine Welt.

(Only in the ecstasy of linguistic procreation does a world emerge out of chaos.)' (F 329–30: 25)

This redemptive process is more fully elaborated in an extended aphorism of October 1911, in which Kraus seeks to express the function of literary creativity through a delicate interweaving of biblical motifs with lines from Goethe's ballad 'Der Zauberlehrling' (F 333: 11–13). Art seeks to restore meaning to a God-forsaken world. And for satire in particular Kraus claims a redemptive function: 'Es gibt keinen so Positiven wie den Künstler, dessen Stoff das Übel ist. Er erlöst von dem Übel. Jeder andere lenkt davon nur ab und läßt es in der Welt, welche dann das schutzlose Gefühl umso härter angreift. (There is no one so positive as the artist whose subject is Evil. He redeems from Evil. Every other artist merely diverts attention from it and leaves it in the world, which then attacks the defenceless sensibility all the more fiercely.)' (F 333: 11) Once again we are conscious of the ambiguities of Kraus's position. While repudiating escapist art which ignores social evils, he commits himself to a mode of imaginative transformation which does not *actually* remove those evils from the world, but merely fortifies the mind against them. In this same sequence of reflections Kraus acknowledges that in political terms this must seem to be an evasion — 'eine Ausflucht'. But as satirist he has his eye on a more distant 'cosmic' horizon (F 333: 13).

It is easy to see why Kraus gained a reputation for vanity. When he writes of the artist, he is almost always by implication fashioning his own image. It is significant how easily his aphorisms about the artist slip from third-person form into the first person singular. Seen more critically, this self-image as artist is a mythical disguise through which Kraus conceals — from himself as well as from his audience — his actual social position. For the belief that it was possible to contract out of the political process was an illusion, as Robert Scheu pointed out in his Open Letter of January 1906 (F 194: 3). Kraus's attempt to give artistic values precedence over politics merely led him to formulate political judgements by reference to questionable aesthetic criteria.

In terms of artistic achievement, however, Kraus had grounds for pride. If we take stock of his position in 1910, the credit balance is overwhelming. During ten years of publication, *Die Fackel* had established itself as one of the two or three most significant literary journals of the German-speaking world. Kraus's 300th number, published in April 1910, included contributions by the leading spirits of the day: Richard Dehmel, August Strindberg, Peter Hille, Peter Altenberg, Arnold Schoenberg, Otto Stoessl, Adolf Loos and Stanislaw Przybyszewski (not to mention an exceptionally subtle sequence of aphorisms by Kraus himself). Kraus had also gathered around him a gifted circle of younger authors, like Karl Hauer, Albert Ehrenstein and Berthold Viertel (who acted as his secretary). And through an extremely wide-ranging correspondence he was reaching out to authors in other intellectual centres. Not only did *Die Fackel* fertilize those intersecting circles of creativity which were such a feature of late Habsburg Vienna. Kraus also began, through public readings and personal interventions, to form circles of acolytes in other centres.

In Innsbruck it was the example of *Die Fackel* which inspired the founding of *Der Brenner*, by Ludwig von Ficker. The poet Georg Trakl and the essayists Carl Dallago and Theodor Haecker also fell under Kraus's spell. In Berlin the pioneering Expressionist journal *Der Sturm* could hardly have come into existence without Kraus's intellectual and financial support (as his extensive correspondence with Herwarth Walden shows). And Kraus's example stimulated not only poets of the *Sturm* circle such as Else Lasker-Schüler, but also contributors to the second Expressionist journal *Die Aktion*, like Pfemfert, Georg Heym and Jakob van Hoddis. In Munich Kraus had helped to give *Simplicissimus* a more vigorous literary profile, and for a time was closely associated with the Bavarian satirist Ludwig Thoma. In Prague he became for a short period an inspiration for Franz Werfel, Max Brod and Willy Haas, while Kafka followed his writings with interest. In Leipzig he was soon to become associated with the avant-garde publisher Kurt Wolff. Although some of these links were short-lived, and Kraus was subsequently to retreat into an embattled isolation, there can be no doubt that for a short period around 1910 he helped to galvanize German intellectual life into an unprecedented spasm of creativity. The map of the 'Vienna circles' (p. 8) must thus be complemented by a second diagram which shows how Kraus's influence radiated out to other centres (see Fig. III). So frequently has he been decried as an author who could 'only negate' that this deserves special emphasis. Kraus's image of the artist as hero forms the climax of a great tradition.[12]

The real problems arise when he attempts to substantiate the role of the artist in society as a way of life (rather than a mode of creativity), as in the essay 'Lob der verkehrten Lebensweise' (June 1908). The 'inverted life-style' of an author who works at night and sleeps during the day is a response to a world which is upside-down:

> Das gesunde Prinzip einer verkehrten Lebensweise innerhalb einer verkehrten Weltordnung hat sich an mir in jedem Betracht bewährt. Auch ich brachte einmal das Kunststück zuwege, mit der Sonne aufzustehen und mit ihr schlafen zu gehen. Aber die unerträgliche Objektivität, mit der sie alle meine Mitbürger ohne Ansehen der Person

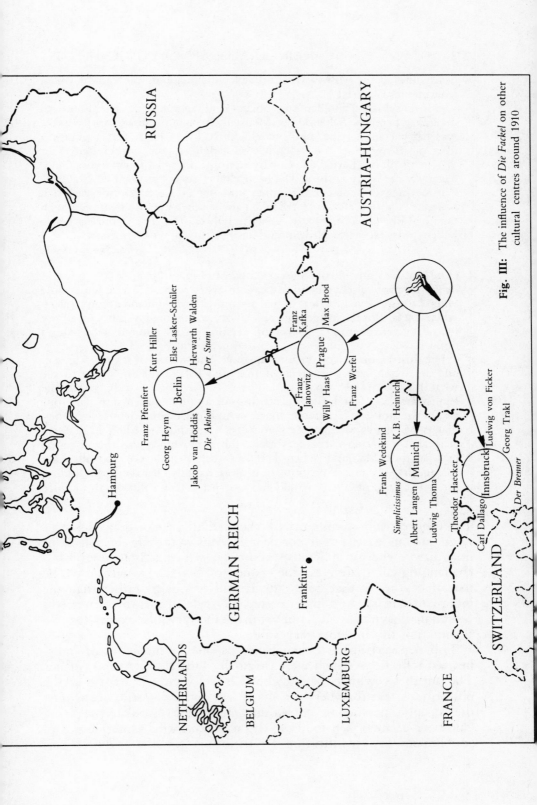

Fig. III: The influence of *Die Fackel* on other cultural centres around 1910

bescheint, allen Mißwachs und alle Häßlichkeit, entspricht nicht
jedermanns Naturell [. . .].

    Darum schlafe ich in den Tag hinein. Und wenn ich erwache, breite ich
die ganze papierne Schande der Menschheit vor mir aus, um zu wissen,
was ich versäumt habe, und bin glücklich. [. . .] Dann aber gehe ich
über die Ringstraße und sehe, wie sie einen Festzug vorbereiten. Vier
Wochen hallt der Lärm, wie eine Symphonie über das Thema vom Geld,
das unter die Leute kommt. Die Menschheit rüstet zu einem Feiertag, die
Zimmermeister schlagen Tribünen und die Preise auf, und wenn ich
bedenke, daß ich all die Herrlichkeit nicht sehen werde, beginnen auch
meine Pulse freudiger zu gehen. Führte ich noch die normale
Lebensweise, so hätte ich während des Festzugs abreisen müssen; [. . .]
(F 257–8: 10–11)

(The healthy principle of an inverted way of life within an inverted world
order has proved its value in my case in every respect. There was a time
when I too achieved the feat of getting up with the sun and going to sleep
when it sets. But the intolerable objectivity with which it shines on all my
fellow citizens without respect of person, on all stunted growth and
ugliness, does not suit everyone's temperament [. . .].

    For this reason I sleep far into the day. And when I wake up, I spread
out the whole paper disgrace of mankind before me, in order to see
what I have missed, and I'm happy [. . .]. Then I walk across the
Ringstrasse and watch them preparing for a jubilee procession. For four
weeks the noise reverberates, like a symphony on the theme of money
that is being put into people's pockets. Mankind is girding itself for a
festival, the master carpenters make the grandstands and the prices as
high as possible, and when I reflect that I shall not see all these
splendours, my pulses begin to beat more happily. If I were still leading
a normal way of life, I would have to leave town during the jubilee
procession; [. . .])

The jubilee celebrations to mark the sixtieth year of Franz Joseph's
reign are an easy target for irony. And yet there is a lack of
imaginative energy in Kraus's response, which fails to establish a
challenging alternative to the values of his fellow citizens. The
narrative voice is that of the disdainful onlooker, rather than the
indignant satirist. And his 'inverted life-style' seems to be merely a
personal idiosyncrasy. It is not yet made the symbolic expression of a
repudiation of contemporary values.

    'Lob der verkehrten Lebensweise' is one of the series of light-
hearted reflections which were originally written for *Simplicissimus*.
The antithesis which they establish is between the artist and the
philistine, rather than between the satirist and the world. Set against
the deeply pessimistic pronouncements of 'Apokalypse', the
cultivated aesthetic sensibility of this narrator forms something of an
anticlimax. The justification Kraus offers for the style of this

narrative is that the quality of the writing is displayed, not in weightiness of subject-matter or heroism of moral stance, but in the ironic stylization of apparently trivial material: 'Für einen ironischen Stilisten ist jenes Thema das wichtigste, das er am glücklichsten gestaltet' (F 203: 19).

It is not, however, the subject-matter of these essays that makes them a lightweight achievement. Their limitation lies precisely in the indulgence of a particular mode of irony. Irony in the hands of an author like Swift may become a highly penetrating instrument. Using narrative personae like that of the 'Modest Proposer' or of the 'Abolisher of Christianity', Swift is able to develop a systematic and cumulative irony of great incisiveness. In Kraus's case, both the concept of irony and the use of narrative persona are quite different. The literary identity he adopts in his essays of this period is not an ironic impersonation of attitudes obliquely under attack, but merely a relaxed projection of his own personality. His conception of ironic stylization results not in a strengthening of the attack by indirect means, but in a relaxation of satirical intensity.

Intensity of perception is, of course, precisely the power that Kraus in his aphorisms has claimed for the artist. The problem is to sustain this heightened consciousness in essayistic narratives dealing with social themes. When in Kraus's writings the artist emerges from the sphere of inner experience to take his stand in a social setting, he becomes a distinctly less impressive figure. Picturing himself walking across the Ringstrasse and watching the activities of the big city, Kraus is assuming an archetypal stance: that of the peripatetic philosopher or (in more modern terms) the *flâneur*.

Walter Benjamin has identified the literary ancestry of the *flâneur* in the writings of Poe and of Baudelaire. He has also indicated the ambiguities inherent in the position: 'The *flâneur* stands on the threshold both of the big city and of the bourgeois class.'[13] The *flâneur* observes the activities of the city without participating in them. Hence his ironic detachment, and the charm and lightness of touch that often characterize his narrative. He prides himself on the independence of his position, setting his individuality as a 'private person' against the anonymity of the masses, hurrying down city streets in pursuit of business interests. But this independence is not without its ambiguities: the commercial activities of the city, which he surveys with disdain, also provide the market in which he sells his wares. Moreover, he cannot escape his social identity as a member of the bourgeois class, however much he may seek to take his stand on the margins of the social order.

The ambivalence of the position is exemplified by one of Kraus's most revealing essays, 'Der Biberpelz' ('The Beaver Coat'):

Mein Wiener Dasein ist jetzt wieder reicher geworden, das ewige Sichdiewanddeslebensentlangdrücken, damit man auf dem Trottoir von keinem Trottel angesprochen wird, hat ein Ende, und jeder Tag bringt neue Abenteuer. Durch all die Jahre keine Gesellschaft, kein Theater, kein Blumenkorso — wie hält man das nur aus? Die Zufuhr der wertvollsten Eindrücke abgeschnitten; und wer weiß, wie lange der innere Proviant gereicht hätte. Selbst die Katastrophen der Saison, Komet und Jagdausstellung, schienen an diesem Zustand nichts ändern zu können. Gewiß, ich wills nicht verhehlen, ich erwartete mir einige Anregung vom Weltuntergang. Wenns aber wieder eine Niete wäre? So lebt man dahin auf dem schmalen Pfad, der von immer demselben Schreibtisch in immer dasselbe Lokal führt, wo man immer dieselben Speisen ißt und immer dieselben Menschen meidet. Froher wird man nicht dabei. Die Welt rings ist bunt, und man möchte sich doch wenigstens an ihr reiben, um zu sehen, ob die Farbe heruntergeht. Man will nicht auf so viel verzichten, ohne zu erfahren, wie wenig man verliert. Nur einmal noch an der vollbesetzten Tafel sitzen, alle Rülpse der Lebensfreude wieder hören, die Schweißhand der Nächstenliebe drücken — ich träumte davon, und eine gütige Fee, wahrscheinlich jene, die den Operettenkomponisten die Lieder an der Wiege singt, hat mich erhört. Ich bin mitten drin, die Erde hat mich wieder — mein Pelz ist mir gestohlen worden!

(F 305–6: 57)

(My Viennese existence has now become richer again, the eternal creeping-along-the-wall-of-life, so as to avoid being spoken to by some fool on the footpath, has come to an end, and every day brings new adventures. Through all these years no convivial gathering, no theatre, no floral parade — how can one possibly stand it? The supply of the most valuable impressions cut off; and who knows how much longer the inner resources would have lasted. Even the catastrophes of the season — the comet and the hunting exhibition — seemed incapable of altering this situation. Certainly, I will make no secret of the fact that I was hoping for some stimulation from the End of the World. But what if that again turned out to be a dud? Thus one lives out one's days on the narrow path that leads from always the same writing-desk to always the same restaurant, where one eats always the same dishes and avoids always the same people. One doesn't become any happier that way. The world around is full of colour, and one would after all like to rub against it, if only to see if the colour comes off. To sit just once more at the groaning board, to hear again all the belches of the joy of life, to squeeze the sweaty hand of brotherly love — I was dreaming of this, and a good fairy, probably the one who sings the songs at the cradle of operetta composers, has granted my wish. I'm in the thick of it, the earth hath me again — my beaver coat has been pinched!)

In this essay Kraus presents himself not as a satirist, but as an inoffensive private citizen of solitary habits, whose way of life is ironized rather than extolled: 'Ich lebte still und harmlos, ich war ein Privatmann, denn ich übte seit vielen Jahren eine literarische Tätigkeit aus. (I was leading a quiet and inoffensive life, I was a private person, for I had for many years been practising a literary occupation.)' (F 305–6: 58) The theft of his overcoat gives rise to a series of vividly evoked scenes of innocent comedy, in which this harmless recluse is obliged to participate as reluctant hero. He rapidly becomes the victim of the social pressures and procedures which his whole previous way of life has been designed to evade. Through the streets and the coffee-houses of the city he is pursued by the intrusive sympathy and amiable fatuousness of his fellow Viennese. From these unwelcome attentions he can see only one avenue of escape. The essay concludes: 'Ich beschloß, mich aus dem Privatleben zurückzuziehen. Mir war eine Hoffnung geblieben. Daß es mir durch die Herausgabe eines neuen Buches gelingen werde, mich den Wienern in Vergessenheit zu bringen. (I decided to retire from private life. There was one hope left. That by publishing a new book I might succeed in inducing the Viennese to forget me.)' (F 305–6: 63)

In 'Der Biberpelz' it becomes clear that a style of ironical self-mirroring can, at its best, complement and enrich the more intense monologue of the satirist. The colourful elaboration of scene compensates for the easing of stylistic tension. Moreover, this lighter tone, enlivened by touches of self-irony, endows the author with attractive human qualities. We even catch glimpses of that warmth and charm which (we are told) so distinguished Kraus in his private life. In these lighter essays a poised and critical but not misanthropic intelligence observes the Viennese scene with amused disbelief and responds with gentle ridicule. A kind of domestication of the satirist has taken place. In 'Der Biberpelz' this is even made an explicit motif: '[. . .] so hatte ich, nachdem das Unglück geschehen war, nur die eine Sorge: Wie sage ichs meiner Bedienerin? ([. . .] thus, after the misfortune had occurred, I had only one anxiety: How am I to tell my housekeeper?)' (F 305–6: 62)

In one respect, this domestication represents a gain. Kraus's preoccupation after 1905 with the role of the artist had led him to assume positions which, although exemplary in implication, were at times intellectually arrogant and socially marginal. Furthermore, the pathos of the Sittlichkeit und Kriminalität essays sometimes led him to assume a stance utterly remote from the civilization he condemned: 'Ich wohne nur mehr als Saturnbewohner den irdischen Affenkomödien bei, ich bringe die Empörung des Erdensohnes nicht mehr auf, die vielleicht wirksamer wäre. (It is only as a visitor from another planet that I attend these asinine earthly performances. I can no longer summon up the indignation of a dweller upon this earth, which would perhaps be more effective.)' (F 263: 14) The lighter essays of the years 1908–10 provide a salutary counterweight to such

centrifugal tendencies. For here Kraus does assume the position of a
'dweller upon this earth' — the inoffensive private citizen who
gives an account of the way the Viennese milieu impinges upon
sensitive nerves. The humanization of the satirist, however, also
implies a limitation; for it leads to a significant reduction in moral
energy.

A striking change comes over the mood of Kraus's work from
about the middle of 1911 onwards. The tone of ironic persiflage, so
prevalent in *Die Fackel* of the preceding years, increasingly gives way
to invective. It would be a simplification to see this transition from
irony into pathos as a contrast between two distinct 'phases'. The
disconcerting quality of Kraus's work arises from variations of tone
within a single text. It is nevertheless clear that after 1911 the
dominant mood becomes progressively more sombre.

The transformation of mood is not due to any significant change in
Kraus's chosen subject-matter. The reader who compares a number
of *Die Fackel* of 1913 with one issued five years earlier will notice no
great difference in the material on which the satire is based (apart
from the fact that *Die Fackel* now contains no contributions by any
hand other than Kraus's own). The matter of his work remains the
same — not the 'major themes' of European politics, but the trivia of
local affairs in Vienna, culled from the inside pages of the daily
newspapers. What has taken place is an intensification of the satirical
response. The challenging dynamism of the satiric monologue arises
precisely because apocalyptic conclusions are drawn from such
apparently commonplace material and trivial symptoms. The overall
structure of Kraus's discourse becomes hyperbolic: the thousandth
performance of a meretricious operetta may lead the satirist to
foretell the End of the World.

'Apokalypse' (October 1908) is the earliest of Kraus's essays in
which we hear the voice of the visionary satirist. But although this
essay contains some of his most penetrating aphoristic insights, it is
not characteristic of his narrative method, and is ultimately
unsatisfying as an imaginative experience. It is unsatisfying precisely
because it fails to establish that tension between the trivial experience
and the visionary conclusion in which the challenge of Kraus's satire
lies. The essay falls into two distinct halves; but there is no
heightening of the tension as the argument advances. After the
dazzling display of aphorisms which gives such energy to the first,
more apocalyptic part of the essay, the attempt to clarify the
relationship between author and audience which forms the second
part of the essay (and justifies its subtitle 'Open Letter to the Public')
comes as something of an anticlimax. In its first part the essay offers
a panorama of a chaotic and disintegrating world, in which a figure

with features reminiscent of Kaiser Wilhelm II appears as apocalyptic horseman, with power 'to take peace from the earth' (*F* 261–2: 4). Kraus gives additional resonance to this vision by invoking passages from the book of Revelation. But it took no special effort of the imagination to see Wilhelm II in October 1908 as a threat to the peace of Europe. This had, after all, been one of Maximilian Harden's main themes for a number of years.

The point becomes even clearer when we consider 'Apokalypse' in the context of the *Fackel* in which it appeared. This same number contains the essay 'Die Malerischen (Phantasien einer Italienreise)', a feuilletonistic piece on the tribulations of being a tourist:

Der Hotelportier ist eine Person, die namentlich auf Reisen stört. [. . .] Indem er sich wie der leibhaftige Vertreter des Herrn Cook gebärdet — jener sagenhaften Persönlichkeit, unter der man sich etwa einen Columbus von fünf Weltteilen vorstellen mag —, dirigiert er die Passagiere immer dorthin, wohin sie eigentlich nicht gelangen wollten. Ich kann und will es nicht sagen, in wie viel unrechte Züge ich auf den Rat der Portiers gestiegen bin, denen ich auf meinen Reisen zu begegnen das Glück hatte. Was den Hotelportier, der auf der Höhe der Situation steht, vor allem auszeichnet, das ist die Präzision der falschen Auskunft [. . .]

(*F* 261–2: 19–20)

(The hotel porter is a person who particularly incommodes one when one is travelling [. . .]. Comporting himself as if he were the living representative of Mr Cook — that legendary personality whom one may imagine as a kind of Columbus of five continents —, he invariably directs passengers to the place where they didn't really want to go. I cannot and will not say how many wrong trains I have boarded on the advice of the hotel porters whom I had the fortune to meet on my travels. What above all distinguishes the hotel porter who is really at the top of his form is the precision of the false information he gives. [. . .])

The imagination at work in this passage is deficient in satirical energy. And no meaningful connection is established between the resigned irony of the *flâneur* and the despairing cry of the apocalyptic satirist, who in the same number of *Die Fackel* asks the question:

Was vermag nun ein Satirenschreiber vor einem Getriebe, dem ohnedies in jeder Stunde ein Hohngelächter der Hölle antwortet? Er vermag es zu hören, dieweil die anderen taub sind. Aber wenn er nicht gehört wird? Und wenn ihm selbst bange wird?

(*F* 261–2: 7)

(What is the writer of satire capable of in the face of this bedlam, to which in any case at every hour the derisive mirth of hell gives an answer? He is capable of hearing it, whilst the others remain deaf. But what if he is not heard? And if he himself is consumed with apprehension?)

Neither of these two narrative responses is entirely convincing, the one being too indulgent, the other too extreme. Taken together, they show that at this stage, towards the end of 1908, Kraus has not yet achieved an integrated narrative identity. The inoffensive and long-suffering tourist is confronted by a real world (the world of hotels and railway trains), but the most he can summon up is a wry smile. The apocalyptic satirist is gripped by despair, but it is despair that is not yet clearly related to the everyday experiences of the reader. The perspective of the *flâneur* is not yet assimilated into the scrutiny of the visionary satirist.

CHAPTER 11

Dreams and Nightmares: The Visionary Satirist

Satirical Dreams

Kraus's satire is intensified by means of dreams and visions. So prominent are these dreamlike narratives in the final decade before 1914 that it is surprising they have not received more attention.[1] The imaginative freedom which Kraus gains through them is one reason for regarding his writings of this period as his richest achievement. The literal reader would no doubt take it that Kraus happened to be sleeping rather restlessly; and that being a satirist he naturally dreamt satirical dreams. But these narratives are by no means simply a record of actual dreams. Their structure is essentially literary.

In place of the arbitrary image-sequences of the dream we find a complex texture of motifs, culminating characteristically in a satirical point. This is not to deny that on occasion actual dreams may have provided the writer with his starting-point. But the evidence suggests that in a sustained dream-satire like 'Der Traum ein Wiener Leben' (September 1910) Kraus began with an 'idea', which was then 'embedded' in a dream.[2] For this reason we must be wary of drawing from the numerous 'dreams' in *Die Fackel* any clear-cut psychological conclusions: either that they show the mind of the dreamer to be 'strong' and 'healthy' (Werner Kraft), or that they reveal 'masochistic' tendencies (Manfred Schneider).[3] The dream material is shaped by a conscious artistic purpose.

It is certainly plausible that the stylistic mannerisms of Maximilian Harden should have haunted Kraus's sleeping mind. But the 'dream' which he constructs around this motif in an aphorism of November 1908 is a deft example of indirect satirical attack, concluding in a pun (*F* 264–5: 20–21). A more artistically rounded reworking of this same motif in dream form occurs in a gloss of April 1911, 'Hinaus!' The satirist's dream is here precipitated by the action of his housekeeper in placing on his bed a copy of the *Neue Freie Presse* containing an article by Harden. A glimpse of this article plunges the satirist into a 'trancelike sleep' ('betäubungähnlich' already hints at Harden's orthographic affectations). The gloss concludes with an ironic awakening:

> Als Schnellzug fuhr ich durch den Tunnel, den ich mir durch die Presse gegraben hatte. Ich wäre sonst, da ich unter ihr lag, erstickt. Meine Maschine sauste und es roch weit und breit nach Kaffee. Da brachte ihn die Bedienerin, die ihn eben gemahlen und gekocht hatte, herein und fragte, warum ich heute wieder gar so grantig sei.
>
> (F 321–2: 23–4)

> (Like an express train I raced through the tunnel which I had dug for myself through the press. Otherwise I would have suffocated, since I lay underneath it. My machine was roaring, and far and wide there was a smell of coffee. It was then brought in by my housekeeper, who had just ground and made it, and who asked why I was once again so very peevish today.)

Such satirical dreams have literary antecedents, notably in the work of Heine.

The comparison with Heine is one which Kraus would have repudiated. Yet the closeness of the parallel can hardly be denied. Such dreams are a recurrent feature of Heine's writings. The technique is prefigured in *Die Harzreise*, where Heine's sentimental traveller is visited in his dreams by the leading Berlin rationalist of that period, Dr Saul Ascher. And the obvious prototype for the abrupt awakening of Kraus's satirist by his housekeeper is to be found in Heine's 'Seegespenst', where the dreaming poet is rudely awakened by the ship's captain.[4] This is not to suggest that Kraus's gloss is consciously derivative. On the contrary, it is the strongest testimony to the existence of literary archetypes that, at a time when Kraus was so determined to differentiate his work from the Heine tradition, we nevertheless find him using analogous forms.

In Heine, the dream is characteristically a vehicle for self-irony. As a mechanism for the disillusionment of the dreamy poet (and the sentimental reader) it has its satirical value; but its effect is diminished by predictable repetition. Kraus uses the dream with greater economy and control. His dream sequences, although as dramatic as Heine's, are less obviously 'staged'. They have some of the sophistication of modern stream-of-consciousness technique. Where Heine's dreams invite us to take flight into a realm of fantasy, Kraus's are imaginative reworkings of the materials of everyday experience. But the implications of 'Hinaus!' are limited by the Heinesque structure of self-irony. Set against the 'real world' of housekeepers

and coffee pots, the satirist's vision is merely personal peevishness.
The point of the narrative is turned against the dreamer himself. In
order to achieve a fully satirical impact, this subjective susceptibility
must be endowed with more general validity.

This problem forms the theme of a dream-aphorism of February
1911:

> Mir träumte, sie glaubten mir nicht, daß ich Recht habe. Ich
> behauptete, es wären ihrer zehn. Nein, zwölf, sagten sie. So viel Finger
> an beiden Händen sind, sagte ich. Da hob einer die Hand und siehe, sie
> hatte sechs Finger. Also elf, sagte ich und appellierte an die andere Hand.
> Und siehe, sie hatte sechs Finger. Schluchzend lief ich in den Wald.
>
> (F 317–18: 32)

> (I dreamed that they refused to believe that what I said was right. I
> maintained that there were ten of them. No, twelve, they said. As many
> as there are fingers on a pair of hands, I said. Then one of them raised his
> hand and behold it had six fingers. All right then, eleven, I said, appealing
> to the other hand. And behold it had six fingers. Sobbing I ran into the
> forest.)

This time there is no self-irony. Kraus's symbolism invests the
dreamer with a representative significance. He is the protagonist of
the natural order, which he invokes in the shape of the human hand;
and it is in nature that he finally takes refuge. He may be put to flight
by the nightmare logic of adversaries, in whom the order of nature
has been overthrown. But his defeat symbolizes a general dilemma.
This image of anomic disorder is reminiscent of the dream-parables
of Kafka. And Kraus would have endorsed Kafka's dictum: 'Dreams
reveal a reality which is beyond rational conception. That is what is
so terrible about life and so profoundly disturbing about art.'[5] These
nightmares illuminate a reality which the normal eye is too
insensitive to perceive. In this both Kraus and Kafka are disciples of
Strindberg.

Dream structures are well designed to express incipient anomie.
This is the theme of 'Der Traum ein Wiener Leben' (September
1910). It finds even more condensed expression in 'Die Vision vom
Wiener Leben' (May 1911). This collage of sounds and images from
the streets of Vienna is not overtly introduced as a dream: it is
presented as a direct impression of life in this disorganized and
anachronistic city. But it culminates in a surrealistic sequence of
images:

> Die Pferde hängen in der Luft. Oder sie kreuzen fidel die Beine wie die
> Kutscher. Die Ringstraße ist von einem gut gezwirbelten Schnurrbart
> ausgefüllt. Man kann nicht vorbei, ohne anzustoßen. Das Leben vergeht,
> ehe er sich entfernt hat. Der Mann ist höher als das Haus im Hintergrund.

Er verdeckt den Himmel. Das Leben rings ist tot. Ich ging durch die
verlängerte Kärntnerstraße. Eine Rauchwolke stieg in die Nacht.
Allmählich zeigten sich die Konturen. Ein Einspänner stand da und tat es
mitten auf der Straße. Er fragte, ob ich fahren wolle. Ich erschoß mich.
                                                              (F 323: 24)

(The horses hang suspended in mid-air. Or they jauntily cross their legs
like the coachmen. The Ringstrasse is completely filled by a well twirled
moustache. One can't get past without bumping into it. Life will have
gone past by the time it has gone away. The man is taller than the house
in the background. He blocks out the sky. Life all around is dead. I
walked through the extension of the Kärntnerstrasse. A pillar of cloud
rose into the night. Gradually the contours became apparent. A cab-
driver stood there and did it in the middle of the street. He asked if I
wanted a ride. I shot myself dead.)

Clearly, this is hardly the imagery of an actual dream. Kraus even
indicates that the stimulus for his surrealistic images derived from a
visual source — the gauche cartoons of Schönpflug (from the
magazine *Die Muskete*).[6] And again there are echoes of a literary
paradigm. The aphorism concludes with a suicidal gesture
reminiscent of Heine. In a well-known poem, 'Mein Herz, mein
Herz ist traurig', Heine lulls his readers into a mood of false serenity
through a series of idyllic images, only to spring a suicidal impulse
on us in the final line ('Ich wollt, er schösse mich tot').[7] The suicide
of Kraus's satirist is equally implausible.

A more problematic element enters Kraus's dream satire when he
narrows his focus on the Viennese scene to one specific figure — the
'Wagentürlaufmacher'. This 'door-opener' (the man who makes his
living from the tips he receives for opening carriage doors) forms a
leitmotif in *Die Fackel* in the last years before the First World War; and
on several occasions he appears in the satirist's dreams. He is one of the
incidental figures in 'Die Vision vom Wiener Leben'. And in January
1912 he becomes the subject of a satirical vision in his own right:

Vision vom Wagentürlaufmacher

Und sie lebten vom Gruß. Ein Volk von Wagentürlaufmachern, das
ich aber nicht, wie jene tristen Antiösterreicher, wegen seiner Unfreiheit
hasse, sondern wegen meiner Freiheit. Allerwärts sprang einer aus dem
Boden, den man nicht brauchen konnte und der darum den Hut zog.
Fuhr ich, so lief einer nach; denn ich fuhr und er hatte den Schlag noch
nicht geöffnet. War weit und breit kein Wagen zu sehen, so war ein
Mann, der öffnete. Er muß von fernher gekommen sein, atemlos, aber er
hatte geahnt, daß ich ihn nicht werde brauchen können, und erschien wie
der Blitz. Nein, das Pflaster hatte ihn
ausgespieen. Es ist unbegreiflich. Er entstand vor meinen Augen, hier
war er noch nicht und hier ist er schon. So tanzt er vor mir her und macht
ohne Dank die Gebärde, als ob er auf eine Klinke drückte. Sie ist ihm

Unterpfand seiner Hoffnung und alles. Ich fasse die unsichtbare Klinke und wehre mich mit Geistesgegenwart. Ein betrunkener Kutscher muß mich dorthin geführt haben, wohin ich nicht sollte. Er ist mit Dem im Bunde, der von der Klinke nicht läßt. Jetzt klirrt ein Fenster, die Klinke bleibt, an ihr eine Hand, an ihr ein Mann, der mit der anderen Hand unaufhörlich eine Mütze zieht. Er wird nicht müde, denn er wechselt ab. Er erklärt sich zu Überstunden bereit. Nun halte ich einen Leichenwagen an und frage, ob er frei sei. Wer aber beschreibt mein Erstaunen, als ich — oh letzter Gruß!

(F 341–2: 56)

(*Vision of the Door-Opener*/And they lived by salutation. A nation of door-openers, which I, unlike those miserable anti-Austrians, hate not because of its unfreedom, but because of my freedom. Everywhere there sprang out of the ground a person who was quite useless and who for that reason doffed his hat. If I took a ride, one of them ran after me; for I was travelling, and he hadn't yet opened the carriage door. If there was no carriage to be seen for miles around, there was still a man who opened. He must have come from far afield, breathless, but he had sensed that I could not have any use for him, and appeared like lightning. No, it was the pavement that spewed him up. It is incomprehensible. He came into being before my very eyes, one moment he didn't yet exist and the next he is here already. Thus he dances along in front of me and without thanks makes the gesture of one who is turning a door-handle. The handle is for him the pledge of his hope and his everything. I seize the invisible door-handle and with presence of mind resist his attentions. A drunken coachman must have driven me to some place where I don't belong. He is in league with that man who won't let go of the door-handle. Now a window rattles, the handle remains behind, attached to it a hand, attached to that a man who with his other hand is incessantly doffing his cap. He never tires, for he takes it in turns. He declares himself ready to work overtime. Now I halt a passing hearse and ask whether it is vacant. How can I describe my amazement when suddenly — oh final salutation!)

The conclusion is one that has been anticipated in an earlier satirical dream. At the door of the hearse (perhaps of the coffin itself) the obsequious door-opener will still be there (F 315–16: 35).

At first sight Kraus's satirical vision might be taken as an image of alienated labour, showing us a human automaton ceaselessly going through the motions of opening a door and doffing his cap. But the problem is that the centre of sympathy lies not with the door-opener, but with the long-suffering narrator. It is the infringement of *his* freedom that we are invited to deplore, not the unfreedom of others. Poor fellow, to be pursued by the attentions of thinly disguised beggars, when all he wants is to ride in a carriage! The perspective is unmistakably privileged. The lower orders (by implication) are supposed to remain out of sight. Their function is to provide services for the convenience of the bourgeoisie, as cab-drivers, waiters or railway porters. They are to be efficient, but unobtrusive. And this, in Kraus's satirical picture of Viennese life, is the nub of the matter. For in Vienna such servants of the public insisted on asserting their individuality. And this disrupted Kraus's ideal scheme of a society in which smoothly-running public services allow the intellectual *his* freedom to cultivate the mind.

Kraus's door-opener is a Dickensian comic character portrayed without Dickens's human sympathy. He is seen as 'an alien individual with bare feet', who insists on opening carriage doors and letting in the wind and the rain (F 323: 23). There is no flicker of interest in what life might be like out there in the rain with no shoes. The perspective combines bourgeois self-centredness with political mystification. The sudden appearance of the door-opener is 'incomprehensible'; he is simply 'spewed up' by the pavement. This image acquires a bitter irony when one reflects that the down-and-outs of Vienna really did sleep in the subterranean drainage system which ran near the street where Kraus lived.[8]

Kraus was by no means unaware that offers of superfluous services occur when a society fails to provide employment of a more worthwhile kind. The consequences of unemployment had been memorably brought home to him by an episode which he records in May 1914. In the early days of *Die Fackel* an apprentice had been needed to help with administrative duties, and this post had been advertised in the press. As a result, 400 applicants turned up outside the office of *Die Fackel* clamouring for the job. And Kraus records that when he arrived that day, he found that the office was being invaded and a political agitator was making a speech. Characteristically, it is the foreground phenomenon (the agitator's political rhetoric) that Kraus finds significant in this scene, not the social reality of unemployment. The spuriousness of such political rhetoric leads him to the conclusion that *all* politics is a hollow fraud (F 399: 14–17). He thus denies himself the means of analysing the root causes of social phenomena like the door-openers.

Paradoxically, it is precisely this lack of political clarity that gives the 'Vision vom Wagentürlaufmacher' its deeper resonance. For it is far more politically suggestive than Kraus intended. Lacking in social realism, it nevertheless has a fundamental truthfulness. This redeeming quality arises from the consistency with which Kraus sustains the nightmare. There is no awakening. The door-opener may be a pest, but his attentions are inescapable. Both dreamer and door-opener are gripping the same invisible door-handle and neither is willing to let go. And when the narrator denounces the Austrians

as a 'nation of door-openers', he cannot exclude himself, even
though he happens to be on the other side of the door. Hence the
logic with which the satirical dreamer is driven towards suicide. The
situation at the carriage door is portrayed as a complete impasse,
which can only be resolved by the death of one of the antagonists. It
is this extremity of vision that brings Kraus's satirical nightmare into
proximity with Kafka's famous parable of the door-keeper, 'Vor
dem Gesetz', written two years later. But Kraus's nightmare has
political as well as existential implications.

The dream satire becomes most eloquent in Kraus's own favoured
spheres: the critique of mass communications, technological
progress, and sexual hypocrisy. 'Die Welt der Plakate' transposes the
faces and slogans of advertising posters into the grotesque figures of
a nightmare, culminating in the slogan of the arms dealer: 'Murder
yourself!' (F 283–4: 25). Even a brochure advertising the Brockhaus
encyclopaedia acquires (in 'Der kleine Brockhaus') hallucinatory
powers. For Kraus's narrative consciousness, drifting with a touch of
fever across the margins between waking and sleeping, this encyclopaedia constitutes an injury to the spirit:

> Wo wird die Mutter sein, die uns Erwachsenen die Stirn hält, wenn wir
> einmal die ganze Bildung von uns geben! Was mir dort im Leben
> widersteht, nehme ich in meinen Traum herüber, und da hatte ich
> kürzlich etwas Fieber und dachte, jetzt, ach, jetzt müßte ich den kleinen
> Brockhaus brechen.   (F 339–40: 20)

> (Where shall we find a mother to hold us grown-ups by the forehead,
> when the time comes for us to bring up the whole of our education! The
> things that are repugnant to me in life I carry over with me into my
> dreams, and just recently I had a touch of fever and thought, now, ah,
> now I would have to throw up the shorter Brockhaus encyclopaedia.)

Dreams are by implication assigned a therapeutic function. But
what follows in Kraus's text is a kind of arrested dream. It is as if the
material absorbed by the waking consciousness is too indigestible to
be broken down during the processes of sleep. Hence chunks of
information are regurgitated: a publicity blurb singing the praises of
the encyclopaedia in quantitative terms ('2,100 pages, 80,000 entries,
168 supplements, 4,500 illustrations, 128 plates, 431 maps'); fragments of the useless information the encyclopaedia contains (about
the Capitol in Washington or the railway between Listowel and
Ballybunion); a literary cliché which identifies the Brockhaus as 'the
phoenix among works of reference'; a list of people in all walks of life
who allegedly need the encyclopaedia, culminating in 'the travelling
salesman, who never wants to be disconcerted by anything' ('der

Reisende, der sich nicht verblüffen lassen will'); and then a final sentence from the Brockhaus publicity brochure:

'Daher ist sein Platz an der Seite jedes arbeitsamen Menschen, der den Anforderungen seines Berufes gerecht werden will und kein beschämenderes Wort kennt als das Eingeständis: "Das weiß ich nicht".' — — Ich schäme mich zu schlafen, seitdem ich diesen Satz gelesen habe. Denn sie fangen jetzt an, schon zu wissen, wie man zu träumen hat. Und es gibt nicht Nacht mehr und Nebel, nicht Schleier noch Schatten. Und ich schäme mich zu sterben, seitdem ich diesen Satz gelesen habe. Denn ein Reisender, der sich nicht verblüffen lassen will, wird sich über mich neigen und mir die Augen aufreißen.   (F 339–40: 21)

('For this reason its place is at the side of every diligent person, who wants to measure up to the demands of his profession and who can think of no more shameful phrase than the admission: "I just don't know".' — — I am ashamed to sleep since I read this sentence. For they are now beginning to know how one is supposed to dream. And there is no more night or nebula, no shroud nor shade. And I am ashamed to die since I read this sentence. For a travelling salesman, who never wants to be disconcerted by anything, will bend down over me and tear my eyes wide open.)

This seems like the conclusion of a nightmare; but it is the nightmare of a mind which has been prevented from falling asleep by the intrusive pressures of a rationalistic civilization.

In such pieces Kraus succeeds in investing his satirical dreams with a representative significance. In other contexts he inverts the relationship between dream and reality, asserting that reality itself has assumed the aspect of a dream. The dream structure in 'Der Traum ein Wiener Leben' is inverted in the same number of Die Fackel by a gloss with the title 'Das Wiener Leben ein Traum', which reprints verbatim fragments of newspaper reports about Viennese traffic accidents (F 307–8: 34–5). There is in this text no subjective contribution by the narrator (apart from one comic interpolation identified as 'Anm. des Träumers' — 'Dreamer's Footnote'); the recapitulated facts themselves are grotesquely dreamlike. The implications of this motif are made even more explicit in Die Fackel of 1 April 1911, where inflated newspaper reports about Austrian nonentities are glossed with the words: 'Dieses Staatswesen ist ja ein Angsttraum, gewiß; aber solche Übertriebenheiten kommen selbst in einem Angsttraum nicht vor. (The state in which we live is a nightmare, certainly; but even in a nightmare one does not find exaggerations on this scale.)' (F 319–20: 17)

Factual reports about Austrian affairs can plausibly be reprinted under headings like 'Ein Fiebertraum' (F 324–5: 28), 'Fiebertraum im

Sommerschlaf' (F 331–2: 30) and 'Was man im Traum aufsagen kann' (F 338: 3). This becomes a recurrent motif in Kraus's writings in the final years before 1914. Indeed he originally intended to give *Die letzten Tage der Menschheit* itself the subtitle 'Ein Angsttraum' (F 406–12: 166). This inversion of the dream–reality relationship is an ingenious device for putting familiar materials into satirical perspective. The newspaper clichés which the normal reader absorbs unthinkingly at the breakfast table are revealed as a trance-inducing ritual with horrendous consequences.

The satirist may claim that his only function is to cut out the nightmare images of contemporary life from the daily newspapers, and to reproduce them in a typographically appropriate form (F 366–7: 32). But this must not blind us to the importance of Kraus's subjective contribution. Alongside the many glosses which owe their impact to direct quotation, we find other passages where he assumes the subjective voice of the visionary satirist. There is a marked intensification as the dreamer becomes the visionary, who perceives all around him portents of destruction.

Apocalyptic Visions

'Das Erdbeben' (February 1908) is the first of Kraus's full-scale satirical visions. This light-hearted piece illustrates the heightening of narrative response towards apocalyptic premonition. It arises from the contrast between the frivolity of the carnival and the reverberations of a minor earth tremor: 'Schon vom Faschingsabend des Männergesangvereins hatte ich mir alles Mögliche versprochen, und ich finde einigen Trost bei dem Gedanken, daß wenigstens ein schwaches Erdbeben die Antwort auf die Enthüllungen war, die dieses Fest unseren entsetzten Blicken geboten hat. (I was already expecting the worst after the fancy-dress ball of the Vienna Male Voice Choir, and it gives me some consolation to think that at least a slight earth tremor was the answer to the revelations which this festivity offered to our horrified gaze.)' (F 245: 16) There follows a list of characteristic costumes and charades: a married couple dressed up as vegetables, the daughter of an industrialist representing the 'growing coal shortage' ('wachsende Kohlennot'). All of this was reported at fulsome length in both the liberal and the nationalist press, and nonentities with incongruous names like Koritschoner are given credit for leading the song and dance.

One snatch of song in particular provokes the satirist into a response which echoes the tragic pathos of the final act of *King Lear*:

Wiener Mode, Wiener Schick,
Wiener Pülcher, Burgmusik,

> Wiener Würsteln, Wiener Madeln,
> G'stellt vom Kopf bis zu die Wadeln — —
> 'Ist dies das verheißne Ende? Sind's Bilder jenes Grauens?' Bezeichnet dies
> Durcheinander von Pülchern, Würsteln und Madeln, wie Wiens beste
> Schätze zu liegen kommen werden, wenn das Unabwendbare eintreten
> wird? . . . Ich sah nach der Magnetnadel. Und richtig, sie zeigte eine
> merkliche Abweichung der Gehirne. Kaum war der Bericht im
> 'Deutschen Volksblatt' erschienen, gab's ein Erdbeben. Nun, dachte ich
> mir, aber jetzt wird für ein Weilchen Ruhe sen. Wir sind gemahnt
> worden.   (F 245: 18)

> (Vienna's clothes, the smartest trend,
> Vienna's tramps, the palace band,
> Vienna sausage, Viennese girls,
> With lissom calves and saucy curls — —
> 'Is this the promised end? Or image of that horror?' Does this chaotic
> mixture of tramps, sausages and girls indicate how Vienna's most
> precious treasures will be strewn around, when the inevitable occurs? . . .
> I checked the magnetic needle. Sure enough, it registered an aberration
> amounting to softening of the brain. Hardly had the report appeared in
> the *Deutsches Volksblatt*, when an earthquake occurred. Now, I said to
> myself, now at last we'll have a bit of peace. We have received a solemn
> warning.)

If the satirist really believes that the earthquake will be taken as a warning, he is soon undeceived. For an earthquake, to the inhabitants of his Vienna, merely provides a further pretext for a carnival, this time played out in the form of letters to the press. Everyone who has felt the slightest tremor gets his name in the newspapers, right down to the chauffeur of the librettist of *The Merry Widow*. And the satirist finally himself joins in the fray. Under the name of 'Zivilingenieur J. Berdach, Wien II, Glockengasse 17', he concocts a letter full of pretentious pseudo-scientific jargon distinguishing 'tellurian' from 'cosmic' earthquakes. This letter was sent to the *Neue Freie Presse*, where it actually appeared. Now at last we seem to have the satirist placed; to make his critical point, he is prepared to become a practical joker and himself assume a false identity in this carnival of stupidity.

Once again, however, the mood of the narrative changes. Delight over a successful hoax gives way to the pathos of a visionary peroration:

> Nein, das war doch kein tellurisches, das war ein kosmisches
> Erdbeben. Das war die Dummheit! Und es war eine Probe, wie sich der
> Wiener beim Weltuntergang, der in diesem Jahr bestimmt stattfindet,
> benehmen wird. Das kann schön werden! Wir werden uns wieder einmal
> so benehmen, daß wir uns vor dem Ausland schämen müssen. Eine

Schlamperei wird herrschen, die ohne Beispiel sein dürfte. Die Flüsse
werden zu spät stehen bleiben und die Erde wird sich unpünktlich öffnen.
Und alle werden auf einmal dabei sein wollen. [. . .] Wiener Pülcher,
Wiener Würsteln, Wiener Madeln, alles liegt durcheinander. Die
wachsende Kohlennot erscheint, und noch einmal zieht der Dr.
Koritschoner mit G'spiel und Musi vorüber. Und das Verhängnis kommt
mit dem großen Reibsackl . . . Alles tot. Nur der letzte Mensch, ein
Lokalredakteur, ruft mit gellender Stimme in das Chaos: Man bemerkte
u.a. Angelo Ei —— Weiter kam er nicht.   (F 245: 24)

(No, that was surely no tellurian, that was a cosmic earthquake. That
was Stupidity! And it was a rehearsal for how the Viennese will behave
when the End of the World comes, as it surely will this year. That will be
a pretty sight! Once again we shall behave in a way that will put us to
shame in the eyes of foreign observers. There will be a muddle of
unprecedented proportions. The rivers too late will cease their flow and
the earth will not open punctually. And everyone will start clamouring at
once to be among those present. [. . .] Vienna's tramps, Vienna
sausage, Viennese girls, everything is strewn around in confusion. The
growing coal shortage appears, and once again Dr. Koritschoner comes
parading past with song and dance. And Destiny comes with its great
duster to wipe the board clean . . . Everyone dead. Only the last man
alive, a sub-editor responsible for the social page, shouts with a voice
which pierces through Chaos: Prominent among those present was
Angelo Ei —— That is as far as he got.)

How seriously is this vision to be taken? Its playfulness of tone,
culminating in a kind of parody of the Day of Judgement, suggests
that it belongs to the realm of comedy rather than satire. Images of
the Viennese incorrigibly misbehaving themselves, when transported into the presence of higher beings, belong after all to the
stock-in-trade of Austrian popular comedy. 'Das Verhängnis mit
dem großen Reibsackl' seems to be a figure straight off the stage of
the popular theatre. And for the juxtaposition of a supernatural
Destiny with the blithely insouciant Dr Koritschoner it would be
easy to find parallels in the comedies of Raimund and Nestroy. Yet it
is no denial of the comic qualities of 'Das Erdbeben' to insist on its
underlying seriousness. The theme expressed here in the language of
visionary fantasy is an imaginative transposition of Kraus's
fundamental critique. The cult of bread and circuses, institutionalized in carnival and operetta, and the saturation coverage
accorded to these matters in the press, will render his contemporaries
incapable of a sober and realistic response when something really
important turns up.

In this relatively early piece, Kraus is trying on the costume of the
visionary satirist, without yet having fully committed himself to the
role. There is still an element of playfulness in the gestures with which

the satirist consults his compass, anticipates the earthquake, and foresees the end of the world. In 'Apokalypse' (October 1908) and 'Die chinesische Mauer' (July 1909) the visionary perspective is more forcefully sustained and the pathos is no longer tinted with parody. The new urgency of tone in 'Apokalypse' (which appeared on 13 October 1908) reflects the political crisis caused by the annexation of Bosnia and Hercegovina. The annexation of the two provinces had been proclaimed just eight days earlier. It put an end to a decade of relative tranquility in Austrian affairs; and it led to a rapid darkening of the horizon of European politics, as a succession of crises (the *Daily Telegraph* affair, Morocco, the Balkans, Sarajevo) brought the nations increasingly close to conflict. The apocalyptic stance now finds a sanction in technological developments and political events. The airship becomes the key symbol of that conquest of the skies which seems to the satirist so ominous. An airship, and the storm which has brought it down, acquire archetypal implications:

> Aber siehe, die Natur hat sich gegen die Versuche, eine weitere Dimension für die Zwecke der zivilisatorischen Niedertracht zu mißbrauchen, aufgelehnt und den Pionieren der Unkultur zu verstehen gegeben, daß es nicht nur Maschinen gibt, sondern auch Stürme! 'Hinausgeworfen ward der große Drache, der alle Welt verführt, geworfen ward er auf die Erde . . . Er war nicht mächtig genug, einen Platz im Himmel zu behaupten.' [. . .]
> Die Natur mahnt zur Besinnung über ein Leben, das auf Äußerlichkeiten gestellt ist. Eine kosmische Unzufriedenheit gibt sich allenthalben kund [. . .].   (*F* 261–2: 1–2)

> (But behold, Nature has rebelled against the attempt to exploit a further dimension for the purposes of a despicable form of civilization, and has given the agents for the destruction of culture to understand that it is not only machines that exist, but also storms! 'The great dragon was cast out, which deceiveth the whole world; he was cast out into the earth . . . And he prevailed not, neither was his place found any more in heaven.' [. . .]
> Nature admonishes us to reflect upon a life that is devoted to externals. A cosmic dissatisfaction manifests itself on all sides [. . .].)

The satirist here speaks in the language of biblical prophecy, invoking the famous passage from the Book of Revelation, chapter 9, about War in Heaven.

In October 1908 Kraus had not yet integrated this visionary perspective with the more casual stance of the *flâneur*. But increasingly his discourse acquires archetypal undertones. Complementary to his critique of technological civilization is his apotheosis of the forces of nature. This reaches its climax in the final years before 1914 in a visionary assault on sexual hypocrisy. The archetype of Pandora, avenging spirit of love, is fused with that of Ephialtes, the demon of nightmares (F 354–6: 4). These visions of retributive nature reach their climax in 'Die chinesische Mauer', published in *Die Fackel* in July 1909 and in book form with lithographs by Kokoschka in March 1914.

This satire is a response to a sexual scandal in New York, which revealed that a white woman missionary had had a series of love affairs with members of the Chinatown community, whom she was supposed to be converting to Christianity.[9] This elicits a grandiose indictment of the hypocrisy of western civilization:

> Hier ist alles problematisch geworden, was sich seit zwei Jahrtausenden von selbst versteht. Auf einem Krater, den wir erloschen wähnten, haben wir unsere Hütten gebaut, mit der Natur in einer menschlichen Sprache geredet, und weil wir die ihre nicht verstanden, geglaubt, sie rühre sich nicht mehr. Sie aber hat durch all die Zeit ihre heißen Feste gefeiert und an unserer gottseligen Sicherheit ihren Erdenbrand genährt. Wir haben die Sexualität für verjährt gehalten; wir haben die Konvention getroffen, von ihr nicht mehr zu sprechen. [. . .] Wir haben uns vermessen, an dem heiligen Feuer, das einst den männlichen Geist zu Taten erhitzte, unsere Füße zu wärmen. Nun zündet es uns das Haus an.
>
> (F 285–6: 2–4)

> (All that has been taken for granted for two thousand years has here become problematic. Upon a crater, which we deludedly believed to be extinct, we have built our huts, have spoken to Nature in a human voice, believing, because we did not understand hers, that she was no longer active. Through all this time, however, she has been celebrating her hot festivals and nourishing her terrestrial fire on our pious sense of security. We have considered sexuality to be out of date; we have established the convention of not talking about it any more. [. . .] We have had the temerity to warm our feet at the sacred flame that once fired the manly spirit to deeds. Now it is setting our house ablaze.)

In earlier essays on sexual themes Kraus had been the advocate of enlightened reform. In 'Die chinesische Mauer', he speaks as one who welcomes the destruction of western civilization. His visionary peroration forsees the shattering of the Great Wall erected by Christian morality and the unleashing of the forces of chaos:

> Da schlägt die Menschheit an das große Tor und ein Weltgehämmer hebt an, daß die chinesische Mauer ins Wanken gerät. Und das Chaos sei willkommen; denn die Ordnung hat versagt. Eine gelbe Hoffnung färbt den Horizont im Osten, und alle Glocken läuten Sturm. Und überall ein Gewimmel. 'Aus dem Rauche des Schlundes kamen Heuschrecken über die Erde und ihnen ward Macht gegeben, wie die Skorpionen auf Erden Macht haben . . . [. . .] Und die Zahl des Heerzuges der Reiterei war zweihundert Millionen. Ich hörte ihre Zahl . . .'   (F 285–6: 16)

(And now mankind beats at the great gate and a universal hammering begins that makes the great Chinese wall start to tremble. And let Chaos be welcome; for Order has failed. A yellow hope tinges the horizon in the east, and all the tocsins are ringing. And a swarm on all sides. 'And there came out of the smoke locusts upon the earth: and unto them was given power, as the scorpions of the earth have power . . . [. . .] And the number of the army of the horsemen were two hundred thousand thousand: and I heard the number of them . . . ')

Once again, the language of Revelation (chapter 9) is used to portend chaos. Civilization, in its attempt to tame sexuality, has 'spoken to Nature in a human voice'. The satirist replies in the voice of apocalyptic prophecy. This vision, which Kraus repeatedly declaimed from the public platform in the years 1911–14, made his reputation as the prophet of the decline of the west. And the Asiatic hordes, which for the satirist tinge the eastern horizon with hope, were vividly rendered in visual terms by Kokoschka's lithograph (see Pl. 25).

The Book of Revelation does more than merely provide a source of quotation. Its language colours Kraus's own style, his use of prose rhythms, his invocation of mythic forces: 'But behold, Nature has rebelled'; 'And now mankind beats at the great gate.' This prophetic voice also has antecedents in a more specifically German tradition. It is scarcely a coincidence that we find Kraus in this period expressing such admiration for the work of Jean Paul. He admired not only the reverential attitude in Jean Paul's descriptions of nature, but also the imaginative power of his visionary writings — the *Traumdichtungen*. In a public reading of November 1912 Kraus recited the most celebrated of these writings, 'Rede des toten Christus vom Weltgebäude herab, daß kein Gott sei'. And there are clear echoes of Jean Paul in Kraus's own visionary style. The 'Rede des toten Christus' reaches its climax in phrases like: 'alles wurde eng, düster, bang – und ein unermeßlich ausgedehnter Glockenhammer sollte die letzte Stunde der Zeit schlagen und das Weltgebäude zersplittern.'[10] Kraus's use of phrases like 'Bis das Weltgebäude zusammenkracht' and 'ein Weltgehämmer hebt an, daß die chinesische Mauer ins Wanken gerät' reveals his indebtedness. Heine's dreams have now been displaced by Jean Paul's visions.

The most striking feature of this style is its expressive range: from biblical prophecy and impassioned invective to caustic wit and crude colloquialism. Contemporary events are transfigured at one moment by the visionary language of Luther, the next by the anarchic fantasy of Petronius (*F* 241: 11). Kraus avoids the trap into which Nietzsche fell when he adopted the stance of the Seer. In *Also sprach Zarathustra* Nietzsche uses a diction so elevated that it rapidly becomes monotonous. It is a work lacking in stylistic tension and, for all its renown,

25   *The Invaders:* Kokoschka's lithograph for *Die chinesische Mauer*

one of the least incisive of Nietzsche's writings. By contrast, Kraus's prophetic voice retains variety, flexibility, unpredictability. The reader can never be sure whether the satirist's response will take the form of pathos or of pun.

A writer with a prophetic vision needs a community to which he may appeal. Nietzsche could address only a future generation, but Kraus was more fortunate. In Vienna he found an audience uniquely receptive to his work. After 1910 the circulation of *Die Fackel* soared; and at his public readings the auditoriums were packed with enthusiastic listeners. The public reception of his work (both his books and his readings) is fully documented in *Die Fackel*. Kraus has often been reproached for devoting so much space to these reviews (many of them fulsome in their praise). Even his admirers have accused him of vanity on this account.[11] No doubt he was gratified (after the ten-year conspiracy of silence with which his work had been surrounded by the Viennese press) to find himself so widely praised. But the question of personal vanity hardly concerns us.

The reprinting of these reviews established not simply his personal fame, but his public role. A social role achieves its significance only through interaction with an audience. In Kraus's earliest form of 'Selbstbespiegelung', we find his identity — that of the 'artist' — reflected only in the mirror of his own style. The circulation of *Die Fackel* even declined during the 'artistic' period, so that in the autumn of 1908 Kraus was contemplating its closure (F 261–2: 1). But now, as visionary satirist proclaiming his message from the public stage, he found his identity endorsed by the community. The self-indulgent artist has become the archetypal satirist — a publicly acknowledged role with its roots in heroic tradition.

It is this paradox of identity and role that Walter Benjamin had in mind when he wrote (of Kraus's public readings): 'It is only here that the true face, or rather the true mask of the satirist becomes visible.'[12] For Benjamin, Kraus's whole enterprise as a publicist was shaped by his indebtedness to Shakespearean paradigms — the Fool, Caliban, above all Timon, the implacable enemy of mankind. Like Shakespeare, Kraus was both author and actor of his own roles. He may not have been fully conscious of the process, since it was inherent in his histrionic temperament (what Benjamin calls Kraus's *daimon*). Although Benjamin is writing of a later period, it is important to recall that Kraus gave his first public reading from *Timon of Athens* as early as December 1914. At a time when censorship inhibited individual utterance, he was content to define his own position through Shakespeare's imprecations against mankind.

This self-assimilation to literary paradigms is even more potent when Shakespearean lines are integrated into Kraus's own text. A notable instance occurs in May 1913. Responding to a caricature which has accentuated his deformed left shoulder, Kraus replies with an impassioned declamation which reaches its climax in words borrowed from *Richard III*:

> And therefore, since I cannot prove a lover,
> To entertain these fair well-spoken days,
> I am determined to prove a villain
> And hate the idle pleasures of these days.
> For I, in this weak piping time of peace,
> Have no delight to pass away the time,
> Unless to spy my shadow in the sun
> And descant on mine own deformity.

                                                                (F 374–5: 38)

Schlegel's translation of these lines is assimilated almost imperceptibly into Kraus's monologue, so that the contemporary audience must have had difficulty in telling which voice they were actually hearing — Kraus or Shakespeare? The answer is that they were hearing the archetypal voice of satirical discourse.

The most explicit definition of Kraus's identity as satirist occurs in his tribute to Nestroy, 'Nestroy und die Nachwelt', read before an audience of 1500 on 2 May 1912. By general consent it is the finest of his literary-critical writings. The account which he gives of Nestroy's satirical genius has influenced the reception of that writer's work ever since.[13] In this essay Kraus achieves an exemplary synthesis between a dissertation on Nestroy and a mirroring of his own identity. His concern is with the problem of 'the satirist', as he later explicitly insisted (F 351–3: 42). Nestroy too was an author who wrote his own roles and performed them on stage with great histrionic flair. For Kraus, the satirist of Biedermeier Vienna can be seen in 1912 as the prophet of Austrian decline. A deep sense of affinity enables him to elicit from his contemplation of Nestroy a definition of the satirist which emphasizes this prophetic function:

> Der satirische Künstler steht am Ende einer Entwicklung, die sich der Kunst versagt. Er ist ihr Produkt und ihr hoffnungsloses Gegenteil. Er organisiert die Flucht des Geistes vor der Menschheit, er ist die Rückwärtskonzentrierung. Nach ihm die Sintflut.
>
> (F 349–50: 23)

> (The satirical artist stands at the end of a development which denies itself to art. He is its product and despairing opposite. He organizes the flight of the spirit from mankind, he is the concentration of energy in reverse. After him the deluge.)

The apocalyptic role which Kraus had begun to adopt in his visionary essays of 1908 and 1909 is here explicitly defined. But the apocalypse is both imminent and immanent. Surrealistic images of the present — as a realm of the living dead — enhance the forebodings of future disaster.

CHAPTER 12

Dance of Death and the Two Runners

The Death of Man

'Death' is the most ominous of the satirist's armoury of metaphors. We are not here concerned with Kraus's personal attitude to dying (though it has been argued that for him, as for Swift and Nestroy, this was an intense preoccupation).[1] Death is a symbolic motif – so prominent in literary satire that there appear to be affinities with primitive soothsaying (Archilochus was reputedly able to pronounce imprecations so potent that his victims actually died).[2] The symbolic 'slaying' of a polemical opponent echoes this tradition. Swift proclaims the 'death' of Partridge the astrologer, Kraus that of Maximilian Harden. 'Death' in this sense signifies the destruction of a reputation.

In Kraus's satire of the final years before 1914 this motif becomes pervasive. It is applied not simply to individual opponents, but to civilization as a whole. The satirist is pictured standing at 'the death-bed of the age' ('Vor dem Totenbett der Zeit', F 400–3: 46). The scene of his artistic activity is 'the death-chamber of mankind' ('das Sterbezimmer der Menschheit', F 360–2: 22). The function of satire is to transcend a 'dead age' ('die tote Zeit', F 349–50: 23). In his visions, the satirist proclaims that 'life all around is dead' ('Das Leben rings ist tot', F 323: 24); and that both the human mind and its cultural ideals are dying a wretched death ('der Geist krepiert', F 368–9: 39). Sexually, too, the white race has become a mere expendable corpse; and the time has come to accompany this corpse to its grave (F 354–6: 4, 70).

The most remarkable expression of this theme is the poem 'Tod und Tango', one of Kraus's first ventures in verse (November 1913). The poem was prompted by reports of a murder, committed by a young man of good family with a responsible position in a bank.

This man together with his wife had been one of the most elegant dancers at the balls of the Viennese social élite. When his wife had sought to divorce him in order to marry another man, the husband had shot her dead with a revolver. He had then turned the weapon against himself, but had survived his wounds. The surprising aspect of the case was that the judicial authorities, having considered psychiatric reports, decided not to proceed against him. He was released and resumed his position at the bank, where he was promptly promoted.

Kraus's initial response to this case (in a gloss of May 1913) is muted. He seems ready to concede that the authorities were right to treat the crime compassionately. And he contents himself with contrasting the case with that of a student who, having survived a suicide pact, finds himself sentenced to death for murder. He pleads for the student to be pardoned and released (F 374–5: 52–4). In this gloss Kraus is not writing as a satirist. He simply argues that the administration of justice should be consistent, as well as humane. But within the next six months his attitude to the first case decisively changes. For it has come to his hearing that the husband who went scot-free after murdering his wife is again to be seen dancing in public. It is now that the perspective of the critical journalist gives way to that of the visionary satirist.

The title 'Tod und Tango' juxtaposes the traditional idea of the dance of death with the most modish of contemporary dance rhythms. The motif of the dance gives unity to what might otherwise be a rambling poem, extending to almost two hundred lines. The basic form is unrhymed iambic pentameter, breaking at crucial moments into rhyme. The style is uncompromisingly colloquial, the movement of the poem implicitly dramatic. The austere voice in which the narrative begins is soon interrupted by interpolations from voices representing other points of view: the trivial comments of the newspapers, the voice of bourgeois self-interest, the gossipy attitude of public opinion.

The narrator's voice too passes through variations of pitch; it rises from irony of understatement to dramatic declamation, as the story of the two dancers (husband and wife) is contrasted with another contemporary case: that of a hysterical woman who, during the change of life, has killed her husband when he tried to leave her. She for her deed is condemned to death, where the rising young man at the bank is promoted:

> Seht hin, o seht, wer für dieselbe Tat
> zum Tod verurteilt, wer befördert wird.
> Seht dieses Jammerbild der greisen Wollust,
> seht, wie der Tod den Lebemann verschont.

(F 386: 23)

(Look there, oh look who for the selfsame deed
is sent to death and who received promotion.
Look at this pitiable case of aging lust,
and look, how Death absolves the Hedonist.)

The language here carries echoes of a medieval morality. The figures
of 'der Tod' and 'der Lebemann' seem to be straight out of Holbein's
Dance of Death.

Kraus attributes the discrepancy in the administration of justice to
the bias of male-oriented courts against women. But in 'Tod und
Tango' he reinforces the critical indictment by means of the
symbolism of the dance. The dance represents the charmed circle of
the upper bourgeoisie. Viennese society cannot afford to lose one of
its best dancers. Kraus extends the image to suggest that the court
procedures themselves form part of the dance. And Themis, goddess
of Justice, finds herself reduced to the status of an indulgent
chaperone. Should this man be excluded, while the world whirls all
around him in the ancient dance? It is at this point that Kraus's blank
verse breaks into heroic couplets:

Wo ist die Tänzerin? 's ist bald ein Jahr,
da fiel sie hin, da lag sie auf der Bahr.
Und er tanzt weiter, Menschen sehen zu,
das Sinnverwirrende läßt ihnen Ruh.
Wer ist es? Wer? Wer betet dort? Wer lebt?
Wer tanzt dort mit dem Knie? Wer springt und schwebt?
O unerhörte Möglichkeit der Welt,
die nicht dem Chaos in die Arme fällt,
die so ermüdet, weiter dazu singt
und so erschüttert, nicht in Splitter springt!
Unschuldig ist der Tänzer, schuld die Zeit,
nicht zu vergehn bei solcher Lustbarkeit!
Die Nacht entflieht vor solchem Solotanz,
doch wird es Tag, und solch ein Tag bleibt ganz.
Und er hat Stunden. Keine aber weckt
das Leben zum Gebet und keine schreckt
die Sünde, keine mahnt und keine klagt
und keine dumpf ihr vivos voco sagt
und keine Glocke weint ihr mortuos plango.
Das Leben starb. Die Mörder tanzen Tango.

(F 386: 24)

(His partner, where is she? 'Tis but a year
that she fell down and lay upon the bier.
And on he dances, people calmly stand
and watch a scene that could unhinge the mind.
Who is it? Who? Who's praying? Who's alive?
Who's kicking up his heels in leap and jive?

> Unprecedented prospect that the world
> into the arms of chaos is not hurled.
> A world so tired, continuing to sing,
> so shaken, and yet never shattering!
> Guiltless the dancer, guilty is the age
> not to expire at such an escapade!
> For such a solo dance drives out the night,
> but day breaks, and the day's not put to flight.
> The hours of day pass by, but none awakes
> life to the need for prayer, no sinner quakes,
> no hour of warning strikes, none of lament,
> and none to its *vivos voco* gives vent
> and no bell sheds the tears of *mortuos plango*.
> Life died. The murderers dance the tango.)

The lines memorably describe a form of life in which the frenzied pursuit of pleasure is accompanied by the death of human feeling. Dancing is portrayed, not as an occasional folly (as in the work of a traditional moralist like Sebastian Brant),[3] but as the symbol of a hedonistic civilization. The visionary perspective opened up in these lines of October 1913 finds its fulfilment in *Die letzte Nacht* (November 1918), where the dance of the Hyenas around the corpses on the battlefield is also set to the rhythm of the tango (*W* v. 750).

In this vision of existence as a living death, what is the position of the satirist himself? At first sight the answer appears simple. He is the seer in the country of the blind. In this realm of the dead, it sometimes seems that the satirist alone is still alive: 'Wer lebt noch außer mir?' is his plaintive cry, towards the end of the visionary poem 'Mein Weltuntergang' (*F* 389–90: 44). Yet the question is more complex. For if Kraus had left the matter there, the satirist would merely be a figure of rhetoric. His self-image is not simply a rhetorical device, however, but a quest for viable identity. And the truthfulness of his vision lies not least in the fact that he does not exclude the satirist from the dance.

This becomes clear when we compare Kraus's conception of himself as artist (in his writings of the period 1905–10) with his self-image as satirist around 1912. The artist is conceived as a self-sufficient figure. His sensitivity sets him apart from the philistinism of the surrounding world. And he tends to stand disdainfully aloof from the nexus of human society. He is essentially an inner-directed figure. This does not however place him in a position of misanthropic isolation; for his artistic endeavour is shared with other creative spirits, whose work finds a forum in *Die Fackel* alongside his own. The figure of the artist is positively orientated towards the future. He is the full man, living ahead of his time. In this sense there is justice in Adolf Loos's tribute to Kraus as a man standing 'at the threshold of a new age'.[4]

As satirist, it is no longer in terms of the inner life that Kraus defines his identity. The satirist's role is one of confrontation. He may denounce and defy the pressures of modern civilization, but he is not able to evade them. For all his aggressive posture, he represents an ideal of human personality that has been forced on to the defensive. *Die Fackel* ceases at this point to be the forum for a community of artists and becomes the solitary place of refuge for a satirist who bears the unmistakable stigma of his age. It is this symbolic self-identification which elicited Brecht's celebrated tribute to Kraus: 'When the age came to die by its own hand, he was that hand.'[5]

Kraus's theme of the death of man achieves its greatest poignancy when it is the satirist himself who succumbs. Where denunciations of the spiritual deadness of his contemporaries are mere invective, the enactment of this theme in his own person has something of the pathos of tragedy. The heroic adversary of the age becomes its hapless victim: 'Die Zeit [. . .] hetzt ihren satirischen Widerpart' (*F* 349–50: 6). And the motif of suicide becomes increasingly prominent, particularly in satirical visions like 'Die Welt der Plakate'. At times Kraus overworks this device by identifying as a 'motive for suicide' some minor irritation. An advertisement showing people guzzling their food and drink is glossed as 'ein Selbstmordmotiv' (*F* 241: 12). So too is a feuilleton by Paul Goldmann, a theatre critic with an inflated reputation (*F* 244: 20). Here the notion of suicide is reduced to a hyperbolic gesture. And the reader may be tempted to reply, as the humorist Roda Roda did in an effective epigram in *Die Muskete*:

> Was ist der Offensive
> Doch für ein seltsamer Gauch!
> Er sammelt Selbstmordmotive
> Und macht davon keinen Gebrauch!
>
> (*F* 253: 22)

> (This man who's so quick to deride
> Is such a peculiar lout!
> Collecting motives for suicide,
> He never carries it out!)

This thrust finds its way through the considerable gap which Kraus leaves between his actual position as a writer and his satirical self-dramatization. At this stage, he has not yet fully committed himself to the role of the satirist; nor has the theme of the death of man assumed central significance.

This theme finds its most explicit expression in the poem 'The Dying Man' ('Der sterbende Mensch', September 1913). It takes the form of a poetic dialogue between 'The Man' and a sequence of interlocutors: Conscience, Memory, The World, Spirit, Doubt, Faith, Wit, The Dog, The Bourgeois, The Whore, and finally the voice of God. In its allegorical form this poem is reminiscent of the final scene of a medieval morality play. Indeed, a parallel may be drawn with Hofmannsthal's German version of *Everyman* (published in 1911).[6] But although Kraus is clearly concerned to invest 'The Man' of his poem with a representative significance, he is not simply an Everyman figure. The poem has a confessional timbre.

Its composition may have been influenced by memories of an actual person – conceivably Kraus's closest friend, Ludwig von Janikowski, who had died two years earlier (F 331–2: 64). But the traits associated with 'The Man' are above all those with which Kraus endows his own self-image: orientation towards the past, rejection of the world, commitment to the spirit, wit and doubt. These qualities are no longer defiantly affirmed. The mood of the poem is defeatist. Composing his thoughts in the hour of death, 'The Man' testifies to the values of an inner world which are impossible to realize here and now. The voice of God does indeed hold out the promise of consolation to one who has remained true to the inner source of his being ('der Ursprung'); but it is only to be attained in the realm of Light, which the Man is about to enter.

This poem about Man at the point of death seems symbolically to express a rather traditional message: that it is necessary to die to the world, in order to live in the realm of the spirit. In traditional religious terms, this would imply the need for some kind of monastic withdrawal into the life of contemplation. But in Kraus's poem the matter is more complex. This three-page poetic dialogue is, after all, printed at the end of a triple number of *Die Fackel* in which, for more than seventy pages, we have seen the satirist wrestling with the evils of the world. In the figure of 'The Dying Man', Kraus can therefore hardly be implying a death-to-the-world in the sense of a literal withdrawal. And the solution which we find implied in his poem is indeed more sophisticated. It occurs in two lines spoken by 'The Man' which draw an explicit conclusion from the dilemmas explored in the dialogue:

> Wer wäre, was er ist, wo Trug und Wesen
> Die Welt vertauscht in jämmerlicher Wahl!

(F 381–3: 76)

> (Who would be what he is, when fraud and being
> are interchanged by this world's dismal choice!)

The antithesis here drawn between 'Trug' and 'Wesen' may seem to echo the medieval polarity of Essence and Accidence. In the theology of traditional Christianity, it is axiomatic that essential being is unattainable in a fallen world. But Kraus's formulation must also be seen against the background of European humanism. Where Christian pessimism presupposes that man must always fall short of the image in which he was created, the fundamental goal of humanism is self-fulfilment in the secular world. The ideal of the whole man is felt to be attainable. Kraus is one of the inheritors of this humanist ideal, transmitted through the writings of Weimar classicism. The ideal of self-cultivation exemplified by Goethe is one of the presuppositions of Kraus's work. And the aesthetic movement of the late nineteenth century, with Wilde as its pivotal figure and the 'artist' as its ideal, provides another channel through which the concept of self-cultivation nourishes his work.

By 1913, however, this vision of self-fulfilment has been abandoned. It is felt to be precluded by the pressures of a hostile world. The lines quoted from 'The Dying Man' indicate that 'fraud' and 'being' have become 'interchanged'. The inner self must die to the world, which can only be confronted in a manner that displays, not the true self, but a kind of protective mask.

The Divided Self

In 'The Dying Man' such a solution is only obliquely implied. The poem proclaims the death of man; but it does not show how, after the necessity of this death-to-the-world has been recognized, one is to go on living. A more explicit clue is provided by a slightly earlier poem, the epigrammatic 'Two Runners' ('Zwei Läufer'). This unpretentious poem was first published without a title in April 1910:

> Zwei Läufer laufen zeitentlang,
> der eine dreist, der andre bang:
> Der von Nirgendher sein Ziel erwirbt;
> der vom Ursprung kommt und am Wege stirbt.
> Der von Nirgendher das Ziel erwarb,
> macht Platz dem, der am Wege starb.
> Und dieser, den es ewig bangt,
> ist stets am Ursprung angelangt.
>
> (F 300: 32)

> (Two runners down time's road have sped,
> one bold, the other full of dread:
> The one from nowhere who reaches his abode;
> the one from the source of life who dies on the road.
> The one from nowhere, after he's arrived,
> has to make way for the one who died.

> The latter, though his days are full of fear,
> knows that the source of life is always near.)

For all its simplicity of construction, this parabolic poem, which epitomizes Kraus's conception of life, lends itself to several levels of interpretation. It offers a variation on the traditional conception of life as a course to be run. And as in the fable of the Tortoise and the Hare, it ends with a reversal of the anticipated outcome. Kraus's two runners seem to represent two very basic human personality types, familiar to us from the language of religion as well as that of social psychology: the children of this world and the children of light; or the other-directed and the inner-directed personality. The inner-directed runner, whose personality is nourished by closeness to the sources of life but whose attitude to experience is apprehensive to the point of dread, is not able to stay the course that leads to the achievement of external goals. The other runner, whose identity has no inner source but whose attitude to life is bold to the point of impudence, easily attains external success. The poem's evaluation of the outcome echoes the traditional religious view: The first shall be last.

It has been suggested that Kraus's concept of 'Ursprung' may be Judaic in origin.[7] But a more specific source may be identified in the sermons of Johannes Tauler, a Dominican monk of the fourteenth century. A new edition of Tauler's sermons was published in 1910, the year that Kraus's poem was composed. And a passage in the very first of these sermons may have caught Kraus's eye. Certain phrases (italicized here for ease of identification) seem to have supplied him with the key images of his poem:

> Darumb ist des himels louf alre edelste und volkomeneste, wan er alre eigenlicheste wider in sinen ursprung und in sinen begin get, do er uzging; alsus ist *des menschen louf* alre edelste und aller volkomenste, wan er aller eigenlichest *wider in sinen ursprung get*. [. . .] Die sele ist geschaffen zwuschent zit und ewikeit. Nu mit iren obersten teile so gehort su in ewikeit, und mit irme nidersten teile so gehort su in die zit, mit iren simelichen vihelichen kreften. Nu ist *die sele bede* mit iren obersten und nidersten kreften *uzgelouffen in die zit* [. . .]

> (For this reason Heaven's course is most noble and perfect when it truly returns to the eternal Source from which it came. So too man's course is most noble and perfect when he too truly returns to his Source. [. . .] The soul is a creation standing between time and eternity. Only with its higher part does it belong to eternity, whereas with its lower part it is bound up with time and with its animal impulses. Now both the soul's higher and its lower energies run their course through time [. . .])[8]

It has not been possible to establish from external evidence that Kraus was reading Tauler at this time. But it is striking that not only are specific images common to the sermon and the poem, but the whole movement of the imagination. Life is pictured as a course to be run through time between two contending impulses. And for both authors the race is won by the runner who turns back to the original source of being. Even the opening image of Kraus's poem: 'laufen zeitentlang', which appears to fuse the dimensions of time and space, may have been suggested by a phrase in this same sermon in which Tauler speaks of 'zitlichen uzloffungen'. But where Tauler's conception of time (worldly experience of the here-and-now) is counter-balanced by the soul's aspiration towards eternity, Kraus's runners run through a dimension of time bereft of theological reassurances. Hence the mystical concept of the original Source gains even greater significance than it has in Tauler's sermon.

Kraus's poem has often been interpreted too externally. It tends to be read as an epigram contrasting the merits of the author's own view of life with the worthlessness of that of his rivals. It is true that Kraus uses the terminology of this poem in polemics against writers lacking in reverence for nature and for the German language – for example, Stefan George or Heine. But if the tension between 'Ursprung' and 'Ziel' were merely a polemical antithesis, the interest of the poem would be less. If Kraus is simply to be identified with the values of 'Ursprung', the significance of 'Zwei Läufer' would be that of a writer giving himself a poetic pat on the back. Acting as judge in a race in which he is himself backing one of the contestants, he solemnly awards the prize to the runner he happens to favour. Read in this way, the poem would simply be a moral fable, in the manner of Lessing or Goldsmith.[9]

A second interpretation takes the runners as bearers of a larger allegory – the race of mankind through time. One runner stands for the technological and purposive element in civilization, the element racing ahead and achieving its goals. This runner comes from 'nowhere', since his origins have no sanction in the original Creation. The second runner represents the spiritual impulse, which lags behind and fails to stay the course, but is sustained by closeness to nature. Read in this way the poem epitomizes the disjunction between spirit and machine, which is one of Kraus's central themes around 1910. And it may be related to a more explicit epigram on the paradoxes of 'Progress' ('Fortschritt') published fifteen years later:

> Was haben wir nur in all der Zeit
> getrieben?
> Wir sind mit dem Fortschritt vorausgeeilt
> und hinter uns zurückgeblieben.
>
> (F 697–705: 72)

(With all this frenzied activity
what did we have in mind?
Racing ahead with progress
we have left ourselves behind.)

Neither of these readings does justice to Kraus's inner theme. For it seems likely that the two runners (in his poem as in Tauler's sermon) represent conflicting impulses within a single personality. The very pace of modern life (accentuated by the image of running) exacerbates this tension. The social role one is obliged to adopt is experienced as alien (coming 'from nowhere'); but it is a necessary expedient if one is to achieve success. And it secures a position which may later make it possible for the inner self (which has had to be suppressed) to reassert its prior claims. Thus Kraus's allegory of modern civilization is also, on the psychological level, a parable of the divided self.

What light does this interpretation of the poem shed on the position of the author himself? The answer must be that we can now no longer identify Kraus exclusively with the runner from the source of life. The dilemma of the divided self is one which he too cannot escape. Must not he too accept the need for a front runner? Might not 'Zwei Läufer' be a confessional poem which mirrors two aspects of his own personality? There is plenty of circumstantial evidence to support this. This poem first appeared in the 300th number of *Die Fackel* at a time when both Kraus's reputation and the circulation of his magazine were growing spectacularly. There could hardly be a more obvious example of the achievement of the goal of external success, such as is associated with the bold runner of the poem. And looking back over these first eleven years of *Die Fackel*, we may legitimately ask: which would be the more plausible epithet to describe Kraus's stance as publicist: 'bang' or 'dreist'? The answer is hardly in doubt. In the whole history of German polemical journalism no writer has ever shown such impudence towards his contemporaries. What from the public viewpoint has died on the way is the author's inner self – that apprehensive inwardness of which we are given glimpses in Kraus's aphorisms (and later in his poetry), especially in his reminiscences of childhood. The death of this inner self (in 'Zwei Läufer' and 'Der sterbende Mensch') symbolizes the self-destructive pressures of civilization. There are affinities here with the lament for the death of childhood which we find in the poetry of Georg Trakl – for example the poem 'An den Knaben Elis', which Kraus included in the programme of his public reading on 16 December 1914.

In Kraus's work the archetype of the divided self finds highly individual expression. It is not one of those schematic dualisms

which form such a recurrent feature of German literature: Goethe's
'zwei Seelen', the *Doppelgänger* motif in Jean Paul and
E. T. A. Hoffmann, the 'Zerrissenheit' cultivated by Heine and
ironized by Nestroy, the 'schizophrenic' heroes of Hofmannsthal in
the 1890s, the antithesis of 'Künstler' and 'Bürger' in Thomas Mann
or of 'Genauigkeit' and 'Seele' in Robert Musil, the 'split selves' of
German Expressionism, the Steppenwolf motif in Hermann Hesse.
It is closer to the cryptic vision of W.B. Yeats:

> I call to the mysterious one who yet
> Shall walk the wet sands by the water's edge
> And look most like me, being indeed my double,
> And prove of all imaginable things
> The most unlike, being my anti-self.[10]

But where for these writers the division of the self becomes a
foreground theme, with Kraus the opposite occurs. The inner
spiritual self takes refuge in privacy and silence, leaving the brashly
aggressive public self holding the stage. His response to the pressures
of alienation is conceived in the tragic, not the ironic mode. The
division of the self ceases indeed to be a literary theme and becomes a
strategy for survival. This is not merely a personal dilemma; it has
wider anthropological implications (which are explored in the
writings of Michel Foucault).[11] But for Kraus this acceptance of the
division of the self has specific personal consequences. These consequences will become clear when we consider his response to the two
most profound experiences of the inner self: religious faith and
romantic love.

CHAPTER 13

Between Jerusalem and Rome: The Dilemma of the Baptized Jew

The poem 'Two Runners' provides a key to the most perplexing aspect of Kraus's career – the dichotomy between satirical discourse and religious conviction. Kraus was brought up in the Jewish faith. But on 20 October 1899 he formally renounced his allegiance to Judaism and became 'konfessionslos'. Twelve years later, on 8 April 1911, he was received into the Catholic Church. He remained a Catholic until 7 March 1923, when he once again formally renounced his religion. This chronology abounds in contradictions. And when we examine its implications, we find that the relation between belief and utterance is even more paradoxical. The two runners seem to run along separate paths, at times even in opposite directions.

The Renunciation of Jewishness
It is clear that Judaism had little significance for Kraus as a set of religious beliefs. His early writings reflect his disillusionment with the dogmatic religious instruction received at school (F 13: 30). Shortly after taking the formal step of leaving the 'Israelitische Kultusgemeinde' in October 1899, he invoked in Die Fackel Herder's idea of the 'purely humanized' Jew, who has renounced his Jewishness in favour of a humanistic ideal (F 21: 31). And this is followed in November 1899 by dire warnings of the 'excesses' which the Jews will suffer in the twentieth century, if they fail to renounce their 'ghetto' attitudes. Kraus's programme is 'through assimilation to redemption' – 'Durch Auflösung zur Erlösung!' (F 23: 7).

So emphatic are Kraus's attempts to discard his Jewish identity that he has been associated with the notion of 'Jewish self-hatred'.[1] It was not, however, hatred of the self, but the desire to liberate the self from compromising affiliations, that was his primary motive. The preponderance of men of Jewish origin in the commercial and financial life of Vienna, on the stock exchange and in journalism, had led to the notion of Jewish identity becoming contaminated by mercantile and opportunistic values. All the more reason for Kraus, the sworn opponent of those values, to distance himself from the Jewish community and assert the distinctness of his own identity. The problem was how to achieve this without endorsing the arguments of antisemitism. In November 1903 we find him insisting that his own intellectual outlook is 'honest and "aryan"' ('ehrlich und "arisch"', F 147: 23). The inverted commas are intended to distance his terminology from that of the racialist theories of the day. Following Houston Stewart Chamberlain, Kraus sees 'Jewish' and 'aryan' attitudes in terms of an ideological rather than racial conflict. But such formulations reveal an acute crisis of identity.

Chamberlain argued in *Die Grundlagen des neunzehnten Jahrhunderts* (1899) that the twentieth century would be dominated by a decisive struggle between 'German' and 'Jewish' forces. Kraus read that book soon after it appeared and seems to have endorsed its principal propositions. On the one hand, the book offered a solution to Kraus's personal dilemma. For Chamberlain (following Herder) suggested that enlightened Jews could change sides and purge themselves of their supposedly negative characteristics (F 21: 31). On the other hand Chamberlain's identification of Jewry as a world-historical force undermining traditional European civilization seemed to square with the prominence of Jews in Viennese journalism and finance. Kraus was clearly impressed by Chamberlain's blend of ideology and erudition, and was proud to count him among early contributors to *Die Fackel*.

The alliance between them is epitomized by Chamberlain's article 'Katholische Universitäten', published in *Die Fackel* in January 1902 and subsequently reissued as a pamphlet. In this article Chamberlain identifies the two arch-enemies of Christian–Germanic culture as 'Rome' and 'Jerusalem'. His primary target is the influence of the Roman Catholic Church, and he denounces the whole concept of a Roman Catholic university. But two-thirds of the way through the article, the attack suddenly turns against a second, more elusive enemy:

> Dem zweiten Feind ist es nicht so leicht, ins Angesicht zu schauen: seine Physiognomie wechselt wie seine Gestalt, er verbirgt sich, er schlüpft einem aalglatt durch die Finger; er trägt heute Hoflivrée und drapiert sich morgen in die rote Fahne; Fürstendiener und Freiheitsapostel, Bankier, Parlamentsredner, Professor, Journalist [. . .] wollten wir den zweiten Feind ebenfalls in ein einziges Wort zusammenfassen, wir könnten ihn allenfalls *'Jerusalem'* nennen.

(F 92: 24–5)

(The second enemy is not so easy to identify: his physiognomy changes like his figure, he conceals himself, slips through one's fingers slippery as an eel; today he is dressed for Court, tomorrow he decks himself out in the red flag; lackey of princes and apostle of freedom, banker, parliamentarian, professor, journalist [. . .] If we wanted similarly to sum up this second enemy in a single word, then it would have to be 'Jerusalem'.)

There is something uncanny about this passage. The concept of 'Jerusalem' as a world-historical principle certainly derives from *Die Grundlagen*. But the mode of expression is far removed from Chamberlain's turgid prose. Both the preoccupation with faces and the vivid satirical disjunctions are more characteristic of Kraus's style. How could such a Krausian passage find its way into Chamberlain's disquisition?

The answer is provided by their unpublished correspondence. When he sent Chamberlain the proofs of his article, Kraus pointed out that it was too short for the 32-page format of *Die Fackel*. It was actually Kraus who suggested that the section on 'Jerusalem' should be expanded to show that (because of the power of the press) this was by far the more dangerous enemy. And Kraus even enclosed his own rough draft ('brouillon') of this passage on 'Jerusalem', to be inserted in the text.[2] Chamberlain readily agreed. So the vivid indictment of the 'Jewish' physiognomy is indeed a synthesis of Chamberlain's Germanic ideology with Kraus's satirical animus.

This illustrates the contradictions of Kraus's position, as a Jewish author helping to propagate the Germanic vision of a civilization threatened by Jewish influences. Like Otto Weininger, he seems to have internalized the antisemitic tendencies of his age. But where this led Weininger to bring his life to an end, it becomes associated in Kraus's writings with symbolic invocations of suicide (*F* 386: 2–3). His strategy was to renounce those disintegrative 'Jewish' characteristics and present to the world a resolutely ethical identity. First as moral crusader, later as artist, finally as satirist, he sought to define for himself a role that transcended racial (as well as social) affiliations. But he was living in a society implacably opposed to such a strategy. On the one hand were the antisemites who proclaimed that Jewishness was a racial destiny which could never be repudiated. On the other were his fellow Jews, who would console themselves, after enduring one of his diatribes, by saying: 'He really is one of us.'

'Er ist doch ä Jud' (October 1913) is Kraus's most vehement repudiation of Jewish identity. Here he declares:

daß ich nicht nur glaube, sondern wie aus der Erschütterung eines Offenbarungserlebnisses spüre, daß mir nichts von allen den Eigenschaften der Juden anhaftet, die wir nach dem heutigen Stand der

Dinge einverständlich feststellen wollen. [. . .] Ich glaube von mir sagen
zu dürfen, daß ich mit der Entwicklung des Judentums bis zum Exodus
noch mitgehe, aber den Tanz um das goldene Kalb nicht mehr mitmache
[. . .]

(F 386: 3)

(that I not only believe, but that I feel as if with the overwhelming force
of a revelation, that I am entirely free of all those characteristics of the
Jews, which in the present state of affairs we may by common consent
identify. [. . .] And I think I may say of myself that I go along with the
development of Jewry as far as Exodus, but quit at the point where the
dance around the golden calf begins [. . .]).

In this sharply formulated eight-page declaration, Kraus expresses
scepticism as to whether there are any specifically Jewish characteristics. The traits most commonly attributed to Jews, cov-
etousness and the lust for power, are in his view distributed equally
among all the peoples of the west – 'auf alle Völker des Abendlandes
gleichmäßig' (F 386: 3). It is nevertheless his explicit aim to purge his
identity of those negative characteristics currently associated with
Jews. The essay shows Kraus struggling with a dilemma which he
cannot resolve, certainly not by invoking the pseudo-scientific
discrimination in favour of 'blond' (and hence ethnically admirable)
Jews proposed by his admirer Lanz von Liebenfels (F 386: 7).
Liebenfels, the propagator of racialist myths, proved to be an even
more compromising ally than Chamberlain.[3]

To disentangle Kraus's links with this reactionary ideology would
require a full-scale study.[4] It was certainly not a formal alliance.
Kraus's contacts with Chamberlain faded after 1904 and his
comments on Liebenfels are guarded. He found the 'Christian–
Germanic' ideology as problematic as the 'Jewish' influences which it
opposed. But traces of Chamberlain's world-historical scheme can
still be detected during the second decade of Die Fackel. And a
tendency to construe the role of the Jews in mythopoeic terms
persisted. The force which Chamberlain identified as 'Jerusalem' is
denounced almost two decades later as 'Israel' in one of Kraus's most
problematic poems of the First World War ('Gebet an die Sonne von
Gibeon', May 1916).

As Kraus reacted against 'Jerusalem', so he gravitated towards
'Rome'. His conversion to Catholicism is perhaps the most
surprising event of his whole career. For it occurred at a time when
he was still campaigning with unremitting vigour against the
repressive Christian attitude towards sexuality. And when he was
baptized, on 8 April 1911, he passed over the event in silence.

In Die Fackel there are few signs of this fundamental reorientation.
The uninitiated reader could never have guessed that he was being

addressed by a Christian author, let alone by a recent convert to Catholicism. If there are hints of a religious orientation, they are drowned by the ferocity of the satire. It is hard to imagine a body of writing more unchristian in tone than Kraus's work of the years after 1911. It includes some of his most vituperative polemics. The commitment to the Christian faith remained a private matter and imposed no constraints on the satirist. It was only in 1922, when he was on the point of leaving the Catholic Church, that Kraus disclosed to his readers that he had been baptized.

This silence is surprising. For it was precisely the confessional tone of Kraus's discourse which gave his writings such authority. The audiences at his public readings were carried away by what appeared to be the 'compelling unity of work and personality'.[5] But in practice the private convictions were kept quite separate from the public role. For this there seem to be two explanations – one circumstantial, the other structural. An open profession of Catholic faith was precluded partly by historical circumstances, partly by the structural determinants of satire.

Catholic Revival and Baptized Jew

The final years before the First World War witnessed a widespread Catholic intellectual revival. In Austria it was signalled by the founding of *Der Brenner* (1910), a periodical in which religious issues were vigorously debated.[6] In England it was associated with Hilaire Belloc's *The Road to Rome* (1902) and with the writings of G. K. Chesterton. In France it commanded the allegiance of a whole generation of writers, with Claudel, Péguy and Barrès as the principal figures. Reacting against the disintegrative tendencies of materialistic civilization, some of the most prominent members of the European intellectual élite resorted to a militant Catholicism as a means of shoring up the old order. And this was accompanied (not only in Germany and Austria) by an antisemitism which professed to be high-minded but was largely a gut reaction.[7]

Kraus's conservative tendencies after 1910 (and his decision to become a Catholic) must be seen within this historical framework. He was aware that writers like Paul Claudel were eloquently reaffirming Christianity as a defence against secular modernism. And the value of Claudel's Catholicism is acknowledged in *Die Fackel*, in an article by one of Kraus's contributors (F 317–18: 24–31). But Kraus was too much of an individualist to align himself openly with the Catholic revival. Religious conviction was for him a matter of private conscience, rather than of public profession. And the last thing he wanted was to ally himself with his ancient adversary Hermann Bahr, who in this same period was trumpeting his return to the Catholic fold in the columns of the *Neues Wiener Journal*.

A further factor inhibited Kraus from openly embracing Catholicism with the fervour of a Péguy or a Claudel – his Jewish origins. He found himself trapped in a paradox. Becoming a Catholic was the surest way of setting a seal upon his decision to renounce his Jewish heritage. But openly to announce his conversion would have exposed him to the charge of having changed his faith for opportunistic reasons. Too many German Jews before him had converted to Christianity in order to advance their careers. The most celebrated example was Heine, who had become a Lutheran in the hope of gaining professional advantages. Baptism (in Heine's famous phrase) was 'the entrance ticket to European culture'.[8] In Habsburg Austria the pressure on Jews to accept baptism was even more intense. Mahler could never have become director of the Vienna Opera if he had not changed his faith. But the 'baptized Jew' soon became a target for opprobrium, from Jewish as well as antisemitic quarters.

Kraus must have been aware of the blistering attack on 'The Baptized Jew' in Fritz Wittels's pamphlet *Der Taufjude* (1904). The Jewish conversion rate was higher in Vienna than in any other European city. Jewish renegades are repeatedly remarked on in Schnitzler's diaries as one of the most disturbing signs of the times.[9] Kraus too, in 'Er ist doch ä Jud', bitterly denounces this 'Renegatentum', which betrays an honourable Jewish tradition to the enemy for short-term social gains (*F* 386: 4). The agonized formulations of this essay betray his anxiety to avoid being tarred by this same brush. His conversion to Christianity had to remain an act of 'secret altruism' ('heimlicher Altruismus', *F* 386: 4).

Kraus's tone in *Die Fackel* remains uncompromisingly satirical. If he is in any sense a 'religious' author, it is by virtue of a natural piety which often takes explicitly anti-Christian forms. God is certainly invoked with some force and frequency in *Die Fackel* after 1911. But these references owe less to the Christian gospel than they do to the Judaic myth which contrasts the purity of original Creation with the fallen state of man. In this sense Kraus's Judaic upbringing may have had a more enduring influence than he realized. The concept of God is not personalized, in the figure of Jesus, but becomes a generalized ontological reference, associated with (and often interchangeable with) concepts like 'Ursprung', 'Natur', 'Schöpfung', 'Geist', 'Wort' and 'Kunst'. It is not the Holy Trinity that Kraus invokes, but triads of his own invention like 'Gott, Kunst und Menschenwert' (*F* 378–80: 30).

After the sinking of the *Titanic* he denounces a civilization which has 'betrayed God to the Machine' ('Sie haben Gott an die Maschine verraten', F 347–8: 6). But it is the awesome mystery of the Creation that he is defending against commercial and technological exploitation, rather than specifically Christian values. It is significant that the name of Christ so rarely occurs in *Die Fackel*. If there is any redeemer figure in Kraus's text, it is the satirist himself. But in place of the Christian gospel of redemption he enacts the Judaic prophetic role of predicting divine retribution.

It is this prophetic undertone which distinguishes Kraus's satire from the writings of a secular social reformer like Bernard Shaw. Kraus himself underlines the contrast when he identifies Shaw as 'an English clown of godlessness' ('Clown der Gottlosigkeit', F 363–5: 25). Kraus's own religious position is hinted at when he writes (in a tribute to Strindberg): 'Die wahren Gläubigen sind es, welche das Göttliche vermissen. (The true believers are those who are aware of the absence of the divine.)' (F 351–3: 1) But he never invokes the Christian gospel in a positive spirit. It is only in his private letters that we find Kraus endorsing St. Paul's homily on Christian charity (*BSN* I. 177).

The obliqueness of his allusions is exemplified by his response in October 1912 to a name encountered in a newspaper, Dr Julius Preßfreund: 'Was es für Sachen gibt! Ich las einst von einem Steuerbeamten, der Josef Christenheit hieß. Ich mochte ihn nicht. Nun aber denke ich oft mit Trauer an ihn. (What a strange world we live in! I once read of a tax official called Joseph Christendom. I didn't like him. Now however I often think of him with sadness.)' (F 357–9: 69) This as as near as Kraus comes to acknowledging that he has revised his view of Christianity. And his references to the question of baptism are equally cryptic:

> 'Sich taufen lassen': das klingt wie Ergebung. Aber sie wollen nie lassen, sondern immer tun; darum glauben sie's selbst dem nicht, der ließ, und glauben, daß er getan hat, und sagen: 'Er hat sich getauft!'
>
> (F 333: 9)

> ('To accept holy baptism': that sounds like an act of submission. They never want to submit, however, but only to take initiatives; thus they are not prepared to credit it when a person submits, and they believe that he took the initiative, and say: 'He's gone over to Rome!')

By casting the problem as an aphoristic reflection upon language, Kraus conceals his personal dilemma.

The Christian Satirist: Homo Duplex

Kraus had a further, structural reason for concealing his conversion to Catholicism. An open profession of faith would have impaired the effectiveness of his satire. Monologue satire is a mode of discourse with its own existential concomitants. It precludes Christian charity: 'Nur kein Mitleid' is the satirist's motto (*F* 324–5: 50). Under specific historical circumstances this imposes upon a writer of religious disposition a dualistic identity. Once we recognize that Kraus had an overriding mission to write satire, the fact that in the years following his conversion there is so little Christianity in *Die Fackel* need no longer surprise us. For the positions of satirist and Christian are incompatible. One cannot simultaneously serve two masters – Jesus and Juvenal.

Satire is by definition uncharitable. If Kraus in his literary practice had begun to follow the precepts of the Sermon on the Mount – loving his enemies and refraining from judgement – he would have ceased to be a satirist. Moreover public commitment to a set of religious beliefs would have inhibited the free play of his imagination. A satirist who aligned himself with some form of religious orthodoxy would lose his freedom for manoeuvre, his disconcerting unpredictability of perspective and right to challenge received ideas. The archetypal satirist (as Kraus insists in 'Nestroy und die Nachwelt') is 'verwirrend gesinnungslos' – disconcertingly uncommitted to any ideological allegiance (*F* 349–50: 17). The satirist's independence would be forfeited if he wrote as propagandist for a set of doctrines, let alone for a church which (as Kraus subsequently put it) 'was not capable of cursing, but only of blessing' ('nicht fluchen, nur segnen konnte', *F* 601–7: 4).

The Christian author who is temperamentally inclined towards satire is thus caught in a dilemma. This is characteristically resolved by the adoption of a satirical persona – a distinct satirical voice which is in marked contrast to the voice of Christian piety. The classical example is provided by Erasmus. In his manual of Christian conduct, the *Enchiridion*, he guides the reader towards a reverent spiritual life. But in his celebrated *Praise of Folly* he adopts an ironic persona which enables him to launch into a satirical diatribe against the malpractices of Christendom. He concedes in his preface that this kind of satire is 'lighter than may become a divine and more biting than may beseem the modesty of a Christian'. But he circumvents this difficulty by adopting the voice of 'Folly, speaking in her own person'. The versatility with which Erasmus deployed the contrasting voices of satirical and of Christian discourse led him to be identified as the archetypal 'homo duplex'.[10]

A similar pattern may be discerned in the work of more modern satirists. Alexander Pope was a Catholic, but this could scarcely be gathered from his poetry. The frame of reference within which his satire operates is provided by eighteenth-century European humanism (of which the *Essay on Man* is the classical statement).

Pope's scheme (as one critic has put it) 'is purposely non-Christian, but it cannot be called non-religious'. And in the structure of his most powerful satire, the *Dunciad*, religion 'exists in reserve'. The literary persona that he adopts in his poetry is that of the satirist or 'wit'. But Pope himself (in a private letter) draws attention to the dualism which separates his literary character from his private personality: 'as a Christian, a friend, a frank companion, and a well natured fellow, and so forth.'[11] Once again the Christian, when he comes to write satire, adopts a non-Christian posture.

More striking still is the case of Jonathan Swift. Swift's Anglicanism does not inhibit the free play of his imagination. In his satire (as opposed to his sermons) he never speaks directly as 'a Christian priest'. Instead, he habitually uses some form of ironic or fictitious persona. Even in the 'Argument to prove that the Abolishing of Christianity in England [. . .] may be attended by some Inconveniences', Swift does not address us directly as a Christian. The complexity of his satirical perspective arises precisely from this ironic persona. 'I hope no Reader imagines me so weak as to stand up in the Defence of *real* Christianity,' he writes. If he had, the piece would have been not a satire but a religious tract. As a priest, Swift preached edifying sermons (on themes like 'The Excellence of Christianity' and 'Brotherly Love'). As a churchman, he put forward 'A Project for the Advancement of Religion and the Reformation of Manners'. But the pious orthodoxy of these pronouncements is quite distinct from the subversive irony of his satire. The *Tale of a Tub* undermines all beliefs and certainties. So striking is this division of the self that Swift's sermon on 'The Excellence of Christianity' and his venomous 'Character of the Earl of Wharton' seem to have been written by two different people.[12]

There is thus an inverse relationship between satire and Christianity. The two may at some deeper level be connected (through shared assumptions about the fallen state of man and the primacy of the ethical). And within the spectrum of persuasive discourse there is certainly a middle ground where the more jocular satirist and indulgent Christian may meet. The Viennese popular theatre provided a stage both for Nestroy's satirical comedies and Raimund's moral fables. And Kraus was indebted to both traditions. But it is Nestroy's satirical animus that he carries to the ultimate extreme. And at the extremes of the spectrum the positions of satirist and Christian are incompatible.

This was most clearly perceived by Kraus's admirer, Theodor Haecker. In younger days Haecker had himself been the author of satirical essays. His early contributions to *Der Brenner* have affinities with Kraus's own work. But when in 1921 Haecker converted to

Catholicism, he felt obliged to abjure his satirical tendencies and anything that might infringe Catholic doctrine.[13] The tension between satirical and Christian impulses, which provides the theme of his *Dialog über die Satire* (1928), is unequivocally resolved in favour of the Christian. And in a diary entry of 7 December 1939, looking back over his literary career, Haecker draws a very clear dividing line between the satirical and the Christian phases of his work.[14] His position is thus the converse of Kraus's. Faced with the choice between writing as a Christian and writing as a satirist. Haecker suppressed his satiric gifts in deference to his Christian calling.

Haecker provides the extreme case. For him, the choice between Christianity and satire is an Either/Or. Hence his doubts as to whether either Swift or Kraus can truly have been Christians.[15] But perhaps the best summary of the paradox with which we are concerned is provided by the writer whom Haecker most admired: Søren Kierkegaard. There can be no doubt about Kierkegaard's commitment to Christianity. He sees it as his life's work 'to reintroduce Christianity [. . .] into Christendom'. The question is: How is this to be brought about? The answer Kierkegaard gives, in *The Point of View for My Work as An Author*, is instructive:

> If it is an illusion that all are Christians – and if there is anything to be done about it, it must be done indirectly, not by one who vociferously proclaims himself an extraordinary Christian, but by one who, better instructed, is ready to declare that he is not a Christian at all.[16]

The parallel with the method that Swift adopts in the 'Argument' is striking. Kierkegaard does not, of course, even in his early aesthetic works, write as a satirist. And many of his writings do in fact take the more direct form of edifying discourses. But what he says here about the need for 'indirect' methods of persuasion has an important bearing on the tactics adopted by writers of satire. If Kierkegaard can adopt a non-Christian persona (for example, in the first part of *Either/Or*) in order to 'deceive his readers into the truth', we should hardly be surprised to find a similar principle at work in the more explicitly satirical writings of less fervently Christian authors. For Haecker (*F* 395–7: 19), Kraus is Kierkegaard's successor.

Against this background the paradoxes of Kraus's position at the time of his baptism become comprehensible. However strong his new-found Christian convictions, he was inhibited from disclosing them by a configuration of factors. His silence served the strategy of strengthening his position as a satirist. But this led inevitably to a division of the self, so that he too became 'homo duplex'. His private religious beliefs were so shielded from the eyes of the world that they elude definition. Only his letters to Sidonie Nadherny, which record his attendance at Mass and include an extended sequence of excerpts from the writings of St. Paul, give glimpses of his devotional life (*BSN* I. 112, 176–8). In public, he remained true to his satirical vocation, which required him to subordinate Christian charity to a purgatorial purpose. This sacrifice of heart is summed up in 1919 in the autobiographical poem 'Nach zwanzig Jahren':

> Sei Zucht und Strafe, Licht zugleich und Brand;
> durch Liebe sind sie nimmermehr zu halten:
> so opfere dein Herz den Haßgewalten

(*F* 508–13: 1)

> (Be rod and punishment, both light and fire;
> through love their folly you will ne'er abate:
> so give your heart up to the powers of hate).

Only very rarely does Kraus's Christianity show through in his published work. It is held 'in reserve', and shows only by implication, in his choice of targets. In the years 1911–14, the targets of satirical attack are taken predominantly from the secular, liberal, progressive, anti-clerical side of the ideological spectrum. Conservative and Catholic organizations largely escape his attentions. The great enemy is the superficial Positivism of the day, with its shibboleths of Progress, Enlightenment and Scientific Advance and its faith in the spiritual efficacy of Journalism, Sociology, Psychiatry and Eugenics. The Christian side is only attacked when it seems to be succumbing to the corrupting influences of the modern world. But even then Kraus speaks (intuitively following Kierkegaard's precept) not as one who vociferously proclaims himself an extraordinary Christian, but (more ambiguously) with the voice of 'one who was born a Jew!' ('eines, der als Jude geboren ist!', *F* 381–3: 67).

Only on one occasion do we find Kraus coming out into the open and directly exhorting his readers towards Christianity. This is in the gloss 'Die Kinder der Zeit' ('The Children of the Age', August 1912), in a passage of some complexity:

> Vor der Sehnsucht alles Geistes, daß dieser Planet abdanke, und selbst vor der Hoffnung, daß dem weißen Leichnam, der auf die Erde drückt, Ratten und Neger das letzte Geleite geben mögen [. . .]: steht eine Sorge. Wir Toten haben hienieden noch manches vorzukehren. Da kann denn kein Zweifel obwalten, daß ich von Standpunkt des Staates, der die Pflicht hat, sich gegen das Unaufhaltsame zu rüsten, manches befürworte, was einer höheren Ordnung so mißfällig ist wie das Gegenteil.[. . .] Viel ist nicht zu retten, aber eine Befestigung des konservativen Willens könnte noch dieser und der folgenden Generation Luft schaffen, und würdelos wie sie gelebt hat, stirbt die Kultur nicht,

wenn sie den Priester kommen läßt.[. . .] Seid Christen aus Notwehr!
Glaubet an Kraft, wo sich die Schwäche analytisch rächt, an Seele, wo
nicht Raum ist für Psychologie! Salbt euch mit den Vorurteilen, deren
Wunderkraft die Urteilsfähigkeit bezweifelt. Geweiht sei jedes Wasser,
von dem die Wissenschaft sagt, es sei H_20 mit Bazillen. Der Säbel, der ins
Leben schneidet, habe recht vor der Feder, die sich sträubt.

$(F$ 354–6: 70–1)

(Before the longing of all the powers of the Spirit that this planet
should abdicate, and even before the hope that rats and negroes should
accompany the white corpse which burdens the earth to its grave [. . .]:
stands one matter for concern. We dead men still have certain
precautionary measures to take here on earth. Thus there can be no doubt
that from the standpoint of the State, which has the duty to arm itself
against the inevitable, I advocate certain things which are just as
displeasing to a higher order as their opposites.[. . .] Not much remains
to be saved, but a consolidation of the conservative will might be able to
gain a breathing space for this and the following generation, and a culture
does not perish as miserably as it has lived, if it sends for the priest.[. . .]
Become Christians in self-defence! Believe in power, where weakness
takes its analytical revenge, and in soul, where there is no room for
psychology. Anoint yourselves with the prejudices whose miraculous
power is doubted by maturity of judgement. Consecrated be every kind
of water of which science maintains that it is H_20 with bacilli. Let the
sword which cuts into life take precedence over the reluctant pen.)

'Die Kinder der Zeit' is Kraus's most outspoken attack on the brave
new world of the twentieth century (reports documenting the effects
of newspapers on children, the aspirations of eugenics, and
contemporary attempts at the artificial reproduction of human cells
and embryos, are reprinted at the beginning of this gloss). This is
however not simply an outburst of revulsion at the dehumanizing
tendencies of the age. The structure of the passage is dualistic,
corresponding to two different viewpoints which are explicitly
identified. The first is the perspective of visionary satire, associated
with the absolute principles of 'Spirit' and of a 'higher order'. Seen in
this perspective, the Europeans of the early twentieth century are
already dead, and all that remains is to accompany the white corpse
to its grave. But cutting across this extreme perspective is a second,
more relative point of view: that of the State. And when Kraus
switches to this second point of view, he is writing as a citizen, not as
a satirist. As satirist, he may still take the attitude: 'And let Chaos be
welcome; for Order has failed ' $(F$ 285–6: 16). But as citizen, he is
concerned to prop up what remains of the existing order. The mask
of the satirist is allowed to slip and we glimpse the anxious features
of the fallible individual, glancing to the right in the hope that
political salvation may come from that quarter.

Few commentators have faced the full implications of 'Die Kinder der Zeit' (analysed in greater depth in Part Four). Kraus's critics merely denounce it as politically reactionary. His apologists, while conceding that it betrays a lack of political judgement, insist that it was a sincere expression of his convictions. But the sincerity of this declaration is its major defect. Sincerity unmediated by irony ceases to be satire. The crucial error of 'Die Kinder der Zeit' is one not of political but of artistic judgement. Authentic satire draws on suprapersonal resources of the human spirit – wit, fantasy, scepticism, ethical radicalism and imaginative subversion. In 'Die Kinder der Zeit' Kraus temporarily abandons the satiric perspective and begins to preach. But Christian exhortation is incompatible with archetypal satire.

In this essay, which Kraus repeatedly read from the public platform, he abandoned the 'gesinnungslos' position of the satirist and aligned himself with an ideological faction. But fortunately his irrepressible imagination led him to attack Christian orthodoxy almost in the same breath as he espoused it. In the number of *Die Fackel* which contained 'Die Kinder der Zeit' Kraus also included 'Weiße Frau and schwarzer Mann'. Here Christian sexual morality, identified as a kind of natural decay, comes under visionary attack (*F* 354–6: 1–4). Kraus belongs to that line of satirists who (though Christian by personal conviction) become most persuasive when they turn their pens against institutionalized Christianity. The satirist shares with the saint the conviction that true Christianity will never be introduced into Christendom.

CHAPTER 14

Silent Heart and Sacred Garden: The Realm of Sidonie Nadherny

The Satirist in Love

It is not only in the sphere of religion that the calling of the satirist involves a sacrifice of heart. If the roles of satirist and Christian are incompatible, what of those of satirist and lover? The nature of satire is defined not least by the aspects of human experience it excludes. The question is how Kraus's experience of love impinges upon his published writings and to what extent it mitigates the harshness of his satirical vision.

In September 1913 Kraus fell in love with Sidonie Nadherny (Pl. 26). The record of their love is preserved in a sequence of over a thousand letters, cards and telegrams which he wrote to her between 1913 and 1936. Sidonie's replies have not survived, but her response can be gauged from her notes and diaries (some of which she wrote in quaint English). It seems to have been love at first sight: 'nach 10. Min. gekannt', writes Sidonie in a diary note of 12 September 1913 which records the intensity of their first encounter. Their first evening together culminated in a star-lit drive through the Prater, and the following day Kraus entertained her at his apartment, after an excursion to Hainbach in the Vienna Woods (*BSN* II. 113).

The intensity of their feelings seems related, on both sides, to the experience of bereavement. Sidonie had grown up on the family estate at Janowitz in Bohemia as one of three children. Her elder brother Johannes was born in 1884, followed by Sidonie and her twin brother Karl in 1885. The siblings seem to have felt a close emotional attachment, particularly as their father died in 1895 and their mother in 1910. The income from their estates enabled them to lead a life of cultivated ease, travelling widely and meeting some of the leading writers and artists of the day (in 1906 Sidonie met the poet Rilke at Rodin's studio in Paris). But their cosmopolitan

26   Sidonie Nadherny

existence seems to have created an underlying strain. In May 1913
Sidonie's brother Johannes committed suicide in Munich, where he
had been receiving medical treatment. It was in the aftermath of this
bereavement that she was introduced to Kraus, who seems to have
been able to comfort her at a moment of great spiritual desolation
('Wüste' in their correspondence is the code word for her initial
emotional state) (*BSN* II. 49). He sees it as his mission to replace her
dead brother in her affections.

From November 1913 onwards Kraus was a frequent guest at
Schloss Janowitz, the Nadherny family home. Sidonie also visited
him in Vienna, and they spent memorable holidays together, touring
Switzerland and Italy by car (in the company sometimes of her
brother Karl, sometimes of the family's Irish-born companion Mary

Cooney). They shared moments of intensely privileged experience,
but could never escape a sense of social constraint. The intensity of
their feelings had to be concealed, and Sidonie was never able to
resolve the tension between this clandestine love affair and the need
to make a socially acceptable marriage. In February 1914, she
received an elaborate letter from Rilke arguing against her alliance
with Kraus on grounds of personal (and perhaps racial)
incompatibility.[1]

Given the social prejudices of the period, the contrast between
Catholic aristocrat and Jewish intellectual must indeed have seemed
incongruous, even though Kraus's conversion had removed the
formal obstacle to marriage. Sidonie's brother Karl seems to have
been strongly opposed: 'Ch. is against dear K.K., it is very sad', she
writes in her diary of 11 November 1914 (*BSN* II. 52). Under these
pressures she announced her engagement to a Florentine nobleman,
Count Carlo Guicciardini. She tried to reassure Kraus that this
marriage of convenience would not impair their relationship; but his
letters betray his profound anxiety. In the event the marriage, which
was due to take place on 6 May 1915, was prevented by the
impending war between Austria-Hungary and Italy.

The social complications were compounded by fluctuations in
Sidonie's own feelings. In August 1914, after their holiday in the
Dolomites, she describes Kraus in her diaries as 'the greatest,
dearest, kindest, best, most noble & most worthful man that exists
[. . .]. He has given me all happiness that was possible to give. He
is the only man living. I never knew so strong a heart, so true a
character [. . .] K. K. shall always remain the *glory & crown* of my
life!' (*BSN* II. 51) But with the passage of time she seems to
have found the intensity of Kraus's feelings constricting. 'K. K., I
wish he'd love me less', she writes in her diary on 8 November
1917, 'for in my heart are other dreams & faithful I cannot be & no
man should want that of a woman, for it must make her fade' (*BSN*
II. 54).

Their gradual estrangement culminated in a decisive break in
October 1918: 'There was a goodbye for ever between K.K. and me
— he who loves as no man ever did' (*BSN* II. 54). It is perhaps not
surprising that she sought refuge in a less demanding relationship.
'He asks for no word of love & he claims no love nor promise, gives
none, therefore we agree,' she observed of her aristocratic
acquaintance Max Graf Thun und Hohenstein (*BSN* II. 55). On 12
April 1920 she and Max Thun were married. But the marriage lasted
only a few months, and in December of that same year she and Kraus
were reunited. In 1924 there followed a further period of
estrangement, for which Sidonie later blamed herself. But they were

reconciled again in September 1927, and the warmth of their relationship continued to sustain Kraus during the final years of his life.

Kraus's emotional turmoil is reflected in his letters. He writes as the passionate petitioner, pressing upon Sidonie the claims of his love with a remarkable eloquence and urging her to have faith in their relationship as the natural fulfilment of her self. Sidonie's replies were clearly more guarded. The imploring tone of Kraus's letters has led a psychoanalyst to diagnose a 'masochistic neurosis' — a 'tendency to self-laceration' which he was able to convert in his satirical writings into aggression against the external world. For another critic the letters reveal a 'narcissistic personality'.[2] But the complexities of human emotion elude such reductive categories. And speculation about unconscious motives is bound to remain inconclusive. The most striking feature of this love relationship is that it made so *little* impression on Kraus's published writings. The private experience of tenderness is not allowed to impinge upon the public stance of satirical aggression. The satirist in love adopts a strategy of concealment.

The Strategy of Concealment

There is no significant change in the tone of *Die Fackel* between September 1913 and the outbreak of war in August 1914. Even the most discerning member of Kraus's audience would not have guessed that the satirist who addressed him from the printed page or the public platform had just fallen passionately in love. Nor was there any break in the rhythm of publication. Eleven issues of *Die Fackel* appeared during that period, comprising twenty-three numbers in all. And Kraus gave no less than twenty-nine public readings, including in his programme many of his most forceful pieces. The temper of his work in this period, although not quite as ferocious as in the year following his baptism in 1911, remains unyieldingly satirical. Only ten days after his first meeting with Sidonie he published the number of *Die Fackel* which contains the poem 'Der sterbende Mensch'. The poem was probably written before that meeting, but it is nevertheless paradoxical that a poem proclaiming the death of man should be published by a person who is just experiencing an emotional rebirth. The poem was also given prominence in his public readings, in Vienna on 22 October and in Berlin on 22 November 1913.

It is clear from the subsequent numbers of *Die Fackel* that Kraus was consciously excluding all traces of his inner experience from his published work. References to relationships between the sexes tend to be profoundly pessimistic in tone:

Er mit dem Geist und sie mit der Schönheit mußten auseinander und
hinaus. Es mit der Technik schafft da und dort Ersatz.

(F 389–90: 34)

(He with his mind and she with her beauty had to separate and depart.
It with its technology supplies a substitute for both.)

This aphorism appeared in the number of *Die Fackel* dated 15
December 1913. At the end of November Kraus had been reunited
with Sidonie at Janowitz. And their letters during December vividly
reflect their shared delight and happiness (*BSN* I. 10–11). The
impression we are given in *Die Fackel*, however, is of a writer so
completely dedicated to his calling that he never has a moment of
leisure to himself. If he wants to read a book, he can do so only 'in
the first free hour' that he has enjoyed for months ('in der nach
Monaten ersten freien Stunde', *F* 391–2: 31). This passage occurs in
Die Fackel of 21 January 1914. Kraus had (according to Sidonie's
record) just spent Christmas and New Year at Janowitz.

The only hint of their relationship occurs in *Die Fackel* of 10 July
1914. Here Kraus prints in facsimile a Grillparzer manuscript, with
the attribution: 'Zum 400. Heft der Fackel übersendet von den
Geschwistern Freiherrn Carl und Freiin Sidonie Nadherny von
Borutin'. This is the only occasion when Sidonie's name occurs in
Die Fackel, and Kraus's acknowledgement suggests no more than
that she and her brother are disinterested admirers of his work. In
this same number of *Die Fackel* we also find the polemical essay
'Sehnsucht nach aristokratischem Umgang'. Rumours had been
circulating in Vienna about Kraus's acquaintance with members of
the landed aristocracy; and he had come under attack from Franz
Pfemfert in *Die Aktion* for betraying his erstwhile admirers on the
radical left. In his reply, Kraus restricts himself to a discussion of the
political implications of the charge. And he concedes that his aim as a
writer, if he has one and if it can be reduced to a political formula, is
'rechtsradikal'. The question of his aristocratic acquaintances is left
ambiguous: 'Ja, ich aspiriere auf aristokratischen Umgang; aber ich,
ewig unbelohnter Streber, finde ihn allzu selten' (*F* 400–3: 94).

It is disingenuous of Kraus to argue that although he aspires to
aristocratic company, he 'all too rarely finds it'. By this date his
acquaintanceship included not only the Nadhernys but other
members of their circle, such as Max Graf Thun and his brother
Felix, Baroness Niny Mladota von Solopisk, Countess Maria
Theodora Pejacsevich, Baron Friedrich Hess-Diller and his wife
Gisela. Kraus would have justified his evasiveness by insisting on the
need for a strict separation of public and private life. But Pfemfert's
attack had shown that that position had become untenable, since

Kraus's social allegiances were unmistakably influencing his stance as a publicist. This was indeed resoundingly confirmed by his declaration in favour of Franz Ferdinand, which appeared in the same (July 1914) number of *Die Fackel*. Franz Ferdinand's estate at Konopiste in Bohemia lay only twenty kilometres from Janowitz, and Kraus had recently visited the famous rose-garden at Konopiste in Sidonie's company (*BSN* II. 135). The division in his life was not between the public and the private, but between a stance defined in defiantly anti-social terms and the author's actual experience of sociability and affection. These private experiences are reflected not only in Kraus's correspondence but in photographs which show him relaxing with Sidonie in the park at Janowitz (see Pl. 27).

At this stage in Kraus's career, as perhaps at no other, we see the two runners running their separate courses. The impudent public self of *Die Fackel* continues to pursue his successful career. The apprehensive inner self, revitalized by the experience of love, remains dead to the world. For this strategy of silence Kraus once again finds a Shakespearean paradigm. It is provided by the relationship between the Fool and Cordelia in *King Lear*. In the text of the play we are given only the most oblique indication of the Fool's feelings: 'Since my young lady's going to France, the Fool hath much pined away' (I iv). For Kraus, however, the Fool's unexpressed devotion to the destiny of Cordelia forms 'the silent heart of the action' — 'das schweigende Herz der Handlung: des Narren Hingegebenheit an Cordeliens Schicksal', *F* 484–98: 89). For contemporary readers this phrase seemed to relate only to Shakespearean dramaturgy. With hindsight it is clear that Kraus is hinting at the secret structure of his own writings. In his private letters too he refers to Sidonie as 'Shakespearean princess' and to himself as a 'Shakespearean Fool' (*BSN* I. 426, 428). Like the Fool in *King Lear*, Kraus discourses satirically on the folly of the world without betraying the tender feelings which form the 'silent heart of the action'.

Kraus did however begin to write lyric poetry. And in these poems, many of them directly inspired by Sidonie, we might expect to find the expression of this new experience of love. In *Die Fackel* of October and December 1915 we do indeed find, in addition to satirical verses, the poems 'Verwandlung' and 'Vor einem Springbrunnen', 'Abschied und Wiederkehr' and 'Wiese im Park'. 'Aus jungen Tagen' follows in April 1916. And all of these poems are included in the first volume of *Worte in Versen*, published early in 1916 and dedicated to Sidonie. Surely, it will be argued, the feelings of the heart are articulated with great lyrical power in such poems as these. Kraus's lyrical work (in the words of one critic) 'shows his satire to be merely the imploring gesture of a lover who

27 Kraus and Sidonie at Janowitz, summer 1915

seeks to guard what he loves from the evil of the world closing in upon it'.[3]

The matter is more complex. For the experience of the lover is almost as elaborately disguised in these poems as it is in the essay 'Sehnsucht nach aristokratischem Umgang'. This is evident both from the poems themselves and from the light which the letters shed on their composition. Kraus's letters to Sidonie contain many indications of his concern that the exact nature of their relationship should not be betrayed. Discussing poems of a specifically personal nature, he speaks of the need for 'some form of *disguise*' ('irgendeine *Verkleidung*', 10 December 1915, *BSN* I. 277). The most obvious method is the retitling of manuscript poems, so that in their published form the personal references are concealed. Thus we are told that the poem published under the title 'Verwandlung' originally bore the title 'Zu Sidis Hochzeitstag' (written at the time of her intended marriage to Guicciardini). 'Vor einem Spring-

brunnen' is substituted for 'Mit Dir vor einem Springbrunnen', and
— most striking of all — 'Aus jungen Tagen' is substituted for the
original title 'Sidi'.

All of this is revealed by Sidonie herself in her notes on the poems.
The purpose of these changes (as Kraus confides in a letter of 4
December 1915) is to mislead the reader: 'die Irreführung des Lesers'.
The title 'Aus jungen Tagen' is chosen in order to give the reader the
clear, inescapable impression that the poem relates to a much earlier
experience ('die deutliche, unverschiebbare Beziehung zu einem alten
Erlebnis', *BSN* I. 255). To Sidonie, however, Kraus justifies the title
as a reference to the rejuvenation which their relationship has
brought him. And in a letter referring to another of these more
personal poems, he expresses his confidence that by such changes the
riff-raff of the world will be deceived ('Das Weltgesindel wird sich
noch nie so wenig ausgekannt haben', 13/14 December 1915, *BSN* I.
288). So successful, indeed, was the strategy of concealment that in
1951 a doctorate was awarded by the University of Vienna for a
dissertation in which these love poems are analysed under the
misapprehension that they all relate to Annie Kalmar.[4]

What is the explanation for this rigorously sustained disguise? The
obvious answer is that it was dictated by social considerations — by
the need to protect Sidonie's reputation. The continuation of their
relationship was possible, it seems, only under conditions of secrecy:
'weiß ganz genau, wie viel wir verbergen müssen, um so viel für uns
frei zu machen!', writes Kraus on 8/9 December 1915 (*BSN* I. 274).
Her brother, her aristocratic neighbours, the servants at Schloss
Janowitz, even the village postmaster have to be deceived about the
nature of their relationship. Repeatedly Kraus expresses his
unhappiness that circumstances impose such constraints upon them.
He is quite emphatic, however, that even the most personal of poems
forms part of his *oeuvre* and must find its way into print: 'Ein Gedicht
ist entstanden. [. . .] Das Allerpersönlichste. Aber es muß doch
einmal Druck finden, denn das gehört zum Werk. Wie nun sollte das
möglich sein?' he writes on 3/4 December 1915 (referring to
'Sidi'/'Aus jungen Tagen'; *BSN* I. 254). Hence the compromise
solution of disguising present experiences under a poetic form which
suggests that they belong to the *past*: 'niemand wird ein
Gegenwärtiges vermuthen,' he writes reassuringly on 8 November
1915 (with reference to 'Abschied und Wiederkehr'; *BSN* I. 218).

The need to preserve social appearances does not, however,
provide the complete answer. For there are hints in Kraus's letters
that, even if social pressures had been removed, he might still have
refrained from publicly celebrating the experience of love. In a
comment of 7/8 December 1914 about the irksome need for

discretion when they meet in Vienna, he writes: 'Wir wollen Liebe verbergen, weil sie zu schön ist, nicht weil sie verboten ist. (Let us conceal love because it is too beautiful, not because it is forbidden.)' (*BSN* I. 104) And a sentence in his letter of 9/10 December 1915 is even more suggestive: 'Ach, ich mache mir gewiß dumme Sorgen, verkleide mich selbst in die Welt, deren ganze Engherzigkeit ich auf mich nehme, nehmen *muß*. (Oh dear, I am certainly foolish to worry so much. I am adopting the disguise of the world, the whole of whose narrowness of heart I am taking upon myself, *must* take upon myself.)' (*BSN* I. 277)

These passages imply that concealment of the experience of love is not only a social but also an existential necessity. It is determined not simply by Sidonie's position in the eyes of society, but by Kraus's position in the eyes of the world. It is a world in which love is too beautiful to be openly celebrated and fullness of heart must be disguised. It is not only when he writes as satirist that Kraus assumes an identity that is the product of his age. When he wishes to express his feelings as a lover, he can do so only under a disguise imposed by the narrow-heartedness of the world.

Poetry of Elegiac Affirmation

This point becomes even clearer when we turn from the motives for concealment to their consequences — the poems themselves. Volume I of *Worte in Versen* contains the poetic precipitate of this love relationship during the period of its greatest intensity, between September 1913 and December 1915. Seven of the poems in this volume arise out of Kraus's relationship with Sidonie. But in none of them do we find a celebration of the experience of love. Both 'Vor einem Springbrunnen' and 'Wiese im Park' are intimately associated with Sidonie. But in both cases the mutuality of human relationships is displaced by reverent contemplation of nature; and the poet is pictured in complete solitude, as he gazes upon the fountain and the meadow. The 'Ich — Du' dimension of interpersonal relations is withheld (Kraus's letters show how wary he was of allowing the intimate 'Du' to become too obtrusive in his poems) (*BSN* I. 275).

The rather differently conceived poem 'Die Krankenschwestern' was also inspired by an incident in which Sidonie tells us she was involved (she was one of the nurses); but here again it is nature that supplies the central theme. In the final poem of the volume, 'Sendung', she does figure more explicitly (as 'die Freundin'); but the central figure of the poem is 'der tote Bruder' (Johannes), and the poet himself figures not as lover but as messenger from the dead. Here as in other poems the experience of love is assimilated into an ill-defined religiosity.

Three further poems reflect Kraus's feelings for Sidonie:
'Verwandlung', 'Aus jungen Tagen' and 'Abschied und
Wiederkehr'. To call these poems love lyrics, however, would be
misleading. They are not lyrical but elegiac in tone. And their
predominant imagery is sombre — the imagery of loss, of death and
the grave. This is particularly the case with 'Abschied und
Wiederkehr'. The poem was occasioned (Sidonie tells us) by an
incident that took place at the end of October 1915. She had paid a
visit to Vienna, and Kraus had accompanied her on her return
journey as far as Iglau, where they parted. The sadness of parting
was relieved for Kraus by an encounter with a little dog, whose
features apparently reminded him of her. Out of this seemingly
slight and even incongruous material Kraus makes a poem of great
pathos. The parting is represented as a death, a final and irretrievable
loss; the return takes the form of a kind of transmigration of souls.
The whole experience is cast in a mode of melancholy: love survives
only through the mystical perception of the poet. No reader of the
poem (without inside knowledge) could fail to suppose that it relates
to the *actual* death of the beloved. Kraus's letter of 9 November 1915
makes it clear, indeed, that this is the effect he intended (though for
him the parting was a 'death' only in a metaphorical sense). The
experience of love is transposed into its opposite — an elegiac
epitaph.

A similar effect is achieved in the poem 'Aus jungen Tagen'. Here
the elegiac perspective is suggested by the substituted title. And
although the initial mood is one of affirmation, the language of the
poem still hints strongly at the death of the beloved. It is only by
treasuring the memory of someone who has sacrificed herself to an
ungrateful world that a sense of affirmation is achieved. This
impression is further strengthened by the fact that in *Worte in Versen*
'Aus jungen Tagen' and 'Abschied und Wiederkehr' are grouped
with the poem 'Widmung des Wortes', which shares with them this
sacrificial theme. The difference is that 'Widmung des Wortes' *does*
refer to an actual death — that of Annie Kalmar. The poem, written
more than two years before Kraus met Sidonie Nadherny, was
published in *Die Fackel* in February 1911 (under a slightly different
title) (*F* 317–18: 33). Thus although the volume of poems is formally
dedicated to 'Sidonie Freiin Nadherny von Borutin', its whole poetic
strategy suggests an emotional allegiance to a woman who has died.

The unfortunate author of the dissertation mentioned above had
therefore some grounds for supposing that poems like 'Aus jungen
Tagen' and 'Abschied und Wiederkehr' were inspired by Annie
Kalmar. Indeed, there may paradoxically be some justification for
such a reading. The poems themselves must have the final word on

their own meanings. They are elegiac affirmations. That is, they represent a synthesis of two forms of experience normally thought of as mutually exclusive. What appears to have happened is this: the elegiac pattern — of tragic sacrifice and transcendent memory — established by Kraus's experience with Annie Kalmar has such a strong hold on his imagination that it superimposes itself upon his relationship with Sidonie Nadherny. A poetic synthesis of the two experiences takes place. It may be facetious to say that the beloved of these poems, like the heroine of *Die Leiden des jungen Werthers*, has the eyes of one woman and the nose of another. But Kraus himself strongly hints at the possibility of such a composite figure in the poem 'Vergleichende Erotik', included in this same volume (*W* VII. 11). And this is entirely in accord with his emphasis on the primacy of consciousness: the ability of the imagination to fuse experiences of past and present, memory and actuality, into a single mental image. It is this that provides us with a final explanation for the discrepancy between the tone of Kraus's love letters and the tone of his poetry. The letters formulate his feelings for Sidonie; the poems express a composite experience of love, with echoes of an earlier bereavement.[5]

Only in the poem 'Verwandlung' does Kraus's relationship with Sidonie Nadherny find more direct expression. This poem is perhaps the finest in Volume I of *Worte in Versen*:

Verwandlung

Stimme im Herbst, verzichtend über dem Grab
auf deine Welt, du blasse Schwester des Monds,
süße Verlobte des klagenden Windes,
schwebend unter fliehenden Sternen —

raffte der Ruf des Geistes dich empor zu dir selbst?
nahm ein Wüstensturm dich in dein Leben zurück?
Siehe, so führt ein erstes Menschenpaar
wieder ein Gott auf die heilige Insel!

Heute ist Frühling. Zitternder Bote des Glücks,
kam durch den Winter der Welt der goldene Falter.
Oh knieet, segnet, hört, wie die Erde schweigt.
Sie allein weiß um Opfer und Thräne.

(*W* VII. 11)

Transformation

Voice in autumn, renouncing over the grave
your world, pale sister of the moon,
sweet bride of the lamenting wind,
floating beneath fugitive stars —

did the call of the spirit raise you up to yourself?
did a desert storm draw you back into your life?
Behold, it is thus that a first human pair
are led by a god on to the sacred island.

Today is spring. Trembling messenger of happiness,
a golden moth has come through the winter of the world.
Oh kneel, bless, listen, how the earth is silent.
It alone knows about sacrifice and tears.)

From Sidonie's note, we know that this poem was written (in March 1915) with the idea of its being set to music and performed at her wedding to Guicciardini. She also elucidates some of the specific references behind the poem: the death of her brother, the starry night of her first meeting with Kraus in Vienna, their first conversation (about experiences in the desert), the island in the lake of the park at Janowitz which they often visited together, and finally the war as the 'winter of the world'.

Once again, we have the characteristic mood of elegiac affirmation. Less declamatory than 'Aus jungen Tagen', free of the overwrought pathos of 'Abschied und Wiederkehr', the poem achieves its effect through an elliptical economy of expression reminiscent of Trakl. Three phases of the love relationship are rehearsed: the beloved's renunciation of life under the impact of bereavement; her reawakening to life, amounting to a kind of paradise regained; and finally (by muted implication) the self-sacrifice of the lovers, accepted in a spirit of reverence, with the golden moth as a token of a frail but enduring happiness. For all the specifically personal circumstances of its composition, the poem achieves a certain universality through its delicate balancing of the gain and the loss arising out of emotional experience. As it advances dialectically from renunciation and renewal to reconciliation, the lament of autumn gives way to a muted affirmation of spring.

What is absent from this poem, as from all those we have considered, is any celebration of the joys of summer. The positive experience of love, though not completely suppressed, finds only veiled expression. The image of a paradise regained in the second strophe of 'Verwandlung' is left ambiguous; here as elsewhere the preponderant emphasis is on sacrifice and sorrow. What is lacking is that note of rejoicing in the experience of love that can be detected in the letters, even though they so often express frustration and anxiety. Their relationship is 'das Aller-Allerschönste', writes Sidonie in December 1913 (*BSN* I. 11). 'Vielen Dank dass es solche Freuden noch gibt,' replies Kraus in a telegram of August 1914 (*BSN* I. 68). And despite the tensions and equivocations there is a profound sense of emotional and spiritual togetherness: 'So umschlungen sind wir!'

(*BSN* I. 223). The letters assign to the experience of love an existential value which finds only a distant echo in the published work.

If social constraints had inhibited the expression of their love during its early months, the outbreak of war imposed an even more severe restriction. The happiness which Kraus and Sidonie enjoyed in their sanctuaries at Janowitz or in Switzerland could not be openly celebrated when so many human lives were being destroyed by the war. The ugliness of the world does not permit the poet to write about the beauty of flowers, Kraus writes in July 1915 (*BSN* I. 167). And as the political tragedy became more ovewhelming, his sense of the need for reticence about personal happiness became more acute. In June 1918, appalled by the death of an acquaintance who has been killed during a military operation, he feels that he must deny himself the personal happiness he has experienced with Sidonie: 'eigenes Glück darf es jetzt nicht geben' (*BSN* I. 459). He thus anticipates the feeling that Brecht was to express twenty years later: of living in 'Bad Times for Lyric Poetry'.[6]

It is difficult to assent to the judgement that Kraus's lyrical work 'shows his satire to be merely the imploring gesture of a lover'. In a sense the reverse is the case: the love poetry is the imploring gesture of the satirist. The lyric poetry is cast in a form which subordinates it to the overriding structure of satire. Love does not figure in *Die Fackel* as a potent force, unreservedly affirmed. This is not the place for a full account of Kraus's later poetry (where occasionally, as in 'Fahrt ins Fextal' from Volume II of *Worte in Versen*, a stronger note of affirmation is sounded). But even if we look at it from a wider perspective, it is still true that the experience of love finds only muted expression in his writings.

Some of Kraus's love poems addressed to Sidonie remained unpublished during his lifetime; others were withheld from the pages of *Die Fackel* and reserved for the more intimate context of *Worte in Versen*. But even there the strategy of concealment is sustained (Sidonie's name is smuggled in as an acrostic).[7] Rarely is the experience of love celebrated in its own right; it tends either to be displaced (by celebrations of the purity of nature or the ecstasy of artistic inspiration) or distanced (by being formulated as an elegiac recollection of a love that has been lost). For Kraus, as for Schiller, the elegiac is the correlative of the satirical;[8] and the lover (like the satirist) becomes *laudator temporis acti*.

Retreat into the Garden

In short, Kraus found himself living a double life. He himself notes the parallel with Jonathan Swift, whose love for Stella also remained an impenetrable secret. Kraus is determined that his own secret will remain so impenetrable that his biographer Leopold Liegler will not even be aware that there is any secret! (*BSN* I. 200–1) His public stance remains unyielding, even though his private letters show that his attitude to life — particularly his conception of relations between the sexes — was undergoing a throughgoing transformation. Aphorisms about erotic experience continued to appear in *Die Fackel*, for example in October 1915 (*F* 406–12: 135–6, 148). But they barely hint at the emotional reorientation which is evident in the letters. The 'Mann – Weib' schema of his earlier writings was disrupted by this experience of the all-encompassing mutuality of love. His conception of 'das Weibliche' (he acknowledges in a letter of January 1915) has been thrown into confusion by Sidonie's human qualities (*BSN* I. 120).

Sidonie was clearly an intelligent woman — 'Frau' not 'Weib'. Conversations about literature did not preclude the erotic embrace, on the contrary: 'Du einzige Frau, die man noch in einem Gespräch über Literatur umarmen möchte, Du seltene Geliebte, zu der man sprechen kann, als hätte man sie nie umarmt!' (*BSN* I. 261). She does not seem to have been an intellectual woman (jestingly Kraus observed that the only books with which she felt a real rapport were *Worte in Versen* and the railway timetable!) (*BSN* I. 364). But this did not deter him from trying to involve her in his literary interests. He presented her with books and sent her lists of improving reading: Dostoevsky's *The Brothers Karamazov* and *The Possessed*, Friedrich Schlegel's *Lucinde*, Jean Paul's *Schulmeisterlein Wuz*, Plautus's *Miles gloriosus*, Goethe's translation of Diderot's *Le Neveu de Rameau*, as well as the comedies of Sardou and Scribe (*BSN* I. 317, 341–2). The transformation of Kraus's conception of femininity was far more fundamental in this relationship than that initiated by his affair with Bertha Maria Denk. Yet the patronizing attitude towards 'die gebildete Frau' is maintained in *Nachts*, his third volume of aphorisms, which was published in 1918 (*W* III. 317).

The relationship between his personal experience and literary creativity is paradoxical. It is not the emotional experience that shapes the literary work, but rather the opposite: in the private letters too it is a literary imagination that we see at work. In his letters to Sidonie Kraus shapes his personal experience according to mythopoeic patterns. The park is repeatedly identified as the Garden of Eden: 'jenen Garten, den Gott in Eden gepflanzt hatte' (*BSN* I. 251). Here, at least momentarily, Adam and Eve are reborn in an experience of primal purity (*BSN* I. 93). Sidonie, pictured among the flowers and animals of her garden, is cast in the role of 'Windsbraut', a tempestuous force of nature (*BSN* I. 135). But however eloquent

Kraus's adjurations to her to follow the impulses of her natural self, the Sidonie of reality could not live up to this idealized image. The absoluteness of Kraus's romantic conception of love could not be reconciled with the relative world in which she was actually living, let alone with the fluctuations in her own feelings.

Sidonie's diary shows the discrepancy between Kraus's idealized demands and her actual emotional state: 'the greater his love grows, the less I can return,' she writes in July 1918 (*BSN* II. 54). Kraus's powerful imagination leads him repeatedly to reaffirm the primacy of his own image. He is very conscious of the subjectivity of emotional perception, acknowledging that his relationship with Sidonie belongs to 'the sacred domain of his imaginings' ('die heilige Domäne seiner Einbildungen', *BSN* I. 137). But he insists that this subjective image is not a 'false illusion' ('Fehlillusion' is the extraordinary word he coins, *BSN* I. 587). His subjective image expresses Sidonie's truer, more natural self, which he is seeking to liberate from the pettiness of her social identity.

It is this intense commitment to the role of lover which endows Kraus's letters with dramatic tempo and even tragic undertones. Among the many Shakespearean allusions the most powerful is provided by *Othello* (III. iii. 91): 'and when I love thee not, Chaos is come again' (*BSN* I. 258). There is a continuous awareness that their love relationship has a 'tragic' quality arising from the collision between the claims of passionate feeling and the pressures of a hostile world. This tragic expectation was spectacularly confirmed when in October 1918 the decisive break with Sidonie coincided with the collapse of the Austro-Hungarian Empire.

The 'true illusions' which are affirmed in Kraus's private letters correspond to the 'true masks' of his satirical discourse. In each sphere we are confronted with heightened images of reality: a totally corrupted public world (with the satirist as heroic antagonist), and an idealized sphere of absolute love. For readers attuned to the norms of common sense, Kraus's discourse in both spheres must seem extravagantly unrealistic. But it was precisely those norms that he set out to challenge. And reality is not always on the side of the realists. The apocalyptic prophecies of the satirist were fulfilled in the First World War. And even the illusions of the lover gained a final endorsement. After their estrangement of 1924–7, it was Sidonie who returned as petitioner, seeking readmission to that ideal garden of Kraus's imagination.

The 'garden' becomes one of the central images of Kraus's work during the decisive years 1913–15. Through this image he sought to unify the impulses of his career as a publicist with those of his private experience. It is both an elegiac Eden for the lovers and the

archetypal antithesis to the corruption of the city. In his private
letters as well as in his published work Kraus endows the image of
the garden with the mythic resonance of Creation, Paradise and the
Fall of Man. It is the voice of God which says to 'The Dying Man' (in
Kraus's poem of September 1913):

> Im Dunkel gehend, wußtest du ums Licht.
> Nun bist du da und siehst mir ins Gesicht.
> Sahst hinter dich und suchtest meinen Garten.
> Du bliebst am Ursprung. Ursprung ist das Ziel.
> Du, unverloren an das Lebensspiel,
> Nun mußt, mein Mensch, du länger nicht mehr warten.
>
> (F 381–3: 76)

> (Walking through darkness, you knew about the light.
> Now you are there and standing in my sight.
> Looking behind, you sought the garden gate.
> You stayed close to the source. Source is the aim;
> Refused to give your heart to life's poor game.
> Now, man of God, you have not long to wait.)

Significantly, the quest for a 'garden' — a place of refreshment and
salvation — pre-dates Kraus's first meeting with Sidonie. He visited
Janowitz two months after this poem was published, so the motif of
'not having long to wait' for admission to the sacred garden proved
strangely prophetic.

For the satirist the need to find a place of refuge from an
increasingly hostile world had by 1911 become a leitmotif. *Die Fackel*
is defined as 'Zuflucht' (F 329–30: 5). The satirist 'organisiert die
Flucht des Geistes vor der Menschheit' (F 349–50: 23) and himself
finds consolation in 'so etwas wie die Flucht in den Geist' (F
384–5: 17). The private experience of the park at Janowitz provided
the fulfilment of this public imperative. And Kraus was able to
synthesize the two motifs in the essay 'Sehnsucht nach
aristokratischem Umgang', which concludes with the resounding
declaration:

> daß die Erhaltung der Mauer eines Schloßparks, der zwischen einer
> fünfhundertjährigen Pappel und einer heute erblühten Glockenblume alle
> Wunder der Schöpfung aus einer zerstörten Welt hebt, im Namen des
> Geistes wichtiger ist als der Betrieb aller intellektuellen Schändlichkeit,
> die Gott den Atem verlegt!
>
> (F 400–3: 95)

> (that the preservation of the wall of a country-house park, where between
> a five-hundred-year-old poplar and a bluebell that flowered today all the
> miracles of the creation are salvaged from the wreck of the world, is more
> important in the name of the Spirit than the activity of all the intellectual
> infamy which takes God's breath away!)

These words, the very last that Kraus published before the outbreak of the First World War, epitomize the quandary in which he found himself. They are not simply a declaration of ideological allegiance (although they betray a political dilemma which Kraus was only to resolve towards the end of the First World War). They transpose his political stance into the archetypal language of the satirical imagination.

For the classical European satirists, from Horace through to Pope, the garden forms the positive counterpart to the corruptness of the city.[9] But Kraus recognized (as his private letters show) that the aristocratic culture of Janowitz was too marginal to provide an alternative to the pressures of modernity: 'Aus der Kultur, die ein Park von Janowitz bezeugt, geht freilich kein *Staat* hervor, sondern nur ein Himmelreich. (Out of the culture which is attested by a park like Janowitz there emerges admittedly no *state*, but only a kingdom of heaven.)' (*BSN* I. 59) The garden at Janowitz, though it continues to figure in his poetry, only remotely impinges on his satire. After the first full year of war, the island on which the lovers had found refuge reappears as a place of exile:

> Ich glaube: Daß dieser Krieg, wenn er die Guten nicht tötet, wohl eine moralische Insel für die Guten herstellen mag, die auch ohne ihn gut waren. Daß er aber die ganze umgebende Welt in ein großes Hinterland des Betrugs, der Hinfälligkeit und des unmenschlichsten Gottverrats verwandeln wird [. . .]
>
> (F 406–12: 168)
>
> I believe: That this war, if it does not kill those who are good, may well create a moral island for them, though they were good even without the war. But that it will transform the whole surrounding world into a vast hinterland of deceit, of frailty, and of the most inhuman betrayal of God [. . .])

The garden has withered away. In place of park, poplars and bluebells there is now only an island to which the satirist can retreat with unnamed kindred spirits. The retreat was not merely a metaphor. Kraus's 'silence' in the face of the horrors of war (only two slim numbers of *Die Fackel* appeared between July 1914 and October 1915) represents his most significant retreat from public engagement. The factors underlying this silence are difficult to disentangle. On one side were the pressures of censorship; on the other the absorbing nature of his relationship with Sidonie, which certainly distracted him from his mission as a publicist.

The Private War

Kraus represented his silence in *Die Fackel* as a principled stand against the clamour of war propaganda (F 404) and a 'strategic retreat' from the sphere of public opinion (*F* 405: 15). But his private letters reveal that it was his relationship with Sidonie which absorbed the major part of his time and energy. Virtually half of the period from June 1914 to September 1915 was spent with or near her, at Janowitz or in Vienna, in the Dolomites during the summer of 1914 (where they were overtaken by the outbreak of war), in Italy during the early months of 1915 and later in Switzerland. In addition Kraus wrote no less than 150 letters, cards and telegrams to Sidonie during this period. These biographical details enable us to assess more realistically his own subsequent claim that there were 'no other scenes' in his life, apart from the printed pages of *Die Fackel* ('daß es andere Szenen aus meinem Leben als die zwanzig gedruckten Jahrgänge nicht gibt', *F* 531–43: 196). So powerful was the attraction of these 'other scenes' during 1914–15 that for a time they displaced *Die Fackel*. For almost a year Kraus found himself caught up in a 'private war' of the emotions.[10]

The crisis was caused by Sidonie's impending marriage to Count Guicciardini. Kraus was wrestling with the paradox that this marriage of convenience, supposedly designed to give Sidonie greater freedom to be with him, was likely to have the opposite effect. Could this therefore be her (perhaps unconscious) intention? The series of letters which he wrote to her between January and March 1915 are of exceptional psychological interest. The emotional relationship is transposed into the terms of an epistolary novel involving four main characters: 'Yer', the letter-writer (who occasionally forgets himself and signs 'Karl Kraus'); the 'Baronin', recipient of his letters; 'Bobby', the hero of the narrative; and the beautiful 'Tangy', with whom he is in love (the names were borrowed from animals on the Janowitz estate).

Bobby, the recipient of Tangy's favours in the past, is an incorrigible idealist. Living in a world of memories and illusions, he dreams of reimposing his passionate vision upon the reluctant Tangy. The role of his friend Yer is to argue him out of his passionate despair and intercede with the Baroness on his behalf. The Baroness in her turn acts as confidante to the elusive Tangy. The tone of the narrative vibrates between the poles of passion and lucidity. It is as if the emotions of Goethe's Werther were being presented by the narrator of *Die Wahlverwandtschaften*.

This epistolary 'fiction' was initially adopted to deceive the censorship (particularly strict between Austria and Italy). But Kraus's division of himself into two distinct characters also seems to have had a therapeutic function. It enables him to distance himself from the Wertherian impulses of Bobby. Through the perspective of Yer he is striving to gain greater detachment. Similarly in the figure

of the Baroness he cultivates that aspect of Sidonie's personality
which is more accessible to rational argument. By this means Kraus
seems to have been able to work through an unprecedented emotional crisis. The agonies of separation brought sleeplessness and
thoughts of suicide. It led to a nervous breakdown ('Nervenkrise')
which so affected him that at the end of his public reading on 13
February 1915 he had to be given medical attention in the concert
hall. The emotional turmoil was compounded by the threat of being
conscripted for national service; and Kraus had to rely on sleeping
tablets to carry him through his convalescence.

He also undertook three physically and emotionally exhausting
journeys to Italy, to plead with Sidonie, until finally the wedding
was cancelled under the shadow of war with Italy. The resolution of
his personal crisis coincided with a devastating reverse for Austrian
diplomacy, which must have intensified Kraus's emotional turmoil.
He himself may have been marginally involved in the attempts to
secure Italian neutrality.[11] His chagrin over the incompetence of the
Austrian negotiators was summed up in the satirically coded phrase
which he telegraphed from Rome to a friend in Vienna: 'Verbroigter
Loibusch' (F 668–75: 42).

Despite these traumas, there is a decisive change of tone in Kraus's
letters during his visit to Rome in March 1915 (even before the
cancellation of the wedding). After brief meetings with Sidonie,
Kraus writes her three letters from his Rome hotel, in which the
impassioned tones of Bobby are displaced by the moderation of Yer.
A *modus vivendi* has been found, in which the absolute claims of love
are held in check by a friendship that is prepared to make allowances:
'Ich will's Dir leichter machen — mit der unverlierbaren
Freundschaft, die Rücksicht kennt, und mit der unverlierbaren
Liebe, die Dich ganz so herstellen will wie Du bist' (5 March 1915,
BSN I. 149). Sidonie seems to have acceded, reassuring Kraus that if
he could never have her hand in marriage, he would always have
access to Janowitz. For in his following letter he signs himself 'K.
von Janowitz'. Kraus concedes that his embittered feelings in the past
were an overreaction. He recognizes that Sidonie has to make
concessions to the claims of her social position, and he is prepared to
accept a situation which has now been thoroughly understood (12
May 1915, *BSN* I. 159–60). Even when they are holidaying together
in Switzerland in June, his letters strike a similar note of patience and
renunciation.

Early in July 1915 Sidonie returned to Janowitz and Kraus to
Vienna. With the emotional crisis now resolved Kraus plunged back
into work (5 July 1915, *BSN* I. 167). The relationship which had
inhibited his productivity now reinforced his decision to resume

publication of *Die Fackel*. The Prologue to *Die letzten Tage der Menschheit* was completed by the end of July. And during the following month (spent at Janowitz) this spate of productivity was sustained: 'K. K. left yesterday after a month's stay, in which he wrote so busily for the drama & the Fackel', Sidonie noted in her diary of 2 September 1915 (*BSN* II. 174). Inspired by her support, Kraus was able to maintain this momentum on his return to Vienna right through to the publication of *Die Fackel* no. 406–12 at the beginning of October. He was now fully launched upon what was to prove the greatest enterprise of his career — his satirical campaign against the inhumanity of war.

PART FOUR

THE WAR OF ILLUSIONS
1914–1918

CHAPTER 15

The Unimagined War and the Apparatus of Propaganda

Kraus's writings during the First World War are unique. Despite the constraints of censorship he was able to publish nineteen issues of *Die Fackel*, amounting to almost one hundred numbers in all. After an initial phase of scepticism and guarded opposition, he gradually intensified his campaign against the war until, towards the end of 1917, he was making political pronouncements which might easily have cost him his liberty. *Die Fackel* was the only German–language journal to adopt a critical view of the war in 1914 and to sustain that attitude with increasing vehemence to the bitter end.[1] The fifty public readings which Kraus gave during the war significantly reinforced his campaign. And during this same period he was writing the first version of his play *Die letzten Tage der Menschheit*, which was not published until 1919 after the lifting of censorship.

Die letzten Tage is rightly regarded as Kraus's outstanding achievement. But it is wrong to assume that a play published in 1919 (and in its definitive version in 1922) accurately reflects the author's position between 1914 and 1918. On the contrary, a decisive reorientation in Kraus's political attitude occurred during 1917. And it was only after the collapse of the Habsburg Monarchy that he endorsed socialist and republican values. *Die letzten Tage* will be discussed in Part Five, which deals with his position at the end of the war. In Part Four the aim is to reconstruct Kraus's attitudes as they evolved during the war itself, on the evidence not only of *Die Fackel* and his public readings, but also of private correspondence and unpublished archival sources. The story is complex – and by no means free of ambiguity.

The Failure of Imagination
The key text is 'In dieser großen Zeit' – 'In These Great Times' – which is rightly given pride of place in the best English selection

from Kraus's writings.[2] It is an essay which abounds in both critical insights and political ambiguities. Kraus read it in public on 19 November 1914, prior to its publication in December (*F* 404: 1–19). It did not initially gain the celebrity of other anti-war pronouncements of the period: Shaw's 'Common Sense about the War' or Rolland's 'Au-dessus de la mêlée'.[3] But it exceeds both of them in intellectual acuteness and moral vision.

The title ironizes the view, almost universal at the time, that the war had ushered in an era of heroic grandeur. Kraus by contrast defines it as a time 'in which what can no longer be *imagined* must *happen*, for if one could imagine it, it would not happen' ('in der *geschehen* muß, was man sich nicht mehr *vorstellen* kann, und könnte man es, es geschähe nicht', *F* 404: 1). As an abstract proposition, this claim is open to obvious objections.[4] But the force of Kraus's argument derives from the specific historical situation in which it was formulated.

By mid-November 1914 the contours of the war were becoming clear. During August and September the German armies had gained a spectacular series of victories reminiscent of the campaign of 1870. But the battle of the Marne had halted the German advance and shown that there would be no quick victory for either side. The stalemate of trench warfare had begun. And the casualty figures were horrendous. On the eastern front the initially victorious German armies were also pinned down by sheer weight of numbers. And for Austria-Hungary the loss of Galicia and the failure to occupy Serbia brought an equally sobering loss of life, territory and prestige. The spectacular war of movement had given way to a grinding war of attrition for which there was no precedent.

This is not just a matter of historical hindsight. The changing character of war was clear to any attentive reader who, disregarding the patriotic headlines, took the trouble to read the small print of the *Frankfurter Zeitung* (one of the few German newspapers that sought to maintain some independence). On 24 September 1914, after the French counter-offensive had come to a halt at the river Aisne, the *Frankfurter Zeitung* reports that the front is assuming the character of a war of fortifications ('Festungskrieg'). The lines are so strongly defended by barbed-wire and machine-guns that attacks frequently fail to advance more than half a kilometre a day. An even more elaborate analysis in the *Frankfurter Zeitung* of 27 September describes the trenches and ramparts which have been constructed and reports that the armies have now begun a long and laborious defensive war.[5]

Such is the historical context of Kraus's proposition that precisely those things are happening which people had been unable to imagine. As A. J. P. Taylor puts it: 'As 1914 drew to a close, the pattern had been drawn for the First World War, a pattern not foreseen by anyone in a responsible position before the war started: Not a short war of quick decisions, but a war of deadlock [. . .]. No one had prepared for this; no one knew how to handle it.'[6] Kraus was later to attack individual political leaders (notably Berchtold and Czernin) for their failure to envisage the consequences of their actions. But when he writes in November 1914 of a failure of imagination, it is not individual politicians that he has primarily in mind. In Kraus's theory great mistakes are not made by great individuals. They tend to be made by nonentities. The magnitude of the ensuing disaster is caused by the 'anonymous mass forces' at work in modern society (F 400–3: 58). The failure of imagination which he diagnoses is more amorphous. It is that of the newspaper-reading public which is being deluded into supporting a war of inconceivable horror.

Kraus's argument subsumes the insights gained from his analysis of the Balkan Wars. Though limited in scale, the Balkan conflict with its heavy casualties might have enabled educated Europeans to gain a more realistic grasp of modern warfare. Factual reporting of those wars might have led the newspaper-reading public to make the necessary effort of imagination, to set aside the notion of war as heroic spectacle and to grasp the realities of suffering and carnage. However, the way in which these wars were covered in the Austrian press (as we have seen) precluded any such reorientation. The realities of war remained shrouded in an aura of glamour, and it was impossible to imagine what war on a European scale might be like.

For Kraus, imagination is the solvent which enables the human mind to free itself from rigid, anachronistic ideologies. His theory of the imagination is more cogent than at first it may seem. It is also less idiosyncratic. English readers will be aware of antecedents in the writings of Coleridge, who similarly emphasizes the dangers of 'a debility and deadness of the imaginative power'. For Coleridge (as for Kraus) imagination, clarity of thought and precision of language work together to promote a healthy climate of opinion. Coleridge too warns of the danger of 'floating and obscure generalities', and he emphasizes 'the beneficial after-effects of verbal precision in the preclusion of fanaticism, which masters the feelings more especially by indistinct watchwords'.[7]

Coleridge initiates a tradition of critical thinking which is carried forward by Carlyle, Matthew Arnold and Ruskin. Coleridge's warnings about 'deadness of the imaginative power' and 'indistinct watchwords' are taken up even more forcefully in Ruskin's denunciation quoted earlier of 'masked words [. . .], which everybody uses, and most people will also fight for, live for, or even die for'. To set Kraus's theories against a background of English tradition, however, is not thereby to justify them. For it might be objected that the theories of Coleridge and Ruskin are just as idealistic as those of Kraus. It is not merely the concurrence but the contrast between the two positions which is instructive. Kraus gives his theory of the corruption of consciousness a much firmer historical basis than is the case with the nineteenth-century English critics.

The realism of Kraus's critique derives from his grasp of the dynamics of technological change. 'The airship is invented and the imagination crawls along like a stage coach,' he had written in January 1908 (*F* 241: 14). But technology does not merely constitute, it exacerbates the problem; for there has come into being a whole new technology for the manufacture of public opinion: the modern, mass-circulation newspaper press. It is on the unprecedented efficiency of this new technological apparatus that Kraus focuses, in order to substantiate his abstract propositions about the destruction of the imagination:

> Er [der Reporter] hat durch jahrzehntelange Übung die Menschheit auf eben jenen Stand der Phantasienot gebracht, der ihr einen Vernichtungskrieg gegen sich selbst ermöglicht. Er kann, da er ihr alle Fähigkeit des Erlebnisses und dessen geistiger Fortsetzung durch die maßlose Promptheit seiner Apparate erspart hat, ihr eben noch den erforderlichen Todesmut einpflanzen, mit dem sie hineinrennt. Er hat den Abglanz heroischer Eigenschaften zur Verfügung und seine mißbrauchte Sprache verschönt ein mißbrauchtes Leben [. . .]
>
> (*F* 404: 9)

> (Through decades of practice the newspaper reporter has brought us to that degree of impoverishment of the imagination which makes it possible for us to fight a war of annihilation against ourselves. Since the boundless efficiency of his apparatus has deprived us of all capacity for experience and for the mental development of that experience, he can now implant in us the courage in the face of death which we need in order to rush off into battle. He has the imagery of heroic qualities at his disposal, and his abuse of language embellishes the abuse of life [. . .])

Kraus's critique of 'the destruction of the mind' is by no means a piece of abstract idealism. Its emphasis on the apparatus for the production of consciousness anticipates more recent theories like those of Walter Benjamin, Hans Magnus Enzensberger and Marshall McLuhan. In *Die Fackel* of 1914–18 Kraus analyses this apparatus in action.

Kraus's thesis about the unimagined war can be tested in a number of ways: first, by reviewing the attempts which were made before 1914 to imagine what the coming war would be like; secondly, by considering the testimony of some of those who did 'rush off into battle'; and thirdly by analysing the apparatus of propaganda.

Voices Prophesying War is the title of a book by I. F. Clarke which describes attempts before 1914 to imagine what the anticipated European conflict would be like. In the period 1870–1914 a vast literature appeared on this subject in all the major European languages, partly by military theorists, partly by writers of fiction. Clarke includes over 130 items in a list of theoretical 'War Studies' published in this period and more than 300 works of fiction portraying 'Imaginary Wars'. His study shows that, with very rare exceptions, the writers of these works completely failed to foresee the form a modern war would take.

In the spate of works dealing with a future conflict between Great Britain and Germany, naval supremacy was the dominant theme. It was assumed that the outcome of the war would depend on those spectacular new warships which proved, in the event, to be such an insignificant factor. The importance of submarines, on the other hand, was virtually ignored. As to the war on land, this was pictured as a short series of mobile and decisive battles. In his chapter 'Science and the Shape of Wars-to-Come', Clarke shows that there was an almost universal failure to grasp the implications of modern technology. The only imaginative writers to glimpse the truth were Albert Robida, H.G. Wells and Conan Doyle. The solitary military strategist to foresee trench warfare was Ivan S. Bloch.

Clarke is in no doubt about the influence of this perversely conceived literature:

> There can be no doubt that the authors of the many tales of future warfare shared in the responsibility for the catastrophe that overtook Europe [. . .] helped to raise the temperature of international disputes [. . .] to sustain and foment the self-deception, misunderstanding and downright ill will that often infected relations between the peoples of Europe. During the forty-three years from 1871 to the outbreak of the First World War the device of the imaginary war had become an established means of teaching every kind of aggressive doctrine from the duty of revenge to the need for a bigger fleet.[. . .] The best that can be said of them is that they often stood for high patriotic ideals at a time when few had realized how technological innovations would totally transform the nature of modern warfare.[. . .] At their worst they perpetuated an archaic attitude to war.

Clarke shows in detail how such writers created an archaic myth totally at odds with industrial civilization, by idealizing war 'in the language of gallantry and glory'. And he closely echoes Kraus's formulations when he writes: 'The imagination tolerated the idea of war, since it lacked the capacity to foresee the devastation, the immense casualty lists, the chaos and destruction that lay ahead.'[8]

The patriotic volunteers who rallied to the colours by the hundred

thousand in August 1914 had been brainwashed into expecting a
short war full of action and drama. Even the professional officers
who had conscientiously studied their manuals of military strategy
had no inkling of what awaited them.[9] The pervasive theme in the
memoirs of that generation is disillusionment. They set out, often on
horseback, with heroic expectations and found themselves after a
matter of weeks trapped in the stagnant and slaughterous business of
trench warfare. Their 'disenchantment' is articulately expressed in
the memoirs published under that title in 1922 by C.E. Montague.
Montague, who volunteered for front-line service even though over
military age, originally shared the heroic idealism of August 1914.
This mood of spiritual elation is translated in his first chapter into
specific terms in the experience of raw but enthusiastic recruits. The
theme of his subsequent chapters is the steady erosion of these
'handsome illusions', the way in which the 'romance' of war is
destroyed by the sheer scale of operations and by the futility of using
yesterday's tactics against today's technology. It was (he writes) 'an
unimagined war of flankless armies scratching each other's faces across
an endless thorn hedge, not dreamt of in Staff College philosophy; a
war that was always putting out of date the best that had been known
and thought and invented'.[10] Montague also devotes two chapters to
the newspaper press and the technology of propaganda which was
developed during the war. Like Kraus, he shows that the lack of
realism in prevailing conceptions of the war was systematically
fostered by war correspondents.

References to the 'unimagined' character of the war can be found in
a range of other war memoirs. Montague represents the point of view
of an educated and highly literate middle class, brought up in the firm
belief that yesterday's parasol ought to keep out the rain of today. At
the other end of the social scale we find Heinrich Lersch, the one
German poet who earned Kraus's praise for a humane poem about the
war (F 418–22: 43–4). Lersch was a boilermaker, with grim pre-war
experiences of unemployment. He too initially greeted the war with
quasi-religious enthusiasm (reflected in strongly nationalistic poems).
But after several months of front-line service he wrote to a friend:

> I could never have imagined it would be like *this*, — nobody could, for
> this business is so new that it's never before been part of war.
>   Courage, valour and skill — all that is superfluous. Whoever has the
> bluntest nerves is least aware of what is going on, otherwise it's all the
> same. We're just waiting for the 'right' grenade [. . .][11]

This same refrain crops up in the letters and memoirs of army
officers who had been eagerly awaiting the war but now found
themselves trapped in a murderous campaign of attrition. And

among political leaders too there were many who imagined (like Bethmann Hollweg, the German Chancellor) that the war would be 'a short thunderstorm to clear the air'. It was (as Fritz Fischer has shown in his masterly study of German attitudes to the approach of war) essentially a 'War of Illusions'.[12]

Most difficult of all to foresee were the casualties that would be caused by this unprecedented war of massed troops confronted by mortars and machine-guns. The German victory in the Franco-Prussian War had been gained with relatively few losses. And neither Britain nor France, despite the vast extent of their empires, had ever experienced this kind of war of attrition. During the 1914–18 War military casualties were higher than in any other war ever recorded. Of the 65,000,000 called up for active service, over 8,000,000 were killed in battle. Averaged out over the four and a half years of the war, this means that 6,000 men were killed *every day*. In addition to this 21,000,000 soldiers were wounded. And it is estimated that there were over 12,000,000 civilian deaths from military action, massacre, disease and starvation.[13]

The brainwashing which had occurred before 1914 was insignificant compared with the immense propaganda apparatus set up in every belligerent country during the war itself. Although the casualty figures were strictly censored, lists of those killed in battle were published regularly. In order to make these losses acceptable, it was necessary to saturate the public with propaganda about the ethical purpose of the war and the glory of dying for one's country. When Kraus argued in November 1914 that people's imaginations had been numbed by clichés, he had one word in mind in particular: 'Heldentod' ('dying a hero's death'). In formulations oblique enough to elude the censor, he identifies the most destructive effect of journalistic propaganda as the tendency to reduce all experience to *quantitative* terms. The extraordinary casualty figures, which without doubt break all previous records, leave the mind so numbed that one ceases to realize that 'this vast quantity divides into individual destinies, which are only felt by individuals' ('die große Quantität in Einzelschicksale zerfällt, die nur die einzelnen spüren'). Suddenly one perceives the 'hero's death as cruel destiny' ('Heldentod als grausames Geschick', F 404: 10).

Time and again Kraus reminds his readers of the appalling casualties. Reviewing in April 1916 the horrific apparatus of death, through aerial bombing, poison gas, machine-gun fire, being drowned or buried alive, he insists that 'every hour should resound through the world with the final beat of a thousand innocent hearts' ('jede Stunde mit dem letzten Schlag von tausend unschuldigen Herzen durch die Welt dröhnen müßte', F 418–22: 101).

Moral imagination means for Kraus the ability to grasp that individual human beings are dying a terrible personal death. It means seeing beyond the rhetoric of heroism, beyond the abstract statistics, and glimpsing the expression on the face of a dying soldier. Although the censorship inhibited the discussion of casualties in these terms, Kraus circumvented this difficulty by citing an irreproachable witness, Bismarck: 'Wer aber nur einmal in das brechende Auge eines sterbenden Kriegers auf dem Schlachtfelde geblickt hat, der besinnt sich, bevor er einen Krieg anfängt. (Anyone who has even once looked into the eyes of a dying warrior on the battlefield at the moment of death will think very carefully before he starts a war.)' (F 454–6: 6) Kraus too, despite his lack of military experience, had this capacity to envisage the horror of death. He was in touch with front-line soldiers who kept him informed about what conditions were really like for men under bombardment. His most impassioned satire is directed against propaganda which devalues death.

Who Controls the Apparatus?

Where Kraus's analysis breaks down is on the question: who controls the apparatus of propaganda? The press of Germany and Austria-Hungary was highly susceptible to government influence even before the war; and from 1914 to 1918 it was subjected to systematic censorship and manipulation. To blame the press for the nationalistic propaganda which inflamed public opinion before 1914 was to overlook the politicians and pressure groups who controlled or inspired it. Fritz Fischer has shown that the propaganda campaign for a preventive war against Russia in the German press in February and March 1914 was orchestrated by the German Foreign Office.[14] On the other hand it is clear that the diversity of the German press precluded complete government control. The 'orchestration of patriotism' tended to run out of control, as the more chauvinistic sections of the press became more bellicose than the government intended. And this provoked a chain reaction in the British press, which succumbed to an orgy of 'scaremongering'.[15]

During the war itself the German press came under close political and military control. Through its propaganda sections and through agencies like the Wolff Telegraph Bureau, the government was able to manipulate the news that was released to the public. The German press in this period did not constitute an independent political force. Its failure lay precisely in the lack of a capacity for sustained opposition, indeed in its willingness to collaborate with militaristic and annexationist policies. Some credit is certainly due to the Liberal and Socialist press for attempting to adopt a more independent line, particularly during the later stages of the war. But the majority of German newspapers were the willing agents of an authoritarian system. The press of Austria-Hungary, led by the bellicose *Neue Freie Presse*, was equally willingly converted into an instrument of propaganda.[16]

The glaring deficiency of 'In dieser großen Zeit' is that Kraus ignores the responsibility of governments for the belligerence of the press. As recently as March 1914 he had reminded his readers of the 'Dispositionsfonds' used by the Austrian government to bribe the newspapers (F 395–7: 6). But in November 1914 he seems to assume that the authorities are not to blame. Hence the extraordinary naïvety of his suggestion that in view of the disgraceful rantings of the newspapers, the State might decide to throttle the freedom of the press (F 404: 3). The possibility that those rantings might themselves be orchestrated by the press department of the Austrian Foreign Office is simply not considered. In the same essay Kraus cites Bismarck with the implication that, far from having manipulated the press to promote a belligerent purpose, Bismarck too had had wars forced upon him by irresponsible journalists (F 404: 11). Only at a late stage (May 1918) does he acknowledge the analogy between the manipulation of the media in 1914 and Bismarck's use of the Ems telegram to trigger off the Franco-Prussian War (F 474–83: 21).

Who then exerts political control over the press? Kraus's evasion of this question arises partly from his disdain for political analysis, partly from his right-wing prejudices in the period around 1914. He seems to be operating with a simplified model which attributes the evils of war to irresponsible journalists and greedy profiteers. Members of the conservative political establishment, on the other hand, appear to be decent men who are doing their best to cope with an intractable situation. It is this model which is implicit in the rather surprising comments which Kraus makes in December 1915 about the operations of the most important Austrian agency for the dissemination of war propaganda, the Kriegspressequartier (F 413–17: 32–6).

The article shows that Kraus had a clear grasp of the different sections involved in the Austrian propaganda effort: the Kriegsarchiv (which employed writers on more literary tasks); the Kriegspressequartier (which dealt with the day-to-day dissemination of propaganda); the Kriegsberichterstatter — the war correspondents who were actually sent out to report on progress at the front; and the free-lance writers (like Bartsch or Hofmannsthal) who were sent abroad on semi-official missions. But although he grasps the system, Kraus blames the individuals. It is writers like Bartsch and Ginzkey who are held responsible for fraudulent propaganda, not the military

authorities who employ them. Amazingly, the Director of the
Kriegspressequartier, Generalmajor von Hoen, is treated as if he
were Kraus's ally in his campaign against these disreputable scrib-
blers. Von Hoen allegedly quotes passages from *Die Fackel* in order
to teach his minions better manners. And Kraus implies that von
Hoen is one of those army officers who share his own low opinion
of Austrian war reportage ('meine Ansicht über die
Kriegsberichterstattung teilen', *F* 413–17: 35).

It may be that Kraus had reliable sources for this view of von
Hoen.[17] But he is so keen to suggest that the Director of the
Kriegspressequartier really despises journalists that he fails to grasp
that through von Hoen the Austrian High Command are
systematically exploiting the press. The question: who controls the
apparatus? is evaded. As a result, a power vacuum is created within
the structure of his analysis. And individual editors and journalists —
those who operate the apparatus, but do not necessarily control it —
become inflated into the evil geniuses of the war.

The most prominent individual target of 'In dieser großen Zeit' is
not Berchtold or Bethmann Hollweg, but Moriz Benedikt.
Although not mentioned by name, it is unmistakably Benedikt who
is 'the man who sits at the cash desk of world history' ('der Mann,
der an der Kassa der Weltgeschichte sitzt', *F* 404: 7). And it is
Benedikt who is denounced in Kraus's péroration as the one potential
victor of the war. Kraus's attack on Benedikt may be overstated. But
it provides a salutary corrective to the writings of historians who
simply ignore the problem of public opinion in their account of the
origins of the First World War. The neglect of this problem by
political historians seems all the more extraordinary, when one
recalls that *The Times's* obituarist held that 'Benedikt, more than any
other man, was responsible for the downfall of Austria' (*The Times*,
20 March 1920). The fact that the Austrian parliament was suspended
early in 1914, and not reconvened until May 1917, gave the *Neue
Freie Presse* exceptional importance as a forum for shaping policy.

More important than Kraus's attack on individual journalists is his
critique of the apparatus as a whole. Whether public opinion is being
manipulated by newspaper proprietors, or by politicians, is in a sense
beside the point. His fundamental argument is that an apparatus now
exists with an almost unlimited capacity for corrupting the public
mind. And, reciprocally, the intellectual and imaginative resilience of
public opinion has become so impaired that at moments of crisis it
actively participates in a process of self-mystification. The core of
Kraus's critique lies not in the attack on Benedikt, but in his
identification of 'the mental self-mutilation of mankind through its
press' ('die geistige Selbstverstümmelung der Menschheit durch ihre

Presse', *F* 404: 10). The generating of false consciousness is a collective and reciprocal process.

War euphoria is not created *ex nihilo* by a small number of individual propagandists. In 1914 hundreds of thousands of people participated in the writing of patriotic poems, signing of declarations, sending of letters to the press. But without the newspapers, the escalation of public opinion from justifiable national pride into hysterical xenophobia could never have taken place. The very existence of mass-circulation newspapers, under the given conditions of ownership and control, and with advanced technology at their disposal, meant that the negative tendencies inherent in public opinion would become magnified and distorted. The apparatus of the press (as Kraus prophetically wrote in February 1913 at the time of the Prochaska affair) 'transforms fear into panic' ('die Angst in eine Panik verwandelt', *F* 368–9: 45).

For Kraus, the Prochaska affair provided a model of the manufacture of war hysteria that was even more instructive than the Friedjung case. For in this affair the war scare resulted not from conscious political manipulation but from the in-built momentum of the apparatus itself. Consul Prochaska was the Austrian representative in Albania at a time of increasing political and military tension in the Balkans. As a result of a telephone conversation being overheard and misunderstood, the rumour found its way into one of the lesser Viennese newspapers, the *Neues Wiener Journal*, that Prochaska had been tortured and murdered by the Serbs. This report was automatically taken up and reprinted in later editions of other more influential newspapers, and the affair rapidly escalated into a mood of anti-Serbian hysteria, the papers competing with one another to supply new and even more gruesome details of the alleged events. It soon transpired, however, that these reports had no factual basis and that Prochaska was alive and well.

The moral which Kraus draws is that the journalists concerned are guilty, not of a conscious intention to promote war, but of simple irresponsibility in the handling of an apparatus which has built-in mechanisms for generating hysteria. The greatest danger lies in the combination of a highly developed press technology and the equally developed shamelessness of the journalists themselves ('die entwickelte Technik und die entwickelte Schamlosigkeit', *F* 368–9: 47). Kraus's most damaging charge against these journalists is not that they want war, but that it is a matter of indifference to them whether the event they are launching is a war or an operetta (*F* 363–5: 71). The techniques of processing and packaging the news are in principle the same. The manipulation of consciousness (as he stresses again in November 1914) involves an elaborate series of technical processes

— 'systematisch, telegraphisch, telephonisch, photographisch' (*F* 404: 10). So powerful has this apparatus become that it is possible to define the telegram as 'an instrument of war like the grenade': 'Die Depesche ist ein Kriegsmittel wie die Granate' (*F* 404: 12).

On the receiving end of this system of communication is a mass audience which can obtain only a confused echo of the events leading to the declaration of war. But this echo, through built-in mechanisms of distortion and magnification, produces unprecedentedly powerful reverberations. It awakens latent emotions of patriotism, or of personal insecurity, or of a desire for a more heroic form of existence; and it transforms these emotions into a fanatical war euphoria. Moreover, it promotes a readiness for action on an unexampled scale: a mass enthusiasm to volunteer for military service, and a fierce vindictiveness among the civilian population. For Kraus this interdependence between the printed word and the violence of action is so close that he speaks of 'actions which produce reports, and reports which are responsible for actions' ('Taten, die Berichte hervorbringen, und [. . .] Berichte, welche Taten verschulden', *F* 404: 1).

The example which Kraus himself gives is the way atrocity propaganda causes atrocities: 'Bringt [die Zeitung] Lügen über Greuel, so werden Greuel daraus' (*F* 404:11). Thus the report of an alleged atrocity against German or Austrian citizens resident in Serbia may lead newspaper readers to commit precisely that atrocity against Serbian citizens resident in Austria. In such cases, quite literally, the report precedes the reality. On a larger scale, the report that French aeroplanes had dropped bombs on Nuremberg before war had even been declared led German airmen to start dropping real bombs on French cities. The report was false, as Kraus himself pointed out (*F* 431–6: 78). But it was nevertheless used by Bethmann Hollweg to justify the declaration of war.[18] Kraus had good grounds for claiming that a telegram could be as lethal as a grenade.

Kraus thus offers a persuasive account of the connections between war and propaganda (though with certain omissions). His cryptic analysis of November 1914 subsumes arguments which extend back through the pages of *Die Fackel* for more than a decade. In sum, he identifies four main groups responsible for the input of information into the apparatus: economic interest groups; proprietors and editors with strong commercial and political motives; journalists who are remarkable for combining fluent professional skills with a lack of responsibility; and finally the writers and intellectuals who so readily bent their pens to propagandistic purposes. As the war continued, this betrayal by the German intellectual élite of its ethical responsibilities emerged as one of Kraus's most significant themes.

CHAPTER 16

Treason of the Intellectuals

August 1914

Kraus's critical stance in *Die Fackel* challenged the patriotic euphoria which seized the intellectuals of every belligerent nation in August 1914. In Germany scarcely a single writer of note failed to put his pen to the service of the national cause. The leading German dramatist, Gerhart Hauptmann, burst patriotically into verse. The most sophisticated novelist, Thomas Mann, offered an even more eloquent defence of the German cause in the essay 'Gedanken im Krieg', while Rilke, Germany's most gifted poet, celebrated the resurrection of the God of War in 'Fünf Gesänge'. The finest minds of Germany, as well as its most eloquent poets, joined in a chorus of enthusiasm for the war which seemed to carry with it the aspirations of the whole nation.[1]

Scholars and publicists were even more patriotic than poets. For the ideologists of the Pan-German and Navy Leagues the declaration of war was of course the fulfilment of their wildest dreams. But even leading liberals joined the patriotic chorus. Maximilian Harden, the most persistent critic of the Kaiser, now devoted *Die Zukunft* to war propaganda. *Simplicissimus*, scourge of the establishment, became jingoistic overnight. Sociologists like Werner Sombart and Max Scheler proclaimed the cultural idealism which they believed to be the inspiration of German military power. The more moderate Friedrich Meinecke was equally enthusiastic about the rebirth of an authentic German nationalism. Max Weber, though he recorded his doubts about the war in his private correspondence, was soon arguing the case for German annexations. The ninety-three German intellectuals who signed the 'Appeal to the Civilized World' of October 1914 included internationally celebrated figures in the arts and sciences like Ehrlich and Eucken, Harnack and Röntgen, Hauptmann and Humperdinck, Max Reinhardt and Siegfried Wagner.[2]

One seeks in vain for dissenting voices. At the conferences of the Second International in Basle and Berne in 1912 and 1913, the Social Democrats had been passionate in their proclamations of international solidarity. During the final days of July 1914 they had even organized public meetings to protest against imperialistic war-mongering. But on 4 August they experienced a mystical conversion. 'In the hour of danger we shall not leave the fatherland in the lurch,' declared the Social Democratic spokesman Hugo Haase, in the Reichstag debate which unanimously approved war credits. The two most resolute opponents of German militarism were silenced. Karl Liebknecht, author of *Militarismus und Anti-Militarismus* (1907), voted in favour of war credits out of a sense of party discipline. Rosa Luxemburg, who had recently been sentenced to a year's imprisonment for her campaign against militarism, was helpless in the face of the overwhelming patriotism of the German Socialists. Every socialist party in Europe voted unanimously with its own government in favour of war, with the exception of two Serbian socialists and the Bolshevik caucus in the Russian Duma.[3]

The Austrian Socialists led by Victor Adler would also have voted for war if they had had the chance (the Austrian parliament was not consulted). For in Austria-Hungary too all political and ideological divisions were swept away by the patriotic euphoria. The *Arbeiter-Zeitung* carried an ecstatic editorial on 'Der Tag der deutschen Nation' (by Friedrich Austerlitz) proclaiming solidarity with Germany.[4] To general amazement national minorities such as the Czechs shared in the patriotic fervour. And leading Austrian authors were quick to catch the militaristic mood. Hermann Bahr was among the most bellicose in celebrating the 'blessings of war' (*Kriegssegen* was the title he gave to his volume of war essays). More delicate sensibilities proved equally susceptible. Hofmannsthal's patriotic poem 'Österreichs Antwort' appeared in the *Neue Freie Presse*, and he also proclaimed in prose his support for the Austro-Hungarian army ('Die Bejahung Österreichs'). Csokor, Dörmann, Ginzkey, Schaukal and Wildgans all celebrated the glories of war in verse. Robert Musil declared his solidarity with the German cause in 'Europäertum, Krieg, Deutschtum' (published in *Die neue Rundschau*). Stefan Zweig sacrificed his European ideals to service in the Austrian Kriegsarchiv.

The 'Ideas of 1914' became a catch-phrase.[5] It identified a transcendent German patriotism which linked the Habsburg territories with the German Reich, 'Weimar' with 'Potsdam', 'Military Power' with 'Spirituality'. This mood extended throughout the ideological spectrum, and seems to have embraced all social groups. The Jewish community, treated from time immemorial as second-class citizens, felt for the first time during those ecstatic August days that they were full members of the German nation. So overwhelming was this experience of *Gemeinschaft* that even sworn antisemites temporarily renounced their prejudices.[6] The declaration of war unleashed emotions which found expression in an immense body of poetry. It is estimated that within the first year no less than 450 anthologies of German war poetry were published. And the editor of *Der deutsche Krieg im deutschen Gedicht*, a magazine founded specifically to print poetry about the war, estimated that the total number of poems written during this period probably exceeded 3,000,000.[7]

In England, France and Russia a similar mood of war euphoria prevailed. Virtually no one was left untouched. Even Bertrand Russell, the most principled English opponent of the war, records that he was 'tortured by patriotism'.[8] Others, like Rupert Brooke, were swept away by a mood of spiritual elation comparable to that of the German poets:

> Now, God be thanked Who has matched us with His hour,
> And caught our youth, and wakened us from sleeping,
> With hand made sure, clear eye, and sharpened power,
> To turn, as swimmers into cleanness leaping,
> Glad from a world grown old and cold and weary [. . .][9]

And fifty-three leading English authors signed a patriotic declaration prepared by the British minister responsible for propaganda, which was released on 17 September 1914. Jingoistic patriots, chauvinistic socialists and bellicose Christians were as prominent in England and France as they were in Germany.[10] The failure of the Christian churches to offer significant opposition to the slaughter was particularly extraordinary. But in this respect, as in others, it is Germany that provides the extreme case. German theologians had a deeply ingrained sense of duty to the State, and scarcely anyone questioned the Kaiser's conviction that he had God on his side.[11] Even the feminist organizations abandoned their principles and rallied patriotically to the cause.[12]

In Germany the cult of national unity in time of war placed a powerful taboo on dissent. If anyone attempted to speak against the war, his protest was quickly suppressed. Karl Liebknecht did vote against war credits in December 1914, but his statement was deleted from the parliamentary record (and could only be circulated as an illegal broadsheet). In England, on the other hand, there were cracks in the façade of national unity from the very beginning (two Cabinet ministers resigned in protest at the declaration of war). Although popular enthusiasm was overwhelming and hundreds of thousands immediately volunteered for military service, there was initially no compulsory conscription and it was possible for individuals to opt out. The more liberal climate of Asquith's England allowed a freedom for critical opposition which papers like the *Manchester Guardian* and the *Nation*, writers like Bertrand Russell and Bernard Shaw intermittently exploited. Journals like the *Labour Leader* and the *Cambridge Magazine* provided a forum for dissenting voices. And when Ramsay MacDonald began to speak out against the war, he was faithfully reported at least by the *Aberdeen Free Press*. Moreover individual writers could draw on the support of significant opposition groupings: the Neutrality League, the No-Conscription Fellowship, the Union for Democratic Control and the Independent Labour Party.

The situation in France was more precarious (the assassination of the Socialist leader Jean Jaurès on the eve of the declaration of war signalled the defeat of the critics of military policy). And as German armies advanced towards Paris, it was clear that France really was fighting a battle for survival. But even here there was scope for opposition. The writings of Romain Rolland, although published in Switzerland, were able to circulate fairly freely and provoked a vigorous debate.[13]

In Germany and Austria-Hungary, opposition was almost completely silenced. The serialization of Heinrich Mann's novel *Der Untertan*, which had begun to appear earlier in 1914, was abruptly halted. *Die Aktion* ceased to have a political voice. *Das Forum*, which initially carried articles more critical in tone, was soon suppressed. Only in Switzerland was there scope for protest against the war. But the only German writer in Switzerland who rose to the occasion was Hermann Hesse, who, overcoming his initial impulse to throw himself into the service of the German cause, published in November 1914 his appeal for restraint and international understanding, 'O Freunde, nicht diese Töne!'.[14]

Within the territories of the Central Powers German writers had a threefold censorship to contend with: the official censorship of the government, the unofficial censorship exercised by editors and publishers, and the overwhelming pressure of public opinion. In these circumstances, few German writers had the opportunity, and none the courage, to publish the kind of direct challenge to government policy which Bertrand Russell wrote for the *Nation*. The inertness of the highly organized German Peace Society in 1914 exemplifies this failure of nerve in the face of the overwhelming power of German militarism.[15] The spectacular military victories of 1914 were celebrated as proof of the superiority of German *Kultur*. The irony is that intellectuals in other countries were equally eloquent in portraying the war as a cultural or ethical crusade.[16]

'Treason of the Intellectuals' was the phrase coined by Julien Benda in 1927 to describe the 'intellectual organization of political hatreds'.[17] By that date the reaction against the war had led to a profound disillusionment. The political gains promised by the apologists of war had proved illusory. The cost in human life was all too clear. More than 8,000,000 soldiers died in battle between 1914 and 1918. And millions of civilians perished from the ravages of bombardment or disease. It was these stark facts that the celebrations of war served to conceal, even to glamorize. With hindsight it was clear that the armchair ideologists of war had done no service to their fellow countrymen in the trenches and had helped to inflict an unprecedented disaster upon mankind.

It is easy to be wise after the event. Kraus's signal achievement was to identify this 'Treason of the Intellectuals' *before* the cataclysm occurred. In his analysis of the Friedjung trial (January 1910) he had demonstrated in exemplary form the willingness of one patriotic intellectual to lend his prestige to the cause of war. In autumn 1914, he extended the argument to include almost all the leading German and Austrian intellectuals.

The Two Germanies

In Kraus's declaration of November 1914 six writers are mentioned by name: Gerhart Hauptmann, Richard Dehmel, Hugo von Hofmannsthal, Ernst Haeckel, Ferdinand Hodler and (as a positive contrast) Detlev von Liliencron (*F* 404: 16–17). These figures are not treated as individuals, but have a representative significance. Among literary authors, Hauptmann and Dehmel are representative for Germany, Hofmannsthal for Austria. Haeckel, one of the ninety-three intellectuals who signed the 'Appeal' of 1914, is perhaps the most prominent figure in the German academic community (the responses of which will be analysed in a later chapter). The Swiss painter Hodler raises the question of how the war is viewed from neutral Switzerland, while in citing Liliencron (and reading from his work on 19 November 1914) Kraus is leaving open the possibility that the war might elicit a more authentic imaginative response.

Gerhart Hauptmann was by far the most celebrated German writer of his day. His powerful early plays had earned him international recognition, including the award of the Nobel Prize for Literature (in 1912) and of honorary degrees from various foreign universities (including Oxford). In an era of imperialism and of increasing military rivalry he represented the 'other Germany'. He was the poet of social conscience (*Die Weber*) and of compassion for human suffering (*Hanneles Himmelfahrt*). He portrayed the dignity of the common man (*Fuhrmann Henschel*), and his imaginative powers enabled him to endow the victims of an oppressive social order with a certain tragic pathos (*Die Ratten*). In 1913 he had even written a pacifistic *Festspiel in deutschen Reimen*, which had alienated his more conservative admirers (including Kraus himself) (*F* 378–80: 29–34). It was thus a remarkable volte-face for Hauptmann to publish in August 1914 the poem 'O mein Vaterland!', celebrating the grandeur of the era ('die große Zeit'), defending the sacred cause of Germany, and justifying the slaughter as a necessary harvest of corpses.[18] This kind of poetry (as Kraus noted) was soon to be found in school textbooks corrupting the minds of the next generation (*F* 426–30: 57).

For Kraus the sense of betrayal was all the more grievous because he had from earliest days been an ardent admirer. He had read Hauptmann's *Vor Sonnenaufgang* in 1890 (at the age of sixteen), had attended the Berlin première of *Die Weber* in 1893, and regarded *Hanneles Himmelfahrt* as a poetic masterpiece. He particularly admired what might today be regarded as one of the more questionable aspects of Hauptmann's work: his ability to transpose the theme of social suffering on to the elevated plane of poetic vision (Hannele is redeemed by the Three Angels who liberate her from earthly sufferings). One reason for condemning the *Festspiel in deutschen Reimen* was Kraus's sense that Hauptmann was sacrificing integrity of poetic vision to political sloganizing.

He was thus appalled in August 1914 to find Hauptmann descending to the level of jingoistic journalism. Since the pressures of censorship inhibited outspoken analysis, Kraus adopted a strategy of confronting the language of patriotic slogans with that of poetic inspiration, by printing in parallel columns two passages by Hauptmann from different stages of his career: 1894 — the compassionate verses of the Three Angels in *Hannele*; and 1914 — some wretched doggerel about the Three Robbers (France, Russia, England) who have assaulted Germany (*F* 426–30: 14–15). The aim was to confront the true Hauptmann with the false, the poet with the propagandist. And this provided the central strategy of Kraus's attack on the treason of the intellectuals throughout the war.

Unlike Benda, he does not attempt an abstract definition of the loyalties of a writer. Instead, he repeatedly gives examples of imaginatively sensitive and ethically responsible discourse, quoting Goethe, Schopenhauer, Jean Paul, Stifter and many others. And in his public readings he eloquently juxtaposed the humane vision of these writers with the debased discourse of the propagandists. *Hanneles Himmelfahrt* was also read in public to differentiate the true Hauptmann from the false (*F* 457–61: 62–3). And by this strategy Kraus brings about the confrontation of 'two Germanies': that of the

Kaiser rejoicing in total victory on the Eastern Front; and that of Kant with his vision of 'Perpetual Peace' (F 474–83: 155–6). The dualism exemplified by Hauptmann is expanded into a vision of a nation which has betrayed its better self.

Richard Dehmel provides a second major theme: the betrayal not of the intellect, but of nature. Dehmel too was a representative figure, the most celebrated lyric poet of Wilhelminian Germany. He was seen as a progressive writer, the prophet of a new, dynamic age. And his rhapsodic verses provided a prototype for the declamatory style of the rising Expressionist generation. Dehmel's response to the outbreak of war was even more astonishing than that of Hauptmann. At the age of fifty-one he enthusiastically volunteered for active service. In extravagant verses he celebrated the war as a divine visitation ('die große Gottesstunde'). And in 'Weihnachtsgruß', published in the Neue Freie Presse on 25 December 1914, he even compared the sound of machine-guns to the music of the spheres ('Sphärenmusik'). What particularly caught Kraus's attention, however, was the way Dehmel conscripted to the patriotic cause the helpless animals who were being killed by the thousand on the field of battle (F 418–22: 42–4). This sacrifice of innocent creatures to the destructive power of the machine was to be developed into one of Kraus's most poignant themes.

Responding to Dehmel's travesties of traditional nature poetry, Kraus again sets up a positive counterpoint. Stifter's story 'Der Hochwald' shows how the sanctity of nature may be invoked against the depredations of war (F 418–22: 56–8). But it is Goethe's poem 'Wandrers Nachtlied' which provides his touchstone. In this most celebrated of German poems the contemplation of nature brings serenity and self-transcendence. The war fever however led to the popularization of militaristic travesties of Goethe's hallowed lines. For Kraus this is a satanic betrayal of the German spirit, for which he holds Hauptmann and Dehmel partly responsible (F 454–6: 1–4). He reminds his readers that Goethe had kept aloof from the national hatreds of the German Wars of Liberation of 1813–15 and had described the writing of warlike poetry by non-combatants like himself as 'eine Maske' (F 443–4: 20).

Kraus is tireless in tracking down bellicose littérateurs. Writers like Alfred Kerr, Ludwig Ganghofer, Otto Ernst and Carl Busse command his attention because of their contemporary popularity. Kerr, a radical democrat before the war and an avowed pacifist afterwards, distinguished himself during 1914–18 by writing xenophobic poems under the pseudonym 'Gottlieb' (F 437–42: 7). Ganghofer, author of folksy romances set in the Bavarian countryside, wrote essays in praise of the war that were an appalling blend of sentimentality and cruelty (*F* 426–30: 15–16). The chauvinistic writings of Otto Ernst were so popular with the front-line troops that Kraus was temporarily reduced to speechlessness, merely documenting in *Die Fackel* the adulatory response (*F* 445–53: 80–6). Busse cashed in on the war with patriotic poems and stories (*F* 454–56: 8–10). What incensed Kraus was not simply the spectacle of writers making money out of the sufferings of others. It was the fact that so many writers and journalists produced war propaganda in order to save their own skins. Towards the end of the war he vowed that this infamy should never be forgotten (*F* 474–83: 156–8).

Patriots and Aesthetes in Austria

In Austria-Hungary the conversion of poets into patriots was even more astonishing. For Austria lacked that stern sense of duty to the State which had been a feature of German life well before 1914. Where in the Germany of the 1890s Hauptmann had exemplified the social commitment of Naturalism, in Austria Hermann Bahr was already proclaiming that Naturalism had been 'superseded'. And the precocious writings of Hofmannsthal had established him as the epitome of Austrian aestheticism. Kraus's sympathies with the Naturalists had led him to denounce Hermann Bahr in one of his early contributions to *Die Gesellschaft* (*FS* I. 103–14). And the aesthetes of the Café Griensteidl had been mocked in his early satire *Die demolirte Literatur* (1897). The astonishing thing is that so many of those littérateurs reappear in *Die Fackel* twenty years later as war-mongers: the aesthete masquerading as *miles gloriosus*.

Hermann Bahr and Felix Salten were predictable candidates for this transformation. Their journalistic versatility enabled them to trim their sails to any wind, and they ran willingly before the storms of war. More surprising is the case of Felix Dörmann, the lyricist of febrile femininity (*Neurotica*, 1891; *Sensationen*, 1892), who reappears as the author of xenophobic doggerel (*F* 462–71: 24). Leo Feld is another of the languid habitués of the Café Griensteidl whom we now find exulting in the gore of battle (*F* 418–22: 100–4). And the librettist Viktor Leon, ironized in 1897 as 'ein wirklich Nervöser', is also cashing in on the patriotic euphoria (*F* 418–22: 102). Even Leopold Andrian, who had long abandoned poetry for a diplomatic career, makes a passing reappearance, welcoming Hofmannsthal on a propaganda mission to Warsaw (*F* 431–6: 95–6). But the key figure is Hofmannsthal himself.

During the First World War Hofmannsthal and Kraus represented diametrically opposed positions of patriotism and pacifism. The confrontation between them exemplifies not merely the divergent response of two gifted writers to a specific historical crisis, but also a more fundamental conflict of loyalties. To evaluate their positions, it is necessary to define what is meant by 'loyalty' and what for an intellectual may constitute 'treason'. If patriotism means supporting the use of poison gas and it is treason to regard victories gained by this means with abhorrence, then Kraus willingly declares himself to be one of the greatest traitors of all time (F 474–83: 43). But if the overriding loyalty is to ethical principles, then it is the political leaders of Austria-Hungary and the German Reich who are guilty of high treason (F 484–98: 235).

Hofmannsthal's loyalty was to Austria-Hungary. As an officer in the reserve (aged forty at the outbreak of war) he was immediately conscripted into the army. But he was soon transferred to a desk job in Vienna. While technically still a serving officer, he became the most prominent literary apologist for the Austro-Hungarian cause. He had close links with the Austrian Foreign Ministry and was sent on semi-official propaganda missions to neutral countries like Switzerland and Scandinavia. His writings are free of the blood-thirsty chauvinism which is so characteristic of this period. But he was unequivocal in his support for the Central Powers and became the most eloquent spokesman for Austria's cultural mission. His letters reveal his doubt and despondency about the viability of the Austrian cause. But they also show the strength of his patriotic feelings. Loyalty to his country took precedence over personal doubts and scruples.[19]

In the eyes of the State it was Kraus's loyalty which was in doubt. Although born in the same year as Hofmannsthal, he was exempt from military service on medical grounds, because of his spinal deformity. Through his writings in Die Fackel and his public readings he became identified as the spokesman of 'defeatism' in Austria-Hungary. And he was denounced to the authorities in March 1918 for allegedly making a treasonable appeal to officers present at a public reading to break their swords and defy their superiors. Although Kraus was able to refute this allegation, he was clearly a suspect figure in the eyes of the War Ministry and the Army High Command (F 508–13: 81–104). Heavy prison sentences were being imposed on persons convicted of appealing to soldiers to lay down their arms (F 474–83: 150). And dissidents convicted of treason (such as Cesare Battisti) were ruthlessly executed. Kraus was more cautious. He had a profound respect for the rule of law and never sought the overthrow of the State. His letters suggest that until a late stage in the war he hoped that the old order in Austria-Hungary would be preserved.

The question is whether a writer's overriding loyalty should be to his country or to some other principle. In The Treason of the

Intellectuals Benda poses the question with exemplary clarity. Is it the function of the intellectual 'to secure empires'? Should his loyalty not rather be to 'disinterested intellectual activity'?[20] Kraus's writings during the First World War pose the question in equally radical terms. But like Benda he does not sufficiently allow for the interdependence of intellectual activity and political institutions. It is only within a community governed by the rule of law that the individual can enjoy the freedom of intellectual dissent. When the existence of the State itself is threatened, intellectual intransigence may become self-defeating. Confronted by this same dilemma in 1934, Kraus was to make a very different choice, sacrificing his critical independence to the overriding need to preserve the independence of Austria. But during the 1914–18 war his position was more intransigent. Hofmannsthal suppressed his individual scruples in the interests of the State. Kraus's insistence on the primacy of the ethical led him ultimately to desire the defeat of his own country.

For Kraus, the writer's primary loyalty is to the self, conceived as the stable centre of ethical integrity. It is for their sacrifice of the self that he arraigns Hauptmann, Dehmel and Hofmannsthal in November 1914: 'Die Aufopferung der führenden Geister ist so rapid, daß der Verdacht entsteht, sie hätten kein Selbst aufzuopfern gehabt. (The self-sacrifice of the leading minds has been so rapid that the suspicion arises that they may have had no self to sacrifice.)' (*F* 404: 16) Fundamental to this conception is the notion of consistency. It was the abruptness of the conversions to patriotism in 1914 which aroused Kraus's immediate suspicion. (His own change of viewpoint involved a long period of silence and a protracted reappraisal of earlier attitudes.) Above all, integrity of the self implies intellectual honesty — a close correlation between public utterance and personal conviction, 'Wort und Wesen' (*F* 508–13: 80). An author should not write about the glories of war unless he is willing to volunteer for front-line service.

It is this discrepancy which Kraus criticizes in the case of Hofmannsthal. But it was Hermann Bahr who provided the initial stimulus. In a feuilleton published on 26 August 1914 in the *Neues Wiener Journal*, Bahr had sent his exultant greetings to Hofmannsthal, whom he pictures as a lieutenant somewhere on the eastern front, sitting by his camp-fire armed to the teeth. In this 'Open Letter' Bahr explicitly links the prevailing spirit of German national solidarity with the rarefied intellectual pursuits he and Hofmannsthal had shared twenty years earlier. And he imagines Hofmannsthal in the conquered city of Warsaw, calling on Leopold Andrian who had been Austrian consul there. Andrian will no doubt be striding through the room declaiming Baudelaire in his deep impassioned voice, while the drums of victory reverberate outside. The text of this feuilleton was reprinted and astringently glossed by Kraus in *Die Fackel* of May 1916, and later incorporated into *Die letzten Tage der Menschheit*.

In fact Hofmannsthal, far from being under arms at the front, was safely at the Kriegsfürsorgeamt in Vienna — an office concerned with the servicing and welfare of the troops. Bahr may in August 1914 have been writing in good faith, but he was soon disabused. This did not prevent him from reprinting the feuilleton in *Kriegssegen* in 1915.[21] The incorrigible Hermann Bahr was thus an easy target. But the main thrust of Kraus's comments is directed against Hofmannsthal himself.

Hofmannsthal could scarcely be blamed for Bahr's vacuous patriotic fantasy. The trouble was that Hofmannsthal had allowed Bahr's picture of his military valour to circulate uncorrected. And by 1916 the omission was compounded by the fact that Hofmannsthal had emerged as a prime disseminator of patriotic propaganda. The proper course (Kraus insists) would have been to issue a public repudiation of Bahr's feuilleton and ensure that *Kriegssegen* was pulped. In view of the sheltered and civilian nature of his own war service, Hofmannsthal should also refrain from any form of eulogy of military prowess (*F* 423–5: 50). The kind of honourable silence which Kraus has in mind is that of Arthur Schnitzler, who not only held his peace, but even issued a vigorous *démenti* when a patriotic journalist attributed to him xenophobic sentiments.[22]

Kraus pictures Hofmannsthal writing a forthright letter to Bahr, correcting his misapprehensions and assuring him that he is indeed enjoying the war — precisely because he is *not* at the front but safely in Vienna (*F* 423–5: 47–8). We now know that what Hofmannsthal actually wrote to Bahr was a letter of a more devious kind. He explains that after mobilization at the end of July 1914 he had been transferred ('abcommandiert') to a department of the War Ministry: 'So much for the necessary correction. After all, each man stands where he has been ordered to go, and I accept your kind lines with heartfelt pleasure.'[23] Far from wishing to issue a public denial, Hofmannsthal actually takes pleasure in the legend Bahr has circulated about his military valour. And in the same breath he puts into circulation a second legend for his own personal satisfaction. It was simply untrue that he had been 'ordered' ('befohlen') to return to Vienna. On being mobilized for front-line service in the Balkans, he had pulled strings with friends in high places in order to avoid active service.

It was not difficult for Kraus to guess that Hofmannsthal must have owed his desk job to 'Protektion' (*F* 423–5: 48). But the full story is more compromising than even he could have imagined. In July 1914

Hofmannsthal obtained his transfer to Vienna through the influence of his friend Josef Redlich (a leading Austrian politician) and of Count Hohenlohe, Governor of Trieste. In the spring of 1915 he managed to arrange a complete dispensation from military service. His first idea was to find some eminent psychiatrist who would certify that he was unfit for military service because of his 'really absurd nerves'. But he was able ultimately to mobilize three prominent friends, Redlich, Alexander Hoyos (principal adviser to the Austrian Foreign Secretary) and Johann Chlumecky (another prominent politician), who persuaded Count Stürgkh, the Austrian Prime Minister, to intervene in person and secure Hofmannsthal's release.[24]

Kraus does not reproach Hofmannsthal for saving his own skin. That is a private matter. The trouble is that Hofmannsthal is so zealous in celebrating the glories of front-line service which he himself has been so anxious to evade. Reviewing the salient features of these patriotic publications, Kraus concludes that Hofmannsthal's integrity is as deeply compromised as that of any of the army of littérateurs who have been sent out to glorify events which they are desperately keen not to experience themselves. He is indeed one of the most outstanding culprits (F 423–35: 51).

Kraus mentions specifically only a few of Hofmannsthal's wartime publications: the patriotically conceived Österreichische Bibliothek series which he edited, his Österreichischer Almanach auf das Jahr 1916, and his popularization of the heroic deeds of Prince Eugene. But Kraus must also have been aware of the more overtly militaristic essays which Hofmannsthal contributed to the Neue Freie Presse, such as 'Geist der Karpathen' (23 May 1915) and 'Unsere Militärverwaltung in Polen' (8 August 1915). These two essays in particular give substance to the accusation that Hofmannsthal glamorized the achievements of the Austrian army.[25] Kraus's attention was also caught by a speech which Hofmannsthal delivered in Berlin in February 1916 under the title 'Unser Krieg', reported in the Neue Freie Presse of 3 February 1916. Although the text of this speech has not survived, press reports indicate that Hofmannsthal celebrated 'Our War' (the conflict with Italy) as a beneficial historical mission which had been joyously accepted by the Austrian people.[26]

The patriotic colouring of Hofmannsthal's writings is for Kraus merely skilful theatrical make-up ('sich mit den Landesfarben schminken', F 423–5: 52). They exemplify the hollowness of Austrian aestheticism: 'Der Krieg hat durch die Anziehung, die er auf die schwerpunktlosen Gehirne, auf das Scheinmenschentum, auf die dekorationsfähige Leere ausgeübt hat, Unwerte vernichtet [. . .]' (The war, through the attraction which it has exerted on brains lacking a centre of gravity, on the hollow men, on emptiness endowed with decorative capability, has destroyed false values [. . .].' (*F* 423–5: 51) These words form the culmination of a critique of aestheticism for which Hofmannsthal had since the 1890s provided Kraus's principal example. Hofmannsthal is repeatedly described as a derivative artist lacking in personal inspiration and dependent on pre-existent art forms: 'ein Künstler nach der Kunst und kein Künstler aus sich selbst' (*F* 242–3: 24). His whole mode of production reveals a lack not merely of imaginative resources but also of resoluteness of character: 'Mangel an Persönlichkeit' (*F* 261–2: 13). This analysis had led Kraus as early as October 1908 to suggest a correlation between aesthete and ideologue. Sustained by no inner centre of gravity, the one attitude can easily become inverted into its opposite. In this sense the aesthete's orchid is indistinguishable from the party politician's button-hole (*F* 261–2: 13). Kraus's sense of the dangers which arise when the aesthete begins to editorialize was reinforced in 1912, when Hofmannsthal published in the *Neue Freie Presse* a patriotic reply to the anti-Austrian sentiments of Gabriele d'Annunzio (*F* 343–4: 44–5). And the events of the war confirmed his diagnosis.

It may be objected that despite his equivocations over military service, Hofmannsthal's patriotism was sincere. But for Kraus true patriotism demands intellectual rigour and moral courage. He makes this point in January 1917 by contrasting Hofmannsthal with a more admirable Austrian patriot, Heinrich Lammasch. Lammasch was a noted international lawyer who shared Hofmannsthal's conservative, Catholic and dynastic allegiances, so the comparison is apt. Hofmannsthal had been on a mission to Scandinavia, delivering lectures which place an idealistic gloss on the war aims of the Central Powers. Lammasch, by contrast, in the article which Kraus cites in *Die Fackel*, denies the war's supposed 'sublimity' and insists that it is an 'immense catastrophe'. And he attributes much of the blame to the German Reich, whose representatives had frustrated the efforts of the peace conferences in The Hague to ensure that international disputes were settled by peaceful means (*F* 445–53: 65–7). Lammasch was even willing to risk arrest for his convictions. And he made memorable speeches in the Austrian House of Lords in favour of a negotiated peace.[27] For Kraus he was in a deeper sense an Austrian patriot (*F* 474–83: 46).

After the war, without renouncing his propagandistic writings, Hofmannsthal began to make gestures of international reconciliation. Kraus insists that such gestures have no value, unless they are accompanied by a clear repudiation of past misdeeds (*F* 514–18: 63–4). And his critique of Hofmannsthal is here linked with another ambiguous example, Stefan Zweig.

Even before the First World War Zweig had built himself a considerable reputation as author and essayist, translator and apostle of European cultural exchange. In the autumn of 1914 he joined the Austrian army and was assigned to service in the Kriegsarchiv. He was nevertheless able to maintain his international contacts, above all his correspondence with Romain Rolland, whom he sought to reassure that he was remaining faithful to their internationalist ideals. In 1915 he began work on a play, *Jeremias*, which celebrated the themes of defeat and renunciation. Published at Easter 1917, it enhanced his reputation as writer opposed to the prevailing patriotic bellicosity. From February 1917 onwards, with the approval of the Austrian authorities, Zweig spent substantial periods in Switzerland, where he expressed pacifist sentiments in a number of articles and reviews. He now enjoyed an international reputation as the leading pacifist among Austrian writers — 'the good European Stefan Zweig', as Rolland called him.[28]

Kraus was unimpressed. Well before the war, in January 1913, he had sceptically glossed Zweig's literary versatility, raising doubts about the stability of purpose of a writer who years before his conversion to Europeanism had poetically idealized the love of the German homeland ('die deutsche Heimatliebe verklärt', *F* 366–7: 26). This motif is taken up again in May 1917, after Zweig has become a contributor to *Donauland* — the 'Danubian Realm', the patriotic journal sponsored by the Kriegsarchiv. Zweig is mentioned only briefly, together with other contributors such as Rilke, Bahr and Ginzkey. But by implication he too is to be counted among those who are denounced as parasites of 'Heimatgefühl' and authors of a 'Feuilletonismus der Glorie', who glorify the battle-front in order to escape it (*F* 457–61: 22–5). In October 1918, after the première of *Jeremias*, Zweig is singled out for special attention. Kraus confronts the 'good European' Zweig, who is enjoying such credit in Switzerland, with the propagandist of the Kriegsarchiv, who in Vienna had been prepared to lay down his life for the 'Danubian Realm' (*F* 484–98: 127–8).

This confrontation has been described as a distressing attack on a 'naïvely well-intentioned' person who was 'genuinely opposed to the war'.[29] Was Zweig not the man who (in the words of his autobiography) had 'not succumbed' to the patriotic intoxication of August 1914; whose conciliatory essay of September 1914, 'An die Freunde in Fremdland', had been welcomed by Romain Rolland; who in the midst of the war had published an article praising the pacifist Bertha von Suttner; and who after visiting war-ravaged Galicia in the spring of 1915 had dedicated himself to the battle against war propaganda and false conceptions of heroism?

The answer is no. Research has shown that Zweig's claims to have been a pacifist from the outset are dubious. His greatest ambition (as he wrote in the autumn of 1914 in a private letter) was to be an army officer helping to win military victories in France. And in a series of published articles he praised the ethical energy of the German war effort (August 1914); hailed the moral and political regeneration of Austria-Hungary (December 1914); and defended the German invasion of Belgium (April 1915). Even the article 'An die Freunde in Fremdland' proves to be a highly ambiguous document, whose velleities were immediately seen through by the vigilant Romain Rolland. Zweig's pacifist publications date from a far later stage in the war (the Suttner article appeared on 21 June 1918).

Worst of all, after his visit to Galicia Zweig was himself guilty of writing precisely the kind of war propaganda which in *The World of Yesterday* he claims to have attacked. An article describing his impressions of Galicia appeared in the *Neue Freie Presse* of 31 August 1915. It is characterized by a facile optimism which emphasizes the positive achievements of German and Austrian reconstruction in Galicia and looks forward to a German victory which will bring the war to an end. The high-mindedness of the letters which Zweig was writing to Rolland is difficult to reconcile with this kind of patriotic propaganda. The nadir is reached in a poem entitled 'Der Krüppel', published in the Christmas 1914 number of the *Neue Freie Presse*, which sentimentalizes the figure of a soldier mutilated by war.

Zweig was a pacifist who lacked the courage of his own convictions. His private diaries reveal the dismal spectacle of a writer aghast at the horrors of war, and yet actively collaborating in the writing of propaganda.[30] It was not until July 1918, when he was safely in Switzerland, that Zweig plucked up the courage to proclaim an unequivocal pacifism. Rarely has a writer of such sensitivity shown so little moral resolution.

In short Kraus was right. If he erred in his writings on Zweig, it was on the side of leniency. With economy and restraint he uses the example of Zweig to establish important points of principle. First, that pacifism is devalued if it is based on earlier betrayals which remain unacknowledged; secondly, that an abstract pacifism, however well-intentioned, must remain inert if it flinches from political engagement. The line which Kraus draws in October 1918 between Zweig's position and his own is exemplary (*F* 484–98: 127–8).

Kraus seems to have felt that pacifists who only opposed the war from the sanctuary of Switzerland were evading their responsibilities. This may explain why (in addition to his comments on Zweig) he is so grudging in his recognition of Romain Rolland's achievements (*F* 484–93: 127–8) and fails even to mention Hermann Hesse. Perhaps Kraus was too much absorbed with Germany and Austria-Hungary to do justice to the humane position adopted by certain writers and artists in Switzerland. In autumn 1914 the Swiss painter Ferdinand Hodler had incensed German public opinion by signing a protest against the bombardment of Reims cathedral. The outrage was all the greater because for many people Hodler's historical paintings seemed to epitomize the spirit of self-sacrifice with which the German soldiers of 1914 had marched off to battle (*The Departure of the Jena Students for the War for Freedom of 1813* seemed particularly apt).[31] Kraus's comment in November 1914 implies that Hodler's protest was unjustified, though his motives may be admirable (*F* 404: 17).

Even more surprising is Kraus's failure to acknowledge the integrity of the Swiss writer Carl Spitteler, who stood firm against the pressure to identify himself with the German cause and found dignified words to define the principles of Swiss neutrality.[32] Kraus was almost certainly familiar with Spitteler's position, since he visited him in Switzerland in May 1916 in the company of Sidonie Nadherny (*BSN* II. 53, 223). During the later stages of the war Zurich became the rallying-point for a significant group of intellectual dissidents who had taken refuge there from the rampant militarism of the German Reich. They included René Schickele, Leonhard Frank, Ludwig Rubiner, Hugo Ball, Klabund and Albert Ehrenstein. But Kraus is unwilling to acknowledge the value of their rather abstract humanitarianism, particularly when it is formulated in a turgid Expressionist idiom. The lyrical effusions of Ehrenstein, written from sheltered positions first in the Austrian Kriegsarchiv and later in Switzerland, cannot for Kraus count as a significant act of protest (*F* 514–18: 5–9).[33]

Only one leading Austrian writer escaped Kraus's censure. This is because only one leading Austrian writer refused to join the patriotic chorus: Arthur Schnitzler. Almost alone among European liberals in 1914 Schnitzler stuck to his principles, refusing to make the slightest concession to militarism or xenophobia. As Austria's most celebrated author he came under great pressure to lend his prestige to the German cause. Publishers, editors and theatre directors badgered him to write patriotic essays and plays. His diaries show that even his wife Olga gave him a bad time because he held aloof from the popular fervour. And his bank manager was dismayed by the sudden drop in Schnitzler's earnings, when so many other writers were cashing in on the war. The pressures even filtered through to his dreams, in which the Emperor Franz Joseph admonished him for failing in his patriotic duty.

Schnitzler stood firm. From the very beginning he saw the war as a disaster. 'World war. World ruin', he noted on hearing that Britain had declared war on Germany (5 August 1914). And like Kraus he attributed the popular enthusiasm to a failure of imagination. With the humane eye of a doctor who has attended operations on wounded soldiers he recognized that the essential meaning of war is not 'fame' but 'suffering'.[34] And he severely censures authors who celebrate military heroism while avoiding front-line service themselves. Schnitzler lacked the courage and resourcefulness which enabled Kraus to articulate his protest in public. But his dignified silence nevertheless earned him the following tribute from Kraus in 1918:

> Sein Wort vom Sterben wog nicht schwer.
> Doch wo viel Feinde, ist viel Ehr:
> er hat in Schlachten und Siegen
> geschwiegen.
>
> (*W* VII. 134)
>
> (Though what he wrote of death is poor,
> there's honour to be gained in war.
> Battles were raging without cease;
> he held his peace.)

From the examples discussed it is clear that Kraus's critique of intellectuals who have betrayed their mission is a matter of principles, rather than personalities. His approach is consistent and comprehensive (although there are one or two surprising omissions).[35] This chapter has concentrated on the representative figures. But Kraus is equally vigilant in his scrutiny of minor authors whose cruder mode of utterance often gave their work even greater popular resonance. Ernst Lissauer's notorious 'Haßgesang gegen England' is noted, together with Hugo Zuckermann's resonant 'Reiterlied' (these two poems achieved such immense popularity that Kraus does not even need to identify their authors) (*F* 418–22: 43–4). He condemns the xenophobic brutalism of Ottokar Kernstock's poetry (*F* 437–42: 74–5) and the blood-thirsty prose of Karl Hans Strobl (*F* 431–6: 58–9); the paper-thin patriotism of Siegfried Trebitsch (*F* 406–12: 19–24) and the sadistic utterances of Franz Karl Ginzkey (*F* 413–17: 33).[36] He is aware that Stefan Grossmann, erstwhile anarchist, is now supporting the German war effort in the columns of the *Vossische Zeitung* in Berlin (*F* 426–30: 25).[37] And he keeps an eye on *Donauland*, the most prestigious journal of Austrian patriotism (*F* 457–61 22–5).

Kraus's judgements may seem severe, particularly as he himself (being exempt from military service) did not have to face the problem of being conscripted into a war he abhorred. But he was

also capable of a more generous response to writers caught in this
dilemma. This is clear from his comments on a poem by Rilke,
which had appeared in *Donauland* alongside the work of the blood-
thirsty Franz Karl Ginzkey:

> Wenn ich ein so feiner Mensch in der Literatur wäre wie Rainer Maria
> Rilke (den ich wirklich dafür halte und den Feinheit vor schlechter
> Gesellschaft nicht bewahren konnte [. . .]), mich würde diese
> Anerkennung meiner Lyrik [. . .] zu dem Entschluß treiben, aus der
> Literatur im Allgemeinen und aus dem Donauland im Besonderen
> auszutreten. Oder vielmehr: ich wäre — allen widrigen Umständen zum
> Trotz — nie eingetreten.   (*F* 457–61: 23)

> (If I were as refined a person in literature as Rainer Maria Rilke (whom I
> really do regard as such and whose refinement has not preserved him
> from bad company [. . .]), this recognition of my lyric poetry [. . .]
> would lead me to resolve to retire from literature in general and the
> Danubian Realm in particular. Or rather: I would never — in spite of all
> adverse circumstances — have joined it.)

In this passage the rigour of the satirist is held in check by Kraus's
more generous private judgement (parenthetically interpolated). The
dualism which underlies his satire here for once becomes explicit. In
most cases there is a direct relationship between the two levels: the
personal ruminations of the author, and the condensed judgement of
the satirist which is their literary precipitate. Here however an
unresolved tension between the two modes of judgement breaks
through into the published text. The sources of this tension can be
traced through Kraus's letters to Sidonie Nadherny, though the story
is too complex to be unfolded here.

The chronicle of Rilke's life shows that he was the most reluctant
of recruits to the Austrian Kriegsarchiv. Unlike Stefan Zweig, he
declined to carry out the duty of writing patriotic copy about the
war, and had instead to be assigned to the task of drawing lines in
ledgers. Though Rilke had initially been carried away by the
euphoria of August 1914, his letters show that by the end of that
month he had recovered his inner centre of integrity: 'dann besann
ich mich [. . .] auf mich selbst' (letter of 29 August). On 19 October
1914 we find him refusing a request from the publisher Axel Juncker
to write war poems. His private letters of 1915 show that he retained
his internationalism of outlook and felt alienated from both Germany
and Austria.[38] Kraus's comments on Rilke show that he was able to
discriminate between the poet's poignant dilemma and the more
dubious activities of the patriotic Austrian aesthetes.

Were these writers (as one historian has concluded) merely 'artists
weak in moral fibre'?[39] Kraus's charge is more serious. He argues

that writers like Hofmannsthal and Stefan Zweig traded their intellectual integrity for a safe desk job and became propagandists of a cause for which they were unwilling to risk their own lives. Of the authors mentioned in this chapter only Hugo Zuckermann actually fought in battle. The Austrian authorities were indulgent to their leading writers, who almost without exception found jobs with the Kriegsarchiv or the Kriegspressequartier. The great strength of English poetry of the First World War is that it is written by men who had direct experience of trench warfare, to which they responded with moral as well as imaginative energy. Their finest poems face the full horror of war. But what is revealed in the writings surveyed in this chapter is a fundamental dishonesty: the use of heroic rhetoric to conceal human suffering.

Poets who in August 1914 were sincerely carried away by the first fine frenzy were subsequently only too willing to be conscripted as propagandists. How is it possible (Kraus asks in October 1915) that when during a battle forty thousand human bodies were torn to pieces on the barbed wire in a single day, poets could still find words to celebrate the bloodshed? (F 406–12: 103) The answer must be that it involved acts of conscious dishonesty. The process may be illustrated by a passage from Gerhart Hauptmann's private diary of 1915, in which he records the death in battle of a family friend:

Am 20. Juni ist Willi Stehr ebenfalls an der Lorettohöhe gefallen. Wer den Blick darauf wendet, der sieht nur Verbrechen, Blut, Mord, Schmerz, Tränen; nur wer ihn wegwendet, sieht: Ruhm, Ehre, Vaterland, Zukunft. Wende weg den Blick.

(On 20 June Willi Stehr also fell in battle on the Loretto Heights. If you turn your gaze towards what is happening, you see only crime, blood, murder, pain, tears. Only if you turn your gaze away do you see glory, honour, fatherland, future. Turn your gaze away.)[40]

'Turning your gaze away' became the overriding principle for intellectuals who betrayed the truth for their country. It was to have the most terrible consequences in Germany after 1933, when a whole generation of writers and intellectuals (led again by Gerhart Hauptmann) averted their eyes from what was actually happening.

Kraus's writings analyse this great betrayal. But his analysis penetrates beyond the question of ethical principle to that of ideological function. Well before the war he had identified ways in which literary culture was functioning as a façade. The events of 1914–18 brought it home to him that the ideals propounded by the German cultural élite were serving as ideological camouflage for a war of economic expansion.

CHAPTER 17

Heroes and Shopkeepers: German Idealism and English Pragmatism

The Smokescreen of Ideals

The euphoria of 1914 was not simply jingoism, but a complex and in certain respects admirable blend of patriotic emotions. The German word 'Erhebung', given currency by Friedrich Meinecke's volume of essays, *Die deutsche Erhebung von 1914*, identifies that fusion of liberating emotions: spiritual exaltation, moral uplift and social upheaval.[1] In each of the belligerent countries people believed that they were fighting for an ideal: France for *l'humanité*, Britain for the rule of law, Germany for *Kultur*, Russia for the sacred rights of the Slavs. And this conviction of moral righteousness was not, at least in the early months of the war, simply the product of propaganda. However much it may later have been exploited, initially this sense of mission was altruistic. This becomes clear when one reads not the pronouncements of armchair patriots, but the testimony of those whose actions speak as loudly as their words: front-line volunteers like Rupert Brooke or C. E. Montague, Charles Péguy or Heinrich Lersch.

The idealistic conception of war was particularly characteristic of Germany. The need to fight a war to consolidate Germany's position in Europe seems to have been accepted by the political and military leadership as early as 1912. The primary aim was pre-emptive: to strike before the grandiose Russian armaments programme could create an invincible enemy in the east. There were also cruder material aims: economic expansion and territorial conquest.[2] However, it was *not* in these material and strategic terms that the war was perceived. For the overwhelming majority it was a 'war of illusions'. August 1914 was experienced as a reawakening of ethical idealism, as a crusade in defence of sacred national ideals. The cry that the fatherland was in danger not only swung the votes of the

Social Democrats in the Reichstag, it forms the leitmotif of innumerable poems and pamphlets. In this literature of patriotic euphoria
the fatherland is invoked not simply as a political concept, but as a
source of mystical inspiration. It represents the desire to rise above
self and faction; to transcend the mundane materialism and utilitarianism of modern society; to dedicate oneself to a higher ideal.

To foreign observers (as to Kraus himself) there seemed to be 'two
Germanies': the Germany whose art and music, philosophy and
literature had captured the admiration of the civilized world; and the
Germany whose armies were apparently hell-bent upon its
destruction. The distinction is made above all by western writers
well-disposed towards Germany. Both Romain Rolland and Bernard
Shaw draw a sharp line between Prussian imperialism (which must
be destroyed) and the German people with their humanistic traditions (which must be protected and preserved). This explanatory
model of Germany may seem simplistic. It ignores that 'third
Germany', which constitutes the missing link: the advanced
industrial society whose economic prosperity both financed the
programme of military expansion and funded the intellectuals. But
the model was advanced as a more enlightened alternative to the
crude anti-Hun propaganda which followed the German invasion of
Belgium.

In German-speaking Europe this well-intentioned distinction was
fiercely repudiated. It was seen as a propaganda device designed to
drive a wedge between the aims of the German political leadership
and the aspirations of the educated élite. Scarcely a single writer in
Germany or Austria had the courage and clarity to take up this
distinction and make it the basis for a critique of power politics. Even
Heinrich Mann, whose essay 'Geist und Tat' (1910) had denounced
the tendency of German intellectuals to align themselves with
military power, now remained silent. His veiled critique of the
Imperial regime in the essay 'Zola' did not appear until November
1915.[3] Meanwhile, a shrill chorus of German intellectuals proclaimed
the identity of militarism and morality. The ninety-three signatories
of the 'Appeal to the Civilized World' insisted on the purity of the
German cause, offered a moral justification for the invasion of
Belgium, and dedicated themselves to the ideals embodied in
military power.[4] The socialist press resounded with the claim that
the war, particularly the struggle against Tsarist Russia, was a war in
defence of *Kultur*. Hair-raising arguments were advanced to prove
that the ideals of Kant, Beethoven and Goethe were identical with
those of Falkenhayn and Hindenburg. And the universities competed
to confer honorary degrees on the military leaders. Kraus
sardonically glosses in October 1915 the arguments invoked by the

scholars Delbrück and Wilamowitz to justify the conferring of a doctorate in Philosophy on General von Falkenhayn (F 406–12: 6).

In England, intelligent political commentators justified the war as a means to an end: the liberation of Belgium, the restoration of the rule of law, the containment of Prussian militarism.[5] In Germany, by contrast, we find a recurrent tendency to celebrate the war as an end in itself. This mood is summed up in an essay published in *Die Neue Rundschau* in November 1914:

> Krieg! Es war Reinigung, Befreiung, was wir empfanden, und eine ungeheuere Hoffnung. Hiervon sagten die Dichter, nur hiervon. Was ist ihnen Imperium, was Handelsherrschaft, was überhaupt der Sieg? [. . .] Was die Dichter begeisterte, war der Krieg an sich selbst, als Heimsuchung, als sittliche Not.

> (War! It was purification, liberation that we experienced, and an immense hope. It was of this that the poets spoke, only of this. What do they care for imperial power, for commercial hegemony, even for victory? [. . .] What inspired the poets was the war in itself, as visitation, as ethical exigency.)

The view of war as an end in itself leads the same writer to declare German militarism to be the true expression of German morality. And the military virtues of self-discipline and organization are seen as precisely those which inspire the highest forms of art and culture. The war (this same writer concludes a few months later) is a kind of mystical synthesis of power and spirit:

> Dieser Krieg [. . .] warum hat Deutschland ihn begrüßt und sich zu ihm bekannt, als er hereinbrach? — Weil es den Bringer seines *Dritten Reiches* in ihm erkannte. — Was ist denn sein Drittes Reich? — Es ist die *Synthese von Macht und Geist*.

> (This war [. . .] why did Germany welcome it with such a sense of commitment, when it broke in upon us? — Because it recognized in the war the bringer of its *Third Reich*. — What then is its Third Reich? — It is the *synthesis of power and spirituality*.)

The italics are in the original. The date of publication is May 1915 and the author Thomas Mann.[6]

Mann's spiritual interpretation of the war cannot simply be dismissed as hypocrisy, although he too was compensating for his own lack of valour by his contributions to the war of words.[7] His sense of the righteousness of the German cause persisted until the publication of *Betrachtungen eines Unpolitischen* in the autumn of 1918. Moreover Thomas Mann is merely the most eloquent spokesman for a view of the war that was endemic in Germany. We find it not merely in the writings of littérateurs dabbling in politics, but also in the pronouncements of German scientists, sociologists and political theorists. Mann's ideas recur in more systematic form in Max Scheler's *Der Genius des Krieges und der deutsche Krieg* and in Werner Sombart's *Händler und Helden*, both published in 1915. For both writers, England is fighting a war motivated by commercial ambitions. In Germany, by contrast, the war is idealism in action — a synthesis of Potsdam and Weimar. The soldiers in the trenches are fighting in the spirit of Goethe's *Faust*, of Nietzsche's *Zarathustra*, even of Beethoven's Eroica symphony. It is essentially a war between German heroes and British shopkeepers.[8] In philosophical terms (the terms used by Wilhelm Wundt in a series of lectures and pamphlets) it is a war inspired on the one hand by Benthamite economic utilitarianism, on the other by the Kantian conception of the moral will and the Hegelian view of the State as the realization of the 'ethical Idea'.[9]

The problem embodied in this interpretation of the war is not to be resolved by labelling such writers as 'typically Germanophilic'.[10] Wundt was a pioneering experimental psychologist and one of the leading academic philosophers of his generation. Sombart was an economist with a sophisticated grasp of the international ramifications of capitalism. Scheler was a social psychologist with the intellectual resources to resist the cruder forms of war euphoria. The essay 'Europa und der Krieg' which he published in the pacifistically inclined *Die weißen Blätter* (January–March 1915) explicitly condemns the Pan-German mystics and their 'metaphysically inflated nationalism'. His essay was even praised by Romain Rolland, in a review of 'Littérature de guerre' published in the *Journal de Genève*, 19 April 1915.[11]

The idealistic interpretation of the war had a seductive effect on the finest minds of Germany. Max Weber was the outstanding proponent of political pragmatism. But in 'Deutschland unter den europäischen Weltmächten', a lecture delivered in Munich on 22 October 1916, pragmatic analysis gives way to idealist mystification. Germany is fighting a war for honour, not for territorial expansion or economic gain. The war is Germany's world-historical destiny, and Weber even speaks of the war as a form of 'consecration' — 'die Weihe eines deutschen Krieges'.[12] Walter Rathenau, the great apostle of mechanization and organizer of Germany's war industries, offers in his book *Von kommenden Dingen* (1917) a further variant on this idealistic theme. The highly efficient forms of social and technological organization which he proposes will (he claims) displace the old world which is dominated by rationality and money, and inaugurate the Realm of the Soul — 'das Reich der Seele'.[13]

Even Hermann Hesse was not immune. Though he enjoys the reputation of having been the most principled pacifist among the

German writers of this period, Hesse's pacifism was from the start in conflict with his loyalty to Germany. He does stand firm against the cruder forms of German nationalism. But he too is inclined to view the war as one between heroes and shopkeepers. Victory for Germany, he writes in a letter of 9 September 1914, would leave some hope for the *Kultur* of the future; but defeat would leave Europe in the hands of the 'moneybags' of England (together with the illiterate Russians). Hesse elaborates this antithesis in an 'Open Letter' published in the *Frankfurter Zeitung* of 13 November 1915: Germany is fighting for an ideal — the ideal associated with Bach and Goethe, Kant and Fichte. The main reproach to be levelled against the British is that their power and wealth have produced material goods (together with well-intentioned liberalism), but no ideals — no commitment to mankind as a whole. Hesse's position is thus very similar to that of Max Scheler, whose *Genius des Krieges* he enthusiastically reviewed in September 1915. Germany's mission is to deliver Europe from 'the catastrophe of soulless capitalism' which originates in England.[14]

Kraus's response to this idealistic rhetoric is unequivocal. He insists that evil becomes most powerful when it is concealed by an ideal: 'Das Übel gedeiht nie besser, als wenn ein Ideal davorsteht' (F 406–12: 126). He sees the effusions of the intellectual élite as a kind of smoke-screen. Kraus's characteristic focus on masks and façades admittedly substitutes a simplified model for complex mental processes. This ethical idealism was not simply a propaganda smoke-screen, released by the German Press Bureau or by the hacks of the Austrian Kriegspressequartier. Kraus is able to show that among the ninety-three intellectuals who subscribed to the famous 'Appeal' of autumn 1914 there were some who signed without any knowledge of the text (F 462–71: 50–1). But how was it possible for those who were swept away by the enthusiasm of 1914 to continue blindly to maintain that the war was an ethical crusade?

It was not mere hypocrisy, but a more inward phenomenon, integral to the mental processes of some of the finest minds of Germany. It is a current of thought which derives its strength partly from Christian, partly from Kantian sources. But a subtle contamination of the processes of thinking has taken place. Kraus hit perhaps on the most apposite metaphor when he ascribed the headlong collapse of human dignity to a 'virus of the brain' ('Gehirnbazillus', F 474–83: 41). For purposes of analysis, however, he uses a two-dimensional model: the notion of 'vorgeschobene Ideale', ideals advanced to screen the evil of war, which spreads all the more rapaciously behind this ideological cover (F 406–12: 168). His aim is to reveal the stark realities which are concealed by this ideological mystification.

Battlefields and Markets

Initially Kraus's approach is impressionistic — the response of the *flâneur* who glimpses a profounder truth behind a configuration of three posters displayed in Vienna at the end of July 1914: the Proclamation which appeared over the name of Emperor Franz Joseph announcing the decision to invade Serbia (see Pl. 28); above it a poster larger than life, advertising a popular restaurant (Pl. 29); and next to that the advertisement of a shoe manufacturer (Pl. 30). These visual motifs (*F* 404: 3) announce three major themes of Kraus's war satire: his attitude to political authority; his critique of Austrian hedonism; and his exposure of the commercial motives underlying German political expansionism.

The advertisement for Berson's shoe-rubbers may seem an incongruous starting-point for a critique of economic imperialism. But Kraus's sensitivity to commercial advertising was soon to develop into a more radical analysis of the war with Marxist implications. 'Berson' was the trademark of a company called Beer & Sohn. In the final months before the outbreak of the war, we find Berson advertisements singled out for special attention in *Die Fackel*. In January 1914 Kraus reproduced from the *Arbeiter-Zeitung* an advertisement which facetiously shows Nietzsche writing a testimonial for Bersons (*F* 391–2: 5–6). Later that same month the Berson copy-writers retaliated with a cartoon portraying Kraus himself 'stepping it out on "Bersons"', and they actually smuggled this advertisement into the *Neue Freie Presse* (*F* 393–4: 29–30). These advertisements are not merely illustrations of Kraus's theme of the commercialization of culture. They also connect with his more widely relevant critique of a society in which commerce reduces human beings to advertisements on two legs.

The baby with Berson shoe-rubbers firmly attached to its feet brings home to the satirist a truth which has been more recently expressed in the language of social psychology: that in advanced industrial societies people are born no longer as babies but as 'consumer trainees'.[15] But Kraus also makes the more vital connection with the war itself: 'Menschheit ist Kundschaft. Hinter Fahnen und Flammen, hinter Helden und Helfern, hinter allen Vaterländern ist ein Altar aufgerichtet, an dem die fromme Wissenschaft die Hände ringt: Gott schuf den Konsumenten! (Mankind is a market. Behind flags and flames, behind heroes and helpers, behind every fatherland an altar has been set up, at which pious science wrings its hands: God created the consumer!)' (*F* 404: 5)

Scrutiny of surface here leads to analysis in depth. Behind the heroics of the war lie the imperatives of commercial expansion. The heroes are being sent into the battlefields so that the merchants can secure their markets:

An meine Völker!

Es war Mein sehnlichster Wunsch, die Jahre, die Mir durch Gottes Gnade noch beschieden sind, Werken des Friedens zu weihen und Meine Völker vor den schweren Opfern und Lasten des Krieges zu bewahren.

Im Rate der Vorsehung ward es anders beschlossen.

Die Umtriebe eines haßerfüllten Gegners zwingen Mich, zur Wahrung der Ehre Meiner Monarchie, zum Schutze ihres Ansehens und ihrer Machtstellung, zur Sicherung ihres Besitzstandes nach langen Jahren des Friedens zum Schwerte zu greifen.

Mit rasch vergessendem Undank hat das Königreich Serbien, das von den ersten Anfängen seiner staatlichen Selbständigkeit bis in die neueste Zeit von Meinen Vorfahren und Mir gestützt und gefördert worden war, schon vor Jahren den Weg offener Feindseligkeit gegen Oesterreich-Ungarn betreten.

Als Ich nach drei Jahrzehnten segensvoller Friedensarbeit in Bosnien und der Herzegovina Meine Herrscherrechte auf jene Länder erstreckte, hat diese Meine Verfügung im Königreiche Serbien, dessen Rechte in keiner Weise verletzt wurden, Ausbrüche zügelloser Leidenschaft und erbittertsten Hasses hervorgerufen. Meine Regierung hat damals von dem schönen Vorrechte des Stärkeren Gebrauch gemacht und in äußerster Nachsicht und Milde von Serbien nur die Herabsetzung seines Heeres auf den Friedensstand und das Versprechen verlangt, in Hinkunft die Bahn des Friedens und der Freundschaft zu gehen.

Von demselben Geiste der Mäßigung geleitet, hat sich Meine Regierung, als Serbien vor zwei Jahren im Kampfe mit dem türkischen Reiche begriffen war, auf die Wahrung der wichtigsten Lebensbedingungen der Monarchie beschränkt. Dieser Haltung hatte Serbien in erster Linie die Erreichung des Kriegszweckes zu verdanken.

Die Hoffnung, daß das serbische Königreich die Langmut und Friedensliebe Meiner Regierung würdigen und sein Wort einlösen werde, hat sich nicht erfüllt.

Immer höher lodert der Haß gegen Mich und Mein Haus empor, immer unverhüllter tritt das Streben zutage, untrennbare Gebiete Oesterreich-Ungarns gewaltsam loszureißen.

Ein verbrecherisches Treiben greift über die Grenze, um im Südosten der Monarchie die Grundlagen staatlicher Ordnung zu untergraben, das Volk, dem Ich in landesväterlicher Liebe Meine volle Fürsorge zuwende, in seiner Treue zum Herrscher und zum Vaterland wankend zu machen, die heranwachsende Jugend irrezuleiten und zu frevelhaften Taten des Wahnwitzes und Hochverrates aufzureizen. Eine Reihe von Mordanschlägen, eine planmäßig vorbereitete und durchgeführte Verschwörung, deren furchtbares Gelingen Mich und Meine treuen Völker ins Herz getroffen hat, bildet die weithin sichtbare blutige Spur jener geheimen Machenschaften, die von Serbien aus ins Werk gesetzt und geleitet wurden.

Diesem unerträglichen Treiben muß das Einhalt geboten, den unaufhörlichen Herausforderungen Serbiens ein Ende bereitet werden, soll die Ehre und Würde Meiner Monarchie unverletzt erhalten und ihre staatliche, wirtschaftliche und militärische Entwicklung vor beständigen Erschütterungen bewahrt bleiben.

Vergebens hat Meine Regierung noch einen letzten Versuch unternommen, dieses Ziel mit friedlichen Mitteln zu erreichen, Serbien durch eine ernste Mahnung zur Umkehr zu bewegen.

Serbien hat die maßvollen und gerechten Forderungen Meiner Regierung zurückgewiesen und es abgelehnt, jenen Pflichten nachzukommen, deren Erfüllung im Leben der Völker und Staaten die natürliche und notwendige Grundlage des Friedens bildet.

So muß Ich denn daran schreiten, mit Waffengewalt die unerläßlichen Bürgschaften zu schaffen, die Meinen Staaten Ruhe im Innern und den dauernden Frieden nach außen sichern sollen.

In dieser ernsten Stunde bin Ich Mir der ganzen Tragweite Meines Entschlusses und Meiner Verantwortung vor dem Allmächtigen voll bewußt.

Ich habe alles geprüft und erwogen.

Mit ruhigem Gewissen betrete Ich den Weg, den die Pflicht Mir weist.

Ich vertraue auf Meine Völ'er, die sich in allen Stürmen stets in Einigkeit und Treue um Meinen Thron geschart und für die Ehre, Größe und Macht des Vaterlandes zu schwersten Opfern immer bereit waren.

Ich vertraue auf Oesterreich-Ungarns tapfere und von hingebungsvoller Begeisterung erfüllte Wehrmacht.

Und ich vertraue auf den Allmächtigen, daß Er Meinen Waffen den Sieg verleihen werde.

Franz Josef m. p.

Stürgkh m. p.

29 Advertisement for the Wolf in Gersthof, on a postcard announcing the reopening of the restaurant in 1913. A poster for this same restaurant represented, for Kraus, the spirit of frivolity to which he took such exception during the First World War

So sollte man auf die Welt kommen

Advertisement for Berson's shoe-rubbers, which Kraus found juxtaposed with the Imperial Proclamation of War (*opposite*) in Vienna in July 1914

Ich weiß genau, daß es zu Zeiten notwendig ist, Absatzgebiete in Schlachtfelder zu verwandeln, damit aus diesen wieder Absatzgebiete werden. Aber eines trüben Tages sieht man heller und fragt, ob es denn richtig ist, den Weg, der von Gott wegführt, so zielbewußt mit keinem Schritte zu verfehlen.   (F 404 : 4–5)

(I know very well that it is necessary at times to turn markets into battlefields, so that these can become markets again. But one dismal day we shall see more clearly and ask whether it is really right to follow so purposively and unerringly with every step the path that leads away from God.)

It is a world, in short, which has gone to war because it has lost its way in the labyrinth of economics — 'eine im Labyrinth der Ökonomie verirrte Welt' (F 404: 7).

Kraus's response to the Berson advertisement is far from being (as has been argued) merely a gesture of aesthetic irritation.[16] It leads him to analysis of underlying causes. His argument gains added force from being formulated in the language not of political economy but of a more fundamental ontology — of alienation from God and from the original purposes of creation. His economic realism is firmly welded to an ethical ideal. 'Kultur' for Kraus is not that irrational force which Thomas Mann in this same period was contrasting with the shallowness of western 'Zivilisation'. 'Kultur' is defined by his insistence that people should be treated as human beings, not as consumers (F 404: 5).

It is this fundamentalism which distinguishes 'In dieser großen Zeit' from other anti-war writings of the period. Kraus's analysis is free of that patriotic partisanship which leads to moral equivocation. Romain Rolland's essays of the early months of the war are explicitly partisan in their condemnation of German war operations and Prussian militarism. Hermann Hesse subordinates his plea for international understanding to an overriding German patriotism (he had volunteered for active service but was turned down on the grounds of short-sightedness). Bertrand Russell's patriotism reportedly led him to desire the defeat of Germany 'as ardently as any retired colonel'.[17] Kraus's arguments, by contrast, transcend the norms of nationalism and invoke a universal moral framework.

His gloss on the bombardment of Reims cathedral illustrates this perspective. The French had reportedly used the roof of the cathedral as a military observation post; the Germans had responded with an artillery bombardment which damaged the building severely and resulted in considerable loss of life. The French denied that the building had been used for military purposes, and its bombardment became one of the focal points for propaganda about German atrocities.[18] It thus provided a test case for critical impartiality.

Rolland was so carried away that he drafted a petition of protest again this act of German barbarism, which was circulated in England and quickly gathered two hundred signatures (Rolland was later to regret the Germanophobic tone of this document).[19] Bernard Shaw's reaction shows greater critical detachment. In 'Common Sense about the War' (published on 14 November 1914) he identifies the destruction of Louvain and the shelling of Reims cathedral as 'a strong hint from Providence that though we can have glorious war or glorious cathedrals we cannot have both'. He has no patience with Rolland and 'all this halfpenny newspaper rubbish about Rheims', for reasons which he explains in a letter to William Heinemann:

> If I were a military officer defending Rheims I should have to put an observation post on the cathedral roof; and if I were his opponent I should have to fire on it [. . .]. If this war goes on long enough there will not be a cathedral left in Europe; and serve Europe right too! The way to save the cathedrals is to stop fighting.[20]

Kraus also notes in a private letter that Rolland has allowed himself to be 'carried away' (BSN I. 71). And (as we have seen) he specifically suggests that Hodler's protest against the bombardment is misconceived (F 404: 17). His own response is similar to Shaw's, not least in its incisiveness of formulation:

> Ich weiß wohl, Kathedralen werden mit Recht von Menschen beschossen, wenn sie von Menschen mit Recht als militärische Posten verwendet werden. Kein Ärgernis in der Welt, sagt Hamlet. Nur daß ein Höllenschlund sich zu der Frage öffnet: Wann hebt die größere Zeit des Krieges an der Kathedralen gegen die Menschen!
>
> (F 404: 4)

> (I know well enough that cathedrals are justifiably bombarded by men if men justifiably use them as military positions. No offence in the world, says Hamlet. It's just that a chasm of hell opens at the question: When will that even greater time begin — the time of the war of the cathedrals against men!

Like Shaw, Kraus sees through the fraud of using a cathedral as a military position and then protesting that the building is sacrosanct. But characteristically, he carries the argument beyond Shaw's common-sense conclusion ('stop fighting'), moving from logical analysis to apocalyptic vision: 'the war of the cathedrals against men'. The image effectively conveys the scale of the European disaster and of the retribution which it invites.

What Kraus discerns behind the cultural façade is not militarism, but militarism powered by economic imperialism. He never makes the slightest concession to the theory that the Germans are fighting a war of heroes against shopkeepers. The altar of consumerism is

visible behind the flags of *every* fatherland. The war is the consequence of 'the subjugation of mankind to economic interests' ('die
Unterwerfung der Menschheit unter die Wirtschaft', F 404: 8). Poets
may claim that the sacrifices of war have brought about a rebirth of
the soul; but Kraus suspects that the soul has already been sacrificed
to the service of manufactured goods (F 405: 16).

Kraus develops this theme more explicitly in a series of polemical
aphorisms published in October 1915:

> 'Es handelt sich in diesem Krieg — ' 'Jawohl, es handelt sich in diesem
> Krieg.'   (F 406–12: 111)

> ('In this war we are dealing —' 'Yes, in this war we are dealing.')

Here language is turned back upon itself in order to reveal the
commercial realities behind the idealistic rhetoric. But Kraus goes on
to make more complex discriminations:

> Es gibt Gegenden, wo man wenigstens die Ideale in Ruhe läßt, wenn
> der Export in Gefahr ist, und wo man so ehrlich vom Geschäft spricht,
> daß man es nicht Vaterland nennen würde und vorsichtshalber gleich
> darauf verzichtet, in seiner Sprache ein Wort dafür zu haben. Solches
> Volk nennen die Idealisten des Exports mit Recht eine Geschäftsnation.
>   (F 406–12: 112)

> (There are regions where they at least leave ideals in peace, when
> exports are in danger, and where they talk about business so honestly that
> they wouldn't call it 'Fatherland' and as a precaution don't even have a
> word for 'Fatherland' in their language. Such a people are rightly called a
> nation of businessmen by the idealists of export.)

Kraus takes over the heroes/shopkeepers antithesis and inverts it: the
shopkeepers are at least free of the hypocrisy of the idealist. Indeed,
their language itself serves to protect them from this form of
self-delusion.

The implied compliment to England is over-generous. If Kraus
had been better acquainted with British war propaganda, he would
have known that idealistic cant also proliferated among the
shopkeepers themselves. Shaw's 'Common Sense about the War'
shows up clearly enough the velleities which underlie the moralizing
about gallant little Belgium.[21] But Kraus's distinction does have a
historical basis. In the English debate about war aims there is a
functionalist quality which is less evident on the German side. Political
and economic goals are discussed in the language of politics and
economics. And even the moralizing tone which prevails in British
war propaganda has a basis in political reality: the invasion of
Belgium *was* (as Bethmann Hollweg conceded in his Reichstag
speech of 4 August 1914) an infringement of international law.

English ideologists could thus appeal to the traditional conception of the 'just war'. The justification of war for a specific moral purpose belongs to a different universe of discourse from the Hegelian conception of war as an ethical force in itself. The latter conception found its most influential expression in Nietzsche's celebrated dictum on 'War and Warriors': 'You say it is the good cause that hallows even war? I tell you: it is the good war that hallows every cause'.[22]

This comparison should not be taken as a defence of British propaganda, which was as appalling in its own way as anything on the German side. There were plenty of imperialists and rabble-rousers in England, and the British Empire too was sustained by an ideology of self-righteousness. 'They say "Christ" and mean cotton', as a shrewd nineteenth-century observer of English affairs expressed it.[23] Marxist historians have argued that the British imperialists were just as ready as those in Germany 'to revel in the slaughter of war'.[24] But there is evidence to support Kraus's assertion that the British were *less* likely to confuse 'Christ' with 'cotton'. It is in Germany (he insists) that the aims of stockbrokers are being tricked out in the guise of the valiant soldier (F 426–30: 70–1).

Scholars and Submarines

The contrast with the British may be clarified by focusing on the academic community. Despite the immense contribution by German universities to science and scholarship, it is difficult to find any academic journal in Germany which provided a forum for debate about the war comparable to the *Cambridge Magazine*.[25] The history faculty at Oxford certainly contributed vociferously to the pamphlet war; but these academics debated specific issues: not merely the principles of international law, but also the need to increase agricultural production or the importance of preventing contagious diseases from spreading among the troops.[26] There is a *pragmatic* note running through the eighty-seven 'Oxford Pamphlets' published during 1914–15 which is quite distinct from the *idealistic* rhetoric of the thirty-five public lectures delivered by professors at the University of Berlin in this same period.

This problematic idealism is exemplified by the writings of Wilamowitz-Moellendorf and Gierke, whom Kraus severely censures for their endorsements of German military power (F 406–12: 6; 437–42: 4–5). Wilamowitz-Moellendorf, classical philologist and Rector of the University of Berlin, insisted that the German military victories were the expression of 'the same spiritual and ethical energies' as had been the source of German superiority in peacetime. For the jurist Otto von Gierke too the war is a revelation of the 'ethical strength' of the *Volksseele*. 'German culture is ethical culture. Its superiority is rooted in the unfathomable depth of its ethical character.' England of course is merely using its maritime power to maintain 'economic supremacy'.[27] Such arguments are particularly ironic when one recalls that one of the few German publications which *did* evaluate the war from an ethical standpoint, *Die ethische Rundschau*, was promptly suppressed by the military censorship; and that when Professor Friedrich Wilhelm Foerster expressed pacifistic sentiments in an article in *Die Friedens-Warte*, he was denounced by his colleagues at the University of Munich for 'hemmungsloser Idealismus' (*F* 431–6: 89–90).

There were so many professorial propagandists for massive annexations and unrestricted submarine warfare that no satirist could possibly keep track of them. Kraus had to be content with having identified the 'type' of the 'national-liberal-professorial-radical' — that 'cross between a university chair and a submarine' which is so characteristic of modern Germany (*F* 437–42: 101). But the strength of his argument derives from a fundamental principle: the separation of spheres. Between academic research and military efficiency there should be a 'clear division' ('eine reinliche Trennung', *F* 406–12: 6). Kraus's implicit compliment to England involves a recognition that that alleged nation of shopkeepers has been able to keep the life of the spirit 'strictly separate' from the problems of commerce ('streng zu separieren vermögen', *F* 406–12: 113). In a war fought between two consumer organizations, the survival of ideals depends on the one which has the honesty not to lay claim to them.

Kraus also makes significant discriminations in his analysis of Christian apologias for war. He was aware that in every belligerent country there were propagandists and priests who were claiming to have God on their side. But he suggests that in Germany the appeal to God is not so much a prayer as the assertion of a *fait accompli*. The God who is worshipped has been 'nationalized'. He is firmly annexed to the German cause and apparently even speaks German to his adherents. Kraus vigorously repudiates the attempt to disguise a 'profane reality beneath an aura of holiness' ('eine unheilige Wirklichkeit unter einen Heiligenschein', *F* 413–17: 19–20). The brashness with which this same national Christianity was used as cover for commercial operations was also easily exposed. 'Gottes Allmacht und die Realitäten' is the title which Kraus gives to a gloss of August 1916, in which he reprints the text of two advertisements which a certain Carl Alfons Stein has inserted in a Prague newspaper. In the first Stein advertises a patriotic play he has written under the title *God's Omnipotence*; in the second he identifies himself as an investment broker seeking deals in real estate (*F* 431–6: 33–4). 'Wars and account books', Kraus tersely observes in an aphorism of

October 1917, 'are conducted in the name of God' ('Kriege und Geschäftsbücher werden mit Gott geführt', F 462–71: 172).

From an early stage Kraus recognizes the imperatives of economic expansion which underlie the idealistic rhetoric. And as the months passed, the ideological façade became increasingly hard to sustain. Even Hofmannsthal had ultimately to acknowledge (though only in a private letter) that the German nation had lost its 'aura of holiness' ('Heiligenschein').[28] The claim that Germany was fighting a defensive war was particularly incongruous. Only during the first weeks of August had there been enemy incursions into German territory. The notion of an ethical crusade was also blatantly at odds with the clamour for the annexation of economically valuable areas of Belgium, France, Poland and Russia (particularly when the annexationist proved to be a Professor of Theology) (F 462–71: 18). A third factor which brought increasing disillusionment was the blatant profiteering by manufacturers of essential commodities. It was incongruous enough to discover that German shareholders were benefiting from the profits of Bethlehem Steel, the American company which was supplying armaments to Germany's enemies (F 406–12: 10). But for Kraus the most tragic contrast was the sight of speculators enriching themselves in the hinterland, while soldiers were being helplessly slaughtered at the front. The real enemy for Kraus is this new commercial power which lurks behind the old façade and is exploiting the ancient emblems of military glory (F 457–61: 18).

Once again the satirist's preoccupation with disguise and façade is a source both of strength and limitation. The close links between the military and manufacturers during the First World War were already creating a 'military-industrial complex'. But Kraus in May 1917 is still astonished by the interaction between these two spheres. And he still invokes the naïve image of the decent army officers who ought to be shooting down the repulsive profiteers (F 457–61: 18). Since Jewish enterprises were prominent among firms which were profiting from the war, his critique also has antisemitic undertones. There is thus a certain affinity between Kraus's attacks on war profiteers and those of the super-patriots, who believed that the heroic efforts of front-line troops were being undermined by disloyal elements at home.[29]

The fundamental difference lay in Kraus's ability to see through ideological disguises of all kinds. Spokesmen for the academic community were voluble in their praise of the achievements of the German chemical industry, and celebrated the Zeppelin and the submarine as triumphs of *Kultur*. Kraus by contrast invokes the values of a more humane artist and scientist, Leonardo da Vinci, who explains in his notebooks why he is unwilling to make public his design for a submarine: 'I do not publish or explain this because of the evil nature of human beings, who would use my invention for murderous acts in the depths of the sea, thereby breaking the hull of ships and sinking them with all the human beings who are in them' (F 474–83: 40).

Kraus does not merely attack the rhetoric of ethical idealism. The romantic cult of heroism is equally spurious in a war to increase exports, fought with the most sophisticated weaponry. This cult of heroism created an even more dangerous hybrid which Kraus identified as 'das technoromantische Abenteuer' (F 474–83: 41–5).

CHAPTER 18

Techno-Romantic Adventure and Tragic Carnival

The Politics of Techno-Romanticism

Kraus's denunciation of mechanized warfare is impressive in itself. The horrors of the trenches, the effects of poison gas, the sufferings of the civilian population, the indiscriminate bombing of cities, the ruthless technology of submarine warfare: all these are clearly identified in *Die Fackel*. But his more complex aim is to expose the contrast between technological reality and romantic aura. He attacks the ideology which celebrates the airman who drops bombs on defenceless cities (*F* 418–22: 38–9) and which honours the submarine captain who has sent hundreds of men to their death (*F* 437–42: 121). In such a war (he argues) one cannot speak of the kind of heroism that Hector showed before the gates of Troy. Modern warfare requires 'endurance before the machine' ('Standhaftigkeit vor der Maschine', *F* 426–30: 36).

In November 1914 Kraus had referred only in passing to those who abuse the imagery of heroism in order to glamorize the war (*F* 405: 9). Later this becomes a major polemical theme. The tasteless heroics of Alice Schalek, war correspondent of the *Neue Freie Presse*, are repeatedly ridiculed. But at least the preposterous Schalek was sincere enough in her enthusiasm for the war to wish to visit the front in person ('Die wackre Schalek forcht sich nit', *F* 406–12: 15–17). A more ferocious invective is reserved for writers who portray war as heroic, while themselves enjoying positions of security and ease.

Hofmannsthal's *Prinz Eugen der edle Ritter* (1915) may seem harmless enough — a re-embellishment of the legends surrounding a national hero.[1] But for Kraus such productions perpetuate anachronistic conceptions of military heroism. The popular ballad about Prince Eugene describes him as building a bridge during the siege of Belgrade. Taking up this motif in a jaunty epigram, Kraus neatly identifies the regressive nature of Hofmannsthal's own bridge-building:

> Schwarzgelblicher Haltung blutlosen Trophä'n
> galt, als es galt, seine tapfere Wahl.
> Es schlug eine Brucken zum Prinz Eugen
> der edle Ritter von Hofmannsthal.
>
> (F 472–3: 20)

> (Patriot with trophies bloodlessly won
> was the chosen pose of his courage so keen.
> The noble Sir Hugo de Hofmannsthal
> threw a bridge back to Prince Eugene.)

The balladesque archaism of 'eine Brucken', together with the image of Hofmannsthal as a knight-at-arms, accentuates that author's anachronistic outlook. But the tendency to picture the war in heroic colours was not characteristic only of eclectic writers like Bahr and Hofmannsthal. It was shared by thousands of ordinary people who responded in August 1914 to the call to arms precisely because the war seemed to offer a heroic alternative to mundane routine. And as the fighting continued there was a compelling need for an ethos of heroism which might give meaning to the miseries of trench warfare. An inbred habit of thinking insists on clothing the perceived sobriety of modern life in heroic myths. In this habit Kraus sees one of the fundamental causes of the war — 'eine der Grundursachen dieses Krieges' (F 437–42: 119).

Goethe's condemnation of the primitive ethos of war is quoted in *Die Fackel* in November 1916 (F 443–4: 18–20). But it is Heine who deserves the credit for identifying the romanticization of evolving political institutions as the central problem of German ideology. This insight inspires his uncannily accurate political prophecies.[2] The incipient alliance between German Romanticism and Prussian expansionism is sharply satirized in *Deutschland — Ein Wintermärchen*. Kraus declines however to acknowledge any indebtedness to Heine. His comments on *Deutschland — Ein Wintermärchen* in April 1916 are brusquely dismissive. At the same time they do indicate that he has been re-reading it (F 418–22: 58). And the affinities are unmistakable. Heine satirizes 'das neue Kostüm' — the anachronistic new uniform introduced by Friedrich Wilhelm IV for the Prussian army of the 1840s (Caput III).[3] Kraus inveighs against the 'Kostümatelier' which provides more recent neo-romantics with their disguises (F 437–42: 119). Both writers are attacking the same regressive tendencies. And both share the archetypal satirical preoccupation with costume and masquerade.

In Kraus's hands Heine's theme undergoes an unprecedented intensification. The contrast between new wine and old bottles is now so much more extreme. The wine is poison gas; the ideological labels still derive from heroic myth. This contradiction finds its incisively economical formulation in Kraus's pun on the words 'glorious' and 'chlorinous' in the notion of 'eine chlorreiche Offensive' (F 474–83: 43). The more extreme emergency elicits from him a more intense response. A counterpart to this formal intensification is Kraus's transposition of Heine's theme into a more inward dimension. There is a certain externality in Heine's treatment of neo-romantic motifs: the anachronistic military costume which he mocks consists of actual helmets and uniforms. Kraus is more concerned with mental equipment.

The metaphor of 'drawing the sword' is a telling example. If the human imagination has failed to grasp the technological advances of modern warfare, this is because people have been conditioned to think about war in terms of 'zum Schwerte greifen'. And they continue to do so even when the weapons actually in use are flame-throwers or poison gas (F 406–12: 111; 445–53: 13, 15). Conditioned reflexes are implanted by an educational system whose textbooks encourage a naïvely heroic view of war (F 426–30: 56–63). They are further developed by romantic fiction and poetry, from the rousing ballads of Uhland (F 457–61: 52) through to Gerhart Hauptmann's celebration in 1914 of 'das deutsche Schwert' (F 426–30: 14). Dinned into the minds of newspaper readers day after day, this neo-romantic idiom established itself as one of the dominant modes of thinking and talking about the war (not only in Germany). Newspaper heroics displaced more sober and rational forms of discourse. As Robert Graves records in *Goodbye to All That*: 'England was strange to the returned soldier. He could not understand the war-madness that ran about everywhere, looking for a pseudo-military outlet. Every one talked a foreign language; it was newspaper language. I found serious conversation with my parents all but impossible.' Graves had no patience with the sentimental propaganda that was portraying the war as a return to the age of chivalry.[4]

For Kraus that anachronistic language reveals the collective unconscious of the nation. In five trenchant pages published in May 1918 he identifies the war as 'Das technoromantische Abenteuer':

Die Unmittelbarkeit des Anschlusses einer neuzeitlichen Erfindung, wonach mit einem Griff die Vergiftung einer Front und weiter Landstriche hinter ihr möglich ist, an ein Spiel mittelalterlicher Formen; die Verwendung einer verblichenen Heraldik im Ausgang von Aktionen, in denen Chemie und Physiologie Schulter an Schulter gekämpft haben — das ist es, was die Lebewesen rapider noch hinraffen wird als das Gift selbst.   (F 474–83: 41)

(The directness of the connection between a modern invention, which makes it possible at the touch of a lever to gas a whole front and extensive areas behind it, and a charade of medieval forms; the application of a faded system of heraldry to the outcome of military actions in which chemistry and physiology have fought shoulder to shoulder — it is this which will destroy living creatures even more rapidly than the poison itself.)

The phenomenon leads Kraus to formulate an even more striking paradox. For he sees its influence working in the direction of the 'victorious collapse' of the Central Powers ('in der Richtung des siegreichen Untergangs', F 474–83: 41).

This prediction was published on 23 May 1918, four days before the final German offensive, in which fourteen divisions broke through on the western front and advanced to the river Marne. Kraus's paradox of 'victorious collapse' shows a remarkable perceptiveness. It arises from his increasing awareness of the *political* dimension of the techno-romantic adventure. Hitherto, Kraus had concentrated on the mystification of the *military* realities at the front and of the *economic* ambitions of the hinterland. Now he identifies an even more significant relationship: between anachronistic ideology ('die mitgeschleppte Ideologie') and anachronistic ruling class ('die alte Herrschaft', F 474–83: 44–5).

It is as if Kraus's preoccupation with masks has led him to overlook the obvious. So concerned has he been with the *new* forces (economic and technological) which this ideology conceals, that he has discounted the significance of the *old* order, whose ambitions the ideology directly expresses. In *Die Fackel* of 1917 and 1918 this deficiency is made good. Showing courage as well as political insight, Kraus extends his critique of ideology into an attack on the political leadership. He shows that from the Kaiser downwards political power is in the hands of romantics. It is not just university professors who proclaim that the sword must not be sheathed until the German Empire has been consolidated by vast territorial annexations. The same political aims are held by those who actually have power of decision: the ambiguous Austrian Foreign Minister, Count Czernin, whom Kraus attacks so fiercely for missing the opportunity of making a conciliatory peace with Soviet Russia in the east (F 474–83: 1–22); and above all the Kaiser himself, whose unique blend of religiosity, neo-romanticism and pseudo-Kantian idealism Kraus shows up in the gloss 'Ein Kantianer und Kant' (F 474–83: 155–6). That he read this attack on the Kaiser in public in Berlin in May 1918, at a time when Germany was effectively governed by a military dictatorship, demonstrates Kraus's growing political commitment.

Once again, it is the Kaiser's use of the image of the sword which betrays the romanticism of the German ruling class. In a speech made after the defeat of Russia, the Kaiser proclaims Germany's determination to bring peace to the world 'by smashing in the gates of those who do not want peace with an iron fist and a gleaming sword'. Reprinting this passage in *Die Fackel*, Kraus draws attention to the metaphors through typographic emphasis (*F* 474–83: 155). And in a subsequent number of *Die Fackel* he reproduces a picture postcard portraying the indomitable Kaiser dressed in medieval helmet and chain mail (*F* 499–500, frontispiece; see Pl. 31). That patriotic postcards of this kind could be produced indicates the extent to which this romanticization of German politics had become institutionalized.

Kraus recognized that the techno-romantic adventure had created a political vacuum. Every German victory increased the gap between a highly advanced military technology and an anachronistic system of political control. Hence his final diagnosis of the 'irreconcilability of the power-structure with the means whereby it is asserted' ('die Unvereinbarkeit der Macht und der Mittel, sie durchzusetzen', *F* 474–83: 45). An authoritarian government could not afford to make the political concessions which would consolidate military victory by establishing a peace based not on conquest but on concessions. The political romanticism epitomized by the Kaiser has prevented the emergence in Germany of any faction capable of negotiating a more realistic peace settlement. Even the Social Democrats (as Kraus notes in October 1917) are too deeply implicated in politics of military conquest to offer any realistic political alternative (*F* 462–71: 169–70).

Kraus's critique of romantic ideology is ultimately fused with his attack on imperialistic policy. The vainglorious insistence on territorial annexation is identified as the factor which will turn military victory into political defeat. And this imperialism is traced back to its political as well as economic source: 'obsolete conceptions of power' in league with a 'vigorous predatory greed' (*F* 484–98: 234). This formulation occurs in 'Eine prinzipielle Erklärung', a forceful political statement which Kraus made on the public platform in November 1917 (although it did not appear in print until October 1918). Here he speaks of the opportunity of a negotiated peace so tragically missed, and identifies the alliance of political forces which bear the responsibility: the political romanticism of the Kaiser, the military technology of Krupp, and the diplomatic ineptitude of Czernin. When Kraus attacks those who are 'guilty of high treason against mankind' — 'die Hochverräter an der Menschheit' — his meaning is unambiguous (*F* 484–98: 235).

Deutsche Ansichtskarte

Franz Josef Huber's Kunstverl.-Anst. - München

UNSER KAISER IN HARNISCH!

In Treue und ✠ in Waffen fest!

›Wir Deutsche fürchten Gott
und sonst absolut nichts und
niemanden auf dieser Welt!‹

Aus der Rede S. M. Wilhelm II., gehalten an Bord S. M. S. ›Viktoria Luise‹.

31 Kaiser Wilhelm II in medieval armour: propaganda
postcard

If the Kaiser is himself a traitor, it is because ultimate loyalty is due
not to one's country but to an ethical ideal. In a moving poem of
May 1918 Kraus celebrates Kant as the loyal subject not of the King
of Prussia but of the universe ('eines Weltalls treuer Untertan', *F*
474–83: 160). But the Kaiser's political romanticism is also
contrasted with a more realistic alternative — the policies of
Bismarck.[5] At first sight this may seem incongruous. Kraus's ethical
idealism has little in common with Bismarckian *Realpolitik*, as it is
usually conceived. Bismarck, often thought of as a sabre-rattling
militarist, was certainly responsible for the triumph of
authoritarianism in the Second Reich. But Kraus reminds us of the
other less familiar Bismarck — the statesman who combined shrewd
political judgement with humane moral imagination. In the early

years of *Die Fackel* he repeatedly praises Bismarck as a man who brought to politics the imaginative gifts of an artist. After 1914 Kraus's attitude gains a sharper political focus, and Bismarck becomes a key witness against German war policies. In November 1914 Bismarck is cited in Kraus's critique of the war hysteria of the German press. In February 1915, in addition to quoting further from his utterances against the press, he documents Bismarck's opposition to war with Russia. And in October 1915 he goes a stage further, invoking Bismarck's authority in an aphorism which condemns the political and economic expansion of Germany (*F* 406–12: 112–13).

Retrospectively Bismarck constitutes Kraus's norm. But his analysis of the techno-romantic adventure also has a prophetic dimension:

> Warum sollte es der Technik, die das Wunder von heute zur Kommodität von morgen macht, nicht möglich sein, einen Apparat zu erfinden, durch den es mittelst einer Druck-, Umschalte- oder Kurbelvorrichtung einem Militäruntauglichen gelingen könnte, von einem Berliner Schreibtisch aus London in die Luft zu sprengen und viceversa?
>
> (*F* 474–83: 43)

> (Why should it not be possible for technology, which makes today's miracle into tomorrow's commodity, to invent an apparatus which by means of some button, lever or handle would enable a person unfit for military service sitting at a desk in Berlin to blow London to pieces or vice versa?)

It is not merely the glaring historical contradictions of Imperial Germany that are under attack. Kraus foresees that if military technology is allowed to develop unchecked by ethical controls, and is still sustained by outmoded patriotic ideals, it will bring about the destruction of civilization.

Tragic Carnival and Austrian Face: The Banality of Evil

As Kraus extends his focus beyond the frontiers of Austria-Hungary, he emerges as the great critic of German ideology. But in his glosses on Austrian attitudes he invokes the more traditional motif of the 'Tragic Carnival' (*F* 426–30: 35–9). The emphasis is not simply on the contrast between mask and reality, but on the role-reversals which characterize a world turned upside down.

For the function of German ideology Kraus finds a key word: 'Aufmachung' ('packaging'). Derived from the jargon of design and marketing, this neologism enables him to pin-point the economic aims underlying German military expansion (*F* 406–12: 98, 115, 151). This process is reinforced by the newspeak of organizational efficiency. It is the language of a military machine which grades human beings 'A', 'B' or 'C' according to physical fitness, packages them as 'war material', and delivers them to the battlefield. This same jargon speaks of people who have been sent to the front as 'einrückend gemacht' — not just 'drafted' but 'forcibly enlisted' (*F* 462–71: 112).

When Kraus turns his attention to Austrian affairs, the concept of 'Aufmachung' becomes assimilated into the more traditional paradigm of theatricality. An example is provided by the Berlin production of *Macbeth* by Max Reinhardt, which had used blood-red spotlights and a blood-stained curtain to depict the killing of Duncan. For Kraus there is an uncanny identity between Reinhardt's 'packaging' of Shakespeare and the 'theatrical production' which is responsible for the shedding of real blood (*F* 418–22: 97). The theatre is borrowing its gimmicks from the horrific technology of war. At the same time the way in which the war is being conducted is manifestly theatrical.

The notion of the war as a masquerade suggested itself to other observers. C. E. Montague describes wartime London as a 'fancy-dress ball of non-combatant khaki'.[6] Like Montague, Kraus is bitterly sarcastic at the spectacle of draft-dodgers disporting themselves publicly in military uniforms. Kraus compares the situation in the streets of Vienna to a 'masked ball', at which, if one really wanted to make a sensation, one would wear civilian clothes (*F* 406–12: 140–1). In April 1917 he reprints a newspaper report about a mentally disturbed person who has been arrested after walking solemnly up and down the Kärntnerstrasse wearing a fantastic uniform. Other uniforms seen promenading in the Kärntnerstrasse, Kraus caustically observes, turn out to be civilians in disguise. And he recalls the case of the writer Hans Müller, whose contribution to the war effort has been a patriotic play. Müller actually wore field-grey uniform when he appeared on the stage of the Munich Court Theatre to acknowledge the applause. The writer in fancy dress ('der kostümierte Hans Müller') is a more fraudulent figure than the man in the fantastic uniform. Can it be that in this tragic carnival 'the wearing of masks is obligatory'? (*F* 454–6: 7–8: 'Maskenzwang'). Like the clothing images in *Macbeth*, this masquerade motif gives coherence to Kraus's satire on the usurpation of powers. In October 1918 the emblems of military glory must finally be recognised for what they are: 'Faschingsmasken' (*F* 499–500: 5). And in *Die letzten Tage der Menschheit* Kraus even more emphatically identifies his contemporaries as 'Masken des tragischen Karnevals'.

Looking back in January 1919, Kraus described the whole war as a gigantic imposture, like that perpetrated by the Captain from Köpenick ('eine gigantische Köpenickiade', F 501–8: 111). A gullible world has been duped by a fraudulent display of military power and prestige. It is ultimately the military themselves whom Kraus denounces, not merely the civilians in disguise. But his most impassioned attack is directed against complacent civilians who treat the war as theatrical spectacle. On two occasions he was able to show that this was literally true. In April 1916 a group of soldiers on leave, survivors of the battle of Uszieczko, were prevailed upon to appear on the stage of a Viennese theatre and re-enact the events of the battle. For Kraus, this reduction of the sufferings of war into a spectacle for patriotic citizens in dinner jackets represents the most terrible betrayal of human dignity. The censor agreed. The whole text of the article in Die Fackel, including the original newspaper report, was blanked out (F 426–30: 1–7), although Kraus was able to publish it in October 1917 after an interpellation in parliament (F 462–71: 1–7).

Kraus was able to document a second example (this time in Munich) of soldiers appearing on stage as actors playing the part of soldiers in a play about their own exploits. On this occasion the production was laced with authentic Bavarian humour in a folksy play about trench warfare. Kraus is reminded of the arrival of the players at the Court of Elsinore: 'What players are they?' 'The best actors in the world, either for tragedy, comedy, history, pastoral, pastoral-comical, historical-pastoral, tragical-historical, tragical-comical-historical-pastoral' (F 426–30: 7–10; Hamlet, II ii. 329, 401–4). As in Hamlet, the play within a play is a grotesque mirror of crimes that have been committed in reality. The problem is that the boundaries between reality and theatricality have become blurred: 'die Sphären fließen ineinander' (F 462–71: 5).

Kraus carries the theatrical analogy even further in a passage he quotes from a diary dealing with the revolutionary upheavals in Austria in 1848. The diarist quoted is a conservative and a Christian. But his faith in divine providence begins to falter as he sees history unfolding 'like a frightening theatrical performance' ('wie eine beängstigende Komödie'). Moreover 'none of the actors knows which play is actually being performed and none knows the secret of his own role' ('Keiner der Schauthäter weiß, welches Stück eigentlich aufgeführt wird, wie Keiner das Geheimnis seiner eigenen Rolle kennt'). To emphasize the relevance of these reflections, Kraus reprints them under the title 'Ein Prophet' (F 423–5: 12–13).

The theatricality of the war manifests itself in innumerable ways: in suavely worn dinner jackets which conceal the barbarism of the social élite (F 418–22: 27–8); women disguised in military uniforms which are a betrayal of womanliness (F 426–30: 36); bankers and commodity brokers who have unsurped military rank (F 457–61: 13, 17); the balletic ceremonial of the salute imposed on soldiers who are shortly to face death (F 462–71: 110–11). On the one hand we are shown the spectacle of the governing class enjoying the 'masked ball' of power and privilege. Even more graphically we are confronted with the actual masks which they impose upon their victims. Kraus reproduces photographs to illustrate the grotesque gas masks which have to be worn in the war zone both by soldiers (F 462–71: 13) and by civilians — even women and children huddled around the hearth (F 474–83: 129). In this image Kraus's theme of the disfigurement of the natural human face reaches its climax. He also included a photograph of women in gas masks in the 1919 edition of *Die letzten Tage der Menschheit*. The motif is taken up again in his visionary Epilogue — the dance of the Male and Female Gas Masks in *Die letzte Nacht*.

The visual motifs are underscored by less tangible examples of disguise and role-reversal. The professor who goes to military headquarters to confer an honorary doctorate on a field marshal may not literally put on uniform. But such professors are among the most ridiculous figures in the carnival (F 406–12: 6; 426–30: 37–8). All the more pernicious is the corruption of intellectual and moral standards which such actions imply. If General von Falkenhayn can be made a Doctor of Philosophy, why should the pacifically-minded writer Adalbert Stifter not be enlisted as an apologist for war? It is in such projects that Kraus identifies the 'Fasching der Geister' — the carnival of minds (F 423–5: 28). The carnival is so insidious because it involves both the assumption of false identities and the propagation of false values. For Kraus the leader of the carnival dance is thus inevitably Moriz Benedikt — 'Vortänzer des tragischen Karnevals' (F 431–6: 131). It is Benedikt's protean plurality of roles that qualifies him to lead the dance. The predator disguised in an elegant waistcoat is also the writer of leading articles who 'der Armee seinen Gruß entbietet und, bald Springinsgeld, bald Patriot, zugleich Märchenerzähler und Bilanzknecht, die Leserschaft durch täglich neue Kapriolen entzückt (sends his salutation to the army and, as quick off the mark as he is on the make, a patriot, a teller of tales and simultaneously a soldier of fortune, delights his readers with a different caper every day)' (F 431–6: 130–1). The elevation of Benedikt to the peerage in 1917 forms a climax in the tragic carnival (F 462–71: 58).

Following hard on the heels of Moriz Benedikt is the even more grotesque figure of Alice Schalek. Once again, reality confronts the satirist with a series of metamorphoses. From woman into journalist into feuilletonist into war correspondent — each change of role is a betrayal of that conception of womanliness which Kraus sought to uphold. In this case, satirical stylization is scarcely necessary. Merely by quoting verbatim from Schalek's war feuilletons, Kraus is able to demonstrate the grotesqueness of a figure who inspects the front-line troops with the air of a commander-in-chief and describes the war as if it were a touristic spectacle (F 406–12: 15–19). In the transformation of Alice Schalek Kraus sees the most monstrous exemplification of the tragic carnival. The betrayal of the traditional norms of femininity symbolizes that combination of hysteria and anaesthesia which grips mankind as a whole (F 426–30: 35–9).

In a small figure Kraus once again pins down a large phenomenon. Officially accredited, widely read, applauded by Viennese audiences, defended even by the Socialist press, Alice Schalek was clearly a portent (F 462–71: 134–41). Unlike other war correspondents of this period, she does not seem to have been consciously dishonest. Her feuilletons naïvely describe what she sees and feels. She is significant precisely because she sees the war with the eyes of a sentimental tourist, thrilling with vicarious excitement, humorous and romantic by turns, busily jotting down her impressions and taking snapshots to show the folks back home. The miseries of war as experience are coextensive with the delights of war as spectacle. For Schalek the 'Globetrotterin', touring the Dolomites and then Belgrade, the war really is exciting. She is not simply a manipulator of the public. She *is* that public, the quintessential bourgeoise — a living caricature of the *Zeitgeist* (F 426–30: 36). Benedikt leads the dance; Schalek exemplifies the thousands of utterly suggestible newspaper readers who are swept along in his train.

Alice Schalek forms part of an apparatus of war which inflates nonentities into persons of power and influence. She who has watched men dying through her lorgnon is officially decorated for valour (F 457–61: 84). Swindlers and speculators are honoured, subordinates elevated into positions of power. The social order is topsy-turvy — 'kunterbunt'. Never has 'man, proud man, dressed in a little brief authority' wielded power with such irresponsibility and such terrifying consequences. This Shakespearean motif, already cited by Kraus in his pre-war critique of Austrian institutions, recurs in *Die Fackel* of May 1917 with a new urgency. The most bitter aspect of the carnival lies in the transfer of powers. Actions which would traditionally have appertained to a tyrant are now carried out by the duty officer of the day. He merely has to press the button marked 'death'. The technical apparatus of war both increases the destructive powers of the individual and also — by distancing him from the consequences of his action — diminishes his sense of

responsibility. Kraus's two great critical themes — the destructiveness of technology and the failure of imagination — are thus fused
with the carnival motif of an inverted social order. The 'world-
historical event' which he diagnoses in May 1917 lies in the
anonymity of the modern apparatus of power, the contrast between
its insignificant, faceless operators and its immense destructiveness
('Unser weltgeschichtliches Erlebnis', F 457–61: 95–100).

Kraus's treatment of this problem anticipates a large critical
literature which has grown up around the concept of the 'banality of
evil'.[7] When he first ironized the slogan of 'these great times', he can
hardly have foreseen how complete would be the metamorphosis of
great and small. In the political leadership of Austria-Hungary Kraus
identifies a sinister blend of mediocrity and frivolity. It is exemplified
by the Foreign Minister responsible for the declaration of war on
Serbia, Count Berchtold. A photograph of Berchtold in uniform,
adopting a jaunty pose, forms the frontispiece to Kraus's necrologue
on Austria-Hungary of January 1919. And in this same number
Berchtold is denounced as a 'dandy of the race course' ('Renngigerl',
F 501–7: 116). Kraus thus anticipates Churchill's judgement that
Berchtold 'is the epitome of this age in which the affairs of
Brobdingnag are managed by the Lilliputians'.[8] Even greater is the
incongruity in the case of the 'non-personality' who has presided
over Austrian affairs for seventy years, Franz Joseph. The Emperor's
dignity of bearing, which in November 1914 had still commanded
Kraus's respect, is in retrospect seen as the pose of 'a demon of
mediocrity' — 'ein Dämon der Mittelmäßigkeit' (F 501–7: 6).

Kraus's increasingly critical attitude towards the dynasty leads to the
larger question of the diffusion of power. Incompetence and corruption at the top promote an anonymous ruthlessness lower down the
chain of command. Technology places demonic power in the hands of
mediocrities. A feeble man sitting at a distant desk can blow a whole
city sky high (F 474–83: 43). The danger for Kraus lies not only in the
destructiveness of modern technology but also in the facelessness of
the man at the desk. Subaltern natures are suddenly elevated into
positions where they wield the power of a Genghis Khan. Harmless
Spießbürger, in peacetime the perpetrators of no greater atrocity than a
carnival evening of the Vienna Male Voice Choir, now under cover of
military uniforms become capable of 'anonymous cruelty' (F
501–7: 26–7). Army doctors ruthlessly send invalids back to the front
(F 501–7: 39). Death sentences have been passed by courts martial
presided over by men who are merely solicitor's clerks in disguise
('verkleidete Advokaturskonzipienten', F 462–71: 167).

No one feels any sense of personal responsibility; for all are acting
under 'cover': 'Deckung durch den Akt, durch die Phrase, durch die

Anonymität, durch den Mangel an Beweisen, durch alle Behelfe der Technik und der Lüge (the cover of a dossier, of a slogan, of anonymity, of lack of proof, of all those expedients of technology and deceit)' (*F* 501–7: 119). At this level too there are no responsible faces. Guilt is almost universal and a whole nation must come to terms with its past. What Kraus attempts in 'Nachruf' is a collage in which specific instances are built into a composite picture of overwhelming power. And the title of this picture is 'The Austrian Face' — ' das österreichische Antlitz'.

His indictment of the Austrian ethos is a complement to Kraus's critique of German ideology. In Germany he exposes the cult of heroic strenuousness. In Austria he denounces the ethos of *Gemütlichkeit* — a geniality which conceals an underlying ruthlessness. In October 1916 the Viennese leisured and official class may still be seen parading the fashionable streets of the city, undeterred by the war cripples limping by. In their faces the satirist discerns 'the rigor mortis of *Gemütlichkeit*' ('die Leichenstarre der Gemütlichkeit', *F* 437–42: 125). Visual motifs reinforce this sense of the inescapable 'Austrian face'. A poster illustrating Lehár's operatic theme 'Bist du's, lachendes Glück?' presides over a city decimated by hunger and influenza. And the appetite of the Viennese for operettas continues undiminished by the horrors of war, as Kraus repeatedly shows (*F* 418–22: 25; 426–30: 25; 431–6: 42).

The motif of frivolity impaled by brutality finds quintessential expression in the picture of the 'laughing hangman'. Ten years before the war Kraus had prophetically identified the re-emergence of 'lachende Henker' from the primitive era of the witch-hunt (*F* 168: 16). Now he is able to document this phenomenon by means of an actual photograph (Pl. 32). It shows the scene after the execution of Cesare Battisti, the Italian-speaking irredentist who (although a Habsburg subject) had fought on the enemy side. Above the hanging body of Battisti stands the beaming hangman in a bowler hat. Around him cluster six army officers and two civilians. Their faces grin and gloat like the masks in a nightmarish painting by Edvard Munch or James Ensor. But the picture, printed as frontispiece to the book edition of *Die letzten Tage der Menschheit* (1922), is a historical document, not a satirical invention. Such hangings were carried out in public, as a deterrent to other potential dissidents or deserters, and photographs of them were taken by the military authorities.[9]

The execution of Battisti, who was nominally guilty of treason, had a basis in law analogous to the case of Sir Roger Casement. The special horror of the Battisti hanging lies for Kraus in the attitudes of the executioners: death is treated as a laughing matter, and they gloat over the body of a fellow citizen whose crime resides in his loyalty to

32   The execution of Cesare Battisti: propaganda photograph

his own nation. Equally horrifying is the fact that the image is a propaganda photograph, printed and circulated by the authorities as a picture postcard. It may thus legitimately be seen as a kind of official self-portrait of Austrian petty tyranny. It has representative force. Kraus makes it clear that there are other similar photographs in existence (like that showing the execution of a Polish countess and her maid) (*F* 501–7: 53). During the war there were mass defections by Habsburg subjects, whose ethnic identity (Czech, Polish, Ruthenian, Serbian or Italian) led them to side with Austria's enemies. No less than 11,400 executions (Kraus tells us) took place under the regime of the apparently so genial Archduke Friedrich.[10]

Kraus goes on to suggest that the same grinning face may be glimpsed at almost any point in the hierarchy of petty tyranny: at the window of a railway booking office; on the military policeman who publicly beats a sick woman who objected to her son's arrest; in the fatuous duplicity of Hermann Bahr; the hotelier who hopes that the horrors of the battlefield will lead to an increase in the tourist trade;

the medical orderlies who apply electric shock to soldiers suffering from nervous breakdowns, suspected of malingering; the officers who compel Serbian peasants to dig their own graves before being executed; the gratuitous cruelty of authorities who force the relatives of a condemned man to watch his execution; the staff officer who executed forty-four of his war-weary troops as punishment for an orgy of drunkenness and indiscipline (*F* 501–7: 52–68).[11]

These 'Austrian brutalities' (Kraus uses the English phrase, *F* 501–7: 63) were widely publicized in the western press.[12] Kraus's aim is to identify the frame of mind in which they originate. They are committed by the ordinary person who 'wouldn't hurt a fly' but simply shrugs his shoulders at actions of inconceivable cruelty (*F* 501–7: 102). Such people (as Kraus says of Count Berchtold) respond to Judgement Day as if it were a fairground entertainment ('Praterscherz', *F* 501–7: 117). They find their apotheosis in the army colonel who uses his rank as cover for operations on the black market and writes jocular letters telling his mistresses how pleased he is with the war (*F* 501–7: 117–19). Behind such banal figures, behind the still unruffled smile of officers, administrators and profiteers, there lurks an absolute force of evil. When on the final page of Kraus's 120-page tribute ('Nachruf') to Habsburg Austria the mask is finally discarded, it is Mephistopheles who appears to speak the epilogue.

The specifically Austrian features of this polemic must not distract from its wider applications. The tragic carnival takes its costumes from the Habsburg Empire. But its leading figures, above all that of the jovial hangman, can recur in any society which allows unrestrained authority to pass into the hands of sadistic nonentities. The uniforms change. The gratuitous cruelty towards defenceless minorities remains the same. The phenomenon which Kraus documents was to recur in even more terrible forms in Nazi Germany. Both Hitler and Eichmann spent their formative years in Austria. But the thrust of Kraus's critique is directed at that 'anonymous cruelty' which may occur in *any* corruptly governed state. After the Nazi seizure of power in Germany in 1933 he was able to demonstrate the affinities with the situation in the First World War. And a photograph of a Nazi mob mocking a Jewish lawyer (subsequently shot dead while 'trying to escape') provided a close parallel to that of Battisti's execution (*W* I. 50). The National Socialists were even more zealous than the leadership in the First World War, in making photographic records of their own cruelty. Sadistic reincarnations of Kraus's jovial hangman can be found in the photographic records of Himmler's S.S. The 'Third Walpurgisnacht' after 1933 was to provide the most terrible confirmation of the truths embodied in Kraus's image of the 'Tragic Carnival'.[13]

CHAPTER 19

Between the Sword and the Pen: Stylistic Discipline and Conservative Standpoint

Amid the whirl of the carnival, where does the satirist himself stand? Looking back in January 1919, Kraus identified himself as the sceptical observer of 'human masquerades' (*F* 501–7: 82). But the detachment to which he aspired was a myth. He too was caught up in that 'frightening theatrical performance' in which 'none of the actors knows the secret of his own role' (*F* 423–5: 12). The relationship between Kraus's pacifism and his politics is extremely complex.[1] To disentangle it, the various strands of his conservatism — his attitudes towards army and dynasty, aristocracy and Church, censorship and police, political parties and individual statesmen — must be traced through the pages of *Die Fackel* with a critical eye. To elucidate the opaque utterances of the satirist it will be necessary to draw on unpublished documents which reveal the underlying assumptions of the author.

The Sword and the Pen

During the final years before 1914 Kraus had on several occasions expressed his admiration for the military virtues: for the 'Sword' which is given precedence over the 'Pen' (in 'Die Kinder der Zeit', *F* 354–6: 71); and for the 'manliness' of an audience of officers at the Pola naval base which he visited in November 1913 (*F* 387–8: 32). 'In dieser großen Zeit' seems to signal a radical change of outlook. And Kraus's retrospective self-interpretation has encouraged this view. Writing in January 1919 he identifies 1 August 1914 as the day when he had changed his mind ('umgelernt') (*F* 501–7: 17). And in a later passage he dates his conversion back to 22 July 1914, the day before the Austrian ultimatum was sent to Serbia (*F* 531–43: 106–7).

'In dieser großen Zeit' certainly adumbrates the arguments of Kraus's subsequent more militant pacifism. But politically it is an ambiguous document. Its main targets are the forces of 'progress' —

the Liberal press and the commercial interests it represents. Of course the censorship precluded direct criticism of the political or military leadership, so nothing can be deduced from the essay's omissions. But it is significant that Kraus cites Bismarck's hope that 'the achievements of the Prussian sword' will not again be lost as a result of journalistic propaganda. At a time when German armies had advanced deep into French, Belgian and Russian territory, the use of this quotation hardly implies an anti-militarist position (*F* 404: 10–11).

Kraus's position in November 1914 even attracted the support of the arch-conservative *Reichspost*, which printed a favourable report on his public reading, just as it had earlier praised his essay 'Franz Ferdinand und die Talente'. In its leading article of 19 July 1914 the *Reichspost* had cited *Die Fackel* in support of its argument in favour of a punitive expedition against Serbia. Now that in November 1914 this enterprise is under way, it praises Kraus's public reading, describing him as a man who deserves some credit for the advent of a new and more worthy age: 'der an dem Kommen einer neuen, würdigeren Zeit nicht eben das kleinste Verdienst trägt'.[2] For the *Reichspost* there did not appear to be any break in the continuity of Kraus's writings. But other readers (for example Franz Pfemfert) discerned the pacifistic implications of 'In dieser großen Zeit'.[3] It is certainly a cryptic document.

The text which Kraus chose for his second public reading of the war, on 12 December 1914, makes it clear that he had by no means broken with his conservative allegiances. It was 'Die Kinder der Zeit' — precisely that declaration in which he had proclaimed his preference for the Sword over the Pen and had argued in favour of 'a consolidation of the conservative will' (*F* 354–6: 70). There is no evidence that these sentiments were modified in the version of the text that Kraus read. On the contrary, his programme emphasizes the continuing validity of this declaration (*F* 405: 2–3). A different note was struck when he included in his next public reading, on 13 February 1915, the prophetic pre-war text 'Und in Kriegszeiten', which identifies war as a suicidal enterprise. But even this still ascribes responsibility for the war to the press, not the political and military leadership. And the declaration that Kraus made at the beginning of this reading expresses scepticism about the war, rather than outright opposition (*F* 405: 14–20).

The 168–page number of *Die Fackel* published in October 1915 seems to mark the point where scepticism hardens into opposition. But the pacifistic thrust of the glosses and aphorisms printed there is still politically indeterminate. And although there are strictures on German expansionism, the military command is still treated with respect. In the gloss 'Philosophie' Kraus attributes to the commanders of the German army an objective and functionalist view of life ('sachliche Lebensauffassung'). Among them (he continues) are some who understand how to preserve the intellectual decencies far better than do the professors of philosophy who foist honorary degrees on them.

Such formulations are not merely to be attributed to Kraus's fondness for antitheses. For he singles out one German commander, General Hermann von Stein, for special praise. Stein had been responsible, in August and early September 1914, for the official bulletins issued by German military headquarters on the western front. These bulletins Kraus praises for their truthfulness and their 'stylistic discipline' ('stilistische Zucht', *F* 406–12: 6–7). Moreover he admired the substance as well as the style of Stein's writings. For he goes on to endorse two personal statements in which Stein argues that rapid military victories are culturally deleterious, since they promote a triumphant materialism similar to that which has dominated Germany since 1871 (*F* 406–12: 7–8).

This praise of General von Stein has inescapable ideological overtones. For Kraus, as for the Prussian officer, the achievements of the German army become problematic when they are exploited by a civilian population which is unworthy of them. From this antithesis the army emerges, at least by implication, in a favourable light. Kraus's initial target is not militarism, but economic pressure groups which are exploiting military achievements for materialistic ends. There is thus an affinity between his position and the kind of forthright Prussian conservatism which Theodor Fontane admired. Blood-thirsty German pedagogues (Kraus suggests) could learn a thing or two from decent military men like the Commanding Officer of the Tenth Army Corps (*F* 426–30: 56–7).

The affinity is intimated again in December 1915, when Kraus quotes with approval an article in the Prussian *Kreuzzeitung*. All expectations that the war would bring about a national moral and religious rebirth, the article argues, have been disappointed. The civilian population is consumed with frivolity and the desire for self-enrichment. Thus every victory is bringing the country nearer to ruin: 'wir werden uns ins Verderben hineinsiegen.' Kraus quotes these sentiments with approval. Conservative Germany (he observes) has just begun to realize what he himself had prophesied in conversation with friends in Innsbruck during the first days of August 1914 and expressed in the declaration 'In dieser großen Zeit' (*F* 413–17: 23–4).

At this stage, almost eighteen months after the outbreak of war, Kraus still explicitly aligns himself with the conservatives and the aristocracy, the Church and the army ('die von Beruf oder Geburt Konservativen, Adel, Kirche und der Krieger selbst', *F* 413–17: 26). In both Church and army he found spokesmen with whom he could identify. In a letter to Sidonie of 21/22 November 1914 he notes that the arguments of 'In dieser großen Zeit' are echoed in the Encyclical of the newly enthroned Pope Benedict XV — a very conservative document whose protest is directed more against the materialistic tendencies of the modern age than against the war itself (*BSN* I. 94).[4]

It is clear that Kraus's admiration also extended to members of the Austrian army, for example Generalmajor Maximilian von Hoen, Director of the Kriegspressequartier. Here again he contrasts devious journalists with a forthright army officer. In a reference to professional soldiers like von Hoen, Kraus writes: 'Sie mögen meine Ansicht über die Kriegsberichterstattung teilen — ich bin ganz ihrer Ansicht über den Krieg. (They may well share my view of war reportage — I completely share their view of the war.)' (*F* 413–17: 35) This cryptic formulation indicates that Kraus in December 1915 had not yet lost his admiration for the military virtues. His surprising claim that professional soldiers share his views may well refer to a celebrated letter by an anonymous army officer, published under the title 'Soldatenkrieg und Zeitungskrieg' in *Danzer's Armee-Zeitung*. This letter repudiated the xenophobic propaganda of the press in terms very similar to those of *Die Fackel*.[5]

There is even a hint of Kraus being personally acquainted with von Hoen, in a passage where he refers to the Major General's manner of speaking as 'authentically soldierly and pithy' ('echt soldatisch kernig', *F* 413–17: 34). During the following year Generalmajor von Hoen's organization sent Kraus an invitation to attend a War Exhibition ('Kriegs-Ausstellung'). Kraus replies that he would only accept if it were a 'Kriegs-Einstellung' ('War Termination') (*F* 431–6: 27). The pun clearly establishes his opposition to the war. But the notion of Kraus associating with members of the officer class is not as incongruous as it may seem. A series of private letters survive which show that for more than a dozen years Kraus was on cordial terms with another officer in the Austrian army, Generalmajor Baron Moritz Erwin von Lempruch. During the pre-war years Lempruch was a faithful but not uncritical reader of *Die Fackel*. Some of his copies of the magazine, which happen to have survived, contain vigorous underlinings and marginal comments which suggest that he particularly appreciated the antisemitic undercurrent in Kraus's satire.[6]

During the war itself the links between Kraus and Lempruch became even closer. Serving as an officer on the southern front, Lempruch continued to receive his copies of *Die Fackel*, and his letters express unqualified admiration for Kraus's work. Kraus clearly valued this friendship, indeed it was a private letter of July 1915 to Lempruch which formed the basis of his conception of a 'moral island' on which the virtuous were marooned by the war (*F* 406–12: 168; *BSN* I. 171–2). Lempruch replied on 12 August in terms which reveal the fundamental affinity between soldier and satirist:

> Sie haben den Grundton meiner Ansicht von der heutigen Zeit richtig eingeschätzt: gegen den äußeren Feind werden wir uns schon wehren; gegen den inneren aber sind wir vorläufig machtlos.

> (You have accurately gauged the basic tone of my view of the contemporary age: we can defend ourselves well enough against our external enemy; but for the time being we are helpless against the enemy within.)[7]

The Enemy Within

The 'enemy within' are clearly the journalists and profiteers, who were regarded as pernicious by soldier and satirist alike. Indeed Kraus was delighted to receive from Lempruch in May 1916 a letter describing how Alice Schalek, visiting Lempruch's section of the front, had been snubbed and repulsed by the commanding officer.[8] He recorded this episode in the following number of *Die Fackel*:

> Aber die günstige Nachricht sei weitergegeben, daß die Schalek nicht überall durchbrechen konnte, von der Südwestfront zurückgeworfen wurde und daß wenigstens dieser Teil des Kriegsschauplatzes zu einer unwirtlichen Gegend für den innern Feind geworden ist, von dem uns die Abwehr des äußern keineswegs befreit hat.
>
> (*F* 426–30: 39)

> (But let the good news be passed on that Schalek was not able to break through everywhere, was repulsed from the south-west front, and that at least this section of the theatre of war has become an inhospitable region for that enemy within, from whom the defeat of the external enemy has by no means liberated us.)

This formulation conflates Lempruch's anecdote with the antithesis between 'external enemy' and 'the enemy within' which had occurred in his letter of August 1915. The antithesis provides indeed the paradigm within which Kraus's satire is conceived during the first two years of the war. And it helps us to understand Kraus's remark in December 1915 that he shared the view of professional soldiers about the war.

The 'enemy within' is a catch-phrase for authoritarian politicians of all ages. Under varying historical circumstances it may denote religious heretics, political dissidents, or ethnic minorities. But in the context of 1915–16 its connotations are unmistakable. Kraus shared with the conservative ideologists of his day a tendency to identify the ills of modern society with some form of pernicious Jewish influence. The First World War, in which thousands of soldiers of Jewish origin fought loyally for their countries, saw a vicious upsurge of antisemitism in Austria-Hungary and the German Reich, as the initial euphoria dissolved and a scapegoat was needed to take the blame for defeat and demoralization.[9] The collapse of November 1918 was blamed on socialists and Jews, who had 'stabbed Germany in the back', at a time when her armies were still undefeated in the field. Kraus's writings are also contaminated by this antisemitic undercurrent. But to his credit it must be emphasized that during the later stages of the war he radically revised his position, recognizing that the primary responsibility for the catastrophe lay not with the journalists and profiteers, but with the political and military leadership.

In *Die Fackel* of 1915–17 there are repeated reminders of the 'Jewish' characteristics of these journalists and profiteers. It has already been emphasized that for Kraus 'Jewishness' was not a fixed racial character, but denotes an attitude of mind that may be found among members of any ethnic group or religious confession. Nevertheless there are continuous indications, often in coded form, that the 'enemy within' is Jewish in origin. On the very page where this phrase occurs (F 426–30: 39) we are reminded that Alice Schalek has a long nose (an allusion to her Jewishness as well as to the 'long face' she presumably makes when she finds herself snubbed). Her nose is also mocked in an earlier context, where the suggestion is that it is so long that it is likely to betray an Austrian military position to the enemy (F 413–17: 36). These coded references with their humorous intention may seem harmless in themselves. But Kraus is here exploiting one of the stock devices of antisemitic caricature, to which he took grave exception when he found his own face portrayed with an accentuated 'Jewish' nose (F 374–5: 32).

The role of the Jews in European civilization had preoccupied Kraus ever since he read Chamberlain's *Grundlagen des 19. Jahrhunderts* shortly after its publication in 1899 (F 21: 30–1). In December 1915 we find him quoting a lengthy disquisition by Dostoevsky on the same theme (F 413–17: 49–74). Unfortunately he was also attracted by cruder formulations of antisemitic assumptions, for example Luther's equation of Jews and usurers (F 423–5: 55–6). The prominence of Jewish families in the commercial life of Vienna and Budapest made that equation plausible. Since the founding of *Die Fackel*, the Jewish entrepreneur Rudolf Sieghart had epitomized for Kraus the combined power of the press and the stock exchange. In January 1917 he quotes a balance sheet which shows

that as principal shareholder in the Styrian Armaments Company
Sieghart received a dividend of almost half a million Crowns for the
year 1915–16 (*F* 445–53: 68).

Similarly the Eisig Rubel who featured in a spectacular court case
of 1917 was not a satirical invention. Rubel was a prominent member
of a consortium which had evidently enriched itself at the expense of
the taxpayer and the Ministry of War. In his account of the case
Kraus accentuates the Jewish jargon in the testimony of the accused,
which expresses for him the 'Mystery of (Jewish) profiteering' and
the 'Cabbala of the balance sheet' ('Mysterium des Rebbachs',
'Kabbala des Saldo', *F* 457–61: 11). Such coded linguistic
identifications are characteristic of Kraus's satire on war profiteers.
There is even a suggestion that the vast profits of the Manfred Weiss
munitions factory in Budapest will exclusively enrich the members
of a Jewish family (*F* 474–83: 131). The one-sidedness of this picture
did not escape Kraus's more critical readers. Commenting on this
number of *Die Fackel*, Schnitzler noted in his diary on 16 October
1918 that Kraus seemed 'only to be aware of Jewish war profiteers'.

Kraus's underlying attitude becomes explicit at certain points in
his poetry. A particularly ill-judged formulation of October 1915
describes the faithful old retainer of an aristocratic house (now
converted into a hospital) as worth more than 'ten thousand Jews' (*F*
406–12: 148). And in a long declamatory poem of May 1916, 'Gebet
an die Sonne von Gibeon', 'Israel' is identified as the 'cosmic enemy'
(*F* 423–5: 58–65). This poem, based on an Old Testament motif,
explores themes of some complexity. But for a reviewer who heard
Kraus declaiming it at a public reading in Zurich on 4 May 1916 its
message seemed devastatingly simple. It appeared that Kraus was
'blaming the Jews for the World War'. This was the gist of a report
that was sent to Schnitzler, in whose diary it is again recorded.[10]

Of course the report was misleading. Kraus's reading attacked
pseudo-patriotic sentiments of all kinds (*F* 426–30: 43–4). And in
'Gebet an die Sonne' he is using the myth of the Chosen People, who
are fighting with God on their side, as a means of attacking the
pseudo-religiosity of the German ideology. But this illustrates the
fundamental ambiguity of his mythopoeic method. The simple
allegorical equation — 'Israel' equals 'Germany', 'Jehovah' equals the
'God of the Kaiser' — is obscured by the suggestion that 'Israel' in
this poem really denotes 'Germany which has fallen under malign
Jewish influence'. For all its magnificent closing vision of a world
purified of human corruption, the poem does at one level appeal to
antisemitic sentiment. Thus in acknowledging the value of Kraus's
anti-war satire, we should also recognize its limitations. 'Gebet an
die Sonne' was repeatedly included in his public readings of 1916–17,

usually as the final item, so that the denunciation of 'Israel' appeared to form the climax of his critique.

The contrast between the corrupt profiteers of the *Hinterland* and the stoical soldiers at the front continued to provide Kraus's dominant satirical paradigm. This is summed up by the title given to the Eisig Rubel case, 'Wehr und Wucher' ('Army and Usury'). Even at this late stage (January 1917) Kraus implies that the Minister of War is an honourable man who has been duped by unscrupulous scoundrels (*F* 457–61: 17). Kraus attacks militarism as an attitude of mind, but not as a political institution: 'Militarismus ist kein staatlicher, sondern ein geistiger Zustand' (*F* 454–6: 45).

There is thus an unresolved tension between Kraus's growing opposition to the war and his continuing respect for the army. On 12 May 1916, a week after that problematic reading in Zurich, he once again declaimed 'Die Kinder der Zeit' from the public platform (*F* 426–30: 50). It seems almost incomprehensible that he should still have endorsed the ominous proposition: 'Der Säbel, der ins Leben schneidet, habe recht vor der Feder, die sich sträubt.' To understand his paradoxical position we must take account of two further factors: Kraus's sympathy for the social class to which professional officers tended to belong — the aristocracy; and his susceptibility to what he calls the 'discipline of style' ('stilistische Zucht', *F* 406–12: 7).

The Discipline of Style

Kraus's satire has from first to last a linguistic basis. The programme he had announced in April 1899 was to counteract the destructive effects of political phraseology (*F* 1: 2). An exceptional sensitivity to linguistic symptoms inspires his critique of the hollow rhetoric of public affairs prior to 1914. And during the war itself he emerged as the first great critic of propaganda, anticipating Orwell's vision of a totalitarian society dominated by doublethink and newspeak. There have been numerous studies of this aspect of Kraus's achievement. What concerns us here is Kraus's more problematic positive proposition: that good style may be the guarantor of moral virtue. This is summed up by the celebrated dictum in his essay 'Die Sprache' of December 1932: 'Welch ein Stil des Lebens möchte sich entwickeln, wenn der Deutsche keiner andern Ordonnanz gehorsamte als der der Sprache! (What a style of life might develop if the German were to obey no ordinance other than that of language!)' (*F* 885–7: 3) This view of language had a decisive influence on Kraus's approach to politics and was responsible for certain dramatic errors of judgement. At crucial junctures his aesthetic impressionability attracted him to political positions specifically because they were formulated in exemplary German. In short, he praised the

Sword because of its skill in wielding the Pen.

The outstanding instance is his response to the Imperial Proclamation of war with Serbia, published on 29 July 1914 over the signature of Emperor Franz Joseph (Pl. 28). We have already noted how Kraus in November 1914 satirically juxtaposed this proclamation with two other posters to be seen on the streets of Vienna: advertisements for Berson's shoes and for a popular restaurant (Pls. 29 and 30). In contrast with these images of commerce and entertainment, the declaration of war is identified as 'that sublime proclamation, that poem which introduced this age full of action, the sole poem which the age has produced, the most humane placard which has ever assaulted the eye of the passer-by'. Kraus's German here contains undercurrents of irony, as he was at pains to point out when he was reproached after the war by a left-wing critic for having endorsed the Proclamation (F 531–43: 127–33). This is particularly true of his pun on the word 'Anschlag' (meaning simultaneously 'placard' and 'assault') (F 404: 3). But the positive implications of his response are unmistakable (he even reaffirmed his praise for the Proclamation in October 1915) (F 406–12: 118). And after the war he still maintained that the literary qualities of the Proclamation — particularly of one key sentence — justified his view of it as a great poem.

The text of his apologia of January 1919 is revealing:

> Mit einem Satz, der wahrhaftig die volle Bürde der Altersweisheit trägt und die ganze Würde des Schwergeprüften, [. . .] mit einem Satz, dessen ausgesparte Fülle den Schwall aller Kriegslyrik aufwog: mit einem 'Ich habe alles reiflich erwogen', springt die Vergangenheit, die sich nicht zu helfen weiß, der Welt an die Gurgel. Und doch war nie etwas weniger reiflich erwogen, und Shakespeares altersberatener Monarch, der aus Hitze und nicht aus Kälte ins Verderben raste, ist daneben ein Gipfel staatsmännischer Erkenntnis.
>
> (F 501–7: 7)

> (With a sentence which truly bears the whole burden of the wisdom of age and the whole dignity of a sorely tried man, [. . .] with a sentence whose pithy plenitude outweighs all the lyric poetry of the war: with the phrase 'I have weighed the matter up most carefully', a past age utterly perplexed leaps at the throat of the world. And yet never was anything less carefully weighed up, and Shakespeare's monarch ill-advised by age, whom heat not coolness plunged into destruction, is the apogee of statesmanlike understanding by comparison.)

Even this formulation leaves too much unexplained. Kraus's admiring response to the Proclamation rests on a series of fallacies. Most obviously, a political manifesto, however well written, can never be a poem. And to suppose that the document was actually written by the Emperor himself, and thus expresses 'the wisdom of age', betrays an extraordinary naïvety. It was in fact written by a junior official at the Cabinet Office. Furthermore, the key sentence which Kraus repeatedly praises: 'Ich habe alles reiflich erwogen', does *not* in fact occur in the Proclamation. In short Kraus's judgement, usually so unerring, is in this case completely haywire.

To take first the document's political content: Kraus was by no means the only contemporary observer to be deeply moved by its dignified and sonorous phrasing, which so resonantly expresses the predicament of Austria-Hungary through the voice of a monarch ripe in years. And yet Kraus of all people should have been able to recognize the fraudulence of the *political* claims advanced in the Proclamation. The claim is made that Austria-Hungary has for three decades been pursuing 'the beneficial works of peace' in Bosnia and has 'protected and promoted' the interests of the kingdom of Serbia. But Serbian agitation has been 'undermining the foundations of the state', and the assassination of Franz Ferdinand is attributable to an organized Serbian 'conspiracy'. Austria-Hungary has made a final effort to resolve the ensuing crisis by peaceful means, but Serbia has 'repudiated' its 'moderate and just demands'.

Kraus was in a position to know that these claims were half-truths. The early files of *Die Fackel* abundantly document the corruption and inefficiency of the Austrian administration in Bosnia. Kraus was also aware that the growing hostility of Serbia after 1900 was due to fundamental errors in Austrian foreign policy. As for Serbia being responsible for a criminal conspiracy among Habsburg subjects, his own analysis of the Friedjung case should have led him to treat such allegations with scepticism, at least until the facts were established. Finally, the claim that Serbia had 'repudiated' the Austrian ultimatum was manifestly a half-truth. Serbia had *accepted* almost every Austrian demand and only demurred on two minor points, where clarification or arbitration was requested. The text of the Serbian reply was published in morning papers on 28 July 1914, so it would not have been difficult to check it against the Proclamation issued the following day. But Kraus's judgement seems to have been clouded by an overwhelming sense of dynastic loyalty. His indignation at the murder of Franz Ferdinand was doubtless a contributory factor.

Secondly, there is the problem of authorship. Kraus seems to have believed that the Proclamation was written by the Emperor in person. His conception of the close rapport between political decision and linguistic utterance had been shaped by the example of Bismarck, who did combine admirable political judgement with equally remarkable powers of literary expression. But in an era when politicians were increasingly hard pressed to find the time to write their own speeches, Bismarck was an outstanding exception. The actual author of the Imperial Proclamation was a Jewish journalist from Prague, Moritz Bloch, employed by the Cabinet Office. When Kraus subsequently learnt the identity of the author, he still insisted that the feelings expressed in the Proclamation were 'authentic' ('echt'), because of the self-identification with the destiny of Austria achieved by this 'stylistic artist from the Ministry' ('Stilkünstler aus dem Ministerium', F 501–7: 7). But Kraus also mentions that the anonymous author was an admirer of Die Fackel; and this may be confirmed from other sources.[11] Thus Kraus was hoist by his own petard. A skilful draftsman, schooled in the precepts of Die Fackel, produced a proclamation so eloquent that the teacher himself was carried away.

The circularity of Kraus's argument is further compounded by his extraordinary error in quotation. On countless occasions he cites the key line from the Proclamation as: 'Ich habe alles reiflich erwogen'. In fact the line reads: 'Ich habe alles geprüft und erwogen'. Although the general sense is the same, the different phrasing — particularly the absence of the key word 'reiflich' ('most carefully') — creates a far less resonant effect. But Kraus himself, though he repeatedly uses this phrase with ironic effect during the 1920s, appears never to have realized his mistake. In subsequent commentaries on his work the discrepancy has seldom been noticed and never satisfactorily explained. It is of course conceivable that somewhere there exists a corrupt text of the Proclamation which Kraus happened to read, in which the phrase 'reiflich erwogen' does occur. But in every surviving copy that it has been possible to examine, the phrase reads 'geprüft und erwogen'.[12] Thus the question must be answered: where did the phrase 'reiflich erwogen' originate and who was its author?

The first point to note is that the phrase, although mentioned in passing in October 1915, does not actually appear to have been quoted in Die Fackel until January 1919 (F 501–7: 7). The lapse of time explains the lapse of memory. Kraus is evidently quoting not from a copy of the Proclamation itself, but from his own fallible recollection of that tumultuous week at the end of July 1914. He repeatedly refers to the fact that the Proclamation was to be seen as a poster on the streets of Vienna. But it must be remembered that on 29 July 1914, when the Proclamation was published, Kraus was on holiday with Sidonie in the Dolomites. It thus seems likely that he first read the text not in poster form, but in an Austrian newspaper.

Austrian tourists holidaying in the Dolomites would have found the principal Vienna newspapers on display at any self-respecting hotel. The news of the ultimatum to Serbia was reported in the morning papers of 24 July, and we can assume that Kraus followed the political crisis with rapt attention. The emphasis in all the Austrian newspapers was on the fact that the decision to confront Serbia with an ultimatum had been extremely 'carefully considered' ('reiflich überlegt' was the phrase used in *Die Zeit* in its evening edition of 24 July). Since *Die Zeit* had initially resisted the incipient war hysteria, it is reasonable to suppose that Kraus followed its coverage (as well as that of the *Neue Freie Presse* and the *Reichspost*). The editorial of Sunday 26 July, spectacularly headed 'Krieg!', can scarcely have escaped his attention. Abandoning its liberal principles, *Die Zeit* proclaims the dawning of 'a great heroic age'. And the editorial goes on to emphasize the resolute attitude of Austrian diplomacy: 'In dieser Haltung liegt die Gewähr, daß unsere Regierung bei Abfassung der Note an Serbien alle daraus möglicherweise entspringenden Wirkungen *reiflich erwogen* hat. (In this attitude lies the guarantee that our Government in drafting the ultimatum to Serbia *weighed up most carefully* all the possible consequences.') (*Die Zeit*, 26 July 1914, p. 1; italics added.) When this same newspaper published the Imperial Proclamation three days later, its editorial began by quoting the phrase: 'Ich habe alles geprüft und erwogen' (*Die Zeit*, 29 July 1914). It seems more than possible that *Die Zeit* was the source both for Kraus's knowledge of the Proclamation, and for his focus on one particular sentence, and for the phrase 'reiflich erwogen' which became conflated with it in his memory.

Of course this is only a hypothesis. But it does offer an explanation for the fact that Kraus seems inadvertently to have 'invented' the most celebrated of all his 'documents'. And such was Kraus's authority that his version became universally accepted as the authentic text. When during the 1920s other authors quote this key phrase from the Imperial Proclamation — for example Jaroslav Hasek and Erwin Piscator — they quote it in Kraus's version, not that of the original document.[13] Like the apocryphal 'Scrap of Paper' which Bethmann Hollweg is alleged to have torn up in August 1914 in Berlin, Kraus's phrase somehow acquired a more convincing ring than the text of the original declaration.[14]

How is it that the phrase 'reiflich erwogen' could acquire such resonance for Kraus and his thousands of unsuspecting readers? The answer lies in its appeal to the histrionic imagination. Kraus responded to political events with a mind soaked in Shakespeare. In June 1914 he had lamented Archduke Franz Ferdinand as a Fortinbras who might have saved the state of Denmark (*F* 400–3: 2). And it is Shakespeare again who provides his paradigm for Emperor Franz Joseph, the monarch whose tragic dilemma found expression in one

sentence of pithy plenitude. The monarch is of course King Lear.
And the sentence which seems to have reverberated at the back of
Kraus's mind must surely be that line in which Shakespeare's tragedy
culminates: 'Ripeness is all' ('Reifsein ist alles', v. ii. 12). The passage
from *Die Fackel* of January 1919 shows how closely the figures of
Shakespearean King and Austrian Emperor had become associated in
Kraus's mind (*F* 501–7: 7). The sentence: 'Ich habe alles reiflich
erwogen' conflates the pathos of Shakespeare with half-remembered
phrases from the Austrian political crisis of July 1914. And the
circularity of Kraus's stylistic diagnosis becomes even more
apparent. The sentence which he so effusively praised is a product of
his own syncretic imagination.

The Shakespearean associations help to explain why Kraus should
have described the Proclamation as a 'poem'. And 'erhaben' is a
word more appropriate to the pathos of the theatre than the
pragmatism of politics. But did Kraus in November 1914 really
intend his audience to believe that he found the Proclamation
'sublime'? In his apologia of May 1922 he insists that the phrase was
used ironically. 'Erhaben' was the word that was being used by
pretentious newspaper reporters. In his own text it thus has an ironic
function designed to undermine this kind of inflated style. The word
is placed (as it were) in invisible quotation marks (*F* 531–43: 128–30).
Kraus's argument can scarcely have convinced his left-wing critic.
And it might be thought that this textual crux will never be resolved.
But it so happens that the manuscript of 'In dieser großen Zeit' has
survived. And the reader with the patience to decipher Kraus's
illegible hand (see Fig. IV) will find that the invisible quotation
marks are actually there.[15]

The text of this paragraph in Kraus's manuscript begins thus:

Fig. IV: [*illegible handwritten text*]

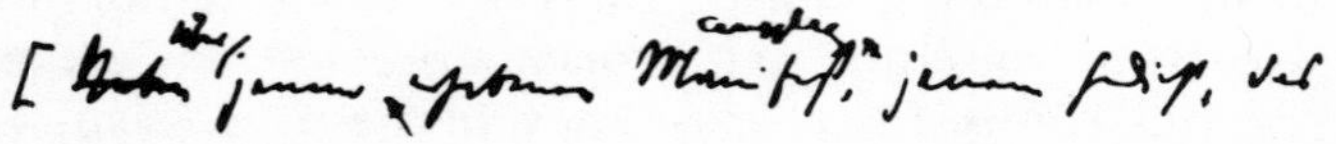

The word 'Anschlag' and the two diagonal strokes deleting the
quotation marks are written in pencil, while the rest of the sentence,
including the emendation of the first word, is in ink. It is clear that
the phrase 'erhabenen Manifest' *was* originally in quotation marks, so
that the ironic intention is unmistakable. Subsequently Kraus must
have realized that in a public reading the quotation marks would not
be audible. So to make his point clear he deleted the quotation
marks, and replaced the word 'Manifest' by 'Anschlag' — a word
with unmistakable critical implications. Preparing the manuscript for
the press, he must have corrected the word 'Anschlag' back to
'Manifest', without restoring the crucial quotation marks (which
would too obviously have betrayed his ironic intentions to the

censor). We may thus conclude that Kraus was absolutely right to claim (in May 1920) that he meant that the Proclamation was 'sublime only as a poem, but as an action an "assault"' ('Nur als Gedicht erhaben, doch als Tat ein "Anschlag"', F 531–43: 129).

It has taken a long time to disentangle a single sentence. But it is worth doing, partly because in the seventy years since Kraus's address appeared this problem has remained unresolved; but mainly because Kraus's praise of the Proclamation exemplifies the fallibility of his whole method of drawing political conclusions from linguistic evidence. Literary style is taken as the correlative of a life-style which is equally admirable, or equally despicable. Well before 1914 we find him expressing his preference for the traditional army officer (Moltke) against the unscrupulous journalist (Harden) in terms of a confrontation of styles (F 234–5: 35–6). And during the war he continues to justify his respect for the Prussian officer class on grounds of style rather than politics. His admiration for the 'disciplined style' of the Prussian general Hermann von Stein betrayed him into political sympathies which proved as untenable as his allegiance to the Habsburg dynasty.

In August and September 1914 General von Stein became a national celebrity. For he was responsible for issuing the official bulletins from German military headquarters. Terse and unadorned, Stein's bulletins are models of concise communication. And it is easy to understand why Kraus admired them. The report of the occupation of Reims, for example,[16] has a no-nonsense quality which is reminiscent of that account of the siege of Milan in 1848 which Kraus had cited in 1912 (F 363–5: 16). Stein, of course, had an easy task. He had victories to record which spoke for themselves, while his Austrian equivalent, General von Höfer, was struggling to find euphemisms to conceal military reverses. But Stein's style is nevertheless refreshingly free of that vainglorious quality which is more characteristic of the Wilhelminian era.

However, from Stein's mastery of style Kraus appears also to draw positive inferences about his political judgement, particularly his comments on the triumph of materialism in modern Germany. And he comes close to endorsing Stein's suggestion that an extended war might have a salutary effect on German culture (F 406–12: 7–8). It was not until three years later, when he found Stein (now German Minister of War) issuing statements that were clearly mendacious, that Kraus retracted his admiration for 'The Quartermaster General of Style' ('Der Generalquartiermeister des Stils', F 484–98: 224–6).

Kraus seems to have longed for a more logical universe in which good style would have guaranteed truthful content. His arguments echo Lichtenberg's dream of a grammar so strict that it would preclude the expression of falsehood.[17] But the world in which he lived came nearer to Orwell's nightmare of a language so systematically perverted that it virtually precluded candour.[18] Kraus's critique is far more convincing when he focuses on negative examples. But it is important to remember that this linguistic focus is a satirical technique, not simply an article of faith. When Kraus condemns a statesman like Czernin, it is not simply because of his faulty punctuation but because of his appalling policies (for which the missing comma becomes the satirical symbol) (F 474–83: 7). Similarly, if Kraus admires officers like von Stein and von Hoen, it is not simply because of their command of German. Their well-structured sentences are the correlative of social forms which also commanded Kraus's allegiance.

The Aristocracy and the Parvenus

Kraus's respect for the professional officer is based on a very traditional model of the social hierarchy. This is elucidated in two extended aphorisms of October 1915, which define the value of the military virtues of 'service' and discipline' ('Dienst' and 'Zucht') — at least in peacetime. The profession of soldier is not simply a way of earning one's living; it has a higher sanction:

> Die militärische Daseinsform verträgt sich mit dem Denken nur als Gelegenheit oder Beruf des edel Gebornen, den Gefahrenlust oder die Empfindlichkeit in jedem und somit auch im vaterländischen Ehrbegriffe zum Schutz des zu solchen Gefühlen untauglichen Bürgers befähigen.
> (F 406–12: 161)

> (The military form of existence makes sense only as opportunity or profession of the nobly born, who through appetite for danger or sensitivity to every concept of honour, including the patriotic concept, become qualified to protect citizens incapable of such feelings.)

In this ideal scheme the authority of the officer over his men is unobjectionable, since it should never happen that a superior person has to take orders from an inferior one. For the hierarchy of rank — at least under the old order prior to compulsory conscription — was a hierarchy of merit: 'Nie konnte ein Subalterner der alten Ordnung unter dem Gefühl, der höhere Mensch zu sein, leiden' (F 406–12: 162). Apart from the statutory period of national service (itself no bad thing for overweight civilians) soldiering was a freely chosen profession. Even during the war a dose of military compulsion might be good for undisciplined intellectuals and insolent men on the make ('den zuchtlosen Intellekt oder die freche Habsucht', F 406–12: 162). The problem is that men of integrity are now also being victimized by the military machine.[19] The advent of a conscript army means that the 'old order' based on nobility of birth is now threatened by 'social and spiritual chaos' ('ein soziales und seelisches Chaos', F 406–12: 162).

Kraus's invocation of a hierarchy based on birth, rank and merit reveals conservative sympathies which are only reluctantly being modified under the pressure of events. He was later to claim that even before 1914 he had seen the braggarts of the Austrian army as 'monsters in peacetime' ('Monstren im Frieden', F 632–9 [October 1923]: 21–2). But this is not borne out by his writings of 1911–14, nor by these aphorisms of October 1915, which begin by specifically emphasizing the value of the disciplined military type: 'Der militärische Typus ist der brauchbarste aller im Frieden vorrätigen Typen der Demokratie' (F 406–12: 160). Of course he is here defining the ideal against which the chaos of the conscript army is being measured. But it is an ideal which he is reluctant to discard.

Kraus remained attached to an antithetical model of society in which the 'old order' has become problematic only because its positions are being usurped by a new class of commercial and journalistic entrepreneurs. As late as January 1917 it is not Field Marshal Conrad von Hötzendorf or Foreign Minister Czernin whom Kraus identifies as 'the two most powerful men in Austria', but Rudolf Sieghart and Emanuel Singer (F 445–53: 131–2). For the satirist of conservative disposition the *nouveaux riches* are a more sinister force than the upholders of the *ancien régime*. It might be said of Kraus (as of Juvenal) that his recurrent theme is 'the appalling influence that mobility of income can have on a static class structure'.[20] His private letters also express his horror at the 'Durcheinander' of Viennese salons, where the old aristocracy are to be seen hobnobbing with social upstarts (BSN I. 305, 331). But if this preoccupation with parvenus is satirically fruitful, it betrays him into judgements which are politically untenable. The landed gentry are conceived as an ideal alternative to the corruption of the metropolis.

In June 1914 Kraus had declared that politically he had 'not yet even reached the French Revolution' ('politisch noch nicht einmal bei der französischen Revolution angelangt bin'). This statement has very precise implications. For it implies the hope that the displacement of the landed aristocracy by the commercial bourgeoisie, which had dominated European history between 1789 and 1914, might yet be reversed. Kraus still dreams of aristocrats secure behind the walls of their country estates, who can resist the depravity of an age whose ideal is membership of the stock exchange with a seat on the board of directors (F 400–3: 90–5). And the outbreak of war, far from destroying this dream, serves initially to intensify its hold on his imagination. The spectacle of delicately nurtured ladies

acting as nurses in military hospitals fills him with complex forebodings about the disruption of social and sexual decorum (*F*
406–12: 142–6). Gloomily he glosses the accelerated *embourgeoisement*
of the aristocracy which results from their participation in war
committees of all kinds. And in April 1916 he admonishes the
aristocracy itself for throwing open the gates of the citadel to the
parvenus ('Die Historischen und die Vordringenden', *F*
418–22: 6–9).

The exchange of social roles ('Rollentausch') has grievous consequences. Ennobled bankers and industrialists now strut up and down
the Kärntnerstrasse, while — the image is worthy of Juvenal — 'the
poor bearer of a noble name, panting under the burden, is the
exploited errand boy of the great industrialist, who compensates him
for the bad treatment he receives by an occasional free meal' ('der
arme "Würdenträger", der unter der Last keucht, ist der mißbrauchte
Dienstmann des Großindustriellen, der ihn für schlechte Behandlung
durch gelegentliches Essen entschädigt') (*F* 418–22: 9). Kraus does
not fail to point out that many of these ennobled *nouveaux riches* are
from Jewish families. Indeed, he exploits the juxtaposition of feudal
and Jewish-sounding titles in his satirical glosses ('Feudales', *F*
431–6: 31).

The special significance of 'Die Historischen und die Vordringenden' is that it is archetypal satire masquerading as political
statement. Kraus gave this piece the subtitle 'Ein Wort an den Adel',
a phrase which carries echoes of Luther. It thus seems to be intended
as a public admonition to the aristocracy to be mindful of the
obligations which their inherited position confers on them. These are
seen primarily as obligations of a spiritual and moral kind ('geistige
Verpflichtung', 'sittliche Verantwortung', *F* 418–22: 7). But Kraus
may also have hoped for a moral stand that would have made a
political impact. He was conscious that members of the Austrian and
above all the Bohemian aristocracy attended his public readings and
admired his work. And in November 1916 he even entertained the
hope, after a particularly successful public reading, that such
aristocrats might be inspired to make a public declaration against the
inhumanity of the war (*BSN* I. 392). This helps us to understand
why Kraus could still — as late as May 1916 — appeal in public for a
consolidation of the conservative forces within the State.

It is now clear that Kraus's 'private war' — his tempestuous
relationship with a woman of aristocratic background — influenced
his perception of the political system. We have noted that in his
letters to Sidonie of April 1915 Kraus signs himself 'K. von
Janowitz'. The formulation betrays his attachment not only to
Janowitz but also to the aristocratic identity it epitomized. Kraus

even took riding lessons so as to be able to participate more fully in the pursuits of a country estate. Moreover, the letters show that the 'Sehnsucht nach aristokratischem Umgang', to which he had cryptically confessed in July 1914, was fulfilled. There was a personal as well as intellectual basis for that admiring attitude which filters through into certain references to the Austrian aristocracy and even the Prussian Junkers (F 462–71: 16–17).

This is not to imply that Kraus was playing a double game, seeking surreptitiously to advance the conservative cause under the flag of radical pacifism. But it is clear that for a large part of the war he remained emotionally attached to an idealized conception of the aristocracy. His position, as he acknowledged in October 1917 at the moment of truth, was a conservative one — 'ein konservativer Standpunkt' (F 462–71: 172). The ferocity of his subsequent polemic against the ruling class may be seen as a compensation for illusions about army and aristocracy which he had indulged too long.

The end of political censorship in November 1918 does not provide a full explanation for the pent-up vehemence of the polemic 'Nachruf'. It must also have been influenced by the lifting of an inner inhibition. In September 1918 Kraus's 'private war' with Sidonie ended in disaster. A moving letter of 18/19 September shows how deeply he was affected by the loss of her love (BSN I. 467–8). But by loosening his ties with the landed aristocracy, this private loss gave him the freedom to form new political affiliations.

CHAPTER 20

From Loyal Satirist to Reluctant Democrat: The Party of Human Dignity

After the collapse of the Habsburg Empire Kraus was accused by a left-wing critic of having shared the militaristic outlook which inspired the war (*F* 531–43: 119–33). And it was later alleged that his anti-war satire was only tolerated because the ruling class did not feel threatened by it (*F* 889: 8). These allegations cannot entirely be discounted, but they are undialectical. For it was precisely the fact that Kraus was regarded by the authorities as a loyal subject of the Monarchy that enabled him to get his humanistic protest into print. It was only towards the end of the war that he came into conflict with the Austrian authorities, as he abandoned his conservative allegiances and ranged himself with the forces of democratic renewal: the Social Democrats, seen as the 'party of human dignity'; and the principles of President Wilson, hailed in October 1918 as a Fortinbras.

Loyal Satirist and Cultured Censor

Kraus's relative freedom from interference by the censorship is one of the most surprising aspects of his position during the war. Recent findings show that freedom to have been based on a special relationship with the censor. The satirist's stance of intransigent opposition proves to be a stylized self-image. The full story is far more revealing.

The censorship in Austria has aptly been described as a system of 'pre-confiscation'.[1] At least eight days before publication of an issue, the editor of a magazine like *Die Fackel* had to present his final proofs to the censor at the Staatsanwaltschaft. If anything was found objectionable, it was simply deleted, and the journal appeared with mysterious blank spaces. This system was in the long run as damaging to the authorities as it was to the press, since the embarrassingly obtrusive blank spaces tended to encourage alarmist rumours.

The exceptional nature of Kraus's relations with the censorship is revealed in a document discovered in the archives of the Austrian Ministry of Justice. It is a report dated 22 January 1918 written by the censor himself, Dr Kurt Hager:

> Several months after the outbreak of war the editor of *Die Fackel*, Karl Kraus [. . .] came to consult the undersigned about formal aspects of the censoring of *Die Fackel*. For a considerable time after the outbreak of war Kraus had suspended publication of *Die Fackel*; now he wanted to issue a further number and was very concerned to avoid confiscation of the printed copies, partly on account of the cost, partly because he would have felt it humiliating to be subject to confiscation, given that he takes such an aggressive attitude towards the daily newspapers. I advised him that for his own magazine he should take the path of pre-censorship, a practice already firmly established and frequently used by the majority of periodicals. This meant submitting the galley proofs, which were then checked through and formally approved by me, while at the same time I marked those passages, articles or notes which could *not* be passed. The galley proofs were returned to him, but he had to submit them again together with the magazine as finally printed. He would thus have the guarantee that the contents that had been checked and approved by me would not suffer further interference, but he had to omit the passages that were not approved. Karl Kraus was in agreement with this procedure and repeatedly acknowledged the accommodating attitude of the censorship authorities.
>
> *In this way all the issues of Die Fackel which have appeared during the war have been censored by me.*
>
> Karl Kraus brought me the proofs in person and also collected them himself; if I found passages or articles which needed to be deleted, I marked these passages, communicated them to Karl Kraus himself, and if requested explained the reasons for their elimination.[2]

This picture of the censor co-operating with the satirist is evidence of an underlying humanity in Austrian institutions. But it depended on Kraus's own willingness to make concessions. Between December 1914 and May 1916 he was able to publish two short issues of *Die Fackel* and four very substantial ones without any trace of interference by the censor. This means that he had been willing to remove phrases or passages to which the censor objected and to have the type reset, so as to eliminate the blank spaces. In a letter to Sidonie he reports that after complicated negotiations over the text of No. 406–12 he was obliged ultimately to alter only a single word in the whole 168 pages (*BSN* I. 199–200). But his success depended upon the good will of the censor, as well as his own subtlety of expression. Looking back on this episode towards the end of his life, Kraus was to describe the Austrian censors during the war as cultured men ('Kulturmenschen', *F* 890–905: 23).

The need to reach an accommodation with the censor may help to explain why Kraus's anti-war satire is not more outspoken. It may also explain why he is initially so restrained towards official Austria. The censor could turn a blind eye to attacks on the likes of Alice Schalek. But when (in the context of a Schalek satire) Kraus also represented figures from the military establishment in a critical light, the blank spaces began to appear (*F* 437–42: 123; cf. *F* 508–13: 62–3). The first blank spaces, in June 1916 (*F* 426–30), indicate that Kraus's gentlemen's agreement with the censor had broken down. By this date the satirist's campaign against the war was becoming more outspoken, and the censor must have been increasingly alarmed at Kraus's success in subverting the patriotic ethos.

Although Kraus is the scourge of Austrian bureaucracy, his private letters show that he was able to gain the co-operation of other official bodies, in addition to the censorship. Count Castell-Rüdenhausen, a senior official in the provincial administration for Lower Austria, seems to have been particularly helpful with arrangements which enabled Kraus to travel to Switzerland during the winter of 1915–16. The timing of Kraus's medical examination in September 1915 was brought forward at Castell's request (Kraus's exemption from military service on medical grounds was again confirmed) (*BSN* I. 199). Sidonie too experienced difficulties in obtaining a visa to travel to Switzerland, not least because her companion Miss Cooney was of British extraction. In this case the decision to grant visas seems to have been taken by the Minister of the Interior himself, Prince Hohenlohe-Schillingsfürst (*BSN* I. 289, 296). Although the bureaucratic procedures regulating travel abroad had become extremely tortuous during the war, Kraus's repeated success in obtaining visas to travel, first to Italy and later (four times) to Switzerland, shows that he was in good standing with the civil authorities.

Confirmation of this is provided by the most surprising of the documents recently brought to light — a hand-written memorandum from the archives of the Kriegsüberwachungsamt dated 2 May 1916. The Kriegsüberwachungsamt, which had overall responsibility for security matters, was evidently becoming suspicious about Kraus's repeated journeys to Switzerland. One of their officials, after checking Kraus's status by telephone with Vienna Police Headquarters, jotted down the following memo: 'Laut telef. Auskunft der Wr Pol Dion ist Kraus vollkommen loyal. (According to telephonic information from Vienna Police Headquarters Kraus is completely loyal.)'[3] The paradox of the loyal satirist thus complements that of the cultured censor. But it is difficult to determine whether the memo is a true reflection of Kraus's official standing, or whether he merely enjoyed the 'Protektion' of some influential figure at Police Headquarters. Kraus was later to pay tribute to the resolute support which he received from the head of the Political Section at Vienna Police Headquarters, Johannes Schober (F 508–13: 98–9).

The Kriegsüberwachungsamt was clearly not entirely satisfied. In August 1916, responding to an enquiry from the military censorship post at Feldkirch on the frontier with Switzerland, they tried to impose a ban on the sending of copies of Die Fackel abroad. Kraus's treatment of certain themes in No. 431–6 was felt to be objectionable. But even this prohibition was soon reversed. It thus seems possible that although the military authorities were beginning to doubt Kraus's loyalty, someone at a higher level was looking after him.

The military authorities ultimately became very suspicious. Kraus's public readings, which had enjoyed a surprising degree of toleration from the civil police, were denounced to General Stöger-Steiner, the Minister of War, in an anonymous letter of April 1918. It must be remembered that at this date it still seemed likely that the Central Powers would win the war. The Treaty of Brest-Litovsk, which imposed crushing terms on the newly-formed Bolshevik government of Russia, had freed thousands of German troops for what was expected to be a final and equally victorious offensive on the western front. Kraus's reading of 27 March 1918 had included outspoken items attacking the German Kaiser and supporting the peace initiative of Heinrich Lammasch (F 474–83: 91). It is not surprising that this reading was denounced as an 'impassioned philippic' against Austrian policy and against the war (F 508–13: 86–90: facsimile of the letter).

The Counter-Propaganda Office of the Army High Command took these accusations seriously, and Kraus was identified in a confidential file as 'the leader of defeatism in Austria' (F 501–7: 91). The Minister of War demanded a full investigation. But Kraus was once again protected by the civil authorities. Schober, who had by now been promoted to Chief of Police in Vienna, submitted a report which exonerated Kraus from the specific allegation that he had called on officers to break their swords. And this was confirmed by Ernst von Seidler, the Austrian Prime Minister. The small print of these official exchanges reveals that the police had been surprisingly tolerant, turning a blind eye to Kraus's practice of reading manuscripts in public which had not yet been submitted to the censor.

By the time the military authorities had been alerted to Kraus's subversive activities, the tide of opinion in Austria was turning in his favour. Even the anonymous informer had to concede that Kraus's pacifist agitation was received with rapturous applause by a large audience, half of whom were army officers. And unlike the German

Reich, Austria-Hungary was not in danger of becoming a military dictatorship.

The final years of the war witnessed a liberalization of the political atmosphere. Parliament had been recalled and Emperor Karl announced a partial amnesty for political detainees. In November 1917 the radical newspaper *Der Abend* was allowed to organize a 'peace referendum', which quickly collected over 50,000 signatures. And in January 1918 the journal *Der Friede* was founded in Vienna to provide a forum for debate on possible terms for peace. Influential public figures such as Heinrich Lammasch and Julius Meinl were trying (as was Kraus) to detach Austria-Hungary from the German alliance and promote a separate peace. Kraus was in contact with this group, particularly with Lammasch.[4] The attempt by the military authorities to curb Kraus's activities was finally overtaken by the collapse of the Monarchy. The file on his alleged treason was closed on 31 October 1918 by the statesman who in Austria-Hungary's final hour was called to be its last Prime Minister — Lammasch himself (*F* 508–13: 81–104).

The Party of Human Dignity

Kraus began the war as a reactionary monarchist and ended it as a radical republican. The question is: When exactly did he renounce his conservative allegiances? It has proved peculiarly difficult to put a precise date to his break with conservative Austria and his commitment to the forces of democratic renewal. The tendency has been to project Kraus's political radicalism after the collapse of the Austro-Hungarian Monarchy back on to his position from 1914 to 1918. It is assumed that his break with the old order occurred relatively early in the war. In fact the break came surprisingly late and was all the more decisive for having been so long delayed.

The difficulty of identifying Kraus's political position arises from the strategy of his satire. He consciously refrains from editorializing. Only rarely do we find him revealing his political opinions — for example, his satisfaction that parliamentary government has been suspended (*F* 406–12 [October 1915]: 104). He studiously ignores the 'great events' which would feature in any political history of the war. The text of *Die Fackel* gives only oblique hints of what Kraus 'really thought' about (say) the Italian declaration of war, the fall of Bethmann Hollweg, the assassination of Count Stürgkh, the death of Emperor Franz Joseph, the Russian Revolution, the American entry into the war, Wilson's Fourteen Points, or the political strikes which convulsed Austria in January 1918. The author's political opinions are disguised by the cryptic stance of the satirist who (as late as May 1918) still claims that he is merely 'a word-fetishist without political interests' ('ein politisch uninteressierter Wortfetischist', *F* 474–83: 14). Only by attending to nuances can one discern the underlying shifts of attitude.

The significance of Kraus's public reading of 12 May 1916 must again be emphasized. After almost two years of horrendous conflict he was apparently still willing to commit himself to the proposition (in 'Die Kinder der Zeit') that the salvation of the State might best be achieved by 'a consolidation of the conservative will' (*F* 426–30: 50; cf. *F* 354–6: 68–70). There is no evidence to suggest that at this public reading he toned down the explicit support given in that pre-war declaration to Church, State and Army. The police report of 2 May certifying that Kraus was 'vollkommen loyal' was evidently not too wide of the mark. His reluctance to hold the Monarchy and the Military Command responsible for acts of inhumanity committed under martial law is also indicated by a gloss of August 1916. Criticisms of the German authorities by Social Democrats in the Reichstag are explicitly repudiated: 'Nichts da! Macht ist nur sich selbst verantwortlich' (*F* 431–6: 88–9). Kraus still seems to be looking for scapegoats for the evils of the war, for example the medical men who connived at inhumanities, rather than blaming the political system.

The authoritarian regime in Austria-Hungary was shaken in the autumn of 1916 by two events which had incalculable consequences. The Prime Minister Count Stürgkh had obdurately refused to reconvene the Austrian parliament, which had been suspended since March 1914. On 21 October 1916 Stürgkh was assassinated by the radical Socialist Friedrich Adler, as a protest against the suppression of democracy. And the death of Emperor Franz Joseph in November 1916 signalled the passing of the old order. Kraus seems however to have felt inhibited from glossing events in these terms. Where we might expect an attempt to gauge the political gravity of the changes, we instead find twenty-five pages devoted to the triviality of the press coverage (*F* 445–53: 34–59).

It is equally difficult to assess Kraus's judgement of the attempts by the new Emperor Karl to reform Austrian institutions and put out peace feelers towards the Entente. The fierceness of his ridicule of Emperor Karl *after* 1919 must not mislead us into supposing that Kraus was equally hostile at the time of Karl's accession. In May 1918, after the signing of a peace treaty with the notionally independent Ukraine, Kraus contrasts a speech by Emperor Karl in favour of peace with the undiminished bellicosity of the German Kaiser. In this juxtaposition Karl appears in a positive light (*F* 474–83: 141–2).

The honest reader must acknowledge that Kraus's postwar denunciations of the Habsburg dynasty are at odds with his respectful

attitude at an earlier date. An essay of May 1917 explicitly acknowledges the climate of reform in Austria. Kraus discerns in the
Austrian governing class 'the strongest possible will to achieve
reforms' and acknowledges their 'honest zeal' (*F* 457–61: 24–5: 'der
redlichste Eifer', 'der stärkste Wille zu Reformen'). Such phrases
echo the sentiments of conservative journals like *Danzer's Armee-
Zeitung*, which had also (in April 1917) praised the 'Wille zur
Regeneration' shown by the Austrian authorities. Both Kraus and
Danzer seem to have been favourably impressed by the resolute
action of the authorities against war profiteers.[5]

The conservatism of Kraus's position at this stage is also evident in
his oblique comments on the Russian Revolution of March 1917, in
the essay 'Unser weltgeschichtliches Ereignis'. The most significant
'world-historical event' for Kraus is not the overthrow of autocracy
in Russia, but the more sinister tendency which he discerns in
Austria-Hungary: 'the tyranny of inferior people' ('die Herrschaft
des niedrigen Menschen', *F* 457–61: 99). We have already noted (in
the section on 'The Banality of Evil') the prophetic accuracy of this
diagnosis. But in the historical context of May 1917 Kraus's analysis
still implies an attachment to a traditional 'order' in which everyone
knew his place. He is guided not by Marx's analysis of class conflict,
but by Shakespeare's vision of an ordered hierarchy, now on the
point of collapse (*F* 457–61: 95–100).

Die Fackel of May 1917 ends on a decidedly conservative note.
Between May and October 1917 there is an unexplained five-month
silence, during which Kraus gave no public readings and issued no
numbers of *Die Fackel*. In part he seems once again to have been
distracted by his 'private war'. Three months were spent with
Sidonie in Switzerland, where he continued to work on the manuscript of *Die letzten Tage der Menschheit*. A battered passport
photograph dated May 1917 shows Kraus in a particularly sombre
mood (Pl. 33). It seems to have been during this period of silence that
his political allegiances underwent radical reappraisal. Despite his
evasive utterances, he does seem to have recognized the world-
historical implications of the year 1917.

While the military struggle continued seemingly interminably
during 1917, with the advantage tipping towards the Central
Powers, the political map of the war was completely redrawn. It was
no longer possible to picture the war (as the German and Austrian
Socialists had done) as a crusade against Tsarist despotism. It was no
longer possible to see it as a struggle for economic supremacy
between rival consumer organizations (as Kraus had suggested in
November 1914). By the summer of 1917 it had become a war

33 Passport photograph of Kraus, dated May 1917

between two political systems: Democracy (represented by President
Wilson and Prime Minister Kerensky) versus Autocracy (the drift
towards military dictatorship in Germany). The speeches of President Wilson in particular underlined this distinction. And the
Bolshevik Revolution of November 1917 was to make the challenge
to the old order in Europe irreversible.

It is against this background that we must interpret the decisive
change of political tone that is evident in *Die Fackel* of October 1917.
It had at last become apparent to Kraus that a choice must be made
not merely between war and peace, but between rival ideological
systems: 'Zwischen den Lebensrichtungen'. In peacetime he had seen
the organizational efficiency of Germany as a milieu more congenial
to the artist than the cultured chaos of Austria. Now that German
efficiency has proved so destructive, that position is no longer
tenable:

> Demnach muß die Frage, 'in welcher Hölle *der Künstler* gebraten sein
> will', abdanken vor der zwingenden Entscheidung, daß *der Mensch* in
> dieser Hölle nicht gebraten sein will, durch die richtende Erkenntnis des
> Künstlers selbst, der nun nicht mehr das Recht und nicht mehr die
> Möglichkeit hat, die sichere Abschließung seines Innern zu suchen,
> sondern nur noch die Pflicht, zu sehen, welche Partie der Menschheit
> gleich ihm um die Erhaltung solchen Glückes kämpft [. . .].
>
> (F 462–71: 76)

> (Accordingly, the question 'in which of these hells *the artist* wants to be
> roasted' must be retracted in the face of the more pressing conclusion that
> the *human being* does not want to be roasted in this hell — through the
> corrective insight of the artist himself, who has no longer the right and no
> longer the possibility of seeking to seal off his inner life securely, but only
> the duty of recognizing which section of mankind is struggling as he is
> for the preservation of happiness.)

The position of Germany must now be seen in a world-wide context
('deutsch-weltlich'). And to identify the new political alternative
Kraus reaffirms Goethe's famous tribute to the potential of the New
World: 'Amerika, das es besser, nein am besten hat' (F 462–71: 78).

This short but crucial essay also expresses Kraus's recognition that
it is necessary to take sides in the internal political struggle in
Austria-Hungary. In a cryptic admission of his own failures of
political judgement he writes: 'I have never repudiated the party of
human dignity' ('Die Partei der Menschenwürde habe ich nie
verleugnet', F 462–71: 78). This hints at a possible alliance with the
Austrian Social Democratic Party. This same number of *Die Fackel*
contains an interpellation signed by thirty-two Social Democratic
members of the Austrian parliament which enabled Kraus to publish,
in the form of excerpts from parliamentary proceedings, a dozen

pages which had previously been deleted from *Die Fackel* by the censor.

Why had Kraus for so long been reluctant to identify himself with the Social Democrats? The answer is that the Party itself had for too long been reluctant to campaign against the war. Under the patriotic leadership of Victor Adler, the Social Democratic organizations had thrown their weight behind the Austrian war effort. As official Party newspaper the *Arbeiter-Zeitung* had also initially supported the war, and it was only gradually that its attitude became more critical. A recent study has shown that it was not until December 1916 that the *Arbeiter-Zeitung* began to argue openly in favour of peace. During 1917 the political line of the newspaper, as of the Party itself, was still patriotic; but there was an increasing emphasis on the inhumanity of the war. From the middle of 1917 onwards it is possible to identify the *Arbeiter-Zeitung* as a 'driving force' in the campaign for peace without annexations.[6] But the failure of the political leadership became spectacularly apparent when they helped to contain the wave of strikes which erupted in Vienna in January 1918, rather than exploiting the situation to force the government to sue for peace.

Kraus evidently followed the coverage of the war in the *Arbeiter-Zeitung* very carefully. In October 1916 he pays tribute to its value as a documentary source and acknowledges that its columns have provided one of the last refuges for 'human dignity'. But he also identifies the tragic contradiction between patriotism and principle which disfigures both paper and Party (*F* 437–42: 30). As the attitude of the *Arbeiter-Zeitung* became more critical, the alliance with *Die Fackel* became closer. Indeed Kraus may himself have contributed to the newspaper's change of tone. For he was on friendly terms with its editor, Friedrich Austerlitz. And we are even told that during the war he used to visit Austerlitz in his office in the depths of the night in an attempt to impose his own 'censorship' on what was to appear in the paper.[7] A deep respect for Austerlitz lies behind the exceptional tribute of October 1917 in which Kraus describes the *Arbeiter-Zeitung* as not simply a newspaper but a 'moral force' (*F* 462–71: 141).

In one sense it may be legitimate to see the campaigns against militarism of *Die Fackel* and the *Arbeiter-Zeitung* as a 'parallel action'.[8] But Kraus continues to differentiate his position from the Social Democratic Party, both in Austria and in the German Reich. Two newspaper clippings document the continuing willingness of the German Party to collaborate with the Kaiser's government (*F* 462–71: 164–5). And on the eve of the Stockholm Conference of November 1917 Kraus pin-points the responsibility of the Socialist International for the war. It lies in the discrepancy between 'party

ideals' and political practice. On paper international socialism has
made splendid proclamations in favour of peace and solidarity. In
reality the organized proletariat has been working flat out in every
country of Europe to build up the armaments industry. The ultimate
absurdity is that the proletariat has manufactured the weapons of its
own destruction (F 462–71: 170).

It is the collaboration between Social Democracy and military
technology which leads Kraus still to distance himself from Marxism. In a belated comment on the case of Friedrich Adler, he
observes:

> Die Problemstellung: Demokratie-Autokratie trifft ins Leere, in das
> Vacuum der Zeit, das hier nur fühlbarer wird als im andern Europa.
> Autokratie als ein technischer Begriff: das könnte es sein.
>
> (F 462–71: 171)

> (The definition of the problem in terms of Democracy versus Autocracy
> is as empty a formulation as the vacuum of the age, which is merely more
> marked here [in Austria] than elsewhere in Europe. Autocracy as a
> technological concept: that would be more plausible.)

Adler, both by his assassination of the Austrian Prime Minister and
by his speech in his own defence, had identified political absolutism
as the greatest enemy.[9] For Kraus this ignores the more sinister fact
that technology seems to have acquired a destructive momentum of
its own. Modern mass politics preclude the solution of Wilhelm Tell,
who slew the tyrant with his crossbow:

> Es gibt keine Armbrust und keinen Tyrannen; es gibt Technik und
> Bürokraten. Es gibt nur den Knopf, auf den das Plutokratische drückt.
> Aber da ist kein verantwortliches Gesicht.
>
> (F 462–71: 171)

> (There is no crossbow and no tyrant; there are technology and
> bureaucrats. There is only the button which plutocracy presses. But there
> is no responsible face.)

Although the democracy-autocracy antithesis left Kraus unconvinced, he was nevertheless moving towards a more democratic
position. The reluctance with which he made this move is evident
from a group of aphorisms published on the very next page of Die
Fackel under the title 'Erfahrungen' ('What one learns from experience'). To liberate the old world it is necessary to support the party
of the new:

> In diesem Sinne muß ein konservativer Standpunkt [. . .] auf Kriegsdauer
> eine Verschiebung erfahren. In Staaten, die dümmer sind als ihre
> Demokratie, muß man für diese sein und ihr gegen den Staat helfen,
> dessen Dummheit sie mobilisiert hat. Sie haben einander untergekriegt.

Die demokratische Tendenz muß im Kampf gegen ihren Folgezustand
unterstützt und die aristokratische zu ihren Gunsten verlassen werden.
(F 462–71: 172–3)

(In this sense a conservative position must for the duration of the war
undergo a displacement. In states that are more stupid than their
democratic forces one must support the latter and aid them against the
state whose stupidity has mobilized them. The warring factions are
wearing each other down. The democratic tendency must be supported
against its own consequences and the aristocratic one abandoned in its
own interest.)

This change of allegiance did not pass unnoticed by Kraus's
conservative admirers. It was registered almost immediately in
Danzer's Armee-Zeitung, the organ of the officer class. An unsigned
note published early in November 1917, probably by Carl Danzer
himself, pays tribute to Kraus's achievements as spokesman for the
conscience of Europe. But it goes on to express regret at the new
position Kraus has adopted in No. 462–71, which is aligning him
with the progressive intellectuals of Berlin.[10]

It is now possible to date Kraus's change of allegiance. The
decisive reorientation seems to have taken place in Switzerland
during the summer of 1917, when he wrote the fiercely anti-
militarist verses of *Die letzte Nacht* (published in November 1918
after the lifting of censorship). And it was in October 1917 that he
abandoned the aristocratic ideal in favour of the new forces of
democracy. But 'abandoned' is too strong a word. His 'conservative
position' is not renounced, but merely 'displaced' — and that only
for the duration of the war. Kraus still seems to have imagined that
the war might end with a reconstitution of the old order. And he still
hesitates to align himself with the Social Democrats. He was aware
that Victor Adler (at the Stockholm Conference) was at last
beginning to speak out against the war.[11] But for political leadership
Kraus turns not to the Social Democrats but to the conservative
statesmen of the Austria-Hungary. His support for Lammasch has
already been emphasized. What is more surprising is that in October
1917 he still had high hopes of the Austrian Foreign Minister, Count
Czernin.

Czernin, a member of the Bohemian landed aristocracy, was one
of that formidable group of conservative politicians cultivated by
Archduke Franz Ferdinand before the war. His proposals for the
internal restructuring of the Dual Monarchy had envisaged a ruthless
programme of 'blood and iron'.[12] But he was clearly more adroit in
the field of foreign affairs. In December 1916, shortly after the
accession of Emperor Karl, he was appointed Foreign Minister — a
post which he held until his enforced resignation in April 1918.

During this period he dominated the Austrian political scene and
became a key figure in the international debate about peace terms.
Czernin recognized as early as April 1917 that the situation of
Austria-Hungary was so desperate that only an early peace could
save the Empire from disintegration. In a series of speeches and
diplomatic notes he responded positively (although with some
equivocation) to the peace initiatives of President Wilson. At the
same time Emperor Karl was putting out secret peace feelers to the
French government through his brother-in-law, Prince Sixtus of
Bourbon.

Kraus seems to have followed Czernin's diplomacy closely. He
was particularly impressed by a speech which the Foreign Minister
delivered in Budapest on 2 October 1917. In this speech Czernin
repudiated war as a means of settling political disputes, proclaimed
the need for international courts of arbitration, and proposed a
system of world-wide disarmament under international supervision.
To this speech Kraus responded with an overwhelming sense of
approbation. This found expression in the opening words of his
'prinzipielle Erklärung', read in public on 11 November and again on
18 November 1917 (F 474–83: 87–8). The text of the declaration was
not published until almost a year later, but it nevertheless vividly
conveys that moment of hope in the autumn of 1917. For the first
time (Kraus writes) the longing of mankind for deliverance from the
curse of militarism and war had found expression in the words of a
Central European statesman. Unfortunately, because of Czernin's
instability of purpose, Kraus's praise had to be retracted almost in the
same breath that it was given. But for a moment (as he later
acknowledges, F 484–98: 232–4) he had believed in Czernin's
sincerity.

Kraus seems to have longed for a statesman with the moral vision
to put an end to the fighting. But Czernin was too closely attached to
the German alliance to develop an independent foreign policy. As
soon as the military balance tilted in favour of the Central Powers,
Czernin abandoned his conciliatory tone and became the advocate of
a peace imposed by force of arms. Kraus was infuriated by the
volte-face between Czernin's proposals for general disarmament (in
his Budapest speech of 2 October 1917) and his commitment four
weeks later to the exact opposite: to 'extending and deepening' the
military alliance with the German Reich.[13] Czernin's pacifism had in
the intervening weeks been dissipated by the spectacular victory of
the Central Powers on the Italian front. Czernin was also instru-
mental in imposing crushing peace terms on Romania and on the
Bolshevik delegation at Brest-Litovsk. And his commitment to the
German alliance was reiterated in two further speeches: to a

Parliamentary Commission in January 1918 and to the Vienna City Council on 2 April 1918 (when the German army seemed on the point of achieving a decisive victory on the western front). Incensed by Czernin's duplicity, especially the contrast between his Budapest and his Vienna speeches (F 484–98: 232 fn.), Kraus denounced the Foreign Minister in an outspoken political polemic, 'Der begabte Czernin' (F 474–83: 1–22), written in February 1918 in Switzerland, although not published until after Czernin's fall from power.[14]

Disillusionment with Czernin seems to have been the final straw which broke Kraus's residual attachment to conservative Austria. Towards the end of 'Eine prinzipielle Erklärung', he speaks out with unprecedented vehemence against the political leadership, who are themselves the 'traitors' ('Hochverräter', F 484–98: 235). During the final twelve months of the war there is a decisive change of tone in Die Fackel, as Kraus in a multitude of astringent glosses attacks the real enemy: the advocates of German military victory and a peace based on annexation. In his public readings too, from November 1917 onwards, he identifies the true culprits: not 'Israel' (by this date 'Gebet an die Sonne von Gibeon' has virtually vanished from his programme), but the Pan-Germans ('Lied des Alldeutschen').

The political focus became even sharper on 27 March 1918, when he gave a reading after a two-month break in Switzerland. Now the German Kaiser himself is ridiculed in 'Ein Kantianer und Kant'. And one can imagine the cumulative impact of texts like 'Das technoromantische Abenteuer', 'Für Lammasch', 'Lied des Alldeutschen', 'Die letzte Nacht' (the scene portraying Moriz Benedikt as Lord of the Hyenas) and 'Zum ewigen Frieden'. That this reading should have led to an investigation by the Austrian military authorities is understandable. In May 1916 they had reasonably concluded that Kraus was a loyal subject of the Empire. Now they were equally justified in believing that his readings had become subversive.

During the final twelve months of the war Kraus's public readings acquired an unprecedented power. This derived not only from the strengthening of his political convictions but also from an accumulation of personal grief. On 8 November 1917 he received the news that Elisabeth Reitler, the woman to whom (after Sidonie) he seems to have felt closest in the world, had committed suicide (BSN I. 444–5). On 16 November he heard that the young poet Franz Janowitz, one of his dearest friends, had died from wounds received in battle (BSN I. 450–1). The shock of these bereavements, which tempted him to cancel his public readings, must in effect have accentuated their power. Officers who attended his reading of 18

November were unable to restrain their tears. Mentioning this in his letter to Sidonie, Kraus continues: 'Wir weinen alle und es geht dennoch weiter' (*BSN* I. 452). It was this sense of the solidarity of grief that gave Kraus his exceptional moral stature. And borrowing words from Goethe, he was now willing to acknowledge that it was the lowest classes who had suffered most from the war and deserved greatest sympathy (*F* 474–83: 71).

In this sense Kraus's claim that he had 'never repudiated the party of human dignity' is justified. But it was not until after the collapse of the Austro-Hungarian Empire that he openly supported the Social Democrats. In a powerful declaration of early November 1918 he welcomed the defeat of the Central Powers as a world-historical retribution for their criminal policies. Since 1 August 1914 (he claims), even from a conservative and patriotic position, he had wished for the triumph of a 'sober, democratic civilization free of illusions' ('nüchterne, fibelfreie, demokratische Zivilisation', *F* 499–500: 32). This is certainly an apt summing-up of his long crusade in favour of a functional civilization and against the masquerade of the Tragic Carnival. But the emphasis on his commitment to 'democratic' principles is clearly an overstatement. Kraus's conversion to democracy was a slow and tortuous process, which was not completed until the old order had collapsed.

A Democratic Fortinbras

Out of the ruins arose a new hero — President Woodrow Wilson. We have seen how reluctantly Kraus responded to Wilson's claim (in his address to Congress on 2 April 1917) that America was entering the war to make the world 'safe for democracy'.[15] In October 1917 the democracy-autocracy antithesis is still repudiated (*F* 462–71: 171). But Kraus seems to have been more favourably impressed by Wilson's claim that America was fighting to liberate the world from German militarism, not to destroy the German people. This argument was advanced in Wilson's reply of 28 August 1917 to the Peace Appeal of the Pope.[16] It is quoted (with implicit approval) in the same number of *Die Fackel* (*F* 462–71: 165).

Kraus's response to Wilson's famous Fourteen Points of January 1918 is still ambivalent. He certainly condemns Czernin for not responding more positively to Wilson's proposals (*F* 474–83: 3–4). But it is only by reading between the lines that Kraus's own attitude towards Wilson can be gauged. One of the Fourteen Points proposed that Austria-Hungary should grant autonomy to its subject peoples and make territorial concessions to Italy. Perhaps a residual loyalty to the Empire inhibited Kraus from giving Wilson his public support. He seems to have preferred the more cautious constitutional reforms proposed by Lammasch (*F* 474–83: 46–9). It was not until October 1918 that Kraus openly declared his support for Wilsonian principles (*F* 499–500: 4). He finally acknowledges that the only person who can restore order to a demented world is Wilson — the 'policeman' (Kraus used the English word in his reading of 13 October; *F* 508–13: 28).

Just as Kraus's writings before 1914 had been structured by apocalyptic prophecy, so now at the end of 1918 they abound in images of closure. The collapse of the Central Powers is pictured as a 'Day of Judgement' on German civilization ('Weltgericht', *F* 499–500: 1). The revolutionary developments sweep away a corrupt political system like a Great Flood bringing retribution to a sinful world ('Die Sintflut', *F* 499–500: 28). The Tragic Carnival is over, and on this historical Ash Wednesday the emblems of military glory are like carnival masks exposed to the glare of sunlight (*F* 499–500: 5). Through these images Kraus emphasizes that military defeat is not some inexplicable disaster, but can be construed within a pattern of guilt and retribution.

The most significant of his images of closure is provided by Shakespearean tragedy. Following Shakespeare, Kraus seeks to discern amid the anarchy of politics a pattern of guilt and retribution — indeed a cosmic moral order. In May 1916 it had still been unclear 'what play was actually being performed' (*F* 423–5: 12). By October 1918 Kraus has succeeded in identifying the play. It is *Hamlet*, the tragedy of a state so rotten that the royal house must be overthrown and order be restored by Fortinbras.

President Wilson is now hailed as the Fortinbras destined to seize power amid the ruins of Europe (*F* 499–500: 4). When one recalls that in July 1914 the role of Fortinbras had been assigned to the reactionary Franz Ferdinand, the full extent of Kraus's political reorientation becomes clear (*F* 400–3: 2). And yet underlying this political transformation is a startling continuity — a continuing reliance on dramatic paradigms. Kraus's position is profoundly paradoxical. He is aware that in the modern world of mass politics and anonymous economic forces, there can be no 'responsible face' (*F* 462–71: 171). And yet he cannot quite suppress the hope that a charismatic hero may emerge to set the world to rights. For a moment, at the turn of 1918/1919, Woodrow Wilson appeared to be that hero. And as Kraus hails him as Fortinbras, so too he finds in Shakespeare's Horatio the paradigm for his own role:

> And let me speak to th'yet unknowing world
> How these things came about; so shall you hear
> Of carnal, bloody and unnatural acts,
> Of accidental judgements, casual slaughters,

Of deaths put on by cunning and forced cause,
And in this upshot, purposes mistook
Fall'n on th' inventors' heads: all this can I
Truly deliver.

(F 499–500: 4; *Hamlet*, V. ii)

These lines set the stage for Kraus's greatest literary enterprise: the attempt in *Die letzten Tage der Menschheit* to reconstruct the horrific events of the war as a tragedy of guilt and retribution. And yet in this play Kraus simultaneously employs the modern techniques of documentary theatre. The tension between traditional moral vision and radical artistic innovation, which is so characteristic of his work, finds in *Die letzten Tage der Menschheit* its ultimate expression.

PART FIVE

THE LAST DAYS OF MANKIND

CHAPTER 21

Documentary Drama and Apocalyptic Allegory

Die letzten Tage der Menschheit is a masterpiece of anti-war satire. But despite the labours of several generations of scholars, the work remains shrouded in mystery. It has rarely been staged — indeed, it seems to defy performance. Its dialogue, mostly based on contemporary documents, is a disconcerting blend of fact and fantasy. It exploits such an astonishing range of linguistic registers that — like Joyce's *Ulysses* — it eludes translation. Moreover English readers have to rely on versions that have been tendentiously edited as well drastically abridged.[1] Even in German there is no critical edition, and the best available commentary misconstrues the author's ideological stance.[2] It is naïvely assumed by almost every critic that the central figure in the play, the Grumbler ('der Nörgler'), represents Kraus's own views during the war. And readers have tended to be baffled by the sheer length and complexity of the play — over 200 scenes, together with a Prologue and Epilogue. The aim of this chapter is to clarify the status of the play by answering three questions: When exactly was it written? What kind of play is it? and How can it be staged?

The Fractured Text

Kraus began work on *Die letzten Tage* during the summer of 1915. It took almost seven years to complete and was not published in definitive form until May 1922. Certain scenes are anticipated in *Die Fackel* prior to the war, notably the skit on Conrad von Hötzendorf (F 366–7: 1–3). And it was during the Balkan Wars of 1912 that Kraus pioneered the technique of turning document into drama. So the play was ten years in gestation. The moment of inspiration may even date back to that summer's day in 1907 when Kraus stood on the slopes of Mount Vesuvius, contemplating the ruins of an earlier civilization. For his title unmistakably echoes Bulwer-Lytton's *The Last Days of Pompeii*.

Kraus records that most scenes of the play were written in first draft between 1915 and 1917. But this must not mislead us into thinking that the completed play gives an accurate picture of his attitudes during those years. The Prologue seems to have been written in July 1915 (*BSN* I. 179). But the only other section completed in definitive form during the war was the Epilogue. It was written in July 1917 in Switzerland and published under the title *Die letzte Nacht* in November 1918, after the lifting of censorship. The play itself underwent further revision before appearing during 1919 in provisional form — in three special numbers of *Die Fackel*. This edition is known as the 'Akt-Ausgabe', because the successive acts of the play appeared at intervals: the Prologue and Act I in April, Acts II and III in June, and Acts IV and V in August 1919. In October 1920 Kraus announced that after numerous revisions the book edition was ready for press (*F* 552–3: 27). But in fact further revisions were made as late as November 1921, and the book did not appear until the following May.

Thus the play does not express a single authorial viewpoint, but reflects Kraus's radical reorientation under the pressure of events. It was initially conceived from that 'conservative position' which was not repudiated until October 1917. Subsequent revisions reflect Kraus's complete disillusionment with the Austrian political establishment in October 1918 and his support for the cause of Social Democracy. And the final process of revision was influenced by his revulsion against the Christian Socialists, who were returned to power by the elections of October 1920. Thus a play begun in 1915 by a 'loyal' satirist was completed by a radical republican with strong socialist sympathies. This resulted in a fundamental change of paradigm midway through the process of composition.

The first draft of the play, written between 1915 and 1917, was shaped by a conservative viewpoint. This is particularly evident in the Prologue, which portrays the muted public mourning for Franz Ferdinand in the summer of 1914. Kraus ironizes in these opening scenes the obsequiousness of Austrian officialdom, and the lethargy of members of the Cabinet, who are observed reading magazines in the coffee-house when they should have dealt with the political crisis. But his main target are the progressives — the journalists and social climbers who can scarcely conceal their satisfaction at the death of the reactionary heir to the throne. Surveying the self-importance of the dignitaries assembled to greet the coffin, the Grumbler pays tribute to the great man who has died and denounces the misshapen faces of the mourners as 'die Judasfratze' (Vorspiel, 10). The antisemitic tone of this phrase underscores the fact that many of Kraus's targets in this scene have Jewish names like Eisenhof, Lippay, Sieghart, and Herzberg-Fränkel.

Kraus's satire is initially directed less against the ruling class than against the 'enemy within'. This ominous phrase from *Die Fackel* of May 1916 (*F* 426–30: 39) recurs in the Grumbler's second verse monologue (II. 10). And Kraus ensures that we catch the antisemitic implications by emphasizing that the 'enemy within' has a 'crooked nose' ('Krummnas''). A multitude of scenes conceived within this paradigm attack the influence of the Jewish press, and of patriots and profiteers whose names and jargon betray their Jewish origin. The critique of propaganda, and of the chauvinistic attitudes it engenders, is sharply angled against the *Neue Freie Presse*, its editor Moriz Benedikt, and its correspondent Alice Schalek. Kraus's right-wing bias is revealed by the fact that the clerical *Reichspost* is initially virtually ignored.

It was only after 1918 that Kraus corrected the imbalance. This becomes clear when we compare the 'Akt-Ausgabe' of 1919 ('A') with the book edition of 1922 ('B').[3] During the final process of revision, between 1919 and 1922, Kraus not only added about fifty new scenes to his play but fundamentally altered its ideological weighting. Thus in the earlier version the chauvinistic influence of the *Reichspost* is touched on only briefly, in a dozen lines (A I. 1). In the book edition that passage is extended to fill more than a page (B I. 1). And two completely new scenes are introduced to drive home the point that the propaganda of the clerical faction is as perfidious in its own way as that of the liberal press (B III. 24 and V. 46). Recent research has shown that this revision was a direct consequence of the close alliance which Kraus formed in 1919 with the *Arbeiter-Zeitung*.[4] It certainly does not reflect his position at the start of the war, when he himself had been a reader of the *Reichspost* and had identified himself (at least in private) with the position of the Catholic Church (*BSN* I. 94).

The effect of these revisions was to extend the range of the play and improve its balance. The right-wing forces come into greater prominence, and political autocracy (not merely the 'enemy within') becomes the target of attack. A new scene is introduced into the book edition (B I. 5) attacking the political irresponsibility of Count Berchtold and the Austrian Foreign Ministry. And Kraus's changing attitude emerges even more clearly from the two scenes portraying Kaiser Wilhelm, the first probably written in 1915, the second in 1919 — after the monarchy was totally discredited. The earlier scene portrays the Kaiser as a harmless buffoon. The main thrust of the satire is directed against the writer to whom he grants an audience,

Ludwig Ganghofer (B I. 23). In the later scene, added after the publication in 1919 of incriminating memoirs by a German admiral, it is the sadistic personality of the Kaiser himself that is attacked (B IV. 37). The target is now not literary posturing, but political despotism. Kraus intensified the attack on the Hohenzollerns by adding to the book edition a completely new scene ridiculing the Crown Prince (B III. 42). And a number of further scenes were added, particularly in Acts IV and V, to expose the brutality of German militarism.

This change of paradigm — from cultural to political satire — is even clearer in a new scene depicting the conditions of factory workers under the military regime (B II. 32). The scene was not written until 1920, when Kraus's alliance with the Social Democrats had become particularly close.[5] It is the scene which comes closest to a Marxist critique of the military–industrial complex. Indeed, it uncannily anticipates the collusion between military and industrialists which culminated in the slave-labour factories of Nazism. The problem is that this scene, so incisive in itself, is completely at odds with the context in which it is inserted. It is immediately followed by the dialogue between Schwarz–Gelber and his wife, which was one of the very first scenes to be written and had been published in Die Fackel in May 1916, during Kraus's conservative phase (F 423–5: 1–11). This satire on Jewish social climbers is clearly shaped by his early paradigm of the 'enemy within'. Juxtaposed with the Marxist perspective of 1920, it generates a radical incongruity.

The process of revision thus resulted in a fractured text. Even Kraus's literary skill could not conceal the discontinuities. His own word for this fissured text (in the Preface to both versions) is 'zerklüftet'. But where he attributes this discontinuity to the anarchy of the events portrayed, we can see that his shifting political perspective exacerbates the impression of incoherence. In addressing the question: When exactly was the play written?, we have already begun to answer the question: What kind of a play is it? It is an unstable text whose disjunctive angles of vision generate a radical incongruity. Moreover these disjunctions in linear sequence are compounded by superimposed levels of signification on the 'vertical' plane. The satirical vision projects documentary materials on to the plane of apocalyptic myth.

Documentary Drama and Apocalyptic Allegory

Die letzten Tage is best described as a documentary drama — one of the first (and perhaps the greatest) ever written. It has often been praised as a panorama of the horrors of war. But its power derives initially from Kraus's resourceful handling of a technical problem. The problem, for any author writing about the First World War, was to find a literary form commensurate with the unprecedented magnitude and horror of events. Those who attempted to encompass events within a conventional narrative often found — like Robert Graves — that they had to abandon the attempt, 'ashamed [as Graves put it] at having distorted my material with a plot, and yet not yet sure enough of myself to retranslate it into undisguised history'.[6] The most effective solutions to this problem are those which combine documentary with imaginative elements, like Barbusse's *Le Feu*, which Kraus had evidently read by October 1917 (*F* 462–71: 175). An even more significant model was provided by Büchner's *Dantons Tod*, to which Kraus refers for the first time in May 1918 (*F* 474–83: 19).

It is uncertain when Kraus first encountered *Danton's Death*, that submerged masterpiece of nineteenth-century drama which (although published in 1835) was not performed until 1902, in Berlin. It is quite likely that Kraus developed independently his technique of recasting documents which 'speak for themselves' into the form of dramatic dialogue. The technique certainly pre-dates the war, although it was in the events of 1914–18 that it found its commensurate subject. For the Great War was — over and above the turmoil of battle — a war of words. And Kraus, as a noncombatant with an argus eye for the duplicities of newsprint, was ideally placed to reconstruct the folly of the war in its own words — without the distortions of literary narrative, superimposed plot, or invented character.

At the time of the play's inception Kraus seems to have wavered between this documentary method and a more subjective mode that would convey the 'nightmare' quality of events. 'Ein Angsttraum' is the subtitle he uses in his earliest references to the play (*F* 406–12: 166; 413–17: 111). The first dialogue scene to be published — the satire on the Schwarz-Gelbers — is also the scene which comes closest to the traditional aesthetic of invented characters speaking fictive dialogue. But as the war continued, Kraus seems to have realized that it would be better to deny himself this creative freedom and rely on the actual words of historical individuals. A multitude of named characters in the play (unlike the Schwarz-Gelbers) bear the names of real contemporaries.[7] And the words which are put into their mouths derive from the text of press reports. Thus when Kraus came to write his Preface, he was able to claim for his play a documentary authenticity. The most improbable conversations (he claims) are actually quotations.

The use of real-life characters was not without its hazards. The Habsburg libel laws were strict, and the representation of living people on stage was specifically prohibited. Kraus had himself invoked this clause in earlier days, against a play which caricatured his own person (*F* 84: 1–10). He can thus hardly have been surprised when, at the height of the war, he was taken to court for defamation of character by two of his most prominent targets — the journalists Hans Müller and Alice Schalek. Schalek's brother even challenged him to a duel. Kraus claimed in his statement to the court that he was not attacking Schalek as a private person. Through the process of satirical transposition names such as 'Schalek' came to represent symbols ('Symbole vorstellen', *F* 521–30: 13). Judgement was finally pronounced not on Kraus, but on Austria-Hungary. The collapse of the Monarchy in November 1918 coincided with the failure of Müller's action, and Schalek withdrew her case shortly afterwards.

These legal actions illustrate the paradoxes of a documentary mode which borrows actual names to represent typical attitudes. The spectacle of characters from a play coming to life and taking revenge on their author sounds like a fantasy by Pirandello or E.T.A. Hoffmann. But there is no doubt that Kraus's method exposed him to real dangers. If the war had ended in German victory, which still appeared possible until the failure of the final German advance in August 1918, Kraus's position would have become untenable. He might well have been condemned by the courts, imprisoned by the military authorities, or hounded into exile by his opponents. His letters show that when he began writing *Die letzten Tage* in July 1915, he had little hope of it being published — except perhaps in Switzerland or the United States (*BSN* I. 179). The fact that after completing the first draft of the play in Switzerland he returned to Austria, risking confiscation of his manuscript at the border, is an index of his courage.

The fundamental strength of Kraus's play derives from his documentary method. Unlike subsequent imitators, he does not play fast and loose with the facts. When challenged on historical grounds, he had no need to equivocate by claiming that he was only expressing a 'poetic' truth. His meticulousness in handling other people's texts meant that he could always cite chapter and verse, when the veracity of an apparently fantastic scene was challenged — as in the case of Kaiser Wilhelm's sadism (*F* 531–43: 196–203). But to praise *Die letzten Tage* for its documentary authenticity is to beg a more fundamental question. The question is not where Kraus got his documents from, but what he does with them.

The Preface which affirms the play's documentary character at the same time gives prominence to a series of imaginative paradigms. The play is defined a a 'tragedy', acted out by 'figures from an operetta'. We are told that in it people from real life are reduced to 'shadows and marionettes' and become the 'masks of the tragic carnival'. We are reminded that even trivial events on a Vienna street corner are related to a 'cosmic' viewpoint. And the sense of an overarching scheme of guilt and retribution is reinforced by the lines of Horatio (quoted in *Die Fackel* of November 1918), which speak of 'purposes mistook/Fall'n on the inventors' heads'. The basic documentary form is thus refracted through a series of intersecting paradigms, which seem mutually incompatible.

The Shakespearean tragic mode was for Kraus the most fundamental. His enduring attachment to it is clear from the Grumbler's final monologue, where Horatio's lines are quoted yet again, setting the seal of moral retribution upon the grotesque panorama of war (A V. 56; B V. 54). But Kraus seems simultaneously to have been aware that the anarchy of events disrupted the closed form of a five-act tragedy. His own division into five acts, loosely corresponding to five successive phases of the war, serves only to show that there is no dramatic development. The action is absurdly repetitive, with the same inane officers mouthing the same meaningless clichés in Scene 1 of each successive Act, regardless of whether the date is August 1914 (Act I), May 1915 (Act II: declaration of war by Italy) or the end of September 1918 (Act V: surrender of Bulgaria). Moreover it was not a war in which there were Shakespearean 'inventors' — heroes and villains who could be held individually responsible for their acts. The notion of collective guilt undermines the possibility of sustaining the traditional dramaturgy, in which 'great men' are responsible for events.

Despite the Shakespearean framework, Kraus's technique is actually closer to Büchner's. The form is fractured and the characters are pictured as the instruments of anonymous historical forces over which they have little control. The juxtaposition of crowd scenes on the streets of Vienna with interiors giving glimpses of political leaders enhances the sense of incongruity. We never see Berchtold drafting his ultimatum to Serbia, merely hear his voice ordering iced coffee (B I. 5). There are no characters of tragic stature, but the actions of these 'figures from an operetta' have catastrophic consequences. Even more radically than Büchner, Kraus subverts the form of tragedy by intercalating elements of operetta and cabaret, carnival and puppet theatre. In certain scenes the characters are specifically identified as 'marionettes'; in others they are surrealistically transformed into animals. The process of visionary transformation is intensified towards the end of the play, especially in Act V, Scene 55, where cinematographic techniques are introduced to project 'apparitions' on to the wall of Divisional Headquarters. And in the visionary Epilogue the colloquial prose of earlier scenes is completely displaced by verse, to form an Expressionistic climax.

The effect of these innovations is breathtaking. The technique of montage, which is the source of the play's documentary authenticity, is also used to deconstruct traditional conceptions of closed form and connected causality. Documents from different linguistic registers are juxtaposed within the scope of a single scene. And the continuous interplay among different dramaturgical codes leaves the audience simultaneously horrified and exhilarated. Of course these divergent perspectives do not generate a systematic political analysis. And Kraus has often been criticized, from a Marxist viewpoint, for failing to give a more realistic account of the dehumanizing effects of capitalism. Those who take this view are welcome to read the collected works of Karl Kautsky (the doyen of Austro-Marxism). But if they choose to read Kraus instead, they must accept the fact that he writes as a satirist, for whom contrasts are more significant than causes, and whose approach even to economic questions is guided by an eye for visual symbols.

Kraus's panorama of the war is shaped by the principle of 'gruesome contrast' ('schauerliche Kontrasthaftigkeit', F 462–71: 171). This principle can be traced through the structure of the play at almost every level: the juxtaposition of scenes — Benedikt (the Pope) praying for peace, and Benedikt (the editor) exulting in war (I. 27 and 28); incongruities within a single scene — the rabble on the streets of Vienna and the purple prose of the journalists assigned to describe it (I. 1); even ambiguities within individual words — 'Bombenerfolg' ('smash hit') applied to an operetta by Victor Leon, as the news vendor announces the bombardment of Belgrade (end of I. 1). The ubiquitous sensitivity to contrasts and discrepancies also generates two of Kraus's most fundamental satirical techniques — reduction and inflation. Great men (like Berchtold, Kaiser Wilhelm or Franz Joseph) are reduced to marionettes or buffoons. And nonentities, like Biach (the inveterate reader of the Neue Freie Presse), are inflated into mythopoeic embodiments of the spirit of the age.

Kraus's mythopoeic method has been criticized as a mystification of the realities of political and economic power.[8] But it must be recognized that he was trying to represent anonymous mass forces in terms of individual characters in a play. They become the archetypal symbols of forces in the collective unconscious. Schalek becomes the suprapersonal embodiment of that perverse rejoicing in slaughter which seized the civilian population. And German war profiteers in Switzerland acquire the apocalyptic names of the giants Gog and Magog (V. 50). The problem is how to create archetypes which are not stereotypes (like 'Oppenheimer' [I. 22], the rapacious Jew of German folklore).[9] The method is perhaps most successful in the Epilogue, where the verse form transcends realistic representation and creates symbolic figures of unprecedented power: the Dying Soldier who defies his superiors; the Death's Head Hussar who epitomizes the sadistic army officer; Engineer Abendrot, who embodies the power of new military technology; and the Lord of the Hyenas — the Antichrist who celebrates the triumph of the media over mankind.

Kraus's documentary drama thus culminates in apocalyptic allegory. The Epilogue ends with the destruction of planet Earth by a bombardment of meteors from Mars. And a 'Voice from Above' pronounces judgement on an irredeemable world. Once again we are confronted by incompatible paradigms. The techniques of deconstruction deployed in the course of the play seem to deny the possibility of any universal meaning. But in the Epilogue (as in the Preface) Kraus seeks to reaffirm a cosmic moral order. The tension between the closed form of the framework and the fractured structure of the play itself remains unresolved. The Epilogue, completed in 1917, is more traditional in conception (even though it uses such imaginative techniques). But as Kraus, during the final processes of revision in 1919–21, added ever more horrifying material to the final scenes of the play, the anarchy of events tended to strain the closed form to breaking point. What finally emerges is an unstable text with three distinct (and mutually incompatible) endings.

The Epilogue, although it ends with the symbolic destruction of the earth, is the most reassuring of Kraus's endings. For it portrays a universe in which God is still in control. And the Antichrist is defeated by divine retribution. The same sense of a transcendent moral order is sustained in the second of Kraus's three climaxes — the final monologue of the Grumbler (V. 54). Here the strands of coherent meaning are stretched closer to breaking point, as the Grumbler recapitulates the unmitigated horrors of the war in an anguished monologue. But this anguish at the death of innocent men finds consolation in the creative act itself. The memory of the dead will be eternally cherished, while the survivors are condemned to perpetual purgatory, as 'shadows' transfixed by the text of the play. The Grumbler, like Horatio, finds consolation in the act of bearing witness to the 'unknowing world'.

The most grandiose of Kraus's culminating scenes, however, portrays the revelry of Austrian and Prussian officers, at the moment of military collapse (V. 55). This scene — perhaps the greatest in the play — has an expressive range which builds up from crude colloquialisms to a horrifying visionary climax, as the helpless victims of military tyranny reappear as 'apparitions' to haunt their tormentors. The idea is borrowed from *Richard III*, where the spirits of those he has murdered return to curse the King on the eve of the battle of Bosworth. Kraus reinforces this motif by means of a more resonant archetype — Belshazzar's Feast, the drunken revel that is brought to an end by the writing on the wall. What Kraus's imagination projects on to the wall of Divisional Headquarters are not words but cinematographic images — documentary in origin but visionary in effect. The scene ends in disintegration and horror — 'total darkness' ('Völlige Finsternis'), a sudden 'wall of flames' ('Flammenwand'), and then the 'screams of death' ('Todesschreie'). This scene, so much more powerful than either the Grumbler's monologue or the Epilogue, ends in a metaphysical void.

The three endings, each conceived in a different spirit and indeed at a different date, cannot be resolved into aesthetic harmony. *Die letzten Tage der Menschheit* is a faulted masterpiece — 'faulted' in a geological sense. The seismic shift of history — and of Kraus's own response — means that the different strata of his play are no longer aligned. And the reader has to dig through accrued layers of meaning to find underlying coherence. Whether this faulted structure is also an artistic defect depends on the criteria we apply. The reader who, contemplating the horrors of 1914–18, is still able to see human history as part of a harmonious pattern will no doubt prefer Hofmannsthal's *Das Salzburger Große Welttheater* to Kraus's *Die letzten Tage*. But it can be argued that even the faults of Kraus's play are the product of a more radical truthfulness — a determination to 'tell it as it was' which is frustrated by the sheer refractoriness of events. For the events themselves would not keep still, while the position of the author was spinning from right to left through 180 degrees. It is in short a play not for a static *theatrum mundi* but for a dynamic revolving stage. And it is here that *Die letzten Tage* must finally reveal its multiple meanings — not on the printed page, but in the living theatre.

Theatrical Effectiveness

The claim that *Die letzten Tage* is unperformable is a myth. The myth originally arose from an over-literal reading of Kraus's Preface, which declares that the play is intended for a 'Martian theatre', since theatre-goers of this world would be unable to endure it. The reason he gives is that it is both too long and too horrendous; and that only the author has the right to exploit the play's paradoxical humour. During his lifetime Kraus did indeed prove a jealous custodian of his text. He permitted performances of the Epilogue and gave public readings from some of the most significant scenes of the play. But when he was approached by the leading directors of the German theatre during the 1920s, Max Reinhardt and Erwin Piscator, he refused to allow them to stage his play. His fear was that their style of production would turn a work of ethical protest into an entertainment. Their emphasis on spectacular stage effects was also completely at odds with Kraus's concept of a 'theatre of poetry', which gave precedence to the spoken word. The paradoxical stage history of Kraus's play thus begins with the fact that in the 1920s it inspired a whole new style of documentary political theatre in Germany, without actually being staged itself.

This self-denying ordinance was maintained by Kraus's literary executor after the Second World War. The play was not premièred until 1964, and then only in a restrained production which played down its theatrical qualities.[10] There are those who argue that the play is simply unsuitable for the theatre, and should be regarded as 'book drama'.[11] But this is a misunderstanding both of Kraus's intentions and his achievement. Kraus himself, though he denied his play to the entertainment theatre of his day, anticipated that theatres of the future might do it fuller justice. He specifically defined his policy of banning productions as 'provisional' (F 834–7: 20). He gave his consent 'in principle' to a planned production by a Socialist theatre in Vienna, which was never realized (F 795–9: 38). And he even prepared his own 'stage version' of the text (F 834–7: 16–17). Thus Kraus's followers have been more purist than the author himself, in insisting that the play is unstageable.

Against this, there are strong counter-arguments. First, the play is essentially acoustic, with its superabundance of contrasting voices, dialects and jargons. Kraus's public readings brought this vividly home to his contemporaries. More recently, the recordings made by Austrian Radio and by Helmut Qualtinger have reminded us of the play's unique acoustic impact. It is certainly not a drama designed for the silence of the printed page. Moreover a close reading of Kraus's stage directions reveals an undeniable emphasis on scenic gesture and visual effect. This is particularly evident in the stage directions which give precise details of costume and appearance.

Certain details may be highlighted to illustrate Kraus's emphasis on visual effect: the wine-stained trousers and bushy beard of the drunkard on the tram (I.13), the cameras, field-glasses and riding breeches of war correspondents (I.21), the pince-nez and side-whiskers of a corpulent field marshal (II. 22). Scene after scene exploits the contrast between different styles of uniform and dress, sometimes crudely (the dwarf in uniform and the giant in civvies, I. 12), sometimes more poignantly (the tattered uniform of a crippled

soldier contrasted with the magnificent medals of an officer, who has
spent the war safely in Vienna, IV. 1). In some scenes, like the one
portraying the irreverent behaviour of visitors to a mosque, the
clothing motifs develop into a complex choreography (III. 19).
Beards and moustaches are also used to point the significance of
situation and character. Conrad von Hötzendorf adjusts his
moustache for the photographer (I. 24), while the points of the
Kaiser's stand vertically on end at moments of frenzy (IV. 37).

Kraus achieves his effects not through naturalistic costume, but
through symbolic accentuation. It is done with economy and
panache, rather in the style of cabaret. How is one visually to
distinguish an Austrian from a Hungarian? Kraus recalls in October
1917 a French cabaret performance, in which Austrian and
Hungarian were identically dressed — but the Austrian wore a top
hat! (F 462–71: 48). His own stage directions have this same gestural
quality. Viennese Municipal Councillors wear top hats (II. 1).
Reporters brandish notebooks, waiters carry napkins, army
commanders are equipped with maps or batons, pretentious ladies
have lorgnettes, effete aristocrats a pocket mirror, while the owner
of a factory under military control carries a whip. Kraus excels in
visual counterpoint. He sets up contrasts between the swagger-stick
of an officer, the crutches of a wounded soldier, and the toothpicks
used by profiteers emerging from the Hotel Bristol (II, 1); the
walking stick of a business man and the wooden leg of a beggar (III.
7); the dignified robes of an Imam, his hands enveloped in his
flowing sleeves, and the cocky young businessmen from Berlin, who
desecrate the mosque by sticking their hands in their pockets and
keeping their hats on (III. 19); the tennis racket of the Crown Prince
and the rifles of soldiers marching to the Somme (III. 42); the picture
of the Emperor in all his splendour hanging on a classroom wall and
the clothing of the schoolchildren which, by the last year of the war,
is made of paper (V. 23).

The counterpoint to these clothing motifs is an emphasis on the
language of the body. Kraus's characters do not merely express
themselves in words. They dance and sing, eat and drink, flirt and
urinate, sweat and stink, laugh and scream. At certain climaxes
bodily functions are given particular prominence. At the empty heart
of the play — and of the city itself — stands the gigantic figure of a
drunken man. He is observed by the Grumbler relieving himself in
public, while uttering the rhythmical words: 'Ein Genuß! – Ein
Genuß! – Ein Genuß!' This pleasure in primitive bodily functions
represents the imperviousness of the man in the street to the
inexorable tragedy of mankind. In this scene (as the Grumbler sees it)
the night is so dark that only a final day of judgement can follow (III.

46). As the tragic gloom intensifies, so the physical appetites of Kraus's characters become ever more incongruous: drunkenness (I. 13), greed (III. 6), gluttony (III. 11), promiscuity (IV. 35), and dreams of what a drunken officer calls his 'piece of tail' ('mein Arscherl', V. 47).

Kraus's characters are not merely (as the Preface has it) 'clichés on two legs'. They have physical appetites which accentuate the fact that they have scarcely an idea in their heads — or at least no idea that has not been put there by the ubiquitous propaganda machine. The Viennese addiction to operetta, music, song and dance forms a recurrent motif. And we are reminded that the body that dances also sweats and stinks (III. 12). There may be hints of Swiftian revulsion at bodily functions. But Kraus's essential theme is that the body has been betrayed to the machine. The subversive allures of the prostitute (II. 29) and the bulging belly of a pregnant woman (II. 18) represent those forces of nature which have been betrayed. In their place we are shown crippled soldiers and the mangled bodies of the dead. And not only the bodies of those killed in battle. Several of the most powerful scenes are set under the shadow of the gallows — an essential feature of the stage set, as the Grumbler reminds us (IV. 29). Sadistic army commanders (we are told) even lay bets as to whether a fourteen-year-old boy, strung up for alleged subversion, will ejaculate at the moment of death (V. 55).

At certain points Kraus's accentuation of physical motifs tends towards the surrealistic. A government official speaking into the telephone is so obsequious that he 'almost crawls inside it' (Prologue, 3); the owner of a coffee-house greets his guests with such ritualistic rigidity that he 'acquires the appearance of the Angel of Death' (II. 17); the 'Austrian face' of a booking-office clerk manifests 'diabolic' satisfaction (IV. 3); on the streets of Vienna the rain 'falls upwards', and 'two leg-stumps in a tattered uniform' block the pavement (V. 1); news vendors crying out their headlines towards the end of the war rush up and down the streets like 'corybants and maenads' (V. 53); the fifth act ends with choruses spoken by animated gas masks, flames, and drowned horses with water 'streaming from their eyes' (V. 55); the beard of Moriz Benedikt is so swarthy that it envelops his face 'like the fur of an animal' (Epilogue).

This tendency towards surrealism culminates in the transformation of human beings into animals, whose figures appear where one might least expect them. Lemurs and billy-goats mingle with the crowds on the main boulevards (IV. 1). A city-centre coffee-house is thronged with 'fauna' bearing names like Mammoth, Walrus, Hamster, Jackal and Baboon (V. 25). The transition from human into animal seems to be associated with certain kinds of clothing. In the same surrealistic scene the girls wear 'insect-like costumes', and we are specifically told that armadillos — 'Gürteltiere' — cross the room. The motif seems to be a development from 'Gürtelrock', a form of clothing associated elsewhere with indecent affluence (V. 43). And ravens and hyenas dominate the climax of Act V and of the Epilogue.

It is the prominence of these visionary motifs which has led some commentators to conclude that the play is unstageable. But for an enterprising director it is precisely this imaginative mummery that would be used to heighten the impact on stage. The visionary 'apparitions' at the end of Act V would be even less of a problem, since they seem consciously conceived in the form of film- or slide-projections. And Kraus himself identified many of the photographs that might be used, for example the grotesque 'female gas-masks' (Pl. 34) reproduced as frontispiece to Acts IV and V of the 'Akt-Ausgabe'. The figures with their monstrous eyes and pendulous snouts epitomize that reduction of mankind to bestiality which is highlighted by animal imagery. A photograph of the fatuous face of Count Berchtold (Pl. 35) is also integrated into the play in a scene (III. 41) which invites the use of photographic projection.

In his use of photomontage and cinematographic motifs, Kraus was a pioneer in technical innovation.[12] Altogether, there are almost a hundred pictorial motifs — film sequences, photographs, posters, picture postcards and even commemorative medals — which might be used as projections in a stage production. Kraus was far less of a purist in practice than he appeared to be in theory. This is clear from the support he gave to the Vienna production of his Epilogue in 1923. This production, designed under his close supervision, used a surrealistic stage set and spectacular lighting to reinforce the impact of the text. Kraus was favourably impressed, and noted how much the Chorus of the Hyenas gained from being presented on stage (F 613–21: 68, 82). He himself recited the long speech of the 'Voice from Above', proclaiming the impending destruction of the Earth. And in certain performances (in an extraordinary exchange of roles) he even played the part of the 'Lord of the Hyenas'. Looking back on this production, he could be justly proud of his own theatrical effectiveness ('eigene Bühnenwirksamkeit', F 613–21: 59).

A further dimension of the play's theatricality lies in the use of music and song. Even the most sensitive reader could not pick up the full resonance of musical motifs from the silent page. They cry out for performance. There are a whole series of set-piece songs used in the manner of Nestroy to introduce comic characters: Ganghofer (I. 23), Hirsch and Roda Roda (II. 15), Commercial Counsellor Wahnschaffe (III. 40) and Emperor Franz Joseph (IV. 31). In some of

34 Women wearing gas-masks

35 (*right*) Count Berchtold in
military uniform

the scenes Kraus even provides a musical score, with ironic effect (Roda Roda's experiences as a war correspondent are sung to the tune of 'O Tannenbaum'). And staff officers record the pleasures of life at brigade headquarters — safely out of range of General Cadorna's artillery — to the rhythm of a waltz (IV. 10). But Kraus more commonly relies on the popular songs of the war itself, which are subtly woven into the dialogue to provide an ironic counterpoint.

The starting-point is documentary. The euphoria of August 1914 is accurately re-created when Kraus shows us crowds singing the 'Prinz Eugen-Marsch' and the 'Wacht am Rhein', while soldiers march through the streets to the strains of 'In der Heimat, in der Heimat da gibts ein Wiedersehn' (I. 1). The documentary material soon acquires a satirical edge. Thus the song 'In der Heimat' is reintroduced at the beginning of every act; but the drafts of soldiers singing it become progressively older, their hair more grey, and the prospect of their returning home increasingly remote. Their sentimental celebration of 'Heimat' is also sharply juxtaposed with what is happening at home: journalists gloating over their exemption from military service, war profiteers gorging themselves in the Hotel Bristol, officers idling their time away in the night-clubs of Vienna, the social élite cruising by in their automobiles.

Kraus's most effective technique is ironic juxtaposition. A news vendor cries that 40,000 Russians have been killed in the fighting round Przemysl, while two black-marketeers stroll past with their ladies, tipsily trilling 'Sterngucker — Sterngucker — nimm dich in Acht' (I. 30). As Czernowitz is recaptured by the Russians, the patrons of the 'Wolf in Gersthof' are entertained with 'Jessas na, uns geht's guat' and (more patriotically) 'Draußen im Schönbrunner Park/ Sitzt ein guater alter Herr' (II. 25). As the blinded soldier of V. 40 is led away by a child who has been collecting cigarette-ends for him, a barrel organ plays the 'Hoch Habsburg-Marsch'.

In certain scenes the juxtapositions of song and situation give way to a more complex musical counterpoint. The dialogue of one night-club scene (III. 45) is interspersed with a dozen different songs, ranging from the saucy 'Ja, mein Herz gehört nur Wien' through the Jewish melody 'Rosa, wir fahren nach Lodz!' to the patriotic 'O du mein Österreich' and finally the bathetic 'Da habts mein letztes Kranl'. The banquet scene at army headquarters which forms the climax of Act V is even more continuously punctuated by musical motifs. As artillery rumbles in the distance, the band plays 'Der alte Noah hats doch gewußt, die schönste Boa wärmt nicht die Brust'. The officers grow increasingly drunk and the singing increasingly discordant as the sounds of battle draw nearer. Just before the moment of total collapse they are singing 'Braunes Isonzomädel', while a Hungarian officer dances a csárdás. This frenetic dance of death is intensified in the verse Epilogue, where two Gas Masks link arms for the masked ball and the Hyenas dance tangos and waltzes around the bodies of dead soldiers.

The vitality and variety of *Die letzten Tage* are inexhaustible. Its fluid transitions ('Verwandlungen') from scene to scene seem designed for the revolving stage. And its anarchic medley of voices and visions cries out for theatrical realization. It combines the satirical vitality of Nestroy with the musicality of *Oh, What a Lovely War*, without forfeiting its underlying documentary power. Of course there is a tension between spectacle and text. Kraus's intensive focus on language will inevitably be dissipated by a production that overemphasizes the play's visual pageantry. And his vast cast — not of rounded characters but of 'clichés on two legs' — will tax the resources of an ensemble attuned to more conventional modes of comedy. But the very superabundance of the play is the source of its stage potential. It is not like Schiller's *Wallenstein* — a play that can hardly be shortened without removing some essential link from the plot. The montage structure of *Die letzten Tage* means that it can be radically cut without damage to its formal integrity.

The incongruities of Kraus's fractured text suggest that the play might gain from a radical pruning. If this seems a heretical denial of Kraus's faith in language, it should be remembered that Shakespeare too was a word-fetishist in his way. Verbal complexity need not preclude theatrical impact. Even the choric duologues of Optimist and Grumbler make vivid use of visual motifs. It is only the strict control of copyright by Kraus and his executor which has prevented *Die letzten Tage* from assuming its rightful place in the German theatre. The Vienna Festival production by Hans Hollmann in 1980 demonstrated how effectively it can be staged by a dynamic dramaturgy in a large auditorium. And even the problems of transposing a play so deeply enmeshed in the German language into terms accessible to an English audience are not insurmountable, as the Edinburgh Festival production of 1983 indicated.[13] Like its model *Danton's Death*, Kraus's play has only begun to make its full impact sixty years after publication. It is the submerged masterpiece of the twentieth-century theatre.

CHAPTER 22

The Tragedy of the Seer

The Identity of the Grumbler

The Grumbler is a character in a play. It is necessary to start with this truism, since most commentators have refused to allow that it is true. The consensus is that we must take him as the *author* of *Die letzten Tage* — 'The Grumbler is, of course, Karl Kraus himself.'[1] This identification seems to be supported by a number of passages in the play. The Grumbler is greeted by bystanders as 'der Fackelkraus' as he walks through the city (I. 25). His speeches often echo the text of *Die Fackel* itself. He tells us that he is writing a play about the war (IV. 2 and 29). On two occasions we see him on a public platform reading poems which Kraus himself published and read during the war (III. 36 and V. 28). And in his final monologue (V. 54) he summarizes the themes of his play, offering it as an act of atonement.

The claim that the Grumbler is Kraus himself raises more problems than it resolves. In the context of a documentary play it must imply that the character's speeches are a reconstruction. But a reconstruction of what? Of views actually published in *Die Fackel* during the war and proclaimed from the platform? Of ideas that the author would have published, but for the censorship? Or of the kind of thing Kraus was saying in private, in conversation or correspondence with friends? Does it allow that he may also have introduced into these speeches opinions formed after the war was over, during the process of revising the text in 1919, or again in 1920–1? Since no previous discussion of the play has attempted to answer these questions, it is necessary to return to first principles.

Any serious study must take account of the differences between the 'Akt-Ausgabe' of 1919 (A) and the book edition of 1922 (B). Even a cursory comparison reveals that during revision the role of

the Grumbler was significantly modified and extended. This is particularly true of his recurrent duologues with the Optimist, which
form a kind of tragic chorus. In 'A' there are thirteen such scenes, in
'B' twenty-four. As a result of these revisions the total length of the
Optimist/Grumbler scenes was increased by about 40 per cent, from
just over 3,600 lines to almost 5,000.[2] A number of scenes portraying
the position of the Grumbler in 1914 or 1915 were actually composed
in 1920 or 1921. However conscientious Kraus may have been in
reconstructing his earlier intellectual outlook, the reconstruction was
inevitably affected by this retrospective process of selection, deletion
and accentuation.

This is not to deny that many of the speeches of the Grumbler have
a documentary kernel, deriving from texts published in *Die Fackel*
during the war. This is particularly true of the longest of the choral
scenes (A I. 12, reprinted virtually unchanged as B I. 29). There are
close correlations between the Grumbler's arguments in this scene
and Kraus's aphorisms of October 1915 (*F* 406–12: 94–168). But
even here there are modifications. In the speeches of the Grumbler,
Kraus's conservatism is toned down, while the comments on both
militarism and capitalism become far more astringent than in *Die
Fackel* of the corresponding period. Kraus's characteristic method is
to build an extended dialogue around what were originally a few
cryptic sentences in *Die Fackel*. In the process he allows himself
considerable imaginative freedom. Although the matter has never
been systematically investigated, it seems likely that only about
one-third of the dialogue spoken by the Grumbler has a textual basis
in *Die Fackel* of 1914–18.

The second possibility, that the speeches of the Grumbler represent what Kraus *would* have published, had he not been inhibited by
the censorship, has some validity; but unfortunately the argument is
speculative. We have virtually no evidence as to what Kraus 'actually
thought' at such moments of crisis as the Austrian ultimatum to
Serbia in July 1914 or the Italian declaration of war on the Central
Powers in May 1915. Ten years later, in August 1924, Kraus was to
recall his revulsion at the spectacle of Austrian soldiers at the
outbreak of war, roaring with enthusiasm for their butchers as they
were carted off to the slaughter (*F* 657–67: 2). But this kind of
retrospective recall, strongly coloured by Kraus's postwar anti-
militarism, lacks the validity of a letter or diary note written at the
time. It is possible that diaries, letters, notebooks or recorded
conversations will still come to light which may elucidate Kraus's
actual position at the beginning of the war. But the evidence as it
stands does not indicate that he was as decisively opposed to the war
in August 1914 as is suggested by the speeches of the Grumbler in the

corresponding scene (B I. 4). Since the scene was added after 1919, this is hardly surprising.

Kraus's position in 1914 was coloured, as we have seen, by an undercurrent of sympathy for the aristocratic and military élite. Of course, aristocratic sympathies did not preclude a pacifist disposition, as his relationship with Sidonie Nadherny shows. There is evidence that Sidonie too 'hated' the war.[3] But it was possible to hate the war for a wide variety of reasons: because it threatened to disrupt the traditional social order; or on the grounds that it was a mistake for Germany and Austria-Hungary to fight a war against Russia, since all three countries were bastions of aristocratic privilege against the democratic tendencies of the West. This last was certainly the view of the two political leaders whom Kraus most admired — Bismarck and Franz Ferdinand. In February 1915 he quotes Bismarck's views on the folly of a war against Russia, with evident approval (F 405: 12–13). What is lacking in the record of Kraus's position in 1914–15 is any unequivocal condemnation of militarism. His letters to Sidonie contain surprisingly few pointers in this direction. The letters to Baron Lempruch, on the other hand, suggest a certain solidarity with the military élite. Thus it is by no means certain that — if there had been no censorship — Kraus's position would have been as radical as the utterances of the Grumbler suggest.

The discrepancies become even more striking when we consider how much Kraus *omits* from the dialogues of the Grumbler. Important aspects of his activity as a publicist during 1914–18 are either toned down or entirely eliminated, notably those public readings or addresses which had a reactionary tendency ('Die Kinder der Zeit', 'Gebet an die Sonne von Gibeon', 'Die Historischen und die Vordringenden'). The same is true of the literary polemics which form a prominent feature of the wartime numbers of *Die Fackel*. And even more striking is the omission from the speeches of the Grumbler of any significant reference to the political campaign — for Lammasch and against Czernin — which so preoccupied Kraus during 1917–18. It is clear that the character of the Grumbler is by no means an accurate reflection of Kraus's own stance as a publicist.

When we turn to the private sphere, the omissions are even more remarkable. We know that Kraus was preoccupied during the first year of the war with the pursuit of an elusive baroness; but the Grumbler appears to have no female friends. We know that in this period he paid three visits to Italy and actually lived through the diplomatic crisis in Rome which preceded the Italian declaration of war. But there is no hint of this in the Grumbler's references to Italy.

Indeed, he adopts a tone of urbane detachment in the scene which follows almost immediately after the news of war with Italy reaches Vienna (A II. 1; B II. 2). We know that Kraus repeatedly took refuge in the depths of the countryside (and published a series of nature poems in *Die Fackel*); but the Grumbler is almost invariably seen in Vienna, and the poems he declaims are exclusively satirical. We know that Kraus had a wide circle of acquaintance, and was in contact during the war not only with writers like Rilke and Spitteler, but also with influential figures like Hager (the censor), Lammasch, Lempruch, Lobkowicz and the Lichnowskys. But the Grumbler is an isolated outsider, his sole companion being his friend the Optimist.

In short, we must abandon the simplistic identification of the Grumbler with Karl Kraus. The figure of the Grumbler, though it does incorporate significant aspects of Kraus's position during the war, is shaped by an overriding literary purpose. There is a parallel with Siegfried Sassoon's *Memoirs of George Sherston* — another account of the war which appears to be a faithful autobiographical reconstruction. Sherston, as Sassoon himself conceded, was 'a simplified version of my "outdoor self"'.[4] In a similar sense the Grumbler may be defined as a simplified version of Kraus's satirical self. He is most significant as a character in the play, not as a mirror-image of the author. And his status is defined by his interaction with a figure that is indubitably fictional — his friend the Optimist.

The Role of the Optimist

Although Kraus in the Preface claims that the most implausible conversations in *Die letzten Tage* were actually spoken word for word, it is clear that the Optimist is an invention. This is not to deny that the Optimist/Grumbler dialogues may owe something to actual conversations: with Ludwig von Ficker, for example, whom Kraus visited in Innsbruck in August 1914; with Adolf Loos, who was so reluctant to accept Kraus's arguments that he became the subject of an epigram addressed 'To a Friend who is Hard of Hearing' ('Einem schwerhörigen Freunde', F 423–5: 16); with the architect Paul Engelmann, who like Loos was patriotic at the outbreak of war, but was gradually converted to Kraus's position; with the publisher Kurt Wolff, who frequently visited Kraus when passing through Vienna on leave from the front; and with Max Lobkowicz, whose allegiance to military ideals Kraus sought to shake in conversations which lasted right through the night.[5] One of the proof sheets for the powerful anti-war declaration on the final age of *Die Fackel* of October 1915 (F 406–12: 168) provides a further clue to the Optimist's identity. For that aphorism originally began with the words: 'Zu einem Optimisten'.[6] Since we know that this aphorism (about the 'moral island') was first formulated in a letter to Baron Lempruch, it is tempting to see him as the primary model for Kraus's literary figure. But on reflection it becomes clear that the Optimist is a synthetic creation, whose literary function — as foil for the Grumbler — is more important than his biographical origin.

If we seek a model for the Optimist, we would be better advised to consider literary ones. Platonic dialogue is one of the oldest literary forms. And the Optimist certainly owes something to those naïve interlocutors who feed Socrates his cues. In satirical writing too the dialogue has distinguished antecedents, from Horace and Lucian to Lessing and Pope. Kraus must have been familiar with this tradition. And we know that he was reading Diderot's *Le Neveu de Rameau* (in Goethe's translation) at the time when he had just begun work on *Die letzten Tage* (*BSN* I. 341–2; letter of 27 May 1916). There are striking similarities of tone between the Optimist/Grumbler scenes and Diderot's satirical dialogue, in which the idealistic illusions of the 'Diderot' figure are continuously subverted by the hyperbolic discourse of Rameau's sceptical 'Nephew'.

The most fruitful way, then, of looking at the Optimist is as a literary creation arising from Kraus's use of dialogue. The imaginary interlocutor whose presence can be discerned in the glosses and aphorisms of *Die Fackel* here comes into his own. But can the Optimist be taken seriously as a dramatic persona? The Grumbler dismisses him as merely the man who provides his cues ('Stichwortbringer für meine Monologe', I. 29). Towards the end of the play he reiterates the view that the chorus scenes are essentially monologues (V. 42). But this view is not borne out by a careful reading of the scenes themselves. Out of the technical requirements of dramatic form dramatic characters are born. And the Optimist certainly is one — a foil for the Grumbler, not merely his stooge — and certainly not just a figment of his imagination. The relationship of Kraus to the Optimist is that of author to fictional character; but the relationship between Grumbler and Optimist is that between two characters in a play. And the meaning of their scenes is to be found not simply in the speeches of the Grumbler, but in the dramatic interplay between two conflicting views of experience.

The contrast between Optimist and Grumbler is established in the first scene in which they appear together. It is evident, above all, in their different modes of discourse. The speech patterns of the Optimist approximate to those of an educated speaker of German;

those of the Grumbler are emphatically aphoristic. He repeatedly responds to the Optimist's objections not with logical argument but with imaginative hyperbole. The good spoken German of the Optimist gives the clue to his dramatic function. He is certainly a patriot who sees contemporary events in an optimistic light and uncritically accepts the political slogans of the moment. But he is by no means a caricature like the Patriot or the various Newspaper Readers who appear in other scenes. Indeed, he represents rather positive qualities. His attitude is balanced, moderate and tolerant, where that of the Grumbler tends towards satirical overstatement:

OPTIMIST: Man darf nicht generalisieren.
NÖRGLER: Ich tu's. Sie können auf meine Ungerechtigkeit bauen.
(I. 29)

(OPTIMIST: You shouldn't generalize.
GRUMBLER: I do. You can count on me to be unjust.)

To the exaggerations and intuitions of the Grumbler he opposes the arguments of common sense: 'Das ist ein Wortspiel. Welche Idee haben Sie im Auge? (That is a pun. What idea do you have in mind?)' 'Sie sagen Derbheiten, aber nicht Wahrheiten. (What you are saying is rude, but not true.)' (I. 29).

The Optimist repeatedly questions his friend's claims about the connection between political disaster and the decay of language. The claims are rejected as far-fetched ('weit hergeholt', I. 29), as an *idée fixe* which is given exaggerated importance (II. 10). It soon becomes apparent that this is a dialogue between unequal partners — not because the Grumbler tends to have the last word, but because the two speak different languages. The Optimist voices in the language of common sense the plain man's objections to satirical argumentation. The Grumbler responds with an intensification of that perspective, in a language which is at times so highly charged that it breaks into verse. This is not simply the language of rational debate. It is nearer to that of tragic vision.

The paradoxical discourse of the Grumbler thus has tragic undertones. At times his arguments are so cogent that they leave the Optimist (and by implication the audience) entirely convinced. Notable examples are the Grumbler's critique of prevailing conceptions of a 'heroic death' (I. 29) and of the slogan of a 'time of greatness' (V. 2), both positions the Optimist is obliged to abandon in the face of unanswerable arguments. Kraus is objective enough in his handling of these scenes not to give the Grumbler an easy victory. The scenes are indeed weighted in his favour. And many of the Grumbler's speeches are reformulations of arguments already familiar to us from *Die Fackel*, above all the emphasis on the crude

economic motives and the mechanized modes of slaughter which
underlie the patriotic rhetoric. The scenes provide an incisive and
unifying commentary on the fragmented action of the play. But their
function is not merely choric. The Optimist and the Grumbler are
after all the most substantial characters in the play. And the conflict
between them adds to Kraus's grotesque panorama a more subtle
dimension of individual tragedy.

What is enacted in these scenes is the tragedy of the seer. Optimist
and Grumbler represent two different ways of looking at life, which
prove to be irreconcilable. Imagery of 'seeing', of 'vision' and of
'perspective' pervades their dialogue. Indeed that imagery
contributes almost as much to the effect of the play as the
preoccupation with sounds and voices which has so often been
identified as the essence of Kraus's satire. In their first great scene, the
Optimist denounces the Grumbler's 'exaggerating perspective'
('übertreibende Perspektive'). But the Grumbler replies that it is a
'true perspective' generated by the 'falsification of life' ('die wahre
Perspektive eines falschen Lebens', I. 29). His nightmare
('Angsttraum') comes closer to the truth than the Optimist's
complacent rationality. But the gap between their two perspectives
leads the Grumbler despairingly to identify himself as the 'dying spy'
of mankind — 'ihr sterbender Spion' (I. 29).
   The conception of the Grumbler as 'seer' is reflected in the abundance of visual motifs, which form pivotal points in his dialogue. The
verbal qualities of these scenes are in this way integrated with the
emphasis on visual effect which has been analysed above. Thus in an
early scene set in front of the War Ministry, the grotesque heads
carved in stone which embellish the façade of that building (Pl. 36) not
only provide a visual backdrop, but are also taken up by the Grumbler
as a satirical motif ('Die Masken an der Fassade dieser Sündenburg', I.
22). Equally important is the emphasis on posters. In I. 29 his eye is
caught by an advertisement for a performance of Mozart's *Requiem*,
which incorporates a conflated image of church window and military
mortar in its design. With characteristically visionary intuition he
deduces from it the godless hypocrisy of the age. The Optimist is not
entirely convinced:

> OPTIMIST (*nach einer Pause*): Ich denke, Sie haben recht. Aber weiß Gott,
> das sehen nur Sie. Unsereinem entgeht es und man sieht darum die
> Zukunft in rosigem Licht. Sie sehen es, und darum ist es da. Ihr Auge
> ruft es herbei und sieht's dann.
> NÖRGLER: Weil es kurzsichtig ist. Es gewahrt die Konturen, und
> Phantasie tut das übrige.

>   (I. 29)

36 Carved head by Wilhelm Hejda on the façade of the
Austrian War Ministry

(OPTIMIST (*after a pause*): I suppose you are right. But God knows, only
   you see that. It escapes people like me and so we see the future in a rosy
   light. You see it, and so it's there. Your eye calls it into being and then
   sees it.

GRUMBLER: Because it is short-sighted. It perceives the outlines, and
   imagination does the rest.)

Although the Optimist can dimly perceive the limitations of his own
horizon, he cannot transcend them. He is ultimately impervious to
the imaginative and moral challenge manifest in the Grumbler's
visionary subjectivity.

   Through the Grumbler Kraus challenges the blindness of normal
vision. The photograph of Berchtold with a quizzical smile
precipitates an impassioned confrontation of the faces of the ruling

class with those whom they have driven to despair and death (III. 41).
And the poster advertising the 'Wolf in Gersthof' is identified as a
portent, indeed as a cause of the holocaust:

> OPTIMIST: Mein Gott, so ein Plakat — das besagt nichts weiter als —
> NÖRGLER: — daß Millionen dahingehen mußten; er aber überlebt, ist
> überlebensgroß! Wenn aufs Jahr die Feinde kommen, die wern schaun!
> OPTIMIST: Ganz vermöchten Sie diese Verbindung zwischen einem
> Plakat und dem Weltkrieg doch nicht auszudenken.
> NÖRGLER: Usque ad finem! Wenn man die Plakate erschossen hätte,
> wären die Menschen erhalten geblieben.
> OPTIMIST: Ich vermag Ihnen auf diesem Gedankengang nicht zu folgen.
> (V. 42)

> (OPTIMIST: My God, a poster like that — it proves nothing except —
> GRUMBLER: — that millions had to go to their death; but the poster
> survives, it is larger than life! When the enemy arrive next year, they're
> in for a surprise!
> OPTIMIST: You wouldn't really be able to think this connection between
> a poster and the world war right through to its logical conclusion.
> GRUMBLER: *Usque ad finem!* If the posters had been shot dead, the human
> beings would have survived.
> OPTIMIST: I can't follow your train of thought.)

There can be no synthesis between the optimism of common sense
and the agonized vision of the satirical imagination. The Optimist
believes to the very end that the Grumbler is wildly exaggerating,
just as he did in Act I, Scene 29, when this same poster was first
discussed. He will never be able to perceive any meaning in the
notion of shooting a poster dead, nor even to guess at the spiritual
impulse which might lie behind so eccentric a formulation. And it
is this that drives the Grumbler into final despair and isolation: not
the folly of politicians, but the imperviousness of a man of good
will.

This is the heart of the tragedy. For these two characters,
apparently so antithetical, are profoundly dependent on each other.
The Optimist seeks of the Grumbler enlightenment as to the
condition of mankind; hence the insistence of his questions. The
Grumbler's need, unacknowledged but implicit in his whole
situation, is to emerge from the isolation to which his prophetic
vision condemns him and re-establish communication with mankind; hence the urgency of his replies. But their duologue issues (in
their final scene) in an unresolved antithesis between blithe optimism
and apocalyptic despair. And we are left with a double tragedy. On
the one hand an optimism born of blindness: 'Ich bin und bleibe
Optimist'; on the other, a vision from which no hope is born: 'Die
Welt geht unter, und man wird es nicht wissen' (V. 49). Thus in the

final isolation of his study (V. 54) the Grumbler describes the play
not as an act of faith in the future, but only as an atonement for the
past.

The tragic pathos of this final monologue certainly has
autobiographical undertones, particularly in the Grumbler's lament
for friends who have been killed in the war. But Kraus does not
identify the friends by name. His aim is to endow the position of the
Grumbler with exemplary significance. He is explicitly identified as
'Thersites' — the archetypal railer against the folly of war who in
Kraus's epic (unlike the Homeric original) is vindicated by events.
The Grumbler's indictment of war has a cumulative power. It begins
(in the Prologue) with a prophecy of divine retribution and ends with
a sense of horror that the prophecy has so gruesomely been fulfilled
(V. 54). But this prophetic stance owes as much to literary paradigms
as to personal experience. Shakespeare's Timon helped to shape
Kraus's initial reaction to the war (public reading of 12 December
1914), just as Horatio provided him with his concluding words in
November 1918 (F 499–500: 4). As a dramatic character the Grumbler bears traces of both these models. The creation of this character
involves a radical self-stylization.

Kraus tones down his own fallible political opinions in order to
enhance the archetypal vision of the seer. Key motifs which in *Die
Fackel* had been shrouded in ambiguity are now, with the wisdom of
hindsight, given a sharper critical focus. The bombardment of the
cathedral of Reims, which Kraus had obliquely justified in December
1914, is seen by the Grumbler as a 'stigma of barbarism' (I. 29). And
in the same scene Kraus's praise of the Imperial Proclamation of
Franz Joseph is now hedged with reservations. In Act IV, Scene 29,
the key phrase from the Proclamation is used with astringent irony
to demolish the paternalistic Franz Joseph myth. In Act II, Scene 10,
the Grumbler's political horizon was still obscured by the conception
of the 'enemy within'. By Act III, Scene 41, he is fiercely denouncing
Berchtold and leading members of the Habsburg dynasty for their
criminal irresponsibility. In the chronology of the drama this scene is
set towards the end of 1916. But it was actually added to the play *after*
the publication of the 'Akt-Ausgabe' in 1919, and reflects the new
conception of political responsibility which Kraus developed after
the fall of the Habsburg Monarchy.

Tragic Guilt and Political Responsibility

Who is to blame? This anguished interrogative runs right through
the Grumbler's speeches, from the Prologue ('War dies die Absicht
[. . .]?') to his final monologue with its myriad question marks (V.
54). These speeches do not offer a consistent answer, partly because

Kraus found the question so intractable, partly because his own attitude altered during the six years which separated the writing of the Prologue from the moment when he put the final touches to the play. The desire for some kind of cosmic answer is never entirely abandoned. The appeal to God in the Prologue ('Du großer Gott') finds at least a faint echo in the closing image of destiny divinely redeemed: 'So wahr Gott lebt — dies Schicksal wird nur durch ein Wunder heil!' (V. 54). But the longed-for miracle does not occur, and such moments of despairing faith are undercut by a Büchnerian sense that the universe has been abandoned by its creator. The *deus absconditus* motif is accentuated by a new passage which Kraus added after 1919 to one of the Grumbler's final scenes (B V. 42; cp. A V. 36). The wicked (the Grumbler declares) are able to mock the judge beyond the stars because his throne is so far away that his arm can no longer reach them.

If there is a suprapersonal pattern of meaning, it lies in the notion of collective guilt, for which the Grumbler finds such eloquent images. The 'Austrian face', ubiquitous embodiment of petty tyranny, leers at him from every side (IV. 29). But even here the argument is not consistent. The Grumbler is torn between this vision of the anonymity of evil and the desire to assign to named individuals a 'responsibility before the court of world history'. The phrase is applied to Emperor Franz Joseph in the very same scene. And this indictment of the Habsburg dynasty is extended (particularly in the final version of the play) to include a rogues' gallery of royal imbeciles. Archduke Friedrich, Commander-in-Chief of the Austro-Hungarian army, is repeatedly portrayed as mentally deficient (II. 28; III. 23); Franz Salvator and Max as frivolous hedonists (II. 25; V. 39); Emperor Karl as capable of uttering only moronic monosyllables (V. 37). And the Grumbler elaborates on these deficiencies, describing Franz Joseph as a 'demon of mediocrity', Friedrich as a 'cretin', Karl as 'simple-minded'. He is equally harsh on minor members of the dynasty: Karl Franz Josef, Augusta, Josef, Salvator, Annunziata, Blanka, Eugen, Max — even the hapless Rudolf, who ended his life at Mayerling (III. 41; V. 42). Franz Ferdinand too is now seen as a 'sombre' figure — 'der finstere Franz Ferdinand' (IV. 29). In these diatribes the only member of the dynasty who is allowed any human dignity is the unnamed homosexual who died in exile in Majorca. In the same scene (V. 42) the Grumbler suggests that the whole world war was fought for this one family — 'einen Weltkrieg für eine Familie'.

There are problems here of both internal and external consistency. Clearly, these speeches are totally different in tone from any reference to the dynasty that had appeared in *Die Fackel* before 1918.

This is due not only to the censorship, but to the fact that Kraus's earlier attitude to the dynasty really had been more respectful. Towards the end of the war his feelings radically altered, though it is difficult to put a precise date to his conversion from monarchist to republican. Of course any writer is entitled to change his mind in the light of changing circumstances. Given the political situation in 1920–1, when conspiracies to restore the Monarchy even led to an attempted *putsch* in Budapest by supporters of Emperor Karl, it was quite legitimate for Kraus to strengthen the anti-Habsburg satire in his play.

The problem of internal consistency is more difficult. How is the insistence on the 'responsibility' of certain named individuals to be squared with Kraus's more fundamental emphasis on collective guilt? The Grumbler's response to this problem is to subsume the individual figure of Franz Joseph under a mythopoeic image of the Habsburg 'daemon' ('Dämon', IV. 29). But this merely adds to the mystery — indeed it appears to do no more than create an anti-myth to set against that legend of Habsburg 'Gemütlichkeit' which the Grumbler has demolished. By invoking the concept of a 'daemon' (ineluctable destiny), the Grumbler seems to preclude more rational political analysis.

Later in the same scene (IV. 29), however, the focus begins to shift – from tragic guilt to political responsibility. This is signalled by the switch from the singularity of satirical discourse to the plural of shared responsibility – from 'ich' to 'wir':

> NÖRGLER: [. . .] Wissen Sie, wofür wir jetzt büßen? Für die Ehrfurcht, zu der uns solche Gestalten herausgefordert haben!
>
> (IV. 29)

> (GRUMBLER: [. . .] Do you know what we are atoning for? For the reverence which such figures [as Archduke Friedrich] provoked in us!)

The use of the word 'we' brings the Grumbler out of his solitude into explicit association with a social class – the educated bourgeoise to which he and the Optimist belong. In the first version of the play the Optimist even emphasizes that the Grumbler has a private income (A III. 3). This detail is eliminated in the book edition (B II. 10), perhaps because Kraus felt that it gave too personal a definition to his satirical persona. But at the same time his revision of the Optimist/Grumbler scenes adds a new emphasis to the political culpability of the educated middle class.

This is made clear by the most important new Optimist/Grumbler scene to be added to the play after 1919 – B III. 41. The scene begins by focusing on the political responsibility of Berchtold. The Optimist's objection that Berchtold cannot be held personally to

blame for the consequences of the decision to invade Serbia leads the
Grumbler to redefine the whole question of political responsibility:

> OPTIMIST: Aber bedenken Sie, er ist doch nicht verantwortlich –
> NÖRGLER: Nein, nur wir sind es, die es ermöglicht haben, daß solche
>   Buben nicht verantwortlich sind für ihr Spiel. Wir sind es, daß wir in
>   einer Welt zu atmen ertragen haben, welche Kriege führt, für die sie
>   niemanden verantwortlich machen kann. [. . .] Größere Kretins als
>   unsere Staatsmänner sind doch –
> OPTIMIST: – die unserer Feinde?
> NÖRGLER: Nein, wir selbst.   (III. 41)

> (OPTIMIST: But surely he is not responsible –
> GRUMBLER: No, only we are, for we made it possible for knaves like
>   him to play a game for which they bore no responsibility. We are,
>   for we were prepared to live in a world which wages wars for which it
>   can make no one responsible. [. . .] Greater cretins than our statesmen
>   are —
> OPTIMIST: – those of our enemies?
> GRUMBLER: No, we ourselves.)

This incisive self-analysis goes beyond the mythopoeic notions of
'Austrian face' and 'Habsburg daemon'. It lays the burden of
responsibility squarely on the shoulders of the Austrian intelligentsia, whose political evasiveness Kraus himself had shared in the
years before 1914.

The change of perspective is fundamental. The satirist of *Die
Fackel*, particularly prior to 1914, is endowed with an aura of
self-righteousness. He characteristically stands aloof from the follies
of his fellow men and repudiates all compromising affiliations. But
the Preface to *Die letzten Tage*, presumably written at the end of 1918
(and subsequently expanded), strikes a different note. Here the
author offers his play as an unqualified confession of complicity in
the guilt of mankind ('ein so restloses Schuldbekenntnis, dieser
Menschheit anzugehören'). Indeed, the very decision to put an image
of his own position, however stylized, into the play implies an
acceptance of shared responsibility. Kraus could after all have cast his
commentary in the form of a 100-page Preface, in the manner of
Bernard Shaw. Instead, he shows that even the most far-sighted
critic cannot escape the social nexus. The Grumbler's role is not
merely that of Chorus. He is also a citizen.

The strands of this self-indictment are drawn together in the final
monologue. At first the Grumbler seems here to be adopting a stance
of authorial superiority. But at crucial points there is again a switch
into the plural form of collective responsibility. The tyranny of the
war (the Grumbler claims) is not that of individual tyrants. Its spirit
derives from the minds of the masses. It is in ourselves, he insists,

that the capacity to create new tyrants lies. Our technological civilization, rendered uniquely vulnerable by its apparatus of propaganda, is in the process of destroying itself:

> Invalide waren wir durch die Rotationsmaschinen, ehe es Opfer durch Kanonen gab. Waren nicht alle Reiche der Phantasie evakuiert, als jenes Manifest der bewohnten Erde den Krieg erklärte? [. . .] Nicht daß die Presse die Maschinen des Todes in Bewegung setzte – aber daß sie unser Herz ausgehöhlt hat, uns nicht mehr vorstellen zu können, wie das wäre: das ist ihre Kriegsschuld!

(V. 54)

> (We were crippled by the newspaper printing presses before the cannons claimed their first victims. Hadn't all the territories of the imagination been evacuated, when that Proclamation declared war on the inhabited earth? [. . .] The war guilt of the press is not that it set the machinery of death in motion, but that it hollowed out our hearts so that we could no longer imagine what it was going to be like!

The argument is familiar to us from 'In dieser großen Zeit'. What is new is the Grumbler's admission of his own guilt. He identifies himself with a whole generation of intellectuals who failed to bring their gifts of mind and imagination to bear on politics until it was too late. And he acknowledges that those who responded to the dignified words of the Imperial Proclamation were just as guilty as those who succumbed to cruder forms of propaganda. Thus the Grumbler reinforces that confession of complicity that Kraus himself offers in his Preface. The voice of *saeva indignatio* now has undertones of *mea culpa*.

The role of the Grumbler does not simply reflect the satirist's preoccupations of 1914–18. It signals that new sense of political commitment which was to inspire Kraus during the second half of his career (to be dealt with in a subsequent volume). From 1919 onwards he abandoned the stance of political ambivalence which characterizes his earlier work and became an uncompromising campaigner for democratic rights and freedoms. His sense of political responsibility led Kraus in February 1919 to throw his support behind the Social Democrats in the elections for the newly constituted Austrian National Assembly (*F* 508–13: 30–2). The Socialists were returned as the largest single party, and a Social Democrat – Karl Renner – was elected first Chancellor of the Austrian Republic.

As a result of the horrific events of the war Kraus had moved from one end of the political spectrum towards the opposite extreme. But we have seen from our analysis – both of the subtext of *Die Fackel* and of the change of paradigm in *Die letzten Tage* – that this ideological reorientation was a protracted and painful process. The outspokenness of Kraus's new republican stance must not lead us to forget how reluctant his conversion had been. His new position was more that of a disillusioned conservative than an unconditional commitment to egalitarian politics. It contained unresolved contradictions which were to re-emerge a decade later when the Austrian Republic was in its turn threatened with collapse. Kraus's support in 1934 for the authoritarian regime of Chancellor Dollfuss was to confirm the underlying truth of his own observation in October 1917 that his conservative standpoint was 'displaced', rather than repudiated. But that is another story.

REFERENCE NOTES
BIBLIOGRAPHICAL NOTE
INDEXES

REFERENCE NOTES

PART ONE

Chapter 1

1 Erich Heller, *The Disinherited Mind* (Cambridge 1952), 200.
2 J. P. Stern, 'Grillparzer's Vienna' in *German Studies. Presented to W. H. Bruford*
   . . . (London 1962), 177. For a fuller account see Dorothy Prohaska, *Raimund and Vienna* (Cambridge 1970).
3 See William Weber, *Music and the Middle Class – The Social Structure of Concert Life in London, Paris and Vienna* (London 1976).
4 *Das Burgtheater und sein Publikum*, ed. Margret Dietrich (Vienna 1976), 216, 238.
5 Bruno Walter, *Theme and Variations* (London 1947), 149–50.
6 Kraus's victims are identified in Dieter Kimpel's edition of *Die demolirte Literatur* (Steinbach 1972).
7 Stefan Zweig, *The World of Yesterday* (London 1943). For more critical accounts, see Carl E. Schorske, *Fin-de-Siècle Vienna: Politics and Culture* (Cambridge 1981); Allan Janik and Stephen Toulmin, *Wittgenstein's Vienna* (London 1973).
8 Arnold Schoenberg, letter to Gustav Mahler, 5 July 1910, in Schoenberg, *Letters*, ed. Erwin Stein, trans. E. Wilkins and E. Kaiser (London 1964), 296.
9 Oskar Kokoschka, *My Life*, trans. D. Britt (London 1974), 28–9.
10 Kokoschka, *My Life*, 35.
11 Café Frauenhuber, 11/12 Nov. 1913: Karl Kraus, Georg Trakl, Philipp Berger and Ernst Deutsch (jointly signed a greeting to Ludwig von Ficker). 20 Nov. 1913: Karl Kraus, Lenz, Georg Trakl, D. Seitz, Albert Ehrenstein, Ernst Deutsch, Henny Herz, Adolf Loos, Dirsztay, Paul Engelmann, Hans Brecka and (?) G. W. Buding signed a similar greeting. See Georg Trakl, *Dichtungen und Briefe* (Salzburg 1969), 308, 310. Casino de Paris, early May 1906: Kraus was sitting with Erich Mühsam and Egon Friedell. The rival group included Henry (director of the Cabaret Nachtlicht), Marya Delvard, Arthur Holitscher and Roda Roda. Peter Altenberg was sitting at a separate table. See press cutting from *Wiener Allgemeine Zeitung*, filed with Kraus's letters to Bertha Maria Denk, Deutsches Literaturarchiv, Marbach (78/458/13).
12 Kraus to Maximilian Harden, 7 Apr. 1899 (Bundesarchiv, Koblenz); Kraus to Frank Wedekind, 21 Oct. 1906 (Stadtbibliothek, Munich).
13 See the pioneering study by Oscar Jaszi, *The Dissolution of the Habsburg Monarchy* (Chicago 1929).
14 For an account which relates the Austro-Hungarian anomalies to a wider European pattern, see Norman Stone, *Europe Transformed 1878–1919* (London 1983).
15 See John W. Boyer, *Political Radicalism in Late Imperial Vienna: The Origins of the Christian Social Movement 1848–1897* (Chicago 1981).
16 For full details see *Die Habsburgermonarchie 1848–1918*, ed. Adam Wandruschka and Peter Urbanitsch, 3 vols. (Vienna 1973–80), III. 56–73, 880–984.
17 See Marsha L. Rozenblit, *The Jews of Vienna 1868–1914* (Albany, N.Y. 1983), ch. 5.
18 Louis Eisenmann, author of the chapter on Austria-Hungary in *The Cambridge Modern History*, vol. XII (Cambridge 1910), 212.

19 Henry Wickham Steed, *The Hapsburg Monarchy* (London 1913), esp. the 'Conclusion'.

20 Zweig, *World of Yesterday*, esp. ch. 1.

21 Ilsa Barea, *Vienna* (London 1966), 332.

22 Emil Kläger, *Durch die Wiener Quartiere des Elends und des Verbrechens* (Vienna 1908). The book contains 75 photographs (by Hermann Drawe) illustrating the appalling living conditions and sleeping quarters of the destitute. It is based on a series of public lectures delivered at the Urania cultural institute.

23 For example Alfons Petzold, *Das rauhe Leben* (Berlin 1920); Adelheid Popp, *Die Jugendgeschichte einer Arbeiterin* (Munich 1930).

24 See Felix Salten, *Das österreichische Antlitz* (Berlin n.d. [1909]).

25 More than 30 different parties were represented in the Reichsrat, which was consequently rendered unworkable. The 87 Social Democrats elected included 50 Germans, 23 Czechs, 7 Poles, 5 Italians and 2 Ruthenes. See C.A. Macartney, *The Habsburg Empire, 1790–1918* (London 1968), 794.

26 See William A. Jenks, *Vienna and the Young Hitler* (New York 1960); P.G.J. Pulzer, *The Rise of Political Antisemitism in Germany and Austria* (New York 1964).

27 Emile Durkheim, *Suicide: A Study in Sociology* (London 1952). This book, first published in 1897, emphasizes the particularly high suicide rate in Vienna (pp. 87–8) and in the Austrian army (p. 238). For Durkheim's account of the social factors leading to 'anomic suicide' see ch. 5 (esp. p. 253).

28 See Albert Fuchs, *Geistige Strömungen in Österreich* (Vienna 1949); William Murray Johnston, *The Austrian Mind: An Intellectual and Social History 1848–1938* (Berkeley 1972); *Das größere Österreich: Geistiges und soziales Leben von 1880 bis zur Gegenwart*, ed. Kristian Sotriffer (Vienna 1982).

29 See Vladimir Dedijer, *The Road to Sarajevo* (London 1967).

30 Ferdinand Tremel, *Wirtschafts- und Sozialgeschichte Österreichs von den Anfängen bis 1955* (Vienna 1969), 369. See also David F. Good, *The Economic Rise of the Habsburg Empire 1750–1914* (Berkeley 1984), which concludes (p. 256) that the Empire was economically successful but failed to adapt its superstructure to modern economic growth.

31 Hermann Bahr, *Austriaca* (Berlin 1911), 34; Adolf Loos, 'Ornament und Verbrechen' (1908), in *Sämtliche Schriften*, ed. Franz Glück (Vienna 1962), 280.

32 See Norman Stone, *The Eastern Front 1914–1917* (London 1975), chs. 4 and 6.

33 Steed, *Hapsburg Monarchy*, 59, 205.

34 Leon Trotsky, *My Life: An Attempt at an Autobiography* (Harmondsworth 1975). Ch. 16 describes Trotsky's exile in Vienna between 1907 and 1914.

35 Friedrich Heer, *Der Kampf um die österreichische Identität* (Vienna 1981), 277.

36 Bruno Bettelheim, 'The Child's Perception of the City', in *Literature and the American Urban Experience: Essays on the City and Literature*, ed. Michael C. Jaye and Ann Chalmers Watts (Manchester 1981), 225.

37 See Germaine Goblot, 'Les Parents de Karl Kraus', *Études Germaniques*, V, no. 1 (Jan.–Mar. 1950), 43–53.

38 Loos, *Sämtliche Schriften*, 153–6.

39 *Das Burgtheater und sein Publikum*, 401–20. So serious were the defects that the theatre had to be closed in 1897 so that the auditorium could be reconstructed and the lyre form eliminated.

40 The buildings of the Ringstrasse are exhaustively described in *Die Wiener Ringstraße: Bild einer Epoche*, 11 vols. (Wiesbaden 1970–80). For a more succinct account see Schorske, *Fin-de-Siècle Vienna*, ch. 2.

41 *Das Burgtheater und sein Publikum*, 99, 177.

42 For details of Sonnenthal's career see *Adolf von Sonnenthals Briefwechsel*, 2 vols.

(Stuttgart 1912), a publication which Kraus extravagantly praised (*F* 391–2: 31–40).

43 *Das Burgtheater und sein Publikum*, 383, 452.
44 Zweig, *World of Yesterday*, 23.
45 Elias Canetti, *Die gerettete Zunge: Geschichte einer Jugend* (Munich 1977), 37–8.
46 Salten, *Das österreichische Antlitz*, 147–50.
47 Hermann Bahr, *Wien* (Stuttgart 1906), 73; *Austriaca*, 197–8.
48 See K. F. Nowak, *Alexander Girardi* (Berlin 1908), 73. The Girardi cult is perceptively analysed in Barea, *Vienna*, 320–2.
49 Hermann Broch, *Hugo von Hofmannsthal and his Time* (Chicago 1984). See also Edward Timms, 'Hofmannsthal, Kraus and the "Theatrum mundi"', in *Hugo von Hofmannsthal: Commemorative Essays*, ed. W. E. Yuill and Patricia Howe (London 1981), 123–32.
50 H. von Hofmannsthal/Eberhard von Bodenhausen, *Briefe der Freundschaft*, ed. Dorothea von Bodenhausen (Düsseldorf 1953), 144 (letter of 30 Apr. 1912).
51 Fritz Stern, 'Bismarck and his Banker', *Times Literary Supplement*, 5 Nov. 1976, 1390. The full story is told in Fritz Stern, *Gold and Iron: Bismarck, Bleichröder and the Building of the German Empire* (London 1977).
52 For a vivid account of the riots in protest against Badeni's language ordinances, see A. J. P. Taylor, *The Habsburg Monarchy* (London 1955), 179–84.
53 See Fritz Fischer, *Krieg der Illusionen* (Düsseldorf 1969), ch. 9.
54 See Frederic Morton, *A Nervous Splendour: Vienna 1888/1889* (London 1980).
55 For the legal background to duelling see Rolf-Peter Janz and Klaus Laermann, *Arthur Schnitzler: Zur Diagnose des Wiener Bürgertums im Fin de siècle* (Stuttgart 1977), ch. 8: Zur Sozialgeschichte des Duells.
56 Arthur Schnitzler, *Die erzählenden Schriften* (Frankfurt 1961), I. 717.
57 Peter Heller, 'A Quarrel about Bisexuality', in *The Turn of the Century: German Literature and Art 1890–1915*, ed. Gerald Chapple and Hans H. Schulte (Bonn 1981), 87–115.
58 Peter Gay, *Freud, Jews and Other Germans* (New York 1978), 32–3.

Chapter 2

1 See Raymond Williams, *The Long Revolution* (London 1961), Pt. ii, ch. 3: The Growth of the Popular Press.
2 See Piers Brendon, *The Press Barons* (London 1982).
3 The Spanish-American War of 1898 was precipitated by the Hearst press, which whipped up such public hysteria after the accidental sinking of the *Maine*, an American ship anchored in Havana harbour, that a reluctant President McKinley was obliged to declare war. See W. A. Swanberg, *Citizen Hearst* (London 1962).
4 See Paul M. Kennedy, *The Rise of the Anglo-German Antagonism 1860–1914* (London 1980).
5 See Stephen Koss, *The Rise and Fall of the Political Press in Britain*, 2 vols. (London 1984); David Ayerst, *Guardian – Biography of a Newspaper* (London 1971).
6 Otto Groth, *Die unerkannte Kulturmacht: Grundlegung der Zeitungswissenschaft*, 5 vols. (Berlin 1960); Kurt Koszyk, *Deutsche Presse im 19. Jahrhundert* (Geschichte der deutschen Presse, Teil II) (Berlin 1966).
7 See Günter Heidorn, *Monopole – Presse – Krieg: Die Rolle der Presse bei der Vorbereitung des Ersten Weltkriegs* (East Berlin 1960).
8 Steed, *Hapsburg Monarchy*, 182–3.
9 Hugo Hantsch, *Die Geschichte Österreichs*, 2 vols. (Graz 1947), II. 473.

10   Joseph Maria Baerenreither, *Der Verfall des Habsburgerreiches und die Deutschen* (Vienna 1939), 137.

11   Hans Tietze, *Die Juden Wiens* (Vienna 1933), 210.

12   Tietze, *Die Juden Wiens*, 211–12. For a detailed account of the corrupt financial operations of the press, see Josef Reich, 'Die Wiener Presse und der Wiener Börsenkrach' (diss., Vienna 1947).

13   Steed, *Hapsburg Monarchy*, 187.

14   Kurt Paupié, *Handbuch der österreichischen Pressegeschichte, 1848–1959*, vol. I (Vienna 1960).

15   Quoted in Barea, *Vienna*, 212.

16   Ferdinand Kürnberger, 'Die Geschichte meines Passes' (*F* 214–15: 7–38).

17   Ferdinand Kürnberger, *Siegelringe* (Munich 1909), 200.

18   Kürnberger, *Siegelringe*, 544; 211–12.

19   See Daniel Spitzer, *Gesammelte Werke*, ed. Max Kalbeck and Otto Erich Deutsch, 5 vols. (Munich 1912), esp. vol. II (which reprints Spitzer's ineffectual feuilletons on the financial scandals of 1873).

20   A letter written by Kraus to a Viennese lady in 1893, asking her to use her influence to gain him a post as theatre critic on the newly founded *Neues Wiener Journal*, is printed in *Forum*, VI, no. 64 (Apr. 1959), 151.

21   See Michael Werner, *Genius und Geldsack: Zum Problem des Schriftstellerberufs bei Heinrich Heine* (Hamburg 1978).

22   The figure of 30,000 copies (*F* 2: 2) means that *Die Fackel* initially outsold newspapers like the *Arbeiter-Zeitung* (24,000 copies in 1900) and the *Reichspost* (only 6,000 copies). The largest circulations were those of the *Neues Wiener Tagblatt* (65,000) and *Neue Freie Presse* (55,000). See Paupié, *Handbuch* I. For Kraus's imitators, see Martina Bilke, *Zeitgenossen der 'Fackel'* (Vienna 1981), 109–40. The cover design of *Die Fackel* had to be abandoned when it was pirated by Kraus's first printer, who had registered it in his own name (*F* 82: 29–31).

23   Jonathan Swift, *Correspondence*, ed. H. Williams, vol. IV (Oxford 1965), 138.

24   Alfred Pfabigan, *Karl Kraus und der Sozialismus* (Vienna 1976), 41–73.

25   Leszek Kolakowski, *Main Currents of Marxism*, vol. II: *The Golden Age* (Oxford 1981). The Marxist debate around 1900 was tremendously rich and varied, but it centred on the 'materialism' of Engels (p. 3).

26   Paupié, *Handbuch* I. 160; Steed, *Hapsburg Monarchy*, 191; Arthur J. May, *The Habsburg Monarchy 1867–1914* (Cambridge, Mass. 1951), 97.

27   Herzl's dandified appearance is emphasized in memoirs of the period (Zweig, *World of Yesterday*, 88). It was not merely a personal foible. Herzl's aim was to make Zionism, which had originated among eastern zealots, respectable in the eyes of western supporters. At the first Zionist conference in 1897 he insisted on delegates wearing top hats and tail-coats (Morton, *Nervous Splendour*, 307).

28   *Urkunden und Akten zur Geschichte der Juden in Wien*, ed. A. F. Pribram, vol. I (Vienna 1918), 582–6.

29   'Prohaska: Nicht eruiert', in Franz Ögg, *Personenregister zur Fackel* (Frankfurt n.d.). 'Prohaska' was the popular nickname for Emperor Franz Joseph.

30   Quoted in Bilke, *Zeitgenossen der 'Fackel'*, 16.

31   Henri Bergson, *Laughter: An Essay on the Meaning of the Comic* (London 1911).

32   J.G. Merquior, *The Veil and the Mask: Essays on Culture and Ideology* (London 1979).

33   See Hans-Heinrich Wilhelm, 'Houston Stewart Chamberlain und Karl Kraus. Ein Bericht über ihren Briefwechsel 1901–1904', in *Zeitgeschichte*, X, no. 11–12 (Aug./Sept. 1983), 405–34.

Chapter 3

1 Jonathan Swift, *The Examiner and Other Pieces* (Oxford 1940), 141.
2 F.R. Leavis, *The Common Pursuit* (London 1958), 86: The Irony of Swift.
3 Matthew Hodgart, *Satire* (London 1969), 12.
4 Compare the persiflage on the name 'Theobald' in Alexander Pope, *Poems* (Twickenham Edition), vol. V (London 1963), 206.
5 For an analysis of similar tendencies in England, see Q.D. Leavis, *Fiction and the Reading Public* (London 1932).
6 *F* 183–4: 40; 156: 11–12. A key witness, Rudolf Holzer, whose case against the director of the Volkstheater Kraus had also taken up, failed to support Kraus in court (he later acknowledged that Kraus had been in the right; *F* 387–8: 24).
7 Robert F. Arnold, *Das deutsche Drama* (Munich 1925), 640–2; *Das Burgtheater und sein Publikum*, 391.
8 Bahr's diary is quoted in Erich Widder, *Hermann Bahr: Sein Weg zum Glauben* (Linz 1963), 90; see also *The Complete Diaries of Theodor Herzl*, ed. Raphael Patai, vol. III (New York 1960), 863.
9 See C. G. Jung, *Four Archetypes* (London 1972), 135–52.
10 See Edward Timms, 'Archetypal Patterns in the Satire of Karl Kraus', in *Karl Kraus in neuer Sicht: Londoner Kraus-Symposium*, ed. Sigurd Paul Scheichl and Edward Timms (Munich 1986), 92–107.
11 Walter Benjamin, *Angelus Novus* (Frankfurt 1966), 375.
12 Arthur Schnitzler, *Tagebuch 1913–1916*, ed. Werner Welzig (Vienna 1983), 240.
13 C. G. Jung, *Psychological Types*, trans. H. Godwin Baynes (London 1944), 555–60: definition of 'primordial image/archetype' ('Urbild/Archetypus'). And see Northrop Frye, *Anatomy of Criticism* (Princeton 1957); *Fables of Identity: Studies in Poetic Mythology* (New York 1963).
14 The motif of the 'Great Boyg' recurs in other contexts in an inverted form (*F* 104: 21; 292: 18). Kraus's attachment to *Peer Gynt* is indicated by the fact that he included scenes from the play in his public readings (for example, 17 Oct. 1921; *F* 577–82: 73).
15 It was at a public reading on 19 Nov. 1914 that Kraus included passages from Revelation. Ch. 8, verse 10 of that Book establishes the connection between *Die Fackel* and apocalyptic prophecy: 'Es fiel ein großer Stern vom Himmel, der brannte wie eine Fackel' (Luther's version) (*F* 404: 20; cf. *F* 546–50: 78). The torch in Kraus's original cover design derives from the emblems of classical mythology. See the torch depicted on the Column of Antoninus, reproduced in *Harper's Dictionary of Classical Literature and Antiquities* (London 1897), 664; also the torch carried by Prometheus, reproduced in *Ausführliches Lexikon der griechischen und römischen Mythologie*, ed. W. H. Roscher, vol. III (Leipzig 1902–9), 3102. The archetypal undertones of Kraus's 'Torch' become clear when one compares it with the cover design of Rochefort's *La Lanterne*, which is said to have influenced his choice of title. Rochefort's yellow cover depicts an actual lantern (an object of practical utility in Victorian households). This point is misrepresented in Werner Kraft, 'Henri Rochefort und Karl Kraus', *Forum*, VI, no. 64 (Apr. 1959), 158.
16 See Henrik Ibsen, *Peer Gynt*, trans. Christian Morgenstern (Volksausgabe von Ibsens Sämtlichen Werken, Berlin n.d.), 459–61. Kraus read the play in this translation and in May 1902 drew attention to the enigmatic figure of 'die Grüngekleidete' (*F* 104: 21).
17 See R. C. Elliott, *The Power of Satire: Magic, Ritual, Art* (Princeton 1960). The Timon archetype is traced back to its source in Gerhard Hay, *Darstellung des Menschenhasses in der deutschen Literatur des 18. und 19. Jahrhunderts* (Frankfurt

1970). Goethe's poem 'Der Zauberlehrling' derives from a motif in the work of Lucian of Samosata (see J. W. von Goethe, *Werke*, ed. Erich Trunz, vol. I (Munich 1981), 666).

18 Mechtild Borries, *Ein Angriff auf Heinrich Heine: Kritische Betrachtungen zu Karl Kraus* (Stuttgart 1971), 88–101.

19 The revival of apocalyptic motifs in modern writing is analysed in Frank Kermode, *The Sense of an Ending: Studies in the Theory of Fiction* (London 1967); Joachim Metzner, *Persönlichkeitszerstörung und Weltuntergang* (Tübingen 1976).

20 The popular panic is documented in Friedrich Archenhold, *Kometen, Weltuntergangsprophezeiungen und der Halleysche Komet* (Berlin 1910); Nigel Calder, *The Comet is Coming* (London 1980).

PART TWO

Chapter 4

1 Christian Broda, 'Legal Reforms', *Austria Today*, IV (Autumn 1978), 26–9.

2 *Arbeiter-Zeitung*, 1 Nov. 1904. Earlier reports appeared on 19, 25 and 26 June and 29, 30 and 31 Oct. 1904.

3 'I Durchschaudi' was the pseudonym used for the first newspaper article on the affair. Kraus met Frau Hervay after her release from prison and was obliged to admit that she was less of a *femme fatale* than he had supposed (F 186: 17).

4 See Mario Praz, *The Romantic Agony* (London 1933); Patrick Bade, *Femme Fatale: Images of Evil and Fascinating Women* (London 1979).

5 A. Schopenhauer, *Sämtliche Werke*, ed. W. von Löhneysen, 5 vols. (Stuttgart 1960–5), V. 719–35 ('Über die Weiber'); F. Nietzsche, *Werke in drei Bänden*, ed. Karl Schlechta (Munich 1966), II. 701–4.

6 Richard Hamann and Jost Hermand, *Naturalismus* (Munich 1972), 65–71: Venus Vulgivaga.

7 See Nike Wagner, *Geist und Geschlecht: Karl Kraus und die Erotik der Wiener Moderne* (Frankfurt 1982).

8 Otto Weininger, *Geschlecht und Charakter* (Vienna 1903), xix, 288.

9 Letter from Marie Wagner, dated 19 Jan. [? 1894], Vienna City Library, Ib 163.325.

10 Zweig, *World of Yesterday*, 72.

11 The story is recorded in a hand-written note by Kraus's friend Mary Dobrzensky, explaining a phrase in a letter he wrote to her on 16/17 May 1935 (Deutsches Literaturarchiv, Marbach, 73.1160/13).

12 Richard Ellmann, *James Joyce* (Oxford 1982), 377.

13 *Minutes of the Vienna Psychoanalytic Society*, ed. Herman Nunberg and Ernst Federn, trans. M. Nunberg, 4 vols. (New York 1962–75), II. 390 (contribution by Max Graf).

14 Wagner, *Geist und Geschlecht*, 102.

15 The list of Annie Kalmar's personal possessions, auctioned after her death, is preserved in the Vienna City Library (IN 137.975). It includes about 30 items of rather elaborate jewellery. Although 15,000 Marks was not a negligible sum, Annie's final illness was aggravated by financial anxieties (which Kraus helped to alleviate).

16 Margarete Mitscherlich-Nielsen, 'Sittlichkeit und Kriminalität: Psycho-analytische Bemerkungen zu Karl Kraus', in *Text + Kritik: Sonderband Karl Kraus*, ed. Heinz Ludwig Arnold (Munich 1975), 27; Manfred Schneider, *Die Angst und das Paradies des Nörglers: Versuch über Karl Kraus* (Frankfurt 1977).

17 Kraus's letter to Annie Kalmar of 2 Jan. 1901 conveys his emotional turmoil: 'Das Wirrsal von Gefühlen – bange Erwartung, Besorgnis, Hoffnung, Verzweiflung, Freude' (Vienna City Library, IN 136. 166). Three other letters from Kraus and ten written by Annie in reply give a vivid impression of the warmth and intimacy of the relationship, and of the great strain placed upon them by separation and illness.

18 Kraus's letters to Bertha Maria Denk are in the Deutsches Literaturarchiv, Marbach, and are referred to hereafter by date and catalogue number. His letters to Wedekind are in the Stadtbibliothek, Munich, and Wedekind's letters to Kraus, printed with some omissions in F 521–30: 101–35, are in the Stadtbibliothek, Vienna.

19 Hugh Salvesen, 'A Pinch of Snuff from Pandora's Box: New Light on Karl Kraus and Frank Wedekind', Oxford German Studies, no. 12 (1981), 122–38.

20 Kraus to Bertha Maria Denk, 10 July 1906 (78/456/17); 28 Sept. 1906 (conjectured date) (78/456/20); book list (78/457/3 – second sheet).

21 Letter of 10 July 1906 (78/456/17).

22 Kraus to Bertha Maria Denk, 9 May 1906 (78/456/14). In addition to Annie Kalmar and Bertha Maria Denk, Kraus is known to have had liaisons with the actresses Irma Karczewska and Kete Parsenow. See Wagner, Geist und Geschlecht, 136.

23 See Frank Wedekind, Gesammelte Werke, 9 vols. (Munich 1920–1), I. 61; picture postcard to Wedekind, 28 Aug. 1905, signed by Kraus and 'Gräfin Potocka'; letter from Kraus to Bertha Maria Denk, 28 Sept. 1906 (?) (78/456/20); book list (78/457/3 – first sheet).

24 Letter to Bertha Maria Denk, 1 Apr. 1907 (78/456/6).

25 This aphorism reformulates a passage from an undated letter to Bertha Maria Denk (? Mar. 1908) (78/457/10).

26 Letters of (?) Mar. 1908 (78/457/10); 7 Apr. 1907 (78/457/6).

27 For the alternative version of the Pandora myth, see Dora and Erwin Panofsky, Pandora's Box: The Changing Aspects of a Mythological Symbol (New York 1965).

28 J. J. Bachofen, Das Mutterrecht (Stuttgart 1861), xix, 241–2.

29 Bachofen, Das Mutterrecht, xviii, 167.

30 Dr Heinrich Grün, Prostitution in Theorie und Wirklichkeit (Vienna/Leipzig 1907). Drawing on his experience as a doctor in one of the less salubrious quarters of Vienna, Grün emphasizes that the low wages paid to women working in restaurants and places of entertainment virtually forced them into prostitution.

31 Loos, Sämtliche Schriften, 157–64.

32 Letter to Bertha Maria Denk, 14/15 Mar. 1908 (78/457/9).

33 Pfabigan, Karl Kraus und der Sozialismus, 99.

34 S. Freud, Gesammelte Werke, ed. Anna Freud et al., 18 vols. (London: Imago Publishing Co., 1940–[1952]), VII 163; Standard Edition of the Complete Psychological Works, trans. . . . J. Strachey et al., 24 vols. (London: Hogarth Press, 1953–74), IX. 200. The two editions are cited hereafter as GW and SE respectively.

35 Germaine Greer, The Female Eunuch (London 1971), 16, 114.

36 Weininger, Geschlecht und Charakter, 452–8.

37 Reinhard Urbach, 'Karl Kraus und Arthur Schnitzler: Eine Dokumentation', Literatur und Kritik, no. 49 (October 1970), 513–30. For Schnitzler's treatment of the position of women, see Barbara Gutt, Emanzipation bei Arthur Schnitzler (Berlin 1978).

38 Schnitzler's diary for the year 1888 repeatedly gives details of his rendezvous with his girl-friend Jeanette Heger and of the number of times they made love, for example: 'August 25th, Saturday, Baden, near Vienna. Evening with Jean.

(5)'. The total recorded for the year as a whole was 400. See Morton, *Nervous Splendour*, 94, 186.
39 Arthur Schnitzler, *Jugend in Wien* (Munich 1971), 150; *Letters of James Joyce*, ed. S. Gilbert and R. Ellmann, 3 vols. (London 1957, 1966), II. 191–2.
40 See Wagner, *Geist und Geschlecht*, 136; Kokoschka, in *My Life*, 42.
41 See Hugh Salvesen, 'The Disappointed Idealist: August Strindberg in Karl Kraus's Periodical *Die Fackel*', *New German Studies*, IX, no. 3 (Autumn 1981), 157–79.

Chapter 5

1 See Thomas Szasz, *Karl Kraus and the Soul-Doctors: A Pioneer Critic and his Criticism of Psychiatry and Psychoanalysis* (London 1977). And see also Mitscherlich-Nielsen, 'Sittlichkeit und Kriminalität' in *Text + Kritik*; and Schneider, *Die Angst und das Paradies des Nörglers*.
2 Freud's letters are in the Vienna City Library, IN 109.723 *et seq.*
3 Pfabigan, *Karl Kraus und der Sozialismus*, 111, arbitrarily denies that Kraus had read Freud's work. Mitscherlich-Nielsen in *Text + Kritik*, 31, makes the opposite but equally unfounded assumption that he had read 'many works by Freud', including the paper on 'A Special Type of Choice of Object made by Men'.
4 Letter to Bertha Maria Denk dated (?) 6 March 1907 (78/457/5).
5 The child of 'psychoanalytical parents' was 'Little Hans', son of the music critic Max Graf, a member of the Psychoanalytic Society who had married one of Freud's patients. Kraus's aphorism refers to the passage in Freud's 'Analysis' where 'Little Hans' is questioned about his feelings on watching a horse defecate. Further instances are identified in Gilbert J. Carr, 'Karl Kraus and Sigmund Freud', *Irish Studies in Modern Austrian Literature*, ed. G.J. Carr and Eda Sagarra (Dublin 1982), 1–30.
6 Freud, *GW* VII. 148; *SE* IX. 185.
7 Freud, *GW* VII. 70; *SE* IX. 44.
8 Ernest Jones, *The Life and Work of Sigmund Freud*, 3 vols. (London 1953–7), II. 9; Szasz, *Karl Kraus and the Soul-Doctors*, 38.
9 *The Freud/Jung Letters*, ed. William McGuire, trans. R. Manheim and R.F.C. Hull (London 1974), 428, 476, 534–5, 541.
10 Wagner, *Geist und Geschlecht*, 136.
11 Schneider, *Die Angst und das Paradies des Nörglers*, 24–7.
12 *Freud/Jung Letters*, 491, 512.
13 Fritz Wittels, *Die sexuelle Not* (Vienna and Leipzig 1909), 83. The book actually appeared in November 1908.
14 *Minutes of the Vienna Psychoanalytic Society*, II. 89.
15 *Minutes*, II. 382–8.
16 Jones, *Life and Work of Freud*, II. 9; Szasz, *Karl Kraus and the Soul-Doctors*, 36; Schneider, *Die Angst und das Paradies der Nörglers*, 23.
17 *Minutes*, II. 391–2.
18 Fritz Wittels, *Ezechiel der Zugereiste* (Berlin 1910). The book contains caricatures of several members of Kraus's circle, including his secretary Karl Hauer (='Josef Windig'), to whom Wittels attributes the venomous words: 'Totschlagen soll man den Saujuden' ('The filthy Jew should be beaten to death') (p. 138).
19 *Minutes*, I. xxxvii; II. 476.
20 Cesare Lombroso, *Genie und Irrsinn*, trans. A. Courth (Leipzig 1887); P.J. Möbius, *Über Kunst und Künstler* (Leipzig 1901); *Goethe* (Leipzig 1903); *Über das*

Pathologische bei Nietzsche (Wiesbaden 1902); Max Nordau, *Entartung* (Berlin 1892); Ferdinand Probst, *Der Fall Otto Weininger: Eine psychiatrische Studie* (Wiesbaden 1904); S. Rahmer, *August Strindberg: Eine pathologische Studie* (Munich 1907). Kraus's comments on the book by Probst indicate that he is aware of the Lombroso–Möbius–Nordau genealogy of this approach to literature; cf. F 169: 6–10 (fn.) and 176: 22–4. The most forceful of his many attacks on Nordau (F 250: 8–10) shows that Kraus had a detailed knowledge of *Entartung*.

21 *Minutes*, I. 65–6 and 257; II. 103–4 and 224–5.
22 *Freud/Jung Letters*, 291.
23 *Minutes*, IV. 16. In a useful article on 'Karl Kraus und die Psychoanalyse', *Merkur*, no. 31 (1977), 158, Edwin Hartl argues that Freud's implicit approval of Graf's book may have been the decisive factor which alienated Kraus from Freud. This seems unlikely. Kraus's aphorism dealing with Graf's book (F 376–7: 21) is notably restrained in tone and contains no reference to Freud. He let Max Graf off more lightly than his fellow pathographers. Graf reciprocated by paying a generous tribute to Kraus on his fiftieth birthday (F 649–56: 112–13).
24 Freud, *GW* VIII. 202–4, 207; *SE* XI. 130–1, 134.
25 Freud, *GW* VII. 160; *SE* IX. 197.
26 Freud, *GW* VIII. 236–7, 417; *SE* XII. 224 and XIII. 187.
27 S. Freud, *Aus den Anfängen der Psychoanalyse: Briefe an Wilhelm Fliess . . . 1887–1902* (London 1950), 261 (letter of 9 Feb. 1898).
28 Pfabigan, *Karl Kraus und der Sozialismus*, 113; Szasz, *Karl Kraus and the Soul-Doctors*, 53.
29 Freud, *GW* I. 278; V. 289, 301–2, 315; IX. 10; XIV. 214. *SE* II. 276; VII. 283, 292, 302; XV. 17; XXX. 187–8.
30 Freud, *Aus den Anfängen der Psychoanalyse*, 254.
31 Freud, *GW* II/III. 518 (my own translation; cf. *SE* V. 514).
32 Freud, *GW* II/III. 237; *SE* IV. 232.
33 Freud, *GW* VII. 429–38; *SE* X. 209–20. Discrepancies between the 'Original Record' of the Rat Man case and the published version reveal the subjectivity of Freud's method. It was Freud himself who 'decided to tell' his patient that the rat is a penis symbol. But the published version suggests that this idea originated with the patient. Compare *SE* X. 214 and 311.
34 The details can be reconstructed from the *Freud/Jung Letters*. Freud and Jung were well aware that the psychological insight of Gross and Honegger was related to their mental instability. Freud's following also included two other suicides: Viktor Tausk (1919) and Herbert Silberer (1922).
35 Jones, *Life and Work of Freud*, II. 153.
36 Mitscherlich-Nielsen in *Text + Kritik*, 31–2, rebukes Kraus for supposing that psychoanalysis ever claimed to be able to explain the unconscious meaning of dreams without the co-operation of the dreamer. This betrays an ignorance of Stekel's work and of the difference between 'active' and 'passive' analysis to which Kraus alludes.
37 Jean Paul's *Levana oder Erziehungslehre* contains the most coherent exposition of his view of childhood (paras. 46–7 draw the contrast between 'Genuß' and 'Freudigkeit'). *Hesperus* and *Die Flegeljahre* contain striking descriptions of the innocence of childhood. The passage quoted here occurs at the beginning of a text which Kraus particularly admired, the 'Rede des toten Christus' from *Siebenkäs*, in *Jean Pauls Sämtliche Werke* (Historisch–kritische Ausgabe), 19 vols. (Berlin 1927–64), VI. 248.

38   Kraus's aphorism echoes the opening lines of a poem by Klaus Groth, which
     had become famous through a musical setting by Brahms:

     > O wüßt' ich doch den Weg zurück,
     > Den lieben Weg zum Kinderland!

     Brahms-Texte, ed. G. Ophüls, 2nd edn. (Berlin 1908), 151 (Opus 63, No. 8).
39   Freud, *GW* I. 497; II/III. 139; V. 127 note; IX. 188. *SE* III. 268; IV. 134; VII. 226
     note; XIII. 156–7 (emphasis added).
40   Freud, *GW* II/III. 127, 613; *SE* IV. 122 and V. 608.
41   'As early as 8 December 1912 he wrote to me that the political situation in
     Austria was stormy and they must be prepared for bad times ahead' (Jones, *Life
     and Work of Freud*, II. 189).
42   Freud, *GW* VII. 91; *SE* XI. 190.
43   Freud, *GW* IX. 171–91; *SE* XIII. 141–59.
44   Jones, *Life and Work of Freud*, II. 198–9.

Chapter 6

1   The Klimt controversy is analysed in Schorske, *Fin-de-Siècle Vienna*, 208–78.
2   Loos, *Sämtliche Schriften*, 153–6. The article first appeared in *Ver Sacrum* in July
     1898.
3   Loos, *Sämtliche Schriften*, 49 (reprinted from *Neue Freie Presse*, 19 June 1898).
4   See Nikolaus Pevsner, *Pioneers of the Modern Movement* (London 1936); Reyner
     Banham, *Theory and Design in the First Machine Age* (London 1960), esp. 88–97.
5   Loos, *Sämtliche Schriften*, 276–88.
6   John Ruskin, *The Seven Lamps of Architecture* (London 1849), 96 and 109–11.
7   Paul Engelmann, *Letters from Ludwig Wittgenstein with a Memoir* (Oxford 1967),
     122–32; Janik and Toulmin, *Wittgenstein's Vienna*; Dagmar Barnouw, 'Loos,
     Kraus, Wittgenstein and the Problem of Authenticity', in *The Turn of the
     Century*, ed. Gerald Chapple and Hans. H. Schulte (Bonn 1981), 249–73.
8   The design which Loos submitted for the new War Ministry is described in
     Ludwig Münz and Gustav Künstler, *Adolf Loos – Pioneer of Modern Design*
     (London 1966), 185–8.
9   Ruskin, *Seven Lamps*, 43 and 110. A similar holistic approach is evident in the
     work of Gottfried Semper, cited by Loos, *Sämtliche Schriften*, 55.
10   Ruskin, *Sesame and Lilies* (London 1865), 31–3; *Sesam und Lilien*, trans. Hedwig
     Jahn (Jena 1900), 53–6.
11   Loos, *Sämtliche Schriften*, 231.
12   Hermann Czech and Wolfgang Mistelbauer, *Das Looshaus* (Vienna 1977). See
     also Burkhard Rukschcio and Roland Schachel, *Adolf Loos: Leben und Werk*
     (Salzburg 1982).
13   Czech and Mistelbauer, *Das Looshaus*, 62–4. The author of this article in the
     Neue Freie Presse, Hugo Wittmann, was singled out by Kraus for special ridicule
     (*F* 313–14: 6).
14   Illustrated in Schorske, *Fin-de-Siècle Vienna*, 94.
15   Adolf Hitler, *Mein Kampf*, 2 vols. (Munich 1939), I. 56–8.
16   August Kubizek, *Young Hitler* (London 1954), 119, 133. Kubizek's account is
     confirmed by documents published in Franz Jetzinger, *Hitler's Youth* (London
     1958), which show that Hitler tried to earn his living in Vienna by copying and
     selling pictures of the monumental buildings on the Ringstrasse.
17   Schorske, *Fin-de-Siècle Vienna*, 24–45; Hitler, *Mein Kampf*, I. 75–6.

Chapter 7

1 Alison Lurie, *The Language of Clothes* (London 1981), 65–8: The Victorian Man and his Beard.
2 Janik and Toulmin, *Wittgenstein's Vienna*, 203.
3 Goethe's encounter with Gottsched is described in *Dichtung und Wahrheit*, Pt. ii, Bk. 7.
4 H. Heine, letter to Moses Moser, 14 Oct. 1826, in *Briefe 1815–1831*, ed. Fritz H. Eisner (Berlin 1970), 265. Herzl's reasons for growing a beard are recorded in *Das größere Österreich*, 90.
5 Intrus, *Deutschland im Spiegel des Marsbewohners Passyrion* (Rostock 1908), iv.
6 T. Carlyle, *Sartor Resartus* (London 1838), 224–5, 73. The affinity may be due to the fact that Carlyle, like Kraus, was indebted to the aesthetics of German Romanticism.
7 'The World of Posters', trans. Harry Zohn, in Karl Kraus, *In These Great Times* (Manchester 1984), 42–7. 'Die Welt der Plakate' has been reprinted as the introduction to an excellent anthology of Viennese posters, *Tagebuch der Straße*, ed. Bernhard Denscher (Vienna 1981).
8 K. Marx, *Capital*, vol. I (London 1977), ch. 1, sec. iv: The Fetishism of Commodities.
9 For a more systematic analysis of this motif, see Karl Riha, '"Heiraten" in der *Fackel*', in *Text + Kritik*, 116–26.
10 Kraus's source has been identified by Leo Lensing as *Österreichs Illustrierte Zeitung*, Kaiserfestnummer (1908): 'Die Österreichische Publizistik'. In this group photograph (itself a photocomposition) Benedikt is shown lording it over his fellow journalists like a monarch over his court.
11 *The Times*, 20 Mar. 1920, 15.

Chapter 8

1 *Quo vadis Austria: Ein Roman der Resignation*, von einem Oesterreichischen Offizier (Berlin 1913).
2 H.G. Wells, *Journalism and Prophecy*, ed. W. W. Wagar (London 1964).
3 See Günther Ramhardter, *Geschichtswissenschaft und Patriotismus: Österreichische Historiker im Weltkrieg 1914–1918* (Munich 1973).
4 See Borries, *Ein Angriff auf Heinrich Heine*.
5 Schorske, *Fin-de-Siècle Vienna*, 9.
6 Ruskin, *Sesame and Lilies*, 33; *Sesam und Lilien*, 56: 'Es gibt verhüllte Worte um uns her . . .'
7 Fritz Raddatz, *Verwerfungen* (Frankfurt 1972), 24–8.
8 *Die Zukunft*, 8 Aug. 1914, editorial; quoted in Hans Joachim Goebel, *Maximilian Harden als politischer Publizist im Ersten Weltkrieg* (Frankfurt 1977), 39.
9 J. W. von Goethe, *Faust*, trans. Bayard Taylor (London n.d.), 51 (ll. 860–3).
10 See William Bragg Ewald, *The Masks of Jonathan Swift* (Oxford 1954).

PART THREE

Chapter 9

1 Leopold Liegler, *Karl Kraus und sein Werk* (Vienna 1920), 403; Caroline Kohn, *Karl Kraus – le polémiste et l'écrivain* (Paris 1962), 336.

2   Georg Moenius, *Karl Kraus – der Zeitkämpfer sub specie aeterni* (Vienna 1937), 11.
3   Erich Mühsam, *Publizistik, Unpolitische Erinnerungen* (East Berlin 1978), 571–5.
4   Moenius, *Karl Kraus*, 11.
5   Kurt Wolff, *Autoren, Bücher, Abenteuer – Betrachtungen und Erinnerungen eines Verlegers* (Berlin n.d.), 98.
6   Friedrich Torberg, 'Zwischen Schmunzeln und Höllengelächter', *Forum*, I, no. 4 (Apr. 1954), 19.
7   Edwin Hartl, in *Austrian Literature*, X, no. 1 (Jan./Feb. 1966), 14; Heinrich Fischer, 'Some Personal Memories of Karl Kraus, Else Lasker-Schüler and Bertolt Brecht', a talk delivered in Oxford, Nov. 1964, unpub. TS, 31.
8   Helene Kann, 'Karl Kraus und sein Alltag', *Forum*, I, no. 4 (Apr. 1954), 21.
9   Helga Malmberg, *Widerhall des Herzens* (Munich 1961), 266.
10 Gina Kaus, *Und was für ein Leben* (Hamburg 1979), 122–32.
11 Letter of 11 July 1906 from Jule Stoeckl, in Vienna City Library, Ib. 163.325: *Briefe von Frauen an Karl Kraus*.
12 Unpub. letter of Kraus to Otto Stoessl, quoted by kind permission of Professor Franz Stoessl.
13 See Sigismund von Radecki, *Wie ich glaube* (Cologne 1953), 22; Berthold Viertel, 'Erinnerungen an Karl Kraus', *Lynkeus*, no. 3 (1948–51), 17.
14 Heller, *Disinherited Mind*, 200.
15 H.M.K. (= Helene Kann), 'Wie Karl Kraus arbeitete', in *Karl Kraus, Dokumente und Selbstzeugnisse* (Zurich n.d.), 17.
16 Heinrich Fischer, 'The Other Austria and Karl Kraus', in *In Tyrannos: Four Centuries of Struggle against Tyranny in Germany*, ed. H. J. Rehfisch (London 1944), 324.
17 Kann, 'Karl Kraus und sein Alltag', *Forum*, I, no. 4, 20.
18 Mitscherlich-Nielsen, 'Sittlichkeit und Kriminalität', in *Text + Kritik*, 24–5; *Minutes of the Vienna Psychoanalytic Society*, II. 391–2.
19 Hans Heinz Hahnl, 'Karl Kraus und das Theater' (diss., Vienna 1948); Hans Weigel, *Karl Kraus oder die Macht der Ohnmacht* (Vienna 1968); Kari Grimstad, *Masks of the Prophet: The Theatrical World of Karl Kraus* (Toronto 1982).
20 Goblot, 'Les Parents de Karl Kraus', *Études Germaniques* V, no. 1, 47; Karl Rosner, *Damals – Bilderbuch einer Jugend* (Düsseldorf 1948), 75–7.
21 Schneider, *Die Angst und das Paradies des Nörglers*, 79, 86, 94, 114.
22 Kokoschka, *My Life*, 47.
23 Willy Haas, *Die literarische Welt* (Munich 1957), 25.
24 Heinrich Fischer, 'Karl Kraus als Privatmann', *Hochland*, XLIV, no. 6 (Aug. 1952), 569ff.
25 Wolff, *Autoren, Bücher, Abenteuer*, 98.
26 Sebastian Brant, *Das Narrenschiff* (Tübingen 1962), 4: 'Vorred'; *The Ship of Fools*, trans. Edwin H. Zeydel (New York 1962), 60.
27 Walter Benjamin, *Illuminationen* (Frankfurt 1961), 397.
28 Quoted by Georg Brandes in Georg Brandes/Arthur Schnitzler, *Ein Briefwechsel*, ed. O. Seidlin (Bern 1956), 119.
29 Kraus's financial position can be reconstructed from unpublished documents in the Vienna City Library. His income for the years 1912–13 can be computed as follows: An agreement dated 1 Mar. 1912 gives his inherited unearned income as 1,000 Crowns per month (IN 169.774). In a letter to the Inspector of Taxes dated 27 Dec. 1913 (B 164.260), Kraus gives the following details of income and expenditure arising from the publication of *Die Fackel*:

Summe der Einnahmen	Ausgaben	
K 29,339.97	Telegramme	79.20
	Porti	85.26
	Zeitungen	51.85
	Spesen	311.95
	Steuern	1,048.61
	Diverse	112.71
	Jahoda & Siegel 14,	797.35

If we subtract his total expenses of 16,486.93 from his total earned income, the result is a profit during the given year of 12,853 Crowns (in addition to his private income of 12,000 Crowns). Kraus's privileged position may be contrasted with that of another aspiring author, Alfons Petzold (1882–1923), who in this same period had to make do with wages of between 20 and 40 Crowns a week as a manual labourer. See Petzold, *Das rauhe Leben* (reprinted Graz 1979), 148.

30 This business letterhead (Vienna City Library, IN 169.751) dates from 1903.
31 For further details of Kraus's financial inheritance, which included a quarter-share in the villa at Ischl, see Vienna City Library, IN 169.775.
32 Letter from Kraus to Bertha Maria Denk, 10 Aug. 1908 (Deutsches Literaturarchiv, Marbach, 78/457/20).
33 See Murray G. Hall, 'Verlage um Karl Kraus', *Kraus Hefte*, no. 26/27 (July 1983), 16.
34 See Ralf Dahrendorf, *Essays in the Theory of Society* (London 1968), ch. 2: 'Homo sociologicus'; Erving Goffman, *The Presentation of Self in Everyday Life* (London 1959).

Chapter 10

1 *The Works of Oscar Wilde*, ed. G.F. Maine (London 1961), 1018–43. The German text which Kraus read, *Der Sozialismus und die Seele des Menschen* (Berlin 1904), was translated (with Hedwig Lachmann) by the Utopian socialist Gustav Landauer.
2 Richard Ellmann, *Yeats: The Man and the Masks* (London 1961), 74.
3 *Works of Oscar Wilde*, 934. Cf. O. Wilde, *Fingerzeige*, trans. Felix Paul Greve (Minden 1903), which contains 'Der Verfall der Lüge', 'Stift, Gift, Schrifttum', 'Kunst als Kritik' and 'Die Wahrheit der Masken'. Kraus specifically commended Greve as translator of *Dorian Gray* (Minden 1903) (F 151: 18).
4 Frank Field, *The Last Days of Mankind: Karl Kraus and his Vienna* (London 1967), 22–3.
5 Field, *Last Days*, 22; *Nietzsche und die deutsche Literatur: Texte zur Nietzsche-Rezeption 1873–1963*, ed. Bruno Hillebrand (Tübingen 1978), 129.
6 Nietzsche, *Werke in drei Bänden*, I. 918.
7 Nietzsche, *Werke*, I. 210.
8 Nietzsche, *Werke*, I. 487; II. 604 (*Jenseits von Gut und Böse,* sec. 2, §40).
9 Nietzsche, *Werke*, II. 168–9.
10 Peter Altenberg, *Leben und Werk in Texten und Bildern*, ed. Christian Kosler (Munich 1981), 112–13.
11 A. Schnitzler, unpub. diary entry of 25 May 1896, quoted in his *Das Wort*, ed. Kurt Bergel (Frankfurt 1966), 7. Hugo von Hofmannsthal, *Gesammelte Werke in Einzelausgaben,* ed. Herbert Steiner, 15 vols. (Frankfurt 1956), Prosa, I. 274–5.
12 See Maurice Beebe, *Ivory Towers and Sacred Founts: The Artist as Hero in Fiction from Goethe to Joyce* (New York 1964).
13 Benjamin, *Illuminationen*, 195.

Chapter 11

1 Werner Kraft, *Karl Kraus: Beiträge zum Verständnis seines Werkes* (Salzburg 1956), contains a useful chapter on Kraus's 'Dream Poems'. But it is vitiated by the assumption that they may be regarded as 'real dreams' (p. 262) rather than literary constructs.

2 Kraus, letter to *Simplicissimus*, 8 July 1910, offering them 'Der Traum ein Wiener Leben', whose inspiration is defined as follows: 'Die Idee: die Unwahrscheinlichkeit des Wiener Daseins eingebettet in einen Traum'. Quoted in Friedrich Pfäfflin, 'Fackelrot am Münchener Himmel: Karl Kraus und Ludwig Thoma 1903–1921', in *Festschrift für Werner Goebel* (Munich 1980), 115.

3 Kraft, *Karl Kraus*, 265; Schneider, *Die Angst und das Paradies des Nörglers*, 110–14.

4 H. Heine, *Sämtliche Werke*, ed. Oskar Walzel, 10 vols. (Leipzig 1910–15), IV. 36–8; I. 204.

5 Gustav Janouch, *Gespräche mit Kafka* (Frankfurt 1961), 30.

6 For examples of Schönpflug's work, see *Die Muskete: Kultur- und Sozialgeschichte im Spiegel einer satirisch-humoristischen Zeitschrift*, ed. Murray G. Hall (Vienna 1983).

7 Heine, *Sämtliche Werke*, I. 107.

8 Kläger, *Durch die Wiener Quartiere des Elends und des Verbrechens*, contains vivid descriptions (with photographs) of the sleeping conditions of dossers in the 'Sammelkanal' and the 'Wienkanal'.

9 The case was sensationally reported in the *New York Times* of June and July 1909 (indexed under 'Chinatown'). It came to light when the body of Else Sigel, a Christian missionary, was found in a trunk in Chinatown.

10 J. W. Smeed, *Jean Paul's 'Dreams'* (London 1966), 94.

11 Hans Weigel, *Karl Kraus* (Vienna 1968), 136–40.

12 Benjamin, *Illuminationen*, 397.

13 See Helmut Rössler, *Karl Kraus und Nestroy: Kritik und Verarbeitung* (Stuttgart 1981).

Chapter 12

1 Paul Schick, 'Der Satiriker und der Tod', in *Festschrift zum hundertjährigen Bestehen der Wiener Stadtbibliothek* (Vienna 1956).

2 See Elliott, *Power of Satire*, ch. 1.

3 Brant, *Das Narrenschiff*, sec. 61: Von dantzen.

4 Adolf Loos, 'Karl Kraus', in *Der Brenner*, no. 3 (June 1913), 841.

5 Quoted in Benjamin, *Illuminationen*, 388.

6 See Timms, 'Hofmannsthal, Kraus and the "Theatrum mundi"', in *Hugo von Hofmannsthal: Commemorative Essays*.

7 The Judaic associations of the word 'Ursprung' are emphasized in Berthold Viertel, *Dichtungen und Dokumente* (Munich 1956), 264.

8 *Die Predigten Taulers*, ed. Ferdinand Vetter (Berlin 1910), 9. An English translation (modified in my own version quoted in the text) is available in *Signposts to Perfection: A Selection from the Sermons of Johann Tauler,* ed. Elizabeth Strakosch (London 1958).

9 Cf. the similar allegory of the journey of Guilt and Shame in Oliver Goldsmith, *The Vicar of Wakefield*, vol. I, ch. 15.

10 W.B. Yeats, *Per Amica Silentia Lunae* (London 1918), 7.

11 See the chapter on 'Man and his Doubles' in Michel Foucault, *The Order of Things: An Archaeology of the Human Sciences* (London 1970).

Chapter 13

1 See Theodor Lessing, *Der jüdische Selbsthaß* (Berlin 1930; repr. Munich 1984).
2 The correspondence between Kraus, Chamberlain, and Chamberlain's first wife Anna is in the Vienna City Library and the Richard Wagner Foundation at Bayreuth. For a preliminary analysis see Wilhelm, 'Houston Stewart Chamberlain und Karl Kraus', *Zeitgeschichte*, X. no. 11–12, 416.
3 Liebenfels's contribution to National Socialist ideology is analysed in Wilfred Daim, *Der Mann, der Hitler die Ideen gab* (Vienna 1984).
4 For a detailed study of Kraus's political position, see Sigurd Paul Scheichl, 'Karl Kraus und die Politik 1892–1919' (diss. Innsbruck 1971).
5 Liegler, *Karl Kraus und sein Werk*, 403.
6 See Gerald Stieg, *Der Brenner und die Fackel: Ein Beitrag zur Wirkungsgeschichte von Karl Kraus* (Salzburg 1976).
7 See Richard Griffiths, *The Reactionary Revolution: The Catholic Revival in French Literature 1870–1914* (London 1965), esp. 306–14.
8 See Jeffrey L. Sammons, *Heinrich Heine: A Modern Biography* (Princeton 1979), 107–10.
9 Rozenblit, *Jews of Vienna*, 132. Schnitzler, in *Tagebuch 1913–1916*, entry for 31 May 1914, denounces the 'katholisierenden Snobismus der neuen Jugend' (p.117).
10 Erasmus, *The Praise of Folly*, trans. John Wilson, 1668 (Ann Arbor, Mich. 1958), 2, 7. And see Manfred Hoffmann, *Erkenntnis und Verwirklichung der wahren Theologie nach Erasmus von Rotterdam* (Tübingen 1972), 1–10.
11 Geoffrey Tillotson, *Pope and Human Nature* (Oxford 1958), 44, 47; 225.
12 Compare J. Swift, *Irish Tracts and Sermons 1720–23*, 241–50, with *The Examiner and Other Pieces*, 175–84.
13 Theodor Haecker, *Satire und Polemik* (Munich 1961), 17: Vorrede, Nov. 1921.
14 T. Haecker, *Tag- und Nachtbücher* (Munich 1947), 26.
15 Haecker, *Tag- und Nachtbücher*, 84–5; and see his *Essays* (Munich 1958), 361: Dialog über die Satire.
16 Søren Kierkegaard, *The Point of View for My Work as An Author*, trans. W. Lowrie (New York 1962), 24.

Chapter 14

1 Rainer Maria Rilke, *Briefe an Sidonie Nadherny von Borutin* (Frankfurt 1973), 215–16.
2 Mitscherlich-Nielsen, 'Sittlichkeit und Kriminalität', in *Text + Kritik*, 34–5; Schneider, *Die Angst und das Paradies des Nörglers*, 65.
3 Heller, *Disinherited Mind*, 200.
4 Elisabeth Kubasta, 'Karl Kraus als Lyriker' (doctoral diss., Vienna 1951), sec. B, 4.
5 In the most convincing section of his book, *Die Angst und das Paradies des Nörglers*, Manfred Schneider shows (pp. 56–66) that the theme of separation carries a particular emotional charge for Kraus, both in his poetry and his letters.
6 Bertolt Brecht, 'Schlechte Zeit für Lyrik', *Werkausgabe*, 20 vols. (Frankfurt 1967), IX. 743–4.
7 Acrostics were smuggled into Volume II of *Worte in Versen* in the poems 'Zum Namenstag' and 'Drei' (*W* VII. 85–6). Poems dedicated to Sidonie which remained unpublished include 'Gespräche' (*BSN* II. 245–6), 'Huldigung der Künste am Namenstag' (*BSN* II. 294), 'Aus Gewohnheit' (*BSN* II. 297) and a further epigram 'Zum Namenstag' (*BSN* II. 298). The poem 'Schäfers

Abschied', which originally incorporated the acrostic SIDI in each of its 24 strophes, was radically revised before publication (compare *W* VII. 244–5 with *BSN* II. 294–7). The effect of these concealments and revisions was to give the poetry what Kraus called a 'double value' ('Doppelwert', *BSN* I. 558): an esoteric personal meaning underlying the manifest literary expression. Kraus's discomfiture when a reviewer did grasp the underlying biographical dimension of his poetry is expressed in a letter of March 1921 (*BSN* I. 497–8).

8   F. von Schiller, 'Über naive und sentimentalische Dichtung', *Sämtliche Schriften*, ed. Karl Goedecke, vol. X (Stuttgart 1871), 457.
9   See Maynard Mack, *The Garden and the City* (Toronto 1969).
10   See Elias Canetti, 'Der neue Karl Kraus', in *Das Gewissen der Worte* (Munich 1975), 234–56.
11   See Paul Schick, *Karl Kraus in Selbstzeugnissen und Bilddokumenten* (Reinbek 1965), 77–8.

PART FOUR

Chapter 15

1   Other journals critical of the war were initially bellicose (Harden's *Die Zukunft*), or restricted to non-political themes (Pfemfert's *Die Aktion*), or obliged to suspend publication (Ficker's *Der Brenner*), forced into exile (Schickele's *Die weißen Blätter*, Fried's *Die Friedens-Warte*), muzzled by censorship (Friedrich Adler's *Der Kampf*), or simply suppressed (Herzog's *Das Forum*). See in particular John Dixon Halliday, 'Karl Kraus, Franz Pfemfert and the First World War: A Comparative Study of *Die Fackel* and *Die Aktion*' (diss., Cambridge 1985).
2   *In These Great Times: A Karl Kraus Reader*, ed. Harry Zohn.
3   See Frank Field, 'Karl Kraus, Bernard Shaw and Romain Rolland as Opponents of the First World War', in *Karl Kraus in neuer Sicht*, 158–71.
4   See J. P. Stern, 'Karl Kraus's Vision of Language', *Modern Language Review*, LXI, no. 1 (Jan. 1966), 71–84.
5   *Der große Krieg: Chronik der Frankfurter Zeitung*, vol. I. (Frankfurt 1915), 473, 499.
6   A. J. P. Taylor, *The First World War: An Illustrated History* (Harmondsworth 1966), 47.
7   S. T. Coleridge, *Biographia Literaria*, ed. J. Shawcross, 2 vols. (London 1939), I. 19; II. 116–17.
8   I. F. Clarke, *Voices Prophesying War 1763–1984* (London 1966), esp. pp. 135, 125, 77.
9   See for example *Hamley's Operations of War*, A New Edition Brought up to the Latest Requirements by Major-General L. E. Kiggell (London 1914). The Russo-Japanese War of 1904–5 had surprised military strategists by the long duration of battles, the strength of entrenchments and the abnormal extension of fronts. But Kiggell assures his readers that a recurrence of this in Europe seems 'most unlikely' (pp. 402–3).
10   C .E. Montague, *Disenchantment* (London 1922), 44–5 (italics added).
11   Heinrich Lersch, *Erzählungen und Briefe*, 2 vols. (Düsseldorf 1966), II. 396.
12   See Fischer, *Krieg der Illusionen*. Bethmann Hollweg's statement is quoted on p. 665, that of a disillusioned officer who had expected a 'fresh and jolly war' on pp. 777–8.
13   See Samuel Dumas and Knud Otto Vedel-Peterson, *Losses of Life Caused by the*

War (London 1923). For updated estimates, see *Encyclopaedia Britannica*, vol. XXIII (London 1963), 775.

14   Fischer, *Krieg der Illusionen*, ch. 17.

15   See Paul Kennedy, *The Rise of the Anglo-German Antagonism* (London 1980); A. J. A. Morris, *The Scaremongers: The Advocacy of War and Rearmament 1896–1914* (London 1984).

16   Günter Heidorn, *Monopole – Presse – Krieg: Die Rolle der Presse bei der Vorbereitung des ersten Weltkriegs* (East Berlin 1960); Kurt Koszyk, *Deutsche Pressepolitik im Ersten Weltkrieg* (Düsseldorf 1968); Dagobert Pokorny, 'Die Wiener Tagespresse und ihre Einflussfaktoren im Ersten Weltkrieg' (diss., Vienna 1950).

17   For a contrasting account of von Hoen, which emphasizes his 'echt österreichische Liebenswürdigkeit', see Karl Hans Strobl, *K.P. Qu.: Geschichten und Bilder aus dem Kriegspressequartier* (Reichenberg 1928), esp. pp. 59–61.

18   See Fischer, *Krieg der Illusionen*, 729–34. The false reports were printed in the national newspapers of 3 Aug. 1914 under headlines like 'Französische Bombenabwürfe in der Umgebung Nürnbergs' (*Die Zeit*) and helped to justify the declaration of war on France the following day.

Chapter 16

1   The predominant mood of 1914 is reflected in the anthology *Deutsche Dichtung im Weltkrieg*, ed. Ernst Volkmann (Leipzig 1934). For a detailed study, see Eckart Koester, *Literatur und Weltkriegsideologie* (Kronberg 1977).

2   See *Aufrufe und Reden deutscher Professoren im Ersten Weltkrieg*, ed. Klaus Böhme (Stuttgart 1975).

3   The dilemma of European Socialism is analysed in James Joll, *The Second International* (London 1968). A detailed account of the left wing of the German Social Democratic Party is given in Peter Nettl, *Rosa Luxemburg* (London 1966).

4   'Der Tag der deutschen Nation' (unsigned editorial, *Arbeiter-Zeitung*, 5 Aug. 1914) celebrates the unanimous vote in favour of war credits in the German Reichstag the previous day. The tone of the *Arbeiter-Zeitung* during the early months of the war is patriotic and even bellicose, with enthusiastic reports of German military advances ('Nach Paris!', 5 Sept. 1914) and patriotic euphemisms to disguise Austrian defeats ('Großer Erfolg bei Lemberg', 13 Sept. 1914).

5   The phrase, originally coined by the economist Johann Plenge, was popularized by the Swedish Germanophile Rudolf Kjellen in *Die Ideen von 1914: Eine weltgeschichtliche Perspektive* (Leipzig 1915).

6   See Egmont Zechlin, *Die deutsche Politik und die Juden im Ersten Weltkrieg* (Göttingen 1969), esp. Pt. i, ch. 4: Die deutschen Juden beim Kriegsausbruch.

7   Quoted in *Deutsche Dichtung im Weltkrieg*, 8.

8   *The Autobiography of Bertrand Russell*, 3 vols. (London 1967), II. 17. See also Jo Vellacott, *Bertrand Russell and the Pacifists in the First World War* (Brighton 1980).

9   Rupert Brooke, *1914 and Other Poems* (London 1915), 11.

10   The mood in France is analysed in Jean-Jacques Becker, *1914 – Comment les Français sont entrés dans la guerre* (Paris 1977) and *Les Français dans la Grande Guerre* (Paris 1980). For the response of British intellectuals see Cate Haste, *Keep the Home Fires Burning: Propaganda in the First World War* (London 1977); M. L. Sanders and Philip M. Taylor, *British Propaganda during the First World War* (London 1982).

11   Karl Hammer, *Deutsche Kriegstheologie (1870–1918)* (Munich 1971) reprints a selection of bellicose sermons, including characteristic addresses by the Kaiser,

who was *summus episcopus* of the Prussian Protestant Church.

12 See Richard J. Evans, *The Feminist Movement in Germany 1894–1933* (London 1976), ch. 7. The tone was set by sickening publications like *Der Krieg und die Frauen* (Leipzig 1915) by Lily Braun, noted for her socialist and pacifist publications prior to the war.

13 See René Cheval, *Romain Rolland, l'Allemagne et la guerre* (Paris 1963).

14 Hermann Hesse, *Politik des Gewissens: Die politischen Schriften*, ed. Volker Michels, 2 vols. (Frankfurt 1977), I. 38–42. The essay appeared on 3 Nov. 1914 in the *Neue Zürcher Zeitung*.

15 See Roger Chickering, *Imperial Germany and a World Without War: The Peace Movement and German Society 1892–1914* (Princeton 1975); Wilfried Eisenbeiss, *Die bürgerliche Friedensbewegung in Deutschland während des Ersten Weltkriegs* (Frankfurt 1980), esp. pp. 100–3 (on the conflict of loyalties in 1914); Fuchs, *Geistige Strömungen in Österreich*, 251–75 ('Pazifismus'); James D. Shand, 'Doves Among the Eagles: German Pacifists and their Government during World War I', *Journal of Contemporary History*, X, no. 1 (Jan. 1975), 95–108. For a comparative study, see F. L. Carsten, *War Against War: British and German Radical Movements in the First World War* (London 1982).

16 For wide-ranging comparative accounts see Roland N. Stromberg, *Redemption by War: The Intellectuals and 1914* (Lawrence, Kans. 1982); and James Joll, *The Origins of the First World War* (London 1984), esp. ch. 8: The Mood of 1914.

17 Julien Benda, *La Trahison des clercs* (Paris 1927), trans. by Richard Aldington as *The Treason of the Intellectuals* (new edn., New York 1969).

18 *Deutsche Dichtung im Weltkrieg*, 62–4. The equivocations of Hauptmann's attitude during the war are revealed by his previously unpublished diaries, analysed in Hans von Brescius, *Gerhart Hauptmann: Zeitgeschehen und Bewußtsein in unbekannten Selbstzeugnissen* (Bonn 1976), 67–95.

19 For a full account, see Heinz Lunzer, *Hofmannsthals politische Tätigkeit in den Jahren 1914–1917* (Frankfurt 1981).

20 Benda, *Treason of the Intellectuals*, 54, 75.

21 Hermann Bahr, *Kriegssegen* (Munich 1915), 9–11.

22 Schnitzler's protest was published in the Munich periodical *Das Forum* (Dec. 1914) and is reprinted in Brandes and Schnitzler, *Ein Briefwechsel*, 206.

23 Quoted in Lunzer, *Hofmannsthals politische Tätigkeit*, 33.

24 Lunzer, *Hofmannsthals politische Tätigkeit*, 26–33, 129–37.

25 Hofmannsthal, *Gesammelte Werke in Einzelausgaben*, Prosa III. 260–78.

26 Lunzer, *Hofmannsthals politische Tätigkeit*, reprints reports from both the *Vossische Zeitung* and the *Neue Freie Presse* (179–80, 359–60).

27 For an account of the career of Heinrich Lammasch see Fuchs, *Geistige Strömungen in Österreich*, 265–70. Fuchs reports that Lammasch would have been arrested, but for the personal intervention of the Emperor. The article from the *Arbeiter-Zeitung* which Kraus praises (*F* 445–53: 66–7) is reprinted in Heinrich Lammasch, *Europas elfte Stunde* (Munich 1919), 92–5. This volume also contains the speeches in favour of a negotiated peace which Lammasch delivered in the Austrian parliament on 28 June 1917, 27 Oct. 1917 and 28 Feb. 1918.

28 See D. A. Prater, *European of Yesterday* (Oxford 1972).

29 Field, *Last Days of Mankind*, 128.

30 The full extent of Zweig's propagandistic writings is disguised by the editors of his 'Complete Works' – *Sämtliche Werke in Einzelbänden*. They exclude articles like 'Galiziens Genesung' from the volume containing his war essays: *Die schlaflose Welt: Aufsätze und Vorträge aus den Jahren 1909–1941*, ed. Knut Beck (Frankfurt 1983). The problem is compounded by the fact that a number of

Zweig's articles appeared anonymously, both in the *Neue Freie Presse* and in the publications of the Kriegsarchiv. Zweig was a leading contributor to patriotic anthologies produced by the Kriegsarchiv: *Unsere Offiziere* (Vienna 1915); *Unsere Soldaten* (Vienna 1915); *Unsere Nordfront* (Vienna 1916); *Unsere Kämpfe im Süden* (Vienna 1917); *Helden des Roten Kreuzes* (Vienna 1915); and *Aus der Werkstatt des Krieges* (Vienna 1915). Zweig's anxiety to avoid active military service and his compensating zeal in the Kriegsarchiv are documented in Klaus Heydemann, 'Der Titularfeldwebel: Stefan Zweig im Kriegsarchiv', in *Stefan Zweig 1881/1981: Aufsätze und Dokumente*, ed. Heinz Lunzer and Gerhard Renner (Zirkular Sondernummer, Vienna 1981), 19–55. The full extent of Zweig's dilemma is apparent from his *Tagebücher*, ed. Knut Beck (Frankfurt 1984). The diaries show that privately he was from the very beginning horrified by the war, sceptical about the prospects of victory, and critical of newspaper propaganda – especially of the *Neue Freie Presse*. But he lacked the moral courage to speak out against the war, and his willingness to collaborate with the Austrian authorities is profoundly at odds with his inner commitment to non-violence. It was not until July 1918 that he openly denounced the war in the article 'Bekenntnis zum Defaitismus', published in *Die Friedens-Warte* (reprinted in *Die schlaflose Welt*, 122–5).

31   See Hans Mühlestein, *Ferdinand Hodler: Ein Deutungsversuch* (Weimar 1914), actually published in 1915, with a postscript dated 18 Feb. 1915 explaining the circumstances of Hodler's apostasy. The painting *Auszug der Jenenser Studenten in den Freiheitskrieg 1813* had recently been installed at the University of Jena, so Hodler's protest placed the authorities in a dilemma. He was denounced by the Rector of the University, Ernst Haeckel (hence Kraus's juxtaposition of their names, *F* 404: 17).

32   Carl Spitteler, *Unser Schweizer Standpunkt* (address delivered in Zurich on 14 Dec. 1914) (Zurich 1915).

33   See Uwe Laugwitz, 'Albert Ehrenstein und Karl Kraus: Entwicklung einer literarischen Polemik 1910–1920' (M.A. diss., Hamburg 1982).

34   Schnitzler, *Tagebuch 1913–1916*, esp. p. 129 ('Der Weltkrieg. Der Weltruin'); p. 143 ('das wesentliche des Krieges [. . .] das Leid'); and p. 172 ('Phantasielosigkeit').

35   Some patriotic effusions seem simply to have escaped Kraus's attention, for example the address which Frank Wedekind delivered in Munich in September 1914, 'Vom deutschen Vaterlandsstolz' (*Gesammelte Werke*, 9 vols. [Munich 1920–1], IX. 411–18). Personal factors may also have inhibited him from attacking prominent spokesmen for the German and Austrian cause such as Houston Stewart Chamberlain and Richard von Schaukal. And Kraus is gentle in his comments on a bellicose poem by his former secretary Berthold Viertel, who in any case soon regretted his outburst (*F* 423–5: 22–3). The really surprising omission is Thomas Mann, whose patriotic writings escape censure, although Kraus does take issue with the 'Kultur versus Zivilisation' antithesis which Mann invoked to justify the German cause (*F* 404: 5–6).

36   Kraus is alluding to Ginzkey's 'Ballade von den masurischen Seen' (printed in *Kriegsalmanach 1914–1915*, ed. Karl Kobald (Vienna 1915), 76–7).

37   Grossmann's memoirs, *Ich war begeistert: Eine Lebensgeschichte* (Berlin 1931), contain a chapter, 'Krieg in der Redaktion', which acknowledges the dishonesty of his propaganda work.

38   See Ingeborg Schnack, *Rainer Maria Rilke: Chronik seines Lebens*, 2 vols. (Frankfurt 1975).

39   Robert A. Kann, 'Trends in Austro-German Literature during World War I: War Hysteria and Patriotism', in *The Habsburg Empire in World War I: Essays on*

the Intellectual, Military, Political and Economic Aspects of the Habsburg War Effort,
ed. Robert A. Kann, Bela K. Kiraly and Paula S. Fichtner (New York 1977),
159–83 (esp. p. 182).

40 Quoted in Brescius, *Gerhart Hauptmann: Zeitgeschehen und Bewußtsein,* 85.

Chapter 17

1   Friedrich Meinecke, *Die deutsche Erhebung von 1914: Aufsätze und Vorträge*
(Stuttgart 1914).

2   See Fritz Fischer, *Krieg der Illusionen,* esp. ch. 9 and 22, and his *Griff nach der
Weltmacht* (Düsseldorf 1961).

3   Heinrich Mann, 'Zola', *Die weißen Blätter* (Oct.–Dec. 1915), 1312–82.

4   'Aufruf an die Kulturwelt' (4 Oct. 1914), reprinted in *Aufrufe und Reden deutscher
Professoren,* 47–9. The tendency to endow the aims of German imperialism with
a 'glittering intellectual veneer' and a 'nimbus of ideals' is analysed in Ludwig
Dehio, *Germany and World Politics in the Twentieth Century* (London 1959),
72–108. For a more comprehensive study see Klaus Schwabe, *Wissenschaft und
Kriegsmoral: Die deutschen Hochschullehrer und die politischen Grundfragen des Ersten
Weltkriegs* (Göttingen 1969).

5   The English equivalent of 'Aufruf an die Kulturwelt' was the declaration which
appeared in *The Times* (18 Sept. 1914), signed by 53 writers including Thomas
Hardy, John Masefield, H. G. Wells, Arnold Bennett, Rudyard Kipling,
Arthur Conan Doyle, Arthur Quiller-Couch and Gilbert Murray. They define
the aim of the war as 'to defend the rights of small nations and to maintain the
necessary law-abiding ideals of Western Europe against [. . .] the domination of
the whole Continent by a military caste' (quoted in Haste, *Keep the Home Fires
Burning,* 25).

6   Repr. in Thomas Mann, *Friedrich und die große Koalition* (Berlin 1916), 14, 21
('Gedanken im Kriege') and 126–7 ('An die Redaktion des *Svenska Dagbladet*').

7   In 1900 Thomas Mann had obtained exemption from military service through
the influence of a senior military doctor (a friend of a friend of the family). In
December 1914 he wrote to Richard Dehmel explaining that although physically unfit for military service, he was determined at least to put his head into
the service of the German cause. See Thomas Mann, *Briefe 1889–1936*
(Frankfurt 1961), 19–20, 93–5, 114–15 (letters to Heinrich Mann and Richard
Dehmel).

8   Werner Sombart, *Händler und Helden: Patriotische Besinnungen* (Munich/Leipzig
1915), 85.

9   Wilhelm Wundt, *Die Nationen und ihre Philosophie: Ein Kapitel zum Weltkrieg*
(Leipzig 1915).

10 Hans Kohn, *The Mind of Germany: The Education of a Nation* (London 1965),
299.

11 Repr. in Romain Rolland, *L'Esprit libre; Au-dessus de la mêlée; Les Précurseurs*
(Paris 1953), 155.

12 Max Weber, *Gesammelte politische Schriften* (Tübingen 1971), 157–77.

13 Walter Rathenau, *Von den kommenden Dingen* (1917), reprinted in *Gesammelte
Schriften,* 5 vols. (Berlin 1925), III. 225, 231–3.

14 Hesse, *Politik des Gewissens,* I. 33, 78, 101.

15 David Riesman, *The Lonely Crowd: A Study of the Changing American Character*
(New Haven 1950), 81.

16 See Max Brod, *Streitbares Leben* (Munich 1960), 152–8.

17 See Cheval, *Romain Rolland, l'Allemagne et la Guerre,* 231–90; Hesse, *Politik des
Gewissens,* I. 33. Bertrand Russell is quoted in Stanley Weintraub, *Bernard Shaw*

1914–1918 (London 1973), 36.

18 See Maurice Landrieux, *The Cathedral of Reims: The Story of a German Crime* (London 1920), which contains many details and photographs of the damage done by the bombardment, together with a denial that the building was used for military purposes.

19 Romain Rolland, *Journal des années de guerre 1914–1919* (Paris 1952), 101, 125–7.

20 Weintraub, *Bernard Shaw 1914–1918*, 58–9.

21 Bernard Shaw, 'Common Sense about the War' (*New Statesman*, 14 Nov. 1914), repr. in *What I Really Wrote about the War* (London 1931), 22–104.

22 Nietzsche, *Werke in drei Bänden*, II. 312. It is 'Zarathustra' who is speaking, but the propagandistic effect was as great as if it had been Nietzsche in his own voice. An edition of 150,000 copies of *Zarathustra* was specially published as a 'field edition' for the troops, as Kraus grimly records in October 1917 (*F* 462–71: 64).

23 The phrase was coined by Theodor Fontane, who puts it into the mouth of one of his characters in ch. 23 of *Der Stechlin* (*Sämtliche Werke*, ed. Edgar Gross, vol. VIII [Munich 1954], 205).

24 Julius Braunthal, *In Search of the Millennium* (London: Left Book Club, 1945), 122. For Braunthal, J. A. Cramb's *Reflections on the Origin and Destiny of Imperial Britain* (1900) are as sinister as anything written by Hegel. Against this we may set the view of the leader of the German Social Democrats, August Bebel. Bebel was so convinced that Prussian militarism was a danger *sui generis* that he sent secret messages to the British Government prior to 1914, urging Britain to maintain her naval superiority. See Helmut Bley, *Bebel und die Strategie der Kriegsverhütung 1904–1913* (Göttingen 1975).

25 The *Cambridge Magazine* (edited by C. K. Ogden) responded to the outbreak of war by publishing a series of critical articles by Bertrand Russell, Romain Rolland, Gilbert Cannan, A. C. Pigou and other supporters of the Union for Democratic Control.

26 See *Why We Are At War: Great Britain's Case*, by Members of the Oxford Faculty of Modern History (Oxford 1914). This was followed by a series of 87 'Oxford Pamphlets' about the war, including studies of *The Farmer in Wartime* (by C. S. Orwin) and *Bacilli and Bullets* (by William Osler).

27 *Aufrufe und Reden deutscher Professoren*, 60, 70, 72, 77. The two lectures quoted were part of a series delivered by professors at the University of Berlin with the aim of boosting patriotic morale, *Deutsche Reden in schwerer Zeit*, 3 vols. (Berlin 1915).

28 Hofmannsthal, letter to Bodenhausen, 10 July 1917, in *Briefe der Freundschaft*, 235–6.

29 See Zechlin, *Die deutsche Politik und die Juden im Ersten Weltkrieg*, esp. Pt. v: *Juden und Antisemitismus im Weltkrieg*.

Chapter 18

1 Hofmannsthal, *Gesammelte Werke in Einzelausgaben*, Prosa III. 290–319.

2 See J. P. Stern, *Re-interpretations* (London 1964), ch. 5: History and Prophecy.

3 Heine, *Sämtliche Werke*, II. 285–6.

4 Robert Graves, *Goodbye to All That* (London 1929), 283; and see Mark Girouard, *The Return to Camelot: Chivalry and the English Gentleman* (London 1981), ch. 18: The Great War.

5 For a detailed account, see Monika Glettler, 'Karl Kraus zwischen Prussophilie und Prussophobie: Bismarck und Wilhelm II in der "Fackel"', *Österreich in Geschichte und Literatur*, XXIII (1979), no. 3, 148–66.

6   Montague, *Disenchantment*, 26.
7   See Hannah Arendt, *Eichmann in Jerusalem: A Report on the Banality of Evil* (London 1963).
8   Winston S. Churchill, *The World Crisis*, vol. VI (London 1931), 54.
9   Three further photographs of complacent hangmen, posing for the camera beside their victims, are reproduced in *Österreich 1918: Zustandsbild eines Jahres*, ed. Karl Bednarik and Stephan Horvath (Vienna 1968), 27, 65, 77.
10 Although it is impossible to establish reliable figures, it is clear that from a very early stage in the war the Austro-Hungarian authorities arrested thousands of potential dissidents among the Serbian population of southern Hungary and the Ruthenians of Galicia, and that many of them were executed. See Josef Redlich, *Das politische Tagebuch*, 2 vols. (Graz 1953), I. 280, 289.
11 Kraus is referring in the last example to the events at Kragujevac in June 1918, which he incorporates into the visionary finale of *Die letzten Tage der Menschheit* (*W* v. 714). Cf. R.G. Plaschka, H. Haselsteiner and A. Suppan, *Innere Front, Militärassistenz, Widerstand und Umsturz in der Donaumonarchie 1918*, 2 vols. (Vienna 1974), I. 388–400; photographic documentation, II. Pls. 24–6.
12 See for example *Austria-Hungary's Effort to Exterminate Her Jugoslav Subjects: Speeches and Questions in the Parliaments of Vienna and Budapest and in the Croatian Diet* (London 1917). The difficulty of knowing whether the allegations were subsequently confirmed or refuted arises from the fact that the official record of Austrian Parliamentary Debates was severely pruned before publication. See *Parlamentarische Chronik*, ed. Karl Meisser (Vienna 1917–18).
13 Reimund Schnabel, *Macht ohne Moral: Eine Dokumentation über die SS* (Frankfurt 1957), esp. p. 489 and p. 493.

Chapter 19

1   For a detailed study, which confirms some of the findings of this chapter, see Sigurd Paul Scheichl, 'Karl Kraus und die Politik'.
2   *Die Reichspost*, 19 July 1914, p.1, and 21 Nov. 1914, p.7.
3   *Die Aktion*, V, no. 7/8 (13 Feb. 1915), col. 95.
4   The document is wrongly identified by the editors of *Briefe an Sidonie Nádherný* as an apostolic letter issued by Pope Pius X in August 1914 (*BSN* II. 149). In fact Kraus is referring to the Encyclical of Pius's successor, Pope Benedict XV, the full text of which was published in *Die Reichspost* on 21 Nov. (the date of Kraus's letter).
5   *Danzer's Armee-Zeitung*, XIX, no. 37 (15 Oct. 1914), 5.
6   A run of 70 copies of *Die Fackel*, many of them rubber-stamped with the name 'Major Baron Lempruch, Wien IV/2, Blechturmgasse 10' or 'Baron Lempruch, Wien IX/1, Porzellangasse No. 45', were acquired from Antiquariat Deutike and are now in the private collection of Dr Edward Timms. Copious annotations show that Lempruch's reading of *Die Fackel* was strongly coloured by antisemitism. This is evident from his habit of underlining Jewish-sounding names, for example Nathaniel Rothschild and Pollack von Parnegg (*F* 218: 27); Barber, Waldberg, Frankl, Pollak, Seligmann, Geiringer, Schlesinger and Herzfeld (*F* 331–2: 20). In a list of 14 names of journalists working for the *Neues Wiener Journal* Lempruch underlines 11 Jewish-sounding names and even tots up the score: '11 gegen 3' (*F* 206: 29).
7   Baron M. E. von Lempruch to Kraus, 12 Aug. 1915 (Vienna City Library, IN 138.782).
8   Lempruch to Kraus, 29 May 1916 (IN 138.785).
9   See Zechlin, *Die deutsche Politik und die Juden im Ersten Weltkrieg*.

10   Schnitzler, *Tagebuch 1913–1916*, 298 (entry of 25 June 1916); *Tagebuch 1917–1919*, 190 (entry of 16 Nov. 1918).
11   See Brod, *Streitbares Leben*, 155. In Redlich, *Das politische Tagebuch* (I. 227), there is a suggestion that the author was Franz Freiherr von Matscheko, Sektionsrat in the Austro-Hungarian Foreign Office. It is possible that Bloch drafted the Proclamation and Matscheko was the department head who put the finishing touches to it.
12   The poster of the Imperial Proclamation may be examined at the Heeresmuseum in Vienna and the Imperial War Museum in London. The text has also been checked as published in the following newspapers: *Arbeiter-Zeitung, Frankfurter Zeitung, Neue Freie Presse, Reichspost, Danzer's Armee-Zeitung, Die Zeit* and the official *Wiener Zeitung*.
13   'Reiflich habe ich alles erwogen' is the phrase which Erwin Piscator puts into the mouth of Emperor Franz Joseph in the supposedly documentary play *Rasputin, die Romanovs, der Krieg und das Volk* (see Piscator, *Das politische Theater* (Hamburg 1963), 166). 'I thought it all over very carefully' is the phrase used by Svejk to explain how he came to purloin a chicken, in the English text of Jaroslav Hasek, *The Good Soldier Svejk and his Fortunes in the World War* (Harmondsworth 1974), 548. I am grateful to Robert Pynsent for pointing out that this is a parodistic echo of the Proclamation, although he fails to realize that the motif derives from Kraus, not from the Proclamation itself. See *The First World War in Fiction*, ed. Holger Klein (London 1976), 147.
14   'Just for a word – "neutrality", a word which in wartime has so often been disregarded, just for a scrap of paper – Great Britain is going to make war,' Bethmann Hollweg is alleged to have said to the British Ambassador Sir Edward Goschen on 4 Aug. 1914. The phrase caught the imagination of the British public, which did indeed picture Bethmann Hollweg tearing up the treaty guaranteeing the neutrality of Belgium as contemptuously as if it were 'a scrap of paper'. See *Oxford Dictionary of Quotations* (London 1981), 42.
15   Original manuscript and typewritten transcript of 'In dieser großen Zeit', Vienna City Library, IN 104.574.
16   See *Worte von Stein: Die amtlichen Berichte aus dem Großen Hauptquartier* (Dessau 1914), report of 4 Sept. 1914: 'Reims ist ohne Kampf besetzt worden'.
17   'Ich habe [. . .] oft gewünscht, daß es eine Sprache geben möchte, worin man eine Falschheit gar nicht sagen könnte, oder wenigstens ein Schnitzer gegen die Wahrheit ein grammatikalischer wäre.' The link between Lichtenberg's aphorism and Kraus's vision of language was first suggested by J. P. Stern in *Lichtenberg: A Doctrine of Scattered Occasions* (London 1963), 163.
18   'It was intended that when Newspeak had been adopted [. . .] a heretical thought [. . .] should be literally unthinkable, at least so far as thought is dependent on words.' George Orwell, *Nineteen Eighty-Four* (London 1983), Appendix: The Principles of Newspeak.
19   Kraus is thinking of his friend Ludwig von Ficker, editor of *Der Brenner*, whose military service placed him in such a demeaning situation that Kraus asked Baron Lempruch to intervene on his behalf (*BSN* I. 171, 175; letters of 20 and 22 July 1915).
20   Juvenal, *The Sixteen Satires*, ed. Peter Green (Harmondsworth 1973), Introduction, 24.

Chapter 20

1   The term was coined by Dr John Halliday, on whose research into Kraus's relations with the censorship this section is based. See John Halliday, 'Satirist

and Censor: Karl Kraus and the Censorship Authorities during the First World War', in *Karl Kraus in neuer Sicht*, 174–208.

2 The German text is reproduced in facsimile by Halliday in 'Satirist and Censor' from the original in the Allgemeines Verwaltungsarchiv in Vienna (JM, IV Druckschriften Allgemein, 1918 Z 3914/157, 2.6.18). The sentence in italics is underlined in the original.

3 Reproduced in facsimile by Halliday in 'Satirist and Censor', from the original in the Kriegsarchiv, Vienna (KÜA, 1916, 68497).

4 Unpublished documents in the Vienna City Library show that on 15 Nov. 1917 Lammasch sent Kraus copies of memoranda drafted by Julius Meinl in favour of a negotiated peace. Kraus reciprocated by sending Lammasch in April 1918 a copy of the declaration 'Für Lammasch' which he had read in public on 30 Mar. (IN 158.822, IN. 158.819). A letter from Meinl to Lammasch dated 14 Nov. 1917 shows that Meinl was particularly keen to enlist Kraus's support. See Heinrich Benedikt, *Die Friedensaktion der Meinlgruppe 1917/18* (Graz 1962), 187.

5 Compare the report of the conviction of the war profiteers Josef Kranz and Eisig Rubel in *Danzer's Armee-Zeitung*, 5 Apr. 1917, p. 4, with Kraus's response in F 457–61 [10 May 1917]: 1–19, 24–5. Unlike Kraus, Danzer does not draw attention to the Jewish background of the people convicted.

6 Norbert Ruske, *Szenische Realität und historische Wirklichkeit: Eine Untersuchung zu Karl Kraus, 'Die letzten Tage der Menschheit'* (Frankfurt 1981), 134–40.

7 Karl Adler, *Der Querulant* (Vienna 1920), 43. This report has been questioned (Pfabigan, *Karl Kraus und der Sozialismus*, 229), but there is evidence in the diaries of Sidonie Nadherny that Kraus did used to visit Austerlitz at his office (*BSN* II. 332; diary of 10 Apr. 1922).

8 See Eckart Früh, 'Die *Arbeiter-Zeitung* als Quelle der *Letzten Tage der Menschheit*', in *Karl Kraus in neuer Sicht*, 209–32.

9 See Ronald Florence, *Fritz: The Story of a Political Assassin* (New York 1971), esp. pp. 223–35.

10 *Danzer's Armee-Zeitung*, XXII, no. 44–5 (1 and 8 Nov. 1917), 7. (I am grateful to Dr John Halliday for drawing my attention to this passage.)

11 Kraus read Adler's Stockholm speech in the *Arbeiter-Zeitung* of 25 Nov. 1917 and commended it to Sidonie (*BSN* I. 437; II. 280). But he did not attempt to build on it in his published work.

12 Czernin's memoranda for Archduke Franz Ferdinand are analysed in Robert A. Kann, *Erzherzog Franz Ferdinand Studien* (Munich 1976), 157–205.

13 Compare the report of Czernin's Budapest speech, *Neue Freie Presse*, 3 Oct. 1917 (Morgenblatt) with the front-page coverage of his commitment to 'extending and deepening' the military alliance with Germany, *Neue Freie Presse*, 30 Oct. 1917 (Morgenblatt). Kraus was particularly provoked by the editor Benedikt's repeated use of the slogan 'Ausbau und Vertiefung' and by the suggestion (in this same editorial) that Czernin's peace proposals at Budapest had been merely a diplomatic manoeuvre ('Handgriff') to deceive the Entente. See F 474–83: 4 and F 484–98: 1–12.

14 For a more detailed analysis of Kraus's polemic against Czernin, see Scheichl, 'Karl Kraus und die Politik', 727–43. Czernin's merits remain a subject for controversy among historians, who have not yet solved 'the riddle of his different faces' (Kann, *Erzherzog Franz Ferdinand Studien*, 205).

15 *America and Freedom: The Statements of President Wilson on the War* (London 1917), 45–59.

16 *America and Freedom*, 71–6.

PART FIVE

Chapter 21

1 Karl Kraus, *The Last Days of Mankind*, abridged and ed. Frederick Ungar, trans. Alexander Gode and Sue Ellen Wright (New York 1974). This edition eliminates from the play antisemitic and anti-capitalist utterances which might give offence to American readers. A similar tendency to transpose the complex ruminations of the satirist into the idiom of democratic anti-militarism mars the translation of selected scenes by Max Knight and Joseph Fabry, included in *In These Great Times: A Karl Kraus Reader*.

2 Karl Kraus, *Die letzten Tage der Menschheit*, ed. (with a commentary, concordance, and index) Kurt Krolop (East Berlin 1978). Although Krolop's commentary is exceptionally detailed, he assumes that in May 1916 Kraus was already repudiating his conservative standpoint (Kommentar, p. 289).

3 The MS of the 'Akt-Ausgabe' survives (Austrian National Library, Codex no. 19.268–19.273). The text has been reprinted in vol. XII of the reprint of *Die Fackel* by Zweitausendeins (Frankfurt [1977]). My analysis, the first to attempt a comparative assessment of the two versions, uses the initials 'A' and 'B' to distinguish them in passages of detailed argument. Where no initial is given, the reference is to the book edition, *Die letzten Tage der Menschheit* (Vienna: Verlag 'Die Fackel', 1922).

4 Eckart Früh, 'Die *Arbeiter-Zeitung* als Quelle der *Letzten Tage der Menschheit*', in *Karl Kraus in neuer Sicht*.

5 Kraus's source (again identified by Eckart Früh) is the *Arbeiter-Zeitung* of 13 Jan. 1920.

6 Robert Graves, *Goodbye to All That*, 410.

7 'Schwarz-Gelber' is a fictive 'speaking name' (black and yellow were the Habsburg colours, so the name has obvious patriotic associations). The husband and wife in the Schwarz-Gelber scene use Jewish jargon expressions. It is possible that Kraus created the name by association with that of a prominent (and ultra-patriotic) member of the Vienna Jewish community, Dr Schwarz-Hiller. See *Kraus Hefte*, no. 4 (Oct. 1977), 4–5.

8 Emil Sander, *Gesellschaftliche Struktur und literarischer Ausdruck: Über 'Die letzten Tage der Menschheit'* (Königstein 1979), 171–5.

9 Kraus originally used the name 'Mannheimer' in this speech by the Grumbler (A II. 8). He later altered it to 'Oppenheimer' to enhance the mythopoeic resonance. The name derives from the notorious Jewish financier, Joseph Süss-Oppenheimer (1692–1738), who was hanged for his alleged misdeeds, giving rise to the 'Jud Süss' figure of German folklore and literary legend. The tendency to subsume war profiteering under a specifically antisemitic myth generates in the monologues of the Grumbler a hybrid form of anti-Jewish anti-capitalism.

10 See 'The Last Days of Mankind: A Neglected Play', by 'Our Special Correspondent' (= Edward Timms), *The Times*, 22 June 1964, p.14 (a review of the Vienna Festival production by Leopold Lindtberg and Heinrich Fischer).

11 Gerhard Melzer, 'Der Nörgler und die Anderen. Zur Anlage der Tragödie *Die letzten Tage der Menschheit*' (diss., Free University of Berlin 1972), 197.

12 See Leo A. Lensing, '"Kinodramatisch": Cinema in Karl Kraus's *Die Fackel* and *Die letzten Tage der Menschheit*', *German Quarterly*, LV, no. 4 (Nov. 1982), 480–98.

13 See Edward Timms, 'The Spectacle and the Text', *Times Literary Supplement*, 11 July 1980, p. 781; and Peter Branscombe, 'Café noir', *Times Literary*

Supplement, 9 Sept. 1983, p. 960 (review of the Citizens Theatre production, trans. and directed by Robert David MacDonald).

Chapter 22

1 Harry Zohn, *Karl Kraus* (New York 1971), 73. A simplistic view of the Grumbler occurs in almost every commentary, for example: 'Karl Kraus selbst ist [. . .] dieser Nörgler [. . .] ohne Stilisierung und Überhöhung ganz real' (Weigel, *Karl Kraus*, 198); 'Alle Anschauungen des Nörglers lassen sich [. . .] mit Ansichten, die Kraus an anderen Orten äußerte, identifizieren' (Melzer, 'Der Nörgler und die Anderen: Zur Anlage der Tragödie *Die letzten Tage der Menschheit*', 8). Even the most recent commentary on the figure of the Grumbler endorses this 'Identifikation dieser Figur mit dem Autor Karl Kraus'; see Wilhelm Hindemith, *Die Tragödie des Nörglers* (Frankfurt 1985), 133.

2 A fairly accurate line count can be made, since the 'Akt-Ausgabe' of 1919 and the first book edition of 1922 were printed by Jahoda & Siegel in the same type face.

3 Sidonie appears to have written in a letter to Rilke of 10 Aug. 1914 that she 'hated' the war. Fragments from this letter are quoted in Rilke, *Briefe an Sidonie Nádherný*, 365.

4 Quoted in Paul Fussell, *The Great War and Modern Memory* (New York 1975), 103.

5 Traces of the conversations with Lobkowicz and Loos can be found in *BSN*; with Ficker, in Stieg, *Der Brenner und die Fackel*; with Kurt Wolff, in his *Autoren, Bücher, Abenteuer*; with Engelmann, in Paul Engelmann, *Letters from Ludwig Wittgenstein with a Memoir*. The striking absence of *contemporary* records of conversations with Kraus makes it extremely difficult to reconstruct his private attitudes during the war.

6 Vienna City Library, IN 153.671–3 (proof sheets for *F* 406–12).

BIBLIOGRAPHICAL NOTE

Full details of works cited in this book are given in the notes. What follows is a check-list of essential sources, together with suggestions for further reading, given for the most part in the order of publication.

A WORKS BY KARL KRAUS
(see also the List of Abbreviations, p.xv)

1 *Frühe Schriften*, ed. J. J. Braakenburg, 2 vols. (Munich 1979): reprints Kraus's essays, reviews and pamphlets published prior to the founding of *Die Fackel*.

2 *Die Fackel* (Vienna 1899–1936), Nos. 1–922: photomechanically reprinted by Kösel Verlag, Munich (1968–76); and by Zweitausendeins, Frankfurt (1977), with an index by Franz Ögg.

3 Original editions of Kraus's writings:
Sittlichkeit und Kriminalität (Vienna 1908)
Sprüche und Widersprüche (Vienna 1909)
Die chinesische Mauer (Munich 1910)
Pro domo et mundo (Munich 1912)
Worte in Versen, 9 vols. (1916–30: vols. I–V, Leipzig; VI–IX, Vienna)
Nachts (Leipzig 1918)
Die letzte Nacht (Epilog zu der Tragödie 'Die letzten Tage der Menschheit') (Vienna 1918)
Weltgericht, 2 vols. (Leipzig 1919)
Die letzten Tage der Menschheit, ['Akt-Ausgabe'] (Vienna 1919)
Literatur oder man wird doch da sehn (Vienna 1921)
Die letzten Tage der Menschheit, book ed. (Vienna 1922)
Untergang der Welt durch schwarze Magie (Vienna 1922)
Traumstück (Vienna 1923)
Wolkenkuckucksheim (Vienna 1923)
Traumtheater (Vienna 1924)
Epigramme (Vienna 1927)
Die Unüberwindlichen (Vienna 1928)
Literatur und Lüge (Vienna 1929)
Zeitstrophen (Vienna 1931)
Die Sprache (posthumous) (Vienna 1937)

4 Translations and adaptations by Kraus:
(a) Works by Johann Nestroy:
Das Notwendige und das Überflüssige (1920)
Der konfuse Zauberer (1925)

(b) Works by Jacques Offenbach:
Madame l'Archiduc (1927)
Perichole (1931)
Vert-Vert (1932)

(c) Works by William Shakespeare:
Timon von Athen (1930)
Shakespeares Sonette (1933)

Shakespeares Dramen, 2 vols. (1934–5): (*King Lear, The Taming of the Shrew, A Winter's Tale; Macbeth, The Merry Wives of Windsor, Troilus and Cressida*)

5 *Werke*, ed. Heinrich Fischer, 14 vols. (Munich 1952–67): the standard edition of Kraus's writings, comprising the following volumes:

    I *Die dritte Walpurgisnacht* (1952)
    II *Die Sprache* (1954)
    III *Beim Wort genommen* (1955)
    IV *Widerschein der Fackel* (1956)
    V *Die letzten Tage der Menschheit* (1957)
    VI *Literatur und Lüge* (1958)
    VII *Worte in Versen* (1959)
    VIII *Untergang der Welt durch schwarze Magie* (1960)
    IX *Unsterblicher Witz* (1961)
    X *Mit vorzüglicher Hochachtung* (1962)
    XI *Sittlichkeit und Kriminalität* (1963)
    XII *Die chinesische Mauer* (1964)
    XIII *Weltgericht* (1965)
    XIV *Dramen* (1967)

6 Correspondence:

Briefe an Sidonie Nádherný von Borutin: 1913–36, ed. Heinrich Fischer and Michael Lazarus, in consultation with Walter Methlagl and Friedrich Pfäfflin, 2 vols. (Munich 1974)

7 Unpublished writings:

This book draws on unpublished letters in the Vienna City Library, the Munich City Library, the German Literary Archive at Marbach, and the collection of Professor Franz Stoessl (Graz). Other unpublished sources, including corrected proof sheets for *Die Fackel*, have been consulted in the Vienna City Library.

B ENGLISH TRANSLATIONS

All passages from Kraus's writings quoted in this book have been translated by the author. The following selections from Kraus's work have been published in English:

Poems: Authorized English translation from the German, trans. Albert Bloch (Boston: Four Seas Press, 1930)
The Last Days of Mankind, abridged by Frederick Ungar, trans. Alexander Gode and Sue Ellen Wright (New York 1974)
In These Great Times: A Karl Kraus Reader, ed. Harry Zohn, trans. Joseph Fabry and others (Montreal 1976; Manchester 1984)
Half-Truths and One-and-a-Half Truths: Selected Aphorisms, ed. and trans. Harry Zohn (Montreal 1976)
No Compromise: Selected Writings, ed. Frederick Ungar, trans. Sheema Z. Buehne and others (New York 1977)

C STUDIES OF KRAUS'S WORK IN GERMAN

There is no definitive study of Kraus's life and work. The following provided significant points of reference for the writing of the present book:

Robert Scheu, *Karl Kraus* (Vienna 1909)
Rundfrage über Karl Kraus, ed. Ludwig von Ficker (Innsbruck 1917)

Berthold Viertel, 'Karl Kraus – Ein Charakter und die Zeit', first pub. in *Die Schaubühne*, 1917; reprinted in Viertel, *Dichtungen und Dokumente*, ed. Ernst Ginsberg (Munich 1956)

Leopold Liegler, *Karl Kraus und sein Werk* (Vienna 1920)

Walter Benjamin, 'Karl Kraus', first pub. in the *Frankfurter Zeitung*, 1931; reprinted in Benjamin, *Illuminationen* (Frankfurt 1961); English trans. in Benjamin, *One-Way-Street and Other Writings*, trans. Edmund Jephcott and Kingsley Shorter (London 1979)

Werner Kraft, *Karl Kraus – Beiträge zum Verständnis seines Werkes* (Salzburg 1956)

Paul Schick, *Karl Kraus in Selbstzeugnissen und Bilddokumenten* (Reinbek bei Hamburg 1965)

Alfred Pfabigan, *Karl Kraus und der Sozialismus – Eine politische Biographie* (Vienna 1976)

Nike Wagner, *Geist und Geschlecht – Karl Kraus und die Erotik der Wiener Moderne* (Frankfurt 1982)

Karl Kraus in neuer Sicht – Londoner Kraus Symposium, ed. Sigurd Paul Scheichl and Edward Timms (Munich 1986; articles in both German and English)

D STUDIES OF KRAUS'S WORK IN ENGLISH

The following publications have contributed to the reception of Kraus in the English-speaking world:

Erich Heller, 'Karl Kraus', in Heller, *The Disinherited Mind* (Cambridge 1952)

J.P. Stern, 'Karl Kraus's Vision of Language', in *Modern Language Review*, vol. LXI, no. 1 (January 1966), 71–84.

Frank Field, *The Last Days of Mankind: Karl Kraus and his Vienna* (London 1967)

Wilma Abeles Iggers, *Karl Kraus: A Viennese Critic of the Twentieth Century* (The Hague 1967)

Harry Zohn, *Karl Kraus* (Twayne World Authors, New York 1971)

C.E. Williams, 'Karl Kraus: The Absolute Satirist', in Williams, *The Broken Eagle: The Politics of Austrian Literature from Empire to Anschluss* (London 1974)

Thomas Szasz, *Karl Kraus and the Soul-Doctors: A Pioneer Critic and his Criticism of Psychiatry and Psychoanalysis* (London 1977)

Kari Grimstad, *Masks of the Prophet: The Theatrical World of Karl Kraus* (Toronto 1982)

E FURTHER BIBLIOGRAPHICAL SOURCES

Otto Kerry, *Karl-Kraus-Bibliographie*. Mit einem Register der Aphorismen, Gedichte, Glossen und Satiren (Munich 1970)

Kerry, 'Nachtrag zur "Karl-Kraus Bibliographie"', in *Modern Austrian Literature* (Special Karl Kraus Issue), vol. VIII, no. 1/2 (1975), 103–210

Sigurd Paul Scheichl, 'Kommentierte Auswahlbibliographie zu Karl Kraus', in *Text + Kritik: Sonderband Karl Kraus*, ed. Heinz Ludwig Arnold (Munich 1975), 158–241

Scheichl, 'Kommentierte Auswahlbibliographie', at intervals in *Kraus Hefte*, ed. Sigurd Paul Scheichl and Christian Wagenknecht (Munich 1977–   )

INDEX OF PRINCIPAL REFERENCES
TO KRAUS'S WRITINGS

GENERAL INDEX